KU-267-304

Freedom of Speech

GRIFFITH COLLEGE DUBLIN
CIRCULAR ROAD DUBLIN 8
TEL: (01) 4150490 FAX: (01) 4549265
email: library@gcd.ie

Second Edition

ERIC BARENDT

OXFORD
UNIVERSITY PRESS

323.443
BAR

OXFORD
UNIVERSITY PRESS

Great Clarendon Street, Oxford OX2 6DP

Oxford University Press is a department of the University of Oxford.
It furthers the University's objective of excellence in research, scholarship,
and education by publishing worldwide in

Oxford New York

Auckland Cape Town Dar es Salaam Hong Kong Karachi
Kuala Lumpur Madrid Melbourne Mexico City Nairobi
New Delhi Shanghai Taipei Toronto

With offices in

Argentina Austria Brazil Chile Czech Republic France Greece
Guatemala Hungary Italy Japan Poland Portugal Singapore
South Korea Switzerland Thailand Turkey Ukraine Vietnam

Oxford is a registered trade mark of Oxford University Press
in the UK and in certain other countries

Published in the United States
by Oxford University Press Inc., New York

© Eric Barendt 2005

The moral rights of the author have been asserted

Crown copyright material is reproduced under Class Licence
Number C01P0000148 with the permission of OPSI
and the Queen's Printer for Scotland

Database right Oxford University Press (maker)

First published 2005
First published in paperback 2007

All rights reserved. No part of this publication may be reproduced,
stored in a retrieval system, or transmitted, in any form or by any means,
without the prior permission in writing of Oxford University Press,
or as expressly permitted by law, or under terms agreed with the appropriate
reprographics rights organization. Enquiries concerning reproduction
outside the scope of the above should be sent to the Rights Department,
Oxford University Press, at the address above

You must not circulate this book in any other binding or cover
and you must impose the same condition on any acquirer

British Library Cataloguing in Publication Data

Data available

Library of Congress Cataloging in Publication Data
Barendt, E. M.
Freedom of speech / Eric Barendt.—2nd ed.
p. cm.
Includes bibliographical references and index.
ISBN 978-0-19-922581-1 (pbk. : alk. paper) 1. Freedom of
speech I. Title.
K3254.B37 2005
342.08′53—dc22

2007004757

Typeset by Newgen Imaging Systems (P) Ltd., Chennai, India
Printed in Great Britain
on acid-free paper by
Ashford Colour Press Limited, Gosport, Hampshire

ISBN 978-0-19-924451-5 (Hbk.)
ISBN 978-0-19-922581-1 (Pbk.)

1 3 5 7 9 10 8 6 4 2

FREEDOM OF SPEECH

...ol'...e Dublin

GRIFFITH COLLEGE DUBLIN

3 9009 00038008 5

323.443
BAR

Preface to the paperback Edition

GRIFFITH COLLEGE DUBLIN
SOUTH CIRCULAR ROAD DUBLIN 8
TEL: (01) 4150490 FAX: (01) 4549265
email: library@gcd.ie

Freedom of speech has been vigorously debated in many countries in the course of the year following the first publication of this book. In particular, the passionate (and sometimes violent) argument over the Danish cartoons depicting the Prophet Mohammed raised a number of important free speech questions. One of them was how far, say, English or French law should take account of the offensiveness of the cartoons to the significant Muslim minorities in those countries, when their publication was acceptable to, or might even have been welcomed by, the majority of the population there. Secondly, does the freedom to demonstrate against the publication of offensive material include, say, the right to burn books or flags, or to threaten a violent response to further publication? Another issue arises from the international dimension of the controversy. Expression lawful in some jurisdictions is proscribed in others as seditious or blasphemous: should we try to resolve these differences by international agreement, or should we simply accept that some countries proscribe material which people in liberal states have a right to publish and read or look at? (For discussion of the problems of global communication over the Net, see pp 468–74.)

In the United Kingdom debate has centred around two new statutes imposing further restrictions on freedom of speech. The Terrorism Act 2006 introduces the offence of encouragement of terrorism, committed by the intentional or reckless publication of any statement 'likely to be understood by some or all of the members of the public to whom it is published as a direct or indirect encouragement . . . to the commission, preparation or instigation of acts of terrorism . . . ': s. 1(1). It is immaterial whether the statement encourages any *particular* act of terrorism, as distinct from terrorism generally, and whether any person is *in fact* encouraged to commit any such act: s. 1(5). The Joint Committee of the House of Lords and House of Commons on Human Rights was unsure whether it was necessary to introduce the offence, given that the criminal law already covered incitement to violence and solicitation to murder; however, the Committee accepted the government had on balance made a case for clarification of the law and the introduction of a narrowly defined offence: 3rd Report of Session 2005–06, HL 75, HC 561, para 25.

What proved particularly controversial was the clause in the Bill indicating that, among the statements likely to be understood as indirectly encouraging terrorism, are included every statement which glorifies the commission or preparation (whether in the past, future, or generally) of terrorist acts, provided it is a statement from which its audience could reasonably be expected to infer that the glorified acts are to be emulated by it: s. 1(3). Critics, including the Joint Committee on Human Rights, argued the provision was too vague; a prosecution might be brought in respect of a speech, for instance, arguing that the public should understand, rather than deplore, suicide bombers. The government argued that such speech would not amount to *glorification* of terrorism, defined as 'any form of praise or celebration' (Terrorism Act 2006, s. 20(2)); further, a speaker in these circumstances would not be regarded as reasonably expecting anyone in the audience to become a suicide bomber.

The government's case is unpersuasive. It ignores the potential 'chilling effect' of the law, the point that speakers might be deterred from saying what they really feel about responses to, say, the invasion of Iraq or Israeli operations in Gaza, because they fear prosecution. To express understanding of, or even general support for, terrorism is political speech, which should only be proscribed when it is clearly intended to incite imminent atrocities. The glorification provision, and perhaps even that proscribing direct encouragement of terrorism, would not pass constitutional muster in the United States. For they would not satisfy the test formulated in *Brandenburg v Ohio* (discussed at pp 165–66) under which extreme political speech may be proscribed only when violence is intended, imminent, and likely.

The second UK measure to attract controversy was the Racial and Religious Hatred Act 2006. For a number of years the government has been attempting to extend the incitement to racial hatred offence to protect religious groups (see p 188). A pledge to take this step was made during the General Election campaign of 2005. The Bill met fierce opposition from writers, concerned that it would be impossible to ridicule or criticize religious faith. As a result of amendments introduced in the House of Lords, the scope of the new offence of stirring up religious hatred, incorporated in the amended Public Order Act 1986 (POA 1986), is much narrower than the racial hatred offence. First, the prosecution must show that the speaker or other publisher used *threatening* words; it is not enough to show, as with the racial hatred offence, that the words were abusive or insulting. Secondly, *intent* to 'stir up racial hatred' against a group of persons defined by reference to religious belief, or lack of it, must be proved: POA 1986, s. 29B. Most importantly, freedom of expression is explicitly protected by a provision (POA 1986, s. 29J) that the new law is not to be:

. . . given effect in a way which prohibits or restricts discussion, criticism or expressions of antipathy, dislike, ridicule, insult or abuse of particular religions or the beliefs or practices of their adherents, or of any other belief system or the beliefs or practices of its adherents, or proselytising or urging adherents of a different religion or belief system to cease practising their religion or belief system.

It is in fact hard to envisage circumstances in which a prosecution for this offence would succeed, where charges could not have been brought for other offences such as incitement to violence, or the use of threatening words within the hearing or sight of a person likely to feel alarm or distress: POA 1986, s. 5, discussed at p 300. Certainly, it is not an offence to ridicule or insult a particular religion or to urge its followers to abandon it because of its absurdity, though they might well feel abused by such speech.

One view, therefore, is that the incitement to religious hatred offence will have little impact on freedom of speech. But that view might well be wrong. Writers and editors may decide to moderate their expression or to withdraw an article, because they fear publication might lead to prosecution, even though it is unlikely it would succeed. The legislation will probably exercise a significant chilling effect on freedom of speech in much the same way as will the proscription of the glorification of terrorism. That would clearly be undesirable, given the importance of the fullest possible freedom of speech on political, social, and religious matters. (See pp 32, 38; 118–19, for discussion of the chilling effect of free speech restrictions.)

Three decisions of the House of Lords should be noted. In *DPP v Collins* [2006] 4 All ER 602 it held that the respondent had committed an offence when he made telephone calls to his MP referring to 'wogs', 'Pakis', and 'black bastards' in the course of expressing strong views on immigration policy. Under the Communications Act 2003, s. 127 he had sent 'by means of a public electronic communications network a message . . . that is grossly offensive . . . '. The House ruled that the test was whether the message was liable to cause gross offence to the people to whom the message related, not whether it grossly offended its recipients—here the MP and his staff. The decision may have significant implications for freedom of speech on the Internet, which is similarly communicated by means of a public electronic network.

The House of Lords was more sympathetic to free speech concerns in the context of a libel action, when it allowed the newspaper's appeal in *Jameel v Wall Street Journal Europe* [2006] 4 All ER 1279 (the judgment of Eady J is mentioned on pp 221–2). When the media publishes a story of real public interest which it has investigated responsibly, it has a defence to a libel action brought in respect of any defamatory allegations contained in the article, unless they were included gratuitously; the law should allow some flexibility to the editor to decide how a story should be reported. The Lords' approach is not dissimilar to that of the European Human Rights Court which has often emphasized that defamatory allegations should be assessed in the context of the whole story (see pp 224–5). In *R (on the application of Laporte) v Chief Constable of Gloucestershire* [2006] UKHL 55, the Lords allowed the appeal of a peace protester who, together with others, had been stopped by the police from proceeding to a demonstration at RAF Fairford against the use of the base by US bombers: see p 150. The House held that the police could only use their common law power to prevent a breach of the peace, when they had reasonable grounds to believe that disorder was really *imminent*; the police action amounted to a prior restraint which called for careful scrutiny.

There is only space in this Preface to mention a few cases from other jurisdictions. In two cases the European Court of Human Rights held that there was an infringement of freedom of expression when publications highly critical of the Catholic Church had been punished for defamation: *Giniewski v France*, Decision of 31 January 2006, and *Klein v Slovakia*, Decision of 31 October 2006. These decisions indicate more concern for freedom of expression than the Court had shown in *Otto-Preminger* (p 192). Of the US Supreme Court cases concerning freedom of speech, the most important was *Garcetti v Ceballos*, decided on 30 May 2006. By a 5–4 majority it held that public employees speaking *pursuant to their official duties* could not claim the protection of the First Amendment against managerial discipline; whistle-blowers do not enjoy constitutional free speech rights. The principle established in *Pickering v Board of Education* (discussed at pp 489–91) under which a public employer's interests have to be balanced against its employees' freedom to speak as citizens on matters of public concern was narrowed. In *Randall v Sorrell*, decided on 26 June 2006, the Court affirmed its decision in *Buckley v Valeo* (see pp 89–90, 481–83) on the incompatibility of election expenditure limits with the First Amendment, and it invalidated the very strict limits imposed by a Vermont statute on contributions to election campaigns.

The current febrile political climate challenges the commitment of liberal societies to freedom of speech. Governments are concerned to reduce the likelihood of acts of terrorism. To that end they consider it important to outlaw both speech which appears to encourage or defend these atrocities and also speech which outrages religious communities and which may weaken their members' sympathy for society at large. But this is not a prudent course. The punishment of peddlers of hate speech or of the glorifiers of terrorism only creates martyrs for their causes, without necessarily averting any serious evil. Alternatively, suppressed material is driven underground, and it becomes impossible then to regulate its circulation. More importantly the dissemination of some harmless, even valuable, ideas may be deterred. It is as important now as it ever has been to defend freedom of speech and affirm its central role in the flourishing of a liberal society.

Eric Barendt

November 2006

Preface

Freedom of Speech was originally published twenty years ago. Since 1985 interest in comparative free speech law has grown appreciably. It has been encouraged recently by the incorporation of the European Human Rights Convention into English law by the Human Rights Act 1998. English courts consider, as they must, decisions of the European Court in Strasbourg; but they also take into account important judgments on free speech in Australia, Canada, and other Commonwealth countries, and rulings of the United States Supreme Court. The House of Lords in *Reynolds* v. *Times Newspapers*, the leading English case on free speech and libel, referred to more than thirty cases from other jurisdictions, including nine rulings of the Strasbourg Court. Comparative free speech law has become a subject of practical importance.

This book is much longer than its predecessor. Free speech law has become more complex in all the jurisdictions considered in this book; there are simply many more cases to discuss. This is true of England, the United States, and Germany. When the first edition appeared, the European Court had only considered a handful of freedom of expression cases; it has now produced a number of important decisions, particularly to resolve conflicts between freedom of expression and reputation or privacy rights. In 1985 Canada had only recently adopted the Charter of Rights and Freedoms; in the last twenty years its courts have produced decisions, for example, on hate speech, pornography, and advertising, which sometimes take a different approach to free speech issues from that of the United States Supreme Court. Since 1992 Australia has also developed a distinctive free speech jurisprudence on the basis of the implied constitutional right to freedom of political communication.

There are other reasons why the contents of this book have expanded. Free speech arguments are increasingly made, and often accepted, in contexts where they might have been dismissed thirty years ago. There has been an explosion in challenges in the United States, and more recently in Canada, to the compatibility of advertising restrictions with freedom of speech. The argument that freedom of speech limits copyright and other property rights is taken more seriously than it used to be. Demonstrators and employees, dismissed for speaking their mind, are increasingly keen to assert rights to freedom of expression, while political parties have mounted further challenges to limits on their election expenditure. Some of their claims raise hard questions about the scope of free speech, as do claims to engage in various forms of protest such as flag-burning or to communicate in the speaker's language of choice. The Internet raises novel issues; they concern the application of familiar free speech principles to a new medium and the question whether it is possible to regulate global communications. In short, there is a wider range of free speech issues to discuss, as well as more cases on the familiar topics of hate speech, pornography, and contempt of court.

As the Preface to the first edition of this book pointed out, courts can only resolve hard free speech questions when they have examined the arguments why freedom of speech (or expression) is guaranteed in the constitution or human rights legislation. The text of the constitution rarely provides clear answers and there may be few, if any, precedents to help judges. That is why this book discusses general philosophical arguments for free speech in its first chapter, and canvasses arguments of principle in many of the others. English courts are less used to handling these arguments than courts in the United States or Germany, but some recent decisions, notably that of the House of Lords in the *Campbell* privacy case, show that they are now prepared to assess the strength of a free speech or press claim when balancing it against another right.

American writers frequently defend a particular free speech theory, contending it provides the best explanation for the decisions of the Supreme Court. I am sceptical of this enterprise. If one single argument must be found, the argument from the right of citizens actively to participate in a democracy provides, I think, the most persuasive justification for freedom of speech. But it does not explain the Supreme Court rulings on pornography and commercial advertising, let alone all the major decisions in other countries. Other free speech arguments have their place. Moreover, the approach of constitutional courts in different countries varies considerably on a range of free speech issues, for example, the validity of hate speech and pornography laws and the compatibility of rights of reply with the guarantee of a free press. These approaches are linked to different perspectives on fundamental questions: the relationship of freedom of speech to equality and human dignity, and whether the freedom always precludes state intervention to promote speech. It is better to examine these different approaches with an open mind, rather than dismiss them because they are incompatible with a preferred free speech theory. As this book shows, some arguments concerning the scope of free speech or its relationship with other rights, for example to privacy or to a fair trial, are sound, while others should be rejected. But these judgments need not entail an ideological commitment to any single theory.

This book has a relatively full discussion of English free speech law. Inevitably, however, discussion of United States decisions and arguments dominates a few chapters, because the courts there have considered free speech questions for longer than those of any other jurisdiction. Only Chapter VI in its analysis of the relationship of free speech and libel law contains anything like a comprehensive comparative survey of leading principles in all relevant countries; a comparable treatment of other areas of law would have necessitated an even longer book. My objective has been to discuss how free speech issues should be, and have been, resolved, giving due consideration to the most important decisions from the legal systems considered in this book. It would be a virtually impossible task to keep up to date with developments in every jurisdiction; but I have endeavoured to cover those in England up to 31 December 2004.

I am indebted to many people for their help in the revision of this book. A number helped with the research, tracking down literature in libraries and from the Net: Maya Anaokar, Deepali Fernandes, Jennifer Johnson, Ron Levy, and Rachel Roberts. I am grateful to colleagues who commented on many of the chapters: David Anderson, Ailsa Chang, Tom Gibbons, Stephen Guest, Dario Milo, and James Weinstein. I would also like to thank Professor Bernd Holznagel for inviting me to spend some time at the University of Münster, where I was able to study recent developments in German law, and University College London for allowing me time away from regular teaching and administrative duties to complete the revision of this book. I thank Sylvia Lough for her help with the preparation of the final text, and Gwen Booth, John Louth, and Louise Kavanagh of Oxford University Press for their encouragement. I owe much to Dominic Shryane for his skilful editorial work.

My greatest debt is to my wife, Sheila, for her support and understanding over the four years it has taken to revise this book. Conversation at home does not need the protection of a free speech clause, but it is the most enjoyable form of communication.

Eric Barendt

January 2005

Outline Contents

Detailed Contents

A Note on Abbreviations

The German abbreviations used in the notes may be unfamiliar, so a short list is appended here.

BVerfGE	Entscheidungen des Bundesverfassungsgerichts (Decisions of the German Constitutional Court)
BVerwGE	Entscheidungen des Bundesverwaltungsgerichts (Decisions of the German Administrative Court)
BGBl	Bundesgesetzblatt (Federal Statute Gazette)
NJW	Neue Juristische Wochenschrift

Secondly, a number of books are referred to frequently, so that, for reasons of space, reference in the footnotes is given only to their author or a short title. They are:

Dworkin	R. M. Dworkin, *Freedom's Law* (New York: OUP, 1996)
Feldman	D. Feldman, *Civil Liberties and Human Rights in England and Wales*, 2nd edn. (Oxford: OUP, 2002)
Freedom of Expression and Freedom of Information	J. Beatson and Y. Cripps (eds.), *Freedom of Expression and Freedom of Information: Essays in Honour of Sir David Williams* (Oxford: OUP, 2000)
Mill	J. S. Mill, *On Liberty and Other Essays* (Oxford: OUP, 1991)
Moon	R. Moon, *The Constitutional Protection of Freedom of Expression* (Toronto: Toronto UP, 2000)
Robertson & Nicol	G. Robertson, QC and A. Nicol, QC, *Media Law*, 4th edn. (London: Penguin, 2002)
Scanlon	T. Scanlon, 'A Theory of Freedom of Expression' (1972) 1 *Phil & Public Affairs* 204, as reprinted in R. M. Dworkin (ed.), *The Philosophy of Law* (Oxford: OUP, 1977), 153
Schauer	F. Schauer, *Free Speech: A Philosophical Enquiry* (Cambridge: CUP, 1982)

Table of United Kingdom Cases

Principal references are shown in **bold** type

Table of United States Cases

Principal references are shown in **bold** type

Table of German Cases

Principal references are shown in **bold** type

CONSTITUTIONAL COURT

Administrative Court

Federal Labour Court

Federal Supreme Court

Table of Decisions of the European Commission and Court of Human Rights

Principal references are shown in **bold** type

EUROPEAN COURT OF HUMAN RIGHTS, STRASBOURG

Cases from Other Jurisdictions

AUSTRALIA

CANADA

IRELAND–
Educational Company of Ireland
v Fitzpatrick (no.2)

Conseil constitutionnel

Cour de Cassation

ITALY

Constitutional Court

Corte di Cassazione, Penal Section

NEW ZEALAND

SOUTH AFRICA

I

Why Protect Free Speech?

1. Introduction

Written constitutions and bills of rights invariably protect freedom of speech as one of the fundamental liberties guaranteed against state suppression or regulation. It is guaranteed by the Universal Declaration of Human Rights and by international conventions, notably the European Convention on Human Rights and Fundamental Freedoms (ECHR). Long before the ECHR was incorporated into its law by the Human Rights Act 1998 (HRA 1998), freedom of speech was regarded in England as an important right; leaving aside established common law restrictions, governments have to produce strong arguments to justify restraints on its exercise. Political philosophers have argued for liberty of opinion and discussion, or for a free speech principle under which speech is entitled to a greater degree of immunity from regulation than other forms of conduct which cause similar harm or offence.[1] Yet philosophers and lawyers disagree about the justifications for a free speech principle or indeed whether there are any good reasons for treating free speech as special. As one leading philosopher has put it, '[f]reedom of expression is a liberal puzzle'. It is prized by liberals for reasons they may not understand.[2]

Public debate in Britain and other liberal democracies about free speech is usually more concerned with the scope of the freedom than with the issue whether the freedom should be protected at all. There are questions how far hard-core pornography or commercial advertising, say, for cigarettes, are covered by freedom of speech. Other subjects of controversy are how much weight should be given to freedom of speech and press freedom when a newspaper article discloses details of a celebrity's private life and whether it is right to limit media publicity before legal proceedings. These matters raise questions of constitutional law in jurisdictions like the United States, Canada, and Germany where courts are required to uphold freedom of expression. The First Amendment to the United States Constitution provides that 'Congress shall make no law . . . abridging the freedom of speech, or of the press . . .'. The text appears simple, but it is left to the courts to decide what

---

[1] See J. S. Mill's classic essay, 'Of the Liberty of Thought and Discussion', in Mill, discussed in s. 2(i) below, and Schauer, ch. 1.

[2] J. Raz, 'Free Expression and Personal Identification' (1991) 11 *OJLS* 303.

constitutes 'speech' and whether, say, a state statute providing for privacy rights can be enforced against the media without infringing its First Amendment freedoms.

A threshold question is the extent to which resolution of difficult free speech issues such as these should be influenced by arguments of political and moral philosophy. In particular, an examination of the theories underlying the free speech principle may suggest solutions to the problems which confront both legislatures and courts. Of course, governments may act largely in response to public pressure, but arguments of principle are often influential in the course of parliamentary debate and should be taken into account by legislators.[3] It may be less obvious, however, that judges should concern themselves with questions of political philosophy, even in jurisdictions where they do have the power to strike down legislation infringing basic rights. The courts' task, it might be said, is to interpret the text, albeit in the light of the constitution as a whole, rather than to engage in philosophical argument.

The function of courts in constitutional cases raises notoriously difficult questions. Free speech litigation is no exception. It is impossible to draw a sharp line between legal and philosophical argument in this context. The literal approach to textual interpretation, of some serviceable use in the construction of detailed statutes, is of little assistance in elucidating the meaning of freedom of speech (or freedom of expression) provisions which are invariably framed in broad, general terms. The courts are perhaps limited to the range of meanings which can be supported on a reading of the text, but the range of possibilities is so wide that this constraint is of little importance. Thus, Black J., a member of the United States Supreme Court who took a literal interpretation of the First Amendment, still had to decide the meaning of 'speech', a matter on which the Constitution provides no help whatever.[4] Naturally there may be a little less difficulty where the free speech clause contains more specific provisions, as Article 5 of the German Basic Law and Article 10 of the ECHR both do. But the courts' task when interpreting and applying any of these provisions remains quite different from that imposed on them when they consider detailed legislation.

An alternative approach is to consider what the framers of the constitution intended. Did the Founding Fathers of the United States Constitution, for example, have in mind that only previous restraints (or censorship) operating before publication were outlawed by the First Amendment, or did they intend it also to proscribe penal sanctions for the publication of, say, seditious speech?[5] For obvious reasons this technique cannot really be sustained. It is rarely clear what

---

[3] UK ministers are required to make a statement that a bill's provisions comply with the European Human Rights Convention or that, though he cannot make a statement of compatibility, the government wishes Parliament to proceed with it: HRA 1998, s. 19.

[4] For the meaning of speech, see ch. III, s. 2 below.

[5] For discussion of this point, see D. S. Brogen, 'The Origins of Freedoms of Speech and the Press' (1983) 42 *Maryland Law Rev.* 429, 439–44.

the drafters of a constitution intended. Preparatory documents frequently evidence conflicting views and aspirations, difficulties which are even more acute in the case of international conventions such as the ECHR. Even when it is possible to infer a particular intent, it should hardly be decisive for litigation arising some decades or centuries after the constitution was framed. Political and social circumstances will have changed so radically that it would be absurd to be limited to the particular conceptions of a freedom entertained by the members of a constitutional assembly. It is unlikely that the delegates to the 1787 Philadelphia Convention anticipated the development of mass commercial advertising or the advent of the broadcasting media, so it would be silly to enquire how they would have applied freedom of speech to these phenomena.

Partly because of these difficulties, it has been urged by Ronald Dworkin that constitutional texts should be viewed as embodying general moral and political *concepts* rather than specific *conceptions*.[6] He pointed out that the US Constitution proscribes 'cruel and unusual punishment', but does not lay down any particular conception of this general concept. Courts must decide whether it should be understood now to outlaw, say, capital punishment; that decision requires reflection on the moral reasons why cruel punishment is forbidden. On this approach a constitution may reflect commitment to a general concept of freedom of speech, but the particular understandings or conceptions of that freedom are best elucidated by an examination of the moral and political reasons justifying its protection and an appreciation of its significance in the constitution as a whole. Moreover, underlying the specific freedoms set out in a bill of rights, there may be even broader concepts concerning immutable basic human rights, for example, rights to equality of respect and concern or of human dignity. The scope of a particular freedom such as freedom of speech, and its meaning in a specific context, may be determined through argument more akin to philosophical reasoning than to conventional legal techniques such as the drawing of inferences from precedents. To some extent, then, the general ideas which justify freedom of speech are of considerable assistance to its interpretation. These ideas are likely to be of a loose, open-ended character, very different from the specific and detailed aims which characterize most modern legislation enacted to deal with a particular problem, say, poor housing or low education standards. Philosophical and political arguments about the justifications for a free speech principle are on this approach highly relevant to constitutional interpretation, insofar as they assist in elucidation of the concept incorporated in the text. If, say, the only sound argument for freedom of speech is that it is essential for citizens to make informed choices between parties at general elections, a court would be wrong to hold the freedom covered sexually explicit material or commercial advertising. Dworkin's approach, building on the distinction between the general concept of free speech and particular conceptions of it, is more likely to resolve hard cases concerning its

---

[6] R. M. Dworkin, *Taking Rights Seriously* (London: Duckworth, 1977), 132–7.

scope than are other techniques which emphasize the meaning of the constitutional text and the intentions of its framers.

This conclusion does not, however, mean that judges ought to resolve hard constitutional cases solely on the basis of *abstract* philosophical argument. For a start, the constitution may be designed to reflect one particular philosophical or moral perspective rather than another. For example, the protection of freedom of expression in most modern constitutions is probably more closely connected with allowing all citizens an equal right to engage in open public discourse than it is with Mill's argument from truth published in 1859. Such a conclusion might emerge more clearly from a look at the overall structure of the constitution than from surmises about the intentions of the framers or the general philosophical concepts which influenced them. Consider a hypothetical constitution, in which the right to freedom of speech is set out in a general chapter entitled 'Political Freedoms', in conjunction with the right to vote, the freedom to form political parties, and rights of access to government information. In that case, it would be hard to deny that freedom of expression concerns only political speech, and that consequently commercial speech and obscenity are not covered. The point may be illustrated by reference to the German Basic Law (*Grundgesetz*). The Constitutional Court has to some extent been influenced in its interpretation of the guarantee of freedom of expression in Article 5 by the specific protection of political parties in Article 21 of the *Grundgesetz*, and so has afforded political speech more protection from government regulation than that it has granted other types of communication.[7]

There is, therefore, a difference between the purely philosophical arguments for a free speech principle, and the specific arguments which courts must consider when they adjudicate constitutional claims to exercise the right. Judicial consideration of the former must be tempered by the constraints imposed by a proper interpretation of the text, and must further be substantially moulded by the concepts adopted by the framers of the constitution, its general structure, and earlier judicial precedents. Constitutional interpretation can be seen, therefore, as a subtle process in which abstract arguments of principle mingle with historical, institutional, and specifically legal factors. As Frederick Schauer, a leading free speech theorist in the United States, has said: '... the task of the courts, in attempting to interpret the open-ended and morally loaded constitutional provisions—freedom of speech ... and so on—is to develop a theory of these clauses, a theory that will be significantly philosophical, but will include a large dose of precedent.'[8] The respective weight of these considerations will naturally vary from one constitution to another. The more specific the legal text and the more detailed and complex the constitution is as a whole, the greater will be the role played by textual and structural arguments. The force of earlier judicial rulings will vary, depending on the doctrine of precedent adopted in the system, and the number and quality of those

---

[7] 61 BVerfGE 1, 9–11 (1982).
[8] 'Must Speech be Special?' (1983) 78 *North Western Univ Law Rev* 1284, 1305.

precedents. Courts should, and will, be more prepared to depart from a single decision which appears inconsistent with the arguments of moral principle underlying a right, than they would be to disregard a line of authority, which might equally be open to challenge on that basis.[9]

Moreover, courts need not wrestle with all the difficulties which beset abstract philosophical argument. While philosophers may remain unsure whether the case for a free speech principle is sound, judges are required to interpret and apply a freedom of speech or a free expression clause. (The terms 'freedom of speech' and 'freedom of expression' are used interchangeably throughout this book, unless the context indicates otherwise.) They must accept the special status of free speech provided in the constitution and must make the best sense of the concept that they can. When freedom of speech or freedom of expression provisions are contained in bills or charters of rights, it is clear that these are rights entitled to some protection from government interference; courts need not explore further the philosophical character of the right. Unlike philosophers, they do not have to worry whether the best arguments for free speech are utilitarian in character or are instead deontological, that is, that free speech is a natural moral right. Moreover, guidance on the scope of free speech may be provided by the constitutional text. Related clauses covering the freedom of assembly and association indicate that courts should protect demonstrations on the streets and other forms of public protest, even though they might consider that on principle such activity falls outside the scope of freedom of speech or of expression.[10] Privacy rights may strengthen controversial claims to free expression rights, for instance, to read pornography at home, which might be hard to justify on the basis of the abstract philosophical arguments for freedom of speech.

Subject to these points, arguments of political theory are often central to the disposition of free speech cases. They are particularly relevant when courts determine the meaning of speech and the scope of the freedom. Courts must decide, for instance, the extent to which freedom of expression covers commercial advertising, sexually explicit material, and expressive conduct such as the desecration of a national flag. They must also determine whether the protection of hate speech directed at racial or religious groups is required by freedom of expression in the light of the underlying moral arguments for guarantee of that freedom, or alternatively whether human dignity supports its proscription. They must rule whether freedom of speech is only a negative liberty, guaranteed against interference by government, or whether it also entails upholding some positive rights, for example, to use public property for speech or to acquire information from public authorities ('freedom of information'). Answers to these questions are rarely provided by the text of the constitution, so judges must decide them on the basis of

---

[9] In *West Virginia State Board of Education* v. *Barnette* 319 US 624 (1943), considered in ch. III, s. 4, the US Supreme Court overruled its decision of three years earlier, *Minersville School District* v. *Gobitis* 310 US 586 (1940).

[10] For the relationship of free speech and freedom of assembly, see ch. VIII, s. 2 below.

the moral and political arguments which underlie its commitment to freedom of speech. They cannot, in short, avoid, confronting difficult questions of political philosophy.

After a brief introduction on the nature of a *free speech principle*, section 2 of this chapter explores the coherence of four justifications for that principle. Each of these arguments assumes different forms, so some simplification is involved in their reduction to four; further, within the context of these justifications for free speech, particular arguments are considered which could be put under an alternative heading. As will be seen, the different arguments for free speech emphasize the interests of either the speaker or of the audience, or perhaps that of the public in an open tolerant society. So section 3 discusses the *free speech interests* of speakers, recipients (listeners, readers, and viewers), and of the general public in the unimpeded communication of information and ideas. These distinctions may have legal significance. Some texts confer rights on both speakers and recipients, while others provide only for freedom of speech or expression, without making it clear whether both groups enjoy rights. In some circumstances, for instance that of commercial advertising, the free speech claims of recipients appear stronger than those of speakers, so it is important how far the free speech or expression clause protects the formers' interests.

Many free speech arguments link the freedom to other rights and values which may be more fundamental in terms of political principle or of the constitution, or both: a right to dignity or the right to equal respect and concern. Equally, these values may circumscribe free speech rights, in particular limiting individual rights to freedom of expression to ensure greater, or more equal, enjoyment of the freedom. In particular, the value of pluralism may justify qualifying the exercise by individuals, notably the owners of media corporations, of their free speech rights. That conclusion would be rejected by many commentators, particularly in the United States, because it seems to entail upholding some government regulation of speech. They contend that it would run counter to the justifications for free speech which underlie its incorporation in the constitution. These arguments are considered in section 4 of this chapter.

2. Four Arguments for a Free Speech Principle

This section explores four arguments commonly put forward to justify a free speech principle, that is a principle under which speech is entitled to special protection from regulation or suppression.[11] The principle must be an independent political principle, distinguishable from general libertarian claims. An anarchist would not need to invoke a free speech principle, since he argues that all attempts by government to regulate his behaviour, including speech, violate his freedom.

---

[11] Schauer, 7–10.

Under the principle, speech is entitled to a degree of immunity from government regulation because of some special quality or value to be attributed to communication and expression. Although the case for free speech protection may be associated with, or rest on, more fundamental claims about human dignity or opportunities for self-fulfilment and development, the principle is only coherent to the extent that speech can be distinguished from other areas of human conduct and activity. Further, a right to free speech must be isolated from other fundamental liberties that may be incorporated in a written constitution, for instance, rights to privacy or to choose a sexual lifestyle, or property rights. This may create difficulties in some contexts. When rights to view hard-core pornographic films or live sex shows are asserted, it is unclear whether these are really claims to free speech, to privacy, or to a broad right to personal liberty in indulging sexual tastes.[12]

A free speech principle need not entail absolute protection for any exercise of freedom of expression. Most proponents of strong free speech guarantees concede that its exercise may properly be restricted in some circumstances, for example, when it is likely to lead to imminent violence. But the principle does mean that government must show strong grounds for interference. It would be inconsistent with any free speech principle, worthy of the name, if a publication could be stopped on the ground merely that it is offensive to some people, or could be penalized because it contributes to disorder or lowers the government's authority or reputation. In short, a free speech principle means that expression should often be tolerated, even when conduct which produces comparable offence or harmful effects might properly be proscribed. And that must be because speech is particularly valuable, or perhaps because we have special reason to mistrust its regulation.

(i) Arguments concerned with the importance of discovering truth

Historically the most durable argument for a free speech principle has been based on the importance of open discussion to the discovery of truth. If restrictions on speech are tolerated, society prevents the ascertainment and publication of accurate facts and valuable opinion. The case is particularly associated with John Stuart Mill, but it had also been made two centuries earlier by Milton, and it has played some part in the theorizing of American judges.[13] There are a number of versions of the argument. Truth may be regarded as an autonomous and fundamental good, or its value may be supported by utilitarian considerations concerning progress and the development of society. A theory resting the special status of speech on the value of truth should, one might think, assume that truth is a coherent concept, and that particular truths can be discovered and justified. That was

---

12 See ch. III, s. 2(iii) and ch. X below for further discussion.
13 J. Milton, *Areopagitica: A Speech for the Liberty of Unlicensed Printing* (1644) in *Prose Writings* (Everyman, 1958). For relevant US judgments, in addition to that of Holmes J. in *Abrams* v. *US* 250 US 616 (1919), see Brandeis J. in *Whitney* v. *California* 274 US 357, 375–8 (1927) and Frankfurter J. in *Kovacs* v. *Cooper* 336 US 77, 95–7 (1949).

Mill's position. Relativists contest this assumption. Their perspective raises philosophical questions outside the scope of this book.[14] But one version of the argument from truth—the marketplace of ideas—associated with Holmes J.'s famous judgment in *Abrams* v. *US* shares to some extent the relativist perspective; it is considered later in this section after discussion of the older, and intellectually more respectable, argument made by Mill.

Mill's truth argument put forward different contentions, dependent on whether the expression at issue is possibly true or is (almost certainly) false. Prohibition of the former category of speech is undesirable because it entails an unwarranted 'assumption of infallibility' on the part of the state. Government naturally acts on its view of what is right when it proscribes certain conduct, for example, unfair trading practices and anti-competitive agreements, but, Mill argued, it is only because opponents of such measures are free to challenge their wisdom that the government can ever be confident that its policies are right and that it is appropriate to legislate.[15] Alternatively, speech may be suppressed because it is objectively false. It is still wrong to take this step, for people holding true beliefs will no longer be challenged and forced to defend their views. They 'ought to be moved by the consideration that, however true it may be, if it is not fully, frequently, and fearlessly discussed, it will be held as a dead dogma, not a living truth'.[16]

Many criticisms can be made of Mill's argument. In the first place, it assumes that in all circumstances (short of an imminent emergency) the publication of a possibly true statement is the highest public good. But there are many situations where legal systems prefer to protect other values, and that choice seems defensible. For example, in many countries racist hate speech is banned, because racial harmony and the protection of the sensitivities of ethnic groups is considered a more important goal than the absolute tolerance in this context of freedom of speech.[17] Similar judgements may be made in other contexts; advertising of tobacco products and dangerous drugs may be prohibited, though some people, not only cranks, may claim it is healthy to use them. Mill's argument that the utility of an opinion cannot be divorced from its truth is unpersuasive. It is not inconsistent to defend a ban on the publication of propositions on the ground that their propagation would seriously damage society, while conceding that they might be true. The interests of truth are, to some extent, protected if the wisdom of the ban can be freely debated.[18]

The best rejoinder to this criticism is that the suppression of speech, however plausible the justification for this course, creates a suspicion of authority and

---

[14] For a defence of the concept of truth, see B. Williams, *Truth and Truthfulness* (Princeton, NJ: Princeton UP, 2002).   [15] Mill, 22–4.
[16] Ibid., 40.   [17] Hate speech is discussed in ch. V, s. 4 below.
[18] See C. L. Ten, *Mill on Liberty* (Oxford: OUP, 1980), 131–2, and see also H. J. McCloskey, 'Liberty of Expression: Its Grounds and Limits' (1970) 13 *Inquiry* 219, 226–7, cf. D. H. Munro, ibid., 238, 252–3.

destroys tolerance. It is better, it is said, to permit the dissemination, say, of hate speech than to curtail the freedom of extremists. The latter course might encourage people to believe the truth of the suppressed speech, which they would otherwise ignore or reject; moreover, it is sometimes dangerous to drive unpleasant ideas underground, for they may surface later in a more dangerous form. There is something in this counter-argument to criticism of Mill. But insofar as the rejoinder rests on a judgement that it is overall misguided to restrict speech, it departs from the argument from truth. That argument is that it is wrong to suppress truth, even though that course is considered useful. Once the utility of suppression is in issue, it is a matter for empirical judgement whether on balance it is right to restrict free expression, and on that matter the judgements of freely elected governments are usually trusted.

A related criticism is that Mill overvalued intellectual discussion and the need for all individuals to be able to debate public affairs vigorously. This feature emerges most clearly in his claim that it would be wrong to prohibit even false speech, because in the absence of opposition the ability to defend true and valuable beliefs will decline. This may be correct, but a government worried that inflammatory speech may provoke disorder is surely entitled to elevate immediate public order considerations over the long-term intellectual development of the man on the Clapham omnibus. At any rate the risk of immediate damage which may occur from the acceptance of falsehood should be balanced against the long-term benefits of constant, uninhibited debate.

However, the greatest difficulty with Mill's argument is its implicit assumption that freedom of discussion *necessarily* leads to the discovery of truth or, more concretely, to better individual or social decisions. That assumption is certainly warranted in environments where there is a shared commitment to the discovery of truth; it is clearly wrong to censor expression in universities and between members of a scientific community, on the ground that it challenges received wisdom. Indeed, a novel idea is much more likely to be accepted in these circles if it is true. Moreover, procedures are in place, for example, peer review of articles submitted for publication, to ensure that their claims to truth are plausible and worth discussion.[19] But it is difficult to make the same assumptions about the role of free speech in society. It is not clear that unregulated speech always leads to the reception of truth. Indeed, some historical experience suggests the contrary; the Nazis came to power in Germany in 1933, although there had been (relatively) free political discourse under the Weimar Republic during the 1920s. This is not to say that truths are more likely to be discovered in the absence of free speech. Freedom of speech may be necessary, if not sufficient, for this purpose, but equally some constraints may be required to ensure that false propositions do not drive out truths.

One question which has been relatively little explored in discussion of Mill's theory is whether his argument applies equally to all types of expression, and in

---

[19] Williams (n. 14 above), 217.

particular whether a distinction should be drawn between claims of *fact* and expression of *opinion*. Mill clearly considered the argument from truth, or at least that aspect of it concerned to justify the tolerance of false opinion, to be more relevant to discussion of political, moral, and social affairs than to mathematical or scientific propositions.[20] His treatment does not explicitly refer to other modes of expression, such as commercial advertising or sexually explicit material, which may consist of both information and ideology or fit into neither category. One interpretation of the truth argument is that it does cover these types of expression, since they form part of a general argument that, say, looking at such material is an aspect of a good lifestyle.

There is perhaps something paradoxical about Mill's thesis. The argument for a free speech principle from truth is said to be particularly applicable to types of expression, which can only rarely, if ever, establish truths with the same degree of assurance that obtains in mathematics or the natural sciences. Truth, of course, is not to be equated with certainty, and the fact that there are better and worse arguments in political and moral discourse is enough to substantiate Mill's conclusion that the prohibition of such discussion by the government is (at least generally) wrong on the truth argument. Less clear is the status of speech which does not assert any coherent proposition or make a claim which could ever be objectively tested. Personal abuse, some emotive political speech (perhaps the 'Fuck the Draft' slogan upheld as protected speech by the US Supreme Court in *Cohen* v. *California*[21]) and hard-core pornography all appear to fall outside the categories of expression which Mill had in mind when he formulated the argument from truth. Yet the legal systems considered in this book to some extent protect these types of expression. That might mean that courts accept justifications for freedom of speech other than the truth argument. In any event, Mill's theory is difficult to apply to types of expression where it seems absurd even to look for an element of truth, or to propositions which are quite obviously factually false, such as 'the moon is made of green cheese'.

A more important question is how relevant the argument from truth is to free speech coverage of the publication of government secrets, or the disclosure of confidential personal information. (Most legal systems impose restrictions on the disclosure of such information in the interests of national security or privacy.) In these circumstances, the speech is not restricted because the government fears the disclosure of information which is false. It is not acting on 'an assumption of infallibility'. The disclosure of information, say, by a civil servant or an employee of a commercial company to a newspaper is outlawed because it reveals true facts which the government or the company wishes to keep confidential. Individuals take privacy actions generally to stop (or secure compensation for) the disclosure of sensitive personal information which is probably accurate. Arguments from truth are not readily applicable in this context; it is better to justify the coverage of such disclosures by free speech clauses with other arguments.

[20] Mill, 51.   [21] 403 US 15 (1971).

Mill's truth argument then applies most clearly to speech stating beliefs and theories about political, moral, aesthetic, and social matters. The position within his theory of factual propositions and scientific or mathematical formulae is less well established. However, this reservation does not seem to affect the judicial interpretation of free speech provisions. Courts are influenced by the other justifications for a free speech principle, especially the argument from its importance in a democracy, which does apply to much factual information.[22] Moreover, some constitutions, such as the German Basic Law, and the ECHR clearly cover the right to impart and receive information, as well as ideas.[23]

As mentioned earlier, the principal weakness of Mill's argument is its questionable assumption that free discussion necessarily leads in a democratic society to the acceptance of truth, or at least the adoption of better or more liberal social policies. Another argument must be made to strengthen the case made by Mill: government is not to be trusted in this context to determine the appropriate procedures for the discovery of truth. One may legitimately doubt whether free speech always leads to truth, but better decisions are likely to emerge from uninhibited discussion than from a process regulated by the state. For government does not share the commitment of a university or the scientific community to the truth, and cannot be relied on to adopt appropriate procedures for its discovery. This is surely a reasonable position, though it needs refinement.[24] At this juncture, the point should be made that the argument runs counter to the majoritarian theory of democracy, under which an elected majority is generally entitled to regulate speech whenever it considers its dissemination is against the overall good or welfare of the community.[25]

Another form of the argument from truth is associated with a famous passage in the dissenting judgment of Holmes J. in *Abrams* v. *US*:

But when men have realized that time has upset many fighting faiths, they may come to believe even more than they believe the very foundations of their own conduct that the ultimate good desired is better reached by free trade in ideas—that the best test of truth is the power of the thought to get itself accepted in the competition of the market, and that truth is the only ground upon which their wishes safely can be carried out.[26]

The 'marketplace of ideas' theory of free speech has been enormously influential in the United States. It is the reason why courts mistrust government intervention, even when it is intended to foster free speech. It provides one explanation for their strict scrutiny of viewpoint or content-based regulation of speech, for arguably such regulation distorts the working of a free market for the exchange of ideas.[27] Just as liberal economists consider it is wrong to interfere with the operation of a free market in goods and services, so in Holmes J.'s view it was equally undesirable to manipulate the market in ideas. The truth would emerge from a 'free trade in ideas' or intellectual competition.

---

[22] See s. 2(iii) below. [23] See ch. II, ss. 4 and 5 below. [24] See s. 5 of this chapter.
[25] See s. 2(iii) below. [26] 250 US 616, 630–1 (1919).
[27] See ch. II, s. 2 below for development of these points.

On one view, Holmes J. thought that unregulated competition in the *actual*, and not just an *ideal*, market is conducive to the discovery of truth.[28] Or he may have taken a relativist (or gloomy) view of truth: whatever emerges from the competitive market in ideas is the truth, and nothing more can be said. That view is far removed from Mill's perspective, which assumes instead a lively discussion of rival views, as if society were conducting a perpetual seminar. In any event, Holmes J.'s version of the truth argument rests on shaky grounds. If it can never be claimed on intellectu- ally defensible grounds that one proposition is stronger than another, the notion of truth becomes more or less empty. In that event, it is hard to see why a democratic- ally elected government should not interfere with the free speech market, just as it may regulate the working of an economic market to ensure, say, open competition and stamp out unfair trading practices. A preference for the marketplace, as opp- osed to governmental regulation, can be justified on many grounds, for example, suspicion of government or a concern for the free speech rights of individuals when their speech is suppressed, but such a choice seems wholly unrelated to Holmes J.'s eccentric views on the impossibility of discovering truth.[29]

Other criticisms can be made of the marketplace theory.[30] First, the market- place is not in practice open to everyone who wants to communicate his ideas. Some views are widely disseminated by the media, others hardly figure in public discussion. Differences in the availability of ideas have little to do with their truth. The marketplace may not therefore provide a forum for the vigorous public debate that Mill and other proponents of free speech envisage. Secondly, insofar as the marketplace theory is an argument about the discovery of truth, it assumes that contributions to the marketplace represent the views of their proponents; ideas should not be put forward primarily because the speaker, say, a tabloid edi- tor, considers they will be popular or that their inclusion will lead to increased sales of his newspaper. For any truth argument assumes attitudes on the part of speakers of sincerity and truthfulness. But we know that newspapers and other publications are often sold or issued to make money, and that, sadly, a concern for truth may be subordinate to other considerations. Finally, the argument assumes that readers and other recipients consider claims made in the marketplace ration- ally, determining whether their acceptance will lead to a better society or an improved lifestyle. That is surely too optimistic an assumption.

Some regulation of the free speech marketplace must surely be conceded, if expression is to be communicated effectively. At the very least, some government intervention is justified, if only to prevent the clash of speech, whether on the streets, on airwaves, or at public meetings. That is widely admitted.[31] Arguably,

---

28 Williams (n. 14 above), 214–15.   29 See Schauer, ch. 2, esp. 19–21.
30 S. Ingber, 'The Marketplace of Ideas: a Legitimizing Myth' [1984] *Duke Law Jo* 1.
31 Even Alexander Meiklejohn, a prominent defender of free political speech, recognized that pro- cedural rules are necessary to regulate the order and length of speech at public meetings: see *Free Speech and its Relation to Self-Government* (New York: Harper, 1948), expanded and retitled as *Political Freedom: The Constitutional Powers of the People* (New York: HarperCollins, 1960), 19–28.

regulation of the mass media is justifiable to ensure that a variety of views can be heard in the marketplace.[32] In some contexts, notably that of commercial advertising where it is difficult for the public to assess the veracity of the claims made to it, intervention is reasonable in order to curtail deception and fraud.[33] On its own the marketplace theory seems a poor argument for freedom of speech. The case has to be made that an unregulated marketplace better serves freedom of speech than other alternatives. And whatever Holmes J. said, it is not really an argument about truth.

(ii) Free speech as an aspect of self-fulfilment

A second major theory of free speech sees it as an integral aspect of each individual's right to self-development and fulfilment. Restrictions on what we are allowed to say and write, or (on some formulations of the theory) to hear and read, inhibit our personality and its growth. A right to express beliefs and political attitudes instantiates or reflects what it is to be human. The argument asserts that there is an individual right to freedom of speech, even though its exercise may be inimical to the welfare of society. Unlike the theories which relate free discussion to the discovery of truth or to the maintenance of a democracy, this rationale is not necessarily consequentialist, although it might be defended in utilitarian terms. The theory might regard freedom of speech as an intrinsic, independent good; alternatively, its exercise might be regarded as leading to the development of more reflective and mature individuals and so benefiting society as a whole.[34] Courts need not concern themselves with this point; however, as will be seen, other difficulties in applying the theory may concern them.

At the level of general philosophy it is reasonable to ask why freedom of speech is particularly important to a person's self-fulfilment. It is far from clear that unlimited free speech is necessarily conducive to personal happiness or that it satisfies more basic human needs and wants than, say, adequate housing and education. Yet unless some reasons can be given for treating expression as particularly significant, the case for a free speech principle made on this basis becomes hard to distinguish from general libertarian claims to do anything which an individual may consider integral to his personality. There is perhaps something uniquely valuable in intellectual self-development. The reflective mind, conscious of options and the possibilities for growth, distinguishes human beings from animals. Freedom of speech is also closely linked to other fundamental freedoms which reflect this aspect of what it is to be human: freedoms of religion, thought, and conscience. But, unlike those freedoms, the exercise of freedom of speech or expression may harm others by, for instance, damaging their reputation or infringing privacy or intellectual property rights; speech is not self-regarding.

---

[32] See ch. XII, s. 2 below for discussion of this topic.

[33] See ch. XI below for regulation of commercial speech.

[34] T. Campbell, 'Rationales for Freedom of Communication', in T. Campbell and W. Sadurski (eds.), *Freedom of Communication* (Aldershot: Dartmouth, 1994) 33–4.

Furthermore, if intellectual development is particularly valuable, rights to education, to cultural goods, and to travel should also be protected. Something more must be said to establish why speech is special.

Admittedly, there are practical reasons why freedom of speech might be singled out for constitutional protection and distinguished from other rights, for example, to an appropriate level of education, which are similarly related to intellectual and moral growth. Freedom of speech is usually regarded as a liberty against the state, or a 'negative freedom', and largely for this reason may be thought more capable of judicial interpretation and enforcement than positive rights to, say, an adequate education. The provision of good schools and universities involves the allocation of resources, and probably public expenditure; framers of constitutions, and courts, may reasonably consider that educational rights should not be legally enforceable, even though they are as closely linked to the self-development of individuals as freedom of speech.

The problems which confront the courts in this context reflect some of these difficulties. Assuming that self-fulfilment arguments do justify a constitutional guarantee of free speech, problems occur in distinguishing between genuine asser-tions of a right to free speech and claims to other freedoms, which might equally be supported by reference to the case from self-fulfilment and development. They are most acute in determining the meaning of 'speech', a topic considered in Chapter III. Is, for instance, an asserted right to incur unlimited election expendi-ture really a claim to free speech or a claim to the unregulated use of money?[35] At first glance, the right might be supported by arguments about self-fulfilment at least in a material sense, but on closer inspection it surely has little connection with the particular view of intellectual and moral development underlying a rights-based view of free speech. A similar question arises when deciding how far pornography qualifies as 'speech' for the purposes of the First Amendment or other free speech provision. A claim for constitutional protection which rests on the role such material plays in satisfying sexual needs can be treated as a free speech argument, but may be more soundly based on a general freedom to moral auton-omy.[36] That general freedom is closely linked to self-fulfilment, as is freedom of speech, but that does not mean that the two freedoms are identical. The self-fulfilment rationale for free speech easily lends support to arguments which are hard to distinguish from general libertarian or moral autonomy claims.

These problems are not removed if, as argued by Ronald Dworkin, the case for free speech protection is grounded on fundamental background rights to human dignity and to equality of concern and respect.[37] Again, this argument does not provide any clear basis for determining the scope of a free speech principle or for

[35] See ch. III, s. 3 below, where it is argued that expenditure restrictions engage freedom of speech because they are intended to limit expression.

[36] See R. M. Dworkin's argument for a right to read pornography on the basis of a broad freedom to moral independence in 'Is there a Right to Pornography?' (1981) 1 *OJLS* 177.

[37] *Taking Rights Seriously* (n. 6 above), 266–78, 364–8.

distinguishing it from a general claim to personal liberty. Take a claim that individuals have a right to choose the manner of their dress or follow their sexual lifestyle free from any public constraint. Should those claims be regarded as aspects of a broad free speech right, of privacy rights, or of a general right to personal liberty? Dworkin's argument is of little help here. Respect for the rights of, say, homosexuals may be based on the same underlying arguments of dignity and equality which support free speech rights, but it would be wrong to conflate the rights. Further, the argument does not show why speech is special, or why it should be singled out from other claims which may be made by libertarians.

There is a further problem which should be noted here, but which will be discussed later in this chapter: it can be argued that the exercise of freedom of speech infringes human dignity or the rights of other persons affected by the speech to be treated with equal respect and concern.[38] This argument is most frequently made to justify the imposition of limits on hate speech and pornography demeaning women. It is not necessary at this stage to say whether it is persuasive. But it is appropriate to point out here that free speech justifications, using as their basis self-fulfilment, dignity, and equality rights are at least vulnerable to this argument.

Quite apart from these criticisms levelled at the intellectual coherence of the theory, it may not explain the terms of particular free speech clauses or the jurisprudence of constitutional courts. On the versions of the theory considered up to this point, it would be hard to justify the application of the free speech principle to the disclosure of *information*, in contradistinction to the dissemination of *ideas* and *opinions*. This point is even more apparent if emphasis is placed on the rights or interests of the speaker. While an unlimited, or at least very wide, freedom to communicate one's own views may be considered an integral aspect of self-development or human dignity, it is surely far-fetched to make the same claim for the disclosure of news and information, unless perhaps the communicator has assembled or is in some way responsible for it. But some free expression provisions, notably Article 10 of the ECHR, explicitly cover the disclosure of information, while in other jurisdictions court rulings have established that disclosure is covered by freedom of speech. Such coverage is better explained under a theory, like the argument from democracy, which emphasizes the interests of the recipients of communications. Similarly the extension of free speech rights to legal persons, such as corporations, makes little sense in terms of self-fulfilment theories, and the same can be said of the application of the free speech principle to the press and other media.[39]

These reservations do not, however, apply to the variant of the argument put forward by Thomas Scanlon.[40] His argument for freedom of expression proceeds

---

[38] See s. 4 below.

[39] For the speech of corporations, see ch. III, s. 3 below, and for free speech and the media, see ch. XII below.

[40] Also see the similar arguments of T. Nagel, 'Personal Rights and Public Space' (1995) 24 *Philosophy and Public Affairs* 83, and of D. A. Strauss, 'Persuasion, Autonomy, and Freedom of Expression' (1991) 91 *Columbia Law Rev.* 334.

from the premise 'that the powers of a state are limited to those that citizens could recognize while still regarding themselves as equal, autonomous, rational agents'.[41] A person is only autonomous if he is free to weigh for himself the arguments for various courses of action that others wish to put before him. The government, Scanlon asserts, is therefore not entitled to suppress speech on the grounds either that its audience will form harmful beliefs or that it may commit harmful acts as a result of these beliefs. The first limb of this conclusion is similar to that reached by John Stuart Mill; Scanlon indeed refers to his own thesis as 'the Millian Principle', though unlike Mill's argument it does not rest on any assumption that truth will emerge from open discussion. Scanlon's thesis is clearly rights-based rather than consequentialist. The individual has a right to hear views and to consider acting on them, even though this process will damage society—although it is conceded that some limits may be imposed during times of extreme emergency. On the other hand, unlike other versions of the self-fulfilment case, it focuses on the rights or interests of the recipients of speech. Another point is worth noting. Scanlon emphasizes that the Millian Principle does not exhaust the arguments for freedom of expression; other theories might, for example, justify a wide right of access to the means of expression. His case is simply that under the Principle the government is unable to use certain grounds for limiting speech.

Compared with some other free speech theories, this argument provides a relatively coherent explanation of much judicial interpretation of free expression provisions. It should be noted incidentally that it is not based on the history and structure of the United States Constitution, and so it may shed light on the interpretation of the free speech clause in any constitution. An important point is that the argument is not limited to political speech, but applies to all speech (or expressive conduct) which provides the audience with information and opinion relevant to the formation of its own beliefs. This is reflected in the case-law of all the jurisdictions considered in this book. Although political speech may be accorded a special degree of protection, artistic and moral discourse, sexually explicit material, and to some extent commercial speech, are also covered. Scanlon's concern with the legitimacy of the government reasons for restricting speech reflects many decisions of the US Supreme Court; measures aimed at the content of particular ideas or discriminating between varieties of political and social communication are subject to strict scrutiny.[42] The theory also distinguishes between the communication of information relevant to the development of political and moral beliefs which is to be protected against regulation, and the revelation of technical information which merely provides the audience with the means to accomplish harmful acts, for example, military and scientific secrets, and which may be prohibited.[43]

The theory has been criticized, to some extent because of the weaknesses of the notion of personal autonomy which lies at its root.[44] It seems that autonomy is

---

[41] Scanlon, 162.   [42] See ch. II, s. 2 below.   [43] Scanlon, 159–60.
[44] Schauer, 67–72, and S. J. Brison, 'The Autonomy Defense of Free Speech' (1998) 108 *Ethics* 312, 323–36.

ascribed to human beings as an element of their essential dignity, rather than an attribute that all people in fact enjoy or appreciate. So the theory might be able to resist the charge that many people are generally incapable of exercising real autonomy. They are unable, it may be said, rationally to consider views and arguments put to them, so unfettered freedom of expression may lead to foolish and dangerous choices, for example, to vote for fascist political parties. Scanlon might be able to dismiss that criticism, because he considers that persons must see themselves as autonomous unless they are prepared to surrender their independent judgement to the state: '[a]n autonomous person cannot accept without independent consideration the judgment of others as to what he should believe or what he should do'.[45] But Scanlon could not so easily reject an argument that autonomous people might deliberately, after careful reflection, choose to allow the state to determine that certain types of speech are too dangerous to be tolerated. Almost everyone would agree, I think, that we should be protected from exposure to false claims by commercial advertisers; hardly anyone is able independently to evaluate such claims before, say, making a disastrous purchase. So the proscription of deceptive advertising is compatible with moral autonomy. But many people might make the same argument about, say, racist hate speech or hard-core pornography. Autonomous people might well agree that some of them find it difficult to evaluate this material, so its availability should be regulated by the state. But they would not surrender their freedom to argue against maintenance of the regulation, and they would require that the scope of any restriction be determined by independent courts.[46]

Scanlon himself reconsidered the soundness of his arguments. In a later article he doubted whether the audience's interest in having a good environment for the formation of its attitudes really justified the broad autonomy principle.[47] Some restrictions on free speech, for example, on saturation advertising by a candidate for office, could be justified in order to foster a climate for rational thought by the public. In some circumstances, he argued, speech may legitimately be restricted on paternalistic grounds, while his original theory had left no room for limitations on, say, cigarette advertising. Another objection to the autonomy thesis is that it does not really do justice to the interests of the *speaker*.[48] It seems odd, for example, to justify the protection of unpopular speech (for example, street demonstrations or underground literature) entirely by reference to the interests of the audience or readership (which may be negligible), but ignore the stronger claims in these circumstances of the demonstrator or publisher. Moreover, Dworkin pointed out that much conventional, political speech hardly offers fresh information or ideas for the public to reflect on and, therefore, would not appear to be covered by the Millian Principle. Despite these points, Scanlon's thesis is

---

[45] Scanlon, 163.

[46] For the significance of judicial review in the free speech context, see s. 5 of this chapter.

[47] 'Freedom of Expression and Categories of Expression' (1979) 40 *Univ of Pittsburgh Law Rev* 519.

[48] Introduction to R. M. Dworkin (ed.), *The Philosophy of Law* (Oxford: OUP, 1977), 14–16.

important. It draws attention to one reason why the suppression of speech is wrong: it prevents free people from enjoying access to ideas and information which they need to make up their own minds.

(iii) The argument from citizen participation in a democracy

This is probably the most easily understandable, and certainly the most fashionable, free speech theory in modern Western democracies. A representative judicial view is this extract from Brandeis J.'s judgment in *Whitney* v. *California*:

Those who won our independence believed that the final end of the State was to make men free to develop their faculties; and that in its government the deliberative forces should prevail over the arbitrary . . . They believed that freedom to think as you will and to speak as you think are means indispensable to the discovery and spread of political truth; . . . that the greatest menace to freedom is an inert people; that public discussion is a political duty; and that this should be a fundamental principle of American government.[49]

In the United States the argument has been particularly associated with the writings of Alexander Meiklejohn.[50] He thought the primary purpose of the First Amendment is to protect the right of all citizens to understand political issues in order to participate effectively in the working of democracy. The Amendment represented the commitment of the people to representative self-government. In some of its leading judgments, particularly in the context of libel proceedings, the German Constitutional Court has similarly recognized the crucial role of freedom of expression in the formation of public opinion on political questions; as a result Article 5 has been particularly broadly construed in this area.[51]

   The argument is attractive largely because it is relatively easy to understand. To some extent it rests on the rules, values, and commitments explicitly stated in the particular constitutional document, as well as on the more abstract philosophical theorizing which characterizes the arguments from truth and the right to self-fulfilment. For courts concerned with legal interpretation this feature is an asset; conceptual shortcomings of the argument are less troublesome for them. One or two aspects of the argument are worth noting. Insofar as the argument is couched in terms of the need to expose citizens to a wide variety of views and to provide it with enough information to hold government to account, a free speech clause would only cover political expression; there would be little justification for extending its protection to literary and artistic discourse, let alone sexually explicit material or commercial advertising. Nor would it cover speech which challenged

---

   [49] 274 US 357, 375–8 (1927).
   [50] See in particular *Free Speech and its Relation to Self-Government* (n. 31 above), and 'The First Amendment is an Absolute' [1961] *Supreme Court Rev* 245.
   [51] See e.g. 12 BVerfGE 113 (1961) (article by a judge replying to criticism of his political attitudes held to be immune from libel proceedings); 61 BVerfGE 1 (1982) (exaggerated attack on a far-right political party held to be political speech immune from libel proceedings).

the existence of democratic government and institutions. The purpose of speech from this perspective is to serve democracy, so it would be wrong to tolerate the circulation of material advocating its overthrow.[52] Yet liberal legal systems do protect non-political speech, although criticism of government and its officials may enjoy a greater degree of protection than, say, commercial speech. That suggests that courts may consider other justifications underpin the free speech clause, in addition to the argument from democracy, or alternatively that argument should be recast to explain why courts do, and should, hold the clause to cover non-political discourse.

In its simplest form the argument from democracy is firmly utilitarian or consequentialist. This has some awkward repercussions, for a government might consider that sometimes the values of a democracy, including its long-term commitment to free speech, can best be preserved by the suppression of some speech. Unlike the case for free speech based on rights to self-fulfilment or moral autonomy, the argument from democracy does not appear necessarily to trump a counterclaim that the exercise of free speech might in some situations be contrary to the public welfare. It is, of course, possible to make further refinements to the basic utilitarian argument in rebuttal of this point: in the long run, it may be said, the maintenance of a confident democracy is best guaranteed by protecting freedom of speech in all (or almost all) circumstances, so temporary regulation might induce political unrest, undermine the acceptability of other laws, and so on.[53]

This difficulty is one aspect of the central weakness of the argument from democracy in the simple form put forward by Meiklejohn. If the maintenance of democracy is the foundation for free speech, how can one argue against the regulation or even suppression of speech by a democracy acting through its elected representatives? As Schauer puts it, 'the very notion of popular sovereignty supporting the argument from democracy argues against any limitation on that sovereignty, and thereby argues against recognition of an independent principle of freedom of speech.'[54] It is difficult to resist this conclusion if the *majoritarian* conception of democracy is accepted, for that allows majorities to determine the limits of the rights individuals are entitled to exercise.

But it is preferable to hold an alternative conception of democracy, under which freedom of speech should be more broadly understood. On what Dworkin terms the *constitutional* conception of democracy, political institutions must respect the right of all citizens to be treated with equal respect and concern.[55] Everyone, including, of course, members of minority groups and parties, is entitled to participate in public discourse and debate, as a result of which temporary political majorities are formed. This right is so fundamental that it cannot be surrendered to the powers of the elected majority. It would be wrong for the majority to

[52] This is the view of R. Bork, 'Neutral Principles and Some First Amendment Problems' (1971) 47 *Indiana Law Jo* 1.   [53] Munro (n. 18 above), 249–53.
[54] Schauer, 41.   [55] Dworkin, 15–26.

suppress the right of minorities to express their dissent. On this perspective, defamatory attacks on public officials, hate speech, and extremist speech challenging the legitimacy of existing institutions must all be tolerated, because the state is not free to determine the boundaries of public discourse.[56] Sexually explicit material is covered by freedom of expression, because it too could claim to be part of public discourse; at least it would be wrong to concede government the authority to exclude it. The relationship of free speech to democracy is quite different in this version of the argument. While under the simpler version associated with Alexander Meiklejohn the commitment to democracy justifies freedom of speech, under this more complex theory it is the equal rights of everyone to participate in society through the exercise of free speech rights and of the related freedoms of assembly and association, which underpin the commitment to democratic government.[57]

This version of the third argument for freedom of speech draws on elements of the other two already considered. The rights of minorities to contribute to political debate should be respected, partly because they may have better ideas than those of the elected majority. The right of all people to equal respect and concern, which underlies their right to engage in public discourse, has close links to the arguments for free speech from dignity and self-fulfilment. It also emphasizes that government should not be permitted to delimit the contours of public discourse; otherwise it could privilege the speech of some individuals by ruling the contributions of others, as it were, out of bounds. To an extent, therefore, it also draws on the fourth 'negative' argument for free speech protection, to be considered shortly.

Although it has to be significantly reformulated to meet theoretical objections, the argument from democracy has been much the most influential theory in the development of contemporary free speech law. The fact that to some extent obscenity and commercial speech, in addition to political discourse, are covered by the freedom of expression provision does not disprove this conclusion. The extension of constitutional protection to these types of expression has been controversial. But courts are understandably reluctant to countenance the regulation of (at least some) non-political speech, either because they distrust the ability of the legislature to distinguish it from genuine discussion of public affairs, or because they fear that the latter will be inhibited by the imposition of restrictions on freedom of expression. Other chapters of this book discuss whether categories of 'speech' can or should be distinguished.[58] Distinctions of this sort, or that between 'speech' and 'conduct', are best made by reflecting on the purposes of a free speech principle, and on this point the argument from democracy offers the most helpful tool for analysis. Admittedly, courts are sometimes influenced in their interpretation of free speech provisions by other rationales for their existence.

---

[56] D. A. J. Richards, *Free Speech and the Politics of Identity* (New York: OUP, 1999), 22–35; R. C. Post, 'The Constitutional Concept of Public Discourse' (1999) 103 *Harvard Law Rev.* 601.

[57] See M. H. Redish, 'The Value of Free Speech' (1982) 130 *Univ of Pennsylvania Law Rev* 591.

[58] In particular, see chs. X (pornography) and XI (commercial speech) below.

This may be understandable, for no argument has a monopoly of truth and constitutional provisions may indeed be framed in the light of various philosophical perspectives.[59] But case-law shows the central importance of political speech, and this in its turn indicates, it is suggested, the pre-eminence of this third argument for free speech.

(iv) Suspicion of government

So far we have examined positive theories for free speech protection. They claim that there is something special about the characteristics or consequences of speech: it enables the discovery of truth, is crucial to the working of a democratic constitution, or is an aspect of human self-fulfilment or autonomy. A fourth theory argues that there are particularly strong reasons to be suspicious of government in this context; it is a negative argument in that it highlights the evils of regulation, rather than the good of free speech.[60] Frederick Schauer places great emphasis on the argument. He points to the history of attempts by governments and other authorities such as the Catholic Church to suppress speech. They have often outlawed speech which turns out to make accurate claims and which eventually becomes widely accepted, even by political or ecclesiastical authority itself. Much misery is occasioned by these efforts. It is difficult to draw a line between speech which might appropriately be regulated and speech which in any liberal society should be tolerated. This point is particularly evident in areas like hate speech or the publication of sexually explicit material, where a law proscribing extremist speech or hard-core pornography can too easily be applied to cover the expression of radical or subversive ideas. Governments, moreover, have strong reasons to fear the impact of these ideas, so they are naturally tempted to repress them. A free speech principle is necessary to counteract this tendency. Schauer concludes his argument in this way:

Freedom of speech is based on large part on a distrust of the ability of government to make the necessary distinctions, a distrust of governmental determinations of truth and falsity, an appreciation of the fallibility of political leaders, and a somewhat deeper distrust of government power in a more general sense.[61]

The argument is a powerful one, and it should be admitted that the positive arguments often use it to bolster their own case. Mill's and Scanlon's arguments, for instance, both contend it is wrong for government to decide whether citizens have access to ideas, though the theories differ with regard to the reasons why that is wrong.

But it is very doubtful whether the argument makes the case for free speech. Two questions should be asked of it. The first is whether government is less to be

---

[59] Schauer, 85–6, and in 'Codifying the First Amendment: *New York* v. *Ferber*' [1982] *Supreme Court Review* 285, 308–17.   [60] Schauer, 80.
[61] Ibid., 86.

trusted in this area than it is in others such as the regulation of sexual conduct or of economic activity. Arguably, popular pressure has meant that even in generally liberal societies, governments are as inclined to penalize minority sexual practices as they are radical speech. Moreover, we need a theory which enables the legislature, courts, and commentators, to distinguish speech which enjoys the coverage of a free speech principle or constitutional clause from conduct which falls outside it and which can therefore be regulated. A purely negative argument cannot do that, since we still need to know when and why government acts improperly, if it, say, outlaws hard-core pornography or the burning of a national flag. Schauer's argument does not provide any reasons why such material or activity should be covered by a free speech or expression clause.[62] The negative case for free speech is parasitic on positive arguments; it reinforces the latter, providing reasons why government should not be trusted to make distinctions in this area, but it does not itself show why speech is special.

The second question is not commonly asked in the United States, but is posed more frequently now in Europe: is there any reason to be particularly suspicious of *government* regulation of free speech, compared with censorship or interference by other bodies such as churches, commercial companies, or even media corporations? Historically, the greatest dangers to the expression of novel political and social ideas have been posed by authoritarian states, admittedly sometimes to protect church doctrine. The Inquisition was able to suppress Galileo's teachings, because Catholic states during the seventeenth century enforced church teaching.[63] Constitutional rights have generally been guaranteed only against state action, because constitutionalism in its intellectual and political origins has been concerned to limit government, not private authority. But there is no necessary reason why they should be so limited. It will be seen in the next chapter that, in Germany, free speech rights and values must be honoured in private law disputes; constitutional courts in Germany, France, and Italy require the law to guarantee the freedom, even if that entails the imposition of restrictions on the interests of private media corporations.[64]

The extension of free speech rights beyond cases of government interference is controversial. The imposition of limits on, say, the rights of broadcasting companies to draw up their own programme schedules certainly restricts the liberty of those companies. As these limits require the institution of public regulatory authorities by government, they may pose dangers to freedom of speech greater than those cured by their imposition. It is unnecessary to resolve this controversy now.[65] But its very existence shows the shakiness of an argument for freedom of speech based on a distrust of government. The claim that government has a duty

---

[62] See the complex arguments of L. Alexander and P. Horton, 'The Impossibility of a Free Speech Principle' (1983) 78 *North Western University Law Rev* 1319, 1329–46.

[63] The continued existence of blasphemy laws is a legacy of cooperation between secular authority and the church: see ch. V, s. 5(i) below.   [64] Ch. II, ss. 4 and 6(i)–(ii) below.

[65] For further discussion, see ch. III, s. 5 and ch. XII, s. 5 below.

to promote the free speech values of widespread uninhibited debate or tolerance is not a trivial one; it argues that free speech is too important to be left to the play of economic forces in an unregulated market. It cannot be met simply by making a rival claim that the reason that we protect free speech in the first place is because we are fearful of government in this context.

3. Free Speech Interests

Another approach to analysis of the justifications for free speech is to explore the interests of people involved in the expression of ideas and information: to what extent do the participants have a real interest in unrestrained communication, and how far do those interests strengthen the arguments for freedom of speech and identify concrete free speech rights? The discussion may afford insights into the arguments of principle considered in the previous section, but more emphasis is placed here on the relations between free speech interests and legal rules. Free speech may be looked at from the perspective of the speaker, the audience (or recipient), and finally, of the bystanders or general public. One general point should be made at the outset. When we refer to the interest of a speaker or audience, we could have (at least) one of three things in mind: the *actual* interest in the communication of a particular idea or piece of information, the *general* interest that a person or group has in the communication of ideas of the character transmitted, and the interest *ascribed* by the law or the courts to that person. The first two statements are descriptive; they assert that a speaker or a listener is really interested in putting across, or considering, a particular idea or type of idea. The third is normative. If it is claimed, for instance, that in the context of broadcasting, it is the interests or rights of listeners and viewers which are paramount,[66] that is probably another way of saying that the law should recognize their claims in priority to those of the broadcasters when they conflict, although the actual interest of a programme-maker in transmitting the broadcast item may be greater than that of viewers as a whole. The law ascribes, for one reason or other, a (greater) free speech interest to one person or group than to another.

(i) The speaker's interest in communicating ideas and information

Intuitively, the speaker's interest seems paramount. This appears most obvious, if rights to free speech are linked with fundamental rights to self-fulfilment and development. Equally, speakers as participators in the political process, say, politicians and political commentators, have important interests recognized by the argument from democracy. Moreover, speakers and other communicators

---

[66] See White J. in *Red Lion Broadcasting* v. *FCC* 395 US 367, 390 (1969).

generally have a close, perhaps an intense, involvement with the content of their message, whether it is political, literary, or artistic. What exactly is the interest? Scanlon has argued that it lies in the speaker's ability to bring ideas and propositions to the attention of a wide audience (though not necessarily the widest possible).[67] The formula, however, raises some questions. Should, for example, the interests of a publisher or distributor be equated with those of the speaker and author, as Scanlon appears to imply?

On one view, some investigation of the speaker's real motives and purposes may be necessary to determine whether his interest should be taken into account in deciding whether free speech protection is appropriate. When book and magazine publishers disseminate their material to make a commercial profit, or a politician makes claims (of doubtful accuracy) purely to enhance his own standing, a claim that freedom of speech should be protected to respect the speaker's interest in communicating his message appears, without more argument, relatively thin. It is certainly weaker than the case which can be made by a writer whose sole aim is to contribute to political or social discussion. Obviously, speech published with this object is the archetypal type of expression to merit coverage by a free speech provision. But there are in fact great difficulties in denying a publication protection, merely because the author was not entirely disinterested. A rigorous examination of motives to exclude speech made for profit would leave little immune from regulation. Moreover, the interests of the recipient should be considered as well. It is often of no concern to him that the author was influenced by the prospect of self-advancement, if the speech contains valuable ideas or information. This point is particularly relevant to political speech, where it should make no difference to the degree of legal protection whether it is disinterested or misleading. Governments are not to be trusted to make this sort of judgement. On the other hand, an economic motive on the part of a publisher might in other contexts lead to the refusal of free speech coverage. One argument for denying commercial speech and hard-core pornography the degree of legal protection afforded political discourse is that much of it is published purely for gain; further, there may be less reservation about the state's ability to draw lines in these contexts, for example, to determine that some types of advertising are inherently deceptive or that extreme hard-core pornography lacks any redeeming merit.[68]

These considerations are also relevant to another question: should a corporation be able to claim freedom of speech? Related questions also arise in the case of newspapers, political parties, and pressure groups, though often the issues there are clarified (and to some extent complicated) by a separate provision in the constitution for freedom of the press and of association. If the right to free speech is primarily viewed as the speaker's right, linked to ideas of human dignity and

---

[67] 'Freedom of Expression and Categories of Expression' (n. 47 above), 521.

[68] For further consideration of the arguments in the context of pornography and commercial speech, see chs. X and XI respectively below.

self-fulfilment, it is hard to see any justification for the protection of corporate speech. But legal systems do consider it covered by freedom of speech or expression provisions.[69] In a leading United States case, the majority of the Supreme Court, invalidating a Massachusetts law which had prohibited banks and business corporations from making contributions to influence referendum campaigns, found the recipients' interests decisive in its decision to hold corporate speech covered by the First Amendment: 'The inherent worth of the speech in terms of its capacity for informing the public does not depend upon the identity of its source, whether corporation, association, union or individual.'[70] The decision shows how important it is to examine interests, other than those of the speaker or publisher, in determining whether to apply a free speech provision.

Would it be right to recognize free speech rights when the claimant has no intention to communicate his ideas to another person? It is arguable that there must be some communication between a speaker and his audience for freedom of speech to be engaged. Free speech theories based on the discovery of truth and from the role speech plays in a democracy both assume communication. Freedom of expression would not be at issue on those theories if, say, a state were to confiscate personal diaries which were kept wholly for the delight of the diarist, though other rights, notably freedom of thought and of property would be. It might, however, be harder to deny a speech claim here, if the self-fulfilment rationale for that freedom were accepted; talking to oneself, as it were, might be as crucial on that argument as communication to others. However, as we have seen, on that rationale free speech claims easily collapse into broader libertarian arguments.

(ii) The audience interest in receiving ideas and information

The audience (or recipient) interest is particularly relevant in the case of information, in contradistinction to opinion and ideas. Restrictions on the free flow of political information are suspect because they invade the audience's interests in having enough material before it to make informed choices and to participate fully in the democratic process. A free speech challenge to official secrets laws based on a civil servant's interest in disclosing the contents of government files is much less attractive. The same point applies to commercial information: the interest of consumers in information about the prices, availability, and attributes of products and services is much stronger than that of the advertiser in their disclosure.[71] The arguments from truth and from democracy attach particular weight to the interests of recipients; ideas, as well as information, should be freely communicable in order to enable recipients to discover the truth and to participate fully in

---

[69] See further ch. III, s. 3(ii) below.

[70] Powell J. in *First National Bank of Boston* v. *Bellotti* 435 US 765, 777 (1978).

[71] In the leading US case, extending the coverage of the First Amendment to informational advertising, the challenge was brought by a consumers' association: *Virginia State Board of Pharmacy* v. *Virginia Citizens Consumer Council* 425 US 748 (1976): see ch. XI below.

public discourse. On the other hand, the speaker's interest may be more involved, if a legislature proscribes controversial political publications which few members of the public are actually interested in reading or viewing. Moreover, a speaker has an interest in putting his ideas across, even if the audience has heard them all before from other sources.

These considerations show how wise it is for free speech provisions, like Article 10 of the ECHR and Article 5 of the German Basic Law, to cover the interests of both speaker and recipient.[72] Each has rights which can be asserted in appropriate cases. In most situations they will equally be affected by restrictions on expression. But sometimes one is in a better position to assert a right, say to receive information, than the other is to claim a right to speak. For example, the speaker may be physically outside the jurisdiction, or unable (or unwilling for various reasons) to face the challenge of initiating litigation. These circumstances do not present any particular legal difficulties where the constitutional (or statutory) text recognizes that both speaker and audience have free speech rights.

The position is much less straightforward where there is an audience interest, but there is no speaker. Larry Alexander suggests that freedom of expression would be engaged if government banned the sale of toy guns, because it considered that children playing with them would acquire militaristic ideas.[73] Yet there is no speaker in this case, and no communication. Or the potential speaker may not want to speak. Is there a free speech right to compel the government, or anyone else for that matter, to disclose information it wishes to keep secret? Attention to the audience's interest alone might suggest that such a free speech right should be upheld. In fact, the jurisdictions considered in this book are unwilling generally to derive a constitutional right to know, or to acquire information, from the free speech clause, though many countries now have freedom of information statutes.[74] This reluctance can be defended. It is one thing to recognize a recipient right to receive speech when the speaker is unwilling to assert his rights or has forfeited his right because, say, he speaks from an environment, such as prison or a military base, where speech rights are restricted.[75] It would surely, however, be a distortion of a free speech principle to invoke it where there is no speaker at all, as in Alexander's toy guns case, or there is no willing speaker. Furthermore, in the latter situation a private individual or company may have an interest in not disclosing its information, which should be recognized in the formulation and interpretation of free speech provisions. In short, recipients do not have a free speech right to compel others to speak.

These points qualify Schauer's argument that recipients are the primary object of free speech concern, and that speakers have derivative rights, recognized only in

---

[72] See ch. II, ss. 4 and 5 below.

[73] 'Freedom of Expression as a Human Right', in T. Campbell, J. Goldsworthy, and A. Stone (eds.), *Protecting Human Rights* (New York: OUP, 2003), 39, 54.

[74] This topic is considered in ch. III, s. 7 below.

[75] For speech in these circumstances, see ch. XIV, ss. 3 and 5 below.

order to protect the formers' interests.[76] If that were the case, the law should uphold constitutional free speech rights of access to information, and recognize that free speech is engaged if government bans toy guns or soldiers to discourage militaristic attitudes. Further, the law would more readily uphold than it does, even in European jurisdictions, the free speech interests of readers and viewers when they conflict with those of the editor or owner of a newspaper or the controller of a television channel. Readers might claim, for example, that a newspaper should give some coverage to foreign affairs, or give more treatment to parliamentary debates than it does to football matches, because their free speech interest is as strongly engaged as that of the editor to determine the contents of his paper. No court would accept that argument. Freedom of speech in this context and press freedom are primarily, perhaps solely, rights of the editor or owner, not those of readers or of the general public.[77]

Schauer, I think, underestimates the extent to which the classic free speech theories rely on speaker interests. Take the argument from democracy. That does not rest primarily on the audience or recipient interest in hearing the ideas of others or acquiring information from them, as if the citizens are to be equated with consumers dependent on the offerings of a few producers and distributors. That demeans the role of citizens. The argument from democracy, as we have seen, is more plausibly framed in terms of active citizens who have an equal right to engage in public discourse and to exchange ideas and information.[78] Secondly, even if Schauer were right in terms of the relative importance of speaker and recipient interests at the theoretical level, courts may be hesitant to draw inferences from his conclusion when they determine concrete free speech cases. A court might properly decide that, although the general argument for free speech attaches as much, or conceivably a little more, weight to the recipient interest than it does to that of speakers, in practice the speaker's interest in a particular communication is stronger than that of the audience. It would be wrong for it to uphold a free speech claim on behalf of the recipient when that would show disrespect for the speaker's interest in, say, not communicating his ideas or sharing information with the recipient.

(iii) The bystanders' (or public) interest in speech

Finally, the public interest should be considered when framing and applying a free speech rule. This may sometimes be hard to distinguish from the audience interest, as is shown by the passage from Powell J.'s judgment in the United States corporate speech case.[79] Mass communications, whether delivered by the media or by corporations, are rarely aimed at a particular group of people separable from the general public. So the argument from democracy could be framed either in

---

[76] Schauer, 105–6, 158–60.   [77] See ch. XII below for further discussion.
[78] See s. 2(iii) above.   [79] N. 70 above.

terms of the rights of individuals to receive information and views pertinent to their political choices, or in terms of the general public interest in the disclosure of such information. The latter claim cannot really be distinguished from the argument that, whatever interest people may actually have in communicating and considering ideas and information, there is an important public good or value to freedom of speech. That argument is considered in the next section of this chapter.

More usually, however, the interest of bystanders or the public is seen as limiting the circumstances in which expression may legitimately be made. Scanlon distinguishes between the bystanders' interest in preventing the harmful side-effects of speech, such as congestion, noise, or litter on the streets, and the important public interests which may sometimes justify restrictions on speech to prevent harms occurring as a result of the audience reactions to speech—for example, engaging in disorder or leaving the armed forces.[80] That distinction is easy to state, but its application may be difficult in practice.

It is far from clear whether a neat distinction can be drawn between the harmful consequences of an audience's reaction to speech and harmful side-effects independent of such reaction. How, for example, should the consequences of speech invading privacy be characterized? Or take the case of a passer-by reacting angrily to a street demonstration, because it is holding up the progress of his car rather than because he dislikes the cause supported by the procession: is his violent response to be treated as an incidental side-effect or a harmful reaction to speech? These comments perhaps only matter if the legal system is more willing to countenance time, manner, and place restrictions on speech imposed to prevent deleterious side-effects than it is to tolerate regulation inspired by hostility to its contents. United States courts and commentators frequently advocate this distinction in discussing the constitutionality of limits on free speech, but it is much harder to apply than to state in abstract.[81] A second point is that limits may be placed on speech to protect either the general public interest or a private right. Public order and national security limitations clearly represent general third-party interests, but expression is also frequently restricted to secure other private rights which may be seen to have stronger weight either generally or in the particular circumstances. Rights to reputation, privacy, and a fair trial are instances of these competing rights. Their weight may depend, of course, on whether they are also constitutionally protected, or exist only under statute or at common law.

The existence of a public interest in the speech might, however, also be seen as a necessary condition for its legal protection. Meiklejohn doubted whether speech about an entirely private matter, that is, a publication of absolutely no concern to the people at large, is covered by the First Amendment.[82] A defamatory remark about a barmaid's chastity, for instance, would not on this perspective engage freedom of speech. It would be difficult to justify its coverage on the basis of the arguments from truth or democracy, but for some people the making of such remarks

---

[80] N. 47 above, 528.   [81] See ch. II, s. 2 below.   [82] N. 31 above, 79.

might be valuable to their self-fulfilment. And the argument from suspicion of government may suggest that it would be wrong to proscribe such comment. The courts might not be able easily to distinguish purely private (defamatory) speech which may be regulated from allegations of public interest which are protected by freedom of speech. As will be seen later in this book, these distinctions have been troublesome in determining the relationship of freedom of speech to the protection of reputation and privacy rights.[83]

Perhaps speech should be *public* in another sense to engage freedom of speech; arguably, it must be communicated to the community or to a section of it to be covered. In contrast, verbal speech or a written note communicated to one person or to a limited group should not be entitled to legal protection under the free speech principle. In favour of that conclusion, it can be said that Mill's thesis and the argument from democracy hardly apply to private speech, insofar as these arguments assume a communication to the general public which can then assess its truth or its relevance to democratic government. The self-fulfilment argument might well justify application of the free speech clause to purely private communications, but in some situations they are more appropriately covered by privacy rights rather than freedom of speech. The censorship by a prison governor of correspondence from a prisoner to his wife, a friend, or his lawyer, more clearly violates the detainee's privacy rights than his freedom of expression;[84] his complaint is that the confidentiality of his correspondence has been infringed, not that he lacks freedom to disseminate information to the public. A need for communication to the public would also explain why the revelation of official secrets to another member of a subversive organization, let alone an enemy agent, would not even engage freedom of speech. The publication is clearly 'speech' in the dictionary sense, but the absence of any public element to the communication weakens any free speech claim. That is not the case when official secrets are revealed to the public: freedom of speech is engaged, though there are powerful arguments for the imposition of restraints.[85]

On the other hand, in some circumstances purely private communications clearly engage freedom of speech. Employers' references are written in confidence to other (prospective) employers, but they enjoy a qualified privilege defence to defamation actions, because it is in the public interest that the writers of references speak freely; equally, the recipients of references have a strong interest in truthful and full disclosure. A spouse or other person involved in an intimate relationship surely has a free speech interest in disclosing details of that relationship to a close friend from whom he seeks advice. (In these circumstances we might indeed be more willing to uphold free speech arguments than we would be when similar

---

[83] See further ch. VI below.

[84] The European Court has usually treated cases of interference with prisoners' correspondence under ECHR, art. 8 (right to respect for private life and correspondence) rather than art. 10 (freedom of expression): see *Silver* v. *UK* (1983) 5 EHRR 347, and *McCallum* v. *UK* (1991) 13 EHRR 597.

[85] The topic is discussed in ch. V, s. 6 below.

details are disclosed to the community, perhaps by the media.) It would be wrong, therefore, to hold that only general or public communications engage freedom of speech. In some instances private speech merits protection, either because there is a clear public interest in unfettered communications between the individuals concerned, or perhaps because the speaker has a strong interest in expressing his feelings to another person. The case for free speech coverage of public discourse, communicated to the general public, is particularly strong. But it would be wrong to exclude private communications altogether from free expression guarantees.

4. Freedom of Speech and Other Values

Free speech arguments typically suggest, if they do not explicitly state, that the freedom entails *rights* to impart and receive ideas and information. The discussion of free speech interests in the previous section shows that the interests of speakers and audience are worthy of protection, and implies that in legal terms their rights should be recognized. This is important. For the claim that individuals have rights to free speech implies that government may not stop them communicating and considering ideas merely because a restraint would benefit, or meet the preferences of most members of, society.[86] Freedom of speech therefore limits the authority of government and its ability to promote what it, and perhaps the majority of citizens, consider to be the public good.

In this section we consider freedom of speech from a different perspective which supplements the arguments made up to this point. It suggests that freedom of speech should be protected because it is a public good, rather than because individuals value it or have a strong interest in its exercise. Joseph Raz argues persuasively that free political expression is integral to the public good of living in a democracy, irrespective of whether individual citizens wish to participate in political debate or to cast their vote.[87] More generally, he argues that freedom of expression is of value because it validates different forms of life—life in a religious community, as a gay person, or engaging in particular hobbies and leisure pursuits. Equally, censorship or suppression of a publication is an insult to the people engaged in the way of life portrayed in that material. Integral to Raz's argument is a belief in pluralism, that is, the value of diverse ways of life which may be incompatible and conflict, but which tolerate each other.[88] A somewhat similar argument has been made by Lee Bollinger, a leading commentator on the First Amendment, against the background of controversial court decisions in the United States protecting extremist speech.[89] He argues that freedom of speech

---

[86] Dworkin (n. 6 above), 190–1.
[87] 'Free Expression and Personal Identification' (n. 2 above).   [88] Ibid., 321–3.
[89] L. C. Bollinger, *The Tolerant Society: Freedom of Speech and Extremist Speech in America* (New York: OUP, 1986).

should be explained and defended as helping to develop a practice of tolerance; hate speech cases provide a good setting for cultivating tolerance, since speech is less damaging than, say, discriminatory conduct, and therefore, these decisions pose relatively few dangers to social cohesion.

Raz points out that the public expression of a way of life is of crucial importance to the well-being of people who have adopted that course.[90] The self-esteem of homosexuals, for instance, is enhanced by the availability of gay literature and magazines, and conversely would be significantly lower in societies where it is suppressed. In this way, freedom of expression establishes and represents a public culture of acceptance and tolerance. This case appears to differ from the rights-based self-fulfilment and autonomy arguments of Dworkin and Scanlon considered earlier in the chapter.[91] They argue for a connection between underlying duties to treat all individuals with equal respect and concern (or to respect their autonomy) and respect for a fundamental liberty of expression. The liberty is derived from that equal concern for all citizens, the 'sovereign virtue of political community'.[92] What, however, all these arguments share is the perception that freedom of speech should be justified by reference to other fundamental values or moral principles, which may be termed equal respect and concern, the self-esteem of individuals, or human dignity. There are also close links between freedom of political expression and democratic values, though Dworkin and Raz would offer different philosophical explanations for those links. Freedom of speech, in short, is integrally connected with other values.

The discussion in the rest of this section explores two topics where the links between speech and other (constitutional) values create problems for philosophers and courts. The first concerns the relationship between free speech, on the one hand, and equality or human dignity, on the other, in the context of extremist speech—either racist speech or hard-core pornography demeaning to women. The second takes up some implications of Raz's views about the importance of pluralism and the suggestion that the law might be used to promote that value. This creates the possibility that freedom of expression might itself be limited in order to foster its underlying values.

(i) Hate speech, dignity, and equality

Defenders of restrictions on hate speech and misogynist pornography justify their imposition to some extent as necessary to protect the equality and dignity rights of members of the targeted groups.[93] In reply, it is said that these restrictions infringe

---

[90] N. 2 above, 312–13. [91] S. 2(ii) above.

[92] R. M. Dworkin, *The Sovereign Virtue* (Cambridge, Mass.: Harvard UP, 2000), 1. Also see *Taking Rights Seriously* (n. 6 above), 272–8.

[93] These are not the only arguments for the imposition of restrictions: see ch. V, s. 4(i) and ch. X, s. 4(v) below.

the rights of the publishers of hate speech to be treated with equal respect and concern; their contributions to public discourse are discounted, which shows them disrespect.[94] Indulging in hate speech may be part of the way of life of racists, so that their self-esteem is damaged if they cannot communicate their views.[95] Further, if government proscribes hate speech, or other speech of which it disapproves, it takes sides on issues of controversy, and so abandons the neutrality it must show if it is to honour equality of respect and concern to all members of the community.

Critics of hate speech laws also argue that a government might abuse its powers to proscribe extremist expression. Its legislation may be applied to curtail subversive or even unpopular speech. Alternatively, writers may be deterred from publishing material of that character, because they fear they would be prosecuted. This is the so-called 'chilling effect' of speech-restrictive laws, the abhorrence of which has substantially influenced the US courts' approach to resolving conflicts between free speech and the protection of reputation rights.[96] As Schauer argues,[97] these dangers certainly provide support for the free speech principle; otherwise it would be too easy for government, or the courts, to use vague laws to curtail speech which is offensive or unpopular. But the argument does not mean that hate speech or pornography laws are necessarily incompatible with freedom of speech; it means that courts should interpret and apply them with regard for the values of free speech, and not allow them to be abused. Hate speech laws only lead to the suppression of radical political speech if courts allow that to happen.

A state should certainly not proscribe hate speech or hard-core pornography merely because their dissemination causes offence or endangers race or gender relations; commitment to a free speech principle means that it is not entitled to legislate for the welfare of society when that involves the infringement of free speech rights. But the argument may be quite different if the hate speech law is defended by reference to a right to human dignity (or perhaps equality rights), particularly if the right has constitutional status. There would then be a conflict between two constitutional principles, the weight of which must be assessed by the court in the light of the particular circumstances. It is not clear that speech should necessarily enjoy priority if its dissemination infringes other rights. Nor should a state always be required to remain neutral about different lifestyles, as Raz himself admits.[98] Should groups who believe that the only valuable form of life is one devoted to committing spectacular murders or to the consumption of dangerous drugs be free to propagate their views of life, taking strength from the knowledge that it is shared by others? There would be no good reason in these circumstances to give freedom of speech an automatic priority over a right to life; if the spread of these beliefs does put life in danger, it would surely be right to curtail their propagation. The relationship of speech and dignity is more problematic, if

---

[94] Dworkin, 234–8; Richards (n. 56 above), 22–35.   [95] Raz (n. 2 above), 320–1.
[96] See ch. VI, ss. 2 and 3(i) below.   [97] Schauer, 83–5.   [98] N. 2 above, 319.

only because human dignity is a such a broad, perhaps indeterminate, concept. But it should be conceded that speech may infringe it: the display of pictures of the recently dead or of acts of bestiality are two such cases. In these circumstances, there is a strong argument that the protection of human dignity should trump any free speech claim.

An assumption underlying arguments for free speech is that human beings are in general able to consider rationally the ideas put to them and determine appropriately their consequent behaviour. That assumption clearly underlies the arguments from democracy and Mill's truth argument; liberty did not apply to 'any state of things anterior to the time when mankind have become capable of being improved by free and equal discussion'.[99] Alternatively, as in Scanlon's autonomy argument, the capacity to make sensible judgements might be ascribed to human beings as an essential aspect of their dignity: liberal societies must accept that by and large people have a capacity for rational thought, although we know that is not always the case. If we did not make that commitment, it would be more difficult to sustain arguments against authoritarian government or the rule of enlightened despots. It is questionable, however, whether these assumptions hold in the context of hate (and perhaps other) speech, where there are strong grounds to doubt whether it will be considered rationally by its audience. Suppose, for example, that racist leaflets are distributed, or graffiti are scrawled, in a neighbourhood where tensions exist between the (white) majority and minority ethnic groups. Many of those who look at the leaflets or graffiti feel vulnerable and threatened as a result, while members of the majority group receive confirmation of their racist outlook. In these circumstances, respect for human dignity perhaps legitimizes the proscription of racist speech, rather than amounting to an argument for its tolerance.

That conclusion can, of course, be disputed. It assumes that racial identity is an essential, rather than a contested, element of individual human dignity. Another perspective can be taken: speech challenging conventional views concerning the meaning of race and of the importance of membership of racial groups should be allowed as an aspect of free public discourse.[100] The proscription of hate speech, it is argued, rests on a presumption that racial identity is an integral aspect of each individual's dignity or personality, which may not be the case. All aspects of individual human dignity are, at least to some extent, determined by social and cultural perceptions which can properly be contested. On this perspective, commitment to freedom of speech requires the tolerance of even personal abuse, however wounding it is to the individual victim.[101]

Equality and dignity are complex moral and political concepts. It is hard to determine their scope in general, or their appropriate weight when it is argued

---

[99] Mill, 15.

[100] R. C. Post, 'Racist Speech, Democracy, and the First Amendment' (1991) 32 *William and Mary Law Rev* 267, esp. 317–26.

[101] This perspective underlies the decision of the US Supreme Court in *Hustler Magazine* v. *Falwell* 485 US 46 (1988), discussed in ch. VI, s. 4 below.

they limit the exercise of freedom of expression. But clearly these values cannot be ignored when they are recognized by the constitution.[102] Neither the legislature nor a court could easily conclude that hate speech has no impact on the dignity of members of racial minorities it targets, irrespective of the particular circumstances. Nor could it comfortably decide that any impact it did have should be ignored, because of the strength of the argument referred to in the previous paragraph. The argument that equality limits the exercise of free speech in this context is much less persuasive; the claim that hate speech, unlike discrimination in the allocation, say, of housing or employment, infringes the equality rights of members of the target ethnic groups is weak and should be rejected. That is certainly true if equality rights are understood in terms of a right to equal treatment; racist speech, however demeaning to members of the victim group, does not infringe that right.

But the argument from human dignity is a strong one. Free speech itself, as we have seen, relies on background claims about the autonomy of human beings or their entitlement to equal respect. It is assumed, further, that they can assess arguments rationally. Extreme hate speech, perhaps some hard-core pornography, and personal abuse all express contempt for the targeted individuals or groups; some publications, for example, the circulation of close-up photographs of a dead or seriously wounded person, demean human dignity and humanity itself. It would appear odd to hold such speech is *always* protected under a principle which itself is grounded on respect for human dignity and rationality. Even if it is admitted, as it should be, that the proscription of, say, extreme hate literature may violate the freedom of speech of racists, based on their right to be treated with equal respect and concern, it is surely equally clear that the publication of such material may infringe the dignity rights of its victims. There is, then, no alternative to balancing freedom of speech and dignity in the context of the particular facts.

(ii) Pluralism and freedom of speech

Implicit in Raz's argument for freedom of expression is the value of pluralism, or variety in types of life and conceptions of welfare.[103] Certainly, a diversity of attitudes, moral beliefs, and ways of life exists in any developed or liberal society; government must respect this diversity, as any attempt on its part to impose uniform standards of behaviour may impose intolerable strains on social cohesion. Freedom of speech reflects and reinforces pluralism, ensuring that different types of life are validated and promoting the self-esteem of those who follow a particular lifestyle. But suppose that the principal media of expression are controlled by particular individuals or corporations and that they deny members of minority

---

[102] Constitutions invariably recognize equality rights, while the German Basic Law, art. 1, guarantees human dignity: see ch. II, s. 4 below.

[103] It is not clear whether Raz regards this variety as intrinsically desirable, as good because it leads to human flourishing, or he accepts that it inevitably exists in liberal societies.

groups the opportunity to express their views, to communicate with other people who share their way of life, or to persuade others to adopt it. Should or may government intervene to promote freedom of expression in the interests of pluralism? Raz appears to contemplate this possibility when he says his views show 'freedom of expression can be supported as part of a pluralist argument for using the law to promote pluralism in the society'.[104] The possibility has been realized in some European jurisdictions. Both the French Conseil constitutionnel and the Italian Constitutional Court have ruled that the free speech rights of media corporations may be limited to ensure that the constitutional value of pluralism is safeguarded.[105]

In contrast, the US Supreme Court is unsympathetic to attempts to promote free speech values or equalize opportunities for speech, if they entail limits on the free speech rights of individuals.[106] However laudable its aims, government cannot be trusted to take decisions in this context. This attitude is influenced by the general suspicion of government and the faith in the marketplace of ideas which characterize the American approach to free speech issues. It may, however, also be shaped by a narrow perspective on free speech which reduces it to a set of individual rights. Those who share this view would presumably consider that free expression exists in a homogeneous society where all adopt the same attitudes and say the same thing, but are *legally free* to say what they think.

From an alternative perspective, free speech not only confers rights, but also reflects the pluralist values of diversity and variety. Freedom of speech does entail the absence of censorship, but also means an actual robust public debate.[107] There is a positive benefit in the expression of a range of views, which is not satisfied when the only people who speak say much the same thing. Free speech is a public good or value in the same way that the arts and good education are. We would not say that a society values the arts, merely because the government does not stop people attending exhibitions or concerts. Why should we conclude that free speech is respected, because there are no legal restraints on publication? A supporter of this alternative perspective might well be prepared to take the risk of government intervention to promote diversity, even when that step limits the 'rights' of some people to disseminate their views.

So it may make some difference whether we think of free speech exclusively in terms of individual rights and interests, or whether we also contemplate it as a public good or value in a pluralist society. Of course, government can do much to promote pluralism and diversity without interfering with individual free speech rights; it can, for instance, subsidize writers and the arts, and establish public broadcasting (to allow the expression of views not given time on commercial media). The advent of the Internet has perhaps weakened the case for media regulation to

---

[104] N. 2 above, 323.   [105] See ch. II, s. 6 below.   [106] Ibid., s. 2.
[107] See J. Lichtenberg, 'Foundations and Limits of Freedom of the Press', in J. Lichtenberg (ed.), *Democracy and the Mass Media* (Cambridge: CUP, 1990), 102, 107.

ensure that minorities and individuals can communicate effectively with each other.[108] And the market may work relatively well to provide for a variety of expression, rich enough to satisfy the needs of a pluralist society. It certainly seems to do that, at least in Britain, in some contexts, for example, the provision of magazines and periodicals to satisfy more or less any taste or lifestyle.

On balance, I prefer the view that free speech not only contains a set of rights, but reflects values which may on occasion require promotion through the law. Those occasions may be rare. Commitment to free speech means that courts must scrutinize carefully any attempt by government to regulate its exercise, however well intentioned that may appear. But an exclusive rights-based approach, and a blind faith in the market, also poses dangers, in particular that of a society in which only a few people can communicate their ideas effectively through the mass media. Moreover, the risks of government intervention may have been exaggerated by commentators, primarily in the United States, who would rule it out in all circumstances. I develop this point in the final section, which discusses the impact of *constitutional* protection on the abstract case for free speech guarantees considered in this chapter.

5. The Constitutional Protection of Free Speech

This chapter has largely been concerned with the coherence of some arguments for a free speech principle, under which expression is entitled to special immunity from regulation. These are abstract arguments developed by political philosophers and jurists, rather than by judges. But courts cannot, it has been argued, ignore them, although in some contexts the text of the constitution they are interpreting and judicial precedents will also shape their decisions, say, on the scope of free speech or how it is to be balanced against privacy, reputation, or other private interests. Each of these abstract arguments makes a good case for freedom of speech. But none of them is immune to criticism. Mill, for instance, assumed that truth, or better decisions, will always emerge from uninhibited discussion, but that seems too optimistic. The argument from self-fulfilment may collapse into a case for a general liberty right. Scanlon's argument from autonomy assumes that people are generally rational, and that autonomous people would never choose to surrender to government the authority to proscribe expression. Though generally acceptable, neither assumption is warranted in all circumstances. The most popular, and perhaps the most attractive, argument is that from citizen participation in a *constitutional* democracy. But that too relies on an argument that citizens have background rights to equal respect and concern, and it may, therefore, be vulnerable to some of the criticisms levelled at other theories, notably that of Scanlon.

As far as the courts are concerned, the constitution or bill of rights makes it plain that speech enjoys special protection. But they must determine why that is

---

[108] See ch. XIII below for discussion of this topic.

so in hard cases concerning, say, the coverage of commercial advertising or pornography by the particular free speech or expression clause.[109] This requirement appears to impose an impossible burden on them. Constitutional courts cannot be expected to decide why free speech is special and what it means, when political philosophers have been unable to agree on answers, and some have concluded that the search for explanation is doomed to failure.[110] Nevertheless, judges cannot escape this task. Perhaps, however, the fact that freedom of speech, or expression, is *constitutionally* guaranteed has some impact on the coherence and strength of the general philosophical arguments for free speech; one of these arguments may be entitled to special weight in hard cases, because the constitutional provision, properly interpreted, reflects a commitment to that justification of free speech. As mentioned earlier, the text of the particular provisions, the structure of the constitution as a whole, and precedents also offer guidance. As a result courts might find it easier to resolve free speech disputes than they would, if they had to rely on abstract philosophical arguments, divorced from any constitutional context.

A few reflections are offered with regard to the significance of the *constitutional* guarantee of free speech. Historically, constitutions, and more particularly their fundamental rights provisions, are drafted to restrain power and to protect citizens against government. Constitutional judicial review limits the power of the majority in the legislature and therefore appears, at first glance, anti-democratic. But the practice can be justified by recourse to one of two arguments. First, judicial review ensures that majorities are properly elected, and that citizens can debate issues intelligently before casting their vote. On this perspective courts protect the democratic process, rather than discrete substantive rights.[111] Alternatively, a second argument urges that it is the equal right of all to participate in the political process which itself justifies democracy, and that courts must protect that fundamental right against infringement by an elected temporary majority or executive government.[112] On both arguments, there is a powerful case for the protection of political speech. The justifications for judicial review support the arguments for freedom of speech from democracy canvassed earlier in this chapter. It is not surprising that these arguments have been the most influential in shaping free speech jurisprudence. Courts are understandably more prepared to strike down restraints on political expression than they are, say, limits on sexually explicit or commercial speech. The former course is justifiable in terms of the courts' constitutional responsibilities. In contrast, they have less, if any good, reason to interfere with a decision of the legislature to limit commercial advertising or other non-political speech.

---

[109] See Schauer (n. 8 above), 1305–6.

[110] For this view, see S. Fish, *There's No Such Thing as Free Speech, and It's a Good Thing, Too* (New York: OUP, 1994), and Alexander, 'Freedom of Expression as a Human Right' (n. 73 above), 72–3.

[111] For a classic exposition of this case, see J. H. Ely, *Democracy and Distrust* (Cambridge, Mass.: Harvard UP, 1980).   [112] Dworkin, 15–26.

The constitutional protection of free speech may also have implications for the strength of the fourth argument for free speech: suspicion of government.[113] That argument asserts that governments are naturally inclined to suppress speech they dislike; further, they are easily tempted to limit radical or dissenting speech when they act to preserve public order. In short, governments abuse their powers. The free speech principle is needed to counteract the dangers of these 'slippery slopes'.[114] This argument explains, for instance, the opposition in the United States to the framing and application of hate speech laws; an ordinance suppressing extremist speech aimed at vulnerable racial groups could easily, it is said, be used to prosecute the expression of other unpopular ideas. And radicals may prefer not to speak, because they fear prosecution under these laws. On one view, this argument strengthens the case for active judicial review to ensure that the legislature, executive government, and the police do not suppress the expression of unpopular ideas. But if the courts discharge their responsibility to check government and to protect free speech effectively, the 'slippery slope' argument loses some of its force. If judges, for example, interpret hate speech laws properly in the light of free speech principles, the laws should not be applied to less extreme radical expression. Dissidents may become more confident that they will not be prosecuted; if so, the 'chilling effect' argument would be less persuasive.

Moreover, the fear of government is less sustainable in other free speech contexts, if we place trust in the courts. As was mentioned at the end of the previous section, there is disagreement whether attempts by government to promote the values of freedom of expression should necessarily be regarded as incompatible with free speech. Courts, and many commentators, in the United States consider they should be, as government motives are always suspect in this context. Even if an independent authority is established, say, to regulate broadcasting, it is feared that its intervention—for example, to improve programme standards—will distort the terms of public debate. But these anxieties assume that the courts are unable to determine in particular cases when the intervention of government or a regulatory authority infringes, rather than promotes, free speech. The argument is, as it were, that all regulation is suspect, because we cannot rely on anyone, even the courts, to distinguish between censorship and measures which encourage speech and its values, for example, pluralism. This argument is incoherent. It is incompatible with the reasons why we rely on courts as the ultimate guarantor of free speech. If courts are trusted to guarantee free speech, to determine its scope and to decide when it may, exceptionally, be limited in furtherance of other interests such as privacy or the right to a fair trial, there is no reason why they cannot equally be trusted to distinguish a measure which promotes free speech from one which improperly suppresses it. The suspicion of government intervention cannot sensibly be extended to distrust of the courts. The guarantee of free speech in a constitution means we must place confidence in them.

---

[113] S. 2(iv) above.
[114] Schauer, 80–5, and in 'Slippery Slopes' (1985) 99 *Harvard Law Rev.* 361.

II

Free Speech in Liberal Legal Systems

This chapter reviews the treatment of free speech in a number of liberal democracies, where it enjoys significant protection. Special attention is paid to free speech principles in four national jurisdictions, England, the United States, Canada, and Germany, and those developed by the European Human Rights Court, interpreting the European Convention on Human Rights and Fundamental Freedoms (ECHR). Briefer reference is then made to the protection of free speech in a few other countries.

The purpose of this chapter is to provide some background to the more detailed discussion of particular free speech topics in later chapters. It sets out the relevant constitutional provisions and examines the approach of the courts in each jurisdiction to their interpretation and application. Inevitably, some general constitutional issues are discussed. Freedom of speech as a legal concept cannot be understood in isolation from other constitutional rights and principles, which may be peculiar to a particular system.

1. England

English free speech law, like other aspects of its civil liberties jurisprudence, has in principle been transformed by the incorporation of the ECHR into United Kingdom law by the Human Rights Act 1998 (HRA 1998). In fact it is doubtful whether the change has so far been much more than cosmetic. The appearance of the law is clearly different, in that courts examine rulings of the European Human Rights Court and sometimes explain their own decisions in terms of the Convention. But it is hard to point with confidence to free speech cases which have been decided differently as a result of the change in the legal landscape brought about by the HRA 1998; the courts could almost certainly have reached the same conclusion on the basis of the common law and the principles of statutory interpretation they had already fashioned. English judges had already begun in the 1990s to develop this law in the light of ECHR rights, even though at that time they were not enforceable in English law. It is important, therefore, to look at common law free speech principles, before discussing a few important cases subsequent to 2 October 2000 when the HRA 1998 became enforceable in English law.[1]

---

[1] The HRA 1998 came into force earlier in Scotland and Wales with regard to devolution issues.

(i) Common law

The absence of any constitutional or legislative statement of freedom of speech used to mean that the liberty was largely residual. In other words, it existed where statute or common law rules did not restrict its exercise. This feature of English law was stressed by Dicey in his classic study of the constitution.[2] He noted that, in contrast to French and Belgian law which frequently made special provision for the protection (or regulation) of the press, English law took little or no notice of such concepts as 'freedom of speech' and 'liberty of the press'. Legal commentary was then as silent, it may be added, as the statute-book: Blackstone, for example, did not mention freedom of speech in his discussion of personal liberties, and the classic passage on previous restraints of freedom of the press occurs in his section dealing with wrongs and libel.[3] Dicey concluded his exposition: 'Freedom of discussion is in England little else than the right to write or say anything which a jury, consisting of twelve shopkeepers, think it expedient should be said or written.' The implications of this for the publication of minority and unorthodox opinion were ignored.[4] He appears to have been satisfied that political speech, approved or tolerated by the majority, was most unlikely to be suppressed.

Fortunately, quite apart from the implications of the HRA 1998, much can now be added to Dicey's treatment of free speech. First, courts have often invoked common law principles of freedom of speech or freedom of the press to limit the scope of other common law rules which inhibit the exercise of these freedoms.[5] This has been particularly true in libel, breach of confidence, and contempt of court cases. For instance, the defences of fair comment and privilege to libel actions have been formulated and applied to promote freedom of speech; in some contexts, courts recognize that it is more important to protect that freedom than the interest of the individual in safeguarding his reputation.[6] To some extent judges were already influenced in the 1980s and early 1990s by UK participation in the European Convention, although its provisions were not at that time binding on them.[7] Secondly, a common law presumption in favour of free speech was used to restrict the scope of an Act of Parliament which otherwise might have been

---

[2] A. V. Dicey, *Introduction to the Study of the Law of the Constitution*, 10th edn. (London: Macmillan, 1959), ch. VI.

[3] W. Blackstone, 4 *Commentaries on the Laws of England*, 16th edn. (London, 1825), 152: see further, ch. IV, s. 1 below.

[4] See I. Jennings, *The Law and the Constitution*, 5th edn. (London: London UP, 1959), 267–9.

[5] A. Boyle, 'Freedom of Expression as a Public Interest in English Law' [1982] *PL* 574.

[6] For further discussion, see ch. VI below.

[7] For judicial discussion of the impact of the ECHR, see Lords Fraser and Scarman in *A-G* v. *BBC* [1981] AC 303, HL, and Lord Denning MR in *Schering Chemicals* v. *Falkman* [1982] QB 1, CA. In *Derbyshire CC* v. *Times Newspapers* [1992] QB 770, the Court of Appeal considered that courts were required to consider the ECHR when the common law was uncertain. It therefore ruled that a public authority could not bring an action in defamation, as that would be incompatible with ECHR, art. 10 (guarantee of freedom of expression). For the House of Lords decision, see ch. VI, s. 2 below.

construed and applied to limit exercise of that freedom.[8] Both in common law cases and in the context of statutory interpretation, courts have been increasingly willing in the last few decades to apply a freedom of speech principle, which would have been repudiated by Dicey and other commentators in the nineteenth and early twentieth centuries.

A third point is that freedom of speech sometimes played a decisive role in dissuading the courts from developing new rules of law or exercising discretionary powers in a novel way. Thus, in one wardship case the Court of Appeal refused to grant an injunction to restrain the publication of a book containing details of the degrading conduct of the ward's father.[9] Publication would have been distressing to the ward, but the judges emphasized the importance of not adding to the numerous restrictions on the circulation of true information. Much the same point was made when an application was made to stop the showing of a television documentary on the work of the Obscene Publications Squad, unless the broadcaster deleted pictures of a man identified as a convicted paedophile. It was argued that, without their removal, the programme would have been distressing to his wife and five-year-old daughter. The Court of Appeal rejected the application, doubting whether it had power to stop a broadcast (or other exercise of free speech rights) in these circumstances; the programme would not have prejudiced any legal proceedings, nor did it relate to the upbringing of a child under court supervision. As Hoffmann LJ put it, '[i]n any area of human rights like freedom of speech, I respectfully doubt the wisdom of creating judge-made exceptions, particularly when they require a judicial balancing of interests.'[10] Press freedom should not be sacrificed, merely because that seemed right on the facts of the case.

English common law, therefore, does not now treat freedom of speech as a merely residual liberty. It is a legal principle, to which courts must pay attention when interpreting, say, public order or obscenity legislation, or when considering the defences to an action for libel or breach of confidence or contempt of court proceedings.[11] Indeed, it has been said that 'there is a constitutional right to freedom of expression'.[12] But the fact that the freedom has not been explicitly spelt out in a constitution or bill of rights (until incorporation of the ECHR) has been significant. It means that freedom of speech has almost invariably been treated as a *defence* or as an *exception* or *qualification* to other well-established legal rights, such as the right to reputation or fair trial rights. The presumption is that those other rights should be protected, unless there is a more powerful free speech argument to support the opposite conclusion. In contrast, where free speech is constitutionally guaranteed, the argument should normally be whether there is a sufficiently

---

[8] A classic example is Lord Reid's speech in *Cozens* v. *Brutus* [1973] AC 854, HL, construing the word 'insulting' in the public order legislation not to cover a demonstration which offended and affronted spectators, but did not abuse them personally; see ch. VIII, s. 4 below.

[9] *In re X (A Minor) (Wardship: Jurisdiction)* [1975] Fam 47.

[10] *R* v. *Central Independent Television plc* [1994] Fam 192, 203, CA.

[11] For the status of freedom of speech, particularly in the context of libel law, see E. Barendt, 'Libel and Freedom of Speech in English Law' [1993] *PL* 449.

[12] Lord Steyn in *Reynolds* v. *Times Newspapers* [2001] 2 AC 127, 207.

strong justification for restricting its exercise; either there is a presumption in favour of free speech, or at least it is assumed that it is entitled to as much weight as the competing interest, say, in personal privacy or in reputation. Further, courts have given relatively little consideration to the scope of the right to free speech outside the familiar contexts of defamation and breach of confidence actions, and contempt of court law. There was no significant challenge, for instance, to the compatibility of copyright law with freedom of speech until the HRA 1998 came into force; copyright is governed by statute, so free speech arguments could not easily be made in that context.[13] Most fundamentally, under the principle of Parliamentary legislative supremacy, courts were required to implement statutes which plainly curtailed freedom of speech, when it was impossible to interpret them to safeguard its exercise.[14] It is these features of freedom of speech at common law which should alter considerably with incorporation of the ECHR and the explicit provision of a right to freedom of expression in the HRA 1998.

It has been unusual for English judges to discuss the philosophical justifications for recognizing a free speech principle or interest. That is hardly surprising, given its limited status at common law. One notable exception was the speech of Lord Steyn in *R* v. *Home Secretary, ex p Simms*,[15] in itself a striking example of judicial boldness in this context. Provisions of the Prison Service Standing Orders appeared on their plain meaning to impose a ban on prisoners giving interviews to journalists, unless the latter undertook not to publish the interview. The House of Lords held the provisions should not be construed to impose such a ban, because that would infringe the prisoners' freedom of speech. Lord Steyn reviewed the objectives of the freedom: it promotes the self-fulfilment of individuals, enables the discovery of truth in the marketplace, and provides the lifeblood for a democracy. The freedom also checks the abuse of power, and it 'facilitates the exposure of errors in the governance and administration of justice'.[16] It was this last justification which was crucial; the prisoners had a free speech right to argue they had been wrongly convicted, and the Prison Service Orders should be interpreted to protect that right. But Lord Steyn doubted whether prisoners had broader free speech rights. But in the absence of clear evidence that the exercise of such rights would endanger prison security or give information to confederates outside jail, there seems no reason why they should not enjoy them.[17]

(ii) The Human Rights Act 1998

The HRA 1998 incorporates into United Kingdom law rights guaranteed by the ECHR, 'the Convention rights' to use the term defined by section 1 of the

---

[13] See now *Ashdown* v. *Telegraph Group* [2002] Ch 149, CA considered in ch. VII, s. 2 below.

[14] In *R* v. *Jordan* [1967] Crim LR 483, the Divisional Court rejected an argument that Parliament could not introduce the offence of incitement to racial hatred, as the law infringed free speech.

[15] [2000] 2 AC 115, HL.   [16] Ibid., 127.

[17] For further discussion, see ch. XIV, s. 5 below.

legislation.[18] Among them is the right to freedom of expression set out in Article 10 of the ECHR. However, the HRA 1998 does not simply provide for incorporation of the Convention rights without qualification. It is unlawful only for public authorities to act incompatibly with a Convention right.[19] Individuals and private institutions are not bound in this way. However, the term 'public authority' includes courts and tribunals, as well as any person 'certain of whose functions are functions of a public nature'.[20] These provisions are complex. It is unclear what functions are covered by this clause and how far private institutions must observe Convention rights when they discharge them. In the context of free speech law, there is room for argument, for example, whether the Press Complaints Commission and the Advertising Standards Authority must comply with the Convention rights to freedom of expression and to respect for private and family life (guaranteed by Article 8 of the ECHR), when they consider complaints against newspapers or advertising agencies. But courts, as public authorities, must ensure the observance of these rights, when they consider actions for breach of confidence to protect personal privacy, actions in libel, or other common law proceedings.[21] Thus, newspapers, broadcasters, and other publishers may argue in an English court that, say, the common law of libel or breach of confidence infringes their free speech (and press) rights under the ECHR, while a claimant may contend that an article in a tabloid newspaper infringes his right to keep personal information confidential, a right which should be developed in conformity with the Convention.

The press in England has for the most part resisted the introduction of explicit privacy rights, which have not been recognized in common law. In order to meet its anxiety that these rights would be introduced into English law by incorporation of the ECHR, the government added what became section 12 of the HRA 1998 to give the press and other media defendants a degree of special protection. The provision applies when a court is considering whether to grant a remedy which might affect exercise of freedom of expression. Procedural steps must be taken to ensure that the press or other defendant is notified of any proceedings, and no prior restraint on publication should be ordered, unless the applicant is likely to succeed at full trial.[22] Section 12(4) is particularly important:

The court must have particular regard to the importance of the Convention right to freedom of expression and, where the proceedings relate to material which the respondent claims . . . to be journalistic, literary or artistic material . . . to—

    (a) the extent to which—

        (i) the material has, or is about to, become available to the public; or

        (ii) it is, or would be, in the public interest for the material to be published;

    (b) any relevant privacy code.

---

[18] See Feldman, 80–104 for general treatment of the HRA 1998.   [19] HRA 1998, s. 6(1).

[20] Ibid., s. 6(3).

[21] *Douglas v. Hello!* [2001] QB 967, CA; *Venables v. News Group Newspapers Ltd* [2001] Fam 430, Dame Elizabeth Butler-Sloss P.; *A v. B plc* [2003] QB 195, CA; *Campbell v. MGN* [2004] 2 AC 457, HL.

[22] HRA 1998, s. 12(2)–(3).

This subsection might appear to give some priority to freedom of expression over competing rights, for example, to privacy or to a fair trial. But the courts have rejected that interpretation. In an early Court of Appeal case to consider the provision, Sedley LJ argued that the reference to 'the Convention right to freedom of expression' included the qualifications to the exercise of that freedom contained in Article 10(2), including the right to reputation and the right to the protection of confidential information.[23] The House of Lords has accepted this view.[24] Freedom of expression is not given any pre-eminence by the HRA 1998, but must be balanced against the competing rights and interests recognized by the Convention.

Courts are required by the HRA 1998 to interpret legislation (whether primary or delegated) so far as possible compatibly with Convention rights.[25] However, it is now clear that observance of this obligation does not entitle them to rewrite statutes, in violation of their plain meaning.[26] It would be wrong, for instance, for a court to rule that the Obscene Publications Act 1959 should not be understood to cover the most explicit hard-core pornography, because its application to that material would be incompatible with freedom of expression. Such a ruling would in effect abrogate the obscenity legislation. But a court may under the HRA 1998 declare that a statutory provision is incompatible with a Convention right.[27]

A few other points should be made. Courts in England (and Scotland) must take account of decisions and other judgments of the European Court of Human Rights, and of opinions and decisions of the European Human Rights Commission, the body which used to determine the admissibility of applications to Strasbourg that national law infringed the rights guaranteed by the ECHR.[28] But English courts are not bound by decisions of the Strasbourg Court or Commission. They are free to take a narrower or wider view of the scope of freedom of expression than that taken by the European Court. Moreover, as will be explained later in the context of discussing free speech principles under the Convention,[29] the European Court has evolved a 'margin of appreciation' doctrine, under which it allows member states, including their courts, some discretion in determining whether it is appropriate to limit the exercise of the rights guaranteed by the ECHR. The doctrine limits the supervisory powers of the Strasbourg Court over the authorities in the states. But it would be inappropriate for, say, the Court of Appeal to apply the doctrine to its own rulings or decisions of other courts in England when they determine what limits may be imposed on the exercise of the right to freedom of expression.[30] The English courts have nevertheless developed similar

---

[23] *Douglas* v. *Hello!* [2001] QB 967, paras. 133–5. See further ch. VI, s. 5 below.

[24] *Campbell* v. *MGN* [2004] 2 AC 457, paras. 55 (Hoffmann), 111 (Hope), 138–41 (Hale).

[25] S. 3; see *Ghaidan* v. *Mendoza* [2004] 3 All ER 411, HL.

[26] *Re S (children: care plan)* [2002] 2 AC 291, HL; *R (on the application of Anderson)* v. *Home Secretary* [2003] 1 AC 837, HL.   [27] HRA 1998, s. 4.

[28] The Commission was merged with the Court in 1999 under Protocol 11 to the ECHR.

[29] See s. 5 below.   [30] See Lord Hope in *R* v. *DPP, ex p Kebilene* [2000] 2 AC 326.

principles of restraint in freedom of expression (and other human rights) cases, under which they allow the legislature and executive some discretion in determining what limits may be imposed on exercise of the freedom within the terms of the Convention.[31]

The HRA 1998 states that reliance on a Convention right does not restrict entitlement to other rights recognized by law.[32] In other words, courts may recognize a common law free speech right, even though it is unclear that it should be upheld as a Convention right, or that it would be upheld by the Strasbourg Court. Courts, for instance, may insist on adherence to the common law principles of open justice—the freedom of the press and public to attend and report on legal proceedings—even when that freedom might be limited under Article 6 of the Convention.[33] In practice courts do not sharply distinguish between freedom of expression at common law and under the ECHR. Indeed, in cases decided before ECHR incorporation took effect, they sometimes said that the approach of the common law to protection of the freedom is similar to that taken under the Convention.[34] A few important recent cases will now be discussed to see whether the HRA 1998 has made much difference to free speech protection in English law.

(iii) Free speech cases after the Human Rights Act 1998

R v. *Shayler* was the first major case to consider the implications of the Convention right to freedom of expression after the HRA 1998 came into force.[35] The issue was the compatibility of the Official Secrets Act 1989 with freedom of expression, given that this legislation did not allow a defendant to argue that his disclosure was in the public interest. The House of Lords held that revelation to the public of official information was covered by the freedom. But the Convention permits restrictions to be imposed on such disclosure, provided they are 'necessary . . . in the interests of national security, territorial integrity, or public safety . . .'. Following a number of European Court rulings, the House considered the key question was whether the restrictions imposed by the 1989 legislation were disproportionate, that is, whether they went further than necessary to safeguard national security. With some hesitation, it held that they did not. The legislation did not impose an absolute ban; it allowed security agents and other civil servants limited opportunities to raise their concerns with appropriate officials or to apply for permission to disclose them to a wider audience. The decision is certainly open

---

[31] This attitude of restraint is sometimes characterized as one of deference to the judgement of the political branches, but see the speech of Lord Hoffmann in *R (on the application of ProLife Alliance)* v. *BBC* [2004] 1 AC 185, paras. 74–7.   [32] HRA 1998, s. 11.

[33] *R* v. *London (North) Industrial Tribunal, ex p Associated Newspapers* [1998] ICR 1212: see ch. IX, s. 4 below.

[34] See *Derbyshire County Council* v. *Times Newspapers* [1993] AC 534, HL; *Reynolds* v. *Times Newspapers* [2001] 2 AC 127, HL.

[35] [2003] 1 AC 247, HL. See ch. V, s. 6 below for further discussion.

to criticism. The government should be required to show why such a broad ban, without provision of any public interest defence, is a necessary restriction on the exercise of free speech rights. But the speeches of the House of Lords did fully consider relevant decisions of the Strasbourg Court and it may well be right to suggest that the defendant's argument would not have been accepted by that Court.

Sometimes the courts have attached more importance to freedom of expression and press freedom than they might have done before incorporation of the ECHR. In one case the Divisional Court allowed the appeal of a demonstrator who had been convicted of an offence under the public order legislation when she desecrated the US flag outside an airbase to the apparent distress of American servicemen.[36] The court held the trial judge had not properly considered whether the demonstrator was protected by the Convention right to freedom of expression, and had wrongly suggested that she could have communicated her views in a less dramatic fashion: that is irrelevant to freedom of speech under which speakers have considerable latitude how they communicate their views. Courts have on occasion vigorously defended press freedom, considering that section 12(4) of the HRA 1998 strengthens the common law principle. In *A* v. *B plc*, Lord Woolf CJ said that any interference with that freedom has to be justified, irrespective of whether the particular publication was in the public interest.[37] So the Court of Appeal allowed a tabloid's appeal against the grant of an interim injunction which had restrained publication of a feature revealing details of a footballer's sexual relationships outside marriage and identifying the footballer. The appellate court attached weight to the point that, if the women with whom he had had affairs had free speech rights to disclose their relationships, so the newspaper had free press rights to make the same disclosures.[38]

Perhaps the most important and, from a free speech perspective, the most disappointing decision was that of the House of Lords in *R (on the Application of ProLife Alliance)* v. *BBC*.[39] The BBC had refused to transmit the election broadcast of the ProLife Alliance, on the ground that its repeated showing of mutilated foetuses would be offensive to viewers, and so violate the 'taste and decency' rule; under this rule the BBC and independent broadcasting authorities are required to ensure that nothing is included in broadcast programmes which offends good taste or decency or which is offensive to public feeling.[40] The Court of Appeal had held that this rule should not be applied, as that would allow the BBC in effect to censor an election broadcast, an important exercise of free political speech.[41] The Lords allowed the BBC's appeal, holding that Parliament (or in the case of the BBC, the government by Royal Charter) had decided that the broadcasting authorities should balance free speech and the protection of viewers from offence.

---

[36] *DPP* v. *Percy* [2002] Crim LR 835, considered in ch. VIII, s. 4 below.

[37] [2003] QB 195, para. 11(iv).   [38] Ibid., para. 43: see further, ch. VI, s. 5 below.

[39] [2004] 1 AC 185: see E. Barendt, 'Free Speech and Abortion' [2003] *PL* 580.

[40] The rule is imposed by the BBC Charter and (at that time) on the ITC by the Broadcasting Act 1990, s. 6(1)(a). See now the Communications Act 2003, s. 319(2).   [41] N. 39 above.

It would be wrong for the courts to uphold a challenge to the judgement of the BBC that the broadcast would infringe the taste and decency rule.

The House of Lords decision showed scant regard for freedom of speech. As the vigorous dissent of Lord Scott pointed out, the broadcasters had not shown that the ban on free political speech, in the form of an election broadcast, met the Convention requirement that it was 'necessary... for the protection of... the rights of others', in this case, the rights of viewers not to be offended. The BBC approach undervalued the importance of free political expression and underestimated the capacity of the public to protect itself, if need be, from shock, by simply turning the television off. Moreover, the refusal to transmit the election broadcast clearly amounted to censorship, or a prior restraint of speech, usually subject to especially strict scrutiny.[42] Lord Hoffmann even doubted whether the ProLife Alliance party was really entitled to claim the Convention right to freedom of expression, granted that it would have had no right of access to use television to get its message across if Parliament had not made arrangements for election broadcasts. That was a particularly bad point. Nobody has a right to broadcast, in the same way in which everybody has a right to talk to his neighbour over the garden fence. But that does not mean that freedom of speech is not guaranteed in this context, at least for those who are licensed or given access to broadcast; of course, legislation may impose greater limits on the exercise of that freedom, than it does in the context of newspaper or book publishing, but it is always arguable that these limits violate freedom of speech. The House of Lords should have construed the broadcasting legislation, as HRA 1998, s 3 requires, not to interfere with freedom of political expression; the taste and decency principle could still have been applied to ban the showing of hard-core pornographic material or gratuitous violence.

Recently the House of Lords has determined the importance or value of the speech when balancing the exercise of freedom of expression against the right to respect for private life guaranteed by the ECHR. In *Campbell* v. *MGN*,[43] it upheld, by a 3–2 majority, the right of the supermodel, Naomi Campbell, to keep details of her therapy from Narcotics Anonymous (NA) private. The *Daily Mirror* infringed this right when they published that information and photographs of her leaving a meeting of NA. The majority did not think the publication merited strong free speech protection. Baroness Hale was particularly clear on this point. Political speech in particular, but also intellectual, educational, and artistic speech and expression are important, because they are crucial for a democracy or a dynamic society, which values individual originality and development. No claims of this kind could be made for the publication of details of a celebrity's private life.[44] It was therefore not entitled to much weight when balanced against Ms Campbell's private life. In contrast, in *Re S (A Child)*[45] the House refused to grant an injunction

---

[42] See ch. IV below.   [43] [2004] 2 AC 457.   [44] Ibid., paras. 148–9.
[45] [2004] 4 All ER 683.

to stop the press revealing the name of a woman charged with the murder of her son, or publishing their photographs, even though publication might damage the psychological health and well-being of another, eight-year-old son. The freedom of the press to report criminal trials fully was fundamental; readers would have little interest in reports which did not disclose the defendant's identity. English courts must therefore consider the value of the particular publication when balancing freedom of expression against other rights.

2. United States of America

It will be helpful to set out the relevant part of the First Amendment:

Congress shall make no law ... abridging the freedom of speech, or of the press, or the right of the people peaceably to assemble, and to petition the Government for a redress of grievances.

Rarely has such an apparently simple legal text produced so many problems of interpretation. The extent to which solutions have been influenced by various free speech theories, or can be justified by reference to them, is explored in later chapters. The rich case-law of the US Supreme Court shows, among other things, its reluctance to commit itself to any of these theories, although particular members of the Court have taken a distinctive approach to free speech issues.[46] As was suggested in Chapter I, the argument from democracy has been the most popular positive justification for the place of freedom of speech in US constitutional law, its influence being shown by the particularly strong protection given to political speech. In comparison, the Court has been more willing to countenance restrictions on commercial speech and advertising,[47] while hard-core pornography may, in theory, still fall entirely outside the scope of free speech coverage.[48] The 'marketplace of ideas' version of the argument from truth, formulated by Holmes J. in his famous dissenting judgment in the *Abrams* case,[49] has also exercised a significant influence on US free speech jurisprudence. While some commentators have found attractive rights-based arguments stemming from fundamental human rights to dignity and self-fulfilment,[50] these arguments have not played a substantial part in shaping Supreme Court rulings on free speech.

By mentioning freedom of speech alongside rights of assembly and petition, the text of the First Amendment itself appears to emphasize the freedom's role in

---

[46] R. C. Post, 'Reconciling Theory and Doctrine in First Amendment Jurisprudence', in L. C. Bollinger and G. R. Stone (eds.), *Eternally Vigilant: Free Speech in the Modern Era* (Chicago: Chicago UP, 2002), 152 draws attention to the incompatibilities between free speech theories and particular doctrines and decisions of the Court.   [47] See ch. XI below.

[48] Ch. X, s. 2 below.   [49] *Abrams* v. *US* 250 US 616 (1919).

[50] See D. A. J. Richards, *Free Speech and the Politics of Identity* (New York: OUP, 1999); C. E. Baker, *Human Liberty and Freedom of Speech* (New York: OUP, 1989); and M. H. Redish, 'The Value of Free Speech' (1982), 130 *University of Pennsylvania Law Rev.* 591.

safeguarding the interests of the opposition and minorities.[51] But relatively little reliance has been placed on this point, except in the development of the linked freedom of association. Textual arguments have been ignored in other respects. The First Amendment literally only applies to the laws of Congress, but it has never seriously been suggested that executive and police orders are immune from judicial review.[52] Even more crucially, since the decision in *Gitlow* v. *New York* in 1925, it has been accepted that freedom of speech and of the press are fundamental personal rights protected from invasion by the *states* (as well as by Congress and the federal government) under the Due Process Clause of the Fourteenth Amendment.[53] But the 'state action' doctrine limits the scope of free speech protection. Under this doctrine, constitutional rights in the United States are only guaranteed against invasion by government and public authorities; these include the courts when they are called on to enforce statutes or common law rights, such as the right to reputation or privacy.[54] But they are not protected against the decisions of private institutions and individuals. For example, the Supreme Court has held that freedom of speech was not violated by the refusal of a private broadcasting company to allow a political group advertising time to protest against conduct of the Vietnam war,[55] or by the decision of owners of a shopping mall not to permit demonstrations on its property.[56]

The US courts have departed from a literal or strict constructionist approach to the interpretation of the First Amendment in one way of particular interest for comparative free speech jurisprudence. Despite the frequent promptings of Black J., a member of the Supreme Court from 1937 to 1971, the Court has never taken literally the injunction 'shall make no law ... abridging the freedom of speech ...'. The absolutist position, advocated by Black and Douglas JJ, is impossible to sustain. Courts are aware of the vital interests that may be threatened by unrestricted speech. As Holmes J. pointed out in the first Supreme Court case seriously to consider First Amendment principles,[57] the 'most stringent protection of free speech would not protect a man in falsely shouting fire in a theatre and causing a panic.' The absolutist position is also untenable because the regulation, and on occasion even the prohibition, of speech may be justified to protect the free speech rights of others. Even Meiklejohn, who took a very wide view of the

---

[51] For the right of assembly and its relationship to freedom of speech, see ch. VIII, s. 2 below.

[52] In the famous *Pentagon Papers* case (403 US 713 (1971)), it was not even argued that the First Amendment did not cover an application by the US federal government to proscribe the publication; see ch. IV, s. 3 below for discussion of the prior restraint in this case.

[53] The observation of Sanford J. in *Gitlow* 268 US 652, 666 (1925) to this effect was first applied to invalidate state legislation in *Fiske* v. *Kansas* 274 US 380 (1927).

[54] See *New York Times* v. *Sullivan* 376 US 254, 265 (1964), considered in ch. VI, s. 2 below. S. Gardbaum, 'The "Horizontal Effect" of Constitutional Rights' (2003) 102 *Michigan Law Rev* 387, argues from this decision that private actors in the US are bound to observe constitutional rights, insofar as they rely on the law for their enforcement.

[55] *Columbia Broadcasting System* v. *Democratic National Committee* 412 US 94 (1973).

[56] *Lloyd Corpn* v. *Tanner* 407 US 551 (1972): see ch. VIII, s. 3 below.

[57] *Schenk* v. *US* 249 US 47, 52 (1919).

protection to be afforded political speech under the First Amendment, recognized that addresses at public meetings could be limited and cut short on valid free speech grounds. Absolutists can try to defend their corner by asserting that 'abridging' does not cover all forms of regulation and that 'the freedom of speech' is not the same as 'speech', so that rightly understood the term does not exclude restrictions on some modes of expression.[58] But really the game is up, the poverty of literalism laid bare.

The United States Supreme Court, therefore, like other constitutional courts, balances free speech and other important rights and interests on the basis of principles it has developed over the last eighty years without guidance from the text of the Constitution. Other interests, such as public order and decency, national security, the rights to reputation and a fair trial are weighed in the scales with free speech. If these interests are found 'compelling', or in some circumstances 'substantial', they may justify restriction on the exercise of speech rights, at least if the government or other authority seeking to justify the limit shows that the restriction has been narrowly formulated, so that it does not restrict more speech than the compelling interest warrants. One form of balancing test is the famous 'clear and present danger' formula, which has the outstanding merit of relative precision, at least in its abstract formulation. Under the current version of the test, speech may only be curtailed when it is directed to producing imminent lawless behaviour and is likely to produce it.[59]

This balancing process need not be incompatible with a strong adherence to the free speech principle, though there is an obvious risk that judges will treat the speech interest as just one factor to be considered in conjunction with others, and so give it less protection than it should enjoy in a liberal society committed to freedom of expression. The Supreme Court has, therefore, formulated a number of principles designed to avoid this danger. One of them is the 'clear and present danger' test, referred to in the previous paragraph. It has been applied to safeguard insulting and inflammatory speech, unless the state can show that as a result imminent disorder is likely to occur.[60] The test has also been used in contempt of court cases; as a result, contempt proceedings which might well succeed in England and other common law jurisdictions would almost certainly fail First Amendment scrutiny.[61] Under another strong principle, courts in the USA must not grant a prior restraint unless the state can show that, without such an order, it would suffer direct, immediate, and irreparable damage.[62] The Court has also formulated a rule under which a public official or figure cannot succeed in a libel action unless he proves that the defamatory allegations were published with the

---

[58] A. Meiklejohn, *Free Speech and its Relation to Self-Government* (New York: Harper, 1948), expanded and retitled as *Political Freedom: The Constitutional Powers of the People* (New York: HarperCollins, 1960), 19–28.

[59] See *Brandenburg v. Ohio* 395 US 444 (1969), discussed in ch. V, s. 2 below.

[60] See ch. V, s. 2 below.   [61] See ch. IX, s. 3(iv) below.

[62] *Pentagon Papers* case, 403 US 713 (1971).

knowledge that they were false.[63] All these principles are designed to give speech more protection than it would enjoy if courts treated it and competing interests as factors of equal weight or importance in the balancing process. There is a strong presumption in favour of free speech.

The most important of these principles states that content-based restrictions on speech should be subject to strict or heightened scrutiny. Under this test the state must show a *compelling* interest to justify the restriction. Further, it must show that it could not have achieved this aim by 'less restrictive means', in other words that a less draconian measure would not have been adequate to safeguard, say, national security or another compelling state interest. In contrast, a content-neutral restriction is subject to intermediate scrutiny, a test much less severe than strict scrutiny, but harder to satisfy than a 'reasonable basis' test under which virtually all restrictions on speech may pass constitutional muster. Intermediate scrutiny requires the state to show that there is a *substantial* interest to support the restriction, and further that the measure was narrowly tailored to achieve that interest, without disproportionately suppressing speech. A further complication is that the Court has sometimes upheld a content-based regulation, taking into account what it regards as the lower value of the speech in question. This development is particularly noticeable in cases concerned with the regulation of sexually explicit material; as Stevens J. said, when upholding the zoning of adult cinemas, 'few of us would march our sons and daughters off to war to preserve the citizen's right to see "Specified Sexual Activities" exhibited in the theaters of our choice.'[64] Unlike hard-core pornography, this material is covered by the First Amendment, but the Court is more prepared to approve its regulation than it would political discourse.

Quite apart from reservations about the complexity of these tests, two difficult questions should be asked: what is the distinction between a content-based and a content-neutral restriction, and does the distinction warrant the different levels of scrutiny? The most clear case of a content-based restriction is one which proscribes the stating of a particular view or idea or the provision of particular information. It would obviously be contrary to the First Amendment for a law to proscribe the publication of any material abusive of Democrats or Catholics, allowing in effect the abuse of Republicans and Protestants. The hostility to viewpoint discrimination may partly explain the controversial Supreme Court decision in *RAV*, invalidating an ordinance which proscribed certain types of speech which the speaker knew would cause anger or alarm to people on the basis, among other things, of their race or religion.[65] As Scalia J. for the Court pointed out, it made it impossible to use extreme language against Catholics, but did not proscribe similar language against anti-Catholics (or for that matter Republicans). The same principle explains why a feminist anti-pornography ordinance was

---

[63] *New York Times* v. *Sullivan* 376 US 254 (1964), discussed in ch. VI, ss. 1–2 below.
[64] *Young* v. *American Mini Theatres* 427 US 50, 76 (1976).
[65] *RAV* v. *St Paul* 505 US 377 (1992): see ch. V, s. 4 below.

struck down; it applied to sexually explicit material demeaning and disparaging women, and therefore discriminated against the dissemination of a particular idea.[66]

It is less clear whether the hostility to content-based restrictions applies to rules which proscribe or limit discussion of particular topics or subject matter, or which discriminate between different speakers, granting, say, facilities or tax advantages for some groups, but not others.[67] The decisions of the Supreme Court on these points are inconsistent.[68] The trend, however, is to treat a rule prohibiting discussion of an entire topic as a content-based rule and subject it to strict scrutiny.[69] The *RAV* decision is instructive on this point. The Court struck down a city ordinance, which penalized extreme hate speech on the basis of the victim's race, colour, creed, religion, or gender, because it prohibited speech with regard to its subject or overall content. Speakers were free to be as abusive as they liked about political topics, or about union members or gays, but they could not communicate their views about 'disfavored subjects'.[70] Scalia J. explained that this selectivity might indicate that the city intended to proscribe the expression of views it disliked. In short, subject-matter restrictions should be covered by the content-based principle, insofar as their clear purpose or effect is to discriminate against the expression of particular views. The same principle would apply to speaker-based restraints, which may well be imposed to give an advantage to the proponents of one view to the cost of others.[71]

These issues are, of course, closely connected to the second question: the reason for the special hostility to content-based rules. It has been argued that this is

---

[66] *American Booksellers Ass'n* v. *Hudnut* 777 F 2d 323 (7th Cir, 1985), considered in ch. X, s. 4(iv) below.

[67] See G. R. Stone, 'Restrictions of Speech Because of its Content: The Peculiar Case of Subject-Matter Restrictions' (1978) 46 *Univ of Chicago Law Rev* 81 for discussion of these questions.

[68] Cases suggesting that the content-based rule applies to subject-matter restrictions include *Police Department* v. *Mosley* 408 US 97 (1972) (improper to ban all picketing, save labour picketing, near state schools), and *Erznoznik* v. *City of Jacksonville* 422 US 205 (1975) (ban on films showing nudity if screen visible from public streets). On the other hand, decisions such as *Lehman* v. *City of Shaker Heights* 418 US 298 (1974) (permissible to allow commercial, but not political, advertising on city buses), *Greer* v. *Spock* 424 US 828 (1976) (permissible to proscribe speech by election candidates on army base, though other speech allowed), and *Young* v. *American Mini Theatres* 427 US 50 (1976) (zoning of adult cinemas on basis of their content permissible, as no viewpoint discrimination) appear to take the opposite approach.

[69] See, for instance, *Simon & Schuster* v. *Members of New York State Crime Victims Board* 502 US 105 (1991), holding that a law requiring income derived from publications by criminals admitting their crime to be used to compensate victims was a content-based restriction on speech which could not survive strict scrutiny, and *Burson* v. *Freeman* 504 US 191 (1992), where the Court exceptionally upheld a rule—outlawing election campaigning within 100 feet of polling stations—although it was characterized by some members of the Court as content-based restriction of speech.

[70] 505 US 377, 391 per Scalia J. (1992).

[71] In fact the Supreme Court has usually upheld these restrictions: see *Perry Education Assn* v. *Perry Local Educators' Assn* 460 US 37 (1983) (constitutional to give union access to mail facilities, which are denied to other unions); *Regan* v. *Taxation with Representation of Washington* 461 US 540 (1983) (constitutional to allow contributions to veterans' organizations to be deductible for tax, but to deny the same privilege for contributions to other charitable organizations which engage in lobbying).

unjustified, and that all restrictions which restrict speech without compelling reasons should be struck down.[72] After all, a total ban on, say, all leafleting and canvassing on the streets would clearly have a more marked impact on political speech than, say, a more limited ban on the distribution of leaflets by political parties, or by Democrats or Baptists. While the second type of ban would be subject to strict scrutiny, the merits of the total ban would be assessed carefully to see whether there are substantial reasons to justify it, for example, the need to prevent litter.[73] Moreover, a community or a state might react to a ruling invalidating content-based restrictions by the imposition of wider, non-discriminatory prohibitions on speech. A number of persuasive arguments can, however, be made to justify the special hostility to content-based restrictions.[74] If a particular viewpoint is outlawed, while others are permitted, the state distorts the terms of public debate. That is true whether the expression of the view is totally forbidden, or is made more difficult by onerous restrictions concerning the time, manner, or place of publication. A law prohibiting canvassing by Republicans on the streets or after 6.00 p.m. leaves them ample opportunities to proselytize in other ways or at other times, but it violates free speech principles by giving them fewer opportunities than Democrats to communicate their ideas. For in these circumstances, clearly the law is framed to limit speech. In contrast, a total ban on all canvassing on the streets might well be imposed in the interests of personal privacy or the smooth flow of traffic, and would then be less objectionable. In short, content-based restrictions should be subject to strict scrutiny, because it is very likely that they were framed to limit the communicative impact of speech.

These points bring out an underlying aspect of United States free speech jurisprudence. Much of it is explicable in terms of a strong suspicion of government, and its motives for imposing restrictions on speech. The principles formulated by the Supreme Court also appear to reveal a distrust of lower state courts, which cannot be relied on, it seems, to uphold freedom of speech when it is balanced against, say, the common law right to reputation or privacy, or important public interests. That is why the Supreme Court has formulated a number of free speech rules and principles which must be followed by state courts. The best example of this occurs in the context of libel actions, where the Court requires public official and figure claimants to prove with convincing clarity that the defamatory allegations were published with knowledge of their falsity.[75] A clear rule or 'definitional' balancing is preferred to ad hoc balancing on the basis of the particular facts of the case.[76]

---

[72] M. H. Redish, 'The Content Distinction in First Amendment Analysis' (1981) 34 *Stanford Law Rev* 113.

[73] See *Schneider* v. *State* 308 US 147 (1939), striking down a ban as going further than necessary to prevent the spread of litter.

[74] G. R. Stone, 'Content Regulation and the First Amendment' (1983) 25 *William and Mary Law Rev* 189.   [75] See ch. VI, s. 3(i) below.

[76] For the merits of this approach, see F. Schauer, 'Categories and the First Amendment: A Play in Three Acts' (1981) 34 *Vanderbilt Law Rev* 265, 296–307.

The strong suspicion of government interference with speech may have influenced US free speech jurisprudence in other ways. First, courts are usually unsympathetic to measures which on one view promote free speech rights or values. The Supreme Court, for instance, has invalidated a statutory right of reply to critical newspaper articles, on the ground that it infringed press freedom.[77] The state court had held the reply right promoted free speech and the free flow of information to the public, but the Court found that enforcement of this right would entail undesirable government intrusion. A Circuit Court of Appeals has accepted the decision of the Federal Communication Commission (FCC) to repeal the Fairness Doctrine, under which broadcasters were required to cover controversial issues of public importance and to present a balanced range of opinion on these issues;[78] it was accepted that the requirement involved unacceptable intrusion by government and the FCC into the freedom of broadcasters to draw up their own schedules.[79] This suspicion of any government regulation, even when it appears intended to promote freedom of speech, is a marked characteristic of US free speech jurisprudence; it is not shared in other jurisdictions.[80]

A second consequence of the strong suspicion of government is that courts are unwilling to interfere with private censorship or control of speech. For example, as already noted,[81] there are no First Amendment access rights to demonstrate or distribute leaflets on private shopping malls. Media corporations are now probably free to merge, and certainly free to refuse to cover important stories, even though these steps impoverish public discourse and the values of free speech. The point is simply that the First Amendment guarantees rights against the state, not against media and other corporations which may be as anxious as government to limit the range of topics and views discussed in public. The merits of this controversy are discussed elsewhere in this book;[82] it need only be emphasized here that one objection to the control of private censorship is that it inevitably requires intervention by government or a specialist public agency, and that is anathema to US courts and many commentators.

The US approach to free speech issues differs considerably, as will be seen, from the jurisprudence in many other countries and jurisdictions. At the risk of considerable oversimplification, freedom of speech is more strongly protected against government regulation in the United States, than it is, say, in Germany and under the ECHR, while other systems, particularly France and Germany, are more willing to countenance restraints on the threats to pluralism from private interests. Courts in the United States distrust detailed, ad hoc balancing of free speech against other competing rights and interests, fearing that the former will inevitably be given too little weight in the scales.

---

[77] *Miami Herald* v. *Tornillo* 418 US 241 (1974): see ch. XII, s. 2(ii) below.
[78] *Syracuse Peace Council* v. *FCC* 867 F 2d 654 (DC Cir, 1989).
[79] For freedom of speech in broadcasting, see ch. XII, s. 5 below.
[80] For the sharply contrasting approaches in Germany, France, and Italy, see ss. 4 and 6 below.
[81] See text at n. 56 above.   [82] In ch. XII below.

A final point should be made. Free speech law in the United States is much more complex than it is in other countries. One reason for this complexity is that the Supreme Court has formulated a number of distinctive free speech doctrines and principles, some of which have been mentioned in this chapter. Others will be explored throughout this book. To some extent these doctrines represent an alternative to the detailed weighing of free speech and other interests which is characteristic in, for example, the courts of Canada and Germany and in the European Human Rights Court. But another reason is simply that the US courts have grappled with free speech issues for much longer than other courts. They have considered these issues for nearly a hundred years, while European courts have for the most part only been engaged with them for the last forty or fifty years. Canada has developed a serious free speech jurisprudence only since enactment of the Charter in 1982, while arguably the courts in England began this development when the HRA 1998 came into force. There is much more American case-law to organize into coherent categories. It is no more surprising that free speech law in the United States is rich and complex, than it is, say, that the law of torts or trusts is difficult in England or Australia.

3. Canada

Until enactment of the Charter of Rights and Freedoms in 1982, as part of the Constitution Act, Canadian free speech law had largely followed the common law approach in England. However, in one notable case, two members of the Supreme Court suggested there was an implicit right to free political speech inherent in the democratic character of Canadian government,[83] while in others the Court struck down by-laws giving local authorities wide powers to stop the distribution of pamphlets and so impose a prior restraint on the exercise of a fundamental freedom to engage in political debate.[84]

The Charter has transformed the legal position. Section 2 provides: 'Everyone has the following fundamental freedoms... (b) freedom of thought, belief, opinion and expression, including freedom of the press and other media of communication.' But unlike the First Amendment it is clear from the text of the Charter that this right is not absolute, for section 1 states:

The Canadian Charter of Rights and Freedoms guarantees the rights and freedoms set out in it subject only to such reasonable limits prescribed by law as can be demonstrably justified in a free and democratic society.

---

[83] *Re Alberta Statutes* [1938] SCR 100, 132–5, 142–6 per Duff CJ and Cannon J. These judgments have influenced the formulation of an implied right to free political expression in Australia: see s. 6 below.

[84] *Saumer* v. *City of Quebec* [1953] 2 SCR 299, 329 per Rand J.; *Switzman* v. *Elbling & A-G of Quebec* [1957] SCR 285.

Other provisions should also be mentioned, notably section 32 which states that the Charter applies both to the federal Parliament and government and to the legislatures and governments of the provinces. Under section 33, however, the federal Parliament and a state legislature can 'override' Charter provisions, including section 2(b), for a period of no more than five years by expressly declaring in its legislation that it is to operate notwithstanding the Charter.

From its first decision on freedom of expression,[85] the Supreme Court has taken a broad view of its scope. It encompasses all modes of expression other than violence or the threat of violence. It included, therefore, in this case peaceful picketing which was intended to induce a breach of contract and to put economic pressure on the respondent. The Court held that freedom of expression covers speech, whether or not it forms part of a dialogue or public debate. In the important *Irwin Toy* case,[86] the Court rejected an argument that restrictions on advertising directed at children did not engage freedom of expression at all, so there would be no need to determine whether the restrictions were justified under section 1 of the Charter. The crucial question was whether the activity at issue attempted to convey a meaning; if it did, it was covered by section 2(b). It is immaterial whether the expression is unpopular or tasteless; there is no difference, it seems, between valuable and less valuable speech.[87] If the purpose of the restriction is to limit expression, section 2(b) is infringed.[88] The effect of this approach has been that the Court has rarely grappled seriously with questions about the meaning of 'expression' for the purpose of the Charter. Invariably, it has spent more time considering whether the restriction imposed on the exercise of the freedom can be justified under section 1.

When it determines whether a restriction on freedom of expression is reasonably justified, the Court applies a complex test which can be broken down into four parts. The first issue is whether the state can show that the restriction fulfils a pressing and substantial objective of sufficient gravity to justify the imposition of limits on freedom of expression. The Court has recognized, for instance, as substantial objectives for this purpose the protection of minorities against the psychological and social harms of hate speech,[89] the protection of women against the injury to their dignity occasioned by pornography,[90] the protection of public health against the risks from smoking,[91] and privacy and fair trial rights in the context of legal proceedings.[92] Secondly, the state must show a rational connection between that objective and the restriction or suppression of the publication.

---

[85] *RWDSU* v. *Dolphin Delivery Ltd* [1986] 2 SCR 573. See Moon, ch. 2 for a critical analysis of the Court's approach to freedom of expression.

[86] *Irwin Toy* v. *A-G of Quebec* [1989] 1 SCR 927.   [87] Ibid., 986 per Dickson CJ.

[88] On the other hand, when a law is not intended to limit speech, but merely has that effect, there is only a violation of section 2(b) if the speech which is constrained advances the purposes of freedom of expression: see Moon, 34–5.   [89] *R* v. *Keegstra* [1990] 3 SCR 697.

[90] *R* v. *Butler* [1992] 1 SCR 452.

[91] *RJR-McDonald Inc* v. *A-G of Canada* [1995] 3 SCR 199.

[92] *Canadian Newspapers* v. *A-G of Canada* [1988] 2 SCR 122; *Dagenais* v. *Canadian Broadcasting Corpn* [1994] 3 SCR 835.

The principle of proportionality, thirdly, obliges the state in principle to show that the legislation amounted to a 'minimal impairment' of speech, or put another way, that it could not have achieved its objective with a more limited intrusion on the exercise of free speech rights. However, when applying this aspect of the proportionality principle, the Court is reluctant to intervene if evidence suggests that the legislature acted reasonably; it is not always required to choose the least intrusive measure.[93] The fourth aspect of the test requires the courts to weigh the benefit of the restriction in terms, say, of promoting public order or racial harmony against the significance of the erosion of free expression rights.

Although the Supreme Court is unconcerned with the value of the particular expression for the purpose of determining the scope of section 2(b), it will take this into account when deciding whether a reasonable limit has been justified under section 1 of the Charter. This was made clear by Dickson CJ in his judgment for the Court in *Keegstra* when it upheld the constitutionality of the proscription of racist hate speech: 'the s. 1 analysis of a limit upon s. 2(b) cannot ignore the nature of the expressive activity which the state seeks to restrict'.[94] Not all speech is of equal value when determining the constitutionality of limits placed on it. In *Keegstra*, Dickson CJ found that hate speech is of limited importance, given that it plays no part in the discovery of truth, that its message injures the self-fulfilment of members of the target groups, and that it deters them from participating in the democratic process. The low value of hate speech was considered at all stages of the balancing process under section 1; in particular, the Court did not apply the 'minimum impairment' test rigorously by requiring Parliament to show the legislation was narrowly drawn only to penalize speech which caused actual hatred of an identifiable group. Unlike McLachlin J. who entered a vigorous dissent, the Court was unconcerned that the legislation might deter or chill some extreme political speech.

The Canadian Supreme Court, therefore, fully considers the context of the particular case and the value of the expression at issue when determining whether the state has made its case for restricting exercise of the freedom. Unlike the US Supreme Court, it is prepared to balance in the light of the particular circumstances and it has not formulated principles, on the basis of which it is difficult for lower courts to uphold limits on speech.[95] Arguably, it would be more logical to rule that, say, hard-core pornography is not covered by section 2(b), than it is to hold that it is covered, but that its prohibition is justified because its impact is to demean the self-esteem of women and to lead men to disparage and perhaps mistreat them. For these harms result from the message or ideas communicated by pornography. If pornography (or racist speech) is covered by freedom of expression,

---

[93] See the judgment of Dickson CJ in *Irwin Toy* (n. 86 above), 992–9.

[94] *R* v. *Keegstra* [1990] 3 SCR 697, 760.

[95] For a critique of the Supreme Court's approach to freedom of expression cases, see J. Cameron, 'The Past, Present, and Future of Expressive Freedom under the *Charter*' (1997) 35 *Osgoode Hall Law Jo* 1.

some very pressing reason beyond this impact should be required to justify its proscription. Put another way, the Supreme Court of Canada does not insist on a substantial justification for the regulation unrelated to the suppression of expression. The content and value of the expression is treated as relevant to the balancing process, so the Court does not share the hostility of the US Supreme Court to content-based regulation.

While its approach is relatively cautious, the Canadian Supreme Court has invalidated a number of restrictions on expression. For instance, it has struck down the prohibition in Quebec of commercial advertising in English,[96] a ban on the publication of details of divorce proceedings,[97] and restrictions on access to a public airport to solicit support for an organization.[98] In perhaps its most controversial decision, it invalidated by a 5–4 majority a comprehensive ban on tobacco advertising, a step which would almost certainly be taken in the United States, but would be unlikely in any European jurisdiction, let alone by decision of the European Human Rights Court.[99] That decision, as do others, brings out the contrasting approaches of different judges to free speech issues; there was disagreement about the appropriateness of ascribing a value to commercial advertising, the relevance of the tobacco manufacturers' profit motive and about the evidence needed to support the ban. Further, McLachlin J. for the Court and La Forest J. in a powerful dissent took sharply divergent lines on the 'minimal impairment' test; it was an important factor in the Court's decision to invalidate the comprehensive ban that it found the legislature could have imposed a more limited ban on lifestyle, and not informational, advertising, while La Forest J. said that Parliament could have opted for a more draconian ban on smoking, so that the advertising rule amounted to 'minimal impairment'.

The jurisprudence of the Canadian Supreme Court is, therefore, already rich and repays comparative study. Its approach to free expression issues and its resolution of particular issues offers a marked contrast to that of the US Supreme Court.[100] This is particularly apparent in the areas of hate speech and pornography where it has upheld restrictions on speech, which would certainly have been struck down in the United States. Whether its approach is similar to or diverges from that of the US courts, the Canadian Supreme Court frequently cites their judgments and even considers academic writing from American scholars. Sometimes different terminology is preferred, perhaps to show a distinctively Canadian approach. When it decided that there is a free expression right to use a public airport (and other comparable facilities) for the purpose of leafleting and soliciting support, the Court rejected the US 'public forum' approach to the

---

[96] *Ford* v. *A-G of Quebec* [1988] 2 SCR 712: see ch. III, s. 5 below for further discussion of this case.

[97] *Edmonton Journal* v. *A-G of Alberta* [1989] 2 SCR 1326.

[98] *Committee for the Commonwealth of Canada* v. *Canada* [1991] 1 SCR 139: see ch. VIII, s. 3(iii) below for further discussion.

[99] *RJR-McDonald Inc* v. *A-G of Canada* [1995] 3 SCR 199: see ch. XI, s. 5 below for further discussion.

[100] For a comparison of US and Canadian free speech jurisprudence from an American perspective, see K. Greenawalt, *Fighting Words* (Princeton, NJ: Princeton University Press, 1995), esp. ch. 2.

categorization of places open to the public for speech; instead L'Heureux Dubé J. asked whether the government had shown good grounds for restricting speech on what she characterized as a 'public arena'.[101]

In theory, Canadian and US free speech law share at least one important feature. In both systems free speech or expression rights are guaranteed only against invasion by government or other public authorities. Section 32 of the Charter makes it plain that Charter rights bind both federal and provincial authorities. But private persons and bodies are not bound to observe freedom of expression in the same way. Nor are the courts directly bound by the Charter when they apply the common law in litigation between private parties; but they should develop 'the common law in a manner consistent with the fundamental values enshrined in the Constitution'.[102] It is far from predictable how far the Charter right to freedom of expression affects common law principles. The Court has held that contempt of court principles designed to protect fair trial rights against prejudicial publicity should be applied in conformity with the Charter, so that the common law preference for the former right should be reformulated to take account of freedom of expression and of the press.[103] On the other hand, in one of its most conservative decisions (from the free speech perspective) the Court declined to hold a libel action brought by a government lawyer was constrained directly by the Charter right to freedom of expression. In the Court's view, there was no government action.[104] Moreover, balancing the values of freedom of expression and reputation rights, Cory J. for the Court gave defamatory statements low value and declined to adopt the US *New York Times* rule under which a public official can only win a libel action if (to oversimplify a little) he proves that the allegations had been made with knowledge of their falsity. In this case, the Charter had no impact on the common law. Canada is now unique in not recognizing the impact of free speech and expression on reputation rights.[105]

4. Germany

Freedom of expression, press freedom, and other related freedoms are guaranteed in Germany by Article 5 of the Basic Law (*Grundgesetz*).[106] It provides:

(1) Everyone shall have the right freely to express and disseminate his opinion by speech, writing and pictures and freely to inform himself from generally accessible sources.

---

[101] *Committee for the Commonwealth of Canada* v. *Canada* [1991] 1 SCR 139, 190.
[102] *RWDSU* v. *Dolphin Delivery Ltd* [1986] 2 SCR 573, 603 per McIntyre J.
[103] *Dagenais* v. *Canadian Broadcasting Corpn* [1994] 3 SCR 835: see ch. IX, s. 3(iii) below for discussion.   [104] *Hill* v. *Church of Scientology of Toronto* [1995] 2 SCR 1130.
[105] See ch. VI, ss. 2 and 3 below.
[106] For commentary on Article 5, see W. Hoffmann-Riem, *Kommunikationsfreiheiten* (Baden-Baden: Nomos, 2002) and D. P. Currie, *The Constitution of the Federal Republic of Germany* (Illinois: Chicago UP, 1994), ch. 4.

Freedom of the press and freedom of reporting by means of broadcasts and films are guaranteed. There shall be no censorship.

(2) These rights are limited by the provisions of the general laws, the provisions of law for the protection of youth, and by the right to inviolability of personal honour.

(3) Art and science, research and teaching shall be free. Freedom of teaching shall not absolve from loyalty to the constitution.

In contrast to the bald terms of the US First Amendment and section 2(b) of the Canadian Charter, the detailed character of these provisions is striking. Not only, as might be expected from a constitution drafted in 1949, are there references to cinema and broadcasting, but there is particular provision for academic and artistic freedom. The rights of speaker and recipient are separately recognized, as they are under the ECHR. The relationship between the freedom to express opinion (*Meinungsfreiheit*) and the right to receive information (*Informationsfreiheit*) has been much discussed by the Federal Constitutional Court; it is clear that they are separate rights, the latter protecting the interests of recipients in unimpeded access to information supplied by sources willing to provide it.[107] There used to be some uncertainty whether the former freedom covers the communication of *facts* as well as the expression of *opinions*. But it is now clear that a distinction between facts and opinions could only be drawn with difficulty, and that *Meinungsfreiheit* covers statements of fact, unless the disseminator knows they are false.[108]

Freedom of the press (*Pressefreiheit*) and broadcasting freedom (*Rundfunkfreiheit*) are treated by the Constitutional Court as distinct from the freedom to express opinions. They protect the institutional independence of newspaper and broadcasting companies from the state, rather than the content of particular articles or programmes from legal restriction.[109] For example, a newspaper's right not to reveal the sources of its information or to have its offices ransacked (without powerful justification) are protected by press freedom, while a primary concern of broadcasting freedom is to ensure that television and radio companies are organizationally free from government influence; the state must not, for instance, appoint all the members of a broadcasting authority. But the Court has also made it clear that broadcasting freedom is subordinate to, or serves, the values of freedom of expression; the interests of viewers in access to a wide variety of programmes and information are more important than the unfettered freedom of a broadcaster to draw up a programme schedule as it pleases.

Censorship is prohibited by the last sentence of Article 5(1). It is an absolute prohibition. But its scope is limited to administrative control exercised before publication or communication. It does not extend to judicial restraints, so its

---

[107] See in particular 27 BVerfGE 71 (1969) where the Constitutional Court held that *Informationsfreiheit* is not a component part of the freedom to express an opinion, but an independent right. It is treated in this way in commentaries: see Hoffmann-Riem (n. 106 above), chs. 4 and 5.

[108] This point is particularly relevant to the treatment of defamatory allegations: see ch. VI, s. 3(iii) below.

[109] See ch. XII, s. 2 below for press freedom and ch. XII, s. 5 below for free speech in broadcasting.

impact is narrower than the principles developed by the US Supreme Court which preclude injunctions save in extreme circumstances.[110]

Some other provisions of the Basic Law should be mentioned. There are separate guarantees for freedom of assembly (*Versammlungsfreiheit*) and for the free establishment of political parties: Articles 8 and 21. These freedoms strengthen the protection of free speech within particular contexts, for example, the conduct of demonstrations and peaceful protest.[111] Other provisions, however, may limit the exercise of freedom of expression. Among them are Article 2 guaranteeing the right to the free development of personality, including privacy rights, and Article 14 guaranteeing property rights. Article 18 provides that freedom of expression and other rights may be forfeited by decision of the Constitutional Court, if they are abused. The most important right is the inviolable dignity of man, guaranteed by Article 1 of the Basic Law which cannot be amended.[112] All other constitutional rights, including freedom of expression, are to be interpreted in the light of this principle. To some extent, commitment to human dignity explains why the Constitutional Court has rejected a challenge to the constitutionality of the statutory provision proscribing Holocaust denial; the provision is rooted in Article 1 of the Basic Law.[113]

In different contexts the Court has emphasized the contribution of the Article 5 freedoms to the development of the individual personality,[114] and their importance to the development of public opinion on political matters. Recognition has, therefore, been given to both the second and third arguments for a free speech principle which were considered in Chapter I. The latter is perhaps the more important; it has influenced the strong protection given to freedom of expression in relation to reputation and personality rights, when the publication concerns a political figure or party or it discusses matters of important public concern.[115] It was emphasized in the seminal *Lüth* case,[116] the first ruling of the Court on Article 5. The case involved a civil action brought by a film director, Harlan, against Lüth, the director of information services in Hamburg who had called for a boycott of a new film made by Harlan.[117] The boycott was called to protest against the director's Nazi associations. The Constitutional Court upheld the argument that the boycott call was covered by freedom of expression; it regarded the freedom as a basic right in a liberal democratic constitutional order which fosters intellectual dialogue and vigorous public debate.[118] When balancing the exercise of this freedom against the film director's private

---

[110] These issues are discussed in ch. IV below.

[111] This topic is considered in ch. VIII below.   [112] Basic Law, art. 79(3).

[113] 90 BVerfGE 241 (1994). See ch. V, s. 4 below.

[114] In 54 BVerfGE 129, 136–7 (1980) the Court stressed the particular importance of the self-fulfilment rationale for verbal speech.

[115] See in particular 61 BVerfGE 1 (1982), treating as political expression the characterization of a political party as neo-Nazi, and the decision of the Federal Supreme Court, NJW 1994, 124, holding as protected political speech a Greenpeace poster campaign which accused the chairman of a chemical company of responsibility for serious pollution.   [116] 7 BVerfGE 198 (1958).

[117] The action was brought under art. 826 of the Civil Code which requires compensation for causing intentional damage 'in a manner offensive to good morals'.

[118] 7 BVerfGE 198, 208 (1958).

economic rights, it was important to note that the speaker in this case was seeking to influence public opinion on German cultural life in the post-war period and its need to rid itself of National Socialist influences.

The *Lüth* case is significant in other respects. Article 5(2) makes it plain that freedom of expression is not an absolute right. Its exercise may be limited by the provisions of general laws (as well as by specific laws to protect young people and by the right of personal honour). In *Lüth* the Court held that these general laws should themselves be interpreted in the light of the fundamental values enshrined in Article 5.[119] Although it is the primary purpose of basic rights to protect citizens against public authority, they are not simply defensive or negative rights. Rather, the rights, in this case freedom of expression, create a system of values which must influence all spheres of law and shape the development of private law. Further, private law itself forms part of the 'general laws' which must be interpreted and applied in conformity with basic constitutional rights.[120] Under these principles, freedom of expression has had a significant impact on defamation and privacy laws, in addition to its influence on the application of statutory provisions enacted to keep public order, to ensure racial harmony, and to regulate unfair competition.

In these respects German free speech law may not be radically different in kind from other systems which allow constitutional rights to shape private law. In both England and the United States, freedom of speech arguments influence in different ways the laws of libel and breach of confidence (or privacy). Even in Canada, Charter values should be considered when courts consider private rights, though this point appears to have been given little weight in the libel context. The German Constitutional Court's approach, however, is distinctive insofar as it may require the state, whether the federal government or a Land (state) government, to take positive steps to protect basic rights. In the context of freedom of expression, this obligation to protect basic rights (*Schutzpflicht*) has been particularly important with regard to the structure and organization of broadcasting authorities and companies. In a number of decisions the Court has required the Länder to ensure that these bodies are free from domination by state and commercial interests and that appropriate programme requirements ensure the provision of a balanced schedule.[121] The Court does not prescribe the exact steps which must be taken to satisfy freedom of expression values, but it does issue guidelines. This degree of intervention would be regarded as dangerous in the United States, where freedom of speech is, as we have seen, protected only against the state; private persons and companies are not bound to observe the free speech rights of others. The imposition of programme requirements would probably infringe the First Amendment rights of broadcasters.

While under Article 5(2) of the Basic Law freedom to disseminate opinions, press and broadcasting freedoms may be limited by general laws, freedom of art

---

[119] 7 BVerfGE 198, 212 (1958).
[120] For a full discussion of these complex aspects of German constitutional law, see P. E. Quint, 'Free Speech and Private Law in German Constitutional Theory' (1989) 48 *Maryland Law Rev* 247.
[121] See ch. XII, s. 5 below.

(*Kunstfreiheit*) and science, and research are apparently unlimited. Article 5(3) does not authorize the imposition of any restrictions or conditions on the freedoms it guarantees, save for teaching freedom which does not grant exemption from loyalty to the constitution, say, for communists or fascists. Nevertheless, it has been established in a number of cases that *Kunstfreiheit* and other freedoms under Article 5(3) must be balanced against other *constitutional* rights and must give way to them when the latter are entitled to greater weight in the circumstances of the case. The leading authority is the famous *Mephisto* decision.[122] The case arose from the republication in 1964 of Klaus Mann's satirical novel, *Mephisto*, originally published in the 1930s. It mercilessly portrayed an actor who courted the favour of Nazi leaders to promote his career; the actor on whom the character was based had died, but his son took proceedings to ban distribution of the novel. The publisher claimed the protection of Article 5(3), apparently an absolute freedom, but the Court ruled that it should be balanced against other *constitutional* rights, in particular the inalienable right to human dignity guaranteed by Article 1 of the Basic Law. A work of art can have social effects and may conflict with privacy and personality rights.[123] A divided Court considered that the civil courts had properly balanced the competing constitutional rights in banning the book's distribution.[124]

This last point brings out two important aspects of German free speech law. First, the courts weigh freedom of expression (or the other right guaranteed by Article 5) against competing rights and interests, whether these are constitutional or reflect legislative objectives. This is a detailed process in which judges may attach greater or less importance to a range of factors. For instance, in *Mephisto* itself, the disagreement between the Court and the dissenting judges concerned the relative weight to be given to a number of factors, including the need to protect the reputation and memory of a dead person, the character of the work which sullied that reputation, and the novel's commentary on how artists had collaborated with the Nazis. The Court gave more weight to the first factor, while the dissents put more emphasis on the character of the work as a daring work of fiction and its contribution to public debate. The process is generally one of ad hoc, factual balancing, quite different from the approach of the US Supreme Court under which complex doctrine and rules are applied to the facts of free speech cases. However, in some areas, notably in defamation and privacy cases, the Court has issued a number of guidelines; there is a presumption in favour of freedom of expression when the publication concerns political and other matters of contemporary debate, while opinion should be more strongly protected than allegations of fact.[125]

---

[122] 30 BVerfGE 173 (1971) (considered further in ch. VI, s. 3(iii) below).

[123] Ibid., 193–4.

[124] Three members of the Court dissented from its decision. Dissenting opinions to Constitutional Court judgments have been permitted since 1971, but are relatively rare.

[125] See further ch. VI, s. 3(iii) below.

Secondly, the role of the Constitutional Court is to ensure that the lower courts—civil, criminal, or other specialist courts such as labour courts—have properly taken the basic rights into account when coming to their decision. It does not intervene unless, say, the civil courts, which heard the case, have, in its view, failed to give adequate weight to freedom of expression or the other basic rights and constitutional provisions at issue. The Court might conceivably have decided the *Mephisto* case differently if it had been acting as an appellate court, as do the US and Canadian Supreme Courts. But it was instead considering a constitutional complaint brought by the publisher that the civil courts had failed to respect his constitutional right.[126] The Court decided that they had taken freedom of expression into account and weighed it properly against competing constitutional rights, although it might itself have considered that freedom of expression trumped the dignity and personality rights of the deceased actor. As a result the Constitutional Court might perhaps intervene less often than an appellate court.

Nevertheless it would be wrong to underestimate the Court's considerable contribution to free speech jurisprudence. It has insisted that freedom of expression covers expressive conduct such as the wearing of badges and the desecration of flags,[127] and it has extended its protection to commercial advertising inasmuch as it raises issues of public concern.[128] It requires lower courts to safeguard freedom of speech in libel and privacy proceedings.[129] And, as already mentioned, on a number of occasions the Court has ruled that broadcasting legislation must reflect the values of freedom of expression by ensuring that public and private radio and television companies are fully independent. In this last area its jurisprudence is unusually fertile, though other constitutional courts in Europe have adopted similar approaches.[130]

5. The European Human Rights Convention

Article 10 of the European Convention on Human Rights and Fundamental Freedoms (ECHR) provides:

(1) Everyone has the right to freedom of expression. This right shall include freedom to hold opinions and to receive and impart information and ideas without interference by public authority and regardless of frontiers. This Article shall not prevent States from requiring the licensing of broadcasting, television or cinema enterprises.

---

[126] Many free speech cases arise under the procedure provided by art. 93 of the Basic Law under which a complaint may be brought directly to the Constitutional Court that a public authority, including a court, has violated a basic or other fundamental right.   [127] See ch. III, s. 2 below.
[128] Ch. XI, s. 2 below.   [129] See ch. VI, s. 3(iii) below.
[130] See E. Barendt, 'The Influence of the German and Italian Constitutional Courts on their National Broadcasting Systems' [1991] *PL* 93, and R. Craufurd-Smith, *Broadcasting Law and Fundamental Rights* (Oxford: OUP, 1997), chs. 6 and 7.

(2) The exercise of these freedoms, since it carries with it duties and responsibilities, may be subject to such formalities, conditions, restrictions or penalties as are prescribed by law and are necessary in a democratic society in the interests of national security, territorial integrity or public safety, for the prevention of disorder or crime, for the protection of health or morals, for the protection of the reputation or rights of others, for preventing the disclosure of information received in confidence, or for maintaining the authority and impartiality of the judiciary.

The most obvious feature of these provisions is the extensive list of circumstances in which limitations to the freedom of expression may be upheld. On a superficial view it appears that Article 10(2) virtually removes the right granted by the first paragraph. But this does not reflect the approach of the European Court of Human Rights, the court sitting in Strasbourg which considers applications by individuals that a state has violated the rights guaranteed them by the ECHR.[131] In addition to the requirement that any permissible restriction must be 'prescribed by law', which excludes arbitrary restraints lacking in legal certainty,[132] the limit must be *necessary in a democratic society* to further the stated aims and goals. The balancing, therefore, starts with a presumption in favour of freedom of expression, the exceptions to which must be narrowly construed. Moreover, the European Court has ruled that an interference with speech should only be treated as 'necessary' if there was a 'pressing social need' for it in the particular circumstances, if the restriction was proportionate to the aim pursued, and the reasons given for it were relevant and sufficient.[133] It is for the state defending the restriction to show that these requirements are satisfied.

In practice, the crucial issue for the Court in Strasbourg is whether the state has met that burden. It rarely considers at length whether the particular speech is covered by Article 10 or, put another way, whether the provision is engaged. However, it is clear from the Court's jurisprudence that freedom of expression covers the dissemination of ideas which shock, offend, and disturb the community, not only those which are acceptable to it.[134] Sexually explicit material may, therefore, fall within Article 10(1), though, of course, it does not follow that its circulation cannot be prohibited compatibly with Article 10(2). The Article also covers commercial speech and professional advertising.[135] Prior restraints or censorship are not wholly forbidden, but are subject to particularly careful scrutiny, because they prevent or delay the exercise of freedom of expression rights.[136] Article 10 is not engaged when an applicant claims a right of access to acquire information; freedom of expression under the ECHR is a negative liberty

---

[131] For a general commentary on the ECHR and the Court, see M. Janis, R. S. Kay, and A. W. Bradley, *European Human Rights Law: Text and Materials*, 2nd edn. (Oxford: OUP, 2002), chs. 1–3.

[132] *Sunday Times* v. *UK* (1979) 2 EHRR 245, 270–3. (The case is discussed in ch. IX, s. 3(i) below.)

[133] Ibid., 275–7. These requirements are frequently restated in European Court rulings on art. 10.

[134] *Handyside* v. *UK* (1976) 1 EHRR 737.

[135] *Casado Coca* v. *Spain* (1994) 18 EHRR 1: see further ch. XI below.

[136] *Observer and Guardian* v. *UK* (1992) 14 EHRR 153: see further ch. IV below.

protected against state interference, though in some circumstances a state may be required to protect its exercise.[137]

Many of the Court's judgments have concerned applications from the press or other branches of the media that libel, breach of confidence, or contempt of court laws are unduly restrictive of their freedom to cover matters of public interest. It has emphasized the vital role of the press as 'public watchdog'; it is incumbent on it to impart information and ideas of public interest.[138] Journalistic freedom allows room for some exaggeration and provocation. But journalists must provide reliable information and act in good faith in accordance with ethical standards;[139] the exercise of free expression under Article 10(2) 'carries with it duties and responsibilities'. As will be shown later in this book, the Court gives somewhat greater weight to freedom of expression with regard to reputation and privacy rights than English courts generally do, though it does not attach the same importance as the US Supreme Court to the exercise of the freedom in this context.[140]

The most distinctive principle formulated by the European Court stems from its position as a supra-national court. It allows member states a 'margin of appreciation' in determining whether it is necessary to impose a restriction on the exercise of freedom of expression. At the same time the Court supervises both the formulation of the restriction and its application by national courts to ensure it is proportionate to the legitimate aim in respect of which it was imposed. While the Strasbourg Court is not an appellate court, it reviews the reasons for the national courts' decisions with great care, often examining the facts of the case in detail. This approach, however, allows it to intervene more readily to protect freedom of expression in some circumstances than in others. States enjoy a wide margin of appreciation when they impose restrictions on the display of sexually explicit material,[141] on commercial speech,[142] or the disclosure of official secrets.[143] In contrast, the Court is more prepared to intervene to safeguard an attack on government or a political figure, even when it takes the form of defamatory allegations.[144]

Three seminal free speech decisions may be discussed briefly. The first two illustrate points made in the previous paragraphs. In the *Sunday Times* case,[145] a majority of the Court held incompatible with freedom of expression the absolute contempt of court rule which had been applied by the House of Lords to stop discussion of the merits of legal proceedings before trial, in this case the trial of the action against a drug company in respect of deformities caused by its thalidomide drug. The United Kingdom had not shown that this restriction was necessary, taking account of the widespread public concern about the level of compensation offered by the drug

---

137 These complex issues are considered in ch. III, s. 6 below.

138 *Observer and Guardian* v. *UK* (n. 136 above), para. 59; *Jersild* v. *Denmark* (1995) 19 EHRR 1.

139 *Bergens Tidende* v. *Norway* (2001) 31 EHRR 16, para. 53.

140 See ch. VI, s. 3 below.   141 *Müller* v. *Switzerland* (1989) 13 EHRR 212.

142 *Markt Intern & Beerman* v. *Germany* (1990) 12 EHRR 161, paras. 33–7.

143 *Leander* v. *Sweden* (1987) 9 EHRR 433, para. 59; *Hadjianastassiou* v. *Greece* (1993) 16 EHRR 219, para. 47.

144 *Lingens* v. *Austria* (1986) 8 EHRR 407; *Castells* v. *Spain* (1992) 14 EHRR 145.

145 *Sunday Times* v. *UK* (1979) 2 EHRR 245, discussed in detail in ch. IX, s. 3 below.

company and the fact that the trial was not imminent. *Lingens* v. *Austria* was the first of many decisions concerning the impact of freedom of expression on national libel laws.[146] The editor of an Austrian magazine had been convicted of criminal libel for failing to prove the truth of its defamatory assessment of the conduct of the former Socialist Chancellor, Bruno Kreisky, in entering into a coalition government with an extreme right-wing political party. The Court unanimously held that this conviction infringed the editor's rights under Article 10. It emphasized the crucial role of the press in promoting public discussion; further, it enjoys wide freedom to criticize political figures who must expect scrutiny from the media when they enter public life. Austrian law wrongly required the defendant to prove the truth of a value judge-ment, an impossible burden. The imposition of that burden would have a deleteri-ous impact on freedom of expression.

The third ruling concerns the interpretation of the third sentence of Article 10(1), allowing states to license cinema and broadcasting. The issue in *Informationsverein* was whether this provision permitted Austria to maintain its public broadcasting monopoly.[147] The Court ruled first, that any broadcast licensing system or monopoly had to meet the general requirements of Article 10(2), in effect, that it was necessary in a democratic society to restrict freedom of expression in this way, say, to ensure a range of good quality programmes. Secondly, the Court argued that a public monopoly represented a far-reaching intrusion on media pluralism which states should guarantee; nobody could communicate his ideas on television unless the public broadcaster granted access. The third step was to point out that this intrusion could no longer be justified, given that broadcasting frequencies were no longer scarce and that other comparable countries allowed public and pri-vate broadcasters to coexist. Austria could take more moderate steps to ensure its objectives were met by, for example, ensuring that licensed private broadcasters had some quality programmes in their schedules. This decision, even more than the other two, shows that the European Court's free speech jurisprudence may have a significant impact on issues of sensitive political and cultural policy.

6. Other Jurisdictions

(i) France

The recognition of freedom of speech in France antedates the First Amendment to the US Constitution. Article 11 of the Declaration of the Rights of Man and of the Citizen of 1789 states:

The free communication of thoughts and opinions is one of the most precious rights of man; hence, every citizen may speak, write, and publish freely, save that he must answer for any abuse of such freedom in cases specified by *loi* (a law enacted by Parliament).

---

[146] N. 144 above, also discussed in ch. VI, s. 3(v) below.
[147] *Informationsverein Lentia* v. *Austria* (1994) 17 EHRR 93.

Article 10 should also be mentioned, although it has not played a significant role in free speech jurisprudence. It provides for freedom of opinion and religion, 'provided their expression does not infringe public policy as established by *loi*.' The Preamble to the Constitution of 1958 recognizes the attachment of the French people to the rights defined by the Declaration of 1789, but the text does not itself guarantee freedom of communication or other fundamental rights. However, one provision is important: Article 34 prescribes that Parliament itself must determine 'the rules concerning . . . civic rights and the fundamental safeguards granted to citizens for the exercise of civil liberties'. As a result it would be unconstitutional for the government or a minister to issue general regulations circumscribing the exercise of a right such as freedom of expression or of the press.[148]

Since 1971 the Conseil constitutionnel, to which bills may be referred before enactment for a judgment on their constitutionality, has established that laws must comply with the 1789 Declaration.[149] Legislation must, therefore, respect freedom of communication as it has been interpreted by the Conseil. But unlike the United States, Canada, and Germany, challenges cannot be made to its constitutionality after the bill has been enacted. That perhaps is one reason why there is less free speech jurisprudence in France than there is in other jurisdictions. Civil and criminal courts also take account of freedom of expression when applying, for example, laws on insult, defamation, and privacy. Privacy rights are strongly protected in France under jurisprudence, confirmed and clarified by a Law of 17 July 1970, but courts have to some extent limited their application to safeguard freedom of expression and press arguments.[150]

One statute should be mentioned. Article 1 of the Law of 29 July 1881 on liberty of the press states that printing and bookselling are free; it explicitly proscribes licensing of newspapers and periodicals.[151] The Press Law, however, contains a range of criminal penalties for various offences, whether committed by written publication, drawings, paintings, or verbally: for example, incitement to crime or to racial or religious hatred, defamation, or insult (*injure*).[152] Article 13 provides for a wide right of reply for anyone named or referred to in a publication; it can be claimed whether or not the publication's treatment of the individual was critical or injurious. Provisions of this kind are common in continental European jurisdictions. They raise difficult free speech questions. From the US perspective, they infringe press freedom, in particular the editor's right to determine the contents of his newspaper, but from another point of view they protect the free speech as well as the personality interests of the correspondent claiming the reply right.[153]

Freedom of communication questions have generally been raised before the Conseil constitutionnel in the course of challenges to laws concerning the press

---

[148] B. Nicholas, 'Loi, Règlement and Judicial Review in the Fifth Republic' [1970] *PL* 251.
[149] For an introduction to judicial review in France, see J. Bell, *French Constitutional Law* (Oxford: OUP, 1992).   [150] Some leading cases are mentioned in ch. VI, s. 5 below.
[151] Art. 5.   [152] Arts. 23–35.   [153] See ch. XII, s. 2(ii) below.

and broadcasting media.[154] In 1984 it considered a challenge to a law limiting newspaper holdings to 15 per cent of the market, and requiring transparency concerning their ownership and financing.[155] It was argued that these provisions inhibited press freedom and commercial freedom. For the most part, the Conseil rejected these arguments.[156] As far as the transparency provisions were concerned, it held that they promoted the effective choice of readers, enabling them to make informed judgements about newspapers. More generally, it ruled that Parliament is entitled to regulate freedom of communication to make its exercise more effective and to balance it with other constitutional rules and values. Among those values is pluralism. Pluralism requires the public to enjoy access to a variety of newspapers, representing different strands of opinion. The Conseil emphasized that Article 11 of the Declaration of Rights of Man conferred on readers rights of choice, which must not be subordinated to private interests or public control, nor left to the market.[157]

This is a seminal ruling. The recipient interest in freedom of speech was fully recognized, although it had not been spelt out in the text of Article 11. Moreover, it trumped the free press and free enterprise interests of newspaper magnates to expand their business without restraint. Media pluralism is a constitutional value, which may justify limits on those interests. Subsequently, the Conseil made it plain that press legislation must comply with these requirements, when it held incompatible with Article 11 of the Declaration provisions in a Bill of 1986 which had relaxed the terms of the 1984 Law without adequately guaranteeing pluralism.[158]

These principles have been applied in the context of broadcasting regulation. In a series of rulings,[159] the Conseil has said that it is for Parliament to balance the exercise of freedom of communication, in the light of technical constraints, with other constitutional values, such as public order, the rights of others, and the need to preserve cultural and social pluralism. It followed that broadcasting legislation could establish an independent authority with powers to issue programme standards and to fine broadcasters who infringed those standards or advertising constraints; further, this legislation should contain adequate safeguards against media oligopolies and concentrations. These rulings are similar to those in other European jurisdictions, notably Germany and Italy.[160] But no other court has fashioned a general principle of pluralism, applicable to all branches of the media. It affirms that individual free speech rights can be limited by a constitutional value, itself intimately connected to freedom of speech.[161] For that reason alone, the French contribution to free speech jurisprudence has been extremely significant.

---

[154] L. Pech, *La Liberté d'Expression et sa Limitation* (Presses Universitaires de la Faculté de Clermont-Ferrand, 2003), paras. 63–8.   [155] Decision 84-181 of 10–11 Oct. 1984, Rec 73.
[156] See ch. XII, s. 3(ii) below for a discussion of press freedom and competition law.
[157] N. 155 above, paras. 35–8.   [158] Decision 86-210 of 29 July 1986, Rec 110.
[159] Decision 82-141 of 27 July 1982, Rec 48; Decision 86-217 of 18 Sept. 1986, Rec 141; Decision 88-248 of 17 Jan. 1989, Rec 18.
[160] See E. M. Barendt, *Broadcasting Law* (Oxford: OUP, 1995), 13–28.
[161] See ch. I, s. 4 above.

(ii) Italy

Reference is made in this book to a few decisions of the Corte Costituzionale on freedom of expression, particularly in the discussion of this freedom in relation to broadcasting regulation. The Italian post-war Constitution of 1948 contains a number of detailed provisions relevant to freedom of speech, of which the most important is undoubtedly Article 21.[162] Its first two paragraphs proclaim (author's translation):

Everyone has the right freely to express his own thoughts (*diritto di manifestare liberamente il proprio pensiero*) verbally, in writing, and by every other means of communication.

The press may not be subject to licensing or censorship. But these freedoms are qualified in other paragraphs; for example, the courts may restrain publication to stop a civil wrong, where this is authorized by a law of Parliament. Paragraph six forbids publications, theatrical and other dramatic events, and all other forms of communication contrary to good behaviour (*buon costume*), authorizing laws to prevent and punish such material.

A few other provisions of the Constitution should be mentioned. Article 15 guarantees the freedom and confidentiality of correspondence and other forms of communication; it covers private communications addressed to individuals or small groups, rather than material addressed to the general public or a section of it.[163] Article 33 guarantees freedom of arts and sciences, and their teaching, while Article 41 protects freedom of private economic enterprise; the latter is particularly pertinent for the protection of commercial advertising and for the rights of private commercial broadcasters. Article 3 of the Constitution recognizes the equal right of all citizens to human dignity as a fundamental principle.[164]

The restriction on public expression contrary to good behaviour has been interpreted by the Constitutional Court to apply to sexually explicit material, the dissemination of which offends standards of decency.[165] It has held that only publications which violate common minimum ethical standards, required by respect for human dignity, may be proscribed; publications which fail to meet these standards may be proscribed, even though they do not have a sexually explicit content.[166] As in Germany, freedom of expression must be weighed against other rights and values prescribed by the Constitution, so the protection of personal honour may support application of libel laws, whether criminal or civil.

---

[162] For commentaries, see C. Esposito, *La Libertà di Manifestazione del Pensiero nell'Ordinamento Italiano* (Milan: Giuffrè, 1958); P. Barile, *Libertà di Manifestazione del Pensiero* (Milan: Giuffrè, 1975); A. Pace, *Problematica delle libertà costituzionali, Parte Speciale*, 2nd edn. (Padua: Cedam, 1992), paras. 87–100. [163] Ibid., para. 55.

[164] Ibid., para. 91, a. Art. 2 recognizes and guarantees the inalienable right of the individual to develop his personality in social relationships.

[165] Ibid., para. 91, e. See Decision 368/1992, [1992] *Giur cost* 2935.

[166] Decision 293/2000, [2000] *Giur cost* 2239.

Religious faith is a constitutional value, so it may be protected by a law penalizing insults addressed to believers, though the law could not punish polemical argument against religious belief.[167] Recently, the Court has ruled that the crime of blasphemy against the Catholic faith (*vilipendio della religione dello Stato*) is incompatible with the equal liberty of all religious communities, guaranteed by Article 8 of the Constitution, in that it only applied to disrespect for the majority religion.[168]

Although the text of Article 21 refers only to the freedom of speakers to express their thoughts, the Court has recognized the rights and interests of the public to receive ideas and information. This is of great importance in the context of broadcasting regulation, where on several occasions it has upheld the constitutionality of restrictions imposed on the freedom of the owners of private commercial channels. These restrictions have usually concerned limits on the number of channels one company may control, a perennial problem in Italy.[169] But the Court has also applied similar principles to approve the constitutionality of standards of objectivity and impartiality imposed on private broadcasters in their treatment of political issues during election campaigns.[170] It was reasonable for Parliament to have attached more weight to the protection of the citizens' rights to full and objective information than to the freedom of private channels to disseminate their own views. External pluralism, that is a variety of private channels, was not necessarily enough to safeguards these rights. The Court has developed the concept of pluralism to require both a measure of pluralism internal to a broadcasting organization, particularly RAI, the public broadcaster, as well as external pluralism. Its jurisprudence on broadcasting regulation is the most significant contribution of the Italian Constitutional Court to free speech law. Unfortunately, it also shows it is pointless to develop free speech principles unless they are respected by the political branches of government. Italian governments have repeatedly failed to implement the Court's rulings; Berlusconi, the longest serving Prime Minister of Italy since the Second World War, has kept his three national commercial channels.

(iii) Australia

There is no explicit guarantee of freedom of speech in the Australian Constitution.[171] Nor is there a bill of rights. The freedom, like almost all civil liberties, has, therefore, been protected by the common law which in its essential

---

167 Decision 188/1975, [1975] *Giur cost* 1508.
168 Decision 508/2000, [2000] *Giur cost* 3965.
169 For a brief account, see Barendt (n. 160 above), 24–8. The most recent significant decision is 420/1994, [1994] *Giur cost* 3716, holding incompatible with arts. 3 and 21 of the Constitution provisions allowing one group to control 25% of national broadcasting licences or three channels. For further discussion, see ch. XII, s. 5 below.   170 Decision 155/2002, [2002] *Giur cost* 1303.
171 Commonwealth of Australia Act 1900. For discussion of Australian law in this area, see M. Chesterman, *Freedom of Speech in Australian Law* (Aldershot: Ashgate, 2000), and G. Williams, *Human Rights under the Australian Constitution* (Melbourne: OUP, 2002), ch. 7.

features is similar to that of England. In some areas, notably contempt of court, Australian law has taken greater account of free speech concerns.[172] But in two cases decided in 1992, the High Court of Australia held there is a freedom of political communication implied in the federal Constitution.[173] Its provisions for the direct democratic election of the Senate and House of Representatives necessarily entail that people should be free to discuss political issues, particularly those which arise in the course of electoral campaigns. In the more important of the two cases, *Australian Capital Television*, the High Court invalidated amendments to Commonwealth broadcasting legislation which had prohibited election advertisements during campaigns, in return for an allocation of free time, largely for the use of established political parties. The Court held the scheme discriminated against independent candidates and new parties, thereby inhibiting free discussion of political issues.

Subsequently the High Court held the implied freedom created a constitutional privilege defence to actions for defamatory allegations made in the context of political debate.[174] The defence covered the discussion of state, as well as federal, politics. Mason CJ took a wide view of the scope of the implied freedom; it covered all speech relevant to the formation of public opinion on issues of general importance. But in *Lange* v. *Australian Broadcasting Corporation*,[175] now the leading decision in this area, the Court made a partial retreat from its earlier rulings. The implied freedom does not create any personal free speech rights; rather, it curtails legislative and executive power. As a consequence, the Court rejected the constitutional defence to libel proceedings it had formulated only three years earlier. But the common law should be developed in the light of the implied freedom, so the Court expanded the qualified privilege defence to cover defamatory allegations communicated to the general public concerning government and political matters, provided that the media (or other defendant) had reasonable grounds to believe the allegations were true and had behaved reasonably, for example, by seeking and publishing the claimant's reply. The Court also confirmed that a law burdening the implied freedom would still be upheld if it was reasonably appropriate to serve a legitimate aim of government, such as national security or public order.

The implied freedom covers expressive conduct, such as a peaceful protest against a state law permitting duck-shooting.[176] But it is confined to political speech, so does not extend to commercial speech or advertising.[177] Equally, a federal court has

---

[172] See *Hinch* v. *A-G (Victoria)* (1987) 164 CLR 15, discussed in ch. IX, s. 3 below.

[173] *Nationwide News Pty Ltd* v. *Wills* (1992) 177 CLR 1; *Australian Capital Television Pty Ltd* v. *Commonwealth* (1992) 177 CLR 106.

[174] *Theophanous* v. *Herald & Weekly Times Ltd* (1994) 182 CLR 104; *Stephens* v. *West Australian Newspapers Ltd* (1994) 182 CLR 211.

[175] (1997) 189 CLR 520. The libel jurisprudence of the High Court is further discussed in ch. VI, s. 3(ii) below.   [176] *Levy* v. *Victoria* (1997) 189 CLR 579: see ch. III, s. 2 below.

[177] *Tobacco Institute of Australia* v. *Australian Federation of Consumer Organizations* (1993) 41 FCR 89, 114, Hill J.

held that the implied freedom does not cover an article explaining shoplifting techniques, even though it also protested against capitalism.[178] In short, the scope of the implied freedom is narrower than that of any explicit right to freedom of expression considered in this book. The Australian development is, however, of considerable theoretical interest. It shows both the strength and shortcomings of an explanation of free speech in terms of its importance for a democracy, at least in its traditional majoritarian formulation.[179] Any liberal democracy must allow some freedom of political speech, unless it disowns its own character. But the argument from democracy must be recast in terms of an equal right to participate in public debate, or other free speech arguments must be deployed, if freedom of expression is to cover the arts, sexually explicit material, or commercial speech.

---

[178] *Brown* v. *Classification Review Board* (1998) 82 FCR 225 (Full Court): see ch. V, s. 2 below.
[179] See ch. I, s. 2(iii) above.

III

The Scope of Freedom of Speech

1. Introduction

What exactly should be covered by a rule protecting freedom of speech? The question is not only of concern to political philosophers, but has to be answered by those courts, such as the United States Supreme Court or the German Constitutional Court, which are required to interpret constitutional guarantees of freedom of speech or of expression. There are two principal issues here. The first concerns the meaning of *speech* for the purposes of the constitutional guarantee, in particular whether it covers forms of conduct which may be understood as communicating a message. The second involves the scope of the *freedom* of speech: does the freedom require recognition of some positive rights to speak or of access to information, or does it necessarily confer only immunities from state bans and other restrictions. For the most part this chapter is concerned with the first issue, but the final three sections discuss some general aspects of the second.

Almost everyone would agree that a verbal or printed attack on the government or other institutions of state should be immune from legal regulation, except perhaps when it is made in circumstances where an immediate outbreak of violence is likely to occur. If the free speech principle does not extend that far, it is difficult to see its point at all. But other types of 'speech' create more problems: for example, no serious commentator thinks perjury or dishonest commercial advertising without political content should be constitutionally protected, while the status of pornography under a free speech principle is far from clear.[1] It may also be difficult to categorize various forms of behaviour and activity, which are intended to convey ideas more usually and conventionally communicated by discussion and writing. Opposition, say, to nuclear weapons or to war in Iraq may be communicated not only by speeches at public meetings and in newspaper articles, but by marches and other forms of protest or by individuals wearing CND or 'No War in Iraq' badges as they go about their daily business. While it is relatively easy to equate these forms of protest with conventional forms of speech, we may instinctively bridle if similar claims are made for mass picketing, the wearing of political uniforms, or the burning of draft-cards and other government documents. Yet in

---

[1] See ch. X below.

some contexts and jurisdictions, modes of conduct such as these have been treated as covered by freedom of expression.

One thing at least is clear. It will not do simply to ask whether a communication falls under the dictionary meaning of 'speech'. Obviously, publication of the printed word is covered, although it is not 'speech' in the ordinary sense of that word. It is sometimes suggested that in this respect there may be a difference between 'speech' and 'expression', with the latter term having a broader scope.[2] If that were the case, one would expect courts such as those in Germany or the European Human Rights Court to give coverage to a wider range of expressive conduct than, say, US courts, since the former are required to apply 'freedom of expression' provisions, the latter the 'freedom of speech' limb of the First Amendment. But there is no evidence that courts draw any distinction between the two concepts, so the two words are used interchangeably in this book.

Equally, some communications, often made verbally, are not usually regarded as covered at all by a free speech principle. Examples of such excluded speech are direct inducements to murder a specific person or to commit some other crime (as distinct from the abstract advocacy of violent political change), bribery, perjury, representations inducing a contract and contractual promises, and the vows exchanged at a wedding ceremony. The point is that 'speech' is really a term of art when it is used in constitutions. Courts must ask whether, in light of the reasons for the protection of free speech or freedom of expression by the constitution, the type of communication in issue is covered by the guarantee.[3] While assertions of fact and statements of value or feelings are covered, because, for instance, they express an individual's beliefs or identity, or contribute to the formation of public opinion, there are no good reasons for protecting 'situation-altering' speech.[4] Marriage vows, contractual promises, and representations, are clearly used to produce a change in legal relations between the parties, rather than to assert a belief about the world; nobody making these statements has any plausible free speech argument for escaping liability when it is appropriate to impose it. Bribery, perjury, and direct inducements to action fall outside freedom of speech protection for similar reasons. Other types of speech are harder to categorize. Begging, for instance, might be regarded, at least in some circumstances, as a type of verbal intimidation or threat, but more generally might be covered, because it implicitly states that the beggar is poor and needs, or would like, financial help.[5]

The distinction between the *coverage* and the *protection* of a free speech clause is relevant to questions about the meaning of speech. As Frederick Schauer has pointed out, it does not follow from the coverage of some type of communication by a free speech clause that a particular instance of it should be protected from regulation in the circumstances of the case.[6] For example, political speech is the

---

[2] Schauer, 50–2.
[3] See K. Greenawalt, *Speech, Crime, and the Uses of Language* (New York: OUP, 1989), ch. 2 for a full discussion of these arguments.　　　[4] This term is used by Greenawalt, ibid., 58.
[5] See further p. 83 below.　　　[6] Schauer, 89–92.

archetypal kind of communication covered by the principle, but often its exercise may be limited, for example, when incitements to illegal conduct are expressed during a national emergency or immediately before a likely riot; in those circumstances the statement would be covered, but not protected from criminal prosecution by the free speech or freedom of expression clause. The distinction between coverage and protection is significant. It enables courts to treat some types of expressive conduct as 'speech', without thereby being committed to its protection in every situation. In contrast, judges like Black J. who took an absolutist view of the construction of a free speech provision—all 'speech' is absolutely immune from abridgement—must rely on a clear distinction between 'speech' and 'conduct'; otherwise it would be difficult for them to uphold the regulation of sit-ins, demonstrations on the streets, and other forms of protest which can be regarded as an exercise of free speech rights.

In fact the trend has been for courts, particularly in the United States of America, to take a broader approach to the scope of free speech coverage. Fewer types of speech are now excluded from the coverage of the First Amendment than used to be the case. Libel and commercial speech are now usually covered, while the definition of 'obscenity' which the states may regulate without constitutional hindrance has been much more narrowly drawn. Only the most extreme hardcore pornography falls outside the scope of the First Amendment.[7] A similar development has occurred in the context of abusive personal speech. In *Chaplinsky* v. *New Hampshire*, decided in 1942, the Court unanimously enunciated a 'fighting words' doctrine, under which certain personal insults were ruled wholly outside the Free Speech Clause: 'such utterances are no essential part of any exposition of ideas, and are of such slight social value as a step to truth that any benefit that may be derived from them is clearly outweighed by the social interest in order and morality'.[8] This principle has, however, been progressively narrowed in the last thirty years, although the actual decision in *Chaplinsky* has not been overruled. The interesting question is whether the underlying rationale for the ruling is still supportable.

On one view the primary reason for protecting free speech from regulation is that there is some special value in the unfettered dissemination of intellectual ideas and of information of political and social importance. Certainly, on the basis of the argument from democracy and Mill's infallibility thesis (considered in Chapter I), the case for including purely emotive speech, or personal insults, within the coverage of the free speech principle seems relatively weak. Only discourse of a political and social character engaging the listener's intellect should be covered. However, while there is much to be said for treating this type of communication as the archetypal category of 'speech', the exclusion of all emotive, nonrational expression from the coverage of the principle would be a mistake. For a start, it will often be hard to disentangle such expression from rational discourse.

---

[7] See ch. X below.   [8] 315 US 568 (1942), discussed in ch. VIII, s. 4(ii) below.

The most opprobrious insult may form part of an otherwise serious criticism of government or of a political figure. Even, however, if it were possible to separate the emotive content from the other parts of a particular publication, it would be wrong to allow its proscription. If speakers could be punished each time they included a colourful, non-rational epithet in their publication or address, much valuable speech would be inhibited. Some margin should be allowed for invective and exaggeration, even if that means some apparently worthless comments are as fully protected as a carefully balanced argument. This principle has been accepted by the United States Supreme Court, the German Constitutional Court, and by the European Court of Human Rights.[9] Moreover, human beings are not entirely rational. For many people it is easier or preferable to communicate in emotive terms; moreover, virtually everyone in some circumstances is influenced by arguments presented in this way. It is, therefore, right for even the most vapid of political slogans ('Fuck the Draft'[10]) to be immune from legal control. Otherwise very deep feelings could not be communicated. While this sort of expression may not always be as valued as highly as a *Times* editorial, it is right to afford it the same legal protection. The benefit of a free speech principle is not the prerogative of the intellectual elite.

In the light of these general observations we can proceed in section 2 of this chapter to examine some hard cases for the application of a free speech provision. In these cases it can be argued that the state was regulating conduct, rather than speech, so they concern the meaning of 'speech' for the purpose of the First Amendment or other free speech/expression provision. But arguably it is pointless to attempt to distinguish speech from conduct; instead, the question might be asked whether the purpose of the law or regulation was to restrict the communication of ideas or information. If that was the government's purpose, then free speech is in issue. This analysis might be applied when the regulation of election expenditure is challenged on freedom of speech grounds: should such regulation be regarded as a limit on the spending of money or on the dissemination of political speech? That question is discussed in section 3 of this chapter. Other issues are whether freedom of speech covers a right not to speak and, more controversially, a right to exclude others from joining a parade or association engaged in speech (see section 4 below). One issue is relatively clear: language rights are covered by freedom of speech (section 5).

All these questions are aspects of the meaning or scope of *speech* for the purposes of a free speech or freedom of expression clause. The other difficulty concerns the character of the *freedom* guaranteed by these provisions. Is freedom of speech solely an immunity from regulation by government and rules of the common law such as the laws of libel and contempt, or may the freedom additionally confer positive rights on individuals, such as a right to use highways and parks for public

---

[9] See *Cohen* v. *California* 403 US 15 (1971); Soraya, 34 BVerfGE 269 (1973); *Bergens Tidende* v. *Norway* (2001) 31 EHRR 16, para. 49.   [10] *Cohen* v. *California* 403 US 15 (1971).

meetings? The scope of legal rights to hold meetings on the streets and other public fora is considered in Chapter VIII below, while Chapter XII discusses another context in which positive free speech rights are frequently claimed: rights of reply and access to the media. Section 6 of this chapter is concerned with general arguments concerning the recognition of positive free speech rights, while section 7 considers *freedom of information*, a right sometimes claimed as one of those positive rights. Section 8 discusses whether freedom of speech limits government discretion in allocating grants, for example, by providing subsidies for the arts or research.

2. Speech and Conduct

(i) General issues

It may seem natural to draw a distinction between *speech* and *conduct* when determining the scope of a free speech provision. Yet courts are prepared to hold that forms of conduct, intended by the actors to communicate opinions and so understood by others, are covered by these provisions. Some commentators go so far as to deny that there is any intelligible distinction between expressive conduct on the one hand, and verbal or written communication—pure speech—on the other: 'The crucial question . . . is simply whether meaningful symbols of any type are being employed by one who wishes to communicate to others.'[11] Even in pure speech cases, the communication of written messages, and perhaps oral ones, does involve the use of symbols, conventionally understood to convey ideas and information.[12] It follows that the use of non-linguistic symbols—the wearing of badges and uniforms or making gestures—should be regarded as speech, particularly when their meaning is as clearly established as a comparable verbal or written message. Everybody understands what a CND badge or a swastika means, so their display should be treated as speech, though there may be good grounds for regulating the use of the latter symbol as dangerous to public order and grossly insulting to members of the Jewish community.[13] To these points should be added a powerful moral argument from equality that, in some circumstances, views can only be expressed effectively to the public by engaging in a course of conduct. Politicians, celebrities, writers, and intellectuals can disseminate their ideas in print and on the broadcasting media, but for most people marching in the streets, wearing badges, and engaging in other activities are the best means of communication.

---

[11] M. B. Nimmer, 'The Meaning of Symbolic Speech under the First Amendment' (1973) 21 *UCLA Law Rev* 29, 61–2.   [12] Ibid., 33–5.
[13] In *Zdrahal* v. *Wellington City Council* [1995] 1 NZLR 700, Greig J. in the New Zealand High Court ruled that the display of swastikas painted on a house could be abated under environment legislation as offensive, though it was covered by freedom of expression guaranteed by the NZ Bill of Rights Act 1990.

As Kirby J. said in a leading decision of the High Court of Australia, '[a] rudimentary knowledge of human behaviour teaches that people communicate ideas and opinions by means other than words spoken or written.'[14] The High Court accepted that the implied right to freedom of political expression was engaged when protesters against duck shooting were prosecuted under regulations making it an offence to enter hunting areas without a licence, although it held these rules were valid restrictions on the exercise of that freedom.

In accord with these principles, the United States Supreme Court has ruled that the wearing of black armbands in school to protest against the Vietnam war was so closely akin to pure speech as to be covered by the First Amendment (and in the circumstances constitutionally immune from prohibition).[15] Courts in the United States and in Germany have held that the wearing of Nazi or other uniforms clearly indicating support for (extreme right) political objectives is covered by freedom of speech, or expression.[16] (But the ban on uniform wearing and display of the swastika in public as an expression of a common political convictions has been upheld in Germany as a public order measure.[17]) In these circumstances it is plain that political views were expressed, that this was the intention of the actors, and that observers understood the behaviour as communicating ideas and opinions. Equally, the wearing of the badge or uniform was stopped because the authorities disapproved of the perspective or ideology expressed in that way. On the other hand, free speech is not engaged where the gesture is not readily understood to communicate a message.[18]

Although some forms of conduct can be characterized as expressive, or to use another term as 'symbolic speech', it would be wrong to equate action or behaviour with speech. For many types of conduct communicate an idea or information to its observers, and may be intended to influence the public in the same way as a political speech or publication. For example, suicide and other terrorist bombs are designed to change political attitudes and may even be interpreted as acts of protest. But acts of terrorism and political assassination cannot possibly claim the coverage of a free speech clause. If the law were to extend to them that benefit, the state would have to justify in each case the application of criminal law as a necessary restriction on the exercise of free speech rights by terrorists. That would be

---

[14] *Levy* v. *Victoria* (1997) 189 CLR 579, 638: for further discussion of the case, see ch. VIII, s. 3(v) below. [15] *Tinker* v. *Des Moines School District* 393 US 503 (1969).
[16] *Skokie* v. *National Socialist Party* 373 NE 2d 21 (1978), and *Collin* v. *Smith* 447 F Supp 676, affirmed 578 F 2d 1197 (7th Cir, 1978).
[17] NJW 1982, 1803, upholding the Uniformsverbot in the Law on Assemblies and Processions of 15 Nov. 1978, BGBl I S 1789, s. 3. Similar bans on the wearing of political uniforms in the United Kingdom are imposed by section 1 of the Public Order Act 1936, applied in *O'Moran* v. *DPP* [1975] QB 864, DC, and by the Terrorism Act 2000, s. 13.
[18] See *Davis* v. *Norman* 555 F 2d 189 (8th Cir, 1977), where the defendant argued unsuccessfully that the parking of a demolished car outside his house was 'speech' protesting against police conduct responsible for the damage. The point is that few observers would understand the gesture to have that meaning.

grotesque. If the distinction between speech and conduct is to be discarded as too crude, some tests or criteria must be formulated to determine when the latter is entitled to benefit from the free speech guarantee.

Before discussing these criteria, a distinction should be drawn between cases of expressive conduct or 'symbolic speech' on the one hand, and on the other, cases where speech or publication in the conventional sense is associated with conduct such as the distribution of leaflets, ringing doorbells to canvass support, or the conduct of meetings and street processions. In all these latter cases there is a clearly understood intention to transmit information or opinions; difficulties only arise because the verbal or written message is communicated in ways which may create a social nuisance or harm unrelated to the content of the speech. For instance, local authorities may regulate leafleting and restrict street canvassing or the holding of processions and protest marches, because of the risks of litter or the disruption to traffic and normal commercial activities. These cases clearly involve free speech issues. It would be wrong, therefore, to regulate on the basis of the views expressed in a leaflet, or its general content, or on the basis of the objects of a street protest. For example, an authority is not free to allow the distribution of leaflets advocating support for the Labour Party, but not for other political parties, or to permit religious, but not political protests. But what are termed 'time, manner, and place' regulations are usually upheld, provided they are no wider than necessary to prevent litter, noise, congestion, or other nuisance.[19] These cases rarely produce much difficulty.

The expressive conduct cases pose much greater problems, because the speech element is generally hard to detect and cannot easily be disentangled from the conduct which the state has a legitimate interest in regulating. The actor's desire to communicate an idea cannot itself be sufficient. Otherwise political assassination, terrorist bombs, and other atrocities would be covered by the free speech provision. Violent conduct is rightly excluded from the coverage of a freedom of speech or expression clause, even if it is partly intended by its perpetrators, and understood by the public, to convey a message.[20] It follows that 'terrorism', as defined in section 1 of the UK Terrorism Act 2000, does not fall within the scope of freedom of expression, although it encompasses violent conduct, or its threat, which is designed to influence the government or to intimidate the general public. In other

---

[19] *Schneider* v. *State* 308 US 147 (1939) and *Martin* v. *Struthers* 319 US 141 (1943) established that not only are content-based restrictions on leafleting and the distribution of circulars incompatible with freedom of speech, but so are time, manner, and place limits which are wider than necessary to prevent noise and other nuisances. More recently the Court has upheld time, manner, and place limits promoting a substantial government interest which would be achieved less effectively without them, a more relaxed standard of review: *Ward* v. *Rock against Racism* 491 US 781 (1989).

[20] Violence, and the threat of violence, is excluded from the coverage of the Canadian Charter guarantee of freedom of expression: see *RWDSU* v. *Dolphin Delivery Ltd* [1986] 2 SCR 573. The United States Supreme Court has held that violent conduct falls outside the First Amendment: see *Wisconsin* v. *Mitchell* 508 US 476 (1993) (no infringement of First Amendment to penalize racially motivated violence with an enhanced penalty).

circumstances what is important, it may be argued, is that the conduct has been understood as a communication not only by the particular people to whom it is addressed, but also by the general public. Sometimes the majority of the public may see the communicative aspects of an act, such as tearing up a draft-card or burning a flag, as subsidiary to the elements of criminal damage integral to an act which it is entitled to prohibit; only a minority of the community may in fact understand that conduct as expressive. Should such conduct be categorized as speech or as conduct?

The leading speech-conduct case in the United States is *United States* v. *O'Brien*,[21] though both the decision and the reasoning are unsatisfactory. The respondent was charged with burning his draft-card under an amendment to the Universal Military Training and Service Act; it made it an offence to destroy or mutilate this document. The majority of the Court, reversing the Court of Appeals, first decided that the behaviour could not be characterized as 'speech' for First Amendment purposes merely because the actor intended to communicate his opposition to conscription for the war in Vietnam. That conclusion is correct. As suggested earlier, the actor's intention to communicate may be a necessary, but is hardly a sufficient, condition for his conduct to be treated as speech. However, at a time when this form of protest against the war was common, the gesture was almost certainly understood as communicating a message, at least by many members of the public. The Court was, therefore, prepared to assume, without deciding, that the communicative element involved in draft-card burning was sufficient to render the conduct 'symbolic speech' entitled to some protection under the First Amendment. On that basis Warren CJ held that government regulation was valid if it furthered an important state interest 'unrelated to the suppression of free expression; and if the incidental restriction on alleged First Amendment freedom is no greater than is essential to the furtherance of that interest'.[22] The government had a legitimate interest in safeguarding the draft registration system, and so there was nothing unconstitutional in the controversial amendment. The respondent was punished for frustrating the registration scheme, not for communicating his opposition to the war in a dramatic fashion.

The decision has been widely criticized.[23] One line of criticism is concerned with the Court's treatment of the amendment to the draft-card legislation, on the assumption that it did limit expressive conduct. It is arguable that the 1965 amendment was so narrowly drafted as to make it plain that Congress's real object was indeed to restrict speech. If the object of the amendment had been to safeguard the registration scheme, it could have made a simple failure to produce the draft-card to the relevant official a criminal offence. The fact that the amendment explicitly prohibited destruction of the card suggests it was aimed at the

---

[21] 391 US 367 (1968).   [22] Ibid., 377.
[23] Nimmer (n. 11 above), 38–44; L. Henkin, 'On Drawing Lines' (1968) 82 *Harvard Law Rev* 63; J. H. Ely, 'Flag Desecration: A Case Study in the Roles of Categorization and Balancing in First Amendment Analysis' (1975) 88 *Harvard Law Rev* 1482.

communication of an idea. Further, the Court's formulation that a ban on expressive conduct is valid, provided it is no greater than essential to *further* an *important* state interest is relatively restrictive of speech. In pure speech cases, even those where the speech is communicated or distributed by conduct, as in leafleting and canvassing cases, a total ban will be invalidated, unless it is *necessary* to safeguard a *compelling* state interest. For example, a comprehensive ban on distributing leaflets in public may not be defended on the ground that it is necessary to prevent litter on the streets. The Court in effect seems more willing to tolerate restrictions on expressive conduct than it is to uphold restraints on more conventional modes of expression.

A more fundamental criticism is that the Court's approach to the categorization of O'Brien's behaviour was misconceived. It is wrong to attempt to distinguish speech from conduct in these circumstances. Burning a draft-card, and other forms of expressive conduct, can equally properly be treated as speech or as con-duct, and it is futile to ask which element predominates.[24] The better approach is to determine the object or purpose of the state's regulation.[25] If its purpose is to punish someone like O'Brien for speaking, then freedom of speech is fully engaged. In contrast, the First Amendment would not be in issue if the object of the regulation were to restrict violent or other undesirable conduct; it is then immaterial whether the regulation is infringed by what might be regarded as expressive conduct. Criminal and tax laws may be violated by individuals protest-ing the injustice of those particular laws or another cause, but the protester's rights to free speech are not violated, unless he is prosecuted in order to silence his protest. That would only occur if the protester were singled out for prosecution under laws not generally enforced, or if the laws had been enacted in order to silence people like him. On this perspective, the suppression, say, of works of art or music, like censorship of literature or plays, engages free speech, because it is impossible to see any reason for suppression other than a wish to prevent the com-munication of offensive images or sounds. But boxing, smoking, or bull-fighting could all be banned, because the government would be acting to protect health or to stop cruelty to animals. But if, say, boxing were banned, because in the view of the government the sport encouraged violent attitudes, freedom of speech would be engaged.

This approach has, it seems, been adopted by the English Court of Appeal in an immigration case.[26] The Home Secretary refused Louis Farrakhan, a US citizen and the leader of a militant Islamic movement, permission to enter the country, on the ground that his presence would create a risk of public disorder. Although the decision was not taken solely, or even primarily, to stop Farrakhan from expressing his views in public, the Court of Appeal accepted that this was one

---

[24] Ely, ibid., 1496–7.

[25] In addition to the literature cited in n. 23 above, see J. Rubenfeld, 'The First Amendment's Purpose' (2001) 53 *Stanford Law Rev* 767.

[26] *R (Farrakhan)* v. *Secretary of State for Home Department* [2002] 4 All ER 289.

object of his exclusion. For that reason the right to freedom of expression was engaged, and it was for the Home Secretary to show, as he did to the Court's satisfaction, that his decision did not disproportionately interfere with the exercise of that right. It was right in this case to concentrate on the reason for the government's decision, since Farrakhan could not be said, at this stage of events, to be engaged in either speech or conduct. Equally, it was clear that the decision to refuse entry had to some extent been taken to stop him speaking.

However, concentration on the government's purpose may not always resolve difficulties in this area. First, it may be no easier in practice, or no less artificial, to determine the government's primary purpose in enacting and enforcing the regulation, than it is to decide whether or not the regulated behaviour should be characterized as expressive conduct. Suppose, for instance, that a local authority prosecutes beggars under regulations which proscribe soliciting money in public, unless the authority has been previously notified and permission given for the activity; but the authority allows charities to raise money in this way, rationing the number of their street collectors only in order to minimize disruption to shoppers and other users of the highway. Begging by individuals is regarded in the community as a serious nuisance, and on one occasion violence was threatened. In these circumstances the government's object is unclear: is it acting to preserve the character of the community and to prevent possible outbreaks of violence, or is it targeting speech on the basis of its content, that is, that it requests money? The answer to that question is no more straightforward than an answer to the question whether begging as such is more speech than conduct. Similar difficulties arise in the context of the regulation of nude dancing and election expenditure, two topics considered later in the chapter. Secondly, even where it is clear that the purpose of the regulation is to restrict the communication of an idea or information, it would not follow that freedom of speech is implicated. Perjury and commercial fraud laws are intended to prevent jurors and investors being misled, but they are not regarded as engaging freedom of speech or expression; they fall outside the scope of clauses guaranteeing the freedom, as this type of speech has nothing to do with the reasons for the guarantee.

Reflection on the purpose of the contested regulation will often help to resolve whether freedom of speech is engaged. But it would be wrong to expect it to do this easily in all circumstances. It is also legitimate to ask how the activity in question is regarded by its participants. Boxing and motor-racing, for instance, are not regarded as communicating views, either by those engaged in the sport or by their spectators, so there could be no free speech objection to their proscription, though a total ban would raise general civil liberties objections. It would be odd to take a different view of the matter, merely because there was evidence that the government acted partly to discourage what it considered unhealthy attitudes to participation in dangerous physical sports. It is when the intentions of actor and observer are opaque that it is right also to ask whether the government's purpose was to curtail the communication of information and ideas.

(ii) Flag desecration

Some of the points in the previous paragraphs are nicely illustrated by the flag-desecration cases which have arisen in the United States, Germany, and England. These cases have been particularly controversial in the United States, where the flag is an object of respect, bordering on veneration. But state laws protecting it against desecration and mutilation have been held incompatible with the First Amendment, since they proscribe expressive conduct through, for instance, taping a peace sign to the flag.[27] The most important decision is that of the Supreme Court in *Texas* v. *Johnson*.[28] The defendant set the flag on fire at a demonstration in Dallas during the Republican Party Convention which was taking place in the city; he was convicted under a state statute which made it an offence to desecrate the national or state flag in a way which would, to the actor's knowledge, seriously offend the public. By a 5–4 majority the Court upheld the Texas Court of Criminal Appeals ruling that the conviction was incompatible with the First Amendment. It was conceded in this case, unlike *O'Brien*, that the act of flag-burning on these facts was 'expressive conduct'; the question was whether the relatively lenient test in that case applied or strict scrutiny should be applied. Brennan J. for the Court argued that the state's purpose in prosecuting Johnson under the desecration statute was crucial. The prosecution could not be defended as necessary to preserve public order, since there was no evidence that his behaviour provoked disorder. The state intended to criminalize the communication of a message about the flag, the view that it does not stand for national unity, but represents other, more questionable values; the statute was explicitly aimed at desecration which the actor knew was seriously offensive. No compelling interest justified the prohibition of expressive conduct which in these circumstances was entitled to the same degree of First Amendment protection as pure speech.

The dissenting judgment of Rehnquist CJ accepted that the law limited freedom of speech, but held nevertheless that it could protect the flag as a unique symbol of national identity. The public burning was not an 'essential part of the exposition of ideas';[29] Johnson could express his contempt for American values in other ways. That view is of course incompatible with the speaker's freedom to choose the form in which his ideas are communicated. Stevens J. equated flag-burning with spraying paint or graffiti on the Washington Monument or Lincoln Memorial, which would be treated as conduct and so fall outside the First Amendment. That is a bad analogy. Those acts could properly be punished under property-damage legislation enacted to protect national monuments. In contrast, the only coherent purpose of flag-desecration statutes is to deter the communication of radical or dissenting views concerning the government and values of the United States. It is immaterial whether the law requires, as the

---

[27] *Spence* v. *Washington* 418 US 405 (1974).   [28] 491 US 397 (1989).   [29] Ibid., 430.

Texas law did, knowledge on the part of the flag-burner that his conduct is seriously offensive.[30]

The German Constitutional Court has adopted a different approach in a case involving the offence of disparagement of the state and its symbols.[31] These include the flag and the national anthem.[32] A prosecution for this offence had been successfully brought in respect of a collage showing a man urinating on a flag displayed at an army swearing-in ceremony. The collage was covered by Article 5(3) guaranteeing freedom of the arts, a provision which is not, unlike Article 5(1), qualified by the provisions of general laws. Nevertheless, the freedom can be limited by constitutional provisions, including those concerned to ensure respect for the fundamental values of the state;[33] these provisions must be balanced against freedom of the arts, whether or not the dissemination of these works directly endangered state security. But in this case, the ordinary courts had ignored the obvious meaning of the collage as an attack on militarism, rather than on the state and its fundamental values. They therefore failed to respect artistic freedom, which must enjoy a degree of licence to question contemporary policies and social values.

An English court was in no doubt that freedom of expression was engaged when a protester was convicted under the public order legislation of using insulting words or behaviour towards US service personnel and their families. In the course of a demonstration outside a US air force base in Suffolk she had defaced the flag by putting a stripe and writing 'Stop Star Wars' across it, and then standing on it. Some of the witnesses gave evidence of their distress. On appeal, the Divisional Court held that the district judge had wrongly stressed that the point of the protest could have been made in other non-insulting ways.[34] That did not give adequate weight to her freedom to express her views through the use of her own property, the US flag. But the court indicated that she might have been properly convicted after a proper consideration of all relevant factors, in particular the point that the demonstrator knew her acts would distress the people to whom it was addressed. An Australian court also assumed that demonstrators were engaged in symbolic speech when they burnt the Indonesian flag outside its embassy in

---

[30] In *US* v. *Eichman* 496 US 310 (1990), the Court, 5–4, struck down the federal 'flag desecration' statute enacted subsequent to its decision in the Texas case, although the statute did not contain a requirement that the demonstrator knew flag-burning was offensive to the public. In effect, the Court considered that the government's interest in protecting the integrity of the flag was inevitably directed at speech.

[31] 81 BVerfGE 278 (1990). See P. E. Quint, 'Comparative Law of Flag Desecration: The United States and the Federal Republic of Germany' (1992) 15 *Hastings Internat and Comparative Law Rev* 613, 627–37, to which I am much indebted.

[32] In 81 BVerfGE 298 (1990), the Court took a similar approach to a case involving a parody of the national anthem. It held that the core of the satire revealed the contradictions between the pretensions of the anthem and social reality, rather than an attack on the values of the anthem itself.

[33] The Basic Law, art. 22 prescribes the colours of the national flag. The Court suggested this provision reflects the state's right to use representative symbols.

[34] *DPP* v. *Percy* [2002] Crim LR 835.

Darwin, although the appeal was allowed on the narrow point that they had been wrongly convicted of the statutory offence of 'disorderly behaviour'.[35] There was no evidence that anyone had been alarmed or frightened by the burning. The important point is that flag-burning and other forms of mutilation of a flag or other symbol is covered by freedom of speech (or expression), and any restrictions on such expressive conduct must be justified under the principles applicable to constraints on pure speech.

(iii) Nude dancing and sexually explicit conduct

Nudity and sexually explicit conduct in public are generally proscribed. Do these bans engage freedom of speech? The Supreme Court has held that nude dancing is expressive conduct, albeit at the outer edge of the First Amendment. In two cases the application of regulations banning public nudity (and other forms of public indecency) to dancing in private clubs has been upheld by a majority of the Court. In the first,[36] four members of the majority, applying the approach in *O'Brien*, found that the object of an Indiana public indecency law was to protect social order and morality, or (in the view of Souter J.) to prevent the undesirable secondary effects of adult entertainment—prostitution and crime. It was not directed at erotic expression. The dancers were free to communicate their erotic message, provided they wore some clothing; that requirement was only an incidental restriction on expressive conduct essential to achieve the order and morality objectives of the ban. Scalia J. went further. As the law did not criminalize public nudity because of its expressive attributes, the First Amendment was not even in issue. With Thomas J. concurring, he repeated that view in the second case, *Erie* v. *Pap's AM*.[37] The other members of the majority in that case upheld the nude dancing ban on the ground that it furthered the legitimate state interest in preventing undesirable secondary effects. The city ordinance had been introduced, in their view, to deal with these consequences of adult entertainment clubs, so the broader public morality argument used to justify the ban in the earlier case was irrelevant.

   As we have seen, the crucial issue in these, and many other, expressive conduct cases may be the object of the challenged ban. The dissenting judgments in both nude dancing cases argued that the object was to limit the communication of erotic expression to adults who would clearly not be offended by it, given that they paid money to view nude dancing. The public order or morality argument could not, therefore, be used to justify prosecution, as that argument was concerned to prevent offence. It was in fact clear in *Erie* that the city ordinance had really been introduced to proscribe nude live entertainment, as the dissent of Stevens and Ginsburg JJ pointed out. They also contended that it was wrong to justify a *total*

---

[35] *Watson* v. *Trenerry* (1998) 145 FLR 159, CA of Northern Territory.
[36] *Barnes* v. *Glen Theatre, Inc* 501 US 560 (1991).   [37] 527 US 277 (2000).

ban on nude dancing by reference to its undesirable secondary effects; that argument would only support confining it to particular areas or the imposition of other limits, rather than a total ban on protected expression. Often, however, the purpose or object of the contested rule will be hard to establish. The state may strongly contend that it intended, say, to avert the consequences of adult entertainment clubs and that banning totally nude dancing is an essential step to achieve that end. But some legislators may have argued in debate that the activity sends the wrong message to young people, or gives the community a bad name, reasons which would suggest that the ban was motivated, at least in part, by hostility to this form of sexually explicit communication. There should be careful scrutiny where the state has not prosecuted nudity in the theatre or stopped the showing of films with explicit sexual content; in those circumstances, the prosecution of nude dancing would seem to be aimed at a particular mode of expressive conduct and so to be directed at speech. Equally, the state can reply that occasional glimpses of nudity during the course of a play are not associated with any undesirable social consequences; further, plays and films, unlike nude dancing, are well established as media of communication.

The treatment of sexual activity in public is surely less problematic. It is covered by nuisance and public decency laws.[38] These laws uphold a moral view that the most intimate sexual relations should be conducted in private. Public sexual activity is not proscribed because it communicates an idea or spectacle which most people find offensive; they consider it wrong for the activity to take place in public, whether or not they witness it. The European Commission of Human Rights rightly rejected an argument that physical homosexual relations are covered by Article 10 of the European Convention on Human Rights and Fundamental Freedoms (ECHR) as a mode of expressing feelings.[39] Sexual conduct is covered by privacy rights, which may extend to protect some forms of such conduct in public. But the argument that all forms of intimate sexual behaviour in public are covered by freedom of speech or expression is wholly misconceived. Its acceptance would erode the speech–conduct distinction in this context, and of course would make it pointless to argue whether, or to what extent, hard-core pornography should be covered by freedom of speech. That argument is troublesome and difficult, precisely because it presents sexually explicit behaviour in the form of (pictorial) speech. That is not the case with actual sexual conduct.

(iv) Conclusions

Drawing the theoretical line between speech and conduct is not easy, nor is the resolution in practice of expressive conduct cases generally straightforward.

---

[38] See the controversial common law offence of outraging public decency, discussed in Feldman, 931–8, and the statutory offence of sexual activity in a public lavatory: Sexual Offences Act 2003, s. 71 (England and N. Ireland).   [39] 7215/75, *X* v. *UK* 19 D & R 66.

The result in the flag-burning cases is obviously right, for there can be no doubt that the laws in all these cases criminalized the dramatic expression of views offensive to majority opinion. It is hard to see any other point to the statute or to the prosecution in the particular cases. But that was not the position in the nude dancing litigation, in *O'Brien*, in the English immigration case, or in the hypothetical begging cases discussed in this section. Nor was it in another important US case, where the Supreme Court rightly upheld a ban imposed by the National Park Service on demonstrators sleeping in Lafayette Park and the Mall near the White House; the Court accepted that overnight sleeping in this context could be regarded as expressive conduct, but held the Park Service had put forward a substantial public interest in maintaining the parks in an attractive state in justification of the ban.[40] The government can often point to good arguments for the regulation which have nothing to do with disapproval of any messages expressed by, or implicit in, the proscribed conduct.

However, courts will fail to do free speech justice if they accept government arguments uncritically. In the first place, some forms of expressive conduct have become so widely practised and are so generally understood as communicating ideas that they should be treated in the same way as pure speech communicated verbally, in writing, or by other conventional forms. The wearing of badges and flag-burning, for instance, have become such familiar means of communication that it is hard to envisage any justification for their regulation, except, of course, those arguments which support the proscription of verbal speech—that it incites violence or is very likely to lead to imminent disorder. Courts should also be willing to examine the government's argument critically to see whether it masks an attempt to suppress or control expression. It is always right to scrutinize government carefully, because a general mistrust of government's capacity to make the right choices is one reason why free speech is strongly protected in liberal constitutions.[41] There are, therefore, powerful reasons for a broad understanding of the meaning of speech, and for courts to be wary when government argues that its object is really to regulate associated conduct.

3. Speech and Money

(i) General issues

Money talks, but is it 'speech'? This question is particularly important in the context of election laws regulating campaign expenditures. Many countries limit the amount of money which may be spent by political parties, candidates, and other people during election campaigns, first, to prevent corruption and secondly, to

---

[40] *Clark* v. *Community for Creative Non-Violence* 468 US 268 (1984).
[41] See the argument in ch. I, s. 2(iv) above.

ensure (so far as possible) that the richer candidates and groups do not have disproportionately more resources with which to influence the outcome of an election. Other restrictions impose ceilings on the level of contributions which may be made to party or candidate funds. These restrictions may be challenged on the ground that they inhibit freedom of speech or, put another way, limit the quantity of speech available to the electorate during campaign periods. Defenders of the restrictions dispute this claim. They argue the restrictions limit expenditure, not speech, and therefore should be regarded as restraints on conduct, which fall outside the scope of the First Amendment or other free expression clause. This fundamental dispute is discussed here, as is the related issue of corporate speech, an issue which often arises in these cases. The justifications for the imposition of limits on the election expenditure and contributions are considered in Chapter XIV.[42]

The Supreme Court addressed these questions in the landmark case of *Buckley* v. *Valeo*.[43] The litigation involved challenges to provisions of the Federal Election Campaign Act (FECA) of 1971, as amended in 1974, limiting the *contributions* which could be made to the campaign of a candidate for office to $1,000, and restricting the *expenditures* which could be incurred by or on behalf of a particular candidate. In particular, individuals and groups could not spend more than $1,000 a year relative to an identified candidate, though the institutional media were exempt from this rule. In an extremely controversial ruling the Court upheld the contributions limitations, but invalidated the FECA provisions imposing limits on campaign expenditure. Both restrictions were regarded as limitations on speech rather than on conduct, although the contribution limitation was considered a less onerous restraint because 'the transformation of contributions into political debate involves speech by someone other than the contributor'.[44] In contrast the $1,000 expenditure restriction entailed, in the Court's view, a substantial restraint on the quantity and diversity of political speech, making it impossible for all people, except the media, candidates, and parties to use any means of communication effectively.

At the outset of its judgment the Court refused to equate expenditure with conduct such as the destruction of the draft-card in *O'Brien*. It then proceeded a little mysteriously to argue that the dependence of speech on money did not itself introduce an element of 'conduct' into the situation so as to reduce the exacting scrutiny which should be conducted to ensure the legislation complied with the First Amendment. Even if the *O'Brien* test, appropriate to cases of expressive conduct or 'symbolic speech' were employed, the relevant government interests involved restrictions on the freedom of individuals and groups to communicate their political opinions and so were directed at speech; unlike *O'Brien* it was not a case where the legislation had another non-speech related object and where freedom of speech was only incidentally affected.

[42] S. 2.   [43] 424 US 1 (1976).   [44] Ibid., 21.

This reasoning is of course open to challenge. The expenditure of money certainly enables more speech to be made, or disseminated on the media. But that link, it can be argued, does not mean that expenditure should be treated as 'speech'. The payment of contributions and the incurring of expenditure do not as such communicate any message or information. When a cheque is written, money changes hands, but no idea is transmitted. It can, therefore, be argued that the FECA limited the use of money, with only an incidental impact on speech.[45] Moreover, insofar as its provisions did limit speech, they did not discriminate on the basis of its viewpoint; the speech of Democrats and Republicans, and of supporters of other parties, was equally restricted.

Nevertheless, the Court's classification of the expenditure restrictions was correct. Speech is dependent on the expenditure of money, so a restriction on the latter amounts to a limit on freedom of speech. It was therefore right to call for compelling arguments to justify the expenditure restrictions, rather than apply the more relaxed level of scrutiny under the *O'Brien* test.[46] The key provision, as interpreted by the Court, precluded expenditure of more than $1,000 on communications which *expressly advocated* the election or defeat of an identified candidate for federal office; it did not prohibit expenditure as such. In effect, it made it impossible for anyone to take out an advertisement in a local, let alone a national, newspaper, supporting a particular candidate, or printing and circulating an election pamphlet. As the Court pointed out, 'virtually every means of communicating ideas in today's mass society requires the expenditure of money'.[47] The fact that the press and other institutional media were exempt from the restrictions shows indirectly that the restraint was aimed at the ability of individuals and groups (other than media institutions) to campaign. Unquestionably the restrictions would have limited the quantity of political speech published during an election period. It is beside the point that political ideas could still be communicated by means such as door-to-door canvassing or public meetings, or that Congress had acted to reduce the electoral influence of wealthy individuals and corporations. Those arguments may make a good case for limiting freedom of speech in the context of elections, a claim considered later in this book.[48] However, they do not deny that freedom of speech is engaged. Rather, they admit that it is, but that there are good reasons for its restraint.

The Supreme Court of Canada had no doubt that freedom of expression was engaged when it was asked to rule on the constitutionality of a ban on expenditure by individuals and groups outside registered national committees and political parties during the course of a referendum campaign.[49] The right to freedom of expression embraces a freedom to choose any methods necessary for communication, other than violence, so it clearly covered incurring expenses.[50] The same

---

[45] See J. Skelly Wright, 'Politics and the Constitution: Is Money Speech?' (1976) 85 *Yale Law Jo* 1001, 1007.   [46] See s. 2(i) above.
[47] 424 US 1, 19 (1976).   [48] Ch. XIV, s. 2 below.
[49] *Libman* v. *A-G of Quebec* [1997] 3 SCR 569.   [50] Ibid., paras. 31–5.

approach was taken by the European Court of Human Rights in *Bowman* v. *UK*.[51] It held that a legislative provision, which made it an offence for an unauthorized person to spend more than £5 during an election period to communicate information to the electorate with a view to promoting a candidate's election, infringed freedom of expression; further, it ruled that it could not be justified as necessary to promote fairness between candidates and to prevent the distortion of election campaigns.[52]

These cases do not establish that limits on election expenditure *necessarily* engage freedom of speech. The provisions challenged in *Buckley* v. *Valeo* and in the *Bowman* case were framed in terms of expenses relating to communication, while the Canadian Supreme Court has taken a consistently broad view of the scope of freedom of expression;[53] in the *Libman* case it was easily satisfied that the expenditure ban engaged freedom of expression. But generally framed limits on expenditure which apply to *every* form of financial support for a candidate or party, for example, registration drives or the provision of transport on polling day, should probably not be treated as equivalent to pure speech restrictions, unless of course they were applied discriminatorily to constrain, say, the placing of advertisements for a candidate. A generally framed limit might more easily pass constitutional muster than one which targets expenses on communication, because it would be clearer that there were legitimate, non-speech related reasons for its enactment: ensuring a more level playing field for the different parties and candidates and avoiding their need to spend excessive time cultivating wealthy financial supporters.[54] In fact, these arguments justify expenditure limits, even when they do limit free speech: see Chapter XIV.

(ii) Corporate speech

In *Bellotti* a 5–4 majority of the US Supreme Court held that a Massachusetts law prohibiting banks and business corporations from spending money on referendum campaigns (other than on issues which materially affected their interests) infringed the First Amendment.[55] The decision largely turned on the question whether corporations were entitled to benefit from the free speech clause; the question whether the expenditure of money was to be treated as 'speech' was relegated to a footnote indicating support for the *Buckley* decision. Since *Bellotti*, a number of Supreme Court decisions have upheld statutory provisions requiring election expenditure by corporations and Chambers of Commerce to come from

---

[51] (1998) 26 EHRR 1.

[52] Following the recommendations in the report of the Neill Committee on Standards in Public Life (Cm 4057, 1998), the £5 limit has been replaced by a less restrictive, more flexible formula: see ch. XIV, s. 2 below. The Committee, with John McGregor, MP dissenting, did not consider that limits on election expenditure were as such incompatible with freedom of speech.

[53] See ch. II, s. 3 above.   [54] Rubenfeld (n. 25 above), 806–7.

[55] *First National Bank of Boston* v. *Bellotti* 435 US 765 (1978).

segregated funds to which shareholders or members have contributed voluntarily. In *Austin* v. *Michigan Chamber of Commerce*[56] six members of the Court approved such a requirement, holding that it prevented the distorting impact of massive corporate expenditure which might have no correlation to public support for the favoured party or candidate. The decision provoked a strongly worded dissent from Scalia J. who accused the majority of engaging in Orwellian censorship. He pointed out that the Michigan law did not prevent the Chamber of Commerce from spending money on general political campaigns, as distinct from campaigns for election candidates, nor did it apply to media institutions. The recent decision of the Supreme Court on the constitutionality of the Bipartisan Campaign Reform Act of 2002 (BCRA) has upheld the extension of the restriction on expenditure from general corporate and union funds to cover expenditure on electioneering communications ('issue advertisements') broadcast within sixty days of a general election, or thirty days of a primary election; corporations and unions can only incur expenditure on these communications from earmarked political funds.[57]

The question of principle is whether restrictions on corporate expenditure really engage freedom of speech at all. Arguably, the free speech principle discussed in Chapter I does not justify the coverage of such expenditure. White J. pointed out in his dissent in *Bellotti* that the arguments from the importance of self-expression as a means to the full development of the individual are clearly irrelevant. A corporation cannot claim a human right as a speaker. On the other hand, the interest of the public in receiving ideas and information is promoted, whether or not a corporation finances their dissemination. Recipients are usually not concerned with the source of the information on which they rely. Further, unless corporations, and other bodies such as trades unions, are free to put over their views effectively, government may be able to dominate public debate through official reports, press releases, and reports of politicians' speeches. Corporations also have real interests in disseminating their views about their products and issues of economic and taxation policy.

Corporations, therefore, should be entitled to claim the benefit of a free speech clause.[58] But it does not follow that their free speech rights are identical to those of individuals. As will be seen in the next section of this chapter, the arguments for recognizing a right not to speak may not apply to corporations. Further, there are good reasons for imposing limits on their electoral or referendum expenditure. As Marshall J. argued for the Court majority in *Austin*, corporations amass enormous wealth, and they can use their resources to swamp voters with advertising and drown out the voice of individuals in the electoral contest. Only individuals are entitled to vote, so regulation of corporate expenditure in this context is much

---

[56] 494 US 654 (1990).   [57] *McConnell* v. *FEC* 157 L Ed 2d 491 (2003).

[58] Under the German Basic Law, art. 19(3), juristic persons are entitled to basic rights to the extent the nature of the right permits. It is clear that companies, political parties, and unions may claim the right to freedom of expression.

more justifiable than it is, say, in the context of the discussion of general political and economic issues. Unlimited corporate expenditure runs counter to the egalitarian principles which underlie the conduct of elections in modern democracies.[59] It is doubtful whether in principle press and other media companies should be wholly immune from the expenditure limits imposed on other corporations during election campaigns. Such immunity confers special privileges on these corporations. In its recent decision on the BCRA, the Supreme Court has, however, upheld the exemption of communications appearing in a news story, commentary, or editorial distributed by a broadcasting station from the ban on the financing of election communications from general corporate funds.[60] The exemption is perfectly justifiable insofar as it applies to the provision of news and commentary on it; it is unclear whether it should give broadcasting companies or the press a right to spend unlimited money on general editorials on issues relevant to an election.

4. Rights Not to Speak

In 1943 some Jehovah's Witnesses challenged the constitutionality of a state requirement that children in public schools salute and pledge loyalty to the United States flag. Their case was principally that the regulation violated the 'free exercise of religion' limb of the First Amendment, but the Supreme Court upheld the challenge on the ground that the students had a right not to be compelled to affirm beliefs they did not hold. In one of the most quoted passages in the history of the Supreme Court, Jackson J. declared:

If there is any fixed star in our constitutional constellation, it is that no official, high or petty, can prescribe what shall be orthodox in politics, nationalism, religion, or other matters of opinion or force citizens to confess by word or act their faith therein.[61]

There are references in the Court's judgment to a 'right of self-determination' and 'freedom of the mind', but it seems clear that Jackson J. considered that a right not to speak, in particular a right not to be forced to say what a person does not accept, is an integral aspect of freedom of speech. A flag salute was treated as an established form of 'symbolic speech', a feature of the ruling which influenced the approach of the Court in the flag-desecration cases discussed earlier in this chapter. It followed that a right not to salute the flag was covered by the right not to speak. Classic examples of the exercise of this right of silence are the 'loyalty oath' cases in which the Supreme Court struck down requirements that state employees affirm allegiance to the national and state constitutions and disclaim membership of the Communist Party and other 'subversive' organizations.[62]

---

[59] See ch. XIV, s. 2 below.   [60] *McConnell* v. *FEC* 157 L Ed 2d 491 (2003).
[61] *West Virginia State Board of Education* v. *Barnette* 319 US 624, 642 (1943).
[62] e.g. *Keyishian* v. *Board of Regents* 385 US 589 (1967).

But the right to stay silent can be invoked in many circumstances far removed from the situations where freedom of speech is in issue. For example, it may be claimed by the defendant in a criminal trial. It is then upheld either under a common law privilege against self-incrimination (as in England) or under a specific constitutional right of silence (as under the Fifth Amendment to the Constitution of the United States). Lawyers, doctors, and priests may refuse to give evidence on the ground of professional privilege, while the press may use the argument that, if it is not allowed a privilege of this kind, its sources of information will dry up and it will not be able to publish stories of real public importance.[63] Insofar as these privileges are recognized in law, they are quite different from the right established by the Supreme Court in the *Barnette* case; they rest on the importance of open and candid communications between, say, lawyers and their clients to which confidentiality is essential.

The right not to speak, or negative freedom of speech, is closely linked with freedom of belief and conscience and with underlying rights to human dignity, which would be seriously compromised by a legal requirement to enunciate opinions which are not in truth held by the individual. The connection is easy to establish. The students in the *Barnette* case clearly had a constitutional right to say and write what they thought about the flag. It would be nonsense to protect that freedom, yet to deny them an accompanying liberty not to adopt in public the officially approved attitude. The close link with freedom of conscience and individual dignity means that the negative freedom can be claimed only by the person claiming the right not to speak. Moreover, it covers a right not to express an *opinion* which the claimant does not hold (as in the *Barnette* case), rather than a general right not to comply with a legal duty to supply *information*, say, to a census officer. The point is that the right not to speak does not rest on the same arguments which support the right to speak: the search for truth, the importance of free speech to a democracy, and the right to self-development.[64] Only the last of these has any relevance for the negative freedom. It is hard to see how individual self-development is furthered by a refusal to give information, while that refusal is, of course, inimical to the other arguments for free speech which assume that the wide dissemination of information is a public good. It is, therefore, much better for a witness, whether in court or at a legislative committee hearing, to justify refusal to answer questions concerning matters of fact by recourse to a privilege against self-incrimination rather than the negative freedom of speech. In this context it is interesting to note that the German Constitutional Court has ruled that the requirement to complete a census form did not violate the applicants' freedom of expression, since *negative Meinungsfreiheit* only covered views and opinions.[65] Nor did an obligation to publish health warnings on cigarette packets engage the

---

[63] For consideration of this aspect of press freedom, see ch. XII, s. 3(iv) below.

[64] See ch. I, s. 2 above.

[65] 65 BVerfGE 1, 40–1 (1984). But the Court found the requirement violated the right of privacy guaranteed by art. 2 of the Basic Law.

producers' freedom not to disseminate their views; it was clear that the warnings could not be attributed to them.[66]

Given the close connection of the right of silence to the freedom of conscience and human dignity, the case for extending coverage of the right to corporations is a thin one.[67] Corporations are entitled to speak, because they may have a distinctive view on matters of political and financial policy, while the public also has an interest in knowing their views on these matters. But that argument can hardly apply to the right not to speak. Nevertheless, the Supreme Court of Canada, without discussing the point, has assumed that corporations do have a right not to speak; for example, it recognized the right of cigarette manufacturers not to be compelled to print health warnings on their products, unless it was clear that they had been required to do this.[68] Otherwise purchasers might assume that manufacturers accepted that smoking is dangerous. Similar issues arise when newspaper editors claim they are entitled not to publish readers' replies to personal attacks previously printed in the paper. Quite apart from an editor's claim to exercise a distinct press freedom in this context,[69] he could also argue that a requirement to publish a reply—a common feature of European press laws—would infringe freedom of speech, including a right not to print views he does not hold.[70] That argument, however, should be rejected. The right of silence is not infringed merely because a newspaper is required by law to publish a proposition it does not agree with. It is only invaded if it is compelled to say or write something which, observers would conclude, would be taken as representing the editor's view. That need not be the case with rights of reply to the press, or the broadcasting media, where it should always be clear that they are published to present the view of the respondent, and do not represent the view of the editor.

It is also important for the court to be satisfied that the right asserted is a right not *to speak*, rather than a right not to engage in a course of *conduct*. The European Court has held that in some circumstances individuals have a right not to be compelled to join a trade union,[71] while the United States Supreme Court in *Abood* v. *Detroit Board of Education* upheld the right of workers (who were not union members) not to be compelled under an agency-shop agreement to finance trade union political activities.[72] The issues in these cases are complicated, partly because the primary right claimed is a freedom not to be compelled to associate, rather than the negative freedom of speech. On one view, however, they concern the scope of the latter freedom: should a refusal to pay financial dues be protected under that

---

[66] 95 BVerfGE 173, 182 (1997).   [67] See Moon, 186–91.

[68] *RJR-McDonald Inc* v. *A-G of Canada* [1995] 3 SCR 199, discussed in ch. XI, s. 5 below. Also see *Slaight Communications* v. *Davidson* [1989] 1 SCR 1038, where the Supreme Court held that a tribunal order requiring a firm to give a former employee a specified reference infringed the firm's freedom not to speak, though the order was regarded as minimally intrusive, since it did not compel it to state an *opinion*.   [69] Ch. XII, s. 2(ii) below.

[70] In *Miami Herald* v. *Tornillo* 418 US 241 (1974), the Court upheld an editor's First Amendment right of editorial freedom not to publish replies to personal attacks.

[71] *Young, James, and Webster* v. *UK* (1982) 4 EHRR 38.   [72] 431 US 209 (1977).

freedom, when the refusal is based on the individual's disapproval of the political causes on which the organization spends its money? The Supreme Court of Canada has taken a different view of the matter from that taken by the US Supreme Court. In *Lavigne* v. *Ontario Public Service Employee Union*[73] it declined to uphold a challenge by a public service employee that his Charter rights to freedom of expression and association had been infringed when he was required to pay union dues, a portion of which was spent on political causes of which he disapproved. The Court did not think the right to freedom of expression was engaged, since the employee remained free to speak out against the union's expenditure and the causes it supported. The principle formulated in the *Barnette* flag-salute case did not apply to the compulsory payment of dues. The US Supreme Court, by bare majority, has reached a similar conclusion in a non-union case: it upheld marketing orders requiring fruit growers in California to pay for generic advertisements for their products against a First Amendment challenge brought by growers who disapproved of the advertisements.[74] Stevens J. for the Court considered the freedom not to speak was hardly implicated, since the marketing orders did not inhibit the growers' freedom to communicate their views; he also thought that they were not compelled to endorse or finance any political views, suggesting in effect that negative freedom of speech does not cover commercial advertising. The crucial question is surely whether the requirement to finance union or other expenditure prevents the individual from communicating his own views or compels him, in effect, to say something he does not believe in. That will normally not be the case.

Further difficulties in the scope of negative freedom of speech arose in two unusual cases from the United States. The first was *Wooley* v. *Maynard*,[75] where the constitutional issues were as subtle as the facts were trivial. The respondents, Jehovah's Witnesses, yet again contributing to First Amendment jurisprudence, objected to a New Hampshire statutory requirement that all non-commercial motor vehicles must bear the state motto, 'Live Free or Die', on their licence plates. So they covered it up. The Court held, with two members dissenting on the point of substance, that New Hampshire was compelling car owners to carry the state's ideological message, and that this requirement unconstitutionally abridged their right not to speak. Rehnquist J. pointed out in dissent, first, that it was far from clear that carriage of the motto was conventionally understood as a mode of 'speech', and second, that in any case nobody would understand the car owner as subscribing to the particular political philosophy so cryptically summarized by it. This second point seems well made. So either the *Wooley* case was wrongly decided, or the rule now is that the state may not require anyone to transmit another person's or the state's own views. Indeed, the Court went so far as to say that an individual has a First Amendment right to refuse to foster any idea he finds

---

[73] [1991] 2 SCR 211.   [74] *Glickman* v. *Wileman Bros and Elliott, Inc* 521 US 457 (1997).
[75] 430 US 705 (1977).

objectionable. But that would go much too far. Citizens could even challenge their liability to pay taxation which is used to finance government programmes and communications of which they disapprove, if negative freedom of speech were extended to cover a broad refusal of that character. It is inconceivable that the Supreme Court would uphold such a challenge, but the possibility shows the danger of extending the right not to speak beyond the circumstances of a case like *Barnette*.

The right not to speak was also upheld when the Public Utilities Commission of California required a utility company to include in its billing envelopes material produced by designated consumer groups, whose views on environmental and other matters was opposed to that of the company. The company was free to continue inserting its own messages and there was no risk of confusion about the source of the enclosed material. Following *Wooley* and its decision in *Miami Herald* v. *Tornillo*,[76] upholding the right of editors not to publish readers' replies, the Court majority held the requirement infringed the First Amendment right of the utility company not to be compelled to carry messages it did not agree with.[77] In the leading dissent, Rehnquist J. pointed out that corporations were hardly entitled to a right of silence, closely linked to freedom of belief and conscience. Further, the obligation to carry other messages did not inhibit the company's freedom to communicate its views in its own messages enclosed in the billing envelopes and in other ways. That is surely correct. The majority decision that the speech of the utility company would be inhibited by the Commission's requirement is unconvincing, as is its view that the order wrongly discriminated between viewpoints by giving access to designated consumer groups. It is correct that the order discriminated in this way, but that was not wrong. Only a small number of groups other than the utility company could use the limited space within the envelope, and it was reasonable to allow organizations which took a different view of environmental matters from that of the company itself to enjoy access to it. There was no more an infringement of freedom of speech than there is when an authority requires a commercial television company to allow political parties or election candidates access to broadcasting time or compels cable operators to make channels available for educational and other public services.[78]

Finally, mention should be made of another set of circumstances when a negative free speech right has been recognized. In *Hurley* v. *Irish-American Gay, Lesbian and Bisexual Group of Boston*,[79] the Court upheld the right of a Veterans Council not to allow a Gay and Lesbian Group to join its St Patrick's Day parade to march under the Group banner, in the face of a court order requiring it to admit the Group under state non-discrimination laws. Souter J. giving the Court's unanimous judgment held the Council was entitled to exercise its right as a speaker to shape

[76] 418 US 241 (1974), discussed in ch. XII, s. 3 below.
[77] *Pacific Gas & Electricity Co* v. *Public Utilities Commission of California* 475 US 1 (1986).
[78] See ch. XII, s. 5 below for regulation of broadcasting.
[79] 515 US 557 (1995).

its expression as it wished and to refuse the claim of the Group to be associated with its parade. The decision was correct. If the Council had been compelled to admit the Group, observers might have inferred that it approved the latter's implicit message; in effect, it would have been compelled to state a position on gay sexuality, a matter on which it preferred to stay silent. Much more difficult to accept is the Court's later ruling in *Boy Scouts of America* v. *Dale*,[80] where a majority held the Boy Scouts could exclude a gay rights activist from membership, contrary to New Jersey non-discrimination law, on the ground that otherwise it would be sending out a positive message about homosexual behaviour. Rehnquist CJ for the Court thought that a group's freedom of 'expressive association' was infringed if, as here, the admission of an unwanted member significantly compromised its ability to advocate its own views. In fact it is unclear that the admission of a gay activist would have interfered with the organization's freedom to state its views. Moreover, enforcement of the non-discrimination law was not aimed at that freedom, any more than general tax laws are aimed at the freedom of dissenters to state strongly that they disapprove of the programmes on which revenue is spent.[81] The law did not compel the Scouts to say it approved of homosexuality; it merely compelled it to admit a gay person to membership, because the state took the view that discrimination on the basis of sexual orientation was wrong. The right not to speak does not cover a right to discriminate or to engage in unlawful practices.

5. Language Rights

In *Ford* v. *Attorney-General of Quebec* the Supreme Court of Canada struck down provisions in a Quebec law requiring the exclusive use of French on signs and posters, in commercial advertising, and for the names of firms.[82] It held that they amounted to a disproportionate restriction on freedom of expression, which includes a right of choice of language. It may seem obvious that freedom of expression covers the right of individuals and corporations to communicate their views, or to advertise their goods and services, in whatever language they like.[83] First, it is difficult to disentangle choice of language from the right of a speaker to choose the *content* of his discourse; if a speaker has a right to use colourful terminology in one language to express his convictions forcefully, it is hard to see why he should be denied the right also to use another language, with which he and listeners may be more familiar, to put across the same message. As the Canadian Supreme Court put it, '[l]anguage is so intimately related to the form and content of expression

---

[80] 120 S Ct 2446 (2000).   [81] Rubenfeld (n. 25 above), 807–17.

[82] [1988] 2 SCR 712.

[83] For a full statement of the argument in this paragraph, see L. Green, 'Freedom of Expression and Choice of Language', in W. J. Waluchow (ed.), *Free Expression* (Oxford: OUP, 1994), 135.

that there cannot be true freedom of expression by means of language if one is prohibited from using the language of one's choice.'[84] Secondly, the choice of language reflects the speaker's individuality and cultural identity as closely as the contents of his speech. Indeed, a speaker might legitimately want to express his feelings, for example, about the rights of a minority by using its language. Equally, the object of laws prescribing the use of a particular language, or restricting or prohibiting the use of others, is to protect the means by which the majority express and assert its identity; these laws are clearly aimed at speech. There can be no doubt then that the choice of language is an integral aspect of freedom of expression, though this freedom might also be covered, to some extent, by other constitutional rights: the right of parents to ensure education for their children in conformity with their convictions,[85] or privacy and general liberty rights.[86]

However, states are entitled to protect the use of an official or other languages in certain circumstances. A language may be prescribed in the Constitution, as it is in France and Spain.[87] Without some protection, the free expression interests of the majority of a community might be endangered by the increasing use of a minority language for important commercial transactions. Indeed, the Supreme Court of Canada did hold in the *Ford* case that it was legitimate for Quebec to protect the French language by compelling advertisers and traders to use it, in addition to English, and to give it marked prominence. But it was disproportionate, additionally, to prohibit English by requiring the exclusive use of French. Similarly the French Conseil constitutionnel upheld provisions of the *loi Toubon* imposing the use of French in business, on public signs, and in other public places, though allowing the use of translations in other languages.[88] These provisions were a legitimate way of reconciling freedom of expression, which includes freedom to choose the language for communicating thoughts, and the constitutional guarantee of French. But the Conseil held incompatible with freedom of expression the more onerous requirements to use specific French words and phrases insofar as they were imposed on the media and on private persons. Those requirements could legitimately be imposed only on public bodies.

[84] *Ford* v. *A-G of Quebec* [1988] 2 SCR 712, 748.

[85] In the *Belgian Linguistic* case (1968) 1 EHRR 252 the European Court upheld a challenge to provisions of the Belgian school system under which children were denied access to education in French on the ground that their parents did not reside in particular communes. But the Court denied there was a general right to education in the language of choice, either under ECHR, art. 8 (right to respect for private and family life) or under art. 2 of the First Protocol (right of parents to ensure education in conformity with their own philosophical convictions).

[86] In *Meyer* v. *Nebraska* 262 US 390 (1923), the Supreme Court struck down a law forbidding schoolteaching in languages other than English as violating the right not to be deprived of liberty without due process.

[87] 'The language of the Republic shall be French': art. 2 of the Constitution of 1958; art. 3 of the Spanish Constitution of 1978 provides that Castilian is the official language which all Spaniards have a duty to know and the right to use.

[88] Decision 94-345 DC of 29 July 1994, RJC I-595, on which see J.-P. Camby, 'Le Conseil constitutionnel et la langue française' (1994) 110 *Revue du Droit Public et de la Science Politique en France et à l' Étranger* 1663.

The speaker's freedom to choose the language for commercial and other private communications, or on the media, should be distinguished from a positive right, say, to provision by the state of information in his language, or a right to use it on official occasions or when completing forms. These positive rights would impose correlative duties on the state to take steps to facilitate the use of the speaker's language and to provide translations of official literature. In many circumstances it is willing to do this; it is usually prepared, for instance, to make important information concerning health available in a number of languages. But that is not a matter of freedom of expression, for that freedom does not usually entail positive rights to help from the state in enabling the speaker to communicate ideas or rights of access to information: see the following sections of this chapter. On the other hand, positive language rights, and corresponding state duties, are sometimes imposed either by the constitution or by statute.[89] Alternatively, the constitution may prescribe two or more official languages, so it would be legitimate to derive a positive right to use them on official occasions. This distinction between the freedom of individuals to use their own language and positive language rights may explain the only English decision in this area. In *Williams* v. *Cowell* the Court of Appeal rejected the applicant's argument that he had a right to have an appeal before the Employment Appeal Tribunal conducted in Welsh, or, in view of his ability to speak English, a right to an interpreter to help him argue his case.[90] He was claiming a positive right to use Welsh in a particular official setting, rather than a freedom to use it in a private or commercial context. Of course, if the claimant had not spoken good English, there would have been a violation of his rights, if no interpreter had been provided. But the violation would have been of his right to a fair trial, not of his freedom of speech rights.[91]

6. What Type of Freedom?

(i) Preliminary issues

The preceding sections of this chapter have examined the meaning of *speech* for the purposes of the legal application of the free speech principle. This section is concerned with an equally intransigent subject: what does *freedom* of speech entail? In particular, legislatures and courts must decide whether commitment to the freedom requires the recognition of only a liberty to speak and write, free from governmental restraint, or whether, at least in some circumstances, it also entails

---

[89] See art. 6 of the Italian Constitution, requiring the state to protect minority languages.

[90] [2000] 1 WLR 187. Under the Welsh Language Act 1993 parties and witnesses may use Welsh in legal proceedings in Wales, but that does not cover appeal proceedings heard in England.

[91] ECHR, art. 6(3)(e) confers a right to the free assistance of an interpreter only in criminal cases; it is arguable that the right extends to all cases if a fair trial could not be conducted in the absence of such assistance.

positive rights to speak. On the latter alternative, the state, and perhaps other institutions and individuals, would sometimes be required to provide opportunities or facilities for speech. It can be argued, for instance, that freedom of speech is only realized if individuals (and organizations) can reply to critical stories about them in the press and on the broadcasting media or, additionally, have some opportunity to use the media to put over their ideas. Equally, claims may be made that there are rights to demonstrate on the streets, in other public places, and even on private property, as otherwise individuals and political groups will lack opportunities to communicate their views effectively to the general public. Or it may be urged that the state should support speech financially by, say, providing subsidies to the press and to the arts, or at least that it would infringe free speech rights if it chooses to support some applicants, but not others, on the basis of the contents of their message.

The debate as to the true character of freedom of speech raises complex issues of political philosophy. It is an aspect of the controversy whether political freedom should be regarded as a *negative* freedom from state control, or may legitimately be taken to comprise *positive* freedoms and rights against the state.[92] At the level of philosophical principle, some light on the question may be shed by reflection on the reasons for the special position of speech. If the main justification for the free speech principle is fear of government regulation in this area, we would be much more reluctant to countenance state measures designed, say, to ensure access to the media or to provide financial support for speech than we would be if the concern is to ensure the dissemination of a wide range of political information and opinion, a goal underlying the argument from democracy.[93] Of course, courts should take into account any indication in the constitution that positive rights of speech should be recognized. Further, it would be reasonable for them to consider institutional factors, in particular the extent to which the regulation of any positive rights is undertaken by independent agencies to minimize the dangers of government control over the content of expression. In fact, constitutions rarely offer guidance on the character of *freedom* of speech, so constitutional tribunals must determine themselves how far, if at all, it is appropriate to recognize positive speech rights.

A lawyer's approach to this subject may be influenced by the writing of the American jurist, Hohfeld. He categorized all legal relationships into the following correlations: right–duty, liberty–no right, power–liability, immunity–disability.[94] The analysis of broad legal concepts, such as 'the right to trade' or 'the right to

---

[92] See I. Berlin, 'Two Concepts of Liberty', in *Four Essays on Liberty* (Oxford: OUP, 1969); C. Taylor, 'What's Wrong with Negative Liberty?', in A. Ryan (ed.), *The Idea of Freedom: Essays in Honour of Isaiah Berlin* (Oxford: OUP, 1979), 175.

[93] See ch. I, s. 2 above for free speech theories and justifications.

[94] W. N. Hohfeld, *Fundamental Legal Conceptions* (New Haven: Yale UP, 1919). Hohfeld used the term 'privilege' rather than 'liberty', but the latter is more illuminating in this, and other civil liberties, contexts.

work', in terms of these relationships would, according to his theory, prevent confusion. One party has a *right* to performance of a contract (or damages in lieu), and the other has a correlative duty to honour the agreement, while 'the right to trade' is really only a *liberty* (or 'privilege' to use Hohfeld's own terminology), as there is no general duty not to interfere with a competitor's trade. It has been suggested, on this analysis, that freedom of speech is only a liberty.[95] It means that the state has no right to intervene. Nobody has a duty to listen, nor is the state, or anyone else for that matter, under a duty to provide facilities for speech. Of course, the liberty may be protected by various claim-rights, where there are correlative duties, for example, the right of a person not to be assaulted when he is speaking or the right of a property owner to hold meetings on his land free from disturbances amounting to the torts of trespass or nuisance, but these rights are only incidentally associated with, and are not integral to, freedom of speech.[96] Hohfeld's analysis is, however, of only limited utility. It states conclusions about legal relationships within a particular system. It may be right to say that free speech is, or was, only a liberty in English law, but that may not be the case in other jurisdictions. (In the United States the First Amendment clearly imposes a disability on Congress to restrict speech and confers on individuals corresponding immunities from regulation when they exercise freedom of speech. But it does not state whether 'the freedom of speech' may only be a liberty, or whether it might, at least sometimes, confer claim-rights to speak.) More importantly, Hohfeld's analysis does not provide any guidance on how courts *ought to* interpret free speech clauses, and it is difficult to apply it to rights and freedoms against the state, in contrast to those which may be claimed in relations between individuals.[97]

The assertion that freedom of speech does confer positive claim-rights against the state carries a number of possible implications. The argument might be that the state is under a duty not to interfere—and not to allow interference by others—with the exercise of the freedom, so that damages are recoverable when interference occurs. The state would, for example, then violate freedom of expression, if it did not protect a newspaper against interference with its operations by opponents of its political line. (Adopting this perspective the European Human Rights Court has held that Turkey was in breach of the guarantee of freedom of expression when it failed to protect a newspaper against sabotage of its operations by critics opposed to its political views.[98]) Claims are often made that there are rights to hold meetings on the streets and in other public places in derogation from the relevant public authority's right to determine the appropriate usage of its

---

[95] G. Williams, 'The Concept of Legal Liberty' (1956) 56 *Columbia Law Rev* 1129, reprinted in R. Summers (ed.), *Essays in Legal Philosophy* (Oxford: OUP, 1968), 121, 138–9.

[96] See H. L. A. Hart, 'Bentham on Legal Rights', in A. W. B. Simpson (ed.), *Oxford Essays in Jurisprudence*, 2nd series (Oxford: OUP, 1973), 171, 179–81.

[97] A. M. Honoré, 'Rights of Exclusion and Immunities against Divesting' (1959–60) 34 *Tulane Law Rev* 453, 459.   [98] *Gündem* v. *Turkey* (2001) 31 EHRR 1082.

property. It may also be argued that the law should uphold rights of access to the media. Further, free speech, on one view, is engaged when the state, or other public funding body, denies financial support for an art exhibition, on the ground that the works to be displayed are offensive or indecent. Or an artist or novelist might make the bold claim that she has a free speech right to financial assistance to enable her to continue working. Of course, the wide range of circumstances in which positive free speech rights may be claimed does not mean they are all necessarily misconceived, and, therefore, that freedom of speech should be treated as only a negative liberty. The range of possible implications should, however, induce some caution in accepting broad propositions of principle about positive free speech rights. This caveat may not matter much in constitutional litigation, for a court need decide only whether it should uphold a *specific* positive right, for example, a right to reply to a personal attack in a newspaper column; it is not required to determine whether free speech generally entails positive rights or what those rights might be.

It is important in this area to distinguish between two levels at which positive free speech rights might be upheld. A court might interpret the constitution to require the recognition of *constitutional* rights, say, of access to the media or to hold meetings on the streets. In that event the legislature (or other body such as a local council or broadcasting regulator) would have an obligation to formulate positive rights, the scope of which might then be challenged in subsequent litigation. Alternatively, the legislature might itself provide for positive access rights, as the United Kingdom Parliament did when it established rights to speak on university campuses—positive rights which are very unusual in English and Scots law.[99] *Statutory* rights of this type are less problematic than constitutional rights. They do not impose duties and associated costs on government which it is unwilling to bear; moreover, insofar as positive rights require detailed formulation, they are framed by a body—the legislature or the executive—which is better suited for this task than a court. But legislative free speech rights may be open to attack. Statutory rights of reply to the press, for instance, may be challenged on the ground that they infringe newspaper editors' free speech or press rights,[100] while a right to hold a meeting in, say, local authority schools or other premises derogates, it could be argued, from its property rights. Alternatively, a constitutional court might take the view that freedom of speech requires the legislature to make provision for, say, the presentation on the media of a wide range of opinion or for adequate financing for public broadcasting, but allow it substantial discretion how this is done. In that event, the court does not formulate constitutional free speech rights or even require Parliament to enact statutory access rights. Rather, it considers that respect for freedom of speech requires the political branches of government to take active steps to foster the values associated with the freedom, but that obligation need not entail the recognition of positive rights.

---

[99] See ch. VIII, s. 3(iii) below.   [100] See ch. XII, s. 2(ii) below.

Positive rights have been recognized most frequently in the context of street protest and meetings in other public places; the particular arguments for their recognition are dealt with in a later chapter.[101] Rights of reply and access to the media are discussed in more detail in Chapter XII.[102] The following pages are concerned with general arguments concerning positive free speech rights, and with two specific issues: first, whether freedom of expression entails a right to acquire information—freedom of information—and secondly, how the law should treat claims to financial support from the state.

(ii) Only a narrow liberty?

Frederick Schauer has argued that 'freedom of speech is best characterized as the absence of governmental interference.'[103] In his view, it does not entail the practical ability or effective opportunities to speak, as proponents of positive speech rights contend. Schauer gives a number of reasons for this view of freedom of speech as a liberty in a narrow sense. In some situations recognition of positive rights would interfere with the free speech, or press, rights of others: this point is, of course, pertinent to the argument whether the law should uphold rights of reply and access to the media.[104] A more general objection is that positive rights could only be effectively protected when a regulatory authority, or the courts, decided it was appropriate to allow, say, a particular group space or time to use the media to communicate its views, or to compel its financial support by a funding authority. The allocation of resources, or broadcasting time, necessarily involves an authority taking decisions to uphold a positive free speech right. Inevitably, that authority might favour one group or strand of opinion to the prejudice of others by decisions which would themselves create unacceptable dangers to freedom of speech. Since one powerful argument for freedom of speech is that government cannot be trusted to take decisions in this area, it would be foolish to give it greater powers in a misguided attempt to give free speech better protection.

Finally, the argument that government should ensure that all individuals and groups are in a position to communicate their views muddles freedom, or liberty, of speech with the conditions for its exercise. The argument would compel enforcement of rights to education, opportunities for travel, or a minimum income (and perhaps some capital) without which goods it is difficult to communicate effectively. It is simply unrealistic to require government to discharge this burden, quite apart from meeting the financial costs of ensuring that everyone, or most people, have real opportunities to engage in freedom of speech. On this perspective,

---

[101] Ch. VIII, s. 3(i) below.

[102] For discussion whether journalists have special access rights to trials and other places, see ch. IX, s. 4 and ch. XII, s. 3(iii) below.   [103] Schauer, 129.

[104] See ch. IV, s. 5 below for private censorship, and ch. XII below for freedom of speech within the media.

the German Administrative Court rightly rejected the claim of a recipient of social assistance to be reimbursed the travelling costs incurred for a journey to Bonn to take part in a political demonstration; there was no interference on these facts with freedom of speech.[105]

These arguments are certainly persuasive against the recognition of *general* positive free speech rights. Freedom of speech is primarily a negative liberty. However, in some contexts, there is a convincing case for upholding narrowly defined positive free speech rights. First, we should examine briefly the general arguments for accepting them. One approach proceeds from the interests of recipients; it is particularly pertinent if the 'participatory democracy' rationale for free speech protection is emphasized in judicial interpretation of the constitutional provision.[106] Arguably, recipient interests in obtaining information and a sufficiently wide range of ideas to enable the making of intelligent political choices are only satisfied if some positive rights to free speech are upheld. The relevance of this point to the case for access rights to radio and television is particularly clear: the electorate should be able to hear on these popular media the views of spokesmen for pressure groups and of ordinary people in addition to those of politicians and professional broadcasters.

But this is not a strong argument. The interests of recipients in hearing a wide range of views and in access to information does not compel the recognition of individual positive *rights*, say, to speak on radio and television. At most there is a free speech case only for ensuring that these media provide a wide variety of programmes and present all relevant strands of political and social opinion. That can be done by establishing a strong public service broadcasting institution such as the BBC and by imposing rigorous programme standards on commercial privately owned channels; it is unnecessary to formulate positive free speech rights in this context.[107] Moreover, the freedom to receive ideas and information is itself usually regarded as only a liberty, rather than a positive right.[108] It would be very odd to use the recipient interest as a foundation or springboard for the recognition of claim-rights to impart ideas and information. Admittedly, a United States case shows the implications of taking a bolder approach. In *Board of Education* v. *Pico*,[109] three members of the Supreme Court were prepared to recognize a First Amendment right of school students to read any book once it had been placed in the school library, so that the governing board were under a correlative duty not to remove it on the basis of its 'offensive' contents. The dissent of Rehnquist J. pointed out that the recognition in this case of a positive right to receive information implied that the communicator had an equally strong right to transmit it. The argument would lead to the strange conclusion that an author or publisher had a right that the school library acquire his work, or at least not delete it from the list.

---

[105] 72 BVerwGE 113, 118 (1985).   [106] See ch. I, s. 2 above.
[107] For further discussion, see ch. XII, s. 5 below.   [108] See s. 7 of this chapter below.
[109] 457 US 853 (1982), discussed below in s. 7.

Similarly, it might be said that if listeners have a right not to have a particular programme taken off the radio, the producers should have an equivalent right to transmit it.[110] These results would be regarded by most people as unacceptable. They show, it is suggested, that it is unwise to treat the freedom to receive information or ideas as more than a liberty, and, further, to build strong speaker rights on this foundation.

The second approach is much more promising. It focuses on the interests of speakers. It is based on the claim that free speech must honour equality. Everyone has an equal right to participate in public discourse; free speech should not be the privilege of the rich and powerful, but all should have at least some opportunity to disseminate their ideas.[111] The more educated may write books and articles, while the very rich may own newspapers or television channels. In contrast, the poor and oppressed can only express their opinions through demonstrations on the streets, and in meetings held in premises they do not own. Equality can only be honoured and some approximation of balance achieved by conferring on minority groups and individuals positive rights such as rights of reply and access to the media, and strong rights to use the streets and other facilities to hold meetings and to demonstrate. In short, freedom of speech requires the recognition of positive rights for speakers, and the imposition of corresponding duties to afford them facilities and grant at least some opportunities for equal exercise of these rights. The legislature and government may fail to formulate positive free speech rights, particularly when they are content for wealthy and powerful interest groups to dominate public debate through, say, their control of the media. In that event courts must intervene to ensure that equality is respected in the exercise of free speech rights.

This is a powerful argument. I am not persuaded that the case made by Schauer and others for a narrow conception of freedom of speech as only a liberty *necessarily* trumps it in *every* situation. Take a free speech dystopia which might exist, even in a generally liberal society. The media are owned by a small number of magnates who allow little or no time or space for the expression of dissenting, let alone socialist views; this is not balanced by a strong public broadcasting system. The government, anxious not to offend these magnates, makes no effort to intervene. Local authorities, for the most part controlled by right-wing political parties, do not allow political demonstrations on the streets or in other public places; on their face the ordinances are content-neutral and do not discriminate against left-wing protest, but the authorities have realized that street protest is the best way for radical views to reach public attention. Of course, radicals could set up their own publishing houses, newspapers, or broadcasting stations, but they lack the means to do this. But the

---

[110] Listeners do not have a constitutional right to compel review by the Federal Communications Commission of programme changes, let alone a right to compel continued showing of the programme: *FCC* v. *WNCN Listeners Guild* 450 US 582 (1981).

[111] See A. Cox, *The Role of the Supreme Court in American Government* (Oxford: OUP, 1976); H. Kalven, 'The Concept of the Public Forum: *Cox* v. *Louisiana*' [1965] *Supreme Court Review* 1, 10–12.

courts remain free and are open-minded about the proper interpretation of the free expression clause of the constitution. In these circumstances, it is surely right for them to construe the clause as conferring rights to demonstrate on the streets and requiring the government at least to make some provision for pluralism in the media. Moreover, if a new government were to enact legislation providing for a right of reply, and perhaps even access to the media, its provisions should be upheld as promoting free speech, rather than regarded as necessarily incompatible with it.

In this free speech dystopia, the conventional arguments against positive speech rights do not outweigh the case for them. In particular, the danger to free speech from government intervention seems trivial compared to the deadening of public discourse brought about by the absence of media pluralism and by the denial of positive rights to use the streets and other public property for peaceful protest. Upholding positive rights would protect the free speech interests of many more people than would an insistence that only, say, the liberties of newspaper editors and media magnates were at issue. Moreover, it would be relatively clear in these cases that the opportunity, space, or time for radical expression had been denied, because the media or the local authority, as the case may be, wanted to curtail its dissemination. Freedom of speech would be fully engaged.

In fact, some positive rights are widely recognized, in particular rights to demonstrate on the streets and in certain other public places or fora.[112] The media and, so far as practicable, members of the public are entitled to attend legal proceedings.[113] In continental European jurisdictions, rights of reply to the press and broadcasting media are upheld as compatible with the free speech and press rights of editors and as respecting the free speech and personality interests of the person exercising them.[114] The Supreme Court of Canada recognized in *Haig* v. *Canada* that positive rights and government duties to act may be necessary in some contexts to make freedom of expression meaningful.[115] Courts should adopt a pragmatic approach. Even if free speech is treated primarily as a liberty, generally demanding non-interference by the state, on occasion legislative intervention should be approved, or even required, when the arguments for that course are compelling. This approach is preferable to a dogmatic insistence on the view that freedom of speech is only a liberty in a narrow sense, or that it is always preferable to treat it in that way.

The drawback of a pragmatic approach is that it may be difficult to determine when the case for recognition of (exceptional) positive rights is made out. One fundamental question, it is suggested, is whether the denial of the positive right is intended to restrict the expression of a particular view, or put more simply, is targeted at speech. On that approach it is easy to see why the blanket denial by an authority of all rights to protest on the streets, let alone a discriminatory refusal

---

[112] Ch. VIII, s. 3 below.   [113] Ch. IX, s. 4 below.   [114] Ch. XII, s. 2 below.
[115] [1993] 2 SCR 995, paras. 68–77.

to allow a particular group to march, engages free speech. Arguably, it is also implicated when an editor refuses to publish a reply to a feature critical of the person claiming it or to publish an article adopting a particular view. But in that event the issue is more complicated, first, because the recognition of reply and access rights would engage editorial freedom, and secondly, because the editor can invoke space constraints: a newspaper cannot publish everything sent to it. In other circumstances it may be plain that the government was not targeting speech. For instance, requests for public assistance to help a claimant attend a meeting or to disseminate his message can properly be turned down to protect social security or other funds; positive rights are not denied in this situation in order to inhibit speech. The same point often applies to decisions rejecting financial support for research or exhibitions; they may be taken for legitimate, non-speech reasons.[116]

Characterization of *freedom* of speech, therefore, may entail some consideration how far the challenged decision engages *speech*, the issue considered earlier in this chapter.

7. Access to Information

This section concerns a particular type of positive right, which on one view falls under freedom of speech or expression: the right asserted by individuals, or by the media, to acquire information, generally known as 'freedom of information'. Associated with the freedom are claims to attend public meetings and events for information-gathering. Freedom of information is now frequently protected in Western democracies by specific statutes.[117] They are enacted to enable citizens to acquire official information which may be of particular concern to them, for example, medical records or discussions concerning planning policy, or which enables them to assess the wisdom of government policies and so participate fully in public discourse. The argument for freedom of information and open government is indeed very similar to one of the principal positive justifications for the free speech principle: the importance of freedom of speech for an active democracy. The negative free speech argument from suspicion of government also supports the case for freedom of information;[118] we rightly distrust government when it keeps information from us, unless there is an extremely strong argument for secrecy. Further, it is correctly pointed out that freedom of speech may be of little value, and certainly in some contexts its exercise will be ineffective, unless the speaker has acquired enough information about political matters to participate in public discourse on equal terms with politicians and officials. The case for 'a right

---

[116] See s. 8 below for further discussion.

[117] e.g. Freedom of Information Act 1966 (USA); Freedom of Information Act 1982 (Australia Cth); Freedom of Information Act 2000 (UK).   [118] See ch. I, s. 2 above for these arguments.

to know' as an aspect of freedom of speech has a long and respectable ancestry,[119] and is supported by some commentators now.[120]

Though the argument is attractive, it should not be accepted, at least without major qualification. What is at issue is the meaning and scope of *freedom* of speech, and in particular whether it covers a constitutional right of access to information from public authorities. One difficulty is that the right would be claimed when in the nature of things there is no willing speaker. Recognition of a right of access would impose a constitutional duty on government or other authority to provide information it did not want to disclose. The government may not, of course, claim a free speech right not to reveal confidential information; it is not entitled to the protection of the First Amendment or other free speech clause. But there would still be something odd in upholding a free speech claim against an unwilling speaker. Another problem is that courts would be required to formulate the scope of constitutional information rights, for example, to determine exactly what information is covered, whether access to it should be free, and whether the authority was in breach if it was not supplied within, say, three weeks. They are understandably reluctant to do this. These matters are much better resolved by legislation or administrative regulations. Nor is it persuasive to argue that without freedom of information speakers are unable to exercise their free speech rights effectively. That proves much too much. The same is true of claims to a certain level of education, to travel, and to a reasonable standard of living, which are clearly not covered by freedom of speech.

A right to receive information and ideas may be explicitly covered by freedom of expression clauses, as it is in Germany and under the ECHR. Alternatively, courts may infer recipient rights from a general freedom of speech clause, as in the United States. These rights have ample content without bringing freedom of information under their umbrella. For instance, the right to receive information, in Germany *Informationsfreiheit*, may be asserted where a speaker has voluntarily supplied information, but is reluctant or unable to protect his constitutional rights. For instance, the intended recipient of imported magazines seized on arrival in the jurisdiction may be in a much better position to initiate litigation than the foreign publisher or author.[121] In these circumstances, the right to receive information is, like freedom of speech itself, primarily a liberty; its protection does not appear to pose difficulties for free speech theory.

The case for freedom of information is a powerful one, and it may be strengthened by the free speech arguments mentioned in the preceding paragraphs.

---

[119] See J. Milton, *Areopagitica: A Speech for the Liberty of Unlicensed Printing* (1644) in *Prose Writings* (Everyman, 1958), 145, and J. Madison, quoted in T. I. Emerson, 'Legal Foundations of the Right to Know' (1976) 54 *Washington Univ Law Quarterly* 1.

[120] Emerson, ibid.; P. Bayne, 'Freedom of Information and Political Free Speech', in T. Campbell and W. Sadurski (eds.), *Freedom of Communication* (Aldershot: Dartmouth, 1994), 199, 204–7.

[121] See *Lamont* v. *Postmaster-General* 381 US 301 (1965) (successful challenge to federal statute requiring addressees of communist propaganda by post to request delivery in writing) and 27 BVerfGE 71 (1969) (successful constitutional complaint brought when literature imported from East Germany confiscated).

So the link between freedom of expression and freedom of information is undeniable.[122] But that does not mean that the latter is covered by the former, so that courts should derive positive rights of access to information directly from a free speech clause. At most, respect for the fundamental values of freedom of expression may require government to enact freedom of information legislation, the scope of which would be subject to review by the courts to ensure that it is compatible with the former, as well as with other constitutional rights, for example, personal privacy. Even when an individual has an exceptionally strong interest in acquiring particular information, a court is more likely to recognize a (constitutional) access right on the basis of privacy, rather than the right to free expression.

United States courts have hesitated to recognize non-statutory, positive information rights. Their existence has been frequently asserted in challenges to the constitutionality of prison regulations prohibiting press interviews with particular prisoners. In two companion cases the majority of the Supreme Court rejected an argument that journalists had access rights to jails in order to interview prisoners.[123] There are obvious objections to allowing all members of the public free access to prisons to interview prisoners or their warders, and the Court majority refused to grant the press any privileges in this context.[124] The question whether there is a First Amendment *right to gather* information was answered in another prison case, *Houchins* v. *KQED*.[125] A Californian broadcasting station argued it was entitled to enter a state prison to inspect and take photographs of that part of the jail where a prisoner had recently committed suicide. The majority of the Court denied the existence of an access right to government information or to information in its control, distinguishing between this claim and the right to communicate information once it had been obtained. Speaking for the three dissenters, Stevens J. considered entry to the prison necessary to protect the public's right to be informed about the conditions there. But that view proves too much, for its acceptance might have led to the pressing of novel First Amendment claims, for example, to attend Cabinet meetings or witness army exercises; press admission to these occasions would equally enhance public knowledge. However, there is one situation where not only in the United States, but also in England and other common law systems, both the media and the general public do enjoy positive rights: access to legal proceedings. This topic is considered in Chapter IX below.[126]

An unusual positive information right was upheld by three members of the US Supreme Court in the plurality opinion in *Board of Education* v. *Pico*.[127] In their view, and probably that of Blackmun J., the right of school students to receive

---

[122] Sir A. Mason, 'The Relationship between Freedom of Expression and Freedom of Information', in *Freedom of Expression and Freedom of Information*, 225.

[123] *Pell* v. *Procunier* 417 US 817 (1974); *Saxbe* v. *Washington Post* 417 US 843 (1974).

[124] For further discussion of these points, see ch. XII, s. 3(iii) below.   [125] 438 US 1 (1978).

[126] S. 4.   [127] 457 US 853 (1982).

information and ideas would be violated by a high school board's decision to remove books from the library on the ground that their content was 'anti-American', 'plain filthy', or in some other way offensive. The difficulties in formulating this novel First Amendment right, and correlative duty on the school authorities, were pointed out by the four dissenters. Would not the recognition of such a right also require the authorities to provide books for the library on the students' request, and could a clear line be drawn between a right to receive ideas in the form of library books and a right to be taught subjects which the students find of particular interest? Another difficulty was pointed out in Rehnquist J.'s dissent. The plurality derived the students' right to receive ideas from the speaker's First Amendment right to transmit them. But no author or publisher has a right that a school purchase his book for its library, or that any public library buy it for that matter. It would be bizarre to uphold a positive right to receive information where the speaker, in this case the author, has none. The alternative basis for the students' recipient rights—that the books contributed to the effective exercise of their own free speech rights—is no easier to sustain. As Rehnquist J. said, the state did not deprive them of access to the books; the claim was that they had to be provided in the *school library*. If that claim is acceptable, it is hard to see any ground for denying, say, the existence of a First Amendment right to have public libraries provided by the state at places reasonably accessible to the public or a constitutional right to read official information in readily available booklets.

The *Informationsfreiheit* specifically covered by Article 5 of the German Basic Law does not confer any constitutional title to acquire information from public authorities. The text makes it plain that the freedom is only to receive information from generally available sources (*aus allgemein zugänglichen Quellen*), and plainly that does not cover government information which has not been publicly released. As is the case with the freedom of expression also protected in the first sentence of Article 5, the freedom of the recipient is fundamentally a negative right, or in Hohfeldian terms a bare liberty; it does not impose duties on the state to provide information or to ensure its provision by others. The German Administrative Court has left open the question whether in some circumstances the press might have a constitutional right of access to information under the separate *Pressefreiheit* provision in Article 5(1), while rejecting a claim by a journalist to participate in special railway journeys which would have enabled him to become better informed about transport plans.[128] The Court indicated, however, that the exclusion of a particular journalist on the basis of the content of his articles might have raised difficulties under Article 5, in conjunction with the Article 3 prohibition of arbitrary discrimination.

The approach to the character of *Informationsfreiheit* taken by both courts and commentators in Germany is similar to the cautious approach of the US Supreme Court to the recognition of positive information rights. But the Karlsruhe Court

---

[128] 47 BVerwGE 247 (1974).

has ruled that the recipient's interests, protected by the freedom of information, must be independently weighed by ordinary courts. Thus, in its leading case in this area,[129] the Court upheld a constitutional complaint brought against the confiscation of literature imported from the (then) German Democratic Republic supporting the proscribed West German Communist Party, because the lower court had not considered the readers' interest in informing themselves from this source. It is where the sender of the information is outside Germany that recipient rights are most likely to be invoked, for the supplier would often not be in a position effectively to assert his freedom to speak. That happened in another important case on *Informationsfreiheit*, where the Court held that it covered the freedom to erect a satellite dish for the receipt of television programmes (from Turkey) and ruled that the ordinary courts had not taken full account of the interest of immigrants in watching programmes from their country of origin.[130]

The ECHR explicitly covers the right to receive information in Article 10(1). But in contrast to both the Universal Declaration of Human Rights and the International Covenant on Civil and Political Rights,[131] it does not cover the right *to seek* information. In a number of cases the European Court has rejected freedom of information claims based on freedom of expression, while recognizing them, to some extent, on the basis of Article 8, guaranteeing the right to respect for private and family life.[132] In *Gaskin* v. *UK*,[133] for example, the Court held that the applicant's rights under that Article had been violated when he was denied access to records held by a local authority concerning decisions it had taken about his care as a child; procedures should be in place to review whether he could be given information without violating anyone else's confidentiality. It is much better to use the privacy right, rather than freedom of expression, as a ground for upholding positive information rights; the case for their recognition is most compelling when the information is of particular concern to the applicant and can be related to his private or family life. Positive free speech rights would not distinguish access to that information from, say, a claim to see general government policy documents.

8. Freedom of Speech and Government Subsidies

To what extent is freedom of speech engaged when government or another public body funds a health programme, research, or the arts? A public subsidy or programme typically imposes constraints on recipients, sometimes requiring them not to engage in activity incompatible with the objects of the programme, which

---

[129] 27 BVerfGE 71 (1969).   [130] 90 BVerfGE 27 (1994).
[131] Art. 19 of both instruments.
[132] *Leander* v. *Sweden* (1987) 9 EHRR 433; *Guerra* v. *Italy* (1998) 26 EHRR 357.
[133] (1989) 12 EHRR 36.

might include advocacy of such activity. On one view, free speech rights are not at issue at all in this context: the government is not under any legal obligation, say, to fund the arts, so if it does provide financial support, it is entitled to do it on its own terms. The greater power not to fund includes the lesser power to impose conditions on the fortunate recipients of its bounty. Equally, if there is no free speech right to claim support from a government unwilling to support the arts in general or, say, postmodern installation art exhibitions, it might follow that no such right would be infringed if funding is unavailable for exhibitions displaying work which is indecent or 'contrary to good taste'. This conclusion is perhaps inevitable if it is assumed that freedom of speech is never more than a negative liberty, protected only against active government regulation or interference. It was the view taken by Scalia J. in his concurring judgment in a leading United States case, *National Endowment for the Arts (NEA)* v. *Finley*.[134] He held that the First Amendment was not even engaged when artists challenged provisions in federal legislation requiring the Chairperson of the National Endowment for the Arts to take into account decency standards and respect for the diverse beliefs and values of the public when he assessed applications. Rejection of an application for arts funding on the ground of indecency should not, in Scalia J.'s view, be treated as an abridgement of freedom of speech.

At first glance this argument may appear sound enough. But suppose a government, angry at the predominantly radical views of modern artists, amends legislation to debar from eligibility for funding all artists whose work satirizes government or its political policies, say, concerning the war in Iraq. Or it might make it a condition of receipt of research funding that recipients do not publish their work in the relevant area, without prior submission to an official for clearance— in other circumstances, a clear prior restraint on speech.[135] Alternatively, funding might be conditional on a commitment by beneficiaries not to speak or write at all on the subject of the research, or on any matter of public concern, conditions requiring them in effect to surrender their freedom of speech. Arguably, in the absence of any judicial control, government would be free to use its considerable funding powers to skew public debate by, say, ensuring that only those whose views are congenial to it are free to publish their work or secure funding in the first place. For these reasons, some American commentators contend that allocation decisions should be subject to much the same degree of free speech scrutiny as the imposition of criminal penalties and other regulation of speech.[136] Owen Fiss, for example, has argued that it is the responsibility of government to use its funding

---

[134] 524 US 569 (1998).

[135] See ch. IV below for prior restraints.

[136] Among the vast literature, see D. Cole, 'Beyond Unconstitutional Conditions: Charting Spheres of Neutrality in Government-Funded Speech' (1992) 67 *New York Univ Law Rev* 675; M. H. Redish and D. I. Kessler, 'Government Subsidies and Free Expression' (1996) 80 *Minnesota Law Rev* 543; O. M. Fiss, *The Irony of Free Speech* (Cambridge, Mass.: Harvard UP, 1996), ch. 2, and 'State Activism and State Censorship' (1991) 100 *Yale Law Jo* 2087.

powers to encourage a rich public debate, so it should support art which challenges social and cultural orthodoxy.[137] From this perspective, freedom of speech is in this context more than a negative liberty in that it imposes some constraints on government when it funds research or the arts; it would violate freedom of expression, for example, if it used its funding powers to support speech which favoured it rather than the political opposition, or gratuitously to curtail the expression of beneficiaries. That would mean that funding conditions could be challenged in some circumstances on free speech grounds, but it need not mean, of course, that an applicant had a First Amendment right to compel government to finance his research or artistic work.

Neither the perspective offered by Scalia J. in his *NEA* judgment nor that of Fiss works well in all circumstances where funding decisions are challenged on free speech grounds. It is surely right to allow a challenge, where, for instance, the government makes it a condition of funding that the recipient surrenders altogether his free speech rights on matters unrelated to the funding. A restriction of this kind is similar to a term of an employment contract requiring civil servants, irrespective of their position, not to speak outside the workplace on matters of public concern.[138] In these cases government is using its power, without good reasons, to remove the free speech rights of individuals who enter into an employment or financial relationship with it. On the other hand, government is entitled to ensure that its grants are not used by recipients for advocating causes the government itself does not wish to support. That was the ground for the decision of the US Supreme Court in *Rust* v. *Sullivan*,[139] upholding regulations of the Secretary of the Health Department, which provided that recipients of grants for the provision of family planning services should not use those funds to promote or encourage abortion or to lobby for more liberal abortion laws. The regulations did not prevent doctors in receipt of these grants from campaigning for abortion, but merely required them not to use the government's money for that activity. That decision was plainly right. The recent decision in *US* v. *American Library Association* is harder to accept.[140] By a 6–3 majority it rejected a challenge to provisions of the Children's Internet Protection Act forbidding public libraries from receiving public assistance for Internet access unless they installed software to prevent the access of anyone to images which are obscene or of child pornography and to stop the access of children to material harmful to them. For the Court, Rehnquist CJ held that Congress was fully entitled to ensure that public money was spent by libraries on providing material of quality for information and educational purposes; in this respect access to the Internet was no different from access to books or magazines. But it would be wrong to allow Congress a completely free hand in allocating public money to libraries. Legislation withdrawing assistance from libraries which

---

[137] *The Irony of Free Speech* (n. 136 above), 37–45.
[138] See ch. XIV, s. 3 below for restrictions on employee speech.   [139] 500 US 173 (1991).
[140] 539 US 194 (2003): for other criticism of the decision, see ch. XIII, s. 2(iii) below.

continued to stock, say, books by Democrats or Communists should surely be struck down on free speech grounds. It would be aimed at speech, rather than ensuring that public money was used to help libraries discharge their traditional functions.

One Canadian case should be mentioned.[141] In 1992 the National Women's Association of Canada (NWAC) challenged the government's decision to fund four Aboriginal associations to enable them to participate fully in constitutional negotiations, but not to provide any funding for it to present the perspective of Aboriginal women. Its argument was that its constitutional rights to freedom of expression and to the equal protection and benefit of the law (guaranteed by Article 15 of the Charter) had been violated. The Supreme Court rejected the challenge, largely on the ground that there was no evidence that the funding arrangements threatened the freedom of NWAC to communicate its views on constitutional reform to the government, either directly or through the four Aboriginal bodies. The point of comparative interest is that, following its own earlier decision in *Haig* v. *Canada*,[142] the Court said that in some circumstances respect for the Charter rights would compel the government to fund or provide a platform for one group in order to ensure it had equal opportunities for expression as those groups which had been subsidized. That would surely apply, for instance, when public money is provided to political parties to assist them fight election campaigns or to prepare their policy. Minority parties should be eligible to receive equivalent funds, whether they take the form of financial grants, reduced postal rates for electoral communications, or free access to broadcasting time.

Equality considerations may, therefore, limit government discretion when it takes funding decisions affecting free speech. But that will not generally be the case. If an arts body decides to fund opera more generously than conventional theatre or to fund one company rather than another, it can do so without engaging freedom of speech, although of course the freedom would be implicated if stage plays or the productions of a particular company were banned. To that extent there is a distinction between the regulation of speech and decisions allocating funds for its support. Decisions on the funding of arts and of scientific and other research inevitably involve substantial discretion in assessing the merits of particular proposals. And that entails some judgement about their content.[143] A greater tolerance should be extended to decisions taken by expert bodies, such as those entrusted with the allocation of arts funds, than to those taken by government itself, since the former are much less likely to attempt to distort public debate. Further, reasonable suspicion of government justifies careful scrutiny of funding arrangements which imperil the advocacy of lawyers or campaigning by organizations whose purpose is to hold government in check; it is in these situations that

---

[141] *National Women's Association* v. *Canada* [1994] 3 SCR 627.   [142] [1993] 2 SCR 995.

[143] F. Schauer, 'Principles, Institutions, and the First Amendment' (1998) 112 *Harvard Law Rev* 84, argues that it is impossible to apply First Amendment principles indiscriminately to funding decisions, irrespective of the character of the institution and the decision concerned.

government may be particularly tempted to use its funding powers to suppress speech.[144] Courts should, therefore, adopt a nuanced approach under which attention is paid to the particular funding arrangements, the independence from government of the allocating bodies, and the impact on speech of their decisions. Ultimately, the most important question is this: were the funding arrangements a reasonable way for government to allocate scarce resources, as in the arts funding cases, or were they instead devised to stifle speech or to distort public discourse? In the former situations freedom of speech is not engaged, but in the latter it is, just as if the speech were inhibited by criminal law.

---

[144] In *Legal Services Corp* v. *Velazquez* 531 US 533 (2001), the Court struck down regulations of the Legal Services Corporation which precluded publicly funded lawyers from participating in lobbying and even from arguing that welfare laws were unconstitutional. It distinguished *Rust* v. *Sullivan* on the ground that lawyers have the distinctive role of arguing against government, which the latter was attempting to limit.

IV

Prior Restraints

It is a commonplace observation that the law regards, and is right to regard, prior restraints on speech and writing with particular hostility. In England, licensing of the press was in effect abolished in 1694, when the annual legislation under which the Stationers' Company used to control the publication of newspapers and pamphlets was not renewed.[1] There has been no general censorship of the press since that time. Indeed, Blackstone considered freedom of the press 'consists in laying no *previous* restraints upon publications, and not in freedom from censure for criminal matter when published'.[2] While the second part of that definition has often been criticized, the first has been treated as gospel, particularly in the United States where prior restraints are rarely countenanced. There is a heavy presumption against their constitutional validity, which is difficult to rebut, even in cases involving the disclosure of government secrets. In Germany, censorship is outlawed by Article 5(1) of the *Grundgesetz*. While the European Court of Human Rights has held that prior restraints on publication are not as such incompatible with Article 10 of the European Convention on Human Rights and Fundamental Freedoms (ECHR), it has emphasized that they do call for careful examination.[3]

English law appears to adopt a more pragmatic approach. Films and videos are subject to statutory censorship, while the government has retained a controversial power to direct broadcasters not to transmit a particular programme or include a class of material in their schedules. Both in England and in other countries, even including the United States, convenors may be required to notify a local authority or the police of their intent to hold a meeting or procession, or to obtain a permit; without a permit the meeting or other form of protest may be illegal. Further, in many jurisdictions courts may grant injunctions to stop the issue of publications which, it is argued, would amount to a breach of confidence, infringe personal privacy, or constitute a contempt of court. In the absence of further legal proceedings, the impact of such an order is to prevent the publication of a newspaper article or transmission of a programme, just as the refusal to grant a film a certificate

---

[1] See W. S. Holdsworth, 'Press Control and Copyright in the Sixteenth and Seventeenth Centuries' (1920) 29 *Yale Law Jo* 841.

[2] 4 *Commentaries on the Laws of England*, 16th edn. (London, 1825), 151.

[3] See in particular *Observer and Guardian* v. *UK* (1992) 14 EHRR 153, 191; *Association Ekin* v. *France* (2002) 35 EHRR 1207.

entails that it cannot be legally shown. But neither permit systems nor, outside the United States, court injunctions attract the same degree of opprobrium as the imposition of prior restraints in other contexts.

Prior restraints in fact present a puzzle. One fundamental question is whether the differences between them and penal sanctions imposed subsequent to publication are sufficiently serious to justify the traditional hostility to the former shown in US jurisprudence and reflected, to some extent, in European legal provisions such as the German Basic Law. Related to that issue is the question whether all forms of prior restraint should be subject to the same degree of suspicion or hostility. It may, for example, be right to view judicial injunctions more benevolently than administrative censorship. Another problem is that it is not always easy to determine whether a particular form of control is a prior restraint. If categorization often proves difficult, attempts to apply a doctrine under which prior restraints on speech are struck down, merely because they appear to operate prior to publication or transmission, should be abandoned. After all, under a free speech clause many restraints on speech may be successfully challenged, even though they operate subsequent to publication. In that event, there would be no need for any special rules concerning prior restraints. These questions of general principle are discussed in the first section of this chapter. The second and third sections deal respectively with the censorship of plays, films, and video, and with the use of prior restraints to prohibit the disclosure of official secrets and other confidential information. Section 4 explores the role of these restraints in two other areas: contempt of court and the allocation of permits to hold public meetings. The final section briefly discusses whether the law should be equally critical of private censorship, for example, a refusal by a publisher to issue a book unless the author removes certain offensive passages.

1. The Varieties and Vices of Prior Restraints

(i) The distinction between prior restraints and penal sanctions

On one view the distinction between a prior restraint and a subsequent penal sanction is little more than one of *form*: the first prohibits speech before publication, exhibition, or transmission, while the second operates subsequent to the event. But in *substance* their effect may be much the same in that both inhibit the exercise of free speech. Indeed, the 'chilling' effect of prospective penal sanctions may in fact be rather greater, as the publisher faces the twin uncertainties of a possible prosecution and an unpredictable sentence. Further, a criminal statute proscribing, say, the publication of hard-core pornography, may deter the issue of a wide range of sexually explicit material, while a court or administrative order directed at a particular book only inhibits publication of that volume. A censorship system at least enables the publisher to have the legality of the book or film determined at comparatively minimal cost; if the work is cleared by the censor, there is little chance of subsequent prosecution, so the publisher may have more confidence in his decision to publish and in his financial investment. For these reasons prior restraints may actually be preferred in some circumstances. For example, some major British film distributors have favoured the censorship system, as they valued the commercial certainty it provided.[4]

Nevertheless, an order prohibiting the release of a particular work arguably has greater and more immediate impact than the general proscriptions of the criminal or civil law. As Alexander Bickel, a leading constitutional scholar, wrote. '[A] criminal statute chills, prior restraint freezes'.[5] An order not to publish material means that it can never legally see the light of day, while a publisher faced only by the prospect of a criminal prosecution may decide to take the risk and release the work, speculating either that he will not be prosecuted or that a jury may acquit. In that sense, prior restraints appear to bite more savagely than the criminal law. But that ignores the point that many publishers will choose not to take the risk of a criminal prosecution, even though they believe that they have a reasonable prospect of acquittal. For a variety of reasons they might prefer not to take that chance. For them criminal law freezes as effectively as prior restraints, as equally may the prospect of a civil action where an award of damages may put a publisher out of business.[6] It is far from clear, therefore, that the prepublication restraints necessarily have a greater impact on freedom of speech than the criminal law.[7] There are, as will be discussed shortly, procedural and other objections to some types of prior restraint. But that is a different ground for hostility than the familiar, but misguided, argument that prior restraints necessarily pose greater dangers to free speech.

In some cases it is difficult to determine whether the method of control is really a prior restraint or not. Thus, the minority of the Supreme Court in the leading American decision, *Near* v. *Minnesota*,[8] doubted whether the facts justified the application of Blackstone's principle. Under a Minnesota state statute a county attorney was able to apply for an injunction to restrain *further* publication of a newspaper which had been held to have published defamatory or scandalous material. Unlike censorship in its purest form, proceedings could only be instituted after one publication of the paper in question, and, moreover, they were taken before a court, rather than an administrative official. So Butler J., with the support of the three other dissenting judges, concluded that the Minnesota law should not be treated as a prior restraint. What the majority of the Court found objectionable was the injunction's broad prohibition of further publication of the newspaper. The publisher would have to satisfy a judge that the edition did not

---

[4] See Williams Committee Report on Obscenity and Film Censorship (Cmnd 7772, 1979), paras. 12.5–12.6: see s. 2 of this chapter for further discussion.

[5] *The Morality of Consent* (New Haven, Yale UP, 1975), 61.

[6] This point is particularly pertinent to civil libel actions: see ch. VI, s. 2 below.

[7] See J. C. Jeffries, 'Rethinking Prior Restraint' (1983) 92 *Yale Law Jo* 409, 427–30.

[8] 283 US 697 (1931).

contain any scandalous or libellous matter before he was free to publish it. The majority was right to characterize this as a prior restraint on speech which had not yet been delivered,[9] but the decision on the point was far from straightforward.

Harder cases have arisen subsequently. If a book has already been published, should an *ex parte* injunction to restrain its further publication pending the immediate determination of its obscenity be regarded as a prior restraint? A bare majority of the Court refused to apply the doctrine in this situation,[10] while in the *Bantam Books* case a few years later only Harlan J. dissented from its application when a state Commission had warned publishers that their literature was 'objectionable' and would be referred to the Attorney-General for possible prosecution.[11] In this decision the Court in effect characterized an administrative warning without legal effects as an invalid prior restraint. A possible implication of the *Bantam Books* ruling is that a police warning that a book might be prosecuted would be ruled unconstitutional, although it is hard to see how the publisher's position would be prejudiced by that step. Another difficult situation to categorize is the suspended sentence. Under this procedure a sentence does not take effect unless the convicted person commits another offence punishable with imprisonment within a particular period of time. If, say, the publisher of an obscene book or a person convicted of making a speech likely to lead to breach of the peace were given a suspended sentence, which would take effect on commission of a similar offence, prior restraint issues might arise. Orders under which demonstrators may be bound over to keep the peace or be of good behaviour raise comparable problems.[12] Similarly the magistrates' power to issue a warrant to search for and seize obscene articles under the English obscenity legislation would probably be treated as a prior restraint in the United States.[13]

The German Constitutional Court has also had to resolve difficult questions on the meaning of the *Zensurverbot* imposed by the third sentence of Article 5(1) of the Basic Law: 'There shall be no censorship'. While the exercise of freedom of expression may be limited by general penal and civil laws, there is an absolute ban on censorship, so it is important to determine the scope of the rule. In a leading case, a majority of the Court ruled that it covered only prepublication restraints (*Vorzensur*) under which materials have to be submitted to the authorities for inspection and approval before distribution is permitted.[14] Thus, the requirement to submit a copy of any film imported from Eastern Europe to a government office within one week of its distribution was not covered by the censorship

---

[9] It is another matter whether the Court would now need to apply a special prior restraint principle, given that the statute in effect proscribed the distribution of seditious and group libel: see ch. V, s. 3 below. [10] *Kingsley Books v. Brown* 354 US 436 (1957).

[11] *Bantam Books v. Sullivan* 372 US 58 (1963).

[12] For binding-over powers, see s. 4 of this chapter.

[13] The US Supreme Court has held that there must be an adversary hearing *before* a warrant is granted: *Marcus v. Search Warrants* 367 US 717 (1961); *A Quantity of Books v. Kansas* 378 US 205 (1964).

[14] 33 BVerfGE 52 (1972), followed by 47 BVerfGE 198 (1978) and 83 BVerfGE 130, 155 (1990).

provision. The point was that exhibition of the film did not depend on prior government approval (although all copies of the film might be confiscated subsequently if it were found to amount to propaganda against a free constitution). In view of the absolute character of the ban on censorship, it would be impossible to apply it to restraints operating subsequent to publication (*Nachzensur*). The Court was unimpressed by the dissenters' view that the 'chilling effect' of the deposit requirement was the same as that of a formal censorship process. The majority rightly thought that went too far. On that perspective any threat that criminal sanctions would be imposed *after* publication would be caught by the *Zensurverbot*, so undermining the distinction between prior restraints or censorship and subsequent penalties.[15]

In one case the Administrative Court appears to have taken a broader view of the scope of the censorship ban. It suggested that it might cover decisions taken under a classification system, under which films were graded for the purpose of assessing an entertainment tax.[16] The denial of a certificate that a film was entitled to tax advantages as a film of cultural quality might in practice make its release economically impossible. Even more radically, the Court suggested that the censorship ban would also apply if the tax arrangements, in the context of existing economic circumstances, made the production of documentaries and cultural films difficult, unless they received a certificate. This approach looked at the substance and economic impact of the restraint rather than its form. Of course, tax arrangements may inhibit the publication of newspapers, books, or other material, but they should only be regarded as tantamount to censorship if payment of a tax or levy is required as a condition for obtaining a licence or permit to publish. Taxation aimed at a particular newspaper group, or at the press or other media generally, may conflict with press freedom.[17] But it should not be treated as a prior restraint where it is levied on the profits made from work already published.

The difficulties arising from some of these United States and German cases suggest that a sharp distinction cannot always be drawn between prior restraints and penal sanctions on speech. But that does not mean that it is usually impossible to identify a prior restraint. Censorship systems under which, say, books or films must be submitted for preliminary scrutiny by a government official before they can be issued are clearly identifiable as *prior* restraints on speech. It might be useful to say something about the characteristics of these systems and the procedural defects which justify the critical scrutiny given them. Then we can see how far these features apply in those borderline cases where it may not be so clear that there is really a prior restraint issue. If the procedure shares many of the features of the classic form of prior restraint, it should be subject to similar scrutiny.

[15] In *Josefine Mutzenbacher*, 83 BVerfGE 130, 155 (1990), the Court ruled that a legislative provision indicating that books might be classified as pornography unsuitable for children, so attracting higher penalties if distributed to them, did not amount to censorship.

[16] 32 BVerwGE 194, 199 (1966).

[17] See ch. XII, s. 3(i) below for discussion of United States cases on this point.

(ii) The principal features of classic prior restraints

Under censorship systems—the classic form of prior restraint—control is exercised prior to publication by an administrative official or committee. The censor generally decides whether to grant or deny permission on the basis of vague standards which may themselves not even be published. There is no right of appeal and no opportunity for immediate judicial review. The writer, publisher, distributor, or broadcaster (as the case may be) is required to submit the book, film, or programme in question to a censor for prior scrutiny; it is an offence, which may be summarily punishable, to publish or exhibit material without approval. Moreover, in these summary proceedings the courts may not allow argument about the constitutionality of the censorship system or its application in the particular case. There may be variants of this procedure. Perhaps the government, or an administrative official on its behalf, has authority to direct that any type of material of which it disapproves is not published, without any requirement on the publisher to submit it for preliminary scrutiny. If the direction specifies the proscribed material in detail, the order amounts to a form of prior restraint, similar to a censorship system involving prepublication scrutiny of the contents of a book or film. It is just as clear in this second instance, as it is in the first, that publication of particular material is prohibited.

Administrative censorship has a number of disturbing features, which may be described as the characteristic vices of prior restraints. Something should be said about them. In the first place, an administrative censor, merely by virtue of his position, is likely to adopt an unsympathetic attitude to the publications he is required to inspect. Otherwise his job would be redundant. A government official may be expected to censor material critical of the government. Alternatively, the body entrusted with censorship powers may be anxious about public criticism if it does allow controversial material to see the light of day. That is one reason why in the *ProLife Alliance* case the BBC's decision to stop the showing of an election broadcast showing mutilated foetuses on the basis that it violated standards of taste and decency should have been subject to careful scrutiny as a prior restraint; if it had allowed the broadcast, viewers might mistakenly have thought the BBC itself was responsible for the content.[18] In addition to these points, there is an infringement of separation of powers principles when decisions about the right to publish are taken by the government or by agents on its behalf.[19] The executive is not only determining conclusively whether an individual is free to speak, but it is also in effect deciding that that person is guilty of an offence if he publishes without the required permit. Under the constitutional principles of the separation of powers these decisions should be taken by the courts.

---

[18] See *R (on the application of ProLife Alliance)* v. *BBC* [2004] 1 AC 185, discussed in ch. II, s. 1 above and ch. V, s. 2 below.

[19] M. I. Meyerson, 'The Neglected History of the Prior Restraint Doctrine: Rediscovering the Link Between the First Amendment and the Separation of Powers' (2001) 34 *Indiana Law Rev* 295.

Moreover, officials are unlikely to be limited by rules of evidence, while the publisher may not have rights of representation or even an opportunity to defend his work. Most importantly, the censor normally operates entirely in secret. Anxiety about these procedural defects in administratively imposed restraints led the Williams Committee to suggest changes to the system of film censorship in Britain.[20] The US Supreme Court in *Freedman*[21] emphasized the importance of procedural safeguards—in particular, prompt judicial determination after a full adversary hearing—as necessary to validate any such system. In its major ruling on prior restraints, the Supreme Court of Canada in the *Little Sisters* case held that the importers of sexually explicit material were entitled to a fair and open customs procedure before it was classified as 'obscene', with the consequence that its import would be illegal.[22] Administrative decisions (and redeterminations on request) should be made promptly, with a full right of appeal to a court under which classification could be made afresh. Further, importers should not be required to prove that the material concerned is not obscene; the state has the burden in administrative proceedings, as in criminal trials, to show that publications are illegal. The strong dissenting judgment of Iacobucci J. urged that the customs legislation as a whole should be struck down as an invalid prior restraint on expression, as it failed to provide adequate procedural safeguards for book and magazine importers.

Another common weakness of administrative censorship systems is the lack of precise standards by which the official is to assess the publication. In their absence it will be difficult for authors and publishers to appreciate what objections are taken to the material and what evidence is admissible to meet them.[23] As far as the substance of a publication is concerned, if the criteria in the relevant statute or regulations are vague and unclear, it will be all too easy for constitutionally protected speech to be censored. It is for this reason that the United States Supreme Court has struck down permit systems under which local authorities have broad discretion whether to allow a meeting to take place or not. In contrast, if the standards, on the basis of which such decisions are to be taken, are tightly drawn, and cannot be used to ban meetings of which the authorities disapprove, the Court is much more likely to uphold the system.[24]

A further vice of censorship is the comparative ease with which the restrictions may be enforced. It will typically be an offence under the relevant regulations to publish or exhibit without having been granted a permit. The publisher may not be permitted to raise in his defence arguments about the unconstitutionality of

---

20 Williams Committee Report (n. 4 above), paras. 12.21–12.32.

21 *Freedman* v. *Maryland* 380 US 51 (1965), discussed further in s. 2 below.

22 *Little Sisters Book and Art Emporium* v. *Minister of Justice and A-G of Canada* [2000] 2 SCR 1120. For commentary, see B. Ryder, 'The *Little Sisters* Case, Administrative Censorship, and Obscenity Law' (2001) 39 *Osgoode Hall Law Jo* 207.

23 See the decision of the European Human Rights Court in *Gaweda* v. *Poland* (2004) 39 EHRR 4, holding an imprecise and vague law incompatible with ECHR, art. 10, because it enabled courts to refuse registration of a periodical on the ground that its title was inaccurate or provocative.

24 For further discussion, see s. 4 of this chapter.

the permit system as a whole or its application to the particular book or film. This bar on collateral challenge may also apply to judicial prior restraints where the court grants an injunction; the defendant may not challenge this order in subsequent contempt proceedings, but must seek judicial review immediately after the injunction is issued.[25] Some commentators in the United States have gone so far as to argue that this is now the principal defect of prior restraints imposed by court injunctions.[26] This variety of prior restraints is considered shortly.

Of course, some of the vices of administrative prior restraints may be cured. Arrangements might be made for 'censorship' decisions to be taken by an impartial tribunal (appointed by an independent commission rather than by the government), which would be required to apply detailed and precise standards and to conduct an open hearing at which the publisher is legally represented. The initial decision might be made subject to full and prompt review.[27] Such arrangements would meet many of the objections to censorship systems raised in the preceding paragraphs. It would even be possible to arrange, as Chafee suggested in his classic book, *Free Speech in the United States*, for a 'play jury' to assess a dramatic performance before it was commercially staged.[28] In these eventualities, it is hard to see any significant difference between a previous restraint and a subsequent penalty, unless there is some sort of right to have an idea or piece of information enter the marketplace at least once. Such a right hardly seems of great value, and in any case—unless the penalties for refusing to go before the censor are severe—is no more effectively abridged by a prior restraint than by the prospect of a criminal prosecution. But this sort of reformed system of censorship exists only in Utopia. In the real world these improvements lead to the disappearance of the system altogether, because its typical advantages—speed, cheapness, and lack of publicity— are lost. Thus, film censorship in the United States virtually collapsed when the Supreme Court imposed severe procedural requirements in *Freedman* v. *Maryland*.[29] In practice administrative prior restraints inevitably present procedural features which call for special scrutiny. Moreover, in principle it is wrong for bodies other than courts to determine whether an individual has a right to speak.

(iii) Judicial prior restraints

To what extent, if at all, should injunctions or other court orders issued to stop a publication be subject to the prior restraint principle? This is now the most

---

[25] *Walker* v. *City of Birmingham* 388 US 307 (1967).

[26] In particular, see S. R. Barnett, 'The Puzzle of Prior Restraints' (1976) 29 *Stanford Law Rev* 539.

[27] Procedural improvements were made to the system under which the Minister of the Interior in France had had power to ban foreign publications under the Law of the Press 1881, art. 14. Nevertheless, the European Court of Human Rights held a ban imposed on public order grounds on the circulation of a book published in Spain to be incompatible with ECHR, art. 10; there was an inadequate legal framework for exercise of the power, and judicial review was not prompt and effective to cure its abuse: *Association Ekin* v. *France* (2002) 35 EHRR 1207.

[28] Z. Chafee, *Free Speech in the United States* (Cambridge, Mass.: Harvard UP, 1941), 533–40.

[29] 380 US 51 (1965).

difficult question in this area of free speech law. English courts have been very reluctant to grant injunctions to stop the repetition of defamatory allegations pending full trial where the defendant is prepared to argue that the allegations are true or amount to fair comment on a matter of public interest.[30] For the court to order an interim injunction in this situation would be to usurp the entitlement of the jury to decide whether the allegations are well founded; moreover, it would infringe freedom of speech.[31] It is also very difficult to obtain a *quia timet* injunction in advance of the publication of defamatory allegations. But the courts on occasion are prepared to grant an injunction, as well as damages, after the claimant has brought a successful libel action. Further, they have frequently granted interim injunctions in copyright and breach of confidence cases, and occasionally to stop a publication in contempt of court.[32] Equivalent remedies may be granted by the courts in France to avert infringements of the laws on defamation and privacy, while the prohibition of censorship in the German Basic Law has never been applied to preclude the granting of a temporary judicial order (*einstweilige Verfügung*) to prevent a publication. In contrast, the general hostility in the United States to prior restraints does extend to judicial injunctions and other temporary orders. This was most famously exemplified in the *Pentagon Papers* case, when the majority of the Supreme Court discharged temporary orders which had been granted against newspapers not to publish confidential State Department papers relating to the war in Vietnam.[33] It is only in very rare circumstances that the US courts are prepared to hold injunctions compatible with the First Amendment.

It is doubtful whether judicial injunctions should usually be subject to a prior restraint doctrine, under which court orders, otherwise compatible with freedom of speech, are struck down merely because they are imposed prior to publication, for they do not suffer from the same procedural defects or vices as administrative censorship. An injunction will usually only be granted after a full argument in an open hearing on the basis of legal standards established in a statute or by previous case-law. There are, for example, a number of precedents in English law establishing what amounts to a breach of confidence, so an argument that an injunction in this context might be granted on the basis of imprecise standards could not easily be sustained. Most importantly, there is no reason to expect courts to be predisposed to the grant of injunctions to restrain publications; their role is not to censor, but to apply legal principles impartially to the parties. There is, therefore, little justification generally for applying the prior restraint doctrine to injunctions or other court orders inhibiting speech.[34] Of course, particular injunctions may be

---

[30] *Bonnard* v. *Perryman* [1891] 2 Ch 269, CA. The Court of Appeal has recently held that the rule in this case is unaffected by the Human Rights Act 1998 (HRA 1998), s. 12(3), discussed below: *Greene* v. *Associated Newspapers Ltd* [2005] 1 All ER 30.

[31] See Lord Denning MR in *Fraser* v. *Evans* [1969] 1 QB 349, 363, CA, and Brooke LJ in *Greene* v. *Associated Newspapers* (n. 30 above), para. 57.

[32] Some of the leading cases in these areas of English law are considered below in ss. 3 and 4 of this chapter.   [33] *New York Times* v. *US* 403 US 713 (1971), considered in s. 3 of this chapter below.

[34] See Jeffries (n. 7 above).

too broad, banning not only the publication in respect of which the proceedings had been taken, but also all further publications of the respondent dealing with the same subject matter, or even binding the whole world.[35] In the House of Lords ruling in the *Sunday Times* contempt case, for example, the newspaper was enjoined from publishing *any* article which prejudged the issue of negligence or dealt with the evidence relating to *any issue* arising in any actions brought against Distillers in respect of the thalidomide drug.[36] This was a much more draconian remedy than a criminal prosecution; a conviction is entered only in respect of a *particular publication* of the article, and so the accused or another person may republish it somewhere else without necessarily being charged or, if charged, without being convicted.[37] But this point does not mean that every injunction should necessarily be subject to stricter scrutiny than that applied to post-publication sanctions, merely because it is imposed before the material is published.

However, some procedural requirements should be observed before a court imposes a previous restraint on publication. If it does not allow the publisher a full opportunity to contest the imposition, in particular to challenge its compatibility with freedom of speech, there is a danger that the judge will grant an injunction on inadequate grounds. A court might ban a publication which should be protected as an exercise of free speech and free press rights. On this basis there would be little reason to apply prior restraint principles to permanent injunctions granted after a full hearing on the facts and law, but the issue of interim or preliminary orders, or temporary stays, before full trial is much more problematic, at least when there is no opportunity to challenge that step.[38] In principle these orders only delay, but in practice may permanently inhibit, the publication of material which on examination would be protected by the free speech clause.

Section 12 of the HRA 1998, reforming UK law in this area, nicely brings out some of these points. First, no order is to be made affecting the exercise of the right to freedom of expression against a party who is neither present nor represented, unless the court is satisfied that the applicant has taken all practical steps to notify him or there were compelling reasons not to take that step.[39] This safeguards the right of the media and other publishers to contest injunctions and comparable remedies inhibiting freedom of speech. More importantly, no interim order may be made to stop publication before trial 'unless the court is satisfied that the applicant is likely to establish that publication should not be allowed.'[40] The House of Lords has said this provision means that a court should not make an interim order

---

[35] In *Venables* v. *News Group Newspapers Ltd* [2001] Fam 430, Dame Elizabeth Butler-Sloss P. granted a permanent injunction binding the world to prevent any disclosure of information likely to lead to identification of two child killers whose safety might be endangered by such disclosure. It should be noted that there was full argument on the facts and the law.

[36] *A-G* v. *Times Newspapers Ltd* [1974] AC 273, considered further in ch. IX, s. 3 below.

[37] See the dissent of Douglas and Black JJ in *Kingsley Books* v. *Brown* 354 US 436, 446–7 (1957).

[38] M. H. Redish, 'The Proper Role of the Prior Restraint Doctrine in First Amendment Theory' (1984) 70 *Virginia Law Rev* 53, 55.   [39] HRA 1998, s. 12(2).

[40] Ibid., s. 12(3).

'unless satisfied the applicant's prospects of success at the trial are sufficiently favourable to justify such an order being made in the particular circumstances of the case.'[41] Generally, that requires the applicant to show that it is more likely than not that he will win at trial, but in some cases a lesser degree of likelihood will be enough. The judge has to make some assessment of the legal and factual merits of the claim, whereas previously he had only to be persuaded that there was a serious issue to be tried and that the balance of convenience favoured grant of an interim injunction.[42] So the reform has undoubtedly made it more difficult to get an interim injunction than it used to be. But it is important to emphasize two reasons why the House of Lords rejected the argument that section 12 required an applicant always to show that it is more probable than not that he would win at full trial. First, the imposition of such a high threshold test might make it very difficult for an applicant to secure an interim order, even though the consequences of not granting such an order might be extremely serious, for instance, a risk of personal injury resulting from identification of the applicant's whereabouts. The gravity of the consequences for the applicant should be taken into account, as well as the likelihood of his success at trial. Secondly, a 'more likely than not' test would mean that a court might not even be able to grant a temporary stay or order to ensure that it had time to consider arguments from the parties. Unless at the outset of legal proceedings the applicant could show that its case would probably succeed, the press would be free to publish.

A similar point to the last emerges from the US *Pentagon Papers* case.[43] When the Supreme Court granted *certiorari* to take the government's appeal from the lower federal courts, it imposed a temporary stay, ordering the newspapers not to publish confidential State Department papers while it considered the arguments. However, four members of the Court doubted whether even these temporary orders should have been made, given the strong presumption against prior restraint. Four days after hearing argument, the Court by a 6–3 majority held the government had not discharged the heavy burden of discharging a prior restraint, and lifted the stays on publication. But Burger CJ, Harlan and Blackmun JJ in separate dissenting judgments protested that the stays should have continued in force to allow fuller consideration by the Court of the legal and other arguments. They turned a standard argument against the grant of interim injunctions on its head. While the press or other defendant should enjoy full procedural safeguards so it can contest the grant of an injunction, equally the government or other claimant should have adequate opportunity to justify the imposition of a prior restraint, at least if it is able to show at the outset that its case raises serious issues. Temporary stays should be tolerated to allow the courts properly to consider the arguments, even though their grant will at least delay publication. Provided the

---

[41] *Cream Holdings* v. *Banerjee* [2004] 4 All ER 617, para. 22.

[42] This was the test formulated by Lord Diplock in *American Cyanamid* v. *Ethicon Ltd* [1975] AC 396, HL. [43] *New York Times* v. *US* 403 US 713 (1971).

defendant has adequate opportunity at all stages of the proceedings to contest the initial grant or argue for the lifting of the order, injunctions do not suffer from the vices which characterize administrative censorship.

(iv) Conclusions

Prior restraints vary so markedly in their form and effect that it may not be right to apply a uniformly hostile attitude. As Paul Freund remarked: 'What is needed is a pragmatic assessment of [the doctrine's] operation in the particular circumstances. The generalization that prior restraint is particularly obnoxious in civil liberties cases must yield to more particularistic analysis.'[44] Some of the factors relevant to this analysis have been indicated in the preceding paragraphs. Clearly, the most important of them is the character and procedure of the censoring body. Judicial restraints are more tolerable than administrative. Permanent restraints should be subject to much closer scrutiny than a temporary order which may delay publication by only a few days or weeks. But the delay has to be balanced against the importance and urgency of the postponed communication. A temporary ban, whether imposed by administrative order or interim injunction, on the transmission of an election broadcast, as in the *ProLife Alliance* case, may mean that it cannot be shown until the campaign is over; even if the ban is subsequently lifted on appeal, it may well be too late for the broadcast to go out before the election is held. In these circumstances, a prior restraint is much more objectionable than the imposition of a penalty after its transmission.[45] This point does not apply to the imposition of a temporary ban on the publication of pornography. As Harlan J. once remarked, 'Sex is of constant but rarely particularly topical interest.'[46]

The extent to which the harmful consequences of speech can be determined prior to publication may also be a relevant factor. While a prosecution may be brought when it has become clear that, say, inflammatory speech has actually led to public disorder, it is much harder to justify stopping such speech on the ground that it is likely to cause disorder. That harm may be too speculative to warrant a prior restraint, whether it is imposed by the police or by court order.[47] There may not be sufficient evidence to justify an anticipatory ban. Of course, a ban might be justified on the ground that the publication in question is inherently likely to provoke a harm the state is entitled to avert. One such instance may be the use of contempt laws to prevent the publication of material likely to prejudice forthcoming legal proceedings (see section 4 below). Moreover, it may be contended that the imposition of a prior restraint is the only realistic means of preventing the harm.

---

[44] 'The Supreme Court and Civil Liberties' (1950) 4 *Vanderbilt Law Rev* 533, 539.

[45] This point was ignored by the House of Lords in *R (on the application of ProLife Alliance)* v. *BBC* [2004] 1 AC 185: see E. M. Barendt, 'Free Speech and Abortion' [2003] *PL* 580, 588.

[46] *A Quantity of Books* v. *Kansas* 378 US 205, 224 (1964).

[47] See V. Blasi, 'Toward a Theory of Prior Restraint: The Central Linkage' (1981) 66 *Minnesota Law Rev* 11, 48.

Two examples are injunctions to restrain the disclosure of highly damaging confidential information, whether concerning affairs of state or sensitive personal secrets (see section 3 below), and the use of permits to prevent the clash of rival meetings and processions when it is clear that violence is inevitable (see section 4 below). In these circumstances only free speech absolutists would rule out the use of prior restraints altogether. But it is always right to insist on full procedural safeguards for the publisher, so he may resist the imposition of such a restraint. These safeguards are not provided in systems of administrative censorship. So they should be scrutinized very carefully. They are rarely compatible with freedom of speech. But it is harder to explain why the prior restraint doctrine should be applied with equal rigour to invalidate court injunctions merely because they are imposed prior to publication.

2. Theatre, Film, and Video Censorship

At various times the live theatre and the cinema have been seen as presenting special problems, which justify some measure of previous restraint. This is now almost unknown in Western democracies in the case of stage plays, but cinema censorship is still common, and in the United Kingdom received the approval of the Williams Committee on Obscenity and Film Censorship. It is, however, far from clear that plays and films are so different from books or newspapers that this special means of control can be justified. To some extent the reasons for their separate treatment may be historical. New forms of expression may initially be thought more dangerous than those which have enjoyed traditional acceptance.[48] This perhaps explains the anxiety about video recordings, subject under statute in the United Kingdom to legal censorship and classification by the British Board of Film Classification (BBFC). Additionally, these means of communication may be regarded as providing entertainment rather than disseminating political and social ideas. So it would be inappropriate to bring them under the protection of freedom of speech. This was a common perspective on the cinema in the first decades of the twentieth century.[49] In contrast these arguments, of course, hardly applied to live drama, a much more ancient art form than the novel or the press column. Nevertheless, theatre has at times been regarded as subversive and a vehicle for the spread of radical ideas, all the more dangerous because of the immediacy of its impact on the audience. That was certainly true in the eighteenth century, when theatre was a popular medium and could be used to satirize or ridicule political figures and institutions.

[48] This may explain the special legal regulation of the broadcasting media discussed in ch. XII, s. 5 below: see the classic article by L. C. Bollinger, 'Freedom of the Press and Public Access: Toward a Theory of Partial Regulation' (1976) 75 *Michigan Law Rev* 1, 17–26.

[49] See McKenna J. in *Mutual Film* v. *Industrial Commission of Ohio* 236 US 230, 244 (1915), and I. H. Carmen, *Movies, Censorship, and the Law* (Ann Arbor: Michigan UP, 1966), ch. 1.

The long survival of theatre censorship in Britain is well known.[50] Put on a statutory basis in 1737 and reformulated in 1843, the powers of the Lord Chamberlain were not abolished until 1968. The Theatres Act of that year implemented the recommendations of a Joint Select Committee of the House of Commons and House of Lords, which had found there was no sensible justification for treating plays differently from books.[51] The Lord Chamberlain had exercised powers which exhibited many of the characteristic vices of censorship: the standards he applied were uncertain and imprecise, allowing a degree of political censorship. Authors had no procedural rights, and there was no appeal from his decisions. But his ability to produce quick and inexpensive decisions on the suitability of plays for performance was appreciated by theatre managers: an interesting parallel to the support for censorship expressed by film distributors. The Select Committee rejected the suggestion that there might be a system of voluntary censorship, under which authors could, if they wished, submit plays to a body, approval by which would secure immunity from subsequent prosecution. One reason for that conclusion was that this body might be less liberal than the Lord Chamberlain had been in practice. A stronger objection to its institution is that its very existence would encourage caution and so inhibit artistic expression.

The Theatres Act 1968 therefore subjects 'plays', naturally subject to careful definition, to the ordinary criminal law of obscenity, incitement to racial hatred, and provocation of a breach of the peace. The law in the United Kingdom was thus brought into line with the rules applying in other countries. The Committee found that there were no prior restraints in this area in France, Germany (where it is constitutionally proscribed), Canada, New Zealand, and most Australian states.[52] Not surprisingly it has not been countenanced in the United States. Indeed, in one of its bolder decisions the US Supreme Court ruled that a municipality imposed an invalid prior restraint when it refused a permit for the musical *Hair* to be staged at a civic theatre.[53] The basis for the ruling was that the procedural requirements mandated by the Court in its earlier decision in *Freedman* v. *Maryland* in the context of film censorship had not been observed, but the Court virtually ignored the point that the municipality was regulating the use of its own property and not simply acting as a general theatre censor. In that context the imposition of a subsequent punishment is hardly a viable alternative, so one of the arguments against use of prior restraints is inapplicable. The Court was really upholding a First Amendment right of access to use public property for speech, a positive right which, outside the context of public meetings, is rarely recognized by United States courts.[54]

For a variety of reasons the cinema continues to pose more difficulties. In Britain there is a system of censorship under which legally decisions are taken under statute, now the Cinemas Act 1985, by local authorities, but in practice by the informally

---

[50] Robertson & Nicol, 189–98.   [51] (1966) HL 255, HC 503.
[52] Ibid., Appendix 24.   [53] *South-eastern Promotions* v. *Conrad* 420 US 546 (1975).
[54] See ch. III, s. 6 above for general discussion of positive free speech rights, and ch. VIII, s. 3 below for the right to hold meetings on public property.

constituted BBFC. The delegation of effective censorship and classification power to the BBFC has now been recognized by statute; it requires local authorities to impose restrictions on admission of children to films which have been designated by the authority itself or *by another body* (specified in the licence of the cinema premises) as unsuitable for them.[55] But the local authority must retain the right to take the final decision.[56] Sometimes an authority allows the showing of a film, despite the refusal by the BBFC to issue a certificate, or (as is more usually the case) it bans its exhibition in the area, despite the grant of a certificate by the Board. The BBFC takes decisions on the basis of published Classification Guidelines, prepared after public consultation.[57] It will not issue a certificate if it considers the film is likely to infringe the criminal law. However, it may also refuse a '15' or even an '18' certificate on broader grounds. For instance, the portrayal of 'dangerous combat techniques' must be cut, if a film is to be released with a '15' certificate, and it may refuse to issue any certificate for a film which shows illegal drug use 'in instructive detail' or which contains explicit images of sexual conduct or the encouragement of drug use. In practice, it is most unusual for a film to be rejected entirely for classification, but that does not mean there is no censorship. Cuts are frequently required for a film to receive a '15' or lower certificate, and on occasion for an '18' certificate.[58] Moreover, it is likely that the system discourages the making or exhibition of some types of film, in particular with hard-core pornographic content, which would certainly be denied a certificate, but which might escape prosecution under the Obscene Publication Act 1959.[59]

Is there any case now for censorship of the cinema, given that it has been abandoned for the theatre and has not existed for over three hundred years for the print media? The Williams Committee concluded that the system of film censorship should be continued, emphasizing that the question was whether the existing arrangements should be abandoned, rather than whether it would be right to introduce them from scratch.[60] Whatever its theoretical weaknesses, the system had worked satisfactorily. Most cinema distributors appreciated its advantages of certainty, speed of decision, and cheapness. It is hard to quarrel with the experience of Committee members that some films are exceptionally nasty and sadistic. The more difficult question is whether film is such a powerful medium that it is right to regulate it more tightly than the theatre and television, where there is also now no general system of censorship.[61] The Williams Committee thought

---

[55] Cinemas Act 1985, s. 1(3).   [56] *Mills* v. *LCC* [1925] 1 KB 213, DC.

[57] The Guidelines were revised in August 2002, principally to make the '12A' rating for films advisory, so that children under twelve may view such films, provided they are accompanied by an adult.

[58] In 2001, 2.8% of '18' films, and in 2002, two such films were cut: see the BBFC annual report for these years.

[59] This legislation covers cinema films (Criminal Law Act 1977, s. 53) and videos: see *A-G Reference (No. 5) of 1980* [1981] 1 WLR 88, CA.

[60] Williams Committee Report (n. 4 above), paras. 12.1–12.11.

[61] Under broadcasting codes, however, television channels will not show films which have not received a certificate from the BBFC, and in practice additional cuts are sometimes made.

this difference in treatment could be justified. One point, understandably not emphasized by the Committee in view of its elitist connotations, is surely that generally cinema caters for a mass audience, less inclined to be selective about what it watches. Its relative cheapness means it is accessible to children. On the other hand, dangers can be reduced by the display of prominent warnings about the character of the films shown and the application of stricter controls on the ages of cinema audiences to ensure that young children do not attend obviously unsuitable shows. Harm to children could be averted without resort to a general censorship system. An Ontario court has held that comprehensive film censorship can not be justified as compatible with freedom of expression when a scheme to safeguard children could be set up, which would be less intrusive on that freedom.[62] A comprehensive censorship system might not be upheld as 'necessary' under Article 10(2) of the ECHR to safeguard public order or to protect morals, if it were challenged under the Convention.[63] Finally, the Williams Committee attached importance to the preference of film distributors, notably the Society of Film Distributors, for the censorship system, as providing them with greater commercial security; once a certificate was given, they knew that in practice no legal proceedings would be taken in respect of the film. But that is a weak argument. It ignores the interests of directors and of the general public in the distribution of uncensored films.

The Williams Committee did, however, suggest some reforms to the censorship system, which regrettably have never been implemented. In particular, it recommended the abolition of local authority control. Differing decisions on the films that could be shown in particular localities could not be justified, since there was little evidence that attitudes varied substantially from one area to another. It may also be said that in principle it is wrong for a civil liberty—the right to communicate and receive artistic expression—to be more fully respected in some areas than in others.[64] The Committee recommended that the BBFC should be replaced by a statutory body, which would enjoy legal authority and the power to enforce its decisions. Its proposed Film Examining Board would formulate the criteria to be applied, subject to some legislative constraints, and hear appeals from decisions on particular films taken by its examining staff. The absence of any formal appeals procedure is a major weakness of the existing system; a film company can ask the Board to reconsider a decision or can apply to a local authority, where it wishes to show the film. But in contrast to decisions on videos, there is no appeal to an independent committee.

The BBFC emphasizes that it is ultimately accountable to the public, as well as to the film industry which finances it. It has consulted the public on amendments

---

[62] *R v. Glad Day Bookshops Inc* (2004) 239 DLR (4th) 119, para. 157, Russell Juriansz J.

[63] But see the unsatisfactory decision of the European Court in *Otto-Preminger-Institut* v. *Austria* (1994) 19 EHRR 34, where it upheld the seizure and ban of a film as necessary to protect the sensitivities of Catholics in the Tyrol.

[64] For further discussion of this point in the context of obscenity laws, see ch. X, s. 3 below.

to the classification scheme, most recently on the change to an advisory '12A' certificate. Moreover, it is independent of government. So it does not share that predisposition to censor which is a major defect of classic administrative censorship systems.[65] Nevertheless, it inevitably has some of the other characteristic shortcomings of those systems. There are no open proceedings, at which, say, the press and other members of the public can hear argument about why certain cuts should be made for a film to be given a particular certificate. Decisions may be inconsistent. There is no requirement for formal reasons to be given. In practice cuts may be negotiated with producers and exhibitors, without the director of the film having any real opportunity to argue that they infringe its artistic integrity. In short, the system remains questionable in principle, although it may work relatively satisfactorily in practice.

Film censorship remains a common feature of other Western legal systems. In Europe it appears from the Appendix to the Williams Report that only Belgium, the Netherlands, and Denmark at that time managed without it altogether. In France, for example, a permit (*visa*) must be obtained from a government minister, currently the Minister of Culture, for a film to be shown or exported, while in exceptional circumstances a local authority may ban the showing a film to prevent disorder, even though a *visa* has been issued.[66] Germany has a system of self-regulation operated by bodies representative of the film industry, since formal legal censorship, as we have seen, is prohibited by Article 5 of the Basic Law. In practice producers submit films for classification, although it is lawful to distribute them without a certificate. This system as a whole does not contravene the *Zensurverbot*, but the confiscation by the classification authority of a film, which had been submitted to it before release, on the ground that its distribution would infringe the penal law did constitute unlawful censorship.[67] The greatest contrast with the system in the United Kingdom is now provided in the United States, where film censorship is in effect a dead letter. It has in fact never been ruled unconstitutional, though the cinema has enjoyed First Amendment protection since the decision of the Supreme Court in *Burstyn* v. *Wilson*.[68] The old-fashioned view that films were mere entertainment and not vehicles for communicating ideas was unequivocally rejected in that case. The Court unanimously refused to approve the ban of a film on the ground that it was 'sacrilegious', a term which was so vague as to enable the state to proscribe a documentary or feature which is clearly covered by the First Amendment.

The Court did have an opportunity to outlaw censorship altogether in 1961, but by a bare majority declined to take it.[69] Characterizing the issue as whether there is a constitutional right to show every type of motion picture at least once, the majority refused to invalidate a Chicago ordinance which empowered the

---

[65] See s. 1(ii) above.

[66] E. Derieux, *Droit de la Communication*, 3rd edn. (Paris: Librairie générale de droit et de jurisprudence, 2000), 237–41. [67] 87 BVerfGE 209, 232–33 (1993).

[68] 343 US 495 (1952). [69] *Times Film* v. *Chicago* 365 US 43 (1965).

commissioner of police to examine all films and to ban those offending certain criteria. The exhibitor had refused to submit his film, in effect challenging the censorship system itself. The litigation did not raise questions concerning the appropriateness of the ordinance's standards or its application to the particular film. The dissent of Warren CJ defined the central question as the constitutionality of an ordinance requiring the submission of *all* films for inspection; this formulation suggests that the minority might have been prepared to tolerate a censorship system under which, say, films portraying sexual activity required approval. But in fact most of Warren CJ's points, in particular his scepticism that films should be treated differently from the press, indicate disapproval of any prior restraints in this area. A few years later in *Freedman* v. *Maryland* the Court in effect outlawed administrative restraints by the imposition of rigorous procedural restrictions.[70] First, the censor had the burden of proof to show that distribution of the film should not be allowed; secondly, only a court could order a permanent ban after an adversary hearing, while a third requirement was that this hearing must take place promptly after the temporary administrative order. These conditions sweep away two of the characteristic advantages of censorship: its informality and lack of publicity. It was, therefore, hardly surprising that a number of states abandoned prior restraints in this area after the *Freedman* ruling.[71] Now the only form of control in the United States is a voluntary classification system operated by the film industry itself. This is used to grade films, largely to assist parents to decide their suitability for children. The effect is that hard-core pornographic movies are easily accessible to adults, as they are in some European countries where censorship systems have been abandoned.

Recently an Ontario judge has ruled that the film censorship system in that province could not be regarded as a justified restriction on the exercise of freedom of expression under the Canadian Charter.[72] He emphasized that as a system of prior restraint it should be scrutinized with particular suspicion; it imposed procedural and financial costs on film distributors, as (with some exceptions) they were required to submit all their work to the Ontario Film Review Board for approval, however innocuous its content. The Ontario statute did set out the standards on which the Board could refuse approval, but they went further than the grounds on which an obscenity prosecution could be brought, compatibly with the Supreme Court's ruling in *Butler*.[73] While a classification scheme would be compatible with freedom of expression, film censorship could not be justified as a reasonable restriction to safeguard society or vulnerable groups against harm; it was relevant that other forms of media were not subject to prior restraint, and the government had not produced any evidence to show why films should be treated differently.

In the United Kingdom, the BBFC has been designated as the authority responsible for determining whether 'video works' are suitable for classification

---

[70] 380 US 51 (1965).   [71] See Carmen (n. 49 above), ch. III.
[72] *R* v. *Glad Day Bookshops Inc* (2004) 239 DLR (4th) 119.
[73] *R* v. *Butler* [1992] 1 SCR 452, discussed in ch. X, s. 4 below.

certificates, having special regard to the likelihood of such works 'being viewed in the home'.[74] It is an offence to supply a video work which has not received a certificate, unless its supply is exempt as a non-commercial supply,[75] or it is a video work exempt from classification. Educational videos, videos concerned with sports, religion, or music, and video games are exempt from classification, unless they depict human sexual activity, torture, or genital organs, etc.[76] The classification categories are similar to those used by the BBFC for cinema films, except that there is a special 'R18' category for videos depicting simulated or actual consenting sexual relations between adults; these videos are only available from licensed sex shops. Section 4A of the Video Recordings Act 1984 requires the BBFC to give special regard to any harm that may be caused to 'potential viewers' or, through their conduct, to society by the way in which the video deals with, among other things, criminal conduct, illegal drugs, or human sexual activity. 'Potential viewers' means the persons, including children, who are likely to view the video if it is given a particular certificate.

Under this censorship system the BBFC applies stricter standards than those it adopts for cinema films. It takes account, as required by the legislation, of the ability of home viewers to replay videos and concentrate on material out of context, as well as of the opportunities for children to view unsuitable material. Moreover, the Board must take account of the unquantifiable (as well as quantifiable) risks of harm that might be occasioned by children who may watch a video depicting, say, criminal conduct or sexual activity. The Board should balance any conjectural risk of harm to children against the interests of adult viewers who would be deprived of access to these videos if a certificate were refused; it is not bound to refuse a certificate until the risks have been quantified.[77]

In principle, video censorship is as much open to question as the older system of film censorship. On the other hand, for reasons indicated in the previous paragraphs, the case for prior restraints recognized by the Williams Committee in the case of the cinema is easier to accept in this context; in particular, the relative ease with which, say, hard-core sexually explicit or very violent videos may be replayed before young viewers potentially makes them extremely harmful. Equally, the makers and distributors of such material may prefer prior restraints than face the uncertainties of subsequent criminal prosecution.[78] Moreover, a distributor does have a right of appeal to the Video Appeals Committee (VAC) from a BBFC decision: a clear improvement on the right to apply to a local authority in the cinema context. Members of the VAC are appointed by an independent panel. The Committee sits in public, allows legal representation, and gives reasoned decisions.[79] In facts it hears very few appeals, but in one important instance it did

---

[74] Video Recordings Act 1984, s. 4(1). 'Video works' include DVDs: see s. 1(2).
[75] Ibid., s. 3(2).   [76] Ibid., s. 2.
[77] See Hooper J. in *R v. Video Appeals Committee, ex p BBFC* [2000] EMLR 850.
[78] Robertson & Nicol, 738.   [79] Ibid., 762.

reverse a BBFC ruling, so permitting an 'R18' certificate to be granted to videos depicting, among other matter, actual sexual intercourse.[80] There is, therefore, some safeguard against arbitrary censorship decisions.

But that safeguard is not always effective. In the best-known case of video censorship, the BBFC refused to issue a certificate for *Visions of Ecstasy*, on the ground that it might be liable to a prosecution for the common law offence of blasphemy.[81] It depicted the erotic fantasies of St Teresa of Avila, as she caressed the body of the crucified Christ. A 3–2 majority of the VAC upheld the Board decision. Perhaps more surprisingly, the European Human Rights Court held that these decisions were compatible with the guarantee of freedom of expression in the ECHR, given that the national authorities have discretion under the margin of appreciation principle to assess what steps are necessary to avoid offence to the public.[82] The Court appreciated that the measure amounted to a prior restraint calling for special scrutiny, but considered that the ban was necessary to avoid infringement of the criminal law through the commission of blasphemy. But in fact it is far from clear that the offence would have been committed. Blasphemy prosecutions are very rare, and if one had been brought, it is quite possible that the jury would have acquitted the defendant. Further, the publicity attendant on the bringing of a prosecution would probably have ensured wider public discussion of both the merits of the particular video and the justifications for maintaining the controversial common law offence. The *Visions of Ecstasy* case brings out one of the vices of prior restraints: they may be imposed to prevent a purely speculative harm, namely that the video would cause sufficient public offence to warrant prosecution and most probably lead to a conviction. In contrast, in this instance the loss to freedom of expression through imposition of the prior restraint was clear.

3. Official Secrets and Confidential Information

One area where there may be a good case for prior restraints is the protection of confidential information. The case may apply as much to government secrets as it does to confidential commercial information, although on the other side there is generally a much stronger argument for free speech in the former context than there is in the case of the disclosure of trade secrets. If the law does not intervene in advance to prohibit disclosure of confidential information of either category, the damage will be done and subsequent penal sanctions are relatively pointless.[83] The same argument might also justify the imposition of a prior restraint on the

---

[80] The application by the BBFC to challenge the VAC ruling by judicial review failed: [2000] EMLR 850.   [81] See ch. V, s. 5(i) below.

[82] *Wingrove* v. *UK* (1997) 24 EHRR 1.

[83] See Jeffries (n. 7 above), 412: 'The harm that may be expected to flow from revealing a state secret is almost exclusively related to the first publication.'

publication of a newspaper feature infringing personal privacy, or conceivably of defamatory material. Harmful speech cannot always in these circumstances be satisfactorily remedied by more speech or by an award of compensatory damages.

However, sometimes the prospect of penal sanctions or a civil action may be enough to deter unacceptable disclosure of confidential information. Much will depend on such factors as the chance of a prosecution being initiated and the likely sentence on conviction, or in civil proceedings the measure of damages. Or an award of damages may be an adequate remedy to redress the harm suffered by the claimants as a result of a publication. This was the position in the notorious *Douglas* privacy case.[84] The Court of Appeal declined to continue the interim injunction to stop publication by *Hello!* magazine of unauthorized photographs of the wedding of Michael Douglas and Catherine Zeta-Jones, because it considered the claimants had largely surrendered their privacy interests by entering into an agreement under which *OK!*, another celebrity magazine, had acquired exclusive rights to publish photographs of their wedding. In those circumstances, the Court thought it inappropriate to impose a prior restraint, as the claimants could be adequately compensated by an award of damages. But that would not be the case if the publication disclosed material which an applicant was entitled and wanted to keep fully confidential or private. An injunction would then be the only effective remedy. Similarly, a prior restraint might provide the only effective recourse for a government, such as the UK government in the 1980s, which wanted to prevent disclosure of official secrets when it was considered too difficult to bring a successful prosecution for breach of the Official Secrets Act 1911.[85]

It would be wrong to apply general principles here without regard to the particular character of the speech and its likely impact. If the information which a newspaper contemplates publishing really does threaten serious damage to the nation's security, only free speech absolutists like Black J. would refuse to countenance a prior restraint. Conversely, neither an injunction nor a subsequent sanction (whether criminal or civil) is appropriate to stop or punish speech which does no more than criticize government or a public official or figure. The real issue in that event is not the form of the restraint, previous or subsequent, but whether any restriction at all could be considered reasonable. There is no need for any special prior restraint doctrine. In some circumstances the justification for a prior restraint may be far from clear at the stage when the injunction is sought. In libel cases, for instance, the publisher may argue at full trial that the allegations are true or are fair comment. If that argument were to fail, an award of damages would be appropriate. The point is that it would be wrong to anticipate the verdict by imposing a prior restraint to prevent further publication before the facts have been

---

[84] *Douglas* v. *Hello!* [2001] QB 967, paras. 138–44 per Sedley LJ, and paras. 169–71 per Keene LJ.

[85] The difficulties are highlighted by the outcome of *R* v. *Ponting* [1985] Crim LR 318, when the jury acquitted the defendant against the direction of the judge (see ch. V, s. 6 below), and the inability to prosecute Peter Wright, the author of *Spycatcher*, under the Official Secrets Act 1911, as he was resident in Australia.

found and the truth of the allegations determined. But if it is virtually certain, or very likely, that publication will occasion irreparable damages to a vital national interest, a prior restraint is justified, as a majority of even the Supreme Court accepted in the *Pentagon Papers* case.[86] The character of the speech and the degree of harm likely to be occasioned by publication should, therefore, both be considered before a prior restraint is imposed.

The approach of the English courts varies, depending on whether the action is brought in libel or breach of confidence.[87] In the former, they refuse to grant an interim injunction to restrain further publication of defamatory allegations, which, the defendant will argue at full trial, are true or amount to fair comment on a matter of public interest. An interim injunction will only be granted if those defences are wholly implausible. A similar approach was advocated by Lord Denning MR for breach of confidence actions,[88] but was rejected by the Court of Appeal in *Lion Laboratories* v. *Evans*.[89] If the courts invariably refused to grant an interim injunction to stop the disclosure of confidential information, disloyal employees could freely leak commercial information to the press. Moreover, while damages may adequately compensate the victim of defamatory allegations, they would not provide a claimant company with adequate redress for loss of its commercial secrets or other confidential information. The defendant must at least be required to show strong grounds for the court to conclude that at full trial publication will be held to be in the public interest. In that case, the Court of Appeal lifted an injunction which had been granted to restrain publication in the *Daily Express* of an article, assembled from confidential documents disclosed to the newspaper by former employees of the claimant, alleging defects in a breath-test machine manufactured by the latter. The judges considered that the public interest in the accuracy of the machine outweighed the plaintiff's interest in confidentiality. Moreover, in this case it would not have been right to expect the information to have been given to the police before press publication, for it was the police who were using the machine.[90] It would now be more difficult for a claimant to secure an interim injunction in these circumstances, since section 12(3) of the HRA 1998 requires a court to be satisfied that at full trial he is likely to show that publication should not be allowed.[91]

English courts are prepared to extend the equitable jurisdiction to restrain breach of confidence to stop the publication of family and political secrets.[92]

---

[86] *New York Times* v. *US* 403 US 713 (1971).

[87] For a critical commentary on this area of law in England and Scotland, see C. R. Munro, 'Prior Restraint of the Media and Human Rights Law' (2002) *Juridical Rev* 1.

[88] *Fraser* v. *Evans* [1969] 1 QB 349, 363, CA.   [89] [1985] 2 QB 526.

[90] Compare the earlier decision of the Court of Appeal in *Francome* v. *Mirror Group Newspapers Ltd* [1984] 1 WLR 892, where it held that tapes of illegally recorded telephone conversations, revealing breaches of the rules of racing by the claimant jockey, should be sent to the police or to the Jockey Club for investigation, rather than disclosed by the press.

[91] HRA 1998, s. 12(4) requires the court to take into account the extent to which it would be in the public interest for the material to be published.

[92] *Argyll* v. *Argyll* [1967] Ch 302 (Ungoed-Thomas J.), *Stephens* v. *Avery* [1988] Ch 449 (Sir N. Browne-Wilkinson, V-C), *A-G* v. *Guardian Newspapers Ltd* [1987] 1 WLR 1248, HL.

The ruling in *Attorney-General* v. *Jonathan Cape* (the Crossman Diaries case) affords a striking contrast to the approach in the United States discussed later in this section. The Attorney-General applied for an injunction to restrain the publication of diaries kept by a deceased Labour Cabinet minister. These dealt in some detail with Cabinet discussions, the deliberations of government committees, and the advice received from civil servants. As the revelations concerned matters which had occurred some ten to eleven years before the date of the proposed publication, Lord Widgery CJ did not think disclosure would undermine the relationship of confidence which existed between government ministers. So on the facts the application was refused. He would, however, have been prepared to grant an injunction if publication had shortly followed the relevant Cabinet meetings. What is particularly interesting is that, while the judge denied he had power to intervene on broad public interest grounds, largely because of the importance of free speech, he paid little attention to this value in extending the equitable jurisdiction to restrain breaches of confidence: 'I cannot see why the courts should be powerless to restrain the publication of public secrets, while enjoying the *Argyll* powers in regard to domestic secrets.'[93] The distinction is, of course, that the former involves political speech of legitimate public interest, while the latter affects privacy interests and is less obviously of public concern. The point was appreciated in the Australian case, *Commonwealth of Australia* v. *John Fairfax*,[94] where Mason J. refused to grant an injunction to restrain breach of confidence merely because the revelations would be embarrassing to the government in the conduct of its foreign policy.

These issues arose again in the notorious *Spycatcher* litigation. In July 1986 the Attorney-General in England obtained interlocutory injunctions pending full trial to stop the *Guardian* and *Observer* newspapers from publishing allegations made by a former MI5 agent, Peter Wright, about security service activities which he proposed to disclose in his memoirs. The newspapers applied in April 1987 for the discharge of these injunctions. They argued that there had been a material change in the circumstances since their grant. In the first place, a number of the allegations had been published during the course of legal proceedings in Australia, which the UK government had taken to stop publication of Peter Wright's memoirs. Secondly, in July 1987 the memoirs were published and freely available in the United States, where no injunction to stop publication could have been obtained by the Attorney-General owing to the First Amendment.[95] Sir Nicholas Browne-Wilkinson V-C granted the newspapers' application, but the Attorney-General's appeal was upheld by the Court of Appeal, and then by a 3–2 majority of the House of Lords.[96] The judges in all the courts were clear that freedom of speech and of the press had to be balanced against the arguments for maintenance of the interim orders: the importance of the public interest in preserving confidentiality

---

[93] [1976] QB 752, 769.   [94] (1980) 147 CLR 39, HC of A.   [95] See p. 142 below.
[96] *A-G* v. *Guardian Newspapers Ltd* [1987] 1 WLR 1248.

in the security service, the morale of other agents which might suffer if publication of the memoirs were allowed, and the need to keep the temporary orders in place until the trial of the action took place with full legal argument. It was clear in this case that damages were not an acceptable alternative remedy. Moreover, the majority was anxious at this stage to resist the argument that, because some of the allegations had now been published in the press, the information could no longer be regarded as confidential. For the minority, Lord Bridge thought it was pointless to continue to impose injunctions which amounted to 'massive encroachments on freedom of speech' and which eventually the European Court of Human Rights would hold contrary to the Convention.[97] He was right in that prognosis.

The English courts, however, refused the subsequent application for permanent injunctions. By the time the case came to the House of Lords, the book *Spycatcher* had been available in the United States and other countries for well over a year; it was easy for anyone in England to buy a copy in the United States and bring it back or to order it from a bookseller there. The Law Lords lifted all injunctions on the ground that the information was now in the public domain.[98] It was too late for the government to argue that it would suffer damage from its disclosure in newspapers. Scott J. at first instance and Bingham LJ in the Court of Appeal made copious references to the importance of the freedom of the press to report matters of public concern, in this case, the allegations made by Peter Wright about the illegal activities of the security service. The position of the press should not be equated to that of Peter Wright himself, or that of any civil servant who broke his terms of employment by divulging official secrets. Moreover, it would have been wrong, according to some of the judges, for the courts to grant an injunction which would prevent the majority of citizens from being aware of allegations available to those who had acquired the book. But it is difficult to detect in any of the judgments, either on the application for the interlocutory injunction or for the permanent order, any special hostility to the imposition of a prior restraint in this context.

Subsequently, the European Court of Human Rights upheld the argument of the two newspapers that the maintenance of the interlocutory injunction after July 1987 was incompatible with freedom of expression.[99] After the book had been published in the United States, there was little chance that the government would win at full trial, so the argument that it was necessary to maintain the temporary order to preserve its rights as a litigant was unsustainable. Moreover, the Strasbourg Court was unimpressed by the argument that it was necessary to grant the interlocutory injunction to promote confidence and morale in the security service. Unlike the English judges, the Court did take into account the character of the injunction as a

[97] *A-G* v. *Guardian Newspapers Ltd* [1987] 1 WLR 1285–6.

[98] *A-G* v. *Guardian Newspapers Ltd (No. 2)* [1990] 1 AC 109. For discussion, see E. Barendt, '*Spycatcher* and Freedom of Speech' [1989] *PL* 204.

[99] *Observer and Guardian* v. *UK* (1992) 14 EHRR 153. But it upheld the initial grant as necessary to protect national security and to prevent the disclosure of confidential information.

prior restraint on speech. While it held that prior restraints were not as such incompatible with the Convention, it added that 'the dangers inherent in prior restraints are such that they call for the most careful scrutiny on the part of the Court.' The imposition of a delay can deprive a story of its value and interest.[100] Further, it suggested that the maintenance of the injunction could not be regarded as a 'necessary' restriction, given the possibility that the Crown could require a newspaper serializing Wright's memoirs to account to it for its profits.[101] The compatibility of a prior restraint with the Convention, on that perspective, should be assessed in the light of the availability of appropriate post-publication remedies. Five members of the Court would have gone further and held that, except in time of war or other emergency, prior restraints are incompatible with the Convention, even when they take the form of court injunctions, temporary or permanent.[102]

This decision of the European Human Rights Court seems to have influenced the UK government when it amended the Human Rights Bill to make it more difficult for an applicant to obtain an interim injunction in cases where freedom of expression is at issue. Section 12(3) of the HRA 1998 provides that no relief affecting the exercise of freedom of expression is to be granted to restrain a publication before trial, 'unless the court is satisfied that the applicant is likely to establish that publication should not be allowed.' It was accepted by the Court of Appeal in the *Douglas* privacy case that the effect of this provision is to make it more difficult than it used to be under the *American Cyanamid* rule to obtain a prior restraint on the press.[103] In *Douglas* it ruled that an applicant now had to show that success at full trial was more likely than not, that there was, in Sedley LJ's words, 'a probability of success'.[104] But in the later *Cream Holdings* case the House of Lords rejected this view. 'Likely' in section 12(3) did not mean 'more likely than not' in every case, for that interpretation would mean that a court could not even grant a temporary stay to enable it to consider argument unless it had already formed the view that the applicant would probably win at full trial. Moreover, the court should take account of the consequences for the applicant if an interim order were not granted as well as his chances of success.[105] On the other hand, the House did not agree with the Court of Appeal which had held that the applicant need only show that it had a 'real prospect of success' at full trial.[106] That requirement would not do justice to

[100] Ibid., para. 60.

[101] Ibid., para. 69. In fact, the House of Lords held that the *Sunday Times* was required to account for its profits in serializing *Spycatcher* in July 1987, but not, Lord Griffiths dissenting, for any profits for serialization after the allegations in the book ceased to be confidential: [1990] 1 AC 109.

[102] See the separate partly dissenting opinion of Judge de Meyer, joined by four other members of the Court, quoting with approval the judgments of Black and Douglas JJ in the *Pentagon Papers* case, 403 US 713 (1971).

[103] Under the *American Cyanamid* rule ([1975] AC 396, 407–8) the applicant only had to show that there was a serious question to be tried and that the balance of convenience favoured grant of an injunction to maintain the status quo. [104] *Douglas* v. *Hello!* [2001] QB 967, para. 134.

[105] *Cream Holdings* v. *Banerjee* [2004] 4 All ER 617, paras. 16–22 per Lord Nicholls.

[106] [2003] 2 All ER 318, CA.

the intention of Parliament to make it more difficult than it had been before the enactment of the HRA 1998 to obtain an interim injunction.

No account of prior restraints in the United Kingdom in this context should ignore the DA Notice system, under which the Defence, Press and Broadcasting Advisory Committee (DPBAC), or in practice its Secretary, may advise editors of newspapers and of television and radio channels not to print or broadcast certain categories of information regarded as secret for national security reasons.[107] This is a system of informal voluntary regulation in which the media fully participate through their membership of the DPBAC. Admittedly, it is clear that clearance (in practice the offering of 'No Advice' on publication) of material does not give the press any immunity from prosecution under the official secrets legislation or from civil action for breach of confidence.[108] On the other hand, positive warnings that the article or broadcast does fall within one of the DA Notices and that publication may endanger national security are invariably observed. It is a nice question whether a maverick publication could challenge the issue of such advice as amounting to a prior restraint on freedom of expression.[109] There would be a number of legal difficulties to a successful challenge, principally whether there was an 'act' of a public authority for the purposes of section 6 of the HRA 1998. Whatever the merits of the legal points, as a matter of principle it would be wrong to defend the system with the argument that the media generally support it. Like the informal system of film censorship, which is generally supported by film distributors, the DA system may not adequately safeguard the interests of recipients, who are deprived of access to information by decisions in which they have no opportunity to participate.

The law in the United States has afforded a strong contrast to the position in the United Kingdom. Admittedly the possibility of prior restraints in this area was left open in *Near* v. *Minnesota*:

The protection even as to previous restraint is not absolutely unlimited. But the limitation has been recognized only in exceptional cases. No one would question but that a government might prevent actual obstruction to its recruiting service or the publication of the sailing dates of transports or the number and location of troops . . .[110]

But no proceedings to restrain the publication of secret government information seem to have been taken before the *Pentagon Papers* case arose in 1971.[111] There the government requested an order to restrain publication in the *New York Times* and the *Washington Post* of secret State Department compilations of papers relating

---

[107] See Feldman, 832–4; D. Fairley, 'D Notices, Official Secrets and the Law' (1990) 10 *OJLS* 430; P. Sadler, *National Security and the D-Notice System* (Aldershot: Ashgate, 2001), esp. ch. 4.

[108] Fairley (n. 107 above), 436–7.

[109] In *Bantam Books* v. *Sullivan* 372 US 58 (1963) the US Supreme Court held an administrative warning of a prosecution to be a prior restraint. But advice issued under the DA systems does not amount to a warning of this kind.   [110] 283 US 697, 716 (1931) per Hughes CJ.

[111] *New York Times* v. *US* 403 US 713 (1971).

to the history of United States involvement in Vietnam. After consideration of the case in a few days, characterized by Harlan J. in dissent as 'almost irresponsibly feverish',[112] the Court, by a majority of 6–3, dismissed the application. All nine Justices delivered separate opinions, and as a result the decision is hard to summarize. But the following observations can safely be made. First, with the exception of Marshall J. (whose judgment turned on the lack of any legal basis for an injunction in the absence of legislation), the majority regarded the prior restraint issue as decisive. Second, while the two absolutists, Black and Douglas JJ reiterated their familiar view that the First Amendment wholly precludes any prior restraints, the case is probably only authority for the more moderate proposition that an injunction will only issue if 'disclosure . . . will surely result in direct, immediate and irreparable damage to our Nation or its people'.[113] Brennan J. would have allowed a prior restraint only where the government could show that publication would inevitably lead to catastrophe or endanger lives—the circumstances suggested in *Near* v. *Minnesota*. A third point is that all members of the majority were influenced by the absence of any Congressional statute authorizing the grant of an injunction in these circumstances, although it is not clear how the existence of a statute would have altered the decision. In the view of White J., a criminal prosecution under the Espionage Act would have been a more appropriate remedy for the government and might succeed in circumstances where a prior restraint could not be imposed.[114] (But other members of the Court were sceptical whether a prosecution could have been brought in these circumstances.[115]) In effect the US government was, therefore, relying on an inherent power to take proceedings to protect national security, a similar argument to that made unsuccessfully by the UK Attorney-General in the *Crossman Diaries* case. The Court was understandably reluctant to grant an injunction in the enforcement of such a broad power, in the absence of an overwhelming justification for the imposition of a prior restraint.

In fact the prior restraint at issue in the *Pentagon Papers* case lacked many of the remedy's characteristic vices. There was an adversary judicial hearing before an impartial court held within a week of the government's application; the burden of proof was on the plaintiff and the application, unlike that in *Near*, related to specified materials of a definite character. The difference between these proceedings and a subsequent criminal prosecution lies in the absence of a jury trial in the former, but it is questionable whether that is enough to justify the strong presumption against prior restraints formulated by the Court in *Pentagon Papers*. In any case, it is likely that a criminal prosecution on these facts would have failed, as the government could not show a compelling interest to justify penalizing publication of the papers; the disclosures were embarrassing, but did not endanger national security. So it was unnecessary to invoke a special prior restraint doctrine,

---

[112] Ibid., 753.   [113] Ibid., 730 per Stewart J., with whom White J. concurred.
[114] Ibid., 737 per White J., with whom Stewart J. concurred.
[115] Ibid., 721 per Douglas J., with whom Black J. concurred.

under which in effect the Court was protecting a right to publish at least once.[116] And it formulated in this context a more severe test for the validity of a previous restraint, in particular the novel requirement of *immediate* damage, than that which it has employed in others, notably the licensing of films and public meetings.

US courts have taken a more cautious stand in some later litigation. A Federal District Court in *US* v. *Progressive, Inc.*[117] granted a temporary injunction, pending full trial, to restrain publication of an article which described in technical detail the manufacture of the H-bomb. On the basis of expert evidence the judge found that the information might enable a medium-power country to make the bomb more expeditiously, and concluded that there was much more justification for the government's view that publication would endanger national security than there had been in the *Pentagon Papers* case. In contradistinction to the position in the earlier case, a statute, the Atomic Energy Act 1954, authorized the government to apply for an injunction against anyone communicating 'restricted data'. It is understandable that the court granted the order, though subsequently the government abandoned its action, when it became clear that much of the information was already in the public domain and its availability did not pose imminent dangers.

More difficult issues were raised in two cases where courts sustained restrictions in CIA employment contracts, arguably amounting to prior restraints. In the first,[118] a Court of Appeals enforced a clause prohibiting publication by an ex-CIA agent of classified information, while in *Snepp*[119] the Supreme Court upheld a contractual provision requiring employees to submit any forthcoming publication for preliminary clearance. It further granted an order imposing a constructive trust for the government's benefit of the profits from the sale of the defendant's book, which had not been submitted for scrutiny. The majority of the Court virtually ignored the prior restraint issue; a term requiring submission for approval of all material, whether classified or not, certainly inhibits the dissemination of speech which in normal circumstances would be constitutionally protected. In the dissenters' view, the contractual term should only have been upheld if there was no other way of preventing disclosures which create a serious risk of direct and irreparable damage.[120] (The government conceded that Snepp's book did not contain confidential information, the disclosure of which endangered national security.)

These cases raise questions about the compatibility of the special restraints imposed on civil servants and government ministers, by contract or otherwise, with their right to freedom of speech. It may be argued that a civil servant has, to some extent, voluntarily surrendered free speech rights by entering into government employment.[121] Even if he retains freedom to state his views on political issues, at least outside the place of work, he has no real free speech interest in disclosing

---

[116] H. Kalven, 'The Supreme Court—1970 Term' (1971) 85 *Harvard Law Rev* 3, 24; Jeffries (n. 7 above), 434–7.   [117] 467 F Supp 990 (1979).
[118] *US* v. *Marchetti* 466 F 2d 1309 (1972), *certiorari* denied by the Supreme Court, 409 US 1063 (1972).   [119] *Snepp* v. *US* 444 US 507 (1980).
[120] See the dissent of Stevens J., with whom Brennan and Marshall JJ concurred, ibid., 516.
[121] See ch. XIV, s. 3 below for full consideration of this topic.

information which has only become available to him as a result of the employment relationship. His employer is clearly entitled to limit his access to sensitive information during the course of the employment; it surely follows that it is equally entitled to require him, as a condition of obtaining access, not to divulge it to third parties. Of course, counter-arguments may be made; the public may be deprived of important information if civil servants are contractually bound not to divulge it. The relevant question here is whether there is anything in this context particularly heinous in the use of prior restraints to prevent disclosure of such information, compared with other remedies for breach of contract (damages or account of profits) or with a prosecution under official secrets legislation. As in other circumstances, the government may apply for an injunction to stop a breach of contract in order to avoid the embarrassment of a criminal prosecution with trial by jury; moreover, a clearance procedure of the type at issue in *Snepp* is conducted in private and in the absence of any clear standards for assessment of the publication. But it is unclear that a civil servant should be able to complain about these procedural points, insofar as he is proposing to publish material to which he would have had no access at all in the absence of government employment.[122] The application of a prior restraint principle in these cases depends on the assumption that a government employee has prima facie freedom to disclose confidential information.

The cases in England and the United States show how hard it is for the courts to formulate clear rules and apply them consistently in this area of confidential government information. An absolutist prohibition on all previous restraints is too dogmatic. It would entail an unqualified right to publish any material once, irrespective of the damage that may occur and no matter the circumstances in which it is acquired. Admittedly, there are very strong reasons for treating these restraints with particular suspicion. Courts are equally open to criticism when they totally ignore those arguments or when, as in the *Pentagon Papers* case, they apply a prior restraint principle unnecessarily and formulate too stringent a test for such a restraint to be upheld.

4. Contempt of Court and Permits for Meetings

(i) Contempt of court

Proceedings for a contempt are usually taken after the offending article has been published.[123] It is relatively rare, at least in England, for an application to restrain publication of a forthcoming article. But this course was taken in the

---

[122] A prior restraint was upheld in *Brown* v. *Glines* 444 US 348 (1980), where the approval of a commanding officer had to be obtained for the circulation of a petition on an air force base or by an officer in uniform.

[123] But courts impose prior restraints when they issue orders under the Contempt of Court Act 1981, s. 4(2) to postpone the reporting of legal proceedings in order to avoid a substantial risk of prejudice to those or to other (subsequent) proceedings.

famous *Sunday Times* case after the editor of that newspaper had sent the Attorney-General the draft of an article he was proposing to publish during his press campaign against Distillers.[124] The newspaper welcomed the institution of proceedings by the Attorney-General, so submission to the prior restraint in this case could be characterized as voluntary. But that does not legitimize it. The interests of newspaper readers in access to comment on pending legal proceedings are prejudiced if an injunction is granted to stop its publication, even though the newspaper itself may prefer that course to the risk of subsequent penal proceedings. In the Court of Appeal, where the injunction was discharged, Scarman LJ drew a contrast between defamation actions and contempt proceedings: in the former an interlocutory injunction would be refused if fair comment on a matter of public interest was pleaded, while in the latter a prior restraint might be imposed.[125] Yet the public interest in free discussion of the issues would be the same. The House of Lords seems to have paid little attention to the prior restraint aspect of the case, though this was accentuated by the extraordinarily wide injunction formulated by the House: all further matter prejudging the issues in the pending trial was enjoined.[126] Nor did the European Court of Human Rights object to the grant of an injunction as a prior restraint on speech, although it found that it could not be sustained in all the circumstances of the case as a necessary restriction on the exercise of the right to free expression.

The issue arose again in *Attorney-General* v. *BBC* ,[127] where proceedings were taken to restrain the repeat of a programme about the Exclusive Brethren. It was claimed the programme would prejudice the hearing of the sect's application for rating relief. The main ground on which the Lords dismissed the contempt proceedings was that a local valuation court was not an inferior court of law for this purpose. But Lord Denning MR dissenting in the Court of Appeal, and Lords Salmon and Scarman in the Lords, referred to the prior restraint issue. Lord Denning MR said the Attorney-General was seeking a 'gagging injunction', and this should not be awarded unless there was a 'clear case where there would manifestly be a contempt of court...'.[128] Lord Scarman was even more forthright. A prior restraint should only be ordered where there is 'a substantial risk of grave injustice', because it was 'a drastic interference with freedom of speech'.[129] Such language and principles are more characteristic of the US Supreme Court; they show a welcome appreciation of the questions involved in this type of proceeding. The Court of Appeal has, however, held in a later case that it would be prepared to restrain publication of newspaper articles on the ground that they infringed the statutory strict liability contempt rule, although an interim injunction could not be granted to stop the publication of defamatory allegations in those articles.[130]

---

124 *A-G* v. *Times Newspapers Ltd* [1974] AC 273, HL: see ch. IX, s. 3 below.
125 [1973] QB 710, 746.   126 [1974] AC 273, 327.   127 [1981] AC 303, HL.
128 Ibid., 311, CA.   129 Ibid., 362, HL.
130 *A-G* v. *News Group Newspapers* [1987] QB 1, CA.

A leading decision of the Supreme Court of Canada in *Dagenais* v. *Canadian Broadcasting Corporation* involved an application to postpone the showing of a fictional television drama series about child abuse in a church school on the ground that it would prejudice contemporaneous and pending trials of members of Catholic religious orders on sexual abuse charges.[131] By a majority, the Court rejected the application, holding that subsequent to the Charter, freedom of expression should be given equal weight with the defendants' fair trial rights. In this case, the risks created by showing the television drama series were too speculative; further, other measures could have been taken to avert them, so it could not be said that it was necessary to order postponement of the television series.[132] The application was clearly for a prior restraint, but there is no indication that the Court would have considered contempt proceedings brought after the screening of the series more sympathetically. However, the Alberta Court of Appeal has recently suggested that the approach in *Dagenais* should not be applied to contempt proceedings, where the existence of alternative measures were only factors to be considered in determining whether a contempt had been committed.[133]

It is far from evident that it is right to treat an application for an injunction more severely than subsequent contempt proceedings. In England both types of application are heard by judge alone, and there does not appear to be any significant procedural difference between them. Further, on one perspective, the injunction does not really bite unless and until it is enforced by separate civil contempt proceedings taken in respect of a publication in violation of it. Arguably, the effect of an injunction, such as that granted in the *Sunday Times* case, is no more inhibiting on freedom of speech than the prospect of subsequent contempt proceedings. It may, however, be more significant if the anticipated penalty for disobedience to the order is greater than that likely to be imposed in subsequent contempt proceedings; the courts might impose heavier fines for deliberate violations of court orders than for the publication of material which amounts to a contempt. In the United States there is another reason why a prior 'gagging order' may be subject to stricter scrutiny than penal contempt proceedings: it may not be permissible to challenge the constitutionality of the 'gagging order' when it is subsequently enforced. If the bar on later collateral challenge were removed, there would be little reason to treat preliminary injunctions with so much suspicion.[134]

The Supreme Court at any rate has had no hesitation in applying its general hostility to prior restraints in this area. In *Nebraska Press Association* v. *Stuart* it unanimously invalidated an order restraining the press and broadcasting media from reporting confessions and other admissions made by a defendant in a murder case and from publishing other facts which implicated him.[135] The judgment of the Court, given by Burger CJ, considered that the heavy presumption against prior

---

[131] [1994] 3 SCR 835.   [132] See ch. IX, s. 3(iii) below.
[133] *R* v. *Edmonton Sun* (2003) 221 DLR (4th) 438.   [134] See Barnett (n. 26 above).
[135] 427 US 539 (1976).

restraints had not been rebutted, but implied that it might be, if there were no other means by which a fair trial could be safeguarded. In a separate judgment, Brennan J., joined by Stewart and Marshall JJ, considered that this extreme remedy could never be justified in this context. The harm to a fair trial was always speculative, and it was an impossible task for the courts to weigh this risk against the public interest in reading newspaper reports such as those covered by the order. In their view the categories of permissible prior restraints formulated in *Near* were exhaustive.[136] In fact Brennan J.'s approach really rests on doubts whether any sort of contempt proceedings can be justified. The argument against judicial balancing applies equally to criminal prosecutions. There is no need to invoke a prior restraint principle, as there is no doubt now that US courts would also hold contempt proceedings taken *subsequent* to publication incompatible with the First Amendment.

In this context, as in others, it is often no easier to assess the harm or damage resulting from speech after it has been published than it is before publication. As will be discussed in Chapter IX, it is almost impossible to determine whether prejudicial pre-trial publicity really endangers the fairness of criminal trials. But it would be nonsensical to deny that in some circumstances a risk of prejudice may arise, since otherwise we would have to assume that media discussion has little or no impact on readers, listeners, and viewers. That assumption is counter-intuitive, and moreover, is inconsistent with the reasons why free speech is valued and guaranteed. The question is how far the risk of prejudice is acceptable and what steps should be taken to minimize it. If the risk of prejudice is regarded as significant, then a prior restraint is much the most effective means of averting it. The United States position of hostility to all restraints on pre-trial publicity is only coherent if it is accepted that no matter what the risks of prejudice may be, it is always better to protect freedom of speech. On that perspective, it makes no difference whether the restraint is prior or penal.

(ii) Permits for meetings

The Supreme Court has shown a more cautious approach in the second area of law considered in this section. Although not specifically listed in the *Near* categories, previous restraints have frequently been upheld in the context of public meetings and processions. Permit requirements to regulate the time, manner, and place of such meetings are generally approved.[137] The object of these requirements is to coordinate the use of, say, a park or the streets, and to ensure financial accountability for any damage to public property, rather than to censor speech on the basis of its contents.[138] On the other hand, an ordinance under which officials

---

[136] 427 US 539, 589–94 (1976).

[137] *Cox* v. *New Hampshire* 312 US 569 (1941); *Niemotko* v. *Maryland* 340 US 268 (1951).

[138] *Thomas* v. *Chicago Park District* 534 US 316 (2002), in which a unanimous Court rejected a facial challenge to a parks ordinance, under which a permit for a meeting could be denied only on specified grounds relating to damage done by previous meetings of the applicant or to the prior grant of permits to other applicants.

have an unfettered discretion to ban the distribution of literature or a peaceful march on any grounds, for example, because they dislike the particular object of the meeting, will be struck down.[139] An ordinance of this character suffers from the characteristic prior restraint vice of a lack of clear standards; if not invalidated, constitutionally protected speech may well be prohibited. More problems are posed in cases in which convenors are prohibited from holding a meeting, because on a previous occasion their demonstrations have led to violence, or because the officials fear a hostile audience will cause disorder. Generally the Supreme Court has disapproved bans issued on these grounds. The best justification for its reluctance to uphold prior restraints in these circumstances is that other means are available to deal with actual disorder at the event; moreover, a serious likelihood of a breach of the peace may be met by extra policing.[140] The argument for the prior restraint then becomes one of cost and administrative convenience, and this is certainly not enough to outweigh the free speech rights of demonstrators and the public interest in hearing their views. It is easy to exaggerate the risks of disorder before a meeting or protest takes place.

Two other arguments may be made against the use of permit systems. First, there is the danger that the licensing authority may not observe fair procedural rules. There has been some suggestion that the procedural requirements laid down in *Freedman* v. *Maryland* in the film censorship field should be applied,[141] but this is not the general rule.[142] They were, however, applied in one case to strike down the grant of an *ex parte* injunction, on the application of city officials, to restrain the further staging of demonstrations by a far-right political party.[143] The case also shows a second reservation about licensing in this area: often it has the effect of postponing or permanently banning political speech of contemporary and vital interest, where even a delay of a few days will dilute its impact. In this respect there is less justification for the use of censorship here than in the case of films and theatre.

Under English law, public protest may be banned or restricted in advance in a number of circumstances. For example, a property owner with land adjoining the highway may apply for an injunction to restrain the nuisance occasioned by a protest demonstration against his business.[144] Under the Public Order Act 1986, notice must be given at least six days before a procession is held on public streets. A chief officer of police may impose conditions on its conduct, including the route to be followed, where he believes it is likely to lead to a serious breach of the peace. Further, if he considers that step insufficient to avert disorder, he may apply

[139] *Lovell* v. *Griffin* 303 US 444 (1938); *Shuttlesworth* v. *City of Birmingham* 394 US 147 (1969).
[140] See the exhaustive discussion of the arguments in V. Blasi, 'Prior Restraints and Demonstrations' (1970) 68 *Michigan Law Rev* 1481.
[141] Seer Harlan J. in *Shuttlesworth* v. *City of Birmingham* 394 US 147 (1969).
[142] In *Thomas* v. *Chicago Park District* 534 US 316 (2002), Scalia J. for the Court said that it was inapposite to apply the *Freedman* requirements to a content-neutral time, place, and manner permit system.   [143] *Carroll* v. *President & Commissioners of Princess Anne* 393 US 175 (1968).
[144] *Hubbard* v. *Pitt* [1976] QB 142, CA.

to the local authority for a ban on all processions for three months.[145] Similarly, the police may apply for an order in some circumstances to ban trespassory assemblies: meetings intended to be held on property to which the public has no or only a limited right of access.[146] The police also have preventive powers to stop a meeting where they consider it is likely to lead to a breach of the peace. The Divisional Court has recognized that they may turn back striking miners from joining a picket a few miles away if they considered that step justified to prevent a real possibility of disorder,[147] while more recently the Court of Appeal has upheld a decision that a senior police officer was entitled to stop coaches proceeding to an RAF base, where he feared that demonstrations against the invasion of Iraq would lead to violence.[148] The courts are rarely troubled that these orders or police actions amount to prior restraints on speech and assembly rights.

Exercise by magistrates of their controversial power to bind demonstrators over to keep the peace or to be of good behaviour can be characterized, at least in some circumstances, as a prior restraint. Sometimes a binding-over order is made after a conviction when it could be regarded as part of the sentence, but it is also on occasion made for a person who has been acquitted, or who has not even been charged with any offence.[149] The European Human Rights Court has held that a binding-over order to be of good behaviour, imposed on anti-hunting protesters who had not committed a breach of the peace, was purely prospective. It was subject to careful scrutiny as a prior restraint; its scope was too vague to satisfy the requirement that restrictions on the exercise of free speech rights be 'prescribed by law'.[150] The Divisional Court has also recognized that an order made after a conviction for the offence of using insulting words likely to cause a breach of the peace may constitute an unreasonable restraint: 'A binding over must not be in such terms as effectively to inhibit a convicted person from exercising his right to free speech within the law.'[151] The Law Commission recommended abolition of the binding-over power for a number of reasons, including the lack of a clear burden of proof and the absence of clear notification to the persons concerned, other than those convicted of a specific offence, of the reason why the order is made.[152] These procedural points are among those which vitiate prior restraints on speech. Certainly, a binding-over order on a demonstrator would now appear vulnerable to challenge on freedom of expression grounds. First, it fails to satisfy the requirement that it is 'prescribed by law'. Secondly, it would be hard to defend the order as necessary to preserve, say, public order, when there are alternative courses to

---

145 Public Order Act 1986, ss. 11–13 (for further discussion, see ch. VIII, s. 5(i) below).
146 Ibid., s. 14A.   147 *Moss* v. *McLachlan* (1984) 149 JP 167, DC.
148 *R (on the application of Laporte)* v. *Chief Constable of Gloucestershire Constabulary* [2005] 1 All ER 473, upholding [2004] 2 All ER 874, DC.
149 See D. G. T. Williams, *Keeping the Peace: The Police and Public Order* (London: Hutchinson, 1967), ch. 4.   150 *Hashman* v. *UK* (2000) 30 EHRR 241.
151 *R* v. *Central Criminal Court, ex p Boulding* [1984] QB 813.
152 Law Commission Report No. 222 (1994), para. 6.27.

take, notably penal sanctions for criminal offences and police intervention to stop further episodes of disorderly behaviour when they are imminent.

But notice and permit requirements can be justified as the most satisfactory method of preventing serious disorder on occasions of public protest. There must be some system for the allocation of times and places for meetings. The threat of penal sanctions may not avert the risks of confrontation between rival groups when each is planning to demonstrate on the same day and in the same neighbourhood. Arguably, the community's interests can really only be protected by permit systems. They should, however, be tightly drawn, so the licensing body does not have power to suppress a meeting on the basis of its objects or of the contents of any speech likely to be made at it. Courts should intervene to check abuse by officials or police authorities of their power to refuse permits, and should also be prepared to strike down licensing systems if they do not adequately circumscribe administrative discretion.

5. Private Censorship

The prior restraint doctrine was developed in the context of official censorship, and subsequently extended, at least in the United States, to subject court injunctions to particularly careful scrutiny. Should similar principles be applied to private censorship? An author might complain of censorship, when a publishing house or an editor of a newspaper refuses to accept his material for publication, perhaps because it is too pornographic or because it adopts a view contrary to the editorial line of the newspaper. Alternatively, an author may consider his work has been censored if private libraries refuse to stock it or remove it from their shelves.[153] It is easy, and common in practice, to use the language of censorship in these circumstances, for undoubtedly the author has been effectively prevented from communicating his ideas to the public, albeit not by law. Conceivably, a writer might bring a similar complaint when he feels the underlying social climate or conventions makes it impossible for her work to find a publisher. Interestingly, Mill argued that liberty of discussion could be as much threatened by social pressure as by legal rules.[154]

The more extreme claims should certainly be resisted. The term 'censorship' is emptied of real meaning if it is applied to any social convention or practice which makes communication for some individuals more difficult. There can be no objection, for example, to an employer in London or New York requiring prospective employees to use English or not to swear when being interviewed for a job. It makes no sense to characterize these requirements as censorship, when effective

---

[153] If the challenge in *Island Trees School District* v. *Pico* 457 US 853 (1982), discussed in ch. XIV, s. 4 below, had been to the removal of books from a *private* school library, would or should that removal be held contrary to the First Amendment?   [154] Mill, 36–8.

discourse is dependent on the observance of linguistic and other conventions.[155] Moreover, to require a publishing house to accept a particular book for publication would interfere with its freedom to choose its own list, perhaps an aspect of its own freedom of speech. Certainly, an editor of a newspaper, or the controller of a broadcasting channel, may claim to be exercising free speech or free press rights when he rejects an article or programme for publication or transmission.[156]

Courts in the United States would almost always reject a challenge to private censorship, because First Amendment (and other constitutional) rights are only protected against state action. Further, a state law requiring newspapers to publish replies to personal attacks in their columns has been struck down as infringing the First Amendment rights of editors.[157] An editor's refusal to publish such a reply, let alone an article submitted for publication, would not be regarded as censorship; the prior restraint principle does not apply to private decisions. That conclusion is defensible, particularly if the principal reason for conferring on freedom of speech a strong measure of legal protection is fear of government control.[158] The regulation of legal rights of reply and other limits on private censorship would necessitate intervention by government, or by a public agency, which might pose greater dangers to freedom of speech than the evil it is intended to control.

Private censorship is qualitatively different from state action, for it does not usually prevent the speaker from seeking other outlets for his ideas. Government bans are more oppressive, as they make it illegal to publish the work anywhere in the jurisdiction. This argument, however, does not carry conviction if the effect of private censorship is to make it impossible, or very difficult, for an author to communicate his views. That may well be the case where the private censor holds a monopoly position, or is a member of a small oligopoly of press barons or media corporations. For example, commercial broadcasters may decide, or agree between themselves, that a documentary made by an independent producer should not be shown because it takes a controversial view on a political issue, and would prove, they think, unpopular to viewers and advertisers. Insofar as freedom of speech is guaranteed for positive reasons, for example, because of the value of the dissemination to the public of a wide variety of opinion on social and political issues, a decision not to show the documentary may be similar in its impact on speech to a government prior restraint.[159] However, it is hard to imagine that in practice a court would intervene in these circumstances. A broadcaster would be able to make a strong argument that it should control its own schedule, or that the documentary was not only controversial, but badly made and unlikely to appeal to viewers.[160]

---

[155] See F. Schauer, 'The Ontology of Censorship', in R. C. Post (ed.), *Censorship and Silencing: Practices of Cultural Regulation* (Los Angeles: Getty Research Institute), 147.

[156] These questions are considered more fully in ch. XII below.

[157] *Miami Herald* v. *Tornillo* 418 US 241 (1974).   [158] Schauer, 124.

[159] See the argument in ch. I, s. 4(ii) above concerning free speech and pluralism.

[160] A court might however entertain a challenge to a policy statement issued by commercial broadcasters that they would not transmit programmes dealing with a particular topic or taking a particular view.

But there are a few situations in which courts should, and outside the United States might, intervene to strike down private censorship. One example, discussed elsewhere in this book, concerns the freedom to speak or hold meetings in commercial shopping malls.[161] Another would be where government or other public authorities delegate censorship powers to private bodies. Arguably, that is what has happened to film censorship in the United Kingdom, though the British Board of Film Classification, a non-governmental body, would probably be treated as a 'public authority' under the HRA 1998.[162] There was a prior restraint in *R (ProLife Alliance)* v. *BBC*,[163] as the BBC is probably also a public authority under the HRA 1998. Further, its decision not to transmit the ProLife Alliance party election broadcast (PEB) was taken under powers conferred on the BBC by its Agreement with government, a measure equivalent to legislation. There was, in effect, government involvement in, or authorization for, the decision. The courts should surely scrutinize with equal care a decision by a private commercial broadcaster not to transmit a PEB, even if it took that decision independently without statutory underpinning. In some circumstances, therefore, the courts should apply the prior restraint principle to scrutinize private censorship. But these are exceptional.

---

[161] See ch. VIII, s. 3(iv) below.
[162] HRA 1998, s. 6(3)(b) provides that a 'public authority' includes 'any person certain of whose functions are functions of a public nature . . .'.   [163] [2004] 1 AC 185, HL.

V

Political Speech

1. Introduction

Perhaps the most significant ruling of the United States Supreme Court since the last war on the scope of the First Amendment has been its decision in *New York Times* v. *Sullivan*.[1] It held that a civil libel action brought by a public official could only be constitutionally sustained if the statement was made with malice, that is, the defendant must have known that it was untrue or have been reckless as to its truth. The precise reasons for this ruling will be explored in the following chapter, but the fundamental rationale may be found in Brennan J.'s much-quoted dictum:

we consider this case against the background of a profound national commitment to the principle that debate on public issues should be uninhibited, robust and wide open, and that it may well include vehement, caustic, and sometimes unpleasantly sharp attacks on government and public officials...[2]

Under this principle, not only civil libel laws, but criminal laws concerning seditious and extreme racist or other hate speech are constitutionally suspect in the United States. While the courts in other jurisdictions may be more inclined to uphold laws proscribing hate speech, they do take care to distinguish them from general proscriptions of political expression, which would almost certainly be regarded as incompatible with freedom of speech.[3]

An initial question is whether it is right to treat speech in the political sphere as more worthy of protection than other types of speech. To some extent this entails reference to the arguments discussed in Chapter I for according freedom of expression special protection against government interference. Some of those arguments do suggest that political speech should occupy what is referred to in American constitutional jurisprudence as a 'preferred position'; courts should be less prepared to countenance abridgements of political and social discussion than

---

[1] 376 US 254 (1964). This was certainly the view of H. Kalven, 'The New York Times Case: A Note on "The Central Meaning of the First Amendment"' [1964] *Supreme Court Rev* 191.

[2] 376 US 254, 270 (1964).

[3] See, for instance, the leading decision of the Supreme Court of Canada in *R* v. *Keegstra* [1990] 3 SCR 697, considered further in s. 4 of this chapter.

they should restrictions on literature, pornography, or commercial advertising. The implications of this differential treatment can then be explored in four areas of political speech discussed in this chapter: seditious speech and related areas of expression, group libel or racially inflammatory speech, blasphemy laws, and finally official secrets laws.

These topics do not exhaust the areas where the courts' special concern for political speech may be relevant. Many of the public order cases discussed in Chapter VIII concern such speech; indeed there is some overlap between the subject matter of that chapter and the issues treated in this. Less obviously some of the varieties of contempt of court considered in Chapter IX, such as criticism of the judiciary, can be regarded as a type of political expression. Attempts to bracket such cases with archetypal instances of political speech, for example, an attack on the government, show the strength of the view that such speech does enjoy a preferred status. They support major themes of this book: courts do generally recognize this status and, moreover, they are right to do so.

2. The Preferred Position of Political Speech

We saw in Chapter II that courts, particularly in the United States and Germany, interpret the relevant constitutional provisions to give particularly strong protection to political speech. Their approach can be explained, and indeed justified, by reference to the weight of the argument from democracy.[4] While the rights-based argument concerning the importance of speech to self-development and Mill's argument from truth suggest that artistic and scientific propositions are equally immune from legislative regulation, the argument from democracy clearly elevates political discourse to a special status. Free political speech encourages a well-informed, politically sophisticated electorate able to confront government on more or less equal terms. It also, as Brandeis J. pointed out in his celebrated judgment in the *Whitney* case, prevents that stifling of debate on political matters, which in the long term might endanger the stability of the community and make revolution more likely.[5]

The simple strength of the argument from democracy may be reinforced by other indications that political speech enjoys a preferred position. Free speech rights may be incorporated in the constitution together with other political freedoms, such as the right to vote and the rights of political parties to play a role in the democratic process. A court may uphold a 'right' of political debate on the ground that it is inherent to a free society, even though no specific constitutional provision guarantees the right. In *Re Alberta Statutes*,[6] three members of the Canadian Supreme Court, which had been asked for an advisory

---

[4] Ch. I, s. 2(iii) above.   [5] *Whitney* v. *California* 274 US 357, 376 (1927).
[6] [1938] SCR 100, 132–5, 142–6, per Duff CJ and Cannon J.

opinion on an Alberta press law, found such a right implicit in the British North America Act 1867, which in their view reflected the spirit of the unwritten British Constitution. More recently, the High Court of Australia has upheld an implied right to freedom of political communication, implicit in the express commitment of the Australian Constitution to the holding of free elections and to democratic government.[7] Indeed, a leading Australian scholar has written that '[t]he guarantee in Australia [of freedom of communication] . . . is based exclusively on the connection between that freedom and democratic institutions'.[8]

The preferred status of political speech may also be defended in another way. Constitutional judges and commentators are constantly called to justify court decisions which conflict with the wishes of the electorate, as represented in the enactments of the democratically elected legislature. The reconciliation of judicial review with democracy is a problem which has baffled generations of scholars.[9] If, for example, the legislature has voted to ban abortion or pornography, can it be right for non-elected judges, unaccountable to the people, to interfere with these decisions? The question is particularly pertinent if there is little or no textual warrant for judicial intervention. Confining freedom of expression to political speech (or at any rate to protect it most rigorously in this context) does reduce the scale of the difficulty. Political speech is immune from restriction because it is a dialogue between members of the electorate and between governors and governed, and is, therefore, conducive, rather than inimical, to the operation of a constitutional democracy. The same is not so obviously true of other categories of 'speech', for which the protection of the free speech clause may be claimed, for example, pornography or commercial advertising.

Sometimes a stronger case is put that the courts should only protect political speech, and that it would be wrong for them to construe the relevant provision as covering, say, literature or pornography. This view has been forcefully urged by Robert Bork.[10] But this argument ignores the other reasons for valuing and guaranteeing freedom of speech, in particular the case from individual self-development and autonomy, without which the democracy rationale for free speech lacks complete conviction.[11] Another objection to Bork's argument is the point that virtually all constitutions explicitly guarantee a number of basic rights in addition to freedom of speech. The existence of these constitutional rights sometimes strengthens the case for protecting speech concerning matters other

---

[7] *Nationwide New Pty Ltd* v. *Wills* (1992) 177 CLR 1; *Australian Capital Television Pty Ltd* v. *Commonwealth* (1992) 177 CLR 106.

[8] L. Zines, 'Freedom of Speech and Representative Government', in *Freedom of Expression and Freedom of Information*, 35, 50.

[9] See in particular A. M. Bickel, *The Least Dangerous Branch* (New York: Bobbs-Merrill, 1962), esp. ch. 1; J. H. Ely, *Democracy and Distrust* (Cambridge, Mass.: Harvard UP, 1980), esp. ch. 3; Dworkin, 1–38.

[10] R. Bork, 'Neutral Principles and Some First Amendment Problems' (1971) 47 *Indiana Law Jo* 1.

[11] Ch. I, s. 2(iii) above.

than political issues. For example, the right of the media to attend and report criminal trials may be supported both by reference to freedom of speech and a constitutional right to a fair trial.[12] Equally, the case for recognizing a right to read or view pornography can be based on privacy rights, as well as on a broad freedom to read ideas and information.[13] Constitutions and bills of rights must be interpreted as a whole, so the scope of freedom of speech can only be understood in the light of the other rights guaranteed in the text.

At all events, the jurisdictions considered in this book do give some non-political speech a degree of protection. The Supreme Court of the United States, for instance, has now extended the coverage of the First Amendment to commercial speech and advertising.[14] The Constitutional Court in Germany has held that commentary on artistic and social questions is covered by the Basic Law,[15] an unsurprising conclusion in light of the explicit protection of 'freedom of art and science, research and teaching' in Article 5(3). The Canadian Supreme Court has also consistently taken a wide view of section 2(b) of the Charter, holding that it covers all activity conveying a meaning, except violence or its threat.[16]

However, the weight given to free speech interests and the degree of their protection may vary significantly according to the characterization of the expression as political, commercial, artistic, and so on. The US, German, and Canadian courts, and the European Court of Human Rights, balance the relevant government interests underlying the challenged law against the speech which the state wishes to punish or restrain. The balancing process may be mandated by the text itself or (as in the United States) represent a judicial technique developed to avoid the difficulties of an 'absolutist' position which asserts that free speech can never be restricted. The weight of considerations such as national security or public order is assessed to determine whether it is enough to justify the suppression or restriction of speech. Sometimes the process involves an ad hoc calculation of the importance in the particular circumstances of the competing interests. But the courts have also formulated general rules, which are adopted to ensure greater consistency in decisions. In some formulations they may also emphasize a presumption in favour of freedom of political speech, unless there are compelling reasons to restrict its dissemination.

One of the rules in United States law has been the 'clear and present danger' test. This famous principle is discussed to illustrate how the Court balances in the area of political speech. It was first formulated by Holmes J. in his judgment for the Court in *Schenk* v. *US*, where the defendants had been prosecuted under the Espionage Act 1917 for circulating leaflets, which urged opposition to the draft and participation in the war, among people called up

---

12 See *Richmond Newspapers* v. *Virginia* 448 US 555 (1980), discussed in ch. IX, s. 4 below.
13 *Stanley* v. *Georgia* 394 US 557 (1969).   14 See ch. XI, s. 3 below.
15 See the *Mephisto* case, 30 BVerfGE 173 (1971) and 54 BVerfGE 129 (1980).
16 *RWDSU* v. *Dolphin Delivery* [1986] 2 SCR 573; *Irwin Toy* v. *A-G of Quebec* [1989] 1 SCR 927.

for military service. Upholding the defendants' conviction, he formulated this general rule:

The question in every case is whether the words are used in such circumstances and are of such a nature as to create a clear and present danger that they will bring about the substantive evils that Congress has a right to prevent.[17]

The test has been applied subsequently in many cases, some of which are discussed in this chapter, and it has also been applied extensively to restrict contempt of court proceedings.[18] Despite, or perhaps because of its progressive refinement in later cases, it remains full of uncertainties. One difficulty of comparative interest is the level at which the test is to be applied. Is the court to ask whether *the legislature* could *reasonably* take the view that a certain type of speech constitutes a clear and present danger to state security (or some other compelling interest). Or is it for the *court itself* to decide whether there was a patent and imminent danger in the particular circumstances of the case?

Holmes J.'s judgment in *Schenk*, with its emphasis on the context of the speech, suggested that the latter approach is the right one. But some influential judicial opinions indicate that deference is due to a legislative assessment, implicit in the statute, that speech of a certain character is per se dangerous.[19] To give a notable example, Frankfurter J. said in *Dennis* v. *US*: 'How best to reconcile competing interests is the business of the legislatures, and the balance they strike is a judgment not to be displaced by ours, but to be respected unless outside the pale of fair judgment.'[20] He concluded, as did a majority of the Court, that it was not incompatible with the First Amendment to convict leaders of the Communist Party of the offence of advocacy of the overthrow of the government by force or violence, created by the Smith Act of 1940. Congress was entitled to take the view that Communist propaganda created a clear and present danger to the survival of democratic political life.

This approach is no longer typical of the US judiciary, as will be shown in the next section of this chapter. It is open to criticism for failing to respect the constitutionally determined presumption in favour of freedom of speech, and for treating the liberty as merely one factor to be considered among many. Moreover, legislation proscribing, say, publications advocating insurrection may have been enacted, as was the Smith Act, during a time of war or national emergency, quite different from the more peaceful circumstances when the court considers its application. Most importantly, it should be remembered that one powerful argument for free speech protection is suspicion of government intervention; the legislature cannot be trusted not to enact broad legislation which indiscriminately suppresses harmless radical speech, as well as really dangerous incitement to insurrection.[21]

---

[17] 249 US 47, 52 (1919).   [18] See ch. IX, s. 3(iv) below.
[19] e.g. *Gitlow* v. *New York* 268 US 652 (1925); *Whitney* v. *California* 274 US 357 (1927).
[20] 341 US 494, 539–40 (1951).   [21] See Schauer, ch. 6.

Both the German Constitutional Court and the European Human Rights Court have insisted that the interests should be balanced in the context of the particular facts. The former has emphasized that the character of the speech, the extent to which it was true or fabricated, and the degree of danger to the relevant state interest should all be considered.[22] In *Lüth*,[23] the leading ruling on the principles to be applied under Article 5, the Court concluded that speech designed to contribute to public debate on a matter of legitimate general concern is entitled to a greater degree of protection than expression in the context of a private dispute or made to protect private economic interests. The issue in this case was whether the grant by a lower court of an injunction, which had prevented the director of public relations of Hamburg from calling for a boycott of a film made by a former Nazi supporter, violated the director's freedom of expression. The Constitutional Court held that the protection of the film-maker's reputation and economic interests was not a sufficiently important objective to justify restrictions on the call for a boycott. The call was treated as speech intended both to influence public opinion and to show that former Nazi sympathizers could not expect an easy rehabilitation in post-war Germany.

The European Court's approach to balancing is strikingly similar to that adopted by the German Constitutional Court and (generally) the Supreme Court in Washington. It enables the judges to give particularly strong protection to political speech, or more generally for speech on matters of public concern, though it is clear that both commercial advertising and publications with sexually explicit content may be covered by Article 10. In the *Handyside* case[24] the Court said the guarantee of freedom of expression was primarily concerned to protect the dissemination of political ideas. Subsequently, in the *Sunday Times* decision[25] it stressed that the extent of each member state's discretion to determine the measures necessary to restrict free speech varies according to the character of the state interest involved. In particular, the state has a greater 'margin of appreciation' in framing measures to protect morals than it does in the case of rules required to maintain confidence in the administration of justice. This distinction is controversial. But it reflects the preferred position of speech concerned with political and public affairs. The *Sunday Times* case involved a newspaper article deploring the conduct of one party to pending litigation which had attracted public comment; it was in a broad sense of the word 'political' and certainly discussed a matter of public concern. The European Human Rights Court in this case expressed its hostility to the *absolute* nature of the English rule, under which any publication prejudging the merits of a forthcoming trial was treated as a contempt of court, irrespective of its contribution to a matter of public discussion.[26] Whether restrictions are 'necessary

---

[22] See in particular Soraya, 34 BVerfGE 269 (1973) (a fabricated press interview is of no value to the development of public opinion); Spiegel, 20 BVerfGE 162 (1966) and 21 BVerfGE 239 (1967) (risk of danger to state security from disclosure of official information is to be assessed on the particular facts).   [23] 7 BVerfGE 198 (1958).
[24] (1976) 1 EHRR 737.   [25] (1979) 2 EHRR 245.   [26] Ibid., 280.

in a democratic society' can only be determined in the light of all the circumstances. This concrete weighing process not only requires judges to determine the importance of the relevant state interest and the degree of danger threatened by the expression, but also enables them to examine the precise character of the speech. As the German *Lüth* case illustrates, it may be significant whether it is calculated to contribute to general public discussion or alternatively is primarily concerned to protect private economic interests. Only the former should be regarded as 'political' speech.

Even under the common law, where freedom of speech has been until recently only a principle limiting the application of other rights, such as the right to reputation or a fair trial, it may be decisive whether the speech involved a matter of public concern. A growing appreciation of the importance of free and open criticism of government has led to the virtual disappearance of the offence of seditious libel. The courts have long recognized a defence of qualified privilege to libel actions for the fair reporting of Parliamentary debates.[27] The scope of the fair comment defence to libel actions enables courts to discriminate between contributions to public discussion on the one hand and purely private character assassination on the other; the fair comment defence protects the expression of opinion on matters of public interest, not gossip which the public considers entertaining.[28] The House of Lords in *Reynolds* v. *Times Newspapers* has, however, refused to recognize in this context a broad common law qualified privilege for non-malicious communication to the public of *political* information. Quite apart from the argument that the recognition of a generic privilege would sometimes fail to give adequate protection to the right to reputation, it would be wrong, in the view of the House, to give stronger protection from libel actions to political revelations than that given other disclosures of public interest.[29]

Two decisions show the willingness of the courts in England to give strong protection to freedom of political speech, and perhaps to elevate that category of speech to something like a preferred position. In *Derbyshire County Council* v. *Times Newspapers* the House of Lords held that it was contrary to the public interest to allow any governmental authority, whether central or local, to sue for libel, as that would fetter freedom of speech. Lord Keith said it was vital 'that a democratically elected governmental body, or indeed any governmental body, should be open to uninhibited public criticism.'[30] In contrast, a commercial company may protect its reputation for honesty and reliability by legal action, although an attack on its probity might be regarded in some circumstances as speech on a matter of general public concern. The Court of Appeal gave strong protection to 'political speech' and 'freedom of political debate', when it held unlawful the refusal of the BBC to transmit a party election broadcast of the ProLife Alliance

---

[27] *Wason* v. *Walter* (1868) 4 QB 73, Lord Cockburn CJ.
[28] *London Artists Ltd* v. *Littler* [1969] 2 QB 375, CA.
[29] *Reynolds* v. *Times Newspapers* [2001] 2 AC 127. See ch. VI, s. 3(iv) below for further discussion.
[30] [1993] AC 534, 547.

on the ground that its content offended good taste and decency.[31] Laws LJ said it would have been much less inclined to interfere with any decision not to show, say, a programme of popular entertainment for this reason. Although the House of Lords upheld the BBC's appeal, its decision did not question the importance of political speech; the BBC was required, in its view, not to transmit any material which offended taste and decency.[32]

While constitutions do not confine freedom of speech to speech concerning public affairs, let alone political matters in a narrow sense, courts do usually give fuller protection to such speech than to other categories of expression. Admittedly, there are circumstances in which political speech may be more tightly restricted than other types of expression; for instance, political advertising on radio and television is often banned in European countries, while commercials are frequently shown. Political speech may be regulated, as here, in the interests of fairness or equality, not because it is less valued than other types of expression.[33] The general preference for political speech can be justified by reference to the underlying arguments of principle for freedom of expression. Liberal constitutions show a commitment to an open participatory democracy, a commitment which precludes, or makes difficult to defend, total bans on public discourse. A preference for public discourse is usually achieved by requiring the state to produce more compelling arguments to justify restrictions on its circulation than it must to defend the regulation of, say, commercial advertising or pornography.

So far the meaning of the terms, 'political speech' or 'public discourse', has been left vague. To some extent their scope can be determined by contrasting them with other types of speech which are generally not so fully protected, in particular commercial speech, the arts, and pornography. Reflection on the implications of the argument from democracy may also shed light, since it underlies the special status of political speech. But it would be wrong to look for too much precision. Courts dislike drawing subtle distinctions in this area, probably because they do not wish arbitrarily to discriminate against certain types of expression on the basis of their contents. Even the familiar frontiers between, say, 'speech' and 'conduct', or between political and commercial speech are frequently contested.[34] In principle, the preferred category should not be confined to communications which directly concern the conduct of government or which seek to influence electoral choices. That would be much too narrow. It would privilege speech on matters raised by political parties and candidates. The public is entitled to discuss a wide range of topics, irrespective of whether they are taken up by government and political

---

[31] *R (on the application of ProLife Alliance)* v. *BBC* [2002] 2 All ER 756.

[32] [2004] 1 AC 185, discussed in ch. II, s. 1(iii) above.

[33] I. Hare, 'Is the Privileged Position of Political Expression Justified?', in *Freedom of Expression and Freedom of Information*, 105 argues persuasively that factors other than the character of the speech are relevant to determining whether it is right to restrict it, but it does not follow that characterization of speech as political or of public concern should be given little weight.

[34] See ch. III, s. 2 above, and ch. XI, s. 2 below.

parties. 'Political speech' refers to all speech relevant to the development of public opinion on the whole range of issues which an intelligent citizen should think about. This proposition was approved by the High Court of Australia in 1994.[35]

In recent cases the High Court of Australia has, however, taken a narrow view of the scope of the freedom of political communication, implied in the Constitution.[36] It held in the *Lange* case that it protects only 'that freedom of communication between the people concerning political or government matters which enables the people to exercise a free and informed choice as electors.'[37] Although the freedom is not confined to speech during election periods and covers criticism of the executive, this is a more limited view of *political* speech than that taken by other courts, including the High Court itself in earlier cases.[38] For instance, an article advocating shoplifting as a means of redistributing resources to the poor could not be regarded as political speech on this narrower view, although it might have been so treated on the broader definition advocated in the previous paragraph. The article did not propose a change in the law or system of taxation, but rather incited its readers to unlawful activity.[39] This perspective is understandable, given that the freedom in Australia is no more than a consequence of the system of representative government established by its Constitution. It is not an express constitutional right, as it is in other jurisdictions where the courts must determine the scope of political speech, or public discourse, in the light of the text of the constitution and the political and moral principles underlying it. The rulings of these courts are discussed in the remainder of this chapter and in the next chapter dealing with the implications of free political speech for the law of libel and privacy.

3. Sedition and Related Offences

A prominent American commentator on the First Amendment, Harry Kalven, observed that the existence of the offence of seditious libel—a hostile attack on government—is the hallmark of an unfree society.[40] If this is the case, there are remarkably few free countries. In England and many Commonwealth countries the offence still exists, although prosecutions are nowadays very rare in some of them, while there are similar offences in the codes of European states.[41] Nevertheless, Kalven's argument is a serious one. What used to be regarded as a

[35] In the judgment of Mason CJ, Toohey and Gaudron JJ in *Theophanous* v. *Herald & Weekly Times Ltd* (1994) 182 CLR 104, 124, HC of A.   [36] Ch. II, s. 6(iii) above.

[37] *Lange* v. *Australian Broadcasting Corporation* (1997) 189 CLR 520, 558.

[38] See M. Chesterman, *Freedom of Speech in Australian Law* (Aldershot: Ashgate, 2000), ch. 2.

[39] *Brown* v. *Classification Review Board* (1998) 82 ACR 225, Federal Court.

[40] Kalven (n. 1 above), 205.

[41] See the French Law of the Press of 29 July 1881, arts. 24 and 30–3; German Penal Code, ss. 90–90b.

clear case of seditious libel in both England and the United States is now generally considered to be merely the vehement expression of political opinion, and therefore the classic instance of constitutionally protected speech. The Privy Council made much the same point when it held incompatible with freedom of expression a provision in Antigua and Barbuda making it an offence to publish any false statement likely to undermine public confidence in the conduct of affairs. As Lord Bridge pointed out, any criticism of government and its members, the archetype of political speech, will have the effect of undermining public confidence in its conduct.[42]

The elements of the common law crime in English law are far from clear. The obscurity made use of the charge dangerous when it was frequently brought, but now probably encourages its obsolescence. The classic definition, approved by Cave J. in his direction to the jury in *R* v. *Burns*,[43] is to be found in Stephen's *Digest of the Criminal Law*.[44] It can be paraphrased as the publication of a speech or writing with intent to bring into hatred or contempt, or excite hostility towards, the Crown, government, Parliament, and administration of justice, or with the aim of inducing reform by unlawful means or of promoting class warfare. Taken literally, this would cover much political argument and oratory, and frequent prosecution and conviction would surely have the effect of stifling any serious criticism of government and other institutions. The offence's survival has only been rendered tolerable in Britain and other Commonwealth jurisdictions by numerous refinements and qualifications.

The classic definition of sedition reflects a traditional, conservative view of the correct relationship between state and society. Governments and public institutions are not to be regarded as responsible to the people, but in some mystical way, as under the doctrine of the Divine Right of Kings, are entitled to the respect of their subjects. At the very most, suggestions concerning the improvement of government may be tolerated, but not open or vehement attack. This attitude was responsible for the frequent use of the charge of sedition in the eighteenth and early nineteenth centuries in England, and has been contrasted, probably too starkly, with the intellectual climate which accompanied the American Revolution and which led to the drafting of the First Amendment. It used to be generally thought that it was the intention of the framers of the Bill of Rights to proscribe prosecutions for seditious libel, because the spirit of American government is that it exists to serve the people.[45] Despite the judicial view that the Sedition Act of 1798 contravened freedom of speech,[46] a noted historian has argued that the First Amendment was only intended to reaffirm the common

---

[42] *Hector* v. *A-G for Antigua and Barbuda* [1990] 2 AC 312, 318.
[43] (1886) 16 Cox CC 333.   [44] Edited by L. Sturge (9th edn., London, 1950), art. 114.
[45] See Alexander Meiklejohn, *Free Speech and its Relation to Self-Government* (New York: Harper, 1948), expanded and retitled as *Political Freedom: The Constitutional Powers of the People* (New York: HarperCollins, 1960); Z. Chafee, *Free Speech in the United States* (Cambridge, Mass.: Harvard UP), esp. ch. 1.   [46] See Brennan J. in *New York Times* v. *Sullivan* 376 US 254, 276 (1964).

law's hostility towards prior restraints or, at most, prevent the federal Congress from enacting sedition laws.[47] The Supreme Court has, however, never regarded itself as confined to implementing the intentions of the Founding Fathers. It may now be said with confidence that the ordinary common law of sedition, or any statute formulated along its lines, would be held unconstitutional as a violation of the central meaning of the First Amendment. But a number of other laws proscribing the advocacy of revolutionary change with these aims have given the US courts more difficulty.[48]

The common law of sedition has been liberalized in a number of respects by the judiciary. Stephen's definition itself drew the important distinction between incitement to revolutionary change on the one hand, and on the other advocacy of lawful reform and the removal of grievances. This difference was crucial in *R* v. *Burns*[49] where the defendant was acquitted after making a passionate speech at a meeting in Trafalgar Square, calling attention to the plight of unemployed workers in London. A number of English cases stress that the speaker must intend to cause violence for the offence to be committed: 'was the language used calculated, or was it not, to promote public disorder or physical force or violence in a matter of State?'[50] The jury must take into account the character of the audience and the current state of public feeling; these factors emphasize the circumstantial nature of the offence in the modern law. The approach is similar to the concrete weighing of interests, which occurs in many jurisdictions where free speech is protected by the constitution. In a leading Canadian case, *Boucher* v. *R.*[51] the Supreme Court held that there must be an intent to disturb the government by force. It was not seditious to incite violence between classes or groups of the population—a matter sometimes covered by the group libel laws discussed in the next section of this chapter. This approach was followed by the Divisional Court in England when it held that Salman Rushdie's novel, *The Satanic Verses*, could not be the subject of a private prosecution for sedition; there must be proof of an incitement to violence, resistance, or defiance for the purpose of disturbing constituted authority.[52] It was not enough that, on one perspective, it created ill-feelings between Muslims and other religious groups in the community. As a result of these developments, public prosecutions for sedition have become virtually unknown, at least in England, so much so that the Law Commission has questioned whether there is any need for the offence.[53]

Nevertheless, at least in theory the common law still draws a distinction between the expression of political opinion on the one hand, and the advocacy or

---

[47] L. W. Levy, *Legacy of Suppression: Freedom of Speech and the Press in Early American History* (Cambridge, Mass.: Harvard UP, 1960).

[48] See e.g. the treatment of the Smith Act of 1940 in *Dennis* v. *US* 341 US 494 (1951), in *Yates* v. *US* 354 US 298 (1957), and in *Scales* v. *US* 367 US 203 (1961).   [49] (1886) 16 Cox CC 333.

[50] See in particular *R* v. *Aldred* (1909) 22 Cox CC 1, 4 per Coleridge J., *R* v. *Caunt* (1947), noted 64 *LQR* 203 (Birkett J.).   [51] [1951] 2 DLR 369.

[52] *R* v. *Chief Metropolitan Stipendiary Magistrate, ex p Choudhury* [1991] 1 QB 429.

[53] Working Paper No. 72 (1977), paras. 76–8.

incitement of violent (or in some formulations, unlawful) political action on the other. The United States Supreme Court has attempted to make a similar distinction in many of its leading decisions in the area of political speech, though the line is now drawn in a different place, so ensuring a wider berth than in England for freedom of expression. In *Gitlow* v. *New York*, where the defendants were prosecuted under the state criminal anarchy statute for advocacy of the forcible overthrow of government, the majority of the Court distinguished between the 'expression of philosophical abstraction' and the 'language of direct incitement'.[54] The state could constitutionally punish the latter because of its *tendency* to lead to crime and endanger other vital community interests. The Court did not think the 'clear and present danger' test relevant where the legislature proscribed the speech itself, as well as the harmful action to which that speech might lead. In this case, the majority of the Court reasoned, the state legislature had in effect determined that the speech constituted a source of danger. The decision, of course, shows remarkable deference to the legislature's abstract assessment of the possible harmful consequences of some types of political speech.

The substitution of the tendency test for the clear and present danger rule was subject to withering criticism by Brandeis J. in his concurring opinion in *Whitney*.[55] Although the decision in *Dennis* v. *US* marked a return to the deference to the legislature shown in *Gitlow*, it is now firmly established that the courts are entitled to determine themselves whether prohibited speech does constitute a serious and imminent danger to state security or other substantial government interest. In *Yates* v. *US*,[56] Harlan J., construing the Smith Act of 1940, which made it unlawful to advocate or teach the duty of violent overthrow of the government or political assassination, distinguished between advocacy of abstract political doctrine, and advocacy designed to promote specific action. Only the latter fell within the terms of the statute. A similar test was then given constitutional status by a unanimous Supreme Court in *Brandenburg* v. *Ohio*:

... decisions have fashioned the principle that the constitutional guarantees of free speech and free press do not permit a State to forbid or proscribe advocacy of the use of force or of law violation except where such advocacy is directed to inciting or producing imminent lawless action and is likely to incite or produce such action.[57]

The two absolutists, Black and Douglas JJ, in separate concurring judgments, considered the 'clear and present danger' test was incompatible with the First Amendment, a position which suggests the majority did have this principle in mind when it formulated the new constitutional requirement for the proscription of inflammatory political speech. There is only a clear and present danger when the advocacy is likely to produce immediate violence or insurrection. The *Brandenburg* test has been applied in subsequent cases, in particular to invalidate

---

[54] 268 US 652, 664–5 (1925) per Sanford J.   [55] 274 US 357, 376 (1927).
[56] 354 US 298 (1957).   [57] 395 US 444, 447 (1969).

a state statute refusing access to the ballot to extreme political parties advocating the overthrow of government by force.[58] The law did not distinguish between abstract support for revolution and incitement to its immediate achievement.

The *Brandenburg* test is certainly much more protective of extremist political speech than the common law of sedition, under which there is no need to prove an incitement to *immediate* violence. Indeed, if it were applied literally, it would have a radical impact. It appears to preclude the application of the ordinary criminal law of incitement to speech in non-political contexts, say, a threat or inducement to murder, unless the state can show that it is likely to lead to immediate unlawful conduct.[59] Section 59 of the United Kingdom Terrorism Act 2000 would certainly be held invalid under the *Brandenburg* test; the provision makes it an offence to incite another person to commit an act of terrorism wholly or partly outside the UK, irrespective of whether the incitement was likely to have immediate impact. In fact the requirement that a state may only proscribe incitement *likely* to lead to the commission of an offence is open to criticism. For it suggests that a prosecution for incitement would be contrary to the First Amendment, where it was clear the police would be able to stop the violence, or where, for some other reason, there was less than a 50 per cent chance that the advocacy would provoke significant disorder.[60]

The most interesting German cases concern the proscription of extremist political parties. Article 21(2) of the Basic Law specifically enables the Federal Constitutional Court to declare unconstitutional political 'parties which, by reason of their aims or the behaviour of their adherents, seek to impair or abolish the free democratic basic order or to endanger the existence of' the Republic. It has been applied in two important cases: the ban, first, of the neo-Nazi Socialist Reich Party and, secondly, of the German Communist Party.[61] There was no reference to Article 5 of the Basic Law in the former case; the legal argument turned exclusively on the constitutional status of political parties under Article 21. But the Court did observe that the constant abuse and insults hurled by leaders of the party against the federal government and the German party system were far removed from constitutionally guaranteed free expression.[62] The relationship between free speech and the Court's power to ban totalitarian political parties was, however, fully examined in the *Communist Party* decision. The party argued that Article 21(2) was incompatible with Article 5 and the fundamental principles of

---

[58] *Communist Party of Indiana* v. *Whitcomb* 414 US 441 (1974).

[59] In *Brown* v. *Classification Review Board* (1998) 82 FCR 225, the Australian Federal Court upheld the Board decision not to allow publication of an article advocating shoplifting and giving advice about techniques for doing this, on the ground that it incited crime. On the basis of the ruling in *Brandenburg*, courts in the United States would presumably hold this protected speech; its proscription would be incompatible with the First Amendment, unless the prosecution proved that the article would immediately and probably lead to outbreaks of shoplifting.

[60] L. Alexander, 'Incitement and Freedom of Speech', in D. Kretzmer and F. Kershman Hazan (eds.), *Freedom of Speech and Incitement against Democracy* (The Hague: Kluwer, 2000), 101, 112–14.

[61] 2 BVerfGE 1 (1952); 5 BVerfGE 85 (1956).   [62] 2 BVerfGE 1, 57–8 (1952).

a liberal constitution. In particular, the propagation of Marxism was constitutionally protected by Article 5(3): '... research and teaching shall be free'. The Constitutional Court, however, drew a distinction similar to that found in many American cases. It was legitimate to preach the inevitable triumph of Marxism and to deny in an abstract way the validity of the present legal order; but an active and aggressive campaign against the Constitution and political system could be proscribed.[63] The interests of free speech and the preservation of the state could, therefore, be reconciled. These cases are as much concerned with freedom of association as free speech itself, but their principles have been applied subsequently to justify the suppression of extremist political speech.[64] In contrast to the *Brandenburg* rule, there is no requirement that the speech is likely to lead to immediate insurrection. The experience of the 1930s has taught that it may sometimes be too late to intervene at the eleventh hour.

Until recently no case had been referred to the institutions of the European Convention on Human Rights and Fundamental Freedoms (ECHR), requiring them to decide the compatibility of sedition or other comparable laws with the freedom of expression protected by Article 10. The report of the Commission in the *Arrowsmith* case did suggest that such laws would be upheld as necessary restrictions to protect national security and public safety or to prevent disorder and crime.[65] The case arose out of the successful prosecution of Pat Arrowsmith under the UK Incitement to Disaffection Act 1934 for distributing leaflets at an army base advocating that soldiers refuse to serve in Northern Ireland or desert the army.[66] She argued that her conviction in effect stifled her freedom of expression in the crucial sphere of political debate. There was no real distinction between the expression of opinion on troop involvement in Northern Ireland, coupled with the supply of information about the treatment of deserters, and direct advocacy that soldiers refuse to fight. The Commission, however, concluded that the prosecution under the 1934 legislation could be regarded as a necessary restriction in view of the *possible* consequences of the applicant's campaign. If it had adopted the *Brandenburg* formula, its report would surely have been favourable to the applicant.

In the last few years the European Court has considered the scope of extreme political speech in a number of cases from Turkey. The background to most of them is the conflict between Kurdish nationalists and the Turkish authorities, and the attempts by the latter to penalize advocacy of a separate Kurdish state or expressions of support for the nationalists. The Court has made it clear that the Convention affords little scope for any restraints on freedom of political speech.[67] But Article 10(2) permits the imposition of restrictions which are necessary in the interests of national security or territorial integrity, so it is compatible with the

---

[63] 5 BVerfGE 85, 141–6 (1956).   [64] 25 BVerfGE 44, 63 (1969).

[65] 7050/75, *Arrowsmith* v. *UK* 19 D & R 5.   [66] [1975] QB 678 (CA).

[67] *Incal* v. *Turkey* (2000) 29 EHRR 449; *Ceylan* v. *Turkey* (2000) 30 EHRR 73; *EK* v. *Turkey* (2002) 35 EHRR 41; *Şener* v. *Turkey* (2003) 37 EHRR 34.

Convention to penalize incitement to violence or the publication of expression understood as justifying it, particularly during periods of terrorist atrocities.[68] Separate judgments, either in dissent or concurring with the majority, have argued that the European Court should adopt the clear and present danger test, as reformulated in *Brandenburg*. In the view of these judges, freedom of expression should prevail where the invitation to the use of force or violence is abstract and intellectual, far removed in time and space from any violence, actual or impending.[69]

Other cases from Turkey have concerned the dissolution of political parties. The decision of the Constitutional Court in Turkey to dissolve the Communist Party was held incompatible with Article 11 of the Human Rights Convention, guaranteeing the right to freedom of association.[70] The Strasbourg Court held that there was no justification for banning a party solely because it attempted to debate the economic and political position of part of the population, including the Kurds. In contrast, by a bare majority, 4–3, the Court upheld the dissolution of the Welfare Party on the ground that its activities and policies were contrary to the secular character of the state.[71] It agreed that a political party may not be banned on the ground that it campaigns for changes in the law or in the constitutional basis of the state, provided it uses legal means and the changes would be compatible with fundamental democratic principles. The Court upheld the ban in this case, because the Party's aims included the introduction of Islamic law, which would threaten the fundamental character of the Turkish state and would endanger freedom of religion, a Convention right. In an important statement of principle, the Court said that Turkey was entitled to prevent the implementation of these policies, even before an attempt was made to introduce them: at the time the Welfare Party was in opposition, but had a good chance of achieving political power.

What then is the right course for a constitutional court to adopt when called upon to determine the extent to which revolutionary political speech should be tolerated under a free speech provision? Should it protect only measured and reasonable criticism designed to influence the electorate to press for reform by lawful means, or does a right of political free speech embrace the advocacy of unlawful, even violent, revolutionary action? One famous judicial answer is really to deny that there is any plausible distinction between these two modes of speech:

> Every idea is an incitement... The only difference between the expression of an opinion and an incitement in the narrower sense is the speaker's enthusiasm for the result.[72]

This is eloquent, but unconvincing. Granted that, often, incitement to action is implicit in political speech, unless perhaps addressed to 'an assembly of professors

---

68 *Zana* v. *Turkey* (1999) 27 EHRR 667.
69 e.g. see Opinion of Judge Bonello in *Arslan* v. *Turkey* (2001) 31 EHRR 264, 290–1.
70 *United Communist Party of Turkey* v. *Turkey* (1998) 26 EHRR 121.
71 *Refah Partisi (Welfare Party)* v. *Turkey* (2002) 35 EHRR 56.
72 *Gitlow* v. *New York* 268 US 652, 673 (1925) per Holmes J.

or divines',[73] the law, even constitutional law, has constantly to draw fine lines which may be hard to justify in abstract philosophical terms. Intuitively, there is a real distinction between criticism, however vehement, of the government on the one hand, and the advocacy of unlawful action and revolution on the other. But does it follow from the truism that a line can be drawn here that this is where the courts should draw it?

Courts may be able to derive substantial assistance in solving this problem from the whole text and spirit of the constitution. Its structure, the historical background, and contemporary political developments, may suggest, for example, that only moderate political expression is immune from government regulation; the law may proscribe speech advocating the overthrow of democratic institutions. That was the view of the German Constitutional Court in the two political party cases. It is understandable that it takes this approach. Germany is what has been termed a 'militant democracy', a principle reflected not only in Article 21(2) declaring the unconstitutionality of anti-democratic parties, but in the terms of Article 20.[74] The European Court has been influenced in its disposition of the Turkish cases by the commitment of the member states, reflected in the Preamble to the Convention, to effective political democracy. Freedom of expression is, in its view, one of the essential foundations of a democratic society, so it would be paradoxical to hold incompatible with the Convention restrictions on speech which is clearly aimed at its destruction.[75]

Robert Bork has argued that the same limits on permissible political speech may be imposed under the United States Constitution. Advocacy of the overthrow of government, even on a theoretical level, may be prohibited because it seeks as its goal the denial of what the majority has democratically decided.[76] The First Amendment does not aim to protect radical speech challenging the conventional political process. While Bork's view may be in accordance with the framers' intentions, it hardly reflects the modern jurisprudence of the Supreme Court; his argument would allow prosecutions for sedition, at least if the terms of a state (or even federal) offence were tightly drawn. Where the text and other relevant explanatory material does not provide an answer, as is the case with the First Amendment, courts have no alternative to determining themselves what the commitment to freedom of speech necessarily entails in this context.

This means that the courts must examine the philosophical and political arguments justifying protection of the right to freedom of expression. The argument from democracy, which, we have seen, provides both the best explanation for the protection of speech and also explains a preferred status for political speech,

---

[73] *R* v. *Aldred* (1909) 22 Cox CC 1, 4 per Coleridge J.

[74] Art. 20(1) provides that Germany is a democratic and social federal state, while art. 20(4) confers on all Germans the right to resist persons seeking to abolish the constitutional order, if no other remedies are possible.

[75] *United Communist Party of Turkey* v. *Turkey* (1998) 26 EHRR 121, para. 52.

[76] Bork (n. 10 above).

hardly warrants the application of these guarantees to discourse posing a serious threat to democracy itself. Two caveats must be entered. First, this conclusion does not justify the maintenance of the common law offence of sedition or other broadly drafted offences punishing all inflammatory political speech. Long-term considerations must be taken into account. As Brandeis J. observed in *Whitney* v. *California*,[77] the suppression of speech may bottle up discontent for so long that eventually really serious violence is inevitable. This reservation may not apply in an emergency, but liberal societies should be prepared to take the risk of some small-scale disorder as a result of intemperate political speech. The second point is that the courts must be prepared themselves to determine whether the particular speech really threatens the stability of the state and its democratic order; these questions should not be determined simply by legislative, let alone executive fiat. Otherwise, it becomes too easy for a repressive, albeit democratic, government to undermine a free speech guarantee, which limits the prerogatives of temporary majorities.[78] These arguments justify a principle like the 'clear and present danger' rule, with its requirement that the harm must be certain and unavoidable for the restriction on speech to be justified.

Another argument supporting the position now adopted by the United States Supreme Court is that of Scanlon, outlined in Chapter I.[79] If it is to respect the moral autonomy of individuals, the state may not prevent their access to speech on the ground that it may persuade them to adopt particular beliefs or to act on those beliefs. That includes incitements to disobey the law or resist the government. On this approach, there would be no legitimate place for the law of sedition, for the UK Incitement to Disaffection Act and section 59 of the Terrorism Act 2000, or for the criminal anarchy statutes now almost certainly unconstitutional in the United States. It is also possible on this perspective to explain the limited exception to free political speech permitted in *Brandenburg*. Where speech is made to an audience which has little or no time for reflection before it decides whether to pursue the course of action urged on it, its members are not to be treated as fully responsible for their conduct; Scanlon's 'autonomy' principle does not apply. Disorder is here both imminent and likely. Mill allowed for this exception when he justified the punishment of rabble-rousers for insulting corn-dealers before a mob assembled outside a corn-dealer's house.[80]

4. Racist Hate Speech

(i) Arguments of principle

While the common law of sedition has fallen into disuse and in most jurisdictions strong criticism of government is now regarded as legitimate, verbal and written

---

[77] 274 US 357 (1927).   [78] See Dworkin, 1–38.   [79] Ch. I, s. 2(ii) above.
[80] Mill, 62.

attacks on racial and other groups have generally been subjected to greater restriction in the last fifty years. This has usually been achieved by group libel statutes and other legislation which make the dissemination of hate speech against racial (and sometimes other) groups a criminal offence. Occasionally, civil remedies are preferred.[81] It is easy to explain these developments. The repercussions of the vicious abuse of Jews (and other ethnic groups) encouraged by the Nazi regime suggested, to put it mildly, that there are worse evils than the suppression of free speech. After the war many European countries have faced the problems of assimilating immigrants into the native culture, while periodically, particularly in the last two or three decades, right-wing political parties and fringe groups have prospered, raising fears of a fascist revival. The prohibition of racially inflammatory speech has been regarded in these contexts as necessary to preserve order between different groups. Bans on hate speech also protect members of minority racial, ethnic, and other groups from psychological injury and damage to their self-esteem, or they may be seen as necessary to reflect their right to equality. Moreover, it has seemed anomalous to proscribe discriminatory practices, for example, in employment and housing, and not to restrict speech advocating discriminatory treatment of minority groups or the compulsory repatriation of immigrants. Sometimes, of course, it is hard to determine whether a publication, for example, the advertisement 'For Sale: Only Whites may apply', is to be regarded as protected speech or as unlawful action.[82] These points reinforce the arguments of principle for regulation of speech likely to cause hatred against discrete communities, particularly racial and ethnic groups. This section examines the treatment of hate speech generally, while section 5 discusses the law of blasphemy and the question whether the proscription of hate speech should be extended to protect religious communities.

Although there are considerable pressures and arguments of principle for legal intervention in this area, it is far from clear that this is justifiable in a society with any serious commitment to the principles of free speech. Under the *Brandenburg* formula, advocacy of imminent unlawful action and violence may constitutionally be prohibited; this would cover incitement to race riots where a breakdown of law and order is likely. But group libel laws and the offence in the United Kingdom of incitement to racial hatred prohibit hate speech, even though there is no suggestion that it is likely to lead immediately to violence and disorder. The argument is, instead, that to tolerate speech abusing racial and ethnic groups is to lend respectability to racist attitudes. Such attitudes may foster an eventual breakdown of public order.[83] But the defenders of free expression reply that such speech

---

[81] See Chesterman (n. 38 above), ch. 5 for a discussion of civil remedies in Australia.

[82] For an example of a case raising this problem, see *Chicago Real Estate Board* v. *City of Chicago* 224 NE 2d 793 (1967) (Illinois S Ct).

[83] See e.g. the speech of Sir B. Janner, MP on the Second Reading of the Race Relations Bill 1965, 711 HC Deb. (5th ser.), cols. 955–62.

is best met by more speech advocating the moral and cultural superiority of a multiracial society. Moreover, the suppression of propaganda may in the long run be as likely to expose society to a risk of violence as tolerance of its dissemination. More fundamentally, many advocates of a liberal free speech position contend that hate speech laws are indefensible on broader grounds of principle, such as the Scanlon moral autonomy reasoning referred to at the end of the previous section. Racist speech, or hate speech against any group, is a form of political speech. The arguments used to justify its proscription can also be adopted to justify banning any speech encouraging the formation of beliefs and attitudes the government dislikes. However despicable its content, racist speech should be tolerated, as otherwise it will prove impossible to resist moves to outlaw other types of less objectionable material.[84]

At least two issues should be disentangled at this point. The first is whether extreme hate speech falls within the scope of a freedom of speech or expression clause. In other words, is racist speech covered by such a clause? The second question, which only arises if it is accepted that hate speech is 'speech' or 'expression', is whether, nevertheless, there are strong enough arguments to justify its restriction as an exception to the presumption that political speech is fully protected (unless perhaps it incites violence). These questions are examined here in the context of extreme hate speech directed against racial groups, but they may also be asked in the context of speech aimed at religious groups and denominations (considered in the following section) and in the context of the feminist arguments for regulating pornography.

There is little doubt that hate speech, even extreme racist speech, is an exercise of freedom of speech, and is rightly regarded as covered by free speech or freedom of expression clauses. That is certainly true of statements of opinion about, say, the attributes of different races, immigration and asylum policy, or the desirability of integrated or segregated employment and housing policies. The German Constitutional Court has, however, held that false factual claims are not covered by Article 5 of the Basic Law, at least if it is known, or has been proved, that they are untrue. This principle, originally developed in the context of libel cases,[85] has been restated in the Court's major decision holding it constitutional to make Holocaust denial a criminal offence.[86] But with this exception courts have accepted that racist speech, however extreme and unpleasant its content, does constitute 'speech' and should not be equated with violent conduct or its threat. That conclusion was reached by the Canadian Supreme Court in *R* v. *Keegstra*,[87] although its majority upheld the constitutionality of the provision of the Criminal Code making it an offence to communicate statements wilfully promoting hatred

---

[84] See J. Weinstein, *Hate Speech, Pornography, and the Radical Attack on Free Speech Doctrine* (Boulder, Col.: Westview Press, 1999) for a comprehensive, broadly sympathetic discussion of these arguments.   [85] 54 BVerfGE 208, 219 (1980); 61 BVerfGE 1, 8 (1982).
[86] 90 BVerfGE 241, 266 (1994).   [87] (1990) 3 SCR 697.

against racial and other groups. Dickson CJ, for the Court majority, recognized that hate propaganda is expression of a type usually characterized as 'political', and had no doubt that it was covered by section 2(b) of the Charter.

However, this conclusion was significantly qualified later in the majority judgment of the Court. In the course of considering whether the restrictions imposed by the Criminal Code were proportionate, it held that hate speech was of limited importance and should not be given much weight when balanced against the arguments for regulation. It undermined democratic values, contributed little to the search for truth, and was inimical to the self-development and fulfilment of individuals. This approach is difficult to accept. It implies, in the first place, that courts are entitled to determine the value of a particular communication, or type of communication, in the context of the justifications for a free speech clause. That would mean that content-based restrictions on speech might be approved, although one of the arguments for freedom of speech is that government is not to be trusted to draw such distinctions between good speech which is free, and bad speech which may be banned or restricted. Secondly, it is hard to reconcile Dickson CJ's view that hate speech is of little importance with his acceptance that it is nevertheless political speech. The dissent of McLachlan J. is persuasive on this point. She emphasized the danger of confining the free expression guarantee to communications regarded as valuable. Inevitably, she pointed out that challenging expression would be prosecuted or, as troubling, speakers and authors would be deterred from communicating their views on political matters for fear of prosecution.

It is in fact unnecessary to characterize the value of hate speech in general, or of a particular communication of this kind, in order to make a strong case for prohibiting it. Apart from public order arguments, two principal justifications are generally put forward. The first is that it is right for a society to indicate its abhorrence of hate speech and the attitudes it reveals and to discourage the spread of racist views, the acceptance of which will in the long run be seriously harmful to good race relations. The difficulty with this argument is, of course, that it runs counter to the principle that speech should not be legally inhibited because the government fears that it will affect popular attitudes or that individuals will act in response to it in disapproved ways—thinking less well of members of different ethnic groups and refusing to mix with them.[88] Moreover, free speech guarantees assume that listeners will generally be able to make rational assessments of the credibility of the claims made to them, whether in the course of election campaigns or in other contexts. Proponents of hate speech laws must show why this is not the case with regard to attacks on racial, ethnic, or other groups.

The second type of justification for these laws is more promising. It argues that racist hate speech should be proscribed because it is highly wounding to members

---

[88] See Scanlon, and D. A. Strauss, 'Persuasion, Autonomy, and Freedom of Expression' (1991) 91 *Columbia Law Rev* 334.

of the targeted group. In some cases it may inflict psychological injury or cause fear of isolation or physical attack. More generally it lowers the self-esteem of those affected, particularly where the targeted group has historically been oppressed, such as blacks and Indians in the United States, or the Jewish communities in Germany and other European countries.[89] Even the dissenting judgment of McLachlin J. in *Keegstra* accepted that hate speech could not be viewed as 'victimless' in the absence of proof that it actually caused hatred or abuse of the target group. It was reasonable to assume that it does cause significant anxiety and distress, which goes well beyond mere offence or annoyance. A stronger variant of these arguments is that racist speech is incompatible with social and legal principles of human dignity and equality, or indeed that it infringes constitutional provisions guaranteeing those fundamental rights.[90] In Germany, for example, group libel laws are defended by reference to the inalienable right to human dignity guaranteed by Article 1 of the Basic Law and the right to the free development of the personality, guaranteed by Article 2. The Supreme Court of Canada in its decision in *Keegstra* found that racist hate speech threatened the self-dignity of members of the target group and their right to equality; the Court accepted the argument that hate speech 'is properly understood as a practice of inequality'.[91] Perhaps the boldest argument, though certainly not the most persuasive, is that hate speech infringes freedom of expression itself by silencing, or by disparaging, the speech of members of the targeted group.

Some of these arguments are stronger than others. The last argument does not make clear how hate speech silences its victims. It may make them less inclined to speak or render their speech less effective, but does not inhibit their legal freedom to communicate their views, in particular their right to reply to racist abuse. In contrast, there is no doubt that hate speech laws infringe the rights of the speaker. Hate speech does not infringe equality in the same way that a discriminatory refusal to allocate housing or provide education to members of the target group clearly does. Racist abuse asserts, perhaps implicitly, that equality and equal rights to housing, education, and welfare should be rejected. But it only infringes equality, if the speaker in the same breath, as it were, refuses a member of the target group a benefit to which he would be entitled if he were a member of the majority. To equate, as the Supreme Court of Canada did in *Keegstra*, hate speech with the practice of inequality is to blur the distinction between speech and conduct. If that is done, then speech is no longer special.

The best argument for restricting racist hate speech is undoubtedly that a state has a compelling interest to protect members of target groups against the

---

[89] M. J. Matsuda, 'Public Response to Racist Speech: Considering the Victim's Story' (1989) 87 *Michigan Law Rev* 2320.

[90] For a vigorous statement of the equality argument for hate speech laws, see C. McCrudden, 'Freedom of Speech and Racial Equality', in P. B. H. Birks (ed.), *Pressing Problems in the Law: Criminal Justice and Human Rights* (Oxford: OUP, 1995), 125.

[91] *R* v. *Keegstra* [1990] 3 SCR 697, 748 per Dickson CJ.

psychological injuries inflicted by the most pernicious forms of extremist hate speech. Suppose, for example, that racist leaflets are put through the letter-boxes of houses occupied by members of the target groups, or left in, or in the vicinity of, churches or other places where they congregate. It is impossible for them to ignore such material and not surprising if they feel devalued and threatened. In these circumstances hate speech surely amounts to an infringement of human dignity. It is unpersuasive to argue that no line can, or should, be drawn between insulting or threatening speech intended or likely to cause racial hatred on the one hand, and speech such as 'Fuck the Draft' or flag-burning on the other.[92] The latter types of speech are undoubtedly very offensive and distressing to many people, perhaps the majority of the community, but they hardly cause the same degree of trauma as anti-Semitic or anti-immigrant hate literature.

But members of the majority ethnic group should be protected against extreme hate speech which denies them their dignity (screaming 'White Trash' on suburban estates), although such speech is unlikely to produce the same trauma or loss of self-esteem which members of historically disadvantaged minorities may experience when they encounter racist abuse. Legislation should be drafted carefully to ensure that only speech which is really wounding to the dignity of the targeted groups is caught by the criminal law. It is the responsibility of the courts to ensure that this boundary is not crossed to permit the proscription of speech which is merely offensive either to minority groups or to the majority.

There remain, of course, a number of good points which may properly be made against this limited acceptance of some hate speech laws. First, there is the risk that the existence of these laws may deter or chill valuable political speech, or even that prosecution may wrongly be brought against such speech. To an extent the risk can be reduced, though not altogether avoided, by circumscribing the terms of the offence, so that it only covers threatening or insulting speech. Further, a provision, like that in England and Wales, which requires a prosecution to have the consent of the Attorney-General or other law officer will effectively preclude private initiatives to suppress speech.[93] It might conceivably be a defence to show that a publication, otherwise caught by the criminal law, was justified in the interests of learning or the arts, or was made in the course of discussion of a matter of public interest.

Secondly, there is the practical point that a prosecution and trial may have the effect of giving hate speech wider currency than it would otherwise enjoy, and indeed make the speaker or publisher a martyr to the cause of free speech. Further, it can be argued that, all things considered, it is better for government to use other means to show society's disapproval of the attitudes revealed in hate speech. It might instead strengthen the institutions and procedures for tackling racial

---

[92] For a different view, see J. Weinstein, 'An American's View of the Canadian Hate Speech Decisions', in W. J. Waluchow (ed.), *Free Expression* (Oxford: OUP, 1994), 175, 206–10.

[93] Public Order Act 1986, s. 27(1).

discrimination, or perhaps provide civil, rather than criminal, remedies for the injuries such speech occasions. But these are not objections of principle to the use of tightly drawn laws to penalize the wounding expressions of hate directed against racial groups.

A particularly controversial question, much debated in the last few years, has been whether Holocaust denial should be forbidden. It has been specifically prohibited in a number of European countries as well as in Israel.[94] A prosecution was brought in Canada in respect of publication of a pamphlet with the title, 'Did Six Million Really Die?', under a provision in the Criminal Code penalizing the publication of statements and news known to be false in circumstances likely to cause public mischief. By a 4–3 majority the Supreme Court allowed the defendant's appeal in the *Zundel* case, upholding his argument that the provision was too broad.[95] McLachlin J., this time giving the majority judgment, held the provision was not intended to combat hate propaganda and racism; but even if that was its objective, it was a disproportionate infringement of freedom of expression, allowing a jury to find guilty anyone who published material it found to be false and likely to cause mischief to a public interest.

On one view, there is little objection to the introduction of such a law. As the German Constitutional Court has held, the dissemination of false information, at least if its publisher knows that it is false or its falsity has been proved, cannot claim the coverage of freedom of expression.[96] Its distribution serves no underlying free speech value and may mislead or deceive the public. On the other hand, it may be sometimes be difficult to disentangle the making of a false historical claim, such as Holocaust denial, from controversial political arguments with which it may be associated and which are entitled to free speech protection, despite their unpalatable and distasteful character. More controversially, McLachlin J. in her judgment in *Zundel* argued that the exaggeration, even the clear falsification, of factual claims may serve the values of freedom of expression, because it can be used to make a case for social reform which should be debated.[97] This claim is not the same as Mill's argument that false opinions should be tolerated in order to compel the holders of true beliefs to defend them with greater vigour.[98] Mill might argue that Holocaust denial should be allowed in order to encourage serious historians to discredit its claims as bogus and so keep the horrors of these atrocities fully in mind.

There are other arguments against proscribing Holocaust denial.[99] The step might have the unfortunate effect of giving its proponents and their claims more publicity than they would otherwise enjoy. That danger would be more acute if

---

[94] For the law in France and Germany, see s. 4(ii) below.
[95] *R* v. *Zundel* [1992] 2 SCR 731.   [96] Auschwitz lie case, 90 BVerfGE 241 (1994).
[97] N. 95 above, 754, criticized by Moon, 48–9 as allowing abuse of the audience interest in accurate and honest communication.   [98] See ch I, s. 2(i).
[99] For discussion from a French law perspective, see L. Pech, *La Liberté d'Expression et sa Limitation* (Presses Universitaires de la Faculté de Clermont-Ferrand, 2003), paras. 685–91.

the defendant were able to dispute the Holocaust in court and the prosecution were required to establish that it occurred. If, however, judicial notice is taken of its occurrence, as is the position in European jurisdictions, and the defendant is precluded from challenging it, he can easily pose as a martyr to the cause of freedom of speech and argue that his trial was unfair. The Canadian Supreme Court took this point; McLachlin J. considered that Zundel's conviction was inevitable, given that he was not permitted to argue that he had been stating an opinion and was not communicating *false* news. There was therefore no trial in the usual sense. Another difficulty is defining the scope of the offence. Should it, for example, be confined to denial of the Holocaust or cover other atrocities which some respectable historians might regard as almost as appalling and as well-established, such as the atrocities in Stalinist Russia, Cambodia, and Rwanda, or the genocide of the Armenians?

It would, therefore, be wrong to introduce a specific offence of Holocaust denial into English law. It is better to rely on education and other measures, for instance, the institution of Holocaust Memorial Day, to deal with the risks created by the dissemination of these claims. An alternative course would be to apply the present incitement to racial hatred provisions, considered in the following paragraphs, to the publication of false claims about the Holocaust. The European Commission has held that Holocaust denial may be regarded as an insult to Jewish people and that the application of criminal laws on incitement to hatred may properly be applied to such publications.[100] This alternative has the advantage that it does not single out Holocaust denial for special treatment; hate speech or group libel laws can be applied to other bogus historical claims which cause psychological injury to particular target groups. But it would be wrong to use the racial hatred offence to penalize such claims, however disreputable they may be. It is strained to suggest that they insult the Jewish community (or other group). They are grossly offensive, but that is an inadequate justification for their proscription.

(ii) Hate speech laws

The modern British legislation in this area is generally defended now in terms of the hurt racist speech causes members of minority groups.[101] It filled a gap in the common law. There was admittedly some old authority that a scurrilous attack on a racial group could amount to ordinary criminal libel.[102] The orthodox definition of sedition certainly covered such writing, but in practice prosecutions for this offence were wholly unsuccessful.[103] In *Boucher* v. *R.*,[104] almost all the

---

[100] 9235/81, *X* v. *Germany* 29 D & R 194; 25096/94, *Remer* v. *Germany* 82 D & R 117.

[101] See Home Office, *Review of Public Order Act 1936 and Related Legislation* (Cmnd 7891, 1980), para. 107.　　　　　　　　　　　　　　　　　[102] *R* v. *Osborn* (1732) 2 Barn KB 166.

[103] See in particular *R* v. *Caunt* (1947), noted 64 *LQR* 203.　　　　[104] [1951] 2 DLR 369.

members of the Canadian Supreme Court took the view that it was necessary to show an intent to disturb constitutional authority. It was not enough to allege an incitement to class or group violence; not only was the common law of little use for securing convictions, it also inevitably lacked the declaratory effect of legislation designed to promote racial harmony.

This was the background to the enactment of section 6 of the British Race Relations Act 1965. The provision made it an offence to publish written matter or make a speech in public, which was threatening, abusive, or insulting, and likely to stir up racial hatred, if the defendant actually intended to cause such hatred. It is also important to see this legislation in the light of the Public Order Act 1936, which had been used to penalize racist speech in previous years, but which required a probable breach of the peace for a prosecution.[105] The new Act removed this requirement. Largely for this reason it was condemned by some Members of Parliament as an unwarrantable invasion of freedom of speech.[106] Prosecutions during the 1960s and 1970s were relatively rare. It is ironic that the legislation was often used to convict militant black spokesmen, and of course (as in some obscenity cases) prosecution secured greater publicity for the publication than it would otherwise have achieved.[107]

Largely because of Lord Scarman's critique of the provision in the 1965 Act in his report on the disorders in Red Lion Square,[108] it was amended by the Race Relations Act 1976. The incitement to hatred provision was incorporated in the public order legislation, now the Public Order Act 1986. Many Members of Parliament understandably thought this a more appropriate place for a criminal law rule than a statute concerned with improvements to race relations. But there is something bizarre about adding to public order legislation a provision, the terms of which have nothing whatsoever to do with a likely breach of the peace. The principal change made in 1976 was the abandonment of the requirement of intention to cause racial hatred; it is enough if, 'having regard to all the circumstances', hatred is likely to be stirred up against any racial group. Despite this amendment, it is doubtful whether the law covers the publication in a 'scientific' journal of an article suggesting that one racial group is inherently inferior in intelligence to another. An article of this character is certainly unpleasant and offensive, but it is unlikely that a court would find it amounts to 'abusive' or 'insulting' speech.[109] 'Racial hatred' refers only to hatred against groups in Britain 'defined by reference to colour, race, nationality... ethnic or national origins',[110] so the provision does not cover hate speech against religious groups and communities, or against people defined by reference to their sex or sexual orientation.

---

[105] See ch. VIII, s. 4(ii) below.
[106] e.g. see the speech of P. Thorneycroft, MP, 711 HC Deb. (5th ser.), cols. 934–6.
[107] P. M. Leopold, 'Incitement to Hatred: The History of a Controversial Criminal Offence' [1977] PL 389, 395–9.   [108] (Cmnd 5919, 1975), para. 125.
[109] In *R* v. *Hancock, The Times*, 29 Mar. 1969, the publishers of a magazine advocating white supremacy were acquitted.   [110] Public Order Act 1986, s. 17.

Arguably, the major weakness of the provision is its requirement that the speech or publication *stirs up hatred* against a target group. That may mean it would be difficult to prosecute successfully the dissemination of hate speech only to members of that group; a restricted publication would be unlikely to stir up hatred against them, although it might cause them considerable psychological distress.[111] In contrast, distribution of hate material among members of an extremist political party would certainly meet the requirement that publication stirs up hatred, although the distress caused to members of the target group would then be indirect. The point is that the offence is probably too narrowly drafted, if its object is to protect members of minority groups against savage hate speech occasioning severe emotional wounds and so infringing their dignity. It might be better if the law simply penalized the publication of hate speech, whether or not it was likely to cause an eruption of hatred against a particular group. Under section 18 of the Public Order Act 1986 it is now enough for the prosecution to show that the publisher used threatening, etc., words intending to stir up hatred, as an alternative to the requirement that, objectively, such hatred is a likely result of the publication. This welcome reform may reduce the difficulties discussed in this paragraph, but it still seems likely that in some circumstances the provision will fail to achieve its objective.

Suggestions have been made to widen the offence to cover any advocacy of discrimination against ethnic groups or of their compulsory repatriation. But the Home Office, in a Green Paper on the review of earlier public order legislation, doubted whether widening the offence in this way could be defended in principle: 'Such an extension of the offence would penalize the expression of opinion as such'.[112] Nor was the Home Affairs Select Committee of the House of Commons any more sympathetic to these proposals in a contemporary report.[113] Such caution is justified. The present British law rightly confines the proscription of hate speech to those cases where it is clear that its dissemination may produce, perhaps indirectly, significant psychological damage and the risk to free political speech is minimal. It would be wrong to extend it in the absence of powerful evidence that a wider ban is necessary.[114]

Interestingly, French law was amended at about the same time as the changes in Britain to give groups stronger protection against racist speech. An amendment in July 1972 to the Law of the Press of 1881 prohibits incitement to discrimination, hatred, or violence with regard to any person or group on account of race, nationality, or religion; it also makes group defamation on racial and religious grounds a specific crime.[115] Convictions have been secured under the latter provision for the

---

[111] In *R* v. *Read*, *The Times*, 7 Jan. 1978, the defendants successfully argued that hate speech using words such as 'niggers' and 'coons' was more likely to excite sympathy for the target group than stir up hatred.   [112] Home Office (n. 101 above), para. 111.

[113] 5th Report of Home Affairs Committee, 1979–80, HC 756, paras. 94–9.

[114] See s. 5(ii) below for extension to cover hatred against religious communities.

[115] Amendments to the Law of the Press of 29 July 1881, arts. 24 and 32, noted by J. Foulon-Piganiol, DS. 1972, Chron. 261.

publication of articles suggesting that France has been invaded by immigrants who came only to claim social security benefits or that their presence has created insuperable social and economic problems.[116] The courts emphasized that the publications in these cases tended to incite hatred against immigrant communities, and that their problems should be discussed objectively, rather than emotively. This approach shows that in practice the French law in this area is more restrictive of free speech than the comparable provisions in Britain.

In 1990 French law was further tightened by a specific provision making it an offence to question whether the crimes against humanity, as defined by the London Agreement of 1945 setting up the Nuremberg War Crimes Tribunal, were really committed—in effect, penalizing Holocaust denial.[117] (It is doubtful whether it was necessary to enact this provision, as revisionist historians had been successfully prosecuted for the offence of group defamation under Article 32 of the Law of the Press.[118]) The most prominent revisionist, Robert Faurisson, has been convicted of the new offence; his argument that the proscription of Holocaust denial is contrary to freedom of expression has been rejected by both the French courts and the United Nations Human Rights Committee.[119] The European Human Rights Commission has held compatible with the ECHR the conviction of a publicist who denied the scale of the Holocaust, holding the French court was entitled not to allow him to contradict historical truth (*une vérité historique notoire*).[120]

There are powerful constitutional and historical explanations for the restrictions imposed by German law on freedom of speech in this area. Section 130 of the Penal Code makes it an offence to incite hatred or provoke violence against groups in the population or against national, racial, religious, or other communities. The criminal law, therefore, not only protects racial and ethnic minorities against offence but also covers religious communities, members of political parties, and cultural associations. There are also a number of provisions penalizing insults and defamation. But two particular provisions have been introduced to give further protection to the Jewish community and other victims of Nazi persecution. In 1985 the Code was amended so that a state prosecution could be brought for *Beleidigung* (insult) without an individual's petition, where the victim of the insult was a member of a group persecuted under the National Socialist regime or other totalitarian systems.[121] Secondly, it is now, as in France, a specific offence to justify, deny, or play down genocide committed under the

---

116 DS 1975. J. 468, Cour d'Appel, Paris, 11th chamber; DS 1975. J. 489, TGI, Grenoble.
117 Law of the Press of 29 July 1881, art. 24 bis.
118 See *Faurisson*, Cour de Cassation (ch. criminelle), 28 June 1983.
119 *Faurisson* v. *France* 2 BHRR 1 (UN HRC).
120 31159/96, *Marais* v. *France* 86 D & R 184.
121 Penal Code, s. 194. For discussion, see E. Stein, 'History against Free Speech: The New German Law against the "Auschwitz"—and Other—Lies' (1986) 85 *Michigan Law Rev* 277, pointing out that the amendment also benefited the members of groups persecuted by other totalitarian regimes, e.g. refugees from the USSR.

Nazi regime.[122] In 1996, two years after its introduction, there were apparently ten convictions for the offence.[123]

Two major rulings of the Constitutional Court in Germany have clarified the standing of these provisions with regard to the freedom of expression guaranteed by the Basic Law. In the first, it upheld the constitutionality of conditions attached to a permit to hold a public meeting, which required its convenors to prevent speeches which denied or doubted the Holocaust.[124] If treated as factual statements, Holocaust denial would not be protected by Article 5, since that provision does not cover claims of fact which are known or proved to be false. Equally, if such claims were treated as background to, or entangled with, controversial statements of opinion, limits could be imposed on their dissemination by general laws, in this case the provisions of the Penal Code prohibiting hate speech and insult. The Jewish community could claim the protection of these provisions. Moreover, the ordinary courts had been entitled to treat Holocaust denial as an insult to the constitutional right of the modern Jewish community to the development of its personality, ultimately rooted in the fundamental right to human dignity guaranteed by Article 1 of the Basic Law. In this context it was constitutionally legitimate to give preference to protection of the latter rights over the protection of freedom of speech. The Court was not troubled by the argument that the claims would inevitably be linked to a discussion of recent German history; the general presumption in favour of free political speech did not apply to insults or to claims which are proved to be false.

The second case led to one of the most controversial decisions of the Karlsruhe Court.[125] It upheld a number of challenges to rulings of the ordinary courts which had convicted defendants of criminal insult under section 185 of the Criminal Code for disseminating, in various forms, the statements, 'Soldaten sind Mörder' or 'potentielle Mörder' ('Soldiers are murderers' or 'potential murderers'). Although this provision could constitutionally be applied in some circumstances to protect the honour and reputation of authorities, institutions, and groups, as well as of individuals, it should not be interpreted to chill effective freedom of political speech. This freedom was of particular importance in the context of criticism of government and control of the abuse of power.[126] It was also important for the courts not to place on a publication, against which a prosecution had been brought, a meaning which would inevitably lead to a conviction, when it might be possible to ascribe to it another more innocuous meaning.

The lower courts had failed to observe these requirements. The statements did not clearly allege that any particular soldier or group of soldiers had committed a murder; rather, they could be interpreted as a general critique of the military role. The Constitutional Court did not think it was necessary, as a matter of constitutional

---

[122] Penal Code, s. 130(3).
[123] See the evidence of Georg Nolte to the Institute for Jewish Policy Research Law Panel (2000), 15.
[124] Auschwitz lie case, 90 BVerfGE 241 (1994).
[125] 'Soldiers are murderers', 93 BVerfGE 266 (1995).   [126] Ibid., 292–5.

law, to interpret the Criminal Code only to cover an insult to a member of a group when he was expressly or implicitly identified by the publication, as in the English civil law of libel. Nevertheless it was important to apply it only to cover publications really infringing the personal honour of individuals. In that context the Court adopted the approach of the Bundesgerichtshof (Federal Supreme Court, the highest court for civil cases), which had imposed two limits on the scope of the offence of group insult. In the first place, the publication must refer to a feature which applies to all members of the group, not just some of its members. Secondly, a prosecution could not be brought for derogatory remarks about a large general group, for example, all Catholics or Protestants, or all women.[127] The Court also referred to its own previous decisions on *Schmahkritik* (abusive remarks) which had been developed in the context of private libel actions.[128] In those cases, freedom of speech gives way to the protection of personal reputation and honour, but it would be inappropriate to apply this general principle to remarks about groups of people, identified by reference to their particular social functions. In those circumstances the remarks are directed not against the character of the individuals who comprise that group, but against its distinctive activity. Finally, the Court rejected the argument that soldiers were entitled to a special degree of protection in view of their duties of obedience.

There have been a few challenges to the compatibility of hate speech and group libel laws with the European Convention. In *Glimmerveen* v. *Netherlands*,[129] the applicants, extremist right-wing politicians, complained that their conviction for possessing racist leaflets violated Article 10 of the Convention. The Commission invoked Article 17 in holding the application inadmissible; this provision states that the Convention should not be interpreted to confer any right to engage in any activity or do anything 'aimed at the destruction of any of the rights and freedoms...' provided in it. It was held to be an abuse of rights to advocate racial discrimination and the repatriation of non-whites from Holland. (Those policies would contravene Article 14 of the Convention, which proscribes the discriminatory treatment of people with regard to their enjoyment of other Convention rights.) Group libel laws have also been defended under Article 10(2) itself, on the ground that they are necessary to prevent disorder or crime, and to protect the reputation or rights of the minority groups concerned. In a case from Germany the Commission upheld the use of defamation laws to prohibit the display of literature denying the historical facts about the Holocaust; the racist pamphlets could properly be regarded as a defamatory attack on each individual member of the Jewish community.[130]

In two cases the European Court itself has indicated that hate speech and Holocaust denial laws are in principle compatible with the Convention,

---

[127] 'Soldiers are murderers', 93 BVerfGE 266, 300–1 (1995).

[128] For discussion of these cases, see ch. VI, s. 3(iii) below.

[129] 8348/78, 18 D & R 187. Also see 25096/94, *Remer* v. *Germany* 82 D & R 117, and 31159/96, *Marais* v. *France* 86 D & R 184.   [130] 9235/81, *X* v. *Germany* 29 D & R 194.

although on the facts it held in both cases that the particular application of these laws infringed freedom of expression. In *Jersild* v. *Denmark*[131] it held that the conviction of a journalist for aiding the spread of racist speech infringed Article 10. The journalist had conducted a television interview with members of an extremist youth group, in the course of which members had made a number of clearly racist remarks. The Court made it clear that the remarks themselves were insulting to members of the targeted groups (blacks and immigrants) and were not protected under Article 10. In the light of its obligations to implement the 1965 International Convention on the Elimination of all Forms of Racial Discrimination,[132] it was legitimate for Denmark to enact legislation proscribing hate speech. But it was wrong to apply the legislation to the journalist who was merely discharging his duty to assist the discussion of matters of public interest. More recently, the Court has said that the proscription of Holocaust denial or any defence of the Nazi atrocities is compatible with the Convention. But it was a violation of the guarantee of freedom of expression to convict a defendant, who had published an advertisement in *Le Monde* in defence of the memory of Marshal Pétain, of an offence of justifying the crime of collaboration with the enemy.[133]

The usual approach of courts and commentators in the United States now affords a strong contrast with the sympathetic treatment of hate speech laws in European jurisdictions, including in this context Britain. The general view is that these laws would, and should, be struck down as incompatible with the First Amendment. However unpleasant and offensive the contents of racist speech, it forms part of political speech or, to use the term of a prominent First Amendment theorist, 'public discourse'.[134] Outside certain contexts such as schools, the workplace, and perhaps universities, the proscription of hate speech on the grounds that it harms groups or individuals or that it corrupts the marketplace of ideas cannot be reconciled with the commitment of the US Constitution to an active democracy serving the value of self-determination. That commitment 'requires that public discourse be open to the opinions of all.'[135] In principle, only hate speech which falls within the narrow category of 'fighting words'—an insult addressed face to face with a member of the target group—may fall outside the scope of the First Amendment.[136] (A state may of course restrict the dissemination of such speech under the *Brandenburg* principle, when it incites immediate and likely lawless action.[137]) Some commentators defend narrowly drawn hate speech laws, largely on the ground that racist attacks infringe the equality and free speech rights of historically disadvantaged

---

[131] (1995) 19 EHRR 1.

[132] Article 4 requires states to declare an offence all dissemination of ideas of racial superiority or hatred.   [133] *Lehideux & Isorni* v. *France* (2000) 30 EHRR 365.

[134] R. C. Post, 'Racist Speech, Democracy, and the First Amendment' (1991) 32 *William and Mary Law* Rev 267.   [135] Ibid., 314.

[136] See *Chaplinsky* v. *New Hampshire* 315 US 568 (1942).   [137] See s. 3 above.

minorities.[138] But this is a minority position and does not receive much support from recent court rulings.

The legal position is in fact complicated by the continued, if shadowy, existence of the decision of the Supreme Court in *Beauharnais* v. *Illinois*.[139] In that case a bare majority of the Court upheld a group libel statute under which the president of a Chicago-based organization had been convicted. He had called for a halt to 'the further encroachment, harassment and invasion of white people, their property, neighbourhoods and persons by the Negro'. Frankfurter J. pointed out, correctly at that time, that ordinary libel laws were not subject to review under the First Amendment. Since an individual's dignity and reputation are associated with that of the group to which he belonged, there was no justification for treating group libel laws differently from the rules of private libel. Although he went on to justify the law in terms of its long-term contribution to the preservation of peace, there is no real suggestion that the statute was upheld on public order grounds; the clear and present danger test was not applied.

The authority of *Beauharnais* has been significantly weakened, now that the Court has held private libel to be covered by the free speech clause. It has been doubted and distinguished in many recent cases.[140] The most important of these is the decision of the Court of Appeals for the Seventh Circuit in *Collin* v. *Smith*[141] where it was ruled that an ordinance prohibiting the dissemination of material, which promoted racial or religious hatred, was unconstitutional. *Beauharnais* was regarded as implicitly overruled by the Supreme Court's decisions on private libel; if not, it was to be explained as turning on public order grounds. The ordinance would have been applied to the march of a Nazi organization through a suburb with a large Jewish population to prevent the infliction of psychological trauma on the residents who included some survivors of the Holocaust. The court ruled it was unconstitutional to prohibit the expression of ideas on the ground of their offensiveness to this community. In effect, a law remarkably similar to the British provisions on incitement to racial hatred was struck down. With two dissenters, the Supreme Court refused *certiorari*,[142] and thus the apparent incompatibility between *Collin* and its own earlier decision remains unresolved.[143]

Although *Beauharnais* has never been overruled, it is unlikely that the Supreme Court would now uphold a group libel law, or even a narrowly drawn hate speech statute protecting vulnerable groups from extremist speech. Its hostility to regulation

---

[138] Matsuda (n. 89 above); R. Delgado and J. Stefancic, *Must We Defend Nazis? Hate Speech, Pornography and the New First Amendment* (New York: New York UP, 1997). For a balanced treatment of hate speech laws in relation to US free speech doctrine, see Weinstein (n. 84 above), esp. chs. 8–10.   [139] 343 US 256 (1952).

[140] *Anti-Defamation League of B'nai B'rith* v. *FCC* 403 F 2d 169, 174 (DC Cir, 1968); *Tollett* v. *US* 485 F 2d 1087 (8th Cir, 1973).

[141] 578 F2d 1197 (1978), affirming the District Court, 447 F Supp 676 (1978).

[142] 439 US 916 (1978).

[143] For a defence of this decision in terms of the value of tolerance, see L. C. Bollinger, *The Tolerant Society: Freedom of Speech and Extremist Speech in America* (New York: OUP, 1986).

in this area was strikingly shown in its well-known ruling in *RAV* v. *St Paul*.[144] The city of St Paul prosecuted the petitioner for infringement of an ordinance making it an offence to place on public or private property any object (including, but not limited to, a burning cross or Nazi swastika) which the accused knew, or had reason to know, arouses anger or alarm 'on the basis of race, colour, creed, religion or gender...'. The petitioner had burned a cross in the backyard of a black family, so he had clearly committed the offence. The Supreme Court held the ordinance was wholly unconstitutional, since in its terms it prohibited speech solely on the basis of its subject matter. It did not cover similar expressive conduct targeting, say, homosexuals or members of a particular political party or trade union. What is startling about this decision is that the Court accepted that the ordinance only covered 'fighting words', that is speech which by its nature was calculated to cause a breach of the peace or injure its addressees.[145] Hitherto, such speech has been treated as falling outside the scope of the First Amendment. But Scalia J., for five members of the Court, held that it was unconstitutional for the law to discriminate on the basis of the particular contents or viewpoint of the 'fighting words', so that, as in this case, the expression of some was forbidden, but not that of others. In short, the Court allowed its hostility to content-based restrictions on speech to prevail over a line of authority which had held that a limited category of aggressive speech, akin to the infliction of verbal injury, was not really 'speech' for the purposes of the First Amendment.

It is hard not to prefer the approach of White J., with whom three other members of the Court concurred. In his view, a state or city is free to ban particular types of 'fighting words' if there is a rational basis for its conclusion that particular hate speech, for example, that relating to target groups identified by their colour or race, created an exceptionally pressing social problem. (He concurred with the decision of the Court, but on the different ground that the ordinance was in fact not confined to 'fighting words'; in his view, it was capable of covering expressive conduct causing no more than offence.) The majority judgment of Scalia J. is best understood as the high-water mark of judicial distrust in the United States of any attempt by government to draw distinctions between types of speech. However, a majority of the Court has recently upheld the constitutionality of a Virginia statute which made it an offence to burn a cross on another's property or on a public place with the intent of intimidating any person or group.[146] For the Court, O'Connor J. held that the state was entitled to ban this type of threatening message, in light of the pernicious history of cross-burning associated with the Ku Klux Klan. Unlike the ordinance at issue in *RAV* v. *St Paul*, the Virginia law did not discriminate between speech on the basis of its content or topic, but singled out a particular form of expressive conduct because of its intimidating character.

---

[144] 505 US 377 (1992).
[145] *Chaplinsky* v. *New Hampshire* 315 US 568 (1942), discussed in ch. VIII, s. 4(ii) below.
[146] *Virginia* v. *Black et al* 155 L Ed 2d 535 (2003).

The decision perhaps leaves open the door to the approval of tightly drawn statutes criminalizing hate speech identified by reference to its threatening character; they may survive First Amendment scrutiny, provided they do not appear to distinguish between, say, racist and other types of hate speech.

5. Blasphemy and Incitement to Religious Hatred

(i) The common law of blasphemy

The common law offence of blasphemy, or in its written form blasphemous libel, goes back to the seventeenth century.[147] In the following two hundred years it was relatively common to prosecute freethinkers and atheists, and even liberal clergymen,[148] who denied in intemperate terms the fundamental tenets of the Christian religion. However, the publication of such material arouses much less controversy in an increasingly secular and tolerant society. There were no prosecutions from 1922 until 1977, so it became possible during that period to consider the offence obsolete. The case of *R v. Lemon* which reached the House of Lords in 1979 showed that this was far from the case.[149] The House upheld the conviction of the editor and publisher of *Gay News* for printing a poem depicting explicit homosexual acts with Christ's body after his death. Although the decision was probably justifiable in terms of the common law precedents, it raised some fundamental questions, in particular, what was the basis or rationale for the offence and whether its existence was compatible with freedom of expression.

The reaction of Muslims in England (and in other countries) to Salman Rushdie's novel, *The Satanic Verses*, which, they alleged, contains several passages blasphemous of God and grossly insulting of the prophet Muhammad, has further sharpened controversy concerning the scope of blasphemy. The common law offence only protects the Christian religion. Indeed, some formulations suggest it would not cover attacks on distinctive doctrines of the Roman Catholic, Orthodox, or Free Churches. The famous judgment of Hale CJ in *Taylor*[150] indicated that the Christian faith is protected against abuse, because it is closely connected with the government of the country, so that only the established Church of England and its formularies are covered. At any rate, a private prosecution against Rushdie and his publisher failed.[151] The Divisional Court held that the common law offence did not extend to religions other than Christianity, and also that there were insuperable problems to widening it to cover them. The result is that the law discriminates in its treatment of different religious communities, offering protection to members of the traditional majority faith, but none to

---

[147] *R v. Taylor* (1676) 1 Vent 293, 86 ER 189.
[148] See *R v. Woolston* (1728) 1 Barnard 162, 94 ER 112.   [149] [1979] AC 617.
[150] N. 147 above.
[151] *R v. Chief Metropolitan Stipendiary Magistrate, ex p Choudhury* [1991] 1 QB 429, DC.

Muslims, Hindus, and Buddhists. The Jewish and Sikh religions are not as such covered by the law of blasphemy, but members of their communities may be protected against scurrilous attacks by the law prohibiting incitement to racial hatred.

It is not, of course, now blasphemous simply to deny God or to repudiate aspects of the Christian faith or teaching.[152] What matters is the manner in which criticism is expressed. A jury may convict 'if the tone and spirit is that of offence and insult, and ridicule, which leaves the judgment not really free to act...'.[153] Rational discussion of religious matters should be free, but not insults which, it was implied, cannot provoke a reasoned response and so contribute nothing to worthwhile debate. It is very difficult to defend this distinction. It runs counter to the refusal of courts now to draw any lines between rational and emotive discourse, or between more and less valuable speech, in freedom of expression cases. Another difficulty from the perspective of freedom of speech is that it is unnecessary for the prosecution to prove that the publisher intended to shock and outrage the feelings of Christians. The House of Lords in *Lemon* held, by a majority of 3–2, that it was enough to show that he intended to publish material objectively found to be blasphemous. It was irrelevant that he may have published the material, genuinely believing that it would, say, provoke Christian believers into fresh insights into their faith.

What is now the most plausible justification, if one exists, for the common law offence? The answer to that question has repercussions both for its scope and for resolving its compatibility with freedom of expression. As with incitement to racial hatred, there is no need for the prosecution to prove that the publication of a blasphemous libel was intended to, or likely to, lead to a breach of the peace. That was made clear in judgments in the Court of Appeal and in the House of Lords in *Lemon*. It can be regarded as a public order offence, only in the sense that, as Lord Scarman said, it may be said to promote tranquillity and harmonious relations between different communities.[154] Nor is it possible now to justify its continued existence as necessary for the protection of the Christian religion as a branch of the constitutional order. Although the Church of England is established, there is no greater justification for protecting it from scurrilous criticism than there is the government or, say, the House of Lords. A much better argument is that society is entitled to, or perhaps even should, protect a sense of the sacred. Something valuable is lost if there are no restrictions at all on what can be said or written about God or religious belief.[155] This view is of course contestable. Many people, perhaps now the majority in England, live by secular values, and may

---

[152] *R v. Ramsay & Foote* (1883) 15 Cox CC 231, 236 per Lord Coleridge CJ.

[153] See the direction of Lord Denman CJ to the jury in *R v. Hetherington* (1840) 4 St Tr NS 563, 590–1.   [154] [1979] AC 617, 658.

[155] Report to the Archbishop of Canterbury of the Bishop of London's Working Group on Offences against Religion and Public Worship (1987), para. 45; Law Commission Report No. 145, *Offences against Religion and Public Worship* (1985), para. 2.12.

prefer that the law makes no attempt to protect what they regard as private, rather than shared, values. But even if this rationale for blasphemy law is accepted, it is hard to see why the law should only protect the Christian perspective of the sacred.

However, the usual rationale for the common law offence is that it is right for the law to protect Christians against the shock and outrage to their feelings provoked by the publication of blasphemous material. This explanation was accepted by the House of Lords in the *Lemon* case, and enjoys wide support.[156] But if this is right, it is hard not to agree with Lord Scarman's criticism of blasphemy 'which is not that it exists but that it is not sufficiently comprehensive.'[157] His point is that in a plural society the law should protect the religious feelings of all citizens against outrage, irrespective of their particular faith. Moreover, the emphasis on the victim group's feelings may explain why the House of Lords was unconcerned with the intention of the writer and publisher of the poem in the *Lemon* case. Writers, it seems, should be sensitive to the sensitivities of religious believers and avoid language which is deeply wounding.

Lord Scarman's argument persuaded two members of the Law Commission to dissent from the view of the other three that the offence of blasphemy should be abolished without any replacement.[158] The dissenters concluded that it was proper for the criminal law to protect religious feelings against outrage, arguing that even non-believers would accept it was right for the state to take that step. They were not persuaded by the majority's objections that it would be difficult to define concepts such as 'religion' or 'matters relating to religion' for the purpose of a broad offence, which would not be confined to the protection of Christianity. The proposals in this Note of Dissent could be implemented by extending the scope of the 'incitement to racial hatred' provisions in the Public Order Act 1986 to cover hatred against groups of persons by reference to religious belief. This is the position in Northern Ireland, where there have been good reasons to make clear society's disapproval of religious hatred.[159] Until recently the Westminster government has been reluctant to take this step for England. A clause to extend the coverage of the incitement offence to religious groups in the Anti-terrorism, Crime and Security Bill 2001 was withdrawn when the House of Lords defeated it, with the argument that it was an unacceptable restraint on free speech. The government has now introduced provisions proscribing incitement to religious hatred against any group defined by reference to religious belief or lack of it.[160]

---

[156] Law Commission Report No. 145, *Offences against Religion and Public Worship* (1985), para. 2.13.   [157] [1979] AC 617, 658.

[158] Note of Dissent to Law Commission Report No. 145.

[159] Northern Ireland (Public Order) Order 1987, art. 9 is broader than the Public Order Act also in that it is an offence to arouse fear, as well as stir up hatred.

[160] Serious Organised Crime and Police Bill 2004, Sch. 10.

(ii) Religious hatred laws and freedom of speech

The ridicule of religious belief or believers is not political speech in the narrow sense, but is part of public discourse, that is speech concerning the organization and culture of society. Public discourse includes discussion of religious questions, whether or not they are matters of dispute between political parties. Blasphemy has indeed often been an element in the protest of radicals and dissenters against the domination of ecclesiastical authorities. It may offer challenging, even disturbing, religious insights. For example, the poem at issue in *Lemon*, presenting the homosexual fantasies of a witness to the crucifixion, intimated that these erotic feelings were valuable to God. The same points may be made in the context of proposals to extend racist hate speech laws to protect religious beliefs and communities. Even the institution of a narrowly drawn incitement to religious hatred offence risks the prosecution and conviction of a writer such as Salman Rushdie. His novel, *The Satanic Verses*, is an imaginative and provocative work of literature, although in the view of many Muslims it amounted to an indecent attack on God and their most fundamental beliefs. It will not do to argue at this point that it is highly unlikely that a court would convict the writer of such a book because it would almost certainly take the view that, although offensive to Muslims, the novel would not stir up hatred against them. For there is a substantial risk that some writers and publishers may be deterred from circulating literary work for fear of prosecution. This risk would be greater if the offence were defined, as the Law Commission dissenters proposed, in terms of the publication of grossly abusive or insulting material relating to religion with intent to outrage religious feelings.

Robert Post has argued that the law of blasphemy in England has traditionally represented the dominance of the cultural perspectives of the Christian majority, while Lord Scarman's judgment in *Lemon* in its support for the protection of all religious groups adopted a pluralist approach.[161] In contrast, United States courts protect the rights of the individual speaker against the interest of churches and other religious groups not to be shocked or offended. Post refers to the decision in *Cantwell* v. *Connecticut*,[162] as an example of a preference for individual against group rights. The Supreme Court held incompatible with the First Amendment guarantees of freedom of speech and free exercise of religion the conviction of Jehovah's Witnesses for disturbing the peace. They had played phonograph records attacking the Roman Catholic Church in offensive terms on a Catholic street. Roberts J. for the Court made it plain that anyone who made indecent or abusive remarks directed to the audience could be convicted of the offence, but in this case there was no threat of violence or personal abuse directed against any individuals. Exaggeration, even vilification, must be tolerated in disputes

---

[161] R. C. Post, 'Cultural Heterogeneity and Law: Pornography, Blasphemy, and the First Amendment' (1988) 76 *California Law Rev* 297. [162] 310 US 296 (1940).

concerning religious faith, as much as in political argument.[163] There is little doubt, therefore, that the common law offence of blasphemy or any broader variant of it, as suggested by Lord Scarman, would be unconstitutional in the United States. Post reports that a number of prosecutions were withdrawn following the decision of a Maryland court in 1970 that the state blasphemy statute infringed the First Amendment guarantee of freedom of religion.[164]

However, it is legitimate to ask whether free speech compels protection for rights of the individual speaker over the group rights of the audience and others insulted by material which ridicules religious belief or believers. If, as was argued in section 4 above, it is reasonable to proscribe publication of material likely to stir up racial hatred, perhaps a strong case may be made to support the extension of that offence to cover incitement to religious hatred. The argument is that an insulting attack on religious belief or, even more clearly, the expression of hatred of religious communities, causes as deep a psychological injury as racist hate speech. Of course, it can be argued that religious belief is a matter of personal choice, while racial (and sexual) identity are immutable characteristics. But that is not entirely convincing. First, it is doubtful whether religious conviction is entirely a matter of personal choice; our religious beliefs are a complex mixture of inherited cultural assumptions and attitudes and individual commitment (or lack of it). But more importantly, the distinction between immutable and chosen characteristics has nothing to do with the extent of the trauma that an attack on those characteristics may occasion. White English Catholics are more likely to experience vicious denigration of their religious convictions as insulting than they are hate speech about their colour.

There are, however, reasons for considering the case for intervention much weaker than it is in the context of racist hate speech. A key point is that there is no common standard of what constitutes hate speech in this context. Some religious communities may feel insulted by speech which would *mutatis mutandis* provoke only indifference in others.[165] It is hard to imagine, for example, that Christians now in England, France, or even the United States, would react to publication of an abusive or satirical book about Jesus Christ and his family in the same way as many Muslims did to Rushdie's novel.[166] Indeed, one noted theologian argues that it is wrong for Christians to take offence when their faith is abused, and that the law should play no part in compelling respect for what should be a matter of personal commitment.[167] It would be difficult for a legal system to accommodate

---

[163] 310 US 296, 307 (1940).

[164] Post (n. 161 above), 316–17, discussing *State* v. *West* 262 A 2d 602 (1970).

[165] C. Unsworth, 'Blasphemy, Cultural Divergence and Legal Relativism' (1995) 58 *MLR* 658, 676–7.

[166] The release of the film of *The Last Temptation of Christ*, and its subsequent showing on television, produced a number of complaints, but did not lead to any prosecution.

[167] K. Ward in *Law, Blasphemy and the Multi-Faith Society* (report of seminar held by CRE and Inter Faith Network of the UK, 1989), 34–6.

the different standards of tolerance allowed, or insult felt, by various religious communities when exposed to vituperative attacks on their faith. Certainly, a law which enabled a prosecution to be brought for blasphemy, extended along the lines proposed by Lord Scarman in *Lemon*, whenever any religious community felt grossly outraged by a publication would seriously infringe freedom of speech. This point explains the preference in the United States for the right of the individual speaker over those of the group claiming to be outraged by religiously provocative speech. While a speaker's right to say what he wants is clearly infringed by blasphemy laws, in the absence of general community standards the injury felt by members of the religious group on experiencing a scurrilous attack will be a matter of conjecture. As Post argues, freedom of religious speech can only be constitutionally curtailed if the particular speech incites violence or amounts to abuse of the person to whom it is directed; in those circumstances there would be widespread agreement that general community norms of civil discourse have been infringed.[168] These arguments also apply to a narrowly drawn hate speech law: it would be very difficult to determine when material would be regarded as 'insulting' or likely 'to stir up religious hatred'.

A second difficulty concerns which groups should be protected by religious hatred laws: should they protect, say, Mormons and Scientologists, as well as the principal religious faiths? The proposals introduced by the government in 2004 would protect, in addition to religious communities, groups defined by reference to lack of religious belief, perhaps a local Humanist Association. But if those groups are covered, it is hard to see why protection should not be extended to other groups with equally strong convictions, such as animal rights protesters. These developments would have serious repercussions for free speech.

In short, it would be misguided for Britain to extend its blasphemy law, or even to introduce an offence of incitement to religious hatred, until a better argument for the step can be found than the well-rehearsed case that such speech wounds members of religious communities and is likely to stir up hatred against them. There are no commonly accepted standards for what amounts to hate speech in this context, so the application of any law would inevitably be uncertain. There is a risk that courts would simply accept the subjective claims of outrage or hurt made by particular religious communities. The result would be the proscription of speech which other groups would cheerfully tolerate or find only mildly offensive when comparable remarks were made about them. It is this point which distinguishes religious from racial hate speech. There is a general, albeit not universal, agreement that racist hate speech may cause serious psychological trauma, injury, and fear among members of the target group. Moreover, the general standards of tolerance and outrage do not vary much from one racial group to another. While it is true that members of historically disadvantaged groups are more likely than members of the white majority to experience hate speech as psychologically

---

[168] Post (n. 161 above), 322–3.

damaging, many people in all communities would find extremist speech directed at their race intimidating. That is not the case in most liberal societies with regard to speech concerning religious belief or identity.

However, the European Court of Human Rights has accepted that a law penalizing or preventing the distribution of religiously provocative films may amount to a necessary restriction on the exercise of the right to freedom of expression. In *Otto-Preminger-Institut* v. *Austria*[169] it upheld the seizure and forfeiture of a cinema film which disparaged Christ, the Virgin Mary, and the Eucharist. In the Court's view these could be regarded as necessary measures to protect the rights of citizens not to be insulted in their religious feelings, so falling within the aims for which restraints on freedom of expression may be imposed under Article 10(2) of the ECHR. Even more controversially, the Court suggested that a public showing of the film would violate the right of believers to have their feelings respected, as guaranteed by Article 9.[170] Similarly, in the *Wingrove* case,[171] it upheld as a necessary restriction on the exercise of freedom of expression the decision of the British Board of Film Classification not to allow the release of a short video portraying graphically the sexual fantasies of St Teresa of Avila. Although their action amounted to a clear prior restraint,[172] the authorities were entitled to prevent what they considered would be a blasphemous insult to the religious feelings of the public. The Court considered it irrelevant that the blasphemy laws did not protect religious communities other than Christians.[173]

These decisions are poorly reasoned. The proposition that citizens have a right not to be insulted in their religious feelings was made without argument. It fits badly with the oft-repeated statement of the Court that freedom of expression includes a right to express ideas which shock and disturb, as well as those which are widely acceptable. The judgments can be read as allowing states to prohibit speech merely on the ground of its offensiveness. There may be good arguments to justify regulation of speech insulting to religious believers, but the Court has not found them; it is very doubtful whether they exist.

6. Disclosure of Official Secrets

(i) General principles

The enforcement of official secrecy laws frequently gives rise to great controversy. This is particularly the case when prosecutions are brought against civil servants

---

[169] (1994) 19 EHRR 34.   [170] Ibid., para. 47.
[171] *Wingrove* v. *UK* (1997) 24 EHRR 1: also see ch. IV, s. 2 above.
[172] See ch. IV, s. 2 above.
[173] In 8710/79, *Gay News* v. *UK* (1983) 5 EHRR 123, the European Human Rights Commission held inadmissible a challenge to the application of the blasphemy law in *Lemon*, brought on the ground that the offence only covered Christians. It was held that freedom of religion did not confer a right to equal protection under the criminal law.

for providing the media with information, the publication of which may embarrass the government, but is unlikely to prejudice national security or other important public interest. Criticism of these prosecutions, or of the use by government of civil actions to restrain a breach of confidence, has frequently been linked with calls for the introduction of freedom of information legislation, granting the public rights of access to official information. The relationship of such rights to freedom of speech is discussed elsewhere in this book;[174] here we are concerned with the implications of the free speech principle, and in particular the protection of political speech, for criminal laws penalizing the communication (and receipt) of government information. The use of injunctions to restrain disclosure under confidentiality rules has been discussed in Chapter IV, as they amount to prior restraints on speech.[175]

One obvious difference between the communication of official secrets and the publication of the political speech considered in the previous sections of this chapter is that the former is concerned with the disclosure of information rather than the assertion of opinion. Admittedly, the distinction between these two categories of speech should not be exaggerated. The communication of information or news is often accompanied by opinion regarding its interpretation, and it may be hard to distinguish them in practice.[176] Political speech advocating violent opposition to government or hostility to racial and ethnic groups may contain claims of fact. But it remains the case that the disclosures considered in this section are restricted because they reveal *information* which the government wishes to keep secret. Suppression is justified in the cause of national security or some other public interest, these arguments often being supported by an assertion of the government's property rights over its own documents and records. It may, therefore, seem difficult to apply Mill's truth argument for freedom of speech to justify a freedom to disclose government information. Disclosure is not forbidden because the state considers the information false or misleading. Indeed, it is standard practice for government to refuse to say whether the allegations made by a civil servant concerning, say, secret service activities are true or false. Many people, probably correctly, accept that leaks by civil servants and secret service agents are generally accurate; government would surely not be anxious to penalize the disclosure of official information if it considered that almost everyone would dismiss it as a fabrication.

A free speech right to disclose official secrets is equally hard to justify on the basis that its exercise is essential to individual self-development or personal dignity and autonomy. This point is associated with another feature of free speech claims in this context: they are generally made on behalf of the recipient of the disclosure or of

---

[174] See ch. III, s. 7 above.   [175] Ch. IV, s. 3 above.

[176] In the contexts of group and private libel the German Constitutional Court has often drawn a distinction between the expression of opinion and factual claims (see s. 4 of this chapter and ch. VI, s. 3(iii) below). But in other circumstances it has refused to accept a sharp distinction between them: see the First Television case, 12 BVerfGE 205, 260 (1961).

the general public, rather than for the speaker.[177] The German Constitutional Court made this point in a case where it upheld the constitutionality of a provision penalizing the disclosure of confidential matters to foreign secret services. In these circumstances, the communicator could hardly assert an individual free speech right derived from a fundamental freedom of self-development.[178] Nor is it easy for civil servants to claim that they have a right, as speakers, to leak confidential information to the press. On the other hand, members of the public clearly have a real interest in receiving as much information as possible to enable them to contribute effectively to political debate. The argument from democracy provides much the strongest support for extending the application of the free speech principle to these cases.

These theoretical points shed some light on the case law. They explain why the First Amendment (and other comparable constitutional provisions) are not engaged when a challenge is made to the validity of espionage laws and other measures prohibiting communication with foreign powers.[179] Disclosures to enemy agents, or to a small group of political associates, are not made as contributions to political discussion. Neither speaker nor recipient has any real free speech interest in these circumstances. Private disclosures and conversations of this sort are not 'speech' for constitutional purposes, so there is no need for the court even to ask itself whether there is any state interest justifying espionage laws. On the other hand, a public disclosure by a politician of confidential government information, or publication of such information by the media, are covered by free speech and press clauses. Both speaker and the general public have a genuine free speech interest in the communication and receipt of information, wide awareness of which may well sharpen political debate. (It does not follow that the particular publication will be protected, where some competing public interest is strong enough to justify restrictions on disclosure.[180])

The position of civil servants, and *a fortiori* secret service agents, is different from that of politicians, since it is hardly part of their role to stimulate public discussion, nor generally do they have authority to disclose information which the government wishes to keep confidential. So it is a difficult question whether a communication by a civil servant to members of the public or a newspaper should be regarded as 'speech' for constitutional purposes. As we have seen, it can hardly be so regarded if it is considered crucial that speakers have a right to divulge such information, derived from an underlying right to self-fulfilment. A civil servant does not have a real free speech interest in disclosing information entrusted to him in confidence, particularly if the information is revealed for

---

[177] For an analysis of free speech interests, see ch. I, s. 3 above.

[178] 57 BVerfGE 250 (1981).

[179] The constitutionality of the United States Espionage Act 1917 was upheld in *US* v. *Rosenberg* 195 F 2d 583 (2nd Cir, 1952).

[180] The interest must be exceptionally strong to justify the imposition of a prior restraint in the United States: see ch. IV, s. 3 above.

financial reward.[181] The best argument for extending the coverage of the free speech principle to disclosure by civil servants is that it enables the press to acquire as much information as possible which it can then pass on to the public. The free speech claim of a civil servant is really parasitic on the relatively strong interest which the public may have in disclosure of the information about the working of government.

(ii) Official secrets laws

Criminal penalties for the unauthorized disclosure of government information in the United Kingdom are now imposed by the Official Secrets Act 1989. It replaced an earlier statute of 1911, described by the Franks Committee in 1972 as a 'mess'.[182] The Official Secrets Act 1911 had made it an offence for a government employee to communicate any official information to anyone without authorization, unless it was his duty to communicate it 'in the interest of the state'. It was also an offence for anyone to receive such information. In principle, a prosecution could be brought for an unauthorized disclosure embarrassing to the government, which posed no danger to national security. A prosecution, for instance, was brought against Clive Ponting, a senior civil servant in the Ministry of Defence, for sending Tam Dalyell, MP, documents concerning the sinking of the Argentine cruiser, the *General Belgrano*, a controversial incident during the Falklands war which Dalyell was investigating to the government's irritation. The judge directed the jury that it was for the government to determine what was 'in the interest of the state' for the purpose of the limited exception to the rule prohibiting unauthorized disclosure. Ponting could not argue that it was in the public interest for facts about the sinking to be revealed to Members of Parliament. Despite this ruling, the jury acquitted the defendant.[183] As a result the government became reluctant to use the criminal law, preferring instead to rely on civil actions to restrain a breach of confidence.

However, the eventual failure of the civil proceedings in the *Spycatcher* case[184] persuaded the government at last to reform the criminal law. The Official Secrets Act 1989 replaces the comprehensive provision in the 1911 enactment with specific prohibitions against the disclosure by civil servants or government contractors of limited types of information, in respect of which there are obviously strong reasons of national security and public safety for preserving confidentiality.

---

[181] The Franks Committee recommended the extension of the corruption laws to penalize a civil servant for revealing information (not otherwise covered by the official secrecy laws) for private gain: *Report of Departmental Committee on Section 2 of the Official Secrets Act 1911* (1972, Cmnd 5104), paras. 201–5. See Y. Cripps, 'Disclosure in the Public Interest: The Predicament of the Public Sector Employee' [1983] *PL* 600, 624–31.

[182] Franks Committee, n. 181 above, para. 88. See Feldman, 869–71 for a discussion of the 1911 provision. [183] *R* v. *Ponting* [1985] Crim LR 318.

[184] Discussed in ch. IV, s. 3 above.

They include information and documents relating to security or intelligence, defence, international relations, and criminal investigations. In most cases the prosecution must prove that the disclosure was 'damaging', a term defined in the legislation in various ways according to the character of the information disclosed. It is only when the disclosure is made by persons who are or have been members of the security and intelligence services that it is immaterial whether it was damaging.[185] Persons other than civil servants, such as journalists, may also be prosecuted if they disclose information covered by the legislation which they know, or have reason to believe, was so covered and where they know, or have reason to believe, that further publication is damaging.[186]

Although the 1989 Act is a considerable improvement on its predecessor, it fails to respect freedom of speech. There is no general defence that publication was in the public interest, as there is to a civil action to restrain a breach of confidence and as there was to a limited extent under the draconian 1911 legislation. Secondly, members and former members of the security and intelligence services commit an offence if they disclose information which they have obtained as a result of their position, even if it is not confidential and so its disclosure would not be damaging to national security or other public interest. It has been strongly argued that it would violate freedom of expression to apply these provisions to the revelation of official secrets in the absence of evidence that disclosure was damaging and of any room for argument that publication was nevertheless in the public interest.[187]

However, the House of Lords has held that the provisions of the Act as a whole are compatible with the guarantee of freedom of expression. In *R* v. *Shayler*,[188] it agreed that the right of the defendant, a former security service member, to freedom of expression was infringed, when he was prosecuted under the Act for disclosing a number of official documents to the *Mail on Sunday* and writing an article in the paper. Moreover, an absolute ban on disclosure without any exception at all could not be regarded as necessary and a proportionate means to safeguard national security. But civil servants and even security service agents are permitted to disclose information 'with lawful authority', so the ban was not an absolute one. There are procedures in section 7 of the Act enabling them to raise their concerns with a staff counsellor and others, including, in extreme cases, the Prime Minister or other ministers, and to ask their permission to make a wider disclosure. A refusal of permission could be challenged by judicial review, so there were proper safeguards to ensure that freedom of expression was not wholly suppressed. Shayler had not attempted to use these procedures, so there was no legal bar to a prosecution. The decision achieves a nuanced balance between respect for freedom of expression and an appreciation of the justifiable needs to protect national security and the confidentiality of the secret and intelligence services.

---

[185] Official Secrets Act 1989, s. 1(1).   [186] Ibid., s. 4.
[187] Feldman, 890–1.   [188] [2003] 1 AC 247.

On the other hand, it is not hard to detect considerable unease, particularly in the speech of Lord Hope, with the restrictions imposed by the legislation, and the absence of a broad public interest defence.[189]

There is little doubt that well-drafted official secrets laws will be upheld by the European Court of Human Rights. States are entitled, for instance, to protect the confidentiality of the operations of the police and security services in fighting terrorism and other criminal activity, provided its measures are a proportionate response to the threats. Under the 'margin of appreciation' principle, states enjoy a wide measure of discretion in their assessment of the dangers of disclosure and in their choice of means by which to combat them.[190] However, the Court held that the Netherlands infringed Article 10 when its courts ordered withdrawal of an issue of a magazine containing a report of the internal security service dated six years before the issue.[191] The Court noted that 2,500 copies of the magazine had already been sold in Amsterdam and that the media had commented on the information in the report. Withdrawal of the issue could no longer be regarded as necessary to safeguard national security, as the information was already in the public domain. Further, the Court doubted whether the contents of a six-year-old report explaining in general terms the work of the security service could be regarded as sufficiently sensitive to warrant steps to prevent publication. This decision indicates it would be willing to review the classification of material by national authorities. The Court might intervene if a case such as *Shayler* were taken to Strasbourg, unless the state could produce evidence to show that publication would prejudice national security or otherwise damage one of the interests which may be safeguarded under Article 10(2).

This would be similar to the approach of the German Constitutional Court. It is prepared to balance the interests of state security or other important public good against the right to free expression. This must be done in the context of the particular circumstances and of the detail disclosed by the publication. The Court emphasized this point in one case when it concluded that the defendant's conviction was not an unconstitutional interference with *Pressefreiheit*; the article had contained a precise description of the site of air force bases.[192] This approach is consistent with that adopted by the German Constitutional Court (and the US Supreme Court) in other areas of political speech.[193] It is surely right to adopt it here. There are unacceptable risks to freedom of speech if the courts allow the political branches of government unfettered discretion to proscribe the disclosure of official secrets.

---

[189] Ibid., paras. 40–5.

[190] See *Klass* v. *Germany* (1978) 2 EHRR 214, para. 48; *Leander* v. *Sweden* (1987) 9 EHRR 433, para. 59; *Hadjianastassiou* v. *Greece* (1993) 16 EHRR 219, paras. 46–7.

[191] *Vereniging Weekblad Bluf!* v. *Netherlands* (1995) 20 EHRR 189.

[192] 21 BVerfGE 239 (1967).   [193] See s. 2 of this chapter.

VI
Libel and Invasion of Privacy

1. Introduction

Few areas of law present such baffling problems for the application of a free speech principle as the law of libel. There is an obvious reason for the difficulties. The law presents conflicts between two well-established rights: freedom of speech and the right to reputation. The latter has a much longer history than the former; reputation has been highly prized and strongly protected for centuries.[1] In most countries great importance is still attached to individual reputation, though it is less highly valued in the United States and some other liberal societies than it used to be. It reflects the supreme value given to individual human dignity, a right which is given special constitutional status in the German *Grundgesetz*,[2] and which plays an important role in international human rights law.[3] Until recently, reputation was regarded as one of the fundamental liberties protected by the Due Process Clause of the Fourteenth Amendment to the United States Constitution.[4] Both the Universal Declaration of Human Rights and the International Covenant on Civil and Political Rights recognize the right to legal protection against attacks on individual honour and reputation, as well as against interference with privacy.[5]

The relationship of free speech and privacy rights or interests creates similar problems. Discrete privacy rights are recognized in the American states, New Zealand, and some Canadian provinces. They are particularly strongly protected in civil law jurisdictions, where they may enjoy constitutional status, either explicitly in the

---

[1] Reputation was protected in Roman law: see J. K. B. M. Nicholas, *An Introduction to Roman Law* (Oxford: Clarendon Press, 1962), 215–18. For a discussion of the foundations of defamation law in England and the United States, see R. C. Post, 'The Social Foundations of Defamation Law: Reputation and the Constitution' (1986) 74 *California Law Rev* 691.

[2] Art. 1. The basic principle of human dignity may not be affected by constitutional amendment: Basic Law, art. 79(3).

[3] See D. Feldman, 'Human Dignity as a Human Value—I' [1999] *PL* 682, 688.

[4] In *Paul* v. *Davis* 424 US 693 (1976) the Court held that reputation alone was not a 'liberty' or 'property' interest protected by the Fourth Amendment. For criticism, see H. P. Monaghan, ' "Of Liberty" and "Property" ' (1977) 62 *Cornell Law Rev* 405, 423–34, but the decision was affirmed in *Siegert* v. *Gilley* 500 US 226 (1991).

[5] Universal Declaration, art. 12; International Covenant, art. 17.

text or by judicial interpretation.[6] Although it is unclear whether English law recognizes a discrete privacy right, it inhibits the disclosure of personal information through the jurisdiction to restrain breach of confidence; privacy interests are protected in English law. How to reconcile freedom of speech with personal privacy is now a matter of considerable controversy in all cultures where people are fascinated by the conduct of celebrities.

In the United States, and to a lesser extent many common law jurisdictions, the clear trend in the last few decades has been to give increasing protection to freedom of speech to the cost of rights or interests in reputation or privacy. Courts have accepted, for example, that the press and other media have a right to publish defamatory allegations about the conduct of politicians and other leading figures, insofar as these stories are of public interest, provided that—to simplify at this point—the media have not disclosed them irresponsibly. Equally, courts may allow the press freedom in some circumstances to disclose the details of the private lives of celebrities, taking the view that freedom of speech and of the press trumps any competing privacy rights.

In section 2 of this chapter we discuss the general arguments for bringing the publication of defamatory allegations, at least in some contexts, within the coverage of freedom of speech. But even if it is accepted that this step is right, it does not follow that free speech should always, or even generally, trump reputation rights. The legal principles for balancing the two rights or interests are considered in section 3; it will be seen that there are a variety of solutions, some of them more solicitous of free speech concerns than others. The legal problems posed by non-defamatory insults and political satire are considered briefly in section 4. Section 5 is concerned with free speech and privacy, where perhaps the most important question is whether the law should adopt similar rules to those appropriate for defamation or should give stronger protection to privacy rights.

2. Is Defamation 'Speech'?

One solution to the problems in this area of law is to deny that defamation is 'speech' for the purposes of a freedom of speech or expression provision. This used to be the view of the United States Supreme Court; an attack on an individual's reputation did not contribute to public discussion, but was rather to be equated with an assault.[7] Even absolutists committed to protecting any mode of speech from restriction might then explain libel laws as a restraint on conduct. This fallacy was not finally exposed until the landmark ruling of the Court in *New York*

---

[6] German Basic Law, art. 10 guarantees privacy of posts and telecommunications; Constitution of Spain, art. 18 protects privacy and honour, while art. 8 of the European Convention on Human Rights and Fundamental Freedoms (ECHR) guarantees the right to respect for private and family life, home and correspondence.   [7] *Chaplinsky* v. *New Hampshire* 315 US 568 (1942).

Times v. *Sullivan*.[8] A defamatory attack on the conduct of a public official—an Alabama commissioner of police—was held to be a form of political speech, the protection of which, as we saw in the previous chapter, is the principal concern of the First Amendment. As a result, the claimant could not bring a libel action unless malice were proved. The crucial step in the Court's reasoning was the analogy drawn between this type of libel and the offence of sedition, which, in the Court's view, would clearly be outlawed by the Amendment. If that analogy were correct, it would inevitably follow that at least some libels are covered by a free speech clause.

Anyone disposed to question this aspect of the Court's reasoning should first consider whether it is consistent with free political speech to allow a government or local authority to protect its governing reputation by means of a civil action for libel in circumstances when no criminal prosecution for sedition or private libel could be brought. (In one extraordinary English case, the judge had ruled that a local authority was entitled to protect its reputation by civil action; it was awarded £2,000 damages, plus £20,000 costs, against a ratepayer who had circulated a strongly critical pamphlet at a public meeting.[9]) Courts in the United States have long appreciated that there is no real distinction in this context between criminal prosecutions for sedition and civil defamation actions.[10] These actions may in fact have more impact on freedom of speech, for there may be no trial by jury, damages may be high, and the onus of proof on the claimant is lighter. The House of Lords has now accepted that to allow government authorities to sue for libel would place an 'undesirable fetter on freedom of speech.'[11] Later decisions in England have extended its ruling to preclude altogether libel actions by public corporations and by political parties.[12] While the libel provisions of the German Penal Code protect the reputation of public authorities, the German Constitutional Court has emphasized that they should not be used to limit criticism of government and should, therefore, be construed to respect the exercise of the constitutional right to freedom of expression.[13]

If civil libel actions by public authorities are incompatible with the protection of free political speech, the same conclusion might be reached where politicians and public officials seek to protect their political reputation by initiating proceedings. Certainly, it makes sense to apply the same principle in cases where, as in the *New York Times* case itself, an individual officer is attacked by implication in an article which is for the most part a protest against the general behaviour of a public authority. English law has not come to this conclusion; politicians may bring

---

    8 376 US 254 (1964).
    9 *Bognor Regis DC* v. *Campion* [1972] 2 QB 169, Browne J., criticized by J. A. Weir [1972] *CLJ* 238.
    10 *City of Chicago* v. *Tribune Co* 139 NE 50 (Illinois S Ct, 1923); *City of Albany* v. *Meyer* 279 P 213 (Calif DC of Appeals, 1929).
    11 *Derbyshire County Council* v. *Times Newspapers* [1993] AC 534, 549 per Lord Keith.
    12 See *British Coal Corpn* v. *NUM*, 28 June 1996, unreported, French J.; *Goldsmith* v. *Bhoyrul* [1997] 4 All ER 268, Buckley J.
    13 'Soldiers are murderers', 93 BVerfGE 266, 291–2 (1995), discussed in ch. V, s. 4(ii) above.

libel actions even if the defamatory allegations are made in the course of a speech of obvious political interest. But the scope of the defences to these actions has recently been expanded, so libel law is clearly not immune from scrutiny in the light of free speech arguments. Similar developments have occurred in most other Commonwealth jurisdictions as well as in Germany and in the jurisprudence of the European Court: see section 3 below for full discussion. The decision of the High Court of Australia in *Theophanous* v. *Herald & Weekly Times Ltd*[14] provides a good example. In earlier cases, it had established that freedom of political commun-ication is implicit in the constitutional provisions guaranteeing free elections to democratic institutions.[15] Inevitably, in its view, such an implied freedom must protect political discussion from onerous criminal and civil liability in defama-tion. Otherwise freedom of political communication would be ineffective; it would make no sense to assert a freedom which could be inhibited by oppressive libel laws.

The US Supreme Court ruling in the *New York Times* case was also justified as an extension of the immunities enjoyed by the politicians and officials themselves. In the United Kingdom Members of Parliament may say anything they like in 'debates or proceedings in Parliament', free from legal challenge.[16] The importance of this freedom has been underlined by the European Court of Human Rights, when it ruled that its exercise could not be challenged by an individual who had been strongly attacked in the House of Commons.[17] The US Supreme Court itself had, only five years before the *New York Times* decision, held that a federal official is absolutely immune from liability in respect of speech made in the course of his offi-cial duties.[18] These privileges are considered necessary for the discharge of their holders' public responsibilities (though it may be doubted whether this applies to false statements made maliciously). The argument from democracy suggests that the criticism of officials and legislators by members of the public is entitled to equal protection under a free speech clause: '. . . it would give public servants an unjusti-fied preference over the public they serve if critics of official conduct did not have a fair equivalent of the immunity granted to the officials themselves.'[19] Just as Members of Parliament and Congressmen may be inhibited from contributing to open debate in the legislature if they fear libel proceedings, so may ordinary people without an immunity from such proceedings be deterred from engaging in polit-ical discussion regarding the merits of particular public figures.

That argument does of course rest on controversial theories about the nature of a democracy. Under the traditional perspective of a representative democracy, it was probably right to allow Members of Parliament wider free speech privileges

---

[14] (1994) 182 CLR 104.
[15] *Nationwide New Pty Ltd* v. *Wills* (1992) 177 CLR 1; *Australian Capital Television Pty Ltd* v. *Commonwealth* (1992) 177 CLR 106: see ch. II, s. 6(iii) above for Australian free speech law.
[16] Bill of Rights 1689, art. 9.   [17] *A* v. *UK* (2003) 36 EHRR 917.
[18] *Barr* v. *Matteo* 360 US 564 (1959).
[19] *New York Times* v. *Sullivan* 376 US 254, 282–3 (1964) per Brennan J.

than those allowed the general public, but that view is much harder to sustain now. However, there are good reasons for caution in this area and for rejecting the view that defamatory speech should always be protected.[20] Some people, particularly those of a sensitive disposition, may be deterred from entering public life if they can never protect their reputation against defamatory allegations.[21] The publication of a libel may destroy the standing and livelihood of someone who is in fact completely innocent of the charges and who will have no redress at all if free speech principles preclude his right to protect his reputation altogether. In the absence of any legal restraints, the media would be free to say what they like about politicians and other public figures, and this would almost certainly encourage a concentration on scandal in preference to a serious discussion of political and social issues. Moreover, in the long term the credibility of the press and other media would suffer, since the public would have no guarantee that their reports were likely to be accurate. The common law of libel does provide some, albeit imperfect, guarantee of truth, as the defendant must justify allegations of fact.

These are powerful points, too readily ignored by enthusiasts for the adoption in England of all US free speech jurisprudence in this area. For these reasons, the House of Lords, and courts in other Commonwealth countries, have rightly rejected that course. But equally these points do not show that the decisions in the *New York Times* case and its progeny (discussed in the next section) are wholly misconceived. The First Amendment and other free speech provisions are framed on the assumption that everyone should be free to contribute to political debate. As the previous chapter showed, political speech is protected unless there is an imminent danger to an important state interest, such as national security or public order. It would hardly be compatible with that line of authority to allow civil actions always to deter the publication of political speech, merely because it defames a politician or official. Courts are, therefore, right to hold that libel laws do not fall outside the *coverage* of a free speech or freedom of expression clause, and that the restraints they impose on the exercise of that freedom must be justified. But it does not follow that every libellous attack on a politician or other person involved in public life should be *protected*, merely because it is an exercise of the right to free speech.

Whatever the merits of these arguments, it is clear that in most Commonwealth countries, as well as in the United States and in Germany, libel law cannot now simply be applied to enforce reputation rights without regard to constitutional free speech considerations. One jurisdiction that has so far not refashioned its libel law is Canada. In *Hill* v. *Church of Scientology of Toronto*[22] the Supreme

---

[20] For a fuller statement of these arguments, see D. A. Anderson, 'Is Libel Law Worth Reforming?' (1991) 140 *Univ of Pennsylvania Law Rev* 487, 524–37.

[21] See H. H. Wellington, 'On Freedom of Expression' (1979) 88 *Yale Law Jo* 1105, 1113–15.

[22] [1995] 2 SCR 1130: see L Leigh, 'Of Free Speech and Individual Reputation: *New York Times* v. *Sullivan* in Canada and Australia', in I. Loveland (ed.), *Importing the First Amendment* (Oxford: Hart, 1998), 51, 58–62.

Court rejected the argument that the rule in *New York Times* should be adopted to provide a defence to a libel action brought by a Crown lawyer who had been wrongly accused of committing a contempt of court. Cory J. denied that defamation law unduly inhibited freedom of expression, considering the existing common law defences of fair comment and privilege adequate to protect its exercise. The case was a poor one with which to launch an argument for incorporation of the *New York Times* rule. Although the allegations implicated a government employee, they did not involve any criticism of government as such or raise a matter of public concern. In a later case where the Court upheld a criminal libel prosecution as compatible with the Charter, it was emphasized that, while defamation is covered by section 2(b), it is expression of 'negligible value'.[23]

English common law has not ignored free speech considerations. Its principal device for balancing them against a claimant's right to reputation has been the defence of fair comment on a matter of public interest. The range of such matters is wide and certainly extends well beyond the topics of political and public life to cover any subject in which members of the public are legitimately interested, for example, theatrical criticism or local questions.[24] Courts have emphasized the importance of protecting free comment on issues of current political interest.[25] This aspect of the defence has given rise to little difficulty; it is at any rate wider in this respect than the *constitutional* immunity enjoyed by the press against actions by 'public figures' in the United States: see section 3 below. The defence, however, can only be sustained if the defamation consists of *comment*, rather than an allegation of *fact*. The distinction is important, because the defendant must prove the truth of libellous factual claims, either under the separate defence of justification or as the basis for the plea of fair comment. The decision of the House of Lords in *Telnikoff* v. *Matusevitch*[26] is important in this context, with some worrying implications for free speech. In a letter to a newspaper, the defendant attacked the writer of an article in an issue of the paper five days previously, accusing him of expressing racist views when he demanded the dismissal of non-Russian staff from the BBC Russian Service. A majority of the House of Lords held that the jury should only consider the terms of the letter, and not additionally the article, in determining whether the accusations amounted to comment or allegations of fact. As a result, editors may feel it sensible to set out extracts from material to which a letter is replying in order for any defamatory remarks in the latter to be treated as comment.

English law has also recognized the importance of free speech in the defences of absolute and qualified privilege. Many of the privileges exist in the political sphere, for example, the absolute privilege of speech enjoyed by Members of

---

[23] *R* v. *Lucas* [1998] 1 SCR 439, para. 57 per Cory J.
[24] See e.g. *London Artists Ltd* v. *Littler* [1969] 2 QB 375, CA; *Slim* v. *Daily Telegraph Ltd* [1968] 2 QB 157, CA.
[25] See Diplock J. in *Silkin* v. *Beaverbrook Newspapers Ltd* [1958] 1 WLR 743, 745.
[26] [1992] 2 AC 343.

Parliament in Parliamentary proceedings and of communications between officers of state, and the qualified privilege for non-malicious fair and accurate reports of Parliamentary and judicial proceedings.[27] But until recently the courts generally rejected the argument that the media should have a defence of qualified privilege to report defamatory allegations on matters of public interest which they believed to be accurate, but which in fact were untrue or at least could not be substantiated in court. Such a defence could only be invoked when the defendant had a duty to make a communication to a person who had a corresponding duty or interest in receiving it, and that was not the case when the media published material to the general public. For example, it was held that there was no such defence in *Blackshaw* v. *Lord*,[28] where a newspaper journalist had wrongly identified the claimant, a former civil servant, as responsible for major incompetence in a government department costing the taxpayer £52 million. It was immaterial that the story was of real public interest. Outside the established categories of privileged occasion (for instance, employers' and teachers' references) the common law has been unwilling to recognize a broad qualified privilege defence rooted in free speech considerations.

That picture has now changed as a result of the landmark ruling in *Reynolds* v. *Times Newspapers* considered in the next section of this chapter.[29] The issue now in English law, as in many other jurisdictions, is how exactly the law should accommodate or balance the two rights to freedom of speech and the right to reputation. While comment on public officials (and perhaps public figures) should be wholly free, it is not so clear that the free speech principle, even interpreted in the light of the argument from democracy, necessitates constitutional protection for false allegations of fact about such people. As Powell J. has said in a leading US decision: 'There is no constitutional value in false statements of fact.'[30] Insofar as it is relevant to constitutional adjudication, Mill's truth theory does not seem to demand tolerance of false allegations of fact, as opposed to questionable political and moral opinions.[31] But we will see shortly that there may be a good reason for allowing unproven factual allegations a degree of protection from libel actions. This position was reached by the US Supreme Court in its landmark decision in *New York Times* v. *Sullivan*, is to some extent taken by the German Constitutional Court, and is now accepted by the House of Lords and other Commonwealth courts.

Another area of difficulty concerns the character of the speech or publication in the course of which defamatory allegations are made. The case for protecting political speech from the spectre of libel actions may not apply equally to all types of defamatory statement. The argument from democracy suggests that defamation

---

[27] See e.g. *Chatterton* v. *Secretary of State for India* [1895] 2 QB 189, CA (absolute privilege for communication from one minister to another); *Cook* v. *Alexander* [1974] QB 279, CA (qualified privilege for fair and accurate Parliamentary sketch). [28] [1984] QB 1, CA.

[29] [2001] 2 AC 127, HL: see s. 3(iv) below.

[30] *Gertz* v. *Robert Welch Inc* 418 US 323, 340 (1974).   [31] See ch. I, s. 2(i) above.

of politicians, public officials, and some other public figures occupying similar positions may be protected, at least if it is an incidental aspect of a contribution to political debate. On the other hand, there seems little, if any, justification for applying a free speech clause to protect casual remarks in a public bar. Other cases are harder to categorize. How should the law treat defamation of film stars, sportsmen, and other people in the public eye, whose activities, however, are of relatively little significance in the conduct of political and public life?[32] Courts must fashion principles on the basis of which free speech and reputation rights are balanced in these different contexts. The process is inevitable, unless either right is wholly sacrificed to the other. That course would surely be unacceptable.

3. Balancing Free Speech and Reputation

In this area of free speech law, the United States courts do not weigh the competing interests in a case-by-case, ad hoc way, or within the framework of a general rule such as the 'clear and present danger' test. In other words, it does not assess for each case the gravity of the damage to the plaintiff's reputation against the value or importance of the *particular* speech or publication. Instead, the Supreme Court has formulated a number of fairly precise rules to cover actions for libel under which the First Amendment affords protection for speech which might otherwise attract defamation liability. (It has adopted the same approach in privacy cases: see section 5 of this chapter below.) In a leading article one commentator explained this preference for 'definitional' balancing in terms of the greater predictability of decisions it secures, and has also argued that it enables the courts to give more weight to speech than is possible under an ad hoc approach.[33] Courts might be inclined on this latter approach to place undue emphasis on the particular harm suffered by the plaintiff and so might ignore the long-term effects on free speech brought about by an award of damages. Courts in Australia and New Zealand have also adopted fairly clear rules, under which libel actions will fail if brought, say, by a politician or election candidate, unless he can prove malice, perhaps subject to the condition that the media or other defendant shows that publication was reasonable. In other jurisdictions, notably England, but also in a different way Germany, a more flexible approach is taken, under which a number of factors are taken into account before determining whether the free speech right trumps the reputation right. That approach may avoid some of the pitfalls of definitional balancing, but equally suffers from other weaknesses, in particular a lack of predictability of result which may inhibit the media.

[32] These questions are now more often asked in the context of the disclosure of private information: see s. 5 of this chapter.
[33] M. B. Nimmer, 'The Right to Speak from *Times* to *Time*: First Amendment Theory Applied to Libel and Misapplied to Privacy' (1968) 56 *California Law Rev* 935.

(i) The United States

It makes sense to start this survey with an exposition of the development of free speech libel principles in the United States, where the issues have been considered for forty years and where the law is now relatively well settled.[34] *New York Times* v. *Sullivan* involved an action brought by an Alabama City police commissioner in respect of allegations in an advertisement carried by the defendant newspaper which suggested, in his view, that he was responsible for the harsh treatment of anti-segregation demonstrators by the local police. As was explained in section 2 above, the Supreme Court held that libel should no longer be treated as immune from scrutiny under the First Amendment. It then proceeded to rule that the state law of Alabama providing for the defence of truth was inadequate to protect free speech. The defendant might not be able to prove that the allegations were justified. Moreover, a newspaper's fear that it might not succeed in persuading the jury of their truth might deter it from publishing stories which were accurate, or which it believed on good grounds to be accurate. To remove this 'chilling effect' of libel law, Brennan J. for the Court imposed as a matter of constitutional law:

[A] federal rule that prohibits a public official from recovering damages for a defamatory falsehood relating to his official conduct, unless he proves that the statement was made with 'actual malice'—that is, with knowledge that it was false or with reckless disregard of whether it was false or not.[35]

Moreover, 'actual malice' has to be shown with 'convincing clarity', a higher standard than the usual requirement in civil actions for claimants to prove their case on the balance of probabilities. The crucial difference between the US rule and the common law is that the latter assumes that the defendant will be able to show the truth of defamatory allegations in court and should accept liability if he does not do this. The *New York Times* rule perhaps more realistically appreciates the imperfections of the legal process.[36] The consequence of the rule is, of course, that sometimes a public official must tolerate the circulation of some untrue statements about him without compensation, unless he can establish 'actual malice'. But that is better, in the Supreme Court's view, than imposing liability for what may in fact be accurate stories which the defendant cannot justify.

Three members of the Court, Black, Douglas, and Goldberg JJ, would have gone further and outlawed all libel actions in respect of defamatory allegations about the official conduct of public officials, whether they had been made maliciously or not. That would be much too extreme a position. To protect from legal

---

[34] This is not an exhaustive treatment of the relationship of free speech and libel in the United States. An important area not covered in this chapter is the statutory provision which provides Internet service providers with immunity from defamation liability: see ch. XIII, s. 4(ii) below.

[35] 376 US 254, 279–80 (1964).

[36] F. Schauer, 'Social Foundations of the Law of Defamation: A Comparative Analysis' (1980) 1 *Jo of Media Law and Practice* 3, 10–12.

action malicious or reckless allegations would be to tolerate a distortion of the democratic process, which could not be warranted under any rationale for the free speech principle.[37] It is probably more pertinent to ask whether the *New York Times* rule goes too far in requiring public official claimants to prove actual malice convincingly. The result is that a newspaper cannot be held liable for defaming a public official even when it has behaved extremely carelessly, no matter how serious the damage to the latter's reputation.[38] Perhaps a more acceptable balance between free speech and reputation rights would be achieved by the imposition on the publisher of a negligence liability for untrue defamatory allegations. Something like this solution was advocated by Harlan J. in respect of libel actions brought by public figures. However, a majority of the Court was prepared, in two cases decided together three years after *New York Times*, to extend its principle to public figures.[39] It was increasingly difficult, in the view of Warren CJ, to distinguish the position of people wielding power in the private sector from public officials; both groups 'shape events in areas of concern to society at large' and enjoy access to the media in order to rebut personal attacks and criticism.[40] The subsequent decision in *Rosenbloom*[41] then further extended the immunity to a libel action brought by an ordinary private person caught up in an event of general public interest, in this case a distributor of nudist magazines charged by the police with publishing obscene materials who sued in respect of a broadcast alleging his guilt of that offence; the material issue on this approach was whether the allegations concerned a matter of public concern, rather than the status or fame of the libel claimant.

That trend was however, halted by *Gertz* v. *Robert Welch Inc*,[42] where the plaintiff, a Chicago lawyer representing the family of a person murdered by a policeman, was defamed in an extreme right-wing publication as a Communist and as responsible for the framing of the police officer. The majority of the Court ruled that Gertz was not a public figure; he was not sufficiently well known in the community to be treated as a public figure in all contexts, while he had not courted publicity to make himself such a figure within the particular context of the police murder. More importantly, the Court abandoned its approach in *Rosenbloom*, holding in Powell J.'s majority judgment that there are powerful arguments for allowing state law to protect the reputation of private individuals, which do not apply when public officials or figures are libelled. Unlike the latter, ordinary individuals do not have access to the media or other opportunities to reply to personal

---

[37] Nimmer (n. 33 above), 949–52.

[38] See, for instance, *Ocala Star-Banner Co* v. *Damron* 401 US 295 (1971), where the newspaper mistakenly published a report that Damron, a candidate for a local office, was facing perjury charges, when in fact it was his brother who had been indicted. *New York Times* precludes recovery even for irresponsible journalism of this type.

[39] *Curtis Publishing Co* v. *Butts, Associated Press* v. *Walker* 388 US 130 (1967).

[40] Ibid., 163–4.   [41] *Rosenbloom* v. *Metromedia, Inc* 403 US 29 (1971).

[42] 418 US 323 (1974).

attacks. Moreover, politicians and celebrities must accept the risk of criticism as a consequence of their entry into public life, but the ordinary citizen should not be held to that risk.

The states were therefore free under the First Amendment to decide their own standards of defamation liability, provided they did not maintain common law strict liability. Further, the Court held that recovery in libel could only be permitted where the claimant proved actual loss or injury. In the absence of any showing of actual malice, there should be no recovery for presumed or punitive damages. In short, the common law was to some extent replaced by a constitutional scheme of fault liability with restrictions on the availability of damages. The Court qualified its decision in *Gertz* ten years later when it ruled that presumed and punitive damages could be recovered in a libel action, without infringement of the First Amendment, where the speech did not involve a matter of public concern.[43] A construction company could therefore recover such damages in respect of an inaccurate and carelessly prepared report by a credit-reporting agency sent to five subscribers, stating that it had filed for bankruptcy. The report was characterized as speech involving only private concerns. Two members of the majority, Burger CJ, and White J., were prepared to overrule *Gertz*,[44] and even to reconsider the *New York Times* decision itself, so that public officials could recover some damages on proof that the allegations were false. The 'public concern' test has been used, less controversially, by the Supreme Court to hold that private figure plaintiffs must prove the falsity of defamatory allegations made on a matter of public concern to succeed in a libel action.[45] (For public official and public figure plaintiffs this requirement is implicit in the established requirement that they must show actual malice, that is, that the statement was published with knowledge that it was false or with recklessness as to its truth; it is immaterial whether the speech is made on a matter of public or private concern.) A final point is that the Supreme Court has rejected the argument that there is a separate constitutional privilege for defamatory opinion, so that an expression of opinion is never actionable;[46] but the claimant must prove that any factual allegation implicit in an opinion is false. That means that an action cannot be brought successfully if, on the proper interpretation of an allegation, it does not state actual facts about the claimant which could be shown to be false.[47]

United States law is, therefore, extremely complex, requiring in the first place lines to be drawn between public officials and figures on the one hand, and ordinary private individuals on the other. With regard to the latter category, a further distinction must be drawn between allegations made in speech of public concern

---

[43] *Dun & Bradstreet Inc* v. *Greenmoss Builders Inc* 472 US 749 (1985).

[44] White J. had dissented in *Gertz*, arguing that there was no justification for constitutionalizing libel law and replacing the common law strict liability rule so far as private individual plaintiffs were concerned.   [45] *Philadelphia Newspapers* v. *Hepps* 475 US 765 (1986).

[46] *Milkovitch* v. *Lorain Journal* 497 US 1 (1990).

[47] For further discussion of these points, see s. 4 of this chapter.

and those made in the course of speech of only private concern. First Amendment considerations have had a radical impact on the incidence and disposition of all types of defamation actions, so much so that 'the law of libel is no longer a major threat to the press in America.'[48] From the perspective of claimants, few actions are fought successfully, with the result that it is virtually impossible for public officials and figures to vindicate their right to reputation, and very difficult for others to do so.

A number of related criticisms may be made of the position in the United States. First, the extension of the *New York Times* rule to cover defamatory allegations concerning public figures, defined in *Gertz* broadly as people of 'pervasive fame or notoriety', is unwarranted.[49] *New York Times* itself held that the libel of public officials should be subject to First Amendment scrutiny because it was integrally linked to political speech and criticism of government. The same cannot be said of defamatory allegations concerning every type of celebrity. Warren CJ in the initial 'public figure' cases suggested that it would be wrong to draw a sharp line between politicians and civil servants on the one hand, and equally powerful people, taking decisions of economic and political consequence, in the private sector.[50] It would indeed be right to treat libel actions by, say, the publisher or editor of *The Times*, the head of the CBI, a leading bank, public company, or trades union, in the same way as an action brought by a Member of Parliament or local councillor. But that is because speech about such people is political speech, usually of real public interest. The same cannot be said of allegations concerning film or football stars, and other celebrities, unless, of course, the notion of political or public interest speech is emptied of any real content.[51] Further, it is simply not true that public figures, or for that matter public officials, necessarily have an effective opportunity to put the record straight when defamatory remarks are made about them. Nor is there any evidence that they cheerfully surrender their reputation rights when entering public life. These arguments were employed by Powell J. in *Gertz* to distinguish the position of public figures from private individuals,[52] but they are hard to sustain.[53]

These points lead to a more fundamental criticism: the US approach, at least in theory, places too much weight on the status of the plaintiff, and too little on the general content of the speech in the course of which the allegations are made.[54]

---

[48] D. A. Anderson, 'An American Perspective', in S. Deakin, A. Johnston, and B. Markesinis, *Tort Law*, 5th edn. (Oxford: OUP, 2003), 721. For an empirical study showing how libel law poses little threat to media freedom in the United States, see D. A. Logan, 'Libel Law in the Trenches: Reflections on Current Data on Libel Litigation' (2001) 87 *Virginia Law Rev* 503.

[49] F. Schauer, 'Public Figures' (1984) 25 *William and Mary Law Rev* 905.

[50] *Butts, Walker* 388 US 130, 163–4 (1967).

[51] This point is more often relevant to privacy actions: see s. 5 below.

[52] *Gertz* v. *Robert Welch Inc* 418 US 323, 344–5 (1971).

[53] Anderson (n. 20 above), 524–30.

[54] M. A. Franklin, 'Constitutional Libel Law: The Role of Content' (1986) 34 *UCLA Law Rev* 1657.

A political party aide is neither a public official nor (generally) a public figure, so falls outside the strict *New York Times* rule,[55] but a popular entertainer may be caught by it and in that case must prove actual malice to recover libel damages.[56] Moreover, a public figure claimant cannot argue that the specific defamatory allegations are of no public concern, because, for instance, they ridicule her in some aspect of her private life: Andrea Dworkin, a prominent feminist advocate of anti-pornography laws, could not complain that she was defamed by a feature portraying her engaged in oral sex.[57] Categorization of the claimant as a public official or figure is decisive. The result of this approach may be that defamatory speech of little or no real public interest is protected from libel proceedings (unless the claimant can show actual malice), while speech of political importance—for example, allegations that a low-level party official is engaged in corruption—might lead to libel proceedings which the claimant will win if he is able to show fault on the part of the press.

Finally, there seems no obvious justification for the Court's decision in *Gertz* to modify as a matter of constitutional law the common law libel rules to require claimants, other than public officials and figures, to show fault and to limit the recovery of punitive and presumed damages. Powell J. for the Court reasoned that this principle recognized the strength of the state's interest in protecting reputation rights, while not exposing the media to strict liability. Fault liability would be appropriate, at least in those cases where it should be clear to an editor from the character of the allegations that she would be liable if the story were untrue.[58] There is of course much to be said for the imposition of the negligence basis of liability in defamation. Strict liability is in some ways an anomalous departure from the general principles of tort liability. But the Court took this step as a matter of constitutional law, implicitly deciding that any defamatory allegation about a private individual is covered by the First Amendment. Libellous remarks made in the course of a heated discussion in a public bar about the morals of the barmaid are apparently to be treated as protected speech, although they are far removed from the publication in *New York Times* or for that matter in *Gertz* itself. White J. rightly protested in the latter case that the Court was using the First Amendment without justification to bring about revolutionary changes in the law of libel.

---

[55] *Lawrence* v. *Moss* 867 F 2d 1188 (10th Cir, 1981).

[56] *Carson* v. *Allied News Co* 529 F 2d 206 (7th Cir, 1976). The Supreme Court has not ruled whether entertainers and celebrities are public figures. It has however held that a social figure involved in well-publicized divorce proceedings was not a public figure, suggesting that it may be prepared to draw a distinction between celebrities and those public figures who occupy a role equivalent to politicians: *Time, Inc* v. *Firestone* 424 US 448 (1976).

[57] *Andrea Dworkin and ors.* v. *Hustler Magazine* 867 F 2d 1188 (9th Cir, 1989).

[58] The Court implied that the *New York Times* malice test might be appropriate where an editor could not anticipate defamation liability from the text, e.g. because she did not intend to refer to the claimant. In a 'look-alike' case an English judge has ruled that common law strict liability for defamation is incompatible with the European Convention: *O'Shea* v. *MGN* [2001] EMLR 943.

(ii) Australia and New Zealand[59]

The principles for balancing reputation and freedom of speech in Australia are naturally shaped by the scope of the freedom of communication implied in the Constitution.[60] In *Theophanous* v. *Herald & Weekly Times Ltd*, the first major case to consider the relationship of the freedom to the common law of libel, the High Court held that the implication of free communication extended to political discussion; it was wide enough to cover discussion of the views and public conduct of persons, such as union leaders and political commentators, engaged in activities which are publicly debated, as well as the behaviour of politicians and candidates for office.[61] The Court accepted that such discussion must be protected from onerous libel laws and, further, that the common law requirement on the media to prove the truth of allegations wrongly chilled freedom of communication. However, the Court rejected import of the *New York Times* rule as undervaluing the right to reputation. In particular, the extension of the rule to cover defamation of public figures was undesirable, while the requirement on claimants to show actual malice convincingly imposed too high a burden.

The Court therefore formulated a constitutional rule under which there is a defence to a defamation action if the defendant shows that it was not aware of the falsity of the allegations, that it was not reckless, and that publication was reasonable, in that, for instance, it took steps to verify accuracy.[62] In contradistinction to the common law, the defendant should not have to prove the truth of the allegations, for that would not do justice to freedom of communication in this context. Mason CJ, Toohey and Gaudron JJ added that the implied constitutional freedom should reshape the contours of common law qualified privilege, so that the public at large would be treated as having an interest in receiving information on political matters.[63]

Subsequently, in *Lange* v. *Australian Broadcasting Corporation*,[64] in an action brought by a former Prime Minister of New Zealand, the High Court clarified some of the uncertainties in *Theophanous*. In a unanimous judgment it accepted that the common law rules of defamation must conform to the Constitution's implication of freedom of political communication, but conformity should be brought about by a restatement of the common law defence of qualified privilege, rather than by the formulation of a separate constitutional defence. The Court declared that 'each member of the Australian community has an interest in disseminating and receiving information, opinions and arguments concerning government and political matters that affect the people of Australia.'[65] But in view of the damage that a defamatory communication to the general public may cause to reputation rights, it was appropriate to require the defendant's conduct to be reasonable, that is, that it had reasonable grounds for believing the allegations

---

[59] See S. F. Fischer, 'Rethinking *Sullivan:* New Approaches in Australia, New Zealand, and England' (2002) 34 *George Washington Internat Law Rev* 101.
[60] See M. Chesterman, *Freedom of Speech in Australian Law* (Aldershot: Ashgate, 2000), ch. 2.
[61] (1994) 182 CLR 104, 124 per Mason CJ, Toohey and Gaudron JJ.   [62] Ibid., 137.
[63] Ibid., 140.   [64] (1997) 189 CLR 520.   [65] Ibid., 571.

were true, took proper steps to check their accuracy, and whenever practicable tried to obtain and publish a response from the claimant.[66]

The important point is that in Australia the reformulated common law defence is confined to defamatory allegations made in the course of speech concerning government and political affairs. Remarks in the *Theophanous* case suggest this category is wide enough to cover speech on any matter of social concern, excluding only commercial speech and scandal,[67] but the clear emphasis in *Lange* is on political speech, albeit not confined to speech during federal election campaigns.[68] What matters is the content of the speech, not the status of the plaintiff. The Australian cases perhaps better reflect the principles underlying *New York Times*, though not the US Supreme Court decision framed, as it was, in terms of speech concerning the official conduct of public officials. *Lange* combines an element of 'definitional' balancing—a rule framed in terms of the type of speech—with a flexible requirement of 'reasonable conduct' which enables courts to pay attention to the circumstances of the case.

The principal New Zealand case also involved an action brought by David Lange.[69] He sued the author and publisher of an article which had criticized his conduct as a politician, including his period in office as Prime Minister, suggesting in particular that he was guilty of a selective memory. The defendants put forward defences of 'political expression' and qualified privilege, arguing with regard to qualified privilege that the author, a lecturer in a political studies department, had a duty to draw the attention of the general public to the allegations and the latter had an interest in receiving them. The privilege argument was accepted by the Court of Appeal after a wide review of the authorities in the Commonwealth, the United States, and under the ECHR. Emphasizing the democratic character of the New Zealand Constitution, the country's commitment to open government, and the recent removal of the offence of criminal libel from the statute book, it held that an appropriate defence of qualified privilege should apply to generally published material concerning the conduct of currently or formerly elected Members of Parliament and candidates, so far as that conduct directly affects their capacity to meet their responsibilities. Unlike the High Court of Australia, the New Zealand Court of Appeal rejected incorporation of any requirement of reasonable care or conduct into the expanded privilege defence. The interest of the recipient, in these circumstances the general public, in becoming aware of the information, existed whether or not the media had taken care to ensure its truth.

The Privy Council considered Lange's appeal in conjunction with that in the English *Reynolds* case: see section 3(iv) below. It referred the case back to the New Zealand Court of Appeal, inviting it to reconsider its ruling in the light of the House of Lords decision in *Reynolds*. In that case the House declined, as will

---

[66] (1997) 189 CLR 520, 572–3.   [67] (1994) 182 CLR 104, 123–4.
[68] (1997) 189 CLR 520, 561.
[69] *Lange* v. *Atkinson* [1998] 3 NZLR 424, CA, affirming the judgment of Elias J. in [1997] 2 NZLR 22.

be seen, to recognize a generic privilege for communications on political matters, while extending qualified privilege to cover any communication to the public on a matter of public interest, provided the media had reported the matter responsibly. The New Zealand Court of Appeal reaffirmed its earlier decision, declining to take the opportunity to introduce any requirement of responsible journalism as a condition for upholding the qualified privilege defence.[70] The imposition of this requirement would, in its view, add to the 'chilling effect' of libel law on freedom of political speech. Further, New Zealand had not experienced 'the worst excesses and irresponsibilities of the English national daily tabloids.'[71]

The New Zealand defence is narrower than the Australian rule, covering only defamatory communications about politicians and candidates. That seems hard to defend on any coherent conception of free speech, since it is undeniable that a defamatory political communication of real concern to the public may equally implicate civil servants and others. There is no strong reason why they should be able to bring libel proceedings successfully, when an action on the same facts brought by a politician would be met by the privilege defence. The Court of Appeal's rejection of a 'reasonable care' requirement is also unpersuasive. Surely the public has an interest in receiving only information which its distributor, generally the press and other media, has good ground to believe is accurate. The imposition of a standard of 'responsible journalism', formulated by the House of Lords in *Reynolds* v. *Times Newspapers*,[72] may deter or chill the exercise of free speech and press rights. But that might be a desirable chill.

(iii) Germany

Under Article 5(2) of the Basic Law the right to free expression is limited by 'the right to inviolability of personal honour' (*Ehre*), as well as by the provisions in general laws.[73] In practice, limits are imposed by the criminal law of insult and defamation (*Beleidigung*)[74] and by provisions of the German Civil Code.[75] But the Constitutional Court has held that reputation is also covered by the constitutional right to the free development of personality (*Persönlichkeitsrecht*) guaranteed by Article 2 and by the inviolable dignity of man (*Die Würde des Menschen*).[76]

---

[70] *Lange* v. *Atkinson (No. 2)* [2000] 3 NZLR 385.

[71] Ibid., para. 34. But a cavalier approach on the part of a journalist might provide evidence of malice which rebuts the qualified privilege defence: see NZ Law Commission Report 64, *Defaming Politicians* (2000). [72] [2001] 2 AC 127, considered in s. 3(iv) below.

[73] For a summary of German law, see J. Fleming, 'Libel and Constitutional Free Speech', in *Essays for Patrick Atiyah* (Oxford: OUP, 1991), 333, 341–5. For a fuller account, comparing German and US law, see G. Nolte, *Beleidigungsschutz in der freiheitlichen Demokratie* (Heidelberg: Springer, 1992).

[74] Penal Code, ss. 185–94.

[75] BGB, ss. 823, 826: see B. Markesinis and H. Unberath, *The German Law of Torts*, 4th edn. (Oxford: Hart, 2002).

[76] See the Böll case, 54 BVerfGE 208 (1980) where the complaint was brought by the novelist under art. 2, in conjunction with art. 1, and the *Mephisto* case, 30 BVerfGE 173 (1971), where it succeeded under art. 1 (the case concerned the reputation of a dead person, so art. 2 could not be invoked).

Under the balancing formula established by the Court in *Lüth*,[77] lower courts must weigh the competing interests in freedom of expression and in personal reputation appropriately in the light of all relevant facts in the case; the Court will uphold a constitutional complaint if the balancing has not been conducted properly. The laws protecting individuals against defamation are not simply to be applied literally to limit the other party's free speech rights, but must themselves be interpreted and applied so they do not unduly restrict freedom of expression.

The same balancing process takes place when two constitutional freedoms are weighed against each other. The famous *Mephisto* case nicely illustrates the Court's approach.[78] The complainant publisher reissued *Mephisto*, a satirical novel by Klaus Mann, which portrayed in a defamatory way the cooperation of a well-known deceased actor with the Nazi regime. An application by the actor's son to restrain its publication was upheld by the Hamburg Supreme Court and the Federal Supreme Court in decisions which, the complainant alleged, violated his freedom of artistic expression (*Kunstfreiheit*), guaranteed by Article 5(3) of the Basic Law. *Kunstfreiheit* is not, unlike freedom of expression, subject to the right of personal honour, as set out in Article 5(2). But the Constitutional Court held that it must be interpreted in conformity with the 'dignity of man', the supreme constitutional value, guaranteed by Article 1 of the Basic Law. Further, human dignity must be respected even after the individual's death. In balancing that obligation and freedom of artistic speech, courts should consider the extent to which the publication at issue was fabricated and the seriousness of the insults. The majority of the Constitutional Court considered that the civil courts had correctly assessed the relevant factors when concluding that in this case the dignity and reputation of the actor should be protected against what was in some respects an inaccurate and distorted impression of him in the novel. The dissenters argued that the historical importance of the general theme of the novel outweighed the damage done to the deceased's memory. One of them, Judge Rupp-v. Brünneck, mentioned the approach in the *New York Times* case to show how, in her view, the balance between free speech and reputation interests should more appropriately be struck.[79]

The detailed consideration of all relevant factors is characteristic in the German cases. While the Constitutional Court has consistently emphasized that this is primarily the responsibility of the ordinary civil or criminal judges, it has issued a number of guidelines to ensure that the constitutional rights are safeguarded. In particular, the Court has emphasized that due weight should be given to the character of the speech or publication and the context in which it was made or issued. Speech should be protected from criminal or civil libel proceedings when the defamatory remarks are made incidentally in the course of a contribution to

---

[77] 7 BVerfGE 198 (1958) discussed in ch. II, s. 4 above.
[78] 30 BVerfGE 173 (1971). For commentary, see P. E. Quint, 'Free Speech and Private Law in German Constitutional Theory' (1989) 48 *Maryland Law Rev* 247, 290–307.
[79] 30 BVerfGE 173, 225 (1971).

public discourse.[80] The presumption in favour of freedom of expression in the context of public discussion, first formulated in the *Lüth* case,[81] applies to libel cases. A lower court, therefore, wrongly convicted for libel the publisher of a leaflet which discussed the involvement of two politicians in the 1939 invasion of Poland; the court had failed to take proper account of freedom of speech when it simply characterized the leaflet as libellous, ignoring its political significance.[82] A statement should be characterized as an insult only when its predominant element is disparagement of the individual, rather than a contribution to political debate.[83] The Court has also emphasized that the status of the libel complainant should be taken into account. Politicians, and *a fortiori* political parties, must expect and tolerate caustic remarks, which might ground a libel action if they were made about ordinary individuals. This principle was applied when the Court held that the judges in the civil courts had failed to respect freedom of expression in stopping an SDP candidate from repeating a charge that the Bavarian Christian Social Union (CSU) party was 'the NPD [a neo-Nazi party] of Europe'.[84] Anyone who engages voluntarily in public debate forfeits to some extent his right to protect himself from attack, while a politician or political party has ample opportunity to reply to insulting and defamatory attacks.

The same principles were applied in a case involving a heated debate between a professor of sculpture and art critics.[85] The former had robustly attacked by name a number of critics and their relationship with gallery and museum directors, to which the critics replied, accusing him of 'hate-filled tirades', motivated by personal resentment and extreme right-wing ideology. The Constitutional Court held that the civil courts had ignored the context of the critics' replies, which might be regarded as making a contribution to a debate concerning the arts. Moreover, the professor had initiated the debate and, therefore, should expect criticism in reply. The decision extends the so-called *Gegenschlag* (retaliation) principle, under which defamatory remarks are protected speech if they form part of a reply to a personal attack. In the Schmid–Spiegel case,[86] a judge accused in an article in *Der Spiegel* of unfitness for office and Communist sympathies wrote a vitriolic reply. Although the reply, as well as the original article, contained factual inaccuracies, it was protected from libel proceedings brought by the magazine editor.

In balancing freedom of expression and reputation rights, the Constitutional Court has emphasized that more freedom should be allowed the expression of opinion than the assertion of facts.[87] As far as the expression of an opinion is

---

[80] 'Soldiers are murderers', 93 BVerfGE 266, 294 (1995). [81] 7 BVerfGE 198 (1958).
[82] Flugblatt, 43 BVerfGE 130 (1976).
[83] Strauss 'coerced democrat' case, 82 BVerfGE 272 (1990).
[84] NPD Europas, 61 BVerfGE 1 (1982).
[85] Römerberg, 54 BVerfGE 129 (1980). Also see 60 BVerfGE 234 (1982) (defamatory attacks on credit houses). [86] 12 BVerfGE 113 (1961).
[87] e.g. 42 BVerfGE 163 (1975); Böll, 54 BVerfGE 208 (1980); NPD Europas, 61 BVerfGE 1 (1982).

concerned, a crucial question is whether it should primarily be regarded as a direct insult or abuse of the person, or whether the defamatory allegations form part of a contribution to public discussion, even though they are polemical or exaggerated. If the personal element predominates, reputation and privacy rights must prevail,[88] but otherwise it is for the court to balance freedom of expression and reputation rights. But factual allegations may also be covered by Article 5, as they provide the basis for the expression of opinion. Further, they cannot always easily be disentangled from the expression of a viewpoint or position, and in those circumstances the whole statement should be characterized as opinion; otherwise the protection of freedom of speech might be too readily curtailed.[89] For the same reason, the ordinary civil and criminal courts must be careful not to characterize as a factual allegation a claim which could equally well be regarded as an expression of opinion.[90] So it was wrong for a civil court to treat the statement, 'the CSU is the NPD of Europe', as a factual allegation that it had Nazi aims, when in its context it could be regarded as a robust political opinion.[91] Further, an opinion need not set out the facts on which it is based to enable listeners or readers to assess its quality.[92]

One important case illustrating the importance of the distinction between an expression of opinion and factual allegations concerned a libel on the author, Heinrich Böll.[93] He brought a civil action in respect of a broadcast quoting him inaccurately as holding the view that the (then) state of West Germany was rotten and that it hunted down terrorists mercilessly. The Constitutional Court characterized the misquotation as in effect the provision of false information. The broadcaster should have made it clear that he was offering an interpretation of the novelist's political beliefs; the allegations might have then been treated as an expression of opinion. An obligation to quote Böll correctly did not inhibit the freedom to express an opinion about his attitudes.

The broadcaster in the Böll case must have known that he was misquoting the author, so he had a very feeble case for free speech protection. Indeed, making untrue allegations of fact, knowing them to be false, is not even covered by Article 5 of the Basic Law; they deceive their readers or listeners and so fall altogether outside a free speech provision.[94] On this point the approach of the Bundesverfassungsgericht is similar to that of the US Supreme Court and other courts.[95] But what about

---

[88] Some leading cases concerning personal insult are considered in s. 4 of this chapter.

[89] The posing of real questions is also covered by art. 5(1), even if the question relates to a matter of fact: see 85 BVerfGE 23 (1991).

[90] 85 BVerfGE 1, 15 (1991); 94 BVerfGE 1 (1996). See D. Grimm, 'Die Meinungsfreiheit in der Rechtsprechung des Bundesverfassungsgerichts', 1995 NJW, 1697, 1699.

[91] NPD Europas, 61 BVerfGE 1 (1982).

[92] Echternach, 42 BVerfGE 163, 170 (1976). Compare *Telnikoff* v. *Matusevitch* [1992] 2 AC 343, where the House of Lords held that a jury could only have regard to the terms of a letter to a newspaper, and not the article to which the letter was replying, when it decided whether allegations in the letter were fact or comment.   [93] 54 BVerfGE 208 (1980).

[94] NPD Europas, 61 BVerfGE 1, 8 (1982).

[95] 'There is no constitutional value in false statements of fact': per Powell J. in *Gertz* v. *Robert Welch Inc* (n. 30 above).

allegations of fact which the writer or broadcaster believes to be true, but which he cannot substantiate or which are later clearly found to be inaccurate? The Constitutional Court accepts that a burden of proof may be imposed (by the ordinary civil courts) on the publisher to substantiate the allegations, but its concern for freedom of expression requires that this burden should not be too high. Individuals should not be required to meet the high standard of care expected of the press and other media, for they do not have the same ability to conduct careful research. They are, therefore, entitled to rely on uncontradicted press reports as a basis for making defamatory statements which turn out to be untrue.[96] It is only if the appropriate duty of care (*Sorfaltspflicht*) is satisfied, that the right to reputation and the exercise of free expression should be balanced; otherwise the former prevails.

In principle the Constitutional Court's role is to ensure that the provisions of the Basic Law are properly interpreted and applied to the facts. It is for the criminal or civil courts to determine what the allegations mean and whether they amount to an insult or are defamatory of the claimant. But an arbitrary decision on these issues by the ordinary courts can prejudice the exercise of free speech rights. The Court, therefore, will intervene if a perverse interpretation has been placed on a statement, so that it falls outside the scope of freedom of speech, or if the judge has excluded, without good grounds, possible meanings which would be protected speech.[97] The Coerced Democrat case illustrates these principles.[98] An article in the magazine, *Der Stern*, alleged that Franz-Josef Strauss, a former Prime Minister of Bavaria, was one of a number of 'coerced democrats' who became democrats out of necessity and who, like the Nazi Führer, satisfied the desire for strong government. If that were taken to mean, as it was by the Bavarian courts, that Strauss himself was a crypto-Nazi, then it could be regarded as a serious insult.[99] But the courts had not given any reason to exclude another meaning: that elements of the German population still hankered for a strongman and put Strauss in that role. On that interpretation, the statement could not have been regarded as disparaging of him. In another case the Court held that the Bavarian courts had wrongly convicted the complainants, protesters at an anti-Strauss rally, because they had interpreted the protesters' banners, 'Strauss covers up Fascists', in the light of the placard of a nearby demonstrator which made the specific allegation that he was protecting a murderer.[100] An individual should be accountable only for opinions he has expressed himself. Further, it is wrong for an expression to be interpreted, as it would be understood by a cursory reader or viewer.[101]

[96] 85 BVerfGE 1, 21 (1991); 99 BVerfGE 185, 197–8 (1998).
[97] For a full statement of these principles, see 94 BVerfGE 1 (1996), where the Court made it clear that it was not its role to impose its own interpretation. [98] 82 BVerfGE 272 (1990).
[99] In fact, even on that interpretation, the Court held the magazine feature amounted to polemical political debate, rather than primarily to an insult to Strauss. [100] 82 BVerfGE 43 (1990).
[101] Flugblatt, 43 BVerfGE 130 (1976); Street-theatre case, 67 BVerfGE 213, 229–30 (1984).

Unlike the American and, to a lesser extent, the Australian and New Zealand approaches, the German case-law makes little attempt to formulate precise rules on the basis of which free speech and reputation rights are to be balanced. No sharp line is drawn, for instance, between defamatory allegations made in the course of political speech or, more narrowly, concerning politicians on the one hand, and allegations made in public discourse generally on the other. Rather, the Constitutional Court lays down guidelines on the basis of which the ordinary civil and criminal courts are required in some circumstances to give priority to reputation or freedom of speech, and in other cases to balance in the light of the particular facts. The preference for this course may partly be influenced by the relationship of the Court to the ordinary courts; it is the role of the former to ensure that constitutional rights and values are respected, but to leave the final decision to the latter. But the US Supreme Court could have adopted a similar approach, leaving the state courts to reshape the common law defences to libel in the light of constitutional principles. Instead, it has replaced the common law with a set of relatively precise rules, notably that requiring public official and figure claimants to show actual malice.[102]

One merit of the German approach, and the solution now adopted in England (considered shortly), is that it removes the need to draw bright lines between, say, a public figure and a private individual. More importantly, it avoids the injustice which may be occasioned, say, a politician in the United States (or it seems now New Zealand) unable to vindicate his reputation following publication of wholly unfounded allegations, because he is unable to prove that they were made knowingly or recklessly. On the other hand, the requirement to balance free speech and reputation rights in the light of all the relevant facts leads to less certainty. And that will inevitably deter the publication of stories which might, in the judgement of the writer or editor, fall outside the protection of freedom of expression.

The Constitutional Court has met this anxiety by emphasizing the presumption in favour of speech which should be applied in those cases when defamatory allegations are made in the course of a genuine contribution to public discourse. It has pointed out that too onerous a requirement on defendants to substantiate the truth of defamatory allegations may have a choking (*einschnürend*) impact on the exercise of freedom of expression,[103] a principle strikingly similar to the 'chilling effect' argument accepted in the *New York Times* case, and now to some extent in England.[104] The German Basic Law, however, recognizes that the right to honour is an aspect of the constitutional rights to dignity and personality. Consequently, it would not be right for the courts to give free expression automatic primacy whenever there is a clash

---

[102] See D. A. Anderson, 'First Amendment Limitations on Tort Law' (2004) 69 *Brooklyn Law Rev* 755.   [103] 85 BVerfGE 1, 16 (1991).
[104] See s. 3(iv) below.

between it and the right to reputation.[105] It is this point which best explains and justifies the German approach to balancing.

(iv) England

Until recently English common law refused to recognize (except in unusual circumstances) a defence of qualified privilege to defamation actions brought in respect of communications to the general public of inaccurate information.[106] A libel action would succeed, unless the defendant could prove the truth of any factual allegations (though the defence of fair comment was available if the publication were characterized as an expression of opinion). The decision of the House of Lords in *Reynolds* v. *Times Newspapers* has now altered the position with regard to allegations of fact.[107] The case involved an action brought by Albert Reynolds, a former Prime Minister of Ireland, in respect of an article in the British edition of the *Sunday Times* about the fall of his government. It suggested he had misled the Irish Parliament and his coalition colleague, Dick Spring, by suppressing important information concerning a controversial appointment of the (then) Attorney-General as President of the High Court. The newspaper failed to satisfy the jury that this allegation was true. On appeal, both the Court of Appeal and the House of Lords held that in certain circumstances a defence of qualified privilege was available to the press and other media in respect of the communication to the public of inaccurate information. But both appellate courts ruled that publication of the particular article was not covered by privilege, largely because it presented serious allegations as statements of fact without mentioning the explanation of events Reynolds had given to the Irish Parliament.

The House of Lords unanimously rejected the newspaper's argument for a broad 'generic' privilege, akin to that established in the United States, Australia, and New Zealand, under which all publications to the general public concerning matters of political interest would be covered by privilege irrespective of the circumstances, or, in the case of Australia, when the publication was reasonable. The Lords considered that step undesirable, because, as Lord Nicholls concluded in the leading speech, it would not give adequate protection to reputation rights. Moreover, it would be wrong to distinguish political discussion from discussion of other matters of general public concern. Lord Steyn, with some hesitation, thought English law should adopt the same approach as that taken in Germany and by the European Human Rights Court, under which balancing between freedom of expression and reputation rights is conducted in the light of all the relevant facts rather than on the basis of the category of speech. All the circumstances should be considered in determining whether the publication was covered

---

[105] Dieter Grimm, at the time of writing a judge on the Constitutional Court, has pointed out that in more cases than not the Court upholds decisions giving priority to reputation: Grimm (n. 90 above), 1704.   [106] See s. 2 of this chapter.

[107] [2001] 2 AC 127.

by privilege because of its value to the public, a matter which depended on the quality of the report as well as its subject matter. Lord Nicholls admitted that this approach might lead to uncertainty and so 'chill' the publication of some material. But he issued a number of guidelines on the basis of which journalists, and at trial the court, could determine whether the standards of 'responsible journalism' have been met.[108] Among them are such matters as the seriousness of the allegations, the extent to which the story involves a question of public concern, the quality of the sources for the story, the steps taken to verify it, and whether the claimant was asked for his comments and his version of events was published in the article. But overall, '[t]he court should be slow to conclude that a publication was not in the public interest and . . . the public had no right to know, especially when the information is in the field of political discussion.'[109] Doubts should be resolved in favour of publication.

These last remarks suggest that *Reynolds* might have had a significant impact on the freedom of the media to investigate and report on matters of public concern by its widening of the qualified privilege defence to defamation actions. However, attempts to rely on the expanded defence have been rejected in a number of cases where the newspaper did not make a serious attempt to check the truth of the allegations before publishing the story or relied on someone with an 'axe to grind' as its source.[110] Sensational stories, in which allegations are presented as though they are statements of fact, are not protected against libel actions. For example, the *Sun* was unable to rely on qualified privilege when it published in a series of issues allegations that Bruce Grobbelaar, a well-known goalkeeper, was guilty of match-fixing by conceding goals; the tone of the articles was sensational, and Grobbelaar had not been given a real opportunity to reply to the allegations when he was confronted with them at an airport immediately before taking a flight.[111]

On the other hand, a Saudi newspaper published in London was free to report allegations that the claimant, one member of the Saudi Arabian community, had spread malicious rumours about another member of the community in London, without itself verifying their accuracy.[112] The newspaper was reporting, not adopting, an allegation made in the course of a political dispute between two prominent members of the Saudi community, and had covered the claimant's version of events; it was inappropriate in those circumstances to require it to check the story, although that is normally required under the guidelines in *Reynolds*. The Privy Council upheld the expanded qualified privilege defence, where a journalist had not anticipated that her article would be understood as implying that the

---

[108] The term 'responsible journalism' was used by Lord Nicholls in *Reynolds* v. *Times Newspapers Ltd* (n. 107 above), 202, and is now often employed to refer to the standard of care required of the media to take advantage of the expanded qualified privilege defence.   [109] Ibid., 205.

[110] See *James Gilbert* v. *MGN* [2000] EMLR 680, Eady J.; *Jameel* v. *The Wall Street Journal Europe (No. 2)* [2004] EMLR 196, Eady J.; *Galloway* v. *Telegraph Group* [2004] EWHC 2786, Eady J.

[111] *Grobbelaar* v. *News Group Newspapers Ltd* [2001] 2 All ER 437, CA.

[112] *Al-Fagih* v. *HH Saudi Research and Marketing (UK) Ltd* [2002] EMLR 215, CA.

claimant had lost his position as managing director of the Jamaican government food importing company as a result of dissatisfaction with his handling of various contracts.[113] If the article had explicitly made that allegation, the journalist would not have been able to claim qualified privilege, as she had failed to check whether that was true. But she had not intended to suggest more than that the claimant's services were terminated after the contracts had been made. On that interpretation, she had met the standards of responsible journalism. The Privy Council also considered that the allegation was not a particularly grave one, indicating that its seriousness, and presumably the damage done to the claimant's standing, should be considered when balancing reputation and free speech rights.

The balancing principles formulated in *Reynolds* have now been clarified by the Court of Appeal in *Loutchansky* v. *Times Newspapers (No. 2)*.[114] The newspaper had published two articles alleging that the claimant, an international businessman, was the boss of a Russian criminal organization and was involved with money laundering and the smuggling of nuclear weapons. The trial judge, Gray J., rejected the qualified privilege defence, holding the newspaper had not taken adequate steps to check the allegations made by its sources and had made no serious attempt to contact the claimant or his solicitor to get their side of the story.[115] No objection was taken to those particular conclusions, but the Court of Appeal allowed the appeal on the ground that the judge's general approach was wrong. Following the familiar duty-interest test for determining whether there was a qualified privilege defence, Gray J. asked whether the newspaper was under a *duty* to publish the allegations in the sense that it would be open to legitimate criticism, if it had failed to do so.[116] The Court of Appeal rightly thought that test was too restrictive. A responsible journalist could decide to publish a story which another newspaper would think prudent not to cover. Lord Phillips MR said it would be wrong for the courts to set the standards of responsible journalism too high, as otherwise newspapers would be deterred from publishing material of public interest.[117] This is a clear recognition that libel law may exercise an undesirable chilling effect on freedom of speech if the balance is not struck properly. Courts should be alive to the implications of their decisions for the media in general.

On the other hand, the judgment of Eady J. in *Jameel* v. *The Wall Street Journal Europe (No. 2)*[118] takes a more conservative approach. In his view, the House of Lords in *Reynolds* did not intend the responsible journalism standard to replace the traditional duty-interest test for determining whether there is a qualified privilege; a judge must consider whether the newspaper had a social or moral duty to publish the particular words complained of to the general public. Grave allegations, in this case that a Saudi businessman and company were involved in

---

[113] *Bonnick* v. *Morris* [2002] EMLR 827. [114] [2002] 1 All ER 652.
[115] [2001] EMLR 898. [116] Ibid., para. 18.
[117] N. 114 above, para. 41. Equally the requirement should not be set too low, as otherwise the public would be misinformed by careless journalists. [118] [2004] EMLR 196.

financial support of terrorists, should only be published after the claimants had a fair opportunity to put their side of the story. The question was not whether the public had a legitimate interest in the prevention of terrorism, but whether it was entitled to be told the claimants' names. The recent decision in *Galloway* v. *Telegraph Group*[119] emphasizes that a newspaper cannot claim qualified privilege if it embellishes serious allegations, without putting them fully to the claimant and without making any attempt to verify them; the newspaper was not entitled to rely on documents found in government offices in Baghdad, which appeared to suggest that George Galloway, MP was in the pay of Saddam Hussein's regime.

Even after *Reynolds*, English libel law may deter the media from publishing allegations which they believe on good grounds to be accurate, when, for instance, there is not enough time to verify them or the claimant is unavailable for comment. In these circumstances libel law continues to chill freedom of speech. But that chill should only be regarded as undesirable if it is accepted that there is a right to publish material damaging to an individual's reputation whenever the allegations are of public interest and there is some basis for believing them to be true.[120] That position would not do justice to reputation rights, respect for which is of concern both to the victim of defamatory allegations and to the general public. The public has a free speech interest in the publication of fair, well-researched stories, not in those which are poorly put together and which gratuitously destroy the standing of people in public life. The House of Lords was, therefore, surely right to insist that the press and other media should be required to observe the standards of responsible journalism, which may often require publication to be delayed until sources have been corroborated and the claimant has been contacted to allow his version of events to be published with the allegations.

(v) The European Convention on Human Rights

The House of Lords in *Reynolds* considered the jurisprudence of the European Court of Human Rights when it decided to formulate an expanded qualified privilege defence. That Court has considered the relationship of freedom of expression and the right to reputation in a number of cases (although some of them would be considered in an English context to involve issues of contempt of court or privacy rather than libel).[121] In line with its general approach in freedom of expression cases, the Court considers whether the restrictions imposed by national defamation law on the exercise of the right to freedom of expression are necessary 'for the protection of the reputation or rights of others'.[122] It takes into account the role of the press and media as 'public watchdogs', holding that journalists must be

---

[119] [2004] EWHC 2786, Eady J.

[120] See Lord Hoffmann in *The Gleaner Co Ltd* v. *Abrahams* [2004] 1 AC 628, para. 72, PC.

[121] See E. Barendt, 'The Impact of the Human Rights Act 1998 on the Law of Libel' (2001/2) *Yearbook of Copyright and Media Law* 141 for a review of these cases.   [122] ECHR, art. 10(2).

allowed some latitude to provide exaggerated and provocative material. Its approach is to look at all the relevant circumstances of the publication before deciding whether on the particular facts it was right for national libel law to curtail freedom of expression.

Three principal points emerge from the Court's rich, but complex jurisprudence. First, it is concerned with the character and subject matter of the defamatory material rather than the status of the libel claimant. Admittedly, the Court has sometimes emphasized that politicians should tolerate more criticism than private individuals, while also making it plain that they do not forfeit their right to protect their reputation even when acting officially. But the greater latitude allowed for criticism of politicians stems from the importance of free political debate to a democracy, a key Convention value. This was first stated in *Lingens* v. *Austria*, which remains a ruling of seminal importance.[123] A former Chancellor, Bruno Kreisky, had successfully brought a criminal libel prosecution in Austria against the editor of a magazine for making allegations that he was guilty of political opportunism in negotiating a coalition government with Peter, the leader of an extreme right-wing party, and in defending Peter against charges of involvement in Nazi atrocities. The Court unanimously held the conviction incompatible with the ECHR, as Austrian law in effect required the defendant to prove the truth of a value judgement on Kreisky's conduct, an impossible task.

Subsequently, it has become clear that the Court will carefully scrutinize constraints imposed by libel law on the discussion of any matter of public concern. Allegations that unnamed police officers had behaved brutally (*Thorgeirson*),[124] that seal hunters had frequently broken hunting regulations and engaged in cruel hunting methods (*Bladet Tromso*),[125] and newspaper reports of alleged incompetent treatment of patients by a cosmetic surgeon (*Bergens Tidende*),[126] have all been characterized as raising matters of real public concern, although none of them concerned politicians or party political issues. (In each case, the Court decided the national libel law imposed unnecessary restraints on freedom of expression.) In *Nilsen and Johnsen* v. *Norway*,[127] it was held that a university professor who engaged in public debate about police conduct in Bergen should expect to tolerate aspersions from police officers about his motives, though he should not be equated with a politician for this purpose. On the other hand, when the Court held compatible with the Convention the conviction in Estonia of a newspaper journalist for publishing insulting expressions, it stressed that the remarks were made about the private life of a woman, who had been a political counsellor to a former Prime Minister, but who was no longer involved in political affairs.[128] Equally, defamatory allegations made in the course of an employment

---

[123] (1986) 8 EHRR 407.　　[124] *Thorgeirson* v. *Iceland* (1992) 14 EHRR 843.

[125] *Bladet Tromso* v. *Norway* (2000) 29 EHRR 125.

[126] *Bergens Tidende* v. *Norway* (2001) 31 EHRR 16.　　[127] (1999) 30 EHRR 878.

[128] *Tammer* v. *Estonia* (2003) 37 EHRR 43. The journalist was convicted of using particularly coarse expressions, so committing the offence of degrading another's honour and dignity.

dispute between the Bank of Spain and one of its officials were not entitled to the same degree of protection as they would have been if they had been made in the context of a public debate on a matter of general concern.[129]

Secondly, the Court gives greater protection to value judgements than to factual allegations. In that respect it adopts the same approach as courts in the United States, Germany, England, and other jurisdictions. Not only is it wrong to expect a defendant to justify a value judgement, it seems that the Court may not require him to show more than a sufficient or some basis of fact to support the comment.[130] Moreover, the Court is willing to interpret the allegations itself; it does not necessarily accept their characterization by the national court as factual claims rather than an expression of opinion.[131] Imputing bad motives to a claimant may be treated as a value judgement, while the common law has sometimes treated such an imputation as an allegation of fact.[132] With regard to allegations of fact, the Court has even been prepared occasionally to hold that a newspaper was free to publish them without proving their truth. Successful libel proceedings in Iceland for the publication of widespread, but unproven, rumours of police brutality were held incompatible with the ECHR.[133] The Court has also held that a newspaper had no duty to verify allegations about seal-hunting methods which had been made in an unpublished government report (though the allegations were later found to be largely untrue),[134] and that a journalist was free to quote extracts from a newspaper article which had defamed government officials without distancing himself from the allegations.[135] All these cases involved the reporting of allegations made by others; in these circumstances it may be reasonable not to require the media to establish the truth of a story for which there is at least some foundation. But the Court has held that the common law presumption of falsity, under which it is for the defendant to prove the truth of defamatory allegations, is not as such incompatible with freedom of expression.[136]

A third feature of the Court's approach to balancing freedom of expression and reputation rights is that it attaches weight to the general purpose of the publication and the relative importance within that context of the defamatory allegations.[137] In *Thorgeirson*, for example, it emphasized that the purpose of the article was to persuade the government to set up an inquiry to investigate police

---

[129] *Nafria* v. *Spain* (2003) 36 EHRR 36.
[130] *Schwabe* v. *Austria*, Series A 242 (1992); *De Haes* v. *Belgium* (1998) 25 EHRR 1.
[131] See *Nilsen* (n. 127 above).
[132] But see *Branson* v. *Bower* [2001] EMLR 800, CA, where it was held that an assertion of motive may be held to be comment at common law, if it is made clear to the reader that it was an inference from the facts.   [133] *Thorgeirson* v. *Iceland* (n. 124 above).
[134] *Bladet Tromso* v. *Norway* (n. 125 above). Also see *Selistö* v. *Finland*, Decision of 16 Nov. 2004, when the Court said reporters had no general duty to verify the truth of statements in a police record: para. 60.   [135] *Thoma* v. *Luxembourg* (2003) 36 EHRR 359.
[136] *McVicar* v. *UK* (2002) 35 EHRR 22.
[137] See *Selistö* v. *Finland* (n. 134 above), where the Court said the purpose of the articles was to discuss the general problem of drinking while working, and that the reference to a particular case was to illustrate the argument: para. 52.

conduct, rather than to make allegations about any particular officers, while in *Bladet Tromso* the newspaper's objective was to investigate and improve methods of seal hunting, not to accuse the crew of any particular boat of cruelty to animals. Defamatory allegations should be seen in the context of a series of articles dealing with matters of public concern. This approach gives greater weight to freedom of speech than that of the common law which typically asks whether there is a defence to the publication of allegations already characterized as defamatory of the claimant.[138] The point is that under the ECHR, as in the United States, the question is whether restrictions on freedom of expression can be justified, rather than whether there is a good free speech defence to vindication of the reputation right.

Overall, the European Court ensures that national courts have balanced freedom of expression and the right to reputation correctly. In its view that entails assessment of all the relevant facts: the character of the publication or discussion in the course of which the allegations have been made, the importance of the allegations within that context and whether they have to some extent been balanced by remarks favourable to the claimant (perhaps published in other articles by the newspaper),[139] the position or status of the claimant, and whether the allegations should be regarded as value judgements or as assertions of fact. The balancing is not between two rights or interests of equal importance. It must be shown that libel law does not impose an unnecessary restriction on freedom of expression. There is, therefore, a presumption in favour of freedom of expression which reflects the status of the freedom under the Convention. The presumption is stronger than it is in Germany, where the courts are required to balance two rights of constitutional weight. It ensures that more weight is attached in this context to freedom of expression than it is in England. Despite the decision of the House of Lords in *Reynolds*,[140] English courts are still inclined to ask whether there are good reasons for the freedom to prevail over reputation rights, rather than whether the need to protect the latter justifies infringement of freedom of expression.

(vi) Conclusions on balancing in libel cases

Free speech and reputation rights may be balanced on the basis of rules to be applied in a fairly mechanistic way or on the basis of a detailed weighing of the particular facts. United States and New Zealand law adopt the former option,

---

[138] *Telnikoff* v. *Matusevitch* [1992] 2 AC 343, HL, holding statements in a newspaper may be characterized as factual claims rather than comment, in isolation from the material in an earlier number of the paper, seems incompatible with the approach of the European Court.

[139] See *Bergens Tidende* (n. 126 above) where it was relevant that the newspaper also published an interview with the claimant and other plastic surgeons, in which attention was drawn to the risks of cosmetic surgery. [140] N. 107 above.

Germany, English law, and the European Court the latter. The Australian position may be regarded as hybrid, in that it formulates a qualified privilege in terms of political discussion, while providing that the defendant must show that publication was reasonable, a provision which requires some regard at trial to the particular circumstances of the publication. Of course this taxonomy may be a little crude. There seems, for example, relatively little difference between the detailed weighing of all the facts required by the House of Lords in *Reynolds* and the hybrid approach of the High Court of Australia in *Lange*. Moreover, both definitional and ad hoc balancing are different ways of accommodating two conflicting rights. The rule in *New York Times* and later cases allows some claimants to recover libel damages, because even in the United States it is recognized that on occasion reputation should trump free speech.

The US preference for definitional balancing is based on the fear that otherwise free speech interests would be subordinated to reputation. If too much discretion is left to trial judges to weigh the strength of the competing interests, there is a danger that the long-term impact of libel law on the media and free speech generally will be ignored.[141] It may be right to award compensation to a claimant whose reputation has suffered from publication of a scurrilous story which the newspaper had not checked. But that result might deter publication in other circumstances where the balance of interests should be struck differently. On the other hand, the US rules mean that deserving claimants, whether public figures or private individuals, can rarely vindicate their reputation, with considerable damage to the individuals concerned and social costs in terms of the declining credibility of the press and the lower quality of public discourse.

Overall, an ad hoc balancing approach is preferable, if only because it is the better way to resolve conflicts between two competing rights. When both rights have constitutional significance, as they do in Germany, this approach must be adopted, unless one right is to be treated as subordinate to the other. In the United States, England, and other systems where freedom of expression has constitutional significance, but reputation does not, there is a stronger case for formulating rules which give the former priority in some contexts. It may be right, for instance, to fashion speech-protective rules to cover the publication of defamatory allegations in the course of political speech. Whichever approach is taken, trial courts and the media should be given guidelines for the assessment of the facts. More importantly, it should be clear, as it is in Germany and is under the Convention, that there is a presumption in favour of freedom of expression. Doubts should be resolved by the trial judge in favour of allowing publication. The media and other publishers should have confidence that if the story is one of real public interest and it has been investigated and prepared responsibly, then they are free to release it without fear of libel proceedings.

---

[141] F. Schauer, 'Categories and the First Amendment: A Play in Three Acts' (1981) 34 *Vanderbilt Law Rev* 265, 301–5.

4. Insults and Satire

Advertisements for Campari have used celebrities who spoke about their 'first time', meaning their first Campari, but with a double entendre reference to their first sexual experience. The US magazine *Hustler* in a parody of the advertisement featured a made-up interview with Jerry Falwell, a prominent evangelical preacher and Moral Majority founder, in which he admitted that his 'first time' was with his mother in an outhouse; he also admitted to being 'sloshed before I go out to the pulpit'. A disclaimer in small print indicated it was a parody, not to be taken seriously. Falwell sued in libel and in the separate tort of intentional infliction of emotional distress. While the jury decided the feature could not be understood as describing actual facts and so could not be defamatory of Falwell, it awarded him substantial damages for the magazine's deliberate infliction of hurt and suffering, a ruling upheld by the Circuit Court of Appeals.[142] However, the Supreme Court, in a rare unanimous decision, reversed.[143] It was contrary to the First Amendment to impose liability in the area of public discussion of public figures, merely because the speaker had a desire to hurt the victim or some other bad motive. The Circuit Court had held the parody was 'outrageous', but that was too subjective a standard to differentiate between acceptable satire on the one hand and a grossly offensive insult on the other. Rehnquist CJ for the Court concluded that public officials and figures could not recover for the intentional infliction of emotional distress, unless they showed the publication contained a false statement of fact, made with 'actual malice', that is with knowledge of its falsity or with reckless disregard whether or not it was true. The ruling in effect precluded a politician or celebrity from recovering damages for any insult of this type, no matter how outrageous its tone.

This case presents a free speech issue, a little different from that involved in a libel action. In libel there is a conflict between freedom of expression and the right of an individual to protect his standing within the community in the face of factual claims or comments on his conduct or attitudes. *Falwell* was concerned with the relationship of individual dignity, rather than reputation, on the one hand to the freedom of political satire on the other. In other jurisdictions the right to parody or satirize may fall under a provision other than that covering free speech. In Germany, it may be covered by the guarantee of freedom of the arts laid down in Article 5(3) of the Basic Law, while in Italy a right of satire has been claimed on the basis of Articles 9 and 33 of the Constitution as well as on freedom of expression.[144]

---

[142] *Hustler Magazine* v. *Falwell* 797 F 2d 1270 (4th Cir, 1986).   [143] 485 US 46 (1988).

[144] Art. 9 requires the development of culture and scientific research, while art. 33 guarantees, without limit, freedom of the arts and sciences and their teaching. For a summary of Italian law protecting personal honour, see R Zaccaria, *Diritto dell' Informazione and della Communicazione* (Padua: Cedam, 1998), 69–86.

The distinction between reputation and dignity cases is not a clear one in English law, partly because under common law, a statement may be actionable as defamatory if it exposes the claimant to ridicule. For example, a majority of the Court of Appeal held that a jury could find defamatory the description of an actor-director as 'hideously ugly'.[145] There is no requirement that, on their proper construction, the words must either explicitly or implicitly make a false statement of fact about the claimant. But in the United States, the Supreme Court has held that if the words are exaggerated or rhetorical hyperbole, the defamation claim must be dismissed as incompatible with the First Amendment.[146] That is why it made sense for Falwell to bring an action under the heading of intentional infliction of mental distress, for it was inevitable under the Court's precedents that a defamation claim would fail.

These legal niceties do not bring out the central question of principle: whether a line can or should be drawn between political satire or parody, fully protected under freedom of speech, and outrageous personal insults which might fall outside it or not be protected when balanced against the right to human dignity. Rehnquist CJ in *Falwell* did not think it possible or sensible to draw a line, either in terms of the writer's real intention or in terms of the degree of insult or outrage perpetrated by the parody. Whatever the merits of that view, the decision has been vigorously defended by Robert Post on the ground that it is fundamentally wrong on general free speech principles for the courts to distinguish between acceptable satire and outrageous personal insults or abuse, no matter how unpleasant the terms used of the claimant. To do this would be to impose on public debate standards of civility, which are contested and the enforcement of which would restrict uninhibited discourse.[147] The decision in *Falwell* on this perspective rightly follows decisions in other areas of free speech law, for instance, those establishing the right to speak offensively of religious communities,[148] or to wear in public the slogan 'Fuck the Draft' on a jacket.[149]

The argument is a strong one, but ultimately unpersuasive. It does not resolve the paradox that, on Post's interpretation, the First Amendment precludes enforcement of standards of civil discourse, when some standards are necessary to hold any rational democratic debate.[150] Free speech arguments are often made on the basis that individuals have fundamental rights to dignity and are entitled to equal respect and concern.[151] The arguments require, at least, that speakers make

---

[145] *Berkoff* v. *Burchill* [1997] EMLR 139.

[146] *Greenbelt Cooperative Publishing Assoc* v. *Bresler* 398 US 6 (1970) (to charge a developer with 'blackmail' was in the circumstances no more than a claim that he engaged in unreasonable negotiating tactics); *Old Dominion Branch No. 496, Letter Carriers* v. *Austin* 418 US 264 (1974) (to charge non-unionists as 'scabs', implying they are 'traitors', was not to be understood as more than an expression of a pejorative opinion).

[147] R. C. Post, 'The Constitutional Concept of Public Discourse: Outrageous Opinion, Democratic Deliberation, and *Hustler Magazine* v. *Falwell*' (1990) 103 *Harvard Law Rev* 601.

[148] *Cantwell* v. *Connecticut* 310 US 296 (1940) (offensive speech about Catholics covered by First Amendment). [149] *Cohen* v. *California* 403 US 15 (1971).

[150] N. 147 above, 642–4. [151] See ch. I, ss. 2(ii) and 4(i) above.

claims which they believe to be true and which they believe the audience should consider seriously in its assessment of a social issue or an individual. Otherwise freedom of speech could be claimed by the pedlars of deliberate lies, aimed at individuals and intended, perhaps, to 'remove' them from public life. These minimal requirements for claiming the protection of freedom of speech were hardly satisfied by the advertisement parody in *Falwell*. On any view, it was a vicious and unpleasant slur on a public figure, admittedly a controversial one whose views were understandably distasteful to many people. Indeed, the small-print disclaimer at the foot of the fake interview revealed its true character. No genuine parody or satire requires that sort of disclaimer, as any reader would know that it was poking fun at its object. The disclaimer was printed in a disingenuous attempt to temper the insult.

The most important point is that the parody was aimed at an individual. Earlier decisions of the Supreme Court upholding a First Amendment right to engage in offensive political and religious speech can be distinguished. It would unduly fetter freedom of speech to impose legal restraints on the terms of that type of discourse; a publisher should not be required to disentangle, say, vituperative criticism of Catholics or socialists as a group from an onslaught on religious belief or left-wing politics. But he can be expected not to engage in abuse of an individual, no matter how much that person is linked with a cause of which the speaker disapproves. That is not to say that Falwell should have recovered damages; it is hard to believe that the parody really caused him any distress. That point, however, is not one of free speech. Gratuitous abuse might cause real hurt, say, on these facts to Falwell's mother, or when racial or sexual insults are directed at an individual. It is unclear that the Supreme Court decision would preclude recovery of damages in these cases.[152] Equally, it did not provide any convincing reason why a public figure should never, as a matter of free speech law, be able to recover for an insult directed at him.

Another solution to this problem is provided by decisions of the German Constitutional Court. Political satire is covered by the Article 5(3) guarantee of *Kunstfreiheit* (freedom of the arts). It protects novel forms of art offering a strong criticism of contemporary events and personalities.[153] The exercise of this freedom is not limited, as is freedom of expression, by the provisions of general laws or the right to reputation, but it must be considered in conjunction with other constitutional rights, notably the right to the free development of personality and human dignity.[154] In the Strauss caricature case,[155] the Court dismissed a case brought by the publisher of cartoons of Strauss, portraying him as a pig copulating

---

[152] Post (n. 147 above), 662 suggests there may be recovery in these cases.

[153] Street-theatre case, 67 BVerfGE 213, 225–8 (1984) in which the Court held that a moving street theatre, in which Franz-Josef Strauss, then a candidate for the Chancellorship, was portrayed in the same float as prominent Nazis, should be protected under freedom of the arts in the absence of evidence that there was a very serious injury to personality rights.   [154] Ibid., 228.

[155] 75 BVerfGE 369 (1987).

with another pig dressed in judicial robes. The publisher argued that his conviction for defamation violated his rights under Article 5(3). The Court was prepared to characterize the drawings as art; there is no distinction for the purposes of the Basic Law between good and bad art. But it dismissed the complaint, as the cartoons were intended to deprive Strauss of his dignity by portraying him as engaged in bestial sexual conduct. Where there was an interference with human dignity, *Kunstfreiheit* must always give way to personality rights. This approach has also been adopted in a case where a satirical magazine had described the claimant as a 'cripple'. Satire can be covered by artistic freedom, but it does not follow that every form of satire should be treated in this way.[156]

The approach taken in the Strauss caricature case is right in principle, even though its application to the facts is controversial. The cartoons would no doubt have angered Strauss, but it is difficult to believe that his reputation suffered or that he was emotionally wounded by them. Political satire should not be protected when it amounts only to insulting speech directed against an individual. If, say, a magazine feature attributes words to a celebrity, or uses a computerized image to portray her naked, it should make no difference that the feature was intended as a parody of an interview she had given.[157] It should be regarded as a verbal assault on the individual's right to dignity, rather than a contribution to political or artistic debate protected under the free speech (or freedom of the arts) clauses of the Constitution.

5. Privacy and Free Speech

(i) Introduction

Many of the arguments considered in the preceding sections of this chapter are now deployed in the context of privacy actions.[158] The law must balance competing rights: to personal privacy on the one hand, and on the other the right of the public to be informed about matters of concern and the freedom of the media to satisfy that concern. Although privacy/free speech issues have hitherto been less often considered at the constitutional level than have those concerning the relationship of reputation and free speech, the former will assume increasing importance. The development is inevitable, given the public's insatiable appetite for details of the personal life of celebrities and the ease with which information can be acquired by long-range photography and the interception of telephone and other communications.

---

[156] 86 BVerfGE 1 (1992).

[157] For an Italian case on the point, see the decision of the Corte di Cassazione, Penal Section, of 20 Oct. 1998, reported in (1999) Il Diritto dell'Informazione e dell'Informatica 369, rejecting appeal of author of a newspaper article which included a cartoon implying that a woman senator fellated Berlusconi. Satire is not protected if does not respect personality rights.

[158] See the essays in B. Markesinis (ed.), *Protecting Privacy* (Oxford: OUP, 1999).

Two general points should be made before comparisons are made between the treatment of privacy issues in various jurisdictions. First, while privacy may conflict with free speech, there are many circumstances in which a right to privacy may support, or even be necessary for, the effective exercise of free expression rights.[159] For example, under the ECHR, the right of prisoners to send and receive letters is typically protected by Article 8 (the right to respect for private life, home and correspondence),[160] but it might equally fall under freedom of expression. The confidentiality of the post, telephone calls, and e-mail correspondence is both an aspect of privacy law (or in English law the jurisdiction to restrain a breach of confidence) and also a safeguard for the freedom to engage in personal conversations.

The second point is more important. It is right to ask whether, or how far, the free speech arguments relevant to libel should be applied to privacy.[161] Speech bringing into question the probity or competence of public officials, and some public figures, is covered by a free expression clause, because it cannot be disentangled from criticism of government. The public is entitled to consider a claim that its leaders have not told the truth (unless the claim is made with knowledge of its falsity or irresponsibly). But it is not so obvious that it has a similar claim to hear details of the intimate, sexual life of a Cabinet minister, let alone of a celebrity soccer player or fashion model, even if they are accurate. The argument from truth, on a casual reading, might appear to cover these disclosures. But that argument, at least as framed by John Stuart Mill, does not apply. He was concerned to prevent the suppression of arguments on the ground that they make false claims, irrespective of whether they are certainly false or whether they may turn out to be true. It is important for society to consider these arguments, however nonsensical they appear to be.[162] But privacy is most often asserted to stop the dissemination of true facts, which the public has no business considering because of their private character. It is a distortion of Mill's argument to conclude that the public is entitled to know everything about everyone.[163] There are some questions to which it is surely appropriate to reply: 'Mind your own business'.

Naturally the issue is trickier when we consider the balance between free speech and the privacy rights of public officials and politicians. Some people, perhaps a majority, may argue that they are entitled to know, for example, whether a candidate for Parliament or the Presidency has committed marital infidelity, is secretly gay, or behaved disreputably as a university student twenty years ago, before deciding how to vote. The arguments for free speech from its role in ensuring effective democracy, and the key importance of uninhibited public discourse,

---

[159] S. M. Scott, 'Protecting Privacy: The Forgotten Value of the First Amendment' (1996) 71 *Washington Law Rev* 683.
[160] *Silver* v. *UK* (1983) 5 EHRR 347; *McCallum* v. *UK* (1991) 13 EHRR 597.
[161] Nimmer (n. 33 above), 956–66.
[162] See ch. I, s. 2 above for discussion of Mill's argument.
[163] See F. Schauer, 'Reflections on the Value of Truth' (1991) 41 *Case Western Law Rev* 699.

make that claim hard to resist.[164] Free speech is clearly in issue. But it is not necessarily a trump card. Otherwise, the law would in effect deny politicians privacy rights, even to stop the publication of stories which have no clear relationship to the discharge of their public duties. Some arguments already mentioned in the context of defamation are pertinent here. Without protection from privacy laws, sensitive people may prefer not to enter public life or may leave it, rather than allow themselves and their family to endure constant tabloid exposures. The media may find it easier to write about personalities and their private life than to explore social issues. That has already happened in England and the United States, where privacy is not well protected, but may have happened less on the continent of Europe, in particular in France where politicians can claim the protection of strong privacy laws.[165]

The relationship of privacy and free speech (or press) rights is therefore complex. It would be wrong simply to apply the arguments relevant to defamation without considering the extent to which the disclosure of private information is covered by freedom of speech. Another difficulty is that privacy claims against the media may be made in a variety of circumstances which may require different treatment: the publication of a photograph, for instance, may be thought a greater invasion of personal privacy and less justifiable in terms of freedom of speech and of the press, than the publication of factual information about the individual concerned. A comparison of free speech/privacy balancing can be made by looking at four types of privacy conflict and then through a discussion of a few cases involving public figures.

(ii) Publication of confidential information

English law has not hitherto recognized a discrete cause of action for privacy against the media, or indeed in other circumstances.[166] But there is a well-established equitable jurisdiction to restrain a breach of confidence, enforceable against the media when it publishes information which it knows, or should have appreciated, is personal or confidential. The courts may therefore protect marital confidences,[167] and the confidential details of a lesbian relationship, from press coverage.[168] The relationship of breach of confidence to press freedom was fully considered by the Court of Appeal in *A* v. *B plc*,[169] when a Premier League footballer attempted to prevent a Sunday newspaper from revealing his identity and

---

[164] F. Schauer, 'Can Public Figures have Private Lives?', in E. F. Paul, F. D. Miller, and J. Paul (eds.), *The Right to Privacy* (Cambridge: CUP, 2000), 293.

[165] For a comparison of French and US privacy law, see J. M. Hauch, 'Protecting Private Facts in France: The Warren & Brandeis Tort is Alive and Well and Flourishing in Paris' (1994) 68 *Tulane Law Rev* 1219.

[166] See the decision of the House of Lords in *Wainwright* v. *Home Office* [2004] 2 AC 406, paras. 15–31.   [167] *Argyll* v. *Argyll* [1967] Ch 302, Ch D.

[168] *Stephens* v. *Avery* [1988] Ch 449, Ch D.   [169] [2003] QB 195.

intimate details of two affairs; the paper had acquired the information from the two women involved. The Court of Appeal discharged the interim injunction granted by Jack J. In a wide-ranging judgment, Lord Woolf CJ held that while public figures are entitled to a private life, they should recognize that even trivial facts relating to them are of great interest to the public. That is particularly the case when the figure has become a role model, whose conduct might be followed by the general public. The question was not whether there was a public interest in the particular information being published, but whether 'the public have an understandable and so a legitimate interest in being told the information'.[170] Further, if newspapers are not free to publish stories in which the public are interested, fewer copies will be sold with repercussions for the survival of the press. Footballers may be regarded as role models whose conduct is open to scrutiny. Further, as the two women were free to disclose details of their affairs to their friends, they should also be free to reveal them to the media. By implication, the media were free to reveal the details to the general public.

Much of this argument is open to criticism. First, the Court of Appeal took a *descriptive* approach to the 'public interest' defence to breach of confidence. From this perspective, the law of confidence (or privacy) cannot inhibit the publication of any material which the public finds interesting. It is immaterial whether the story is one with which the public ought to be concerned, because, say, it involves a matter of political or social controversy, the *normative* approach traditionally taken in both breach of confidence and libel law. Taken to its extreme, the descriptive approach would mean that a privacy or breach of confidence claim could never be made to prevent, or secure compensation for, the publication of, say, explicit details of a celebrity's sexual affairs, since these always seem to interest the public. Secondly, it does not follow from the entitlement of the women to disclose details of the affairs that the press also enjoys a parallel right of public revelation. The two women were exercising their right to free expression as individuals to tell their stories, a right which might conceivably have been exercised to correct false beliefs their friends had formed as a result of local gossip or perhaps to vent their personal anger. But those arguments could not possibly justify media publication of details of the affairs to the general public; the public had no clear entitlement to know anything about the story.

Secret political discussions may be covered by breach of confidence or privacy, though the public should have a greater interest—the normative approach—in their disclosure than it does in the publication of bedroom gossip. Two cases may be compared. In *Bartnicki* v. *Vopper*[171] a majority of the US Supreme Court held that Vopper, a radio broadcaster, had a free speech right to play on his programme a tape of an intercepted telephone conversation in which the caller, Bartnicki, a teachers' union negotiator, had discussed the timing of a proposed strike with the head of the local union. The Court accepted that the interception was unlawful;

---

[170] Ibid., para. 11(xii).   [171] 532 US 514 (2001).

Vopper had not been involved in that illegality, but was aware that the tape sent him had been acquired in that way. But the discussions between the union officials were of considerable public interest to the community, so Stevens J. for the Court decided that Vopper should be free to broadcast them, irrespective of the interceptor's illegal conduct. The state interest in protecting privacy of communication was not strong enough to justify an award of damages against him. In dissent, Rehnquist CJ argued that an award of damages would discourage telephone interception and so protect privacy; further, protection of confidentiality safeguarded the First Amendment rights of the parties to telephone communications. The Court's decision would, in his view, exercise a chilling effect on private conversations.[172]

In contrast, the German Federal Supreme Court ruled that *Stern* magazine infringed the personality rights of two leaders of the Christian Democratic Union (CDU) when it published a transcript of their bugged telephone conversation.[173] It was not simply that the transcript revealed details of some private matters, albeit closely connected to the emergence of one of the participants, Helmut Kohl, as CDU candidate for Federal Chancellor, clearly a matter of public interest. Irrespective of the contents of the communication, there was an infringement of the right of all individuals to use the telephone system without fear that their conversation would be reproduced following its interception. It was immaterial that there was a public interest in the subject matter of much of the conversation; the magazine could have commented on the leaders' attitudes without publishing the transcript.

A more expansive view of freedom of expression, in a slightly different privacy context, was taken by the European Court of Human Rights in *Fressoz and Roire* v. *France*.[174] The applicants, the editor of *Le Canard Enchaîné* and a journalist on the paper, reproduced photocopies of income tax assessments of the head of Peugeot in the context of an article alleging that he had awarded himself a 45 per cent income rise over two years, in the course of which the average pay of its workers during that period rose by only 6.7 per cent. They were convicted of an offence of handling private tax documents, which they had acquired, it was presumed, as a result of a breach of confidence by an official. The European Court held that this conviction amounted to a disproportionate interference with the journalists' freedom of expression, given that the information about the level of earnings was not itself confidential; taxpayers could inspect a list of people liable for tax and find out details of their income and tax liability. It was reasonable to give the story credibility by reproducing copies of the assessments.[175] An argument of this kind might have been used, if necessary, to strengthen the journalist's case in *Bartnicki* v. *Vopper*, or to achieve a different result in the German case. But in those cases the publications (of the tape or transcript) revealed confidential discussions and

---

[172] 532 US 514, 554 (2001).   [173] NJW 1979, 647.   [174] (2001) 31 EHRR 2.
[175] Ibid., paras. 53–4.

information, and so infringed personal privacy; they did not merely give credence to information which was already available.

(iii) Revealing personal identity

Conflicts between privacy and freedom of speech arise when the media identify someone who has a legal right to anonymity or who prefers anonymity to publicity. For instance, legislation may make it an offence to disclose the name of the victim of rape or other sexual assault.[176] A provision of this type has been held compatible with freedom of expression in Canada.[177] But it is unclear whether it would survive constitutional challenge in the United States. The Supreme Court has held that the media were free to identify a rape victim, when they had obtained the name from court records open to public inspection.[178] In *Florida Star* v. *BJF*[179] it ruled by a majority that a state law making it unlawful for media communications to identify the victim of a sexual offence could not be applied to enable a rape victim to recover damages from a newspaper which had named her. Its journalist had seen a police report left in a press room which by mistake mentioned her name. The principal reason for the decision was that the journalist had not acted illegally in his acquisition of the information; the Sheriff's Department had wrongly included the victim's name in the report. But it is hard to see why the lawfulness of the acquisition should mean that the press was free publicly to reveal information which the state had good reason to keep private—in the interests of encouraging rape victims to come forward and of their protection from emotional distress.[180] Further, the Court considered the statute was too narrowly drafted, in that it proscribed the identification of sexual offences only by the mass media, and not by individuals. Admittedly, Marshall J. for the Court declined to hold that privacy could never prevail over press intrusion, or that a state could never criminalize identification of the victim of a sexual offence. White J. in dissent argued that the majority had given the privacy interest too little weight and the public's right to know too much. He doubted whether there was any public interest in publishing the names, addresses, or other details of the victims of crime, a robust expression of the normative approach to the 'public interest' concept. His view is a minority position in the United States, where it is unlikely now that the media could be prevented from identifying the victims of sexual offences, let alone crimes generally.

---

[176] Sexual Offences (Amendment) Act 1992, s. 1 (UK); art. 39(5) of the Law of the Press of 29 July 1881, as amended by Law of 23 Dec. 1980 (France).

[177] *Canadian Newspapers* v. *A-G of Canada* [1988] 2 SCR 122, Supreme Ct of Canada.

[178] *Cox Broadcasting Corpn* v. *Cohn* 420 US 469 (1975). In *Smith* v. *Daily Mail Publishing Co* 443 US 97 (1979) the Court found unconstitutional the prosecution of newspapers for infringing state law which forbade them to identify juveniles charged with offences. Their names had been obtained lawfully. [179] 491 US 524 (1989).

[180] P. B. Edelman, 'Free Press v. Privacy: Haunted by the Ghost of Justice Black' (1990) 68 *Texas Law Rev* 1195, 1204–7.

A different approach to balancing was taken by the German Constitutional Court in its famous *Lebach* decision.[181] The complainant had been convicted as an accessory to an armed robbery of a military arsenal, in which some soldiers had been killed. Shortly before his release from prison, a public broadcaster proposed to show a drama-documentary about the affair, which would have named and shown photographs of Lebach. The state courts refused on free speech grounds to stop the programme, but the Constitutional Court upheld his complaint that their decisions did not take proper account of his privacy rights, based on the constitutional right to the free development of personality guaranteed by Article 2 of the Basic Law. That right had to be balanced against freedom of expression. In weighing them the lower courts should have appreciated that a television documentary could infringe privacy more seriously than a press report. What was crucial was that the documentary did not concern a current event, but revived an earlier matter; further, the broadcast might endanger Lebach's rehabilitation into society on release from prison.[182] The Court took a normative approach to the scope of the free speech defence to privacy claims, when it held that in these circumstances the public interest in revelations about past crimes should give way to the culprit's interest in anonymity.

In two well-publicized English cases, Dame Elizabeth Butler-Sloss P., has protected the interests of past criminals in anonymity. In *Venables* she granted a permanent injunction to prevent the media disclosing any information which would identify or reveal the whereabouts of two young men about to be released after serving a period of detention for the murder of a two-year-old boy.[183] There was substantial evidence that the young men might be attacked on their release, so the injunction was primarily issued to safeguard their right to life, rather than a privacy right. The more recent Mary Bell case does, however, clearly illustrate a conflict between the two rights.[184] As a young girl, the claimant had been convicted of the manslaughter of two children. On her release from detention, she had been given a new identity under the name Mary Bell, formed a stable relationship, and had a daughter. To safeguard the latter's welfare, the anonymity of mother and daughter had been safeguarded by an injunction issued by the court in exercise of its wardship jurisdiction.[185] In the recent case Dame Elizabeth Butler-Sloss P. held that their anonymity should be further protected after the daughter became eighteen. She emphasized that a restriction on press freedom could be justified on the exceptional facts; in the absence of an order, the media would continue to give publicity to the case and to the whereabouts of Mary Bell and her daughter, which would exacerbate the former's mental illness. Moreover, the injunction only

---

[181] 35 BVerfGE 202 (1973).

[182] Ibid., 237–8. For discussion of *Lebach* in comparison with English and US cases, see B. Markesinis, 'The Right to be Let Alone versus Freedom of Speech' [1986] *PL* 67.

[183] *Venables* v. *News Group Newspapers Ltd* [2001] Fam 430.

[184] *X, A Woman formerly known as Mary Bell* v. *O'Brien* [2003] EMLR 850.

[185] *Re X (A Minor) (Wardship Injunction)* [1984] 1 WLR 1422, Balcombe J.

inhibited publication of details which would lead to their identification; the press could continue to comment on the case. It is clear that the judge regarded the case as highly unusual. Generally in these circumstances there is a presumption in favour of press freedom; released criminals normally have no right to protect their anonymity on release. In some cases, for example, involving the publication of photographs of a celebrity, privacy and freedom of expression are now treated in English law as rights to which equal weight should be attached; neither right has pre-eminence or automatic priority over the other.[186] However, privacy must, it seems, generally take second place to freedom of expression, when the case concerns the coverage of legal proceedings or the anonymity of parties or released prisoners.[187]

(iv) Publication of photographs

An individual's right to control reproduction of his photograph is an important aspect of privacy rights in German[188] and French law.[189] (It may also be an aspect of the publicity or patrimonial rights of a celebrity to exploit aspects of her identity for profit.[190]) The publication of a photograph may be very damaging to personal privacy, enabling easy identification of a celebrity, while it may be unclear how far it should enjoy protection under freedom of speech unless it adds something of importance to the information given in the accompanying text. Equally, photographs communicate the significance of an event, say, the damage done by terrorist bombs more effectively than any prose description could. In those circumstances their publication is generally in the public interest, whether that concept is understood normatively or descriptively. But in other cases it would be right to provide a remedy for their publication (or even to prevent it by prior restraint), because of the much greater, and unacceptable, intrusion on individual privacy. It is, for example, obviously in the public interest to report that a celebrity has had a baby, but equally clearly there could be no serious free speech argument to justify publication of a photograph of her in labour, a violation of human dignity as well as her privacy rights.

The courts must balance free speech and privacy in this context as in others. Factors to take into account are whether the photograph was taken of the claimant while he was in a public place or while at home or in another private place, whether the person was captured incidentally in a shot of, say, a street market or

---

[186] *Campbell* v. *MGN* [2004] 2 AC 457, para. 55 (Lord Hoffmann), para. 113 (Lord Hope), and para. 138 (Baroness Hale).

[187] See the recent decision of the House of Lords in *Re S (A Child)* [2004] 4 All ER 683 refusing to grant an injunction to prevent disclosure of identity of a woman charged with the murder of her older son, and publication of their photographs, even though media publicity would infringe the privacy of the woman's younger son.

[188] The leading case involving Princess Caroline of Monaco is discussed in s. 5(vi) below.

[189] See E. Picard, 'The Right to Privacy in French law', in Markesinis (n. 158 above), 49, 84–5.

[190] The relationship of this right to free speech is briefly considered in ch. VII below.

a sports crowd or was singled out, and whether his consent was obtained.[191] These factors were considered by the Canadian Supreme Court when it upheld the decision of the Quebec courts that a woman's right to privacy had been infringed when an arts magazine published a photograph of her sitting on the steps of a public building.[192] No attempt had been made to get her consent. The Court did not consider that any free speech argument could justify publication in these circumstances; the claimant was not a public figure and the photograph did not capture any newsworthy event.

Different approaches to the use of photographs to illustrate newsworthy incidents may be shown by comparing a leading US case with some French decisions. In *Shulman* v. *Group W Productions* the Supreme Court of California held that a woman, permanently and seriously injured in a traffic accident, could not claim that her privacy had been violated by the broadcast of a video made by a television cameraman who had accompanied the helicopter rescue crew to the accident and filmed her in extreme agony.[193] The Court said that a publication is 'newsworthy', or of legitimate public concern, when some reasonable members of the community could take a legitimate interest in its content; news presented as entertainment and the coverage of past events are both covered, an approach which would probably require a California court to decide the German *Lebach* case in favour of the broadcaster. It was immaterial that the broadcast could have been edited to exclude some of the images and words of the claimant, for it would be improper for courts to act as a super-editor of the press.

The Cour de Cassation in France in contrast held there was an infringement of privacy when a weekly magazine published photographs of an actress leaving hospital, where she had been treated for serious injuries incurred in a road accident.[194] It insists that published photographs of a person injured in a bomb blast do not violate human dignity by, for instance, focusing on an individual's wounds or by exposing her to ridicule.[195] A photograph of a police officer who had participated a few days earlier in the eviction of squatters in a parish church was legitimate because it was published a few days after that event in a commentary on it.[196] There must be a clear link between the event and the photograph. When two weekly magazines published photographs showing the Prefect of Corsica moments after his assassination in public, it was held that they violated human

---

[191] For a comparative study of the law in the United States, Canada, and New Zealand, see E. Paton-Simpson, 'Privacy and the Reasonable Paranoid: The Protection of Privacy in Public Places' (2000) 50 *Univ of Toronto Law Jo* 305.

[192] *Aubry* v. *Canadian Broadcasting Corpn.* (1998) 157 DLR (4th) 577.

[193] 74 Cal Rptr 2d 843 (Cal, 1998). But the Court allowed a claim for intruding on the claimant's expectation of privacy by recording her conversations with her rescuers to go to trial, as the media enjoys less constitutional protection for news-gathering than for publication.

[194] *Chantal Nobel* case, Cass civ 1, 6 June 1987, Bull civ I no 191.

[195] Cass civ 1, 20 Feb. 2001, D 2001, 1199.

[196] Ibid., note J.-P. Gridel, 'L'actualité de l'image des personnes impliquées dans un événement relevant de l'information légitime'.

dignity, so it was immaterial that they were taken after his decease. The fact that the photographs would have been of interest to some readers was also irrelevant. A photograph of the Prefect while alive could have been used to illustrate the story without detracting from its content.[197]

The English courts have begun to grapple with these questions in the last few years. In one interesting case the judge was prepared to grant an interim injunction to restrain publication of photographs of a well-known BBC television presenter in a brothel, although he declined to stop publication in a newspaper of the fact that the presenter had visited the brothel and engaged in sexual activity there or of details of those activities.[198] The presenter had laid himself open to publication of the information by openly discussing his private life, while his position with the BBC made it legitimate for the public to take an interest in his lifestyle. But there was no public interest in publication of the photographs which would be particularly intrusive on the presenter's privacy. The *Douglas* case established that photographs may amount to confidential information, so the claimants could recover damages for the unauthorized publication of their wedding photographs; the photographs showed more graphically than any written account how the 'happy couple' appeared on the day.[199]

The leading case in this area is now the ruling of the House of Lords in *Campbell* v. *MGN*.[200] The *Daily Mirror* published a number of articles about Naomi Campbell, a celebrity fashion model. They revealed that she was receiving treatment at Narcotics Anonymous (NA) for drug addiction, and disclosed details of the treatment, with photographs of her leaving a meeting of NA. By a majority of 3–2, the House held that, in conjunction with the photographs, publication of the fact that she was receiving treatment at NA and details of her attendance, as distinct from the bare fact that she was receiving some treatment for her addiction,[201] infringed Ms Campbell's privacy; she was entitled to protect that interest by the breach of confidence action. Lords Nicholls and Hoffmann dissenting did not think the photographs added anything of significance to the disclosure that Ms Campbell was receiving treatment at NA, a revelation the newspaper was entitled to make to fill out its story that she was having treatment for her drug problems. Lord Hoffmann pointed out that the photographs did not portray her in a humiliating situation.[202] In contrast Lord Hope and Baroness Hale for the majority considered that publication of the photographs of Ms Campbell added

---

[197] Cass civ 1, 20 Dec. 2000, D 2001, 885, note J.-P. Gridel, 'Retour sur l'image du préfet assassiné'.

[198] *Theakston* v. *MGN* [2002] EMLR 398, Ouseley J.

[199] *Douglas* v. *Hello!* [2001] QB 967, para. 138 (Sedley LJ), para. 165 (Keene LJ), and *Douglas* v. *Hello! (No. 3)* [2003] 3 All ER 996, para. 186(xiii) (Lindsay J.).   [200] [2004] 2 AC 457.

[201] It was agreed that the newspaper was entitled to disclose that Ms Campbell was receiving treatment for her drug problems, as she had previously denied that she suffered from such difficulties.

[202] N. 200 above, paras. 76–7. The case could be distinguished from *Peck* v. *UK* (2003) 13 BHRC 669, when the European Court of Human Rights ruled that it was an infringement of privacy for a local authority to release CCTV film of a person on a high street carrying a knife shortly before he attempted to commit suicide.

to the loss of privacy occasioned by disclosure of the details of her treatment. For Lord Hope the photographs tipped the balance, making the publication overall an unjustified infringement of the model's privacy. A reasonable person of ordinary sensibility in her position would object to their publication.[203] Baroness Hale explained that Ms Campbell would understandably feel that she had been followed by the photographer to the meeting and as a result would be less likely to attend in future.[204] In contrast, there was no good free speech argument for publication of the photographs; the story could have been illustrated with other images of the model. The majority approach is persuasive. The photographs did not add anything of importance to the story, but their inclusion gave it greater prominence and would have probably added to the distress it caused.

(v) Presenting the claimant in a false light

In a number of cases the German Constitutional Court has ruled that publication of a fictitious interview, or the inaccurate attribution of remarks, violates the privacy rights of the person concerned, and is not protected by freedom of expression.[205] In *Soraya*, where a weekly paper had fabricated an interview with the former wife of the Shah of Iran, purporting to reveal intimate details of her private life, the Court explained that readers have no right to be informed about the lives of celebrities through fictitious stories.[206] French law adopts the same approach.[207] These decisions are straightforward, since it can hardly be argued that such material deserves free speech protection.

More difficult are cases where a well-publicized crime or other episode is made the subject of a novel, play, or film, but some details of the story are embroidered or exaggerated to give it colour. They may put people involved in the episode in a false light, one of the four types of privacy invasion identified by Prosser in his taxonomy of the varieties of privacy infringement.[208] They may also be defamatory. It is therefore hardly surprising that the US Supreme Court applied the principle developed in *New York Times* to false light cases.[209] In *Time, Inc v. Hill* it held an article which in some respects falsely depicted the plaintiff family's involvement in a notorious kidnapping a few years earlier, and so invaded its privacy, was covered by the First Amendment.[210] The New York privacy law could only provide compensation for a false report if it was shown that it had been published with knowledge of its falsity or with reckless disregard of its truth. Arguably, however, it was inappropriate to apply a rule formulated for libel actions brought by public

---

[203] N. 200 above, paras. 119–24.   [204] Ibid., paras. 154–6.

[205] Soraya, 34 BVerfGE 269 (1973); Eppler, 54 BVerfGE 148 (1980) (no privacy violation as not established that complainant had not used the attributed words); Böll, 54 BVerfGE 208 (1980), discussed in s. 3 above.   [206] 34 BVerfGE 269, 283–4 (1973).

[207] *Marlene Dietrich* case, CA of Paris, 16 Mar. 1955, DS 1955, 295.

[208] W. L. Prosser, 'Privacy' (1960) 48 *California Law Rev* 383, 398–401.

[209] 276 US 254 (1964): see s. 2 above.   [210] 385 US 374 (1967).

officials and figures. In 1952 the Hill family had been held hostage by some convicts, an episode which had been given extensive publicity. But they were hardly public figures, and the story was no longer newsworthy, whether that idea is interpreted normatively or descriptively. The free speech argument for rejecting their privacy claim was thin. It would not have been accepted in France, where on facts similar to those in *Time* v. *Hill* the Cour de Cassation has required cuts in a film presenting a fictionalized account of events in order to protect privacy rights.[211]

(vi) The privacy of politicians and other public figures

It seems clear from cases discussed in the preceding pages that the status of the claimant is only one factor, albeit often an important one, in determining whether free speech should prevail over privacy. The crucial question is whether the story, or the reproduction of the photograph, is in the public interest. Of course, the public has a keen interest in the private life of celebrities and of leading politicians and other public figures, so on the descriptive approach their privacy actions will inevitably fail. But apart from the United States that is not the position taken by courts when they balance free speech and privacy. For example, the Court of Appeal in *A* v. *B plc* (the footballer case) said that a public figure is entitled to have his privacy respected in appropriate circumstances.[212] The House of Lords confirmed this view in *Campbell* v. *MGN*.[213] As Lord Hope put it: '. . . it is not enough to deprive Miss Campbell of her right to privacy that she is a celebrity and that her private life is newsworthy'.[214]

In France the privacy rights of politicians and other public figures are strongly protected. While these rights are not infringed when pictures of them performing official functions are published, the use of such pictures for caricature may violate them.[215] In a particularly controversial decision, the widow and sons of President Mitterrand were able to restrain further dissemination of a book, *Le Grand Secret*, by his doctor, which revealed that the late President knew he was suffering from cancer in 1981, a secret he had kept from his family as well as the public.[216] The Paris Court of Appeal rejected a freedom of expression argument based on Article 10 of the ECHR, holding that it was necessary to stop distribution of the book in order to protect confidentiality. The publishers of the book took the case to Strasbourg.

---

[211] Lelièvre, Cass civ 1, 13 Feb. 1985, DS 1985, 488 (real names of victims used in fictionalized account of kidnapping cut); Jeanjacquot, Cass civ 1, 13 Feb. 1985, DS 1985, 488 (fictional scenes in which actress played mistress of notorious criminal violated privacy rights of the mistress, and so to be suppressed).   [212] [2003] QB 195, para. 11(xii).
[213] N. 200 above.
[214] Ibid., para. 120. Lord Hoffmann dissented on the facts, but took the same view that celebrities are entitled to protect their privacy: para. 66.
[215] Courts stopped use of the photograph of President Pompidou for advertising, TGI, Paris, 4 Apr. 1970, JCP, 1970, II, 16328, and reproduction of an image of President Giscard d'Estaing on playing cards, TGI, Nancy, 4 Oct. 1976, JCP, 1977, II, 18526.
[216] CA of Paris, 27 May 1997, JCP 1997, II, 22894, note Derieux.

The European Human Rights Court held that the permanent injunction could not be justified as necessary to protect the rights of the late President to honour, reputation, and privacy. With the passage of time since his death, the interest of his family in protecting those rights weakened, while the importance of public debate over the merits of Mitterrand's terms of office acquired greater weight. Moreover, the information had lost its essential confidentiality, given that 40,000 copies of the book had been sold before the injunction was imposed and its contents were available on the Net and had been the subject of extensive debate.[217]

The most rewarding discussion of the relationship between the privacy rights of public figures and freedom of expression is found in the decisions of the German courts, and now the European Human Rights Court, on actions brought by Princess Caroline of Monaco.[218] She complained that her privacy had been violated by the publication of numerous photographs of her by two popular magazines. The Federal Supreme Court granted her an injunction to prevent further publication of photographs showing her with an actor in a garden restaurant in the south of France, but declined to stop reproduction of other photographs which showed her either alone or with her young daughter in public places.[219] The former photographs intruded on her private romantic life, but as a person of 'contemporary history' (*Zeitgeschichte*)[220] she had to accept that images of her would be taken and published, whether or not she was then performing a public function. The Princess then brought a constitutional complaint, arguing that the civil court decisions had violated her basic rights under Articles 1 and 2 insofar as they permitted publication of the other photographs.

The Constitutional Court upheld her complaint in part, finding that the decisions had not paid attention to Article 6 of the Basic Law concerning the care and upbringing of children.[221] Publication of the photographs showing the Princess with her daughter should have been considered in that light. But it took no objection to publication of the other photographs, showing the Princess alone or dining in public with friends. The Court formulated a number of principles on the basis of which privacy and freedom of expression should be balanced. Public figures, including politicians, are entitled to keep their private life concealed, insofar as it does not affect their duties, and they may be entitled to protect privacy outside their home. On the other side of the scales, freedom of the press covers features about the lives of those celebrities who become role models.[222] It would be wrong

---

[217] *Plon* v. *France*, Decision of 18 May 2004, paras. 49–53. In contrast the Court upheld the temporary injunctions granted in January 1996 only ten days after Mitterrand's death.

[218] Also see the decision of the Federal Supreme Court of 29 June 1999, NJW 1999, 2893, holding that the press was entitled to report details of divorce proceedings disclosing that a great grandson of the last Kaiser, and a friend of Princess Caroline, had committed adultery. His claim for violation of privacy was dismissed.   [219] Decision of 19 Dec. 1995, NJW 1996, 1128.

[220] The term is used in the Law on Copyright in Works of Art and Photography of 9 Jan. 1907, s. 23(1), which allows dissemination of pictures of people from the realm of contemporary history without their consent.   [221] 101 BVerfGE 361 (1999).

[222] Ibid., 390–2.

to require a celebrity to approve the publication of any photograph which showed her in public. German law, unlike that in France, does not afford public figures a veto on the publication of their image.

In a seminal ruling the European Court of Human Rights has now ruled that the German courts' decisions infringed the Princess's right to respect for her private life, guaranteed by Article 8 of the ECHR.[223] It recognized that the national courts had a margin of appreciation in balancing that right against freedom of expression, but emphasized that the case did not involve the dissemination of any ideas, but rather the publication of photographs. Most importantly, it considered that:

a fundamental distinction needs to be made between reporting facts—even controversial ones—capable of contributing to a debate in a democratic society relating to politicians in the exercise of their functions, for example, and reporting details of the private life of an individual who . . . as in this case does not exercise official functions.[224]

The tabloids had published the photographs to satisfy popular curiosity with regard to Princess Caroline's private life; they did not contribute to any debate of general interest. The Court added that the pictures had been taken without her knowledge or consent. It was wrong for the German courts to have given her less privacy protection merely because she is regarded as a figure of contemporary society and because the photographs were taken while she was in public (and not secluded) spaces. These criteria were too vague to give applicants in the position of the Princess enough guidance on how to protect their privacy, and they did not justify the intrusion which had occurred. In conclusion the Court doubted whether the public had a legitimate interest in knowing how the Princess appeared in her private life, albeit in public places; even if it did, it was entitled to less weight than her right to effective protection of her private life.[225]

It is difficult to exaggerate the importance of this decision. It establishes that privacy protection is not confined to the disclosure of information, or the publication of photographs, embarrassing to the claimant. The photographs in this case did not show the Princess in a humiliating position, nor were they published, unlike those in the *Campbell* case, to give greater prominence to a story which revealed confidential information. The Princess simply objected to her constant portrayal in tabloid newspapers and magazines. From the perspective of freedom of expression, the decision draws a crucial distinction between the publication of material of political or other public importance, on the one hand, and of gossip and celebrity pictures on the other. While the latter is more likely to infringe privacy, it is less likely to be protected by free speech arguments. The European Court takes a normative approach to the public interest argument: in its view, it could only be properly invoked as a defence to an action for breach of confidence or

---

[223] *Von Hannover* v. *Germany* (2004) 16 BHRC 545.   [224] Ibid., para. 63.
[225] Ibid., para. 77.

privacy, where the publication discloses material in which the public *ought* to take an interest. The decision has significant implications for the balancing of free speech and privacy in England; *A* v. *B plc*[226] should now be decided differently.

(vii) Conclusions on balancing in privacy cases

The discussion of balancing in libel cases is relevant here.[227] Ad hoc balancing in which the courts weigh all the relevant factors is to be preferred to the application of a rule such as that formulated by the US Supreme Court in *New York Times*. In fact the case for detailed, ad hoc balancing may be stronger in privacy cases than it is in libel, because of the infinite variety of ways in which privacy may be infringed. A rule formulated, say, for false light cases such as *Time, Inc* v. *Hill*[228] is not easily applicable to cases where the press has disclosed true, but embarrassing facts about the claimant. It may be inappropriate to resolve instances of privacy invasion through the publication of photographs by principles developed to deal with the revelation of confidential discussions or other factual stories. These points would be challenged by proponents of definitional balancing, who would argue that, in the absence of a clear rule, too much discretion is left to individual judges and that free speech will be chilled. But equally, application of a strong free speech rule like that in *New York Times* would lead to the unacceptable result that it is almost impossible for politicians and celebrities to protect their privacy.

It is worth pointing out that virtually all privacy claims in the free speech context are made against the press and other media, rather than against individuals asserting free expression rights. Indeed, in some instances the individual interest in free expression may support the privacy claim rather than point to a right to infringe it.[229] The press of course is entitled to the protection of the freedom of speech or expression clause, but its rights are essentially derivative from those of the public.[230] It cannot easily claim a violation of its human rights if it is ordered not to print a story which violates individual privacy. These points should be taken into account in borderline cases, though equally courts should appreciate that the enforcement of privacy might deter the media from publishing some stories which are of public interest, whether this conception is understood descriptively or normatively.

The assessment of the appropriate weight to be attached to privacy and free speech or press interests varies significantly from one society and culture to another. It also changes over time. The former variation is illustrated by the different approaches adopted by US courts on the one hand, and by French and German courts on the other. Privacy used to be more respected in the United States and in Britain than it is now. The press did not disclose stories about

---

[226] [2003] QB 195, CA, considered in s. 5(ii) above.   [227] See s. 3(vi) above.
[228] 385 US 374 (1967).   [229] See the confidentiality cases discussed in s. 5(ii) above.
[230] For fuller discussion, see ch. XII, s. 1 below.

John F. Kennedy's affairs either before or during his Presidency, or Winston Churchill's illness during the Second World War and in his last period as Prime Minister in the early 1950s. It is inconceivable that the press would not publish details of such matters now.[231] In most liberal democracies it is regarded as legitimate for the media to publish details of a politician's health, because there is a reasonable assumption that it may affect the discharge of his duties. There is less agreement whether there is a free speech right to reveal a public figure's sexual orientation or details of his intimate affairs, which is so strong that it should necessarily trump privacy. The case for protecting free speech is stronger in the case of disclosures concerning politicians and public figures occupying positions of power, than it is for comparable revelations about entertainment celebrities. But it would be wrong to hold that free speech arguments should always prevail over the privacy, even, say, of a President or Prime Minister.

A difficulty is whether courts should start with a presumption in favour of freedom of speech and resolve cases of doubt in favour of publication. That should be the position when free speech is balanced against reputation rights, at least when the press can show that publication of the story is in the public interest and that it has behaved responsibly. It is not so clear that this should be the position in privacy cases. As we saw at the beginning of this section, the argument for holding that freedom of speech covers the invasion of privacy is relatively weak. Further, privacy itself may be guaranteed by the constitution, so there may be an equally good case for giving priority to that right and requiring the media to show why it need not be respected.

In abstract the rights to privacy and to freedom of speech appear to be of equal value, as was said by members of the House of Lords in *Campbell* v. *MGN*.[232] A proportionality analysis should be applied to both, so the court should ask itself whether it was necessary to restrict publication in order to protect privacy, and vice versa, whether to allow the publication would disproportionately sacrifice the individual's privacy.[233] The relative importance of the rights in the circumstances and the arguments for restricting them must be taken into account. In time, appellate courts should be able to fashion guidelines which would enable trial judges to balance privacy and free speech in a relatively predictable way. Presumptions might play a limited part in applying the guidelines. One might be that, in cases of doubt, privacy claims by ordinary individuals should be upheld. It would be for the press (or other defendant) to show that there are good grounds for revealing personal information. Under another guideline, claims by political figures might

---

[231] See however the disagreement in the High Court of Australia whether it would be right to protect the privacy of President Franklin D. Roosevelt not to have his impairment revealed. In *Australian Broadcasting Co* v. *Lenah Game Meats Pty Ltd* (2002) 185 ALR 1, Kirby J. thought any restraint on the press would be wrong (para. 219), while Callinan J. would uphold privacy protection in these circumstances (para. 344). [232] See s. 5(iv) above.

[233] In particular see Baroness Hale in *Campbell* v. *MGN* [2004] 2 AC 457, paras. 140–1. Also see Munby J. in *Re Angela Roddy (A Minor)* [2004] EMLR 127, paras. 16–19.

be approached with a presumption in favour of free speech; in borderline cases, it would be for a politician claimant to show that the revelations, say, concerning a relationship with a member of his staff, had nothing to do with his fitness for office and infringed his right to privacy. Of course, these presumptions would be relatively weak. Courts should apply them only when the factors were equally balanced. If the law treated them as firm rules, it would establish a form of definitional balancing, similar to that developed in the United States, and either privacy or freedom of speech would be sacrificed.

VII

Copyright and Other Property Rights

1. Introduction

While the relationship of freedom of speech to copyright protection has increasingly attracted the attention of copyright lawyers,[1] the topic has rarely been discussed by writers on freedom of speech. Courts, even in the United States, have almost always rejected arguments that the scope of copyright is constrained by free speech considerations. When the monopoly right of broadcasters to publish details of their programmes was challenged in Strasbourg, the European Human Rights Commission denied that enforcement of the broadcasters' copyright even engaged freedom of expression; in the Commission's view, only the person who had compiled information had a right under Article 10 of the European Convention on Human Rights and Fundamental Freedoms (ECHR) to impart it.[2] Copyright infringers, in short, do not enjoy free speech rights. This conclusion is surprising. As the previous chapter has shown, courts in many jurisdictions protect free speech and press rights, even when their exercise clearly infringes legal rights to reputation or privacy. Decisions to that effect were generally welcomed as timely recognition of the value and scope of free speech and expression rights. So an initial question is why a similar development has not occurred in the case of copyright law. Are there any good reasons why copyright law should remain immune from free speech scrutiny?

Some explanations for this immunity will be explored in section 2 of this chapter. One is that copyright is a property right. Further, it has a long history and has developed entirely apart from free speech concerns. But these explanations are inadequate to *justify* the present position, under which copyright escapes serious

---

[1] See e.g. P. Samuelson, 'Copyright, Commodification, and Censorship: Past as Prologue—But to What Future?' and P. B. Hugenholtz, 'Copyright and Freedom of Expression in Europe', in N. Elkin-Koren and N. W. Netanel (eds.), *The Commodification of Information* (The Hague: Kluwer, 2002), 63 and 239; N. W. Netanel, 'Copyright and a Democratic Civil Society' (1996) 106 *Yale Law Jo* 283; M. Birnhack, 'The Copyright Law and Free Speech Affair: Making-up and Breaking-up' (2003) 43 *Idea: The Journal of Law and Technology* 233; D. Fewer, 'Constitutionalizing Copyright: Freedom of Expression and the Limits of Copyright in Canada' (1997) 55 *Univ of Toronto Faculty Law Rev* 175; P. Drahos, 'Decentring Communication: The Dark Side of Intellectual Property', in T. Campbell and W. Sadurski (eds.), *Freedom of Communication* (Aldershot: Dartmouth, 1994), 249.

[2] 5178/71, *De Geillustreerde Pers NV v. Netherlands* (1976) 8 D & R 5.

free speech scrutiny. Section 3 argues that at least some infringing works are entitled to the *coverage* of a free speech (or expression) clause, even though in most instances the publication of an infringing work may properly be restrained by the rules of copyright law. In those circumstances the publication is not a *protected* exercise of the right to freedom of speech. Copyright and freedom of speech should be balanced, just as the interests in reputation and personal privacy must be weighed against competing free speech or press interests. Of course, it is often argued that copyright legislation itself accommodates free speech concerns, and that it, therefore, balances those concerns with those of the holders of copyright by making provision for 'fair use' of copyright works. But ultimately it is for the courts to decide whether 'fair use' and other defences give adequate protection to free speech rights in this context; it is not for the legislature to determine the scope of constitutional speech or expression rights. Section 4 discusses balancing copyright and free speech rights.

Much of this chapter is concerned with the relationship of copyright to freedom of speech. But similar problems arise in other areas of law where property rights are recognized, whether under statute or at common law: examples are trade marks, and the rights of publicity which have been widely recognized in the United States, if not hitherto in England. Enforcement of these rights may have repercussions for the exercise of freedom of speech; this topic is briefly discussed in section 5 of the chapter.

2. Why is Copyright Immune from Free Speech Scrutiny?

(i) Doctrinal arguments

This section discusses some arguments of principle which have often been invoked to explain why copyright law does not engage freedom of speech. For the most part they have been developed by commentators, and to some extent the courts, in the United States. In comparison there has been relatively little discussion of these issues in England.[3] That is largely because until enactment of the Human Rights Act 1998 (HRA 1998) it was impossible to argue that freedom of expression rights precluded enforcement of copyright. Now, however, as the decision of the Court of Appeal in *Ashdown* v. *Telegraph Group Ltd*[4] indicates, English courts must consider the coherence of these arguments.

One argument might be that freedom of speech is protected only against *state* infringement, and not against the limits imposed by private individuals or corporations. In the language of the US courts, there is no 'state action' which engages

---

[3] Notable exceptions are the articles by F. M. Patfield, 'Towards a Reconciliation of Free Speech and Copyright' (1996) *Yearbook of Media and Entertainment Law* 199, and by J. Griffiths, 'Copyright Law and Censorship: The Impact of the Human Rights Act 1998' (1999) *Yearbook of Copyright and Media Law* 3.   [4] [2002] Ch 149, considered in s. 3(ii) below.

the First Amendment. Claims of copyright infringements are almost invariably brought by private individuals, film and media corporations, so it may be argued that there is no state action to bring freedom of speech into play. This would be a bad argument. Copyright is a right conferred by statute, interpreted and applied by the courts. So enforcement of copyright inevitably involves state action. US courts have not been troubled by the argument in the context of libel and privacy claims, which like copyright actions are brought by individuals on the basis of rights conferred by statute, or on the basis of the common law. Indeed, the state action argument was specifically rejected by the US Supreme Court in *New York Times* v. *Sullivan*,[5] when it held that the common law of libel in Alabama enjoyed no immunity from First Amendment scrutiny. Nor are English courts troubled by this argument when they adjudicate libel or breach of confidence actions: it is clear that freedom of expression must be considered in determining whether there is a defence to these proceedings,[6] and that should also be the position in copyright cases. So it would be impossible to put forward the state action point as an explanation, let alone a justification, for holding copyright law immune from free speech challenge.

The state action argument is one of general constitutional or human rights law. The other doctrinal arguments concern two distinctive principles of copyright law itself. The first of these is the idea–expression distinction. Copyright does not limit the dissemination of ideas or the spread of news and information, but only the use by others of the *expression* of the holder of copyright. Melville Nimmer, a distinguished writer on many areas of free speech law as well as a great copyright lawyer, contended that in this way First Amendment concerns were met by copyright legislation.[7] The conclusion is unsatisfactory. It does not do justice to the point that sometimes it is important for an infringer to use the very words or other distinctive expression of the copyright holder, if he is effectively to communicate his ideas, perhaps the sentiment that the quoted or parodied work is meretricious.[8] Nimmer himself did not think the distinction worked where an idea and its expression are inseparable, as in a news photograph. Reproduction of film of the assassination of President Kennedy or of the famous photograph of the My-Lai massacre in Vietnam necessarily used a distinctive form of expression in order to communicate the character of the particular news event.[9]

Secondly, it is said that copyright legislation recognizes free speech concerns by providing 'fair use' or, in the United Kingdom, 'fair dealing' defences. That claim is accurate. It was the conclusion reached by the United States Supreme Court in *Harper & Row Publishers* v. *Nation Enterprises*, its leading ruling on the relationship

---

[5] 376 US 254, 265 (1964).

[6] See e.g. with regard to libel, *Reynolds* v. *Times Newspapers* [2001] 2 AC 127, HL, and with regard to privacy and breach of confidence, *Campbell* v. *MGN* [2004] 2 AC 457, HL.

[7] 'Does Copyright Abridge the First Amendment Guarantees of Free Speech and Press?' (1970) 17 *UCLA Law Rev* 1180.   [8] See s. 3(ii) below.

[9] N. 7 above, 1198–9.

of copyright and freedom of speech.[10] A 6–3 majority of the Court denied the defendants, the publishers of *The Nation*, the 'fair use' defence when it published substantial extracts from the unpublished memoirs of ex-President Ford, which were to be serialized in *Time* magazine. The Court rejected the argument that the defendants had a First Amendment right to publish the extracts, even though they covered important political events, notably Ford's decision to pardon President Nixon. (In his dissenting judgment Brennan J. argued the decision did not do justice to free speech: property rights were given precedence over the free use of knowledge and ideas.) The German Federal Supreme Court took a similar approach when it denied a weekly paper a free press right to publish the text of the song 'Lili Marleen' in connection with the release of a film about a prominent singer; the Court held that the copyright statute regulated the conflict between the interests of the rights-holder and those of publishers.[11] Admittedly, the defences provided by copyright legislation may be interpreted broadly to take account of free speech concerns. The US Supreme Court, for example, held a music group could argue 'fair use' when it copied substantial parts of a rock ballad in its parody of that work; a parody inevitably involves borrowing from the core of the imitated work.[12]

The question remains whether reliance on statutory defences will always satisfy the requirements of a constitutional right to freedom of speech (or expression). It has been doubted whether the fair dealing defence in the United Kingdom, as it has been interpreted by the courts, does justice to the freedom.[13] In any case it would be wrong for the courts to hold that the copyright statute *necessarily* safeguards freedom of speech, with the result that no further consideration of the relationship of expression and copyright is required. That would be an abdication of the judicial responsibility to determine the scope of the right to freedom of expression, and how far it is necessary to restrict its exercise to protect copyright. The Court of Appeal in England was, therefore, right to hold in the *Ashdown* case[14] that the Convention right to freedom of expression may conflict with copyright, even though the statute itself sets out a number of 'fair dealing' defences which give effect to that freedom. It rejected the view of Sir Andrew Morritt, V-C in the High Court that the 1988 copyright legislation made exhaustive provision for the freedom.[15]

Similarly, the German Constitutional Court has ruled that the requirements of freedom of the arts (*Kunstfreiheit*), guaranteed by Article 5(3) of the Basic Law, must be considered by ordinary courts when determining whether there is defence to an action for copyright infringement.[16] The case concerned the use of copious

---

10 471 US 539 (1985).
11 Lili Marleen case, [1987] 89 Gewerblicher Rechtsschutz und Urheberrecht 34.
12 *Campbell* v. *Acuff Rose Music, Inc* 510 US 569 (1994).
13 See Griffiths (n. 3 above), 15–20.   14 [2002] Ch 149, fully discussed in s. 3(ii) below.
15 [2001] Ch 685.
16 *Germania 3 Gespenster am Toten Mann*, Decision of 29 June 2000, 1 BvR 825/98.

extracts from two of Berthold Brecht's plays in a dramatic work published in 1996, *Germania 3*. The provisions of the German copyright law did not, on their traditional interpretation, afford the publisher a defence; it required the quotations to be used as a basis for his own work, perhaps in the form of a commentary on Brecht's plays or as a starting point for the presentation of independent ideas. The Constitutional Court held it was too restrictive only to allow a defence in those circumstances. The guarantee of *Kunstfreiheit* required a more generous interpretation of the copyright statute when the infringing work was itself a work of artistic originality which, in this case, had used substantial extracts from Brecht's work as independent elements in a theatrical collage.

Courts should not leave the scope of free speech rights in relation to copyright to be prescribed by copyright legislation itself. The doctrinal arguments are unpersuasive, because they imply that it is legitimate for the courts to leave the last word to the legislature over such matters as the scope of copyright protection, the term of protection, and the range of defences available to copyright infringers. That cannot be right, unless it is clear that copyright infringement is not even covered by freedom of speech. But that is not clear, as will be explained in section 3 of this chapter.

(ii) Historical arguments

If the doctrinal arguments are unpersuasive, perhaps there is a good historical explanation for the traditional immunity of copyright from free speech scrutiny. United States courts and commentators wholly ignored the conflict between copyright and free speech until the 1970s.[17] It is as if they occupied separate legal worlds. The US Constitution explicitly authorized Congress '[T]o promote the Progress of Science and useful Arts, by securing for limited Times to Authors and Inventors the exclusive Right to their respective Writings and Discoveries.'[18] It would be surprising, the argument goes, if legislation specifically authorized by the Constitution, and indeed enacted initially in 1790 shortly after its ratification, could be challenged on the basis of incompatibility with the First Amendment. After all, many of the same people were responsible for framing both the Constitution and four years later its first ten Amendments. This historical case is buttressed by the argument that the very intention and effect of copyright law is to promote the production of literature and other works. In short, to use the familiar metaphor of O'Connor J. in the *Harper & Row Publishers* case, '. . . it should not be forgotten that the Framers intended copyright itself to be the engine of free expression.'[19] The argument is that copyright protection encourages authors,

---

[17] See Birnhack (n. 1 above), 247–51, and D. L. Zimmerman, 'Information as Speech, Information as Goods: Some Thoughts on Marketplaces and the Bill of Rights' (1991) 33 *William and Mary Law Rev* 665, 674–712.
[18] US Constitution, art. I, s. 8, cl. 8 ('the Copyright clause').
[19] 471 US 539, 558 (1985).

artists, and composers to create new work; without the incentive of royalties and licence fees, they would be less productive. Copyright, in short, promotes freedom of speech.

These arguments were plausible in the nineteenth century when the principal beneficiaries of copyright protection were individual authors and dramatists, rather than, as now, recording companies, film producers, and other media corporations. During that century copyright was protected for a relatively short time before the work entered the public domain: in the United Kingdom, fourteen years (with a possible renewal for a further fourteen years) under the Statute of Anne of 1709, or subsequent to legislation in 1842, the author's life plus seven years.[20] After that period works could be freely copied, so the right had much less impact on freedom of speech than it does now when the standard term of copyright is life plus seventy years.[21] Further, during the nineteenth century, copyright was for the most part protected against literal copying, and not against translations and adaptations, where the copier, at least to some extent, adds creative or original features in the preparation of the infringing work. Free speech arguments could not, therefore, easily have been invoked a hundred years ago. In any case, free speech itself was not taken seriously as a constitutional right in the United States until the 1920s, or in England and other European jurisdictions until the last two or three decades.[22] So it is hardly surprising that copyright and other intellectual property rights have until recently escaped free speech scrutiny.

However, this historical account only provides an explanation. It does not *justify* the immunity of copyright law and its principles from careful examination to determine their compatibility with freedom of speech. A comparison with libel law may be helpful. Before the landmark decision of the Supreme Court in *New York Times* v. *Sullivan*,[23] it was generally assumed that the right to reputation was unaffected by the First Amendment: the common law defences of truth, fair comment, and privilege took adequate care of free speech considerations. (English libel law similarly developed apart from constitutional free speech considerations until the House of Lords decided *Reynolds* v. *Times Newspapers*.[24]) Admittedly, the evolution of libel law was influenced by these considerations, but it was not significantly constrained by them. That is now no longer the position. Free speech and libel law do not, as it were, occupy separate legal worlds, coming together only with the permission of the latter. It is the constitutional right to free speech which shapes the contours of the right to reputation. Unless there is a good reason for its different treatment, the same should be true of copyright law.

[20] See L. Bently and B. Sherman, *Intellectual Property Law* (Oxford: OUP, 2001) ch. 7.
[21] Copyright, Designs, and Patents Act 1988 (CDPA 1988), s. 12(2) (UK); Copyright Term Extension Act of 1998, s. 102(b), amending Copyright Act of 1976 (US).
[22] See ch. II, ss. 2–4 above.   [23] 376 US 254 (1964), discussed in ch. VI, s. 2 above.
[24] [2001] 2 AC 127, discussed in ch. VI, s. 3(iv) above.

(iii) Copyright is a property right

It may be important in this context that copyright is a property right. Its status as a property right is explicitly spelt out in the UK legislation.[25] This aspect of copyright was emphasized by both Sir Andrew Morritt V-C and the Court of Appeal in the leading English case, *Ashdown* v. *Telegraph Group Ltd.*[26] The right to property is guaranteed by Article 1 of the First Protocol to the ECHR, so copyright is protected by the Convention.[27] The property character of copyright is also emphasized in the United States,[28] where the right to property is guaranteed by the Fifth Amendment.[29] The German Constitutional Court has held that the use of copyright works is guaranteed under the Basic Law by its Article 14 guarantee of property rights. On this basis it invalidated provisions of the copyright statute which allowed works to be exploited (in the particular cases, in schools and churches) without payment of compensation.[30]

Even granted that copyright is a property right entitled to constitutional protection, it hardly follows that constitutional free speech or expression arguments are, therefore, *necessarily* irrelevant to its scope and enforceability in particular cases. Claims to the exercise of property and free speech rights often conflict, as when a reader claims that he has a free speech right to publish a reply to an editorial in a newspaper against the editor's and owner's property (and free press) rights to deny him space,[31] or when demonstrators claim they have a right to conduct a protest on private property. Courts are usually reluctant to recognize free speech rights in these situations. Both the US Supreme Court and the European Human Rights Court have rejected claims to use a privately owned shopping centre to distribute leaflets or to hold meetings, as incompatible with the owners' property rights.[32] Now it can certainly be argued that copyright infringements similarly involve the abuse of the property rights of private individuals or corporations, so these rights should prevail over any free speech claim by the infringer. But it cannot be argued that a free speech claim must be dismissed, just because it would interfere with a *property* right. That conclusion would give property rights a privileged position in the constitutional order to which they are not entitled. It may be noted that in the recent *Germania 3* case the German Constitutional Court emphasized that property rights were not guaranteed without limit, and must be balanced against freedom of the arts, also protected by the Basic Law.[33] Moreover,

---

[25] CDPA 1988, s. 1(1).　　[26] [2001] Ch 685, Ch D; [2002] Ch 149, CA.

[27] See *Ashdown* v. *Telegraph Group Ltd* [2001] Ch 685, para. 8 per Sir Andrew Morritt V-C.

[28] Zimmerman (n. 17 above), esp. 691–2.

[29] Private property is not to be taken for public use without just compensation.

[30] 31 BVerfGE 229, 239 (1971); 49 BVerfGE 382, 392 (1978).

[31] See ch. XII, s. 3 below.

[32] See the leading US case, *Hudgens* v. *NLRB* 424 US 507 (1976), and the recent decision of the European Court in *Appleby* v. *UK* (2003) 37 EHRR 38, denying rights, against the owners' will, to use private shopping centres for speech, considered in ch. VIII, s. 3(iv) below.

[33] N. 16 above, para. 19.

copyright infringements only reduce the opportunities of the rights-holder to make profits from royalty payments; they do not necessarily entail a major interference with the core of a property right.

In the previous chapter, it was explained that in many jurisdictions courts balance freedom of speech against constitutional rights or interests in privacy and reputation. It is wrong to give one right automatic preference, because that means justice is not done to the other. The same should apply when free speech conflicts with property rights. In fact, property rights may be less strongly protected than fundamental human rights, such as the right to dignity and privacy; the ECHR, for instance, allows states to enforce laws necessary 'to control the use of property in accordance with the general interest...',[34] a broader qualification than that generally found to the exercise of other rights guaranteed by the Convention. In this context, it should also be stressed that copyright is an artificial, not a natural, property right. It was instituted to reward and promote creativity.[35] It would be odd to give it a total immunity against free speech challenge, when an argument is made that in the circumstances its protection would stifle rather than promote creativity.

3. Free Speech Coverage of Copyright Infringement

(i) General arguments for coverage

Section 2 examined the coherence of arguments which are frequently deployed to explain, and perhaps even to justify, the exclusion of copyright from free speech scrutiny. The arguments concerned aspects of copyright doctrine, its history, and its character as a property right. The question considered in this section is whether under free speech principles copyright infringement should be covered by the First Amendment or other relevant constitutional guarantee. The section first examines the general arguments for coverage of copyright infringement by free speech provisions, and then discusses whether under standard free speech principles infringers may sometimes claim free speech rights. The third subsection briefly examines the unusual deference of United States courts to copyright legislation.

Some types of speech or expression which fall within the dictionary meaning of these terms are treated as not covered by the free speech provision. They do not fall within the scope or coverage of the free speech clause, so there is no requirement for the state to justify their regulation before a court. Examples of speech which are not covered at all are perjury, bribes, the making of contractual promises,

---

[34] Protocol 1, art. 1(2). Also see German Basic Law, art. 14 which provides that the content and limits of property are determined by law.

[35] J. Waldron, 'From Authors to Copiers: Individual Rights and Social Values in Intellectual Property' (1993) 68 *Chicago-Kent Law Rev* 840, 850–6.

threats of violence in a face-to-face confrontation, and perhaps some extreme hard-core pornography.[36] As explained in Chapter III, the categories of excluded speech, not even covered by a free speech clause, have diminished, particularly in the United States. For example, defamatory allegations were brought within the coverage of the First Amendment in the historic ruling in *New York Times* v. *Sullivan*,[37] while other cases have established that neither professional nor commercial advertising is wholly excluded from its scope.[38]

The question is whether copyright infringement is, or more pertinently should be, totally excluded from the coverage of free speech. Should it be treated in the same way as, say, an offer of a bribe or a threat of violence? The scope of free speech depends on why it is regarded as a valuable right, and given strong constitutional protection. Bribes, perjury, and threats are excluded from coverage, because there is no good reason on any of the justifications for free speech guarantees, to think that they fall within it. A bribe, for example, does not contribute to public discourse or assert a proposition which may be true; nor is it easy to see it as enhancing the mental or other self-development of the person offering it. It does not merit coverage under any of the three classic justifications for strong free speech protection: Mill's argument from truth, the role of public discourse in a liberal democracy, or the part played by speech in the development and fulfilment of individuals.[39] On these arguments bribes, perjury, verbal threats, and contractual promises, fall outside the scope of free speech or expression guarantees.

But this is not necessarily the case with copyright infringement. If it were the case, copyright laws themselves would not make exceptions for free speech, as they do with the provision of 'fair use' or 'fair dealing' defences. Some infringements are regarded as worthy of protection, because they contribute to the free discussion, say, of the quality of a play or a work of art ('fair dealing . . . for the purpose of criticism or review'[40]). Quite apart from these legal rules, some infringing works should be regarded as an exercise of free speech rights because they are integral to the development of its author or because they enhance the general public understanding of literature or the arts. This is clearly the case with parodies, satire, and appropriation art, all of which may quote or in other ways exploit existing work, and thereby infringe copyright. Indeed, their effectiveness as a parody or appropriation art depends on reproduction or adaptation of significant parts of the earlier work. Copyright infringement in these circumstances is inevitable.[41] So it is wrong to treat a parody as an infringement of copyright without considering the implications for the infringer's own freedom of speech as an author or artist. Similar arguments may apply to the reproduction of documents or letters subject to copyright in an infringing work. The reproduction of such material should

---

[36] See ch. III, s. 1 above for discussion of types of speech excluded from free speech coverage, and ch. X below for pornography. [37] See ch. VI, s. 2 above.
[38] See ch. XI, s. 1 below. [39] See ch. I, s. 2 above. [40] CDPA 1988, s. 30(1).
[41] P. Loughlin, 'Copyright Law, Free Speech, and Self-Fulfilment' (2002) 24 *Sydney Law Rev* 427, 432–8.

often be treated as covered by a freedom of speech clause, because it may provide the public with valuable information and so contribute to public discourse. (In UK copyright law that argument is recognized by the defence of 'fair dealing... for the purpose of reporting current events...'.[42]) In the absence of free speech arguments (or adequate statutory fair use or fair dealing defences), rights-holders could use copyright to withhold important information from the public to the impoverishment of political debate.

The arguments for free speech guarantees, therefore, suggest that at least some infringing works are covered by the guarantee. The case for coverage is strongest when the infringement is a work of satire or a parody or reproduces information or images of political or social importance.[43] It is much weaker, or non-existent, in straightforward commercial piracy, when the copier aims solely to exploit the artistic skills of others for financial advantage.[44] In those circumstances it is easy to persuade the court that there is no real free speech interest at stake, or alternatively that any free speech interest should be trumped by that of the rights-holder. But it is wrong to derive principles from those circumstances and apply them automatically to all instances of conflict between copyright and freedom of speech or expression. Moreover, the importance of free speech suggests there should be a strong presumption in favour of coverage of any communication of ideas or information; without such a presumption there is a danger that valuable speech may be stifled by enforcement of copyright law.[45] It is for those contending that the communication should be excluded from coverage to show it falls outside the scope of the free speech clause.

(ii) The free speech interests of infringers

Copyright law assumes that copyright infringers have no free speech rights. As Nimmer put it, an infringer who pirates the expression of others 'is not engaging in *self*-expression in any meaningful sense' (his emphasis).[46] But this misses two points. First, an infringer may have a free speech right, derived from the interest of the public in access to a work which the rights-holder may have chosen not to distribute or perhaps only to make available at a price which most people cannot afford. More importantly, Nimmer's conclusion does not do justice to the interests of infringers, such as parodists and appropriation artists who deliberately copy others' work in order to make important political or artistic points concerning, say, the clichéd character of the rights-holder's work. Nimmer assumed that a writer is only engaged in self-expression when he expresses his ideas in a unique form and does not borrow from others.[47]

---

[42] CDPA 1988, s. 30(2).   [43] See Patfield (n. 3 above), 208–15.

[44] Birnhack (n. 1 above), 252.

[45] See F. Schauer, 'Categories and the First Amendment: A Play in Three Acts' (1981) 34 *Vanderbilt Law Rev* 265.   [46] Nimmer (n. 7 above), 1192.

[47] See Loughlin (n. 41 above), 432.

These issues were considered by the Court of Appeal in the recent *Ashdown* case.[48] It held that in exceptional circumstances freedom of expression could conflict with the enforcement of copyright law. Paddy Ashdown, then the leader of the Liberal Democrats, claimed infringement of copyright when the *Daily Telegraph* printed substantial extracts from minutes he had kept of confidential discussions with the Prime Minister, Tony Blair, concerning political cooperation between the Labour government and the Liberal Democrats after the general election of 1997. In addition to its unsuccessful argument that the publication amounted to 'fair dealing' for the purpose of reporting current events, the newspaper argued that the right to freedom of expression, incorporated in UK law by the HRA 1998, limited the scope of copyright. In the Court of Appeal, Lord Phillips MR denied that freedom of expression 'extends to the freedom to convey ideas and information using the form of words devised by someone else'.[49] Nevertheless, he held that there might be a public interest that readers 'should be told the very words used by a person, notwithstanding that the author enjoys copyright in them'.[50] In this case the newspaper's interest in publishing the minute was parasitic on the interest the public had in knowing details of the discussions between Blair and Ashdown, but Lord Phillips MR was wrong to imply that an infringer never has a right to use others' words to communicate his ideas. His judgment ignored the argument that social critics, satirists, and political commentators have legitimate free speech interests of their own, which they may exercise by incorporating substantial extracts from the speeches of politicians and others on whose work they are commenting.[51]

The consequence of paying attention exclusively to the interests of readers, and ignoring those of the writer or speaker, is shown in the only important copyright case to be considered in Strasbourg. In *De Geillustreerde Pers NV* v. *Netherlands*[52] the Commission rejected a complaint by a commercial magazine publisher that the copyright held by broadcasting companies in their programme schedules interfered with its freedom of expression also to list these schedules. The Commission considered that only the public's interest in access to the information was involved. Its interest was satisfied through the provision of the schedules by the broadcasters. That latter point might be correct, though it would be contestable, say, if broadcasters were to charge exorbitant prices for their listings magazines. Moreover, the argument assumes that the commercial publisher had no free speech or free press interest of its own. It would clearly have had a strong interest of its own, if it had used presentation of the schedules, say, to make critical points about the quality of Dutch broadcasting. Quite apart from that point, it is surely better to conclude that the commercial publisher was exercising freedom of expression, but that, if it merely reproduced the listings compiled by the broadcasting

---

[48] [2002] Ch 149.   [49] Ibid., para. 31.   [50] Ibid., para. 43.
[51] For a vigorous statement of this view, see Waldron (n. 35 above), 875–7.
[52] 5178/71, (1976) 8 D & R 5.

companies, it was necessary to restrain exercise of the freedom to protect copyright.

It is important to stress that copyright infringers may have free speech rights. Jeremy Waldron has persuasively argued that the standard perception of the copyright-free speech conflict presents copyright as a strong property right, in some cases balanced against weak free speech arguments which emphasize the social interest in communication of information to the public.[53] That perspective implicitly denies that copyright infringers have rights as speakers, or for that matter, that members of the public have individual free speech rights to receive or listen to infringing copies. It also exaggerates the weight of copyright as a property right, which itself is established on the contestable proposition that in all circumstances strong intellectual property rights are required to encourage the production of literary and other works, and so promote the values of free expression. It is in fact much clearer that copyright laws violate the free speech rights of infringers than it is that these laws promote the values which justify recognition of free speech rights.

One aspect of freedom of speech is that speakers are entitled to choose the terms in which propositions are put, as well as the intellectual content or subject matter of their discourse. Under this principle the law improperly interferes with the exercise of that freedom if, for example, it proscribes the use of certain language on the ground that it is shocking or offensive.[54] The principle was applied by the European Human Rights Court when it held that a journalist had freedom under Article 10 to publish documents containing the tax assessments of the head of Peugeot in order to give credibility to a story about his salary; the conviction in the French courts for making unlawful use of tax documents was incompatible with the Convention.[55] The journalist was free to strengthen the story by reproducing confidential documents.

Copyright law departs from this fundamental free speech principle. It asserts that publishers are entitled to communicate an idea or to provide information or news, as long as they do not use the exact words or expression of a rights-holder. This is the idea–expression dichotomy which has already been referred to.[56] Copyright law infringes the principle that a speaker is entitled to choose how he formulates his arguments by proscribing the use of language and other material which have become the subject of intellectual property rights. For example, the Ninth Circuit Court of Appeals held that it was unnecessary to conjure up the Walt Disney characters to parody American life and society, and that, therefore, there was no defence to an action for copyright infringement when they were depicted in adult comic books as figures in a freethinking, anarchist counter-culture.[57]

[53] Waldron (n. 35 above), 856–62.
[54] The classic authority is *Cohen* v. *California* 403 US 15 (1971), where the Court held the words, 'Fuck the Draft', on a jacket worn in a courthouse corridor, protected speech: see ch. VIII, s. 4(ii) below.   [55] *Fressoz and Roire* v. *France* (2001) 31 EHRR 2.
[56] S. 2(i) above.
[57] *Walt Disney Productions* v. *Air Pirates* 581 F 2d 751 (9th Cir, 1978).

But that approach severely circumscribes the right of satirists to use familiar emblems, symbols, and characters to illustrate their critique. It is a real limitation on the manner of speech, if not its rational or intellectual content.

(iii) Deference to copyright legislation

One reason why US courts reject challenges to the enforcement of federal copyright legislation is that they regard it as an affirmative measure to promote the goals of freedom of speech. As the Court of Appeals for the Fifth Circuit has put it: '[t]he judgment of the Constitution is that free expression is enriched by protecting the creations of authors from exploitation by others, and the Copyright Act is the congressional implementation of that judgment.'[58] The Supreme Court expressed the same sentiment in an important recent case. In *Eldred* v. *Ashcroft* it rejected a challenge to the extension of the term of copyright from life plus fifty years to life plus seventy years for published works with existing copyrights.[59] Part of the petitioners' argument was that the extension failed heightened judicial review under the First Amendment. The Court held such scrutiny was unnecessary on the familiar ground that copyright law itself contained 'built-in First Amendment accommodations'. The purpose of copyright 'is to *promote* the creation and publication of free expression' (emphasis of Ginsburg J. for the Court).[60] That is right. But the mere fact that legislation is intended to promote free speech should not have given it immunity from serious First Amendment scrutiny.

The US Supreme Court is normally unwilling to uphold legislative restrictions on freedom of speech (or press freedom) merely because they are intended to promote speech or to enhance equal opportunities for speech. It is distrustful of government intervention, fearing that it will distort the free marketplace of ideas.[61] Examples of its approach are its decision striking down the provision of a right to reply to personal attacks in newspapers,[62] and the decision invalidating restrictions imposed by a federal law on election expenditure; the restrictions were intended to enable lower income groups and candidates to contribute to political debate on a more equal footing with wealthy corporations and individuals, but nevertheless were struck down.[63] A majority of the DC Circuit Court of Appeals accepted the assessment of the Federal Communications Commission that the imposition of positive programme requirements on broadcasters, for example to

---

[58] *Dallas Cowboys Cheerleaders, Inc* v. *Scoreboard Posters, Inc* 600 F 2d 1184, 1187 (5th Cir, 1979).
[59] 537 US 186, 154 L Ed 2d 683 (2003). The Court did in principle leave the door open to First Amendment challenge if Congress were to change the contours of copyright legislation. It is unclear what this means. For commentary, see W. J. Gordon. 'Do we have a Right to Speak with Another's Language? *Eldred* and the Duration of Copyright', in P. L. C. Torremans (ed.), *Copyright and Human Rights* (The Hague: Kluwer, 2004), 109. [60] N. 59, 711.
[61] See ch. I, s. 2 above for the 'marketplace of ideas'.
[62] *Miami Herald* v. *Tornillo* 418 US 241 (1974).
[63] *Buckley* v. *Valeo* 424 US 1 (1976): see ch. XIV, s. 2 below.

show programmes dealing with controversial local political issues, infringed the First Amendment rights of the channels.[64] In all these cases the courts were unsympathetic to the argument that the intention and effect of the measures was to promote the values underlying freedom of speech, by ensuring, for example, that the public heard the views of the person attacked or had access to serious programmes which private broadcasters might be unwilling to schedule for commercial reasons. Yet the Supreme Court has accepted the comparable argument that copyright legislation is immune from scrutiny because it promotes speech.

The approach of the Supreme Court in *Eldred*, as in *Harper & Row*,[65] to the review of copyright legislation can only be explained in terms of its denial that freedom of speech is engaged in copyright litigation or, put another way, that infringers have First Amendment rights. But it is wrong to deny these claims. Copyright infringement is covered by the First Amendment. If the Court were to accept that, it is hard to believe that it would be prepared to uphold copyright legislation merely because it promotes the values of freedom of speech. Not only is that approach inconsistent with that adopted by the Court in other areas of free speech law, it may also be misconceived. It is questionable whether copyright law, as it stands at present, always promotes speech. It is reasonable to doubt, for example, whether authors and publishers need the range of rights conferred by copyright, or a term of protection as long as life plus seventy years, to encourage them to produce literature and other works or to reward them for their past efforts. And even if copyright law promotes the *production* of work, it equally clearly inhibits its *distribution*. Admittedly, the impact of copyright law on freedom of expression raises complex economic and cultural issues. It is understandable that courts are reluctant to interfere with Congressional judgement. The point is that they have not shown the same reluctance in other contexts, notably in considering challenges to complex legislation regulating election expenditure and contributions to political parties and candidates' campaigns. In this respect, as in the others discussed in this section, the courts treat copyright as a special case, giving it 'talismanic immunity' from appropriate First Amendment scrutiny.[66]

4. Balancing Copyright and Freedom of Speech

The coverage of some copyright infringements by freedom of speech provisions does not mean that copyright is unenforceable. It means only that enforcement of copyright should be subject to free speech scrutiny, when this freedom is clearly

---

[64] *Syracuse Peace Council* v. *FCC* 867 F 2d 654 (1989), cert denied 110 S Ct 717 (1990).

[65] Discussed in s. 2(i) above.

[66] The phrase 'talismanic immunity' is taken from Brennan J.'s judgment for the Court in *New York Times* v. *Sullivan* 376 US 254, 269 (1964), holding that libel was not entitled to immunity from the First Amendment.

engaged. That would not be the position in the standard case of commercial piracy, probably because courts would rightly not ascribe free speech rights to those infringers. On an alternative perspective, their rights are entitled to little or no weight when balanced against copyright. But satirists, appropriation artists, and news reporters can often claim to be exercising free speech rights, which should be weighed against the intellectual property right when they make use of copyright works. There is nothing odd, or intrinsically difficult, about this process. After all, it is what courts do when they balance freedom of speech or expression against privacy or reputation rights.

Nevertheless, it is understandable that the process conjures up fears of commercial uncertainty for rights-holders and of endless litigation. They were expressed by the courts in the *Ashdown* case.[67] English judges should, however, soon develop principles on the basis of which it would be relatively easy to determine when freedom of speech arguments would be seriously considered and when, on the other hand, copyright would be regarded as a necessary and proportionate restriction on exercise of that freedom under the HRA 1998. Freedom of expression challenges to the enforcement of copyright should only be sustained when copyright law is used to suppress the dissemination of information of real importance to the public or to stifle artistic creativity, parody, or satire, and moreover, when the legislation itself does not provide adequate safeguards for that freedom. In this context, as in others, deference to the legislature's judgement would be appropriate. The provision of 'fair dealing' and other defences should not preclude an argument that copyright enforcement infringes freedom of speech; but a court can properly require the infringer to provide strong reasons why it should disregard the balance between the rights struck by the legislation.

But there are circumstances in which courts should intervene to protect free speech, for example, cases where a writer or artist creates a work of real originality, but incorporates substantial elements of another work and therefore infringes copyright. In *Rogers* v. *Koons*,[68] a well-known postmodern artist, Jeff Koons, used a popular photograph, 'Puppies', in his sculpture entitled 'String of Puppies'. He deliberately intended in this way to satirize material values, as exemplified in the photograph of a family with its dogs. The Circuit Court rejected the 'fair use' defence because the parody did not make clear to viewers that it was satirizing the separate, original work of another artist, the photographer. In effect, freedom of artistic expression was subordinated to the claimant's copyright, including his freedom to sell rights to make derivative works from the photographs. The decision does not remotely do justice to the sculptor's freedom of artistic and political expression.[69] In comparison, the German Constitutional Court has emphasized

---

[67] [2002] Ch 149, para. 17 per Lord Phillips MR.   [68] 960 F 2d 301 (2nd Cir, 1992).

[69] See in this context *Walt Disney Productions* v. *Air Pirates* 581 F 2d 751 (9th Cir, 1978), where copyright was used to stop the use of Walt Disney cartoon characters in an adult 'counter-culture' comic book. Both fair use and First Amendment arguments were rejected, as the defendant could have expressed his ideas without infringing copyright.

that freedom of artistic expression should be given priority to copyright, when the injury to the latter right is trivial without the risk of significant economic damage.[70]

Even more clearly, copyright should not be enforced when to do so would censor speech, the publication of which could not be prevented by other remedies. But that is what happened in an Australian case, *Commonwealth of Australia* v. *John Fairfax and Sons Ltd.*[71] The High Court dismissed the government's application for an injunction in breach of confidence to restrain the publication of documents concerning foreign affairs and defence policy, but allowed it in copyright. There is no apparent justification for this divergence, except that the label of 'property right' attaches to copyright, but does not to the protection of confidential information.

The use of copyright to protect personal privacy can be regarded as an abuse of the former right. In *J. D. Salinger* v. *Random House*, a Circuit Court granted the reclusive author an injunction to stop the use in a forthcoming biography of extracts from his unpublished letters.[72] Salinger was entitled to protect his opportunity to sell his letters in future for a profit, although nothing suggested he was likely to do this; there was also little evidence that publication of a book containing short extracts from the letters would impair the market for the sale of the letters in full. The court protected copyright, at the cost of public awareness of the content of the author's letters either until he agreed to their publication or until the expiration of the copyright period (at that time, his life plus fifty years).[73] Salinger was, of course, anxious to protect his privacy, rather than his ability to exploit his copyright. He would probably have lost a privacy action, bearing in mind the strong protection courts in the United States give to competing First Amendment rights. Recently, the US Supreme Court has held that the media have a First Amendment right to reveal the contents of a private secretly taped conversation involving the discussion of matters of public concern.[74] Yet a copyright claim brought in these circumstances might have been successful. It is surely wrong to allow a copyright action to succeed, when it acts as a surrogate for a privacy claim which would, rightly or wrongly, almost certainly fail.[75]

It is harder for courts to resolve the issue when a facial challenge is made to a statutory provision giving enhanced protection to copyright to the detriment of the exercise of free speech rights. Such a challenge was made when it was argued that the extension of the term of copyright in the United States for existing works to life plus seventy years (to bring the term into line with that prescribed by the EU Directive) infringed the First Amendment.[76] But even in these cases courts should

---

[70] *Germania 3* (n. 16 above), para. 24.
[71] (1980) 147 CLR 39. See Griffiths (n. 3 above), 5–6 for criticism of this case.
[72] 811 F 2d (2nd Cir, 1987).   [73] Ibid., 100.
[74] *Bartnicki* v. *Vopper* 532 US 514 (2001): see ch. VI, s. 5 above.
[75] See the criticism of Zimmerman (n. 17 above), 670–2.
[76] *Eldred* v. *Ashcroft* 537 US 186 (2003), discussed in s. 3(iii) above.

scrutinize the legislation carefully. Granted that copyright protection may infringe the free speech rights of prospective infringers, readers, and other users (until the work enters the public domain), the legislature should be expected to produce some arguments to justify an increase in the term of protection or other change which benefits rights-holders. Some indication should be given why an extension might act as an incentive to produce more literary and other works, or why it is appropriate to reward authors, composers, directors, etc. and their heirs in this way. Breyer J., dissenting from the Court's judgment in the *Eldred* case, understandably doubted whether Congress had provided enough evidence to justify an extension in the term of protection; the claim that it provided additional incentives to produce new works or republish older works was quite implausible, while the impact of the extension on scholars, teachers, film buffs, database operators, and others would be considerable. In this context, the courts can balance free speech and copyright, ensuring that the legislature does not, as generally happens, sacrifice the former because of its enthusiasm for (or effective lobbying by) rights-holders.

5. Trade Mark and Publicity Rights

Free speech issues similar to those raised in relation to copyright have been canvassed in other contexts, among them trade marks and publicity rights. They are discussed briefly in this section in the context of a few leading US cases. But the same questions can be raised in any jurisdiction where trade marks and patrimonial rights to the protection of personal identity can be vindicated. As in copyright cases, courts in the United States have generally been more solicitous of these property rights than they have of personal privacy and dignity rights. The reasons for this divergence have rarely been explored. One explanation, as with copyright, is historical; these areas of law have developed apart from free speech jurisprudence. But this account is unsatisfactory, particularly with regard to the publicity rights which have developed only recently and which have been closely linked with aspects of the privacy right. In any case, no historical or doctrinal account can *justify* the immunity of these rights from careful free speech scrutiny.

(i) Trade marks and the Gay Olympics case

Trade mark laws confer on the proprietor of a mark an exclusive right to use a particular sign or symbol in connection with specified commercial activities. Trade marks give consumers information about the origin of the goods or services; they, therefore, imply that the products are of an established quality, and in a sense promote or advertise it.[77] For a business to use the trade mark of its competitor to

---

[77] For the functions of trade mark laws, see Bently and Sherman (n. 20 above), ch. 31.

market its own goods misleads consumers and clearly amounts to unfair competition. Even if such use were treated as commercial speech, its restriction would clearly be justified.[78] Harder free speech questions are posed by the use of another's trade mark for the purpose of satire or parody. In principle, that should certainly be covered, and perhaps protected, by a free speech provision. Yet a Circuit Court of Appeals granted an injunction to stop the showing of a film, *Debbie Does Dallas*, on the ground that it infringed the trade mark in the uniform of the Dallas Cowboys Cheerleaders;[79] the film portrayed women granting sexual favours to become cheerleaders for the Dallas football team. It was a satire on an aspect of American culture and deserved the protection of the First Amendment.

The conflict between free speech and a right analogous to a trade mark was at issue in *San Francisco Arts and Athletics Inc* v. *US Olympic Committee*.[80] A provision in the federal Amateur Sports Act of 1978 conferred on the US Olympic Committee (USOC) the right to prohibit the use of the word 'Olympic' and associated symbols for non-authorized commercial and promotional purposes.[81] (USOC was not required to show that an unauthorized use would give rise to confusion before it prohibited it, so its powers went beyond the normal confines of trade mark legislation.) By a majority of 7–2, the Court rejected the argument of the organizers of the Gay Olympics in San Francisco that they had a First Amendment right to use the prohibited words on promotional literature for their games.[82] Powell J., for the majority, classified the Committee's exclusive right as a limited property right, and held it could trump the freedom of the organizers to use the words in their literature. That was treated as commercial speech, entitled to less protection under the First Amendment than political discourse. Moreover, the restriction, in Powell J.'s view, only inhibited the manner or form in which the organizers of the Gay Olympics promoted their games.

But Brennan J. rightly protested in dissent that the legislation did not only, or even primarily, restrict commercial advertising. It inhibited the organizers' choice of language. In effect it permitted bans on the communication of an idea in the most effective form—in this case, the idea that the Gay Olympics are comparable to, and inspired by the same values as, the regular Games held every four years since the end of the nineteenth century. The legislation, therefore, could not be regarded as merely imposing a restraint on the manner and form of the message the organizers wanted to communicate. The provision should have been subject to

---

[78] See ch. XI, s. 4 below for the regulation of commercial speech.

[79] *Dallas Cowboys Cheerleaders* v. *Pussycat Cinema, Ltd* 604 F 2d 200 (2nd Cir, 1979).

[80] 483 US 522 (1987), and see the criticisms of R. N. Kravitz, 'Trade Marks, Speech, and the *Gay Olympics* Case' (1989) 69 *Boston Univ Law Rev* 131.

[81] Comparable UK legislation prohibits unauthorized use of the word 'Olympic' and associated symbol and terms: Olympic Symbol etc. (Protection) Act 1995.

[82] A 5–4 majority of the Court also held there was no 'state action' in the USOC decision to prohibit promotion of the Gay Olympics. This is wholly unconvincing; the decision was authorized by federal law and there is extensive government patronage of the regular Olympics. For the state action argument in copyright, see s. 2 above.

strict scrutiny and should have been upheld only if USOC had established that it protected a substantial interest and that its aim could not have been achieved by other means less restrictive of free speech. That burden was not met; the organizers of the Gay Olympics had offered the publication of disclaimers indicating the absence of any link with the official four-yearly Games. The result of the decision was that the Court legitimized the removal of a commonly used word, 'Olympic', from its use to promote competitive athletic activities by homosexual athletes.

Of course, unlike the position in standard trade marks cases, nobody would have been confused by the use of the word 'Olympics' in these circumstances. What USOC really objected to was loss of dignity. It felt, perhaps on good grounds, that use of the word 'Olympics' by the organizers of the gay games would somehow devalue the term. Some people might think less highly of the regular Olympics. But these are poor reasons to justify a limit on free speech. They would not be accepted in the United States in a privacy action, even though then the claim is brought by an individual who may have suffered real personal distress as a result of the publication. On the evidence of the Gay Olympics case, it seems that while free speech is often considered more important than the privacy or dignity of individuals, it is not as important as the ability of an organization to protect its monopoly right to use particular words and symbols.

(ii) Publicity rights

Publicity rights protect celebrities against the unauthorized use of their name, image, voice, or other attribute, which would damage their own ability to exploit aspects of their personality commercially.[83] They protect, for example, celebrities' rights to endorse (or in some way to be associated with) T-shirts, sports goods, perfumes, drinks, or other goods or services. The right developed in the states of the United States during the 1950s, initially as an aspect of the privacy right against commercial appropriation of an individual's name or likeness, but subsequently as an autonomous right with distinctive attributes. In particular, unlike the rights to reputation and privacy, it is a property right, which may in most states be asserted by the celebrity's heirs, and which can be assigned. An analogous, but more limited personality right has been recognized in Ontario.[84] In England and Australia, the tort of passing off may sometimes protect endorsement rights against unauthorized use of a celebrity's name, likeness, or other attribute, when that use wrongly gives consumers the impression that the celebrity is lending his name to a particular product.[85] This is much narrower than the publicity right recognized in

---

[83] For a comparative study, see H. Beverley-Smith, *The Commercial Appropriation of Personality* (Cambridge: CUP, 2002), esp. chs. 4–6.

[84] Ibid., 115–37. For a sceptical view of the desirability of importing publicity rights, see M. A. Flagg, 'Star Crazy: Keeping the Right of Publicity Out of Canadian Law' [1998–9] *Intellectual Property Jo* 179.

[85] See *Irvine* v. *Talksport Ltd* [2002] 2 All ER 414, Ch D; *Henderson* v. *Radio Corporation Pty Ltd* [1969] RPC 218, HC of New South Wales.

the United States. That right can be protected, irrespective of whether the defendant's use of the celebrity image (or other attribute) created a false message which would induce members of the public to think that the celebrity was endorsing its goods. For example, the heirs of Martin Luther King have been able to assert publicity rights, although there was no evidence that he had endorsed commercial products in his own lifetime, or that the public would think that he, or his heirs, had endorsed the plastic busts of him, which were distributed by the defendants.[86]

US courts have often protected publicity rights, despite arguments that their enforcement infringes the freedom of the media or of advertisers to use the images of celebrities for promotional purposes.[87] Admittedly, there is no liability where a photograph or voice is used in a news report, but that exemption does not cover commercial features and advertising. In one well-known case, the Court of Appeals for the Ninth Circuit refused to recognize that an advertiser had a First Amendment right to parody the distinctive dress, hairstyle, and props of a game-show hostess in promoting its products;[88] the Court did not even trouble to apply the usual tests for determining the constitutionality of restrictions on commercial speech.[89] In the only Supreme Court decision on publicity rights, it denied a First Amendment defence to the claimant's action for damages for the broadcast of his human cannonball act performed at a county fair.[90] In this unusual case, the right protected the performance, rather than the claimant's face or other attribute of his identity; moreover, the television company broadcast the whole of the short (fifteen-second) performance, so it would have been difficult for it to argue a 'fair use' defence comparable to that provided in the federal copyright statute.

However, some recent decisions have upheld constitutional free speech arguments in this context. In *Cardtoons* v. *Major League Baseball Players Association*,[91] the Tenth Circuit Court of Appeals upheld the First Amendment rights of the producer of playing cards against the publicity rights of the footballers, whose images and names were parodied on the cards. The court carefully examined whether application of the Oklahoma publicity right statute in this context would overprotect the right. Parodies of celebrities were clearly valuable means of expression; further, publication of the cards would hardly undermine the footballers' rights, say, to endorse sportswear, as the cards had not been issued to market a substitute product. The important point in this case is that the court was not prepared to treat publicity rights as immune from strict free speech scrutiny. A similar

[86] *Martin Luther King Jr Center for Social Change* v. *American Heritage Products* 296 SE 2d 697 (Ga, 1982).

[87] D. L. Zimmerman, 'Fitting Publicity Rights into Intellectual Property and Free Speech Theory: Sam, You Made the Pants Too Long!' (1999) 10 *DePaul-LCA Jo of Arts and Entertainment Law* 283, 287–8.

[88] *Vanna White* v. *Samsung Electronics America* 971 F 2d 1395 (9th Cir, 1992), rehearing denied 989 F 2d 1512 (9th Cir, 1992).

[89] For restrictions on commercial speech, see ch. XI, s. 4 below.

[90] *Zacchini* v. *Scripps-Howard Publishing Co* 433 US 562 (1977).

[91] 95 F 3d 959 (10th Cir, 1996).

approach was taken by another Circuit Court of Appeals when it allowed the appeal of a Los Angeles magazine against a ruling that it was liable in damages for infringing Dustin Hoffman's publicity rights.[92] The magazine had published, in the context of a feature about Hollywood stars past and present, a manipulated photograph of the actor, giving the impression that he was wearing a contemporary silk gown. The Court of Appeals held the magazine was entitled to full First Amendment protection, since the photograph illustrated a feature article, rather than an advertisement. Further, it was wrong to hold, as the lower court had done, that the feature had been published with knowledge of its falsity; there was no clear and convincing proof that the editors intended to suggest to ordinary readers that they were actually seeing Hoffman's image in the doctored photograph.

From the free speech perspective, these two decisions are surely right. Quite apart from doubts about the wisdom of recognizing publicity rights,[93] there is no reason why they should be given stronger protection than reputation or privacy rights when they are balanced against freedom of speech. Indeed, they should be given much less protection than those basic human rights which are closely connected with human dignity. Further, unlike the position in copyright, there is no free expression case for protection of the publicity right when it is balanced against the free speech interests of the media, parodists, and (to a lesser extent) advertisers. Moreover, the fact that publicity rights have been characterized as property rights, so they can be assigned and passed on at death, should not give them more weight in this context. In short, free speech should often, though not always, trump broad publicity rights. Admittedly, in some circumstances the free speech argument may be weak. Advertisers who use the image of a celebrity without his consent to endorse a product, and so mislead consumers, do not have a strong claim. It may be legitimate in those instances to protect a publicity right, or, in English law, to allow a passing-off action to protect the celebrity's goodwill. But those rights do not deserve protection when there is little risk that the public will be deceived, or when the infringement forms part of a parody or a political or social commentary and is as a result covered by freedom of speech.

[92] *Hoffman* v. *Capital Cities/ABC Inc* 255 F 3d 1180 (9th Cir, 2001), allowing the publisher's appeal from 33 F Supp 2d 867 (CD Cal, 1999).

[93] D. Lange, 'Recognizing the Public Domain' (1981) 44 *Law and Contemporary Problems* 147; M. Madow, 'Private Ownership of Public Image: Popular Culture and Publicity Rights' (1993) 81 *California Law Rev* 127.

VIII

Meetings, Protest, and Public Order

1. Introduction

English lawyers have often denied the existence of a right to hold a public meeting. For Dicey, it was nothing more than the exercise by a number of people of their individual freedom to walk along the streets in conversation with others.[1] In circumstances where that exercise conflicted with the interests of public order, courts generally gave preference to the latter. So it was possible for judges to say of a leading case where a constable had asked a speaker at a public meeting to move on, and on her refusal had arrested her for obstruction of a police officer in the execution of his duty, that it had nothing to do with the law of unlawful assembly.[2] It is now much less common for courts in England to take this narrow view. Moreover, constitutions and the European Convention on Human Rights and Fundamental Freedoms (ECHR) protect freedom of assembly, although it is no more protected absolutely from restrictions than is the freedom of speech with which it is closely associated.

For many people, participation in public meetings or less formal forms of protest—marches and other demonstrations on the streets, picketing, and sit-ins—is not just the best, but the only effective means of communicating their views.[3] Leader-writers, journalists and other writers, politicians, and celebrities can use the mass media, but these opportunities are regularly available only to a small minority. Taking part in public protest, particularly if the demonstration itself is covered on television and widely reported, enables people without media access to contribute to public debate. A right of peaceful assembly is an important freedom, even though individuals can also write letters to newspapers, participate in radio phone-in programmes, and engage in discussion on the Internet. One has only to recall the impact of the worldwide protests and demonstrations before the war in Iraq to appreciate the value of this right to millions of people who might otherwise have felt completely voiceless on a matter of fundamental political significance.

---

[1] A. V. Dicey, *Introduction to the Study of the Law of the Constitution*, 10th edn. (London: Macmillan, 1959), 271–2.

[2] See Lord Hewart CJ and Humphreys J. in *Duncan* v. *Jones* [1936] 1 KB 218, 222, QB.

[3] The points in this paragraph are made at greater length in the author's, 'Freedom of Assembly' in *Freedom of Expression and Freedom of Information*, 161.

These particular demonstrations were in one sense ineffective; they did not stop the war. But other protests may have influenced events. For example, the years of protest in universities and elsewhere surely played some part in persuading the United States to withdraw from engagement in Vietnam. In England the recent protests by anti-hunting saboteurs and by the Countryside Alliance (against a ban on hunting with dogs) may have influenced the approach of the government, which, lacking strong convictions on the matter, became anxious to placate both strands of opinion. Politically, protest is an important phenomenon. It is therefore important to know how far there are legal rights to engage in it.

A number of issues need to be explored. The first is the relationship of freedom of speech and freedom of assembly: what, if anything, does the latter right add to free speech (or expression) rights exercised in the context of meetings and other forms of protest? This question is discussed in section 2 of the chapter. Mass demonstrations typically are held on the streets, while public parks and other open spaces, such as Hyde Park and Trafalgar Square in London or state capitol grounds in the United States, have been common venues for large meetings. On a smaller scale, some groups now use airport terminals, railway and bus stations, and other places where people congregate to solicit support and financial donations. The legal question is whether demonstrators have a right to use these places, or whether the relevant public authority may forbid such use; it may take the view that it is inconvenient to the public and that a property owner may determine the uses to which its land is put. This issue has been explored for several decades in the United States, where the courts have formulated principles under which some property is regarded as a 'public forum' on which there are rights of speech and of assembly. The issue has arisen more recently in Canada, and to some extent, in the United Kingdom. Its resolution is critical to the existence of any effective right to hold public meetings, for otherwise they could only be held on the convenor's own land, or on property where the owner—private or public—allowed them to take place. This crucial topic is discussed in section 3 of this chapter.

Even the strongest advocates of free speech rights concede that restrictions may sometimes be justified in the interests of public order. Mill himself admitted this when he wrote that, '. . . opinions lose their immunity when the circumstances in which they are expressed are such as to constitute their expression a positive instigation to some mischievous act'.[4] So, he continued, views on the iniquitous behaviour of corn-dealers could properly be punished if delivered to a mob assembled outside a merchant's house. Such speech could be proscribed either because it might be regarded as inherently inflammatory or because it is likely in the circumstances to lead to violence or disorder. Alternatively, the police might decide that a demonstration should be halted because they fear that a hostile audience would react violently. These sets of circumstances are considered in section 4, which is concerned with the relationship of freedom of speech and of assembly to public

---

[4] Mill, 62.

order. Section 5 examines two techniques which may be used to limit the scale of the public order problems. The convenors of political demonstrations on the streets may be required to give notice of a proposed march, to allow the police to take steps to avoid disorder and disruption to the life of the community by the imposition of conditions on its route and timing. Secondly, in some sensitive contexts, in particular those of anti-abortion protest, buffer zones may be set up between demonstrators and others who may feel harassed or intimidated by the protest. The use of these techniques enables the courts to strike a balance between free speech and other important interests.

2. The Right to Assemble and Freedom of Speech

Constitutions often provide a distinct guarantee for freedom of assembly. The First Amendment to the US Constitution covers 'the right of the people peaceably to assemble' and 'the right to petition the Government for a redress of grievances' as well as freedom of speech and of the press. In other constitutions, the coverage of freedom of assembly or the right to hold public meeting is kept distinct from that of freedom of expression and related rights. The German Basic Law, for instance, provides for *Versammlungsfreiheit* in Article 8(1): 'All Germans shall have the right to assemble peaceably and unarmed without prior notification or permission.' The Italian Constitution also covers freedom of assembly separately from freedom of expression.[5] Article 11 of the ECHR protects the right to freedom of peaceful assembly and of association, though the exercise of these rights may be qualified or restricted in much the same sets of circumstances as the exercise of the right to free expression guaranteed by Article 10. A possible implication of these provisions is that the assembly right is different in scope from the right to freedom of speech or of expression, and indeed in the case of the ECHR that it may have more in common with association than speech rights.

However, it is far from clear what these differences amount to.[6] Free speech clauses are now interpreted to cover expressive conduct, such as the wearing of badges and armbands, flag-burning, and even non-violent forms of protest, for example, sit-ins and peaceful picketing.[7] If public order or hate speech laws are used to penalize a speech at a public meeting or to prosecute the carrying of a placard with an extremist message, then it seems immaterial whether the orator or protester claims the protection of the free speech or the freedom of assembly provision. Both are implicated. The right to peaceful assembly in this context adds little, if anything, to the free speech right. So it is not surprising that the Supreme Court in an early First Amendment case said that the two rights were 'cognate'. It was incompatible

---

[5] Art. 17 (freedom of assembly) and art. 21 (freedom of expression).
[6] See 'Freedom of Assembly' (n. 3 above), 162–5.
[7] For full discussion of this topic, see ch. III, ss. 1–2 above.

with the Constitution to make it an offence to participate in a meeting of the Communist Party, even though no speech was made there advocating violence or insurrection.[8] On the other hand, while the European Human Rights Court has considered some applications arising from the arrest of the applicants for engaging in diverse forms of protest solely under Article 10 (freedom of expression),[9] in *Rai, Allmond and 'Negotiate Now'* v. *UK*[10] the Commission treated an application challenging the refusal to allow a meeting to be held in Trafalgar Square as raising issues under Article 11 (freedom of assembly). Other Convention provisions, including Article 10, were only relevant to its interpretation.

It does seem that freedom of assembly can be invoked to strengthen claims which could not easily be asserted under freedom of speech. The application in *Rai* is perhaps a good example; it involved a challenge to the government's policy not to allow meetings concerned with Northern Ireland to be held in a prominent place in the centre of London, where the risk to public order was considered particularly acute. It might have been difficult to assert a right to hold a meeting there on the basis of free speech arguments alone. In many contexts, for example, the use of advertising space on public transport, even the US Supreme Court has been unwilling to recognize positive access rights of speech.[11] But it has been more willing to uphold access rights to use certain public spaces for the purpose of meetings and other forms of political protest, where freedom of assembly can be invoked (although in some cases it is unclear whether the Court is placing more weight on that freedom than it does on freedom of speech). In short, a right to assemble may confer positive rights to hold meetings on public property, which might not be recognized as an aspect of freedom of speech.

There may be other differences in the scope of speech and assembly rights. Although, as mentioned earlier, some forms of expressive conduct may be treated as 'speech', recourse to the assembly right removes the need for argument about the point. When the Supreme Court in *Brown* v. *Louisiana*, by a 5–4 majority, reversed the conviction of five blacks under a breach of the peace law for a peaceful sit-in at a public library in protest against its segregation facilities, Fortas J. referred to the First Amendment rights of speech, assembly, and petition. They 'are not confined to verbal expression [but] embrace appropriate types of action which certainly include the right in a peaceable and orderly manner to protest by silent and reproachful presence, in a place where the protestant has every right to be, the unconstitutional segregation of public facilities.'[12] This conclusion could not have been reached, it is suggested, if the right to free speech had not been bracketed in the text with related rights to freedom of assembly and to petition for the redress of grievances. German and European decisions also indicate that freedom of assembly may require public authorities to take positive steps to

---

[8] *De Jonge* v. *Oregon* 90 US 353 (1937).   [9] *Steel* v. *UK* (1999) 28 EHRR 603.
[10] (1995) 19 EHRR CD 93.   [11] *Lehman* v. *City of Shaker Heights* 418 US 298 (1974).
[12] *Brown* v. *Louisiana* 383 US 131, 142 (1966).

protect the rights of demonstrators against disruption. The state must take positive steps to safeguard the effective exercise of this freedom.[13]

These differences in the scope of the two rights reflect an important point: freedom of assembly has an *organizational* dimension, enabling the convenors of meetings and street processions to choose, subject to limits and conditions, the time and place of their demonstration and, of course, most fundamentally their objectives.[14] This dimension is also found in press freedom; editors enjoy organizational and institutional rights to determine the policy of the newspaper, its daily contents, and which journalists and correspondents write for it.[15] Like freedom of the press, freedom of assembly is linked to free speech and is protected because it serves the same values as the latter: the self-fulfilment of those participating in the meeting or other form of protest, and the dissemination of ideas and opinions essential to the working of an active democracy. Public meetings and demonstrations enable those ideas to be communicated more effectively. A common purpose to draw the attention of the public to the protesters' ideas is essential. In the absence of such a purpose, the blockade by Roma gypsies of a motorway near the German/Swiss border fell outside freedom of assembly; the German Constitutional Court ruled that the blockade was intended to force the Swiss authorities to allow them entry and could properly be classified as the crime of coercion.[16]

Courts in the United States, as shown in *Brown*, do not always discriminate carefully whether the right to freedom of speech or the right to peaceable assembly is in issue. In contrast, the German Constitutional Court is more concerned to determine the legal basis for a constitutional complaint or reference. In the Auschwitz Lies case it considered the challenge to the application of conditions on the holding of public meetings solely under Article 5 (freedom of expression) rather than Article 8 guaranteeing freedom of assembly.[17] An extreme right-wing political party had been granted a permit to hold a meeting on condition that its organizer ensured that speakers did not deny the Holocaust, a restriction on the exercise of the right to freedom of expression. Article 8 was not in issue. The point is that the restriction in that case was directed at the *content* of the speeches likely to be made at the meeting. If, on the other hand, a condition has nothing to do with the objects of the demonstration, or the terms of speeches made or placards carried by demonstrators, then freedom of assembly, rather than of expression, is in issue. It is the assembly right which enables the convenor to choose the time, manner, and place of the demonstration, subject to reasonable limits. These principles were applied by the German Constitutional Court when challenges were brought to the application of the criminal law proscription of intimidation (*Nötigung*) to a blockade of the entry to nuclear energy plants.[18] The prosecutions

---

[13] See Brokdorf, 59 BVerfGE 313, 355 (1985); *Platform 'Ärzte für das Leben' v. Austria* (1991) 13 EHRR 204.   [14] Brokdorf, 59 BVerfGE 313, 343 (1985).

[15] See ch. XII, s. 2 below.   [16] 104 BVerfGE 92 (2002), paras. 41–3.

[17] 90 BVerfGE 241 (1994).   [18] 104 BVerfGE 92 (2002).

had been brought in respect of the blockade, rather than the views about nuclear energy the protest drew to public attention; the criminal proceedings were assessed under the Article 8 guarantee of freedom of assembly.[19]

This distinction is, of course, relatively easy to state, but may be much harder to apply. Under the UK Public Order Act 1986, the police may impose conditions on the route of a procession if they fear that a march on the proposed route might lead to disorder or to 'serious disruption to the life of the community'.[20] Suppose that power is exercised to prevent a demonstration against US foreign policy proceeding past the US Embassy or in an area where a number of US citizens are resident, on the ground that it would be seriously offensive to the Embassy staff or the American community, or that it would imperil good order. Insofar as other marches are allowed in this area, it would be seem that the conditions discriminate on the basis of the objectives of this particular demonstration, so free speech is implicated. Equally, the restriction is imposed on the particular venue of a street procession which is free to take other routes. It is unclear whether we are primarily dealing here with a restriction on free speech or a separate assembly right.[21] In practice, however, this difficulty does not much matter. Constitutional clauses are not interpreted in isolation from each other. Nor should they be. What can be said with confidence is that freedom of assembly strengthens arguments which might not carry conviction on general free speech principles. This is most clear when we consider the question whether there are rights to hold meetings on the streets and other public spaces, irrespective of the wishes of the authority which owns or regulates the land.

3. Access to Streets and Other Public Fora

(i) Theoretical issues

Claims that there is a right to hold meetings and conduct protest on the streets, in public halls and parks, or in other public areas such as airport terminals, may meet two related theoretical problems. The first is whether freedom of speech, or the right to peaceful assembly, includes positive rights or should alternatively be treated purely as a liberty which the government should not infringe. This general problem has been discussed earlier in the book,[22] where it was pointed out that it is relevant to a number of controversies concerning the scope and application of free speech provisions. Among them are their coverage of freedom of

---

[19] Ibid., paras. 36–7. [20] S. 12(1)(a).
[21] In principle it is unclear whether the ban at issue in *Rai et al* v. *UK* (n. 10 above) on holding 'controversial' meetings concerned with Northern Ireland in Trafalgar Square was more concerned with the subject of the protests or with the risk to public order in the centre of London. The European Human Rights Commission considered the application under ECHR, art. 11 which suggests that it thought the latter was the principal object. [22] Ch. III, s. 6 above.

information,[23] the constitutionality of conditions attached to government or other public funding of the arts,[24] and whether the press enjoy access rights to attend trial and other legal proceedings.[25] The claim that there are rights to hold meetings or engage in other forms of protest on some types of public property should, therefore, be considered in conjunction with these other controversial arguments about the scope of freedom of speech.

The second difficulty is particularly pertinent to public protest, though it also arises on occasion in other areas of free speech law. The government (or other relevant public authority in whom land is vested) may claim that it should be as free as any private person to determine the appropriate use of its property, so it should be free to ban all meetings on its streets and in its parks. English law has not entirely abandoned this perspective.[26] It used to be shared by US judges, notably by Holmes J. when sitting in the Supreme Court of Massachusetts;[27] a state was entitled to control the use of its property as it likes, and was therefore free to ban all meetings or permit them on its own terms. This view has now been rejected by the US Supreme Court, though there are, as will be seen, significant vestiges of this perspective with its emphasis on property rights.

The first difficulty can be met. Quite apart from the general arguments for recognition of access rights to speak, the case for their acceptance in this context is particularly persuasive. First, the case is stronger because it rests on the right to freedom of assembly as well as the related free speech right. The political protest and activity covered by the assembly right inevitably takes place on streets and in other public places, whether it takes the form of leafleting and canvassing shoppers, of politicians meeting and addressing crowds, or of marches and demonstrations. But it is the second point which is crucial. Some access rights must be recognized if the guarantee of free political speech is to be effective. Political parties, other groups, and individuals cannot exercise their free speech rights without the use of some property, whether a personal computer, printing press or broadcasting studio, a hall or park, or the streets. In particular, meetings and demonstrations, the traditional means of individual and collective protest, can only be held in large open spaces. Freedom of speech would surely be an illusion if there were no enforceable rights to use public spaces in some circumstances to exchange views and voice grievances.[28] The force of this point might be reduced if individuals had access rights, or were freely allowed, to use the mass media for those purposes. But newspapers, television, and radio afford only limited opportunities

---

[23] Ch. III, s. 7 above.   [24] Ch. III, s. 8 above.   [25] Ch. IX, s. 4 below.
[26] But see the decision of the House of Lords in *DPP* v. *Jones* [1999] 2 AC 240, discussed below.
[27] See *Davis* v. *Massachusetts* 162 Mass 510 (1895), approved by the US Supreme Court: 167 US 43 (1897).
[28] See H. Kalven, 'The Concept of the Public Forum: *Cox* v. *Louisiana*' [1965] *Supreme Court Rev* 1. Also see *Committee for the Commonwealth of Canada* v. *Canada* [1991] 1 SCR 139, where it was emphasized that some access to public property for speech must be allowed, for otherwise the right would be valueless.

for people other than public figures and media professionals. Conceivably, the Internet might one day constitute a forum for public discourse similar to that traditionally, though now rarely, provided by political and village hall meetings. But that time has not yet arrived, and it is reasonable to doubt whether Internet discussion groups and chat-rooms will ever perform this role.[29] Demonstrations and meetings still provide the best occasion for political speech, and they can only take place if property owners allow them, or the law provides rights of access.

There should also be little difficulty in overcoming the second objection of principle to recognition of free speech access rights in this context, namely, that they interfere with the property rights of government or other public authorities. First, this objection assumes that property rights are necessarily more important than the rights to freedom of speech and of assembly. But even where government has legal title to land and other property, it does not enjoy strong, constitutional property rights in the same way as private citizens. The reasons which justify and underlie the ascription of property rights to individuals do not apply to public bodies. Government, whether central or local, enjoys property rights on behalf of the community;[30] they are held to meet public interests, among which is the interest in free speech and protest. Of course, land is held for other purposes. Highways are primarily dedicated for transport or, to use the quaint phrase of older English cases, 'to pass and repass'.[31] Parks are maintained for recreation, airport and bus terminals to allow passengers opportunities for relaxation and refreshment while they wait. Recognition of a right to free speech or to assemble in these places may be incompatible with their principal use. It would obviously make nonsense of the purpose of a small public park to allow it to be used every weekend for a mass demonstration; but a large open space such as Hyde Park is often used for public meetings (and for concerts) without excluding its enjoyment for walks and other recreation. It makes much more sense to balance the free speech interests and the other public interests and concerns in this context than it does to give either interest automatic priority, with the consequence that the other is wholly ignored.

These arguments explain why the objections of principle to access rights have for some time been overcome in the United States in the context of the traditional places for meetings and demonstrations—the streets and other open spaces suitable for such activity. Municipal and other public authorities are not now entirely free to ban meetings and demonstrations in these places, known as public fora. On the other hand, the Supreme Court has been more reluctant to recognize rights to hold meetings or distribute leaflets in other public areas, where the freedom of the relevant authority to preclude speech on its property is still respected. It would be wrong to conclude that the theoretical questions have been wholly resolved in favour of freedom of speech and of assembly. As the following sections

---

[29] See ch. XIII, s. 2(iii) below for discussion whether the Internet is a public forum for speech.

[30] This point does not apply in the same way when there is a conflict between free speech and the rights of a private property. For cases concerned with this conflict, see s. 3(iv) below.

[31] Lopes LJ in *Harrison v. Duke of Rutland* [1893] 1 QB 142, 154, CA.

will show, courts balance other interests against these rights in determining how far positive rights to protest should be recognized.

(ii) Traditional public fora: streets, open spaces, and public halls

The argument for positive access rights to hold public meetings is strongest when the claim is made in the context of the streets and public open spaces. First, the convenor of the meeting and the speakers do not ask the public authority to do anything for them. Indeed, unless and until demonstrators are arrested for obstruction or unlawful assembly, or are asked to leave, they are free to be on the land; a free speech claim in these cases could indeed be presented as an argument that the authority should not interfere with a prima facie lawful use of the area. The argument is stronger than it is, say, in the context of public halls, schools, and other enclosed facilities where recognition of the right would require the relevant authority to open the premises at a time when they would probably otherwise be closed. It would certainly be stronger than an extreme claim that the state is under a duty to build premises suitable for public meetings. Secondly, to repeat a point made earlier in this chapter, it is hard to see how the right to freedom of speech and *a fortiori* freedom of assembly could be regarded as coherent rights, unless they could be exercised on the streets and other open spaces; otherwise they would exist in a vacuum. Finally, as the Supreme Court of the United States and other courts have recognized, the streets and parks have traditionally been recognized as suitable fora for public debate and meetings, so the claim is not in this context a novel one. The same point applies with almost as much force to such places as the local village or community hall, for long used for election and other public meetings.

Nevertheless, it has been commonplace in legal writing to observe that there is no *right* to hold a public meeting in England or other parts of the United Kingdom. Meetings and processions may take place when they are not prohibited under the general criminal and civil law, or have not been banned by the police or other authority under their statutory powers to ensure public order.[32] The convenor of a meeting has generally no right to compel a public authority to provide him with facilities, or to permit him to hold it on the streets or other public open spaces. On the other hand, in the absence of any restriction, it is perfectly lawful to hold a meeting as an exercise of the individual's liberty of speech.[33] Moreover, the courts have recently accepted the argument that the law does recognize freedom of assembly and that legislation should be interpreted and applied to respect that right.

To look at English law in a little more detail, it is clear that there is no right to the use of a public building for a meeting. However, candidates for parliamentary

---

[32] For discussion of these powers, see s. 5 of this chapter.
[33] See the robust statement of principle by Lord Denning MR in *Hubbard* v. *Pitt* [1976] QB 142, 178–9, CA.

and local elections are entitled to use schools and public halls for election meetings.[34] So a local authority has no discretion to deny that facility to an extreme right-wing party.[35] With this exception, a public authority is as much entitled to refuse consent as is a private landowner. In practice, however, many local authorities readily give permission to political and other groups to hold meetings in town halls and other public property. But since they are exercising ordinary property rights rather than acting under specific statutory powers in allocating the use of their buildings, there may be nothing to prevent them from discriminating between various political groups. On the other hand, an authority must honour a contract to allow an extremist political party the use of its premises for a conference; when contractual *rights* are at stake, the law will not allow the authority to pick and choose.[36]

With regard to meetings on public open spaces, such as streets and parks, local authorities have no general common law power to ban them in advance.[37] But it does not follow that there is a right to hold public meetings in such spaces. It is an offence, for example, to obstruct the highway.[38] Frequently by-laws or other regulations require the prior permission of the district authority or the consent of a government department. There is no right to hold a meeting in Trafalgar Square, at least insofar as it would interfere with the right of passage through that area.[39] The use of Hyde Park for political and other meetings is controlled by the government. Again, there is no right to hold a meeting there,[40] though there was an outcry when permission was initially refused for a meeting in February 2003 to protest the imminent invasion of Iraq. It was sometimes said that the law has been more generous with regard to processions than it has been for public meetings on the streets. A procession is a use of the highway for its primary purpose of passage, so it is lawful unless it blocks the movement of other users unreasonably.[41] But that does not really amount to a positive right to organize a procession, which could be claimed to challenge a police decision not to allow it along a particular route or a local authority ban.

The usual approach to these questions in English law has recently been modified by the House of Lords in *DPP* v. *Jones*.[42] Section 14A of the Public Order Act 1986 enables the police to apply to a local council to prohibit the holding of 'trespassory assemblies', defined as assemblies held on land to which the public has no right of access or only a limited access right, and held without permission of the

---

[34] Representation of the People Act 1983, ss. 95–6.

[35] *Webster* v. *Southwark LBC* [1983] QB 698, Forbes J.

[36] *Verrall* v. *Great Yarmouth Council* [1981] QB 202, CA.

[37] *M'Ara* v. *Edinburgh Magistrates*, 1913 SC 1059.   [38] Highways Act 1980, s. 137(1).

[39] See *Ex p Lewis* (1888) 21 QBD 191, DC. Authority to grant a permit to hold a meeting in the Square has now been transferred from central government to the Mayor of London: S.I. 2000/801.

[40] *Bailey* v. *Williamson* (1873) 8 QBD 118, DC.

[41] See the classic article by A. L. Goodhart, 'Public Meetings and Processions' (1937) 6 *CLJ* 161.

[42] [1999] 2 AC 240, noted by G. Clayton, 'Reclaiming Public Ground: The Right to Peaceful Assembly' (2000) 63 *MLR* 252.

landowner or outside the limits of any permission or *the limits of any public right of access*.[43] Salisbury District Council had made an order banning assemblies within four miles of Stonehenge, a site at which a number of disorderly meetings had taken place. The defendants had gathered with others on the grass verge of a highway within this area; their conduct was entirely peaceful and no obstruction was caused to any traffic. A police officer took the view that the meeting fell within the terms of the order, so the defendants who refused to move on were charged with the offence of trespassory assembly. The issue was, therefore, whether the public has a right of access to the public highway for the purposes of assembly and whether this meeting exceeded the limits of any access right. By a majority of three to two, the Lords allowed the demonstrators' appeal, holding that under the common law a peaceful non-obstructive meeting on the highway did not necessarily amount to a trespassory assembly. Lord Irvine LC, and more clearly, Lord Hutton recognized a right of public assembly which in some circumstances (as in this case) could be exercised on the streets. In their view the common law right to use the highway was not confined to passage and re-passage and ancillary rights.[44] In contrast, the dissenting Law Lords, particularly Lord Hope, adopted the perspective, long discarded in the United States, that a public authority was as entitled as a private landowner to determine how its property was used; the order meant, in their view, that the demonstrators were trespassers.

Lords Irvine LC and Hutton were influenced by the approach taken by the courts to prosecutions for the statutory offence of wilful obstruction of the highway without lawful authority or excuse. In the leading modern case the Divisional Court had allowed the appeal of animal rights protesters who had been convicted of the offence when they had demonstrated outside a furrier's shop, thereby temporarily blocking the highway.[45] It had held that the peaceful protest in this case was lawful, so there was a 'lawful excuse' for the obstruction. It would have been odd for the Lords in *DPP* v. *Jones* to have held the demonstration was a trespassory assembly, although a prosecution on an obstruction charge would have failed, as the defendants had a lawful excuse for their reasonable use of the highway. It would be wrong, however, to exaggerate the significance of the House of Lords decision. The third member of the majority, Lord Clyde, was not prepared to formulate a general right of assembly to meet on the highway, while Lords Irvine LC and Hutton would not have decided the case in the same way if it had been found that the demonstrators caused an obstruction or public nuisance. It would be wrong to conclude that the rights to free speech and freedom of assembly will always trump other competing rights, for example, those of motorists. But in this case they did trump the

---

[43] Public Order Act 1986, s. 14A(5).

[44] Lord Hutton adopted the argument of Lamer CJ in *Committee for the Commonwealth of Canada* v. *Canada* [1991] 1 SCR 139, 155 to the effect that freedom of expression cannot be exercised in a vacuum, so it requires the recognition of some right to demonstrate on public spaces.

[45] *Hirst* v. *Chief Constable of West Yorkshire* (1987) 85 Cr App Rep 143.

public authority's rights as landowner, and that is a clear advance on previous precedents.

Any discussion of the comparable American law inevitably starts with the much-quoted judgment of Roberts J. in *Hague* v. *CIO*.[46] The Committee for Industrial Organization, a trades union, challenged a New Jersey city ordinance establishing a licensing system for the holding of meetings on the streets and in its parks and public buildings. City officials had refused the applicant permission to hold a meeting in a public park to explain to workers the meaning of the recently passed National Labor Relations Act. There was no evidence of any apprehended breach of peace; moreover, it was clear that other groups had been given permits to hold meetings in public places. The case was, therefore, that the ordinance was itself void in that it did not preclude arbitrary exercise of licensing powers, and, secondly, that it had been applied in a discriminatory manner. A majority of the Supreme Court rejected the city's submission that it was as entitled to use its property freely as a private property owner. The licensing system was both on its face, and as applied, void. The decision itself does not perhaps state anything more radical than other cases outlawing discriminatory permit systems for street demonstrations, though the principle was here applied to public parks. But a passage in Roberts J.'s judgment has been cited to support a general right of access to public places for the exercise of free speech rights:

Wherever the title of streets and parks may rest, they have immemorially been held in trust for the use of the public and, time out of mind, have been used for purposes of assembly, communicating thought between citizens, and discussing public questions . . . The privilege of a citizen of the United States to use the streets and parks for the communication of views on national questions may be regulated in the interest of all; it is not absolute, but relative, and must be exercised in subordination to the general comfort and convenience, and in consonance with good order and peace; but it must not, in the guise of regulation, be abridged and denied.[47]

It is this statement which paved the way for arguments that even non-discriminatory refusals to allow rights of access for free speech and assembly may be unlawful under the First Amendment.

Over the last forty years the Supreme Court has explored the implications of the principles set out in Roberts J.'s judgment: do they confer a right of access, or only a right of equal access so that all that is prohibited is discriminatory treatment of various groups? In what sense is the right 'relative' and what interests are compelling enough to take priority over free speech rights? Finally, should the rules be extended beyond streets and open spaces to cover government offices and buildings or even in some circumstances private property? Only a few of the leading cases need be mentioned to illustrate the various problems. In *Edwards* v. *South Carolina*,[48] in the course of reversing a conviction for carrying in an orderly

---

[46] 307 US 496 (1939).   [47] Ibid., 515–16.   [48] 372 US 229 (1963).

manner anti-segregation banners on state capitol grounds, the Court intimated that there was a right of access to demonstrate in this area. Defiance of a law *reasonably* limiting the hours during which the grounds were open to the public might have led to a different result. The decision in *Brown* v. *Louisiana* is more surprising and certainly more radical in its implications.[49] By a bare majority the Court held that there was a protected right under the First Amendment to sit peaceably in a public library in order to protest against state segregation of the students there. There was no evidence of any disturbance, so the conviction under the state breach of the peace statute was ruled unconstitutional. This provoked a vigorous dissent from Black J. who protested that:

[The First Amendment] does not guarantee to any person the right to use someone else's property, even that owned by government and dedicated to other purposes, as a stage to express dissident ideas. The novel constitutional doctrine of the prevailing opinion nevertheless exalts the power of private non-governmental groups to determine what use shall be made of governmental property over the power of the elected governmental officials.[50]

It may be that Black J.'s remarks read too much into the majority judgment. The case did not establish a right to demonstrate for any conceivable cause in any government building, no matter the disturbance it occasioned the normal usage of that building. It is important to note that the occupiers in *Brown* were protesting against the segregated facilities in that library, not segregation laws generally. Nor were they making other political grievances. Further, there was no evidence of significant interference with normal library use. The decision represents the limit to which the Court has taken the public fora principle under which there are access rights to use government and other public property for speech and peaceful protest. However, later decisions have shown a much more cautious approach to the recognition of positive rights to hold meetings on public property outside the traditional fora identified by Roberts J.

A year before the library case, the Court had expressly refrained from holding in *Cox* v. *Louisiana*[51] that the uniform, non-discriminatory banning of all processions and meetings on city streets and other public spaces under a state obstruction of the highway statute (strikingly similar in its terms to the UK highways legislation) would be unconstitutional. The measure in this case had, however, been held unconstitutional as applied on the facts, because there was evidence that the police had enforced it selectively against the protesters who were demonstrating against segregation by department stores. More conclusively, over the next twenty years the Court decided there is no absolute right of access to speak and hold meetings on prison grounds[52] or on army bases.[53] But it upheld rights to exercise First Amendment freedoms, subject to reasonable regulation,

---

[49] 393 US 131 (1966).   [50] Ibid., 166.
[51] 379 US 536 (1965): for criticism of the cautious approach of the Court, see Kalven (n. 28 above).   [52] *Adderley* v. *Florida* 385 US 39 (1966).
[53] *Greer* v. *Spock* 424 US 828 (1976).

in schools[54] and university campuses,[55] and in the areas immediately outside a school and the Supreme Court building itself.[56]

The Court has struck down measures which on their face tolerated some types of protest or picketing on public fora, but which prohibited others. They fell foul of its traditional hostility to content-based rules favouring the expression of some views or categories of speech over others. Restrictions of this kind on speech on public fora are subject to strict scrutiny, in the same way as the prohibitions imposed by general criminal law. Thus, in *Chicago Police Dept* v. *Mosley*,[57] the Court invalidated an ordinance which had banned all peaceful picketing within 150 feet of school premises during term time, except for picketing of any school involved in an employment dispute. Once a public forum has been opened up for speech, the authorities may not preclude some groups for speaking because of their views or the topics they want to discuss. It is very doubtful now whether they could prohibit a public meeting on the streets and other traditional public fora, unless it would be incompatible with the primary use of the place, for instance, by making the passage of traffic impossible for a significant period of time.[58] On the other hand, reasonable time, manner, and place restrictions have been upheld, provided at any rate that they leave ample alternative channels for communication of the ideas and information.[59] The classification of government property as a public forum is a matter of crucial importance. If the property is not treated as a public forum, the government is entitled to limit speech and protest on it, provided at any rate that it does not discriminate on the basis of the speaker's particular views. But outside the established category of streets, pavements, and other open spaces where meetings and demonstrations have traditionally been permitted, it has been unclear how government and public property should be classified for this purpose.

(iii) New public fora for speech and assembly

Courts in the United States, and more recently Canada, have tackled the classification question (outside the category of traditional speech fora) in a number of different contexts. Most of them concerned claims to distribute leaflets or solicit funds in airport and other transport terminals,[60] or to advertise on hoardings at

---

[54] *Tinker* v. *Des Moines School District* 393 US 503 (1969): protest by students inside the school protected.

[55] *Widmar* v. *Vincent* 454 US 263 (1981): campus a public forum, so college authority not entitled to bar a group wanting to use its facilities for religious worship and discussion.

[56] *Grayned* v. *Rockford* 408 US 104 (1972): noisy demonstration 100 feet from school covered by First Amendment, but subject to reasonable regulation; *US* v. *Grace* 461 US 171 (1983): pavements outside US Supreme Court building a 'public forum' for leafleting and protest.

[57] 408 US 92 (1972).   [58] *Grayned* v. *Rockford* 408 US 104, 116–17 per Marshall J. (1972).

[59] See e.g. *Heffron* v. *International Society for Krishna Consciousness* 452 US 640 (1981), where a state rule confining the distribution of literature and solicitation of funds on fairgrounds to particular booths was upheld.

[60] *Wolin* v. *Port of New York Authority* 392 F 2d 83 (2nd Cir, 1968) cert denied, 393 US 940 (1968), upholding right to distribute in a bus terminal leaflets protesting the war in Vietnam.

such places or at highway junctions.[61] Although freedom of assembly was not directly involved in those cases, categorization of the land in question as a public forum would have significance for the exercise of that freedom by holding protest meetings or engaging in demonstrations. In *Perry Education Assn* v. *Perry Local Educators' Assn*,[62] the US Supreme Court held that there are three types of government property for the purposes of speech rights: a traditional public forum such as a highway or a park commonly used for speech; a non-traditional designated public forum, whether of a limited or unlimited character, which the government has opened to allow all or some people opportunities for expression; and lastly, public property, which neither by tradition nor designation is open for such use. The courts should carefully scrutinize any regulation of speech in the first two categories of property, while the government could entirely close the third type of property to speech, provided it did not discriminate on the basis of the viewpoint of the speaker. At first glance, this approach might seem properly solicitous of freedom of speech. However, the government can easily argue that it had not designated a non-traditional forum for speech by all groups or for discussion of every subject; it could confine the use of its property to particular types of speech. A designated public forum could turn out to be very limited indeed, as it was in *Perry* itself, where the majority of the Court upheld a school district authority's argument that it could allow the recognized teacher's association access to school mailbox facilities, but deny access to a non-recognized union. The category of a non-traditional public forum, only opened by government to certain groups or for the discussion of particular issues, is really quite useless; a public authority is in effect as free to restrict speech on this type of property as it is in non-public fora. Moreover, once an authority has stopped one group or individual from speaking to people or distributing literature, say, at a railway station, it can argue that the station is not a designated public forum for any other expressive activity; the exercise of control in the past justifies further refusals.

The difficulties in this tripartite classification were exposed in the leading modern case, *International Society for Krishna Consciousness (ISKCON)* v. *Lee*.[63] It concerned the application of regulations of the New York and New Jersey Port Authority banning solicitation of money and distribution of literature in airport terminals. A majority of the Supreme Court, in a judgment given by Rehnquist CJ, held that these terminals could not be regarded as public fora for speech. Historically, they had not been used or made available for this purpose, so they could not be regarded as traditional public fora. Nor had the Port Authority designated them as appropriate places for speech. Rather, it took the view that the terminal was for the comfort and passage of travellers. Consequently, the regulations

---

[61] *Lebron* v. *National RR Passenger Corp (Amtrak)* 69 F 3d 650 (2nd Cir, 1995), dismissing claim to advertise on Amtrak billboard at Penn Station; *Sentinel Communications* v. *Watts* 936 F 2d 1189 (11th Cir, 1991), holding that open area at interstate highway rest stop not a public forum.
[62] 460 US 37 (1983).   [63] 505 US 672 (1992).

need only satisfy the test of reasonableness, the lower degree of scrutiny applied to speech in a non-public forum. (On that basis, the ban on face-to-face solicitation for money was upheld, though that on leafleting was invalidated.) In a strong dissent, Kennedy J., joined by three other members of the Court, pointed out the contradictions in the category of 'designated public forum': it allows the government to limit speech by imposing restrictions on the uses to which its property is put. Rather, a place should be treated as a public forum if its objective physical characteristics, and the actual public access and permitted uses on it show that speech would be appropriate there and would not be incompatible with its other (primary) uses. On these criteria, airport terminals should be treated as public fora. They contain broad thoroughfares similar to public highways, and there is easy access to them. Time, manner, and place regulations can ensure that the distribution of literature and other speech-related activity does not significantly interfere with their principal purpose of ensuring that passengers can reach their flights in reasonable comfort.

Kennedy J.'s approach is clearly more attractive than that of Rehnquist CJ for the majority and is certainly more protective of speech. There should probably be no sharp or bright line between traditional public fora and other venues which in some circumstances may be appropriate for the exercise of speech and assembly rights. The Court's judgment in *ISKCON* ignored the changing character of speech venues. More people now congregate and stroll in airport terminals than they do in some city centres. But the character of the place remains important. Airport and many other transport terminals should be treated as suitable venues for speech, because they are spacious and are used for a wide variety of shopping and other commercial purposes. In contrast, a post office or welfare office should not be regarded as a public forum for a meeting, as usually it has limited space and is devoted to one purpose. It has been suggested that it would be better to ask merely whether the speech would interfere with the other purposes to which the government property was put, or with the other public concerns and interests which may be involved, say, the interest of passengers in travel.[64] But that approach should be rejected. If it were adopted, the public forum doctrine would in effect be abandoned. There would be a prima facie right to use any public property for speech, even a local authority office or a government ministry to which the public had access only for particular purposes. It would still be open to the government to argue that there are good grounds for restricting the speech in order to safeguard other concerns, but it would surely be unreasonable to impose that burden on it in every case where an attempt is made to use its property for speech or to hold a meeting.

The leading Canadian case in this area shows the variety of different approaches which can be taken to the public forum problem. The question in *Committee for*

---

[64] S. G. Gey, 'Reopening the Public Forum: From Sidewalks to Cyberspace' (1998) 58 *Ohio State Law Jo* 1535, 1576.

the Commonwealth of Canada v. *Canada*[65] was whether a political group was entitled to distribute literature and solicit for members at Montreal International Airport. Federal regulations prohibited such activity, but the Court unanimously ruled that they infringed the right to freedom of expression and that infringement could not be upheld under section 1 of the Charter as a reasonable limit on its exercise. L'Heureux-Dubé J. took the broadest approach, holding that all non-violent expression on government property was *covered* by section 2(b) of the Charter; the character of the place where the speech occurred was relevant to determining only whether the regulations could be justified. It was not, therefore, for the demonstrators to show that airports are a 'public arena' (the term used by the judge to avoid confusion with the US public forum concept). The character of the place, together with a number of other criteria, is relevant to the constitutionality of time, manner, and place regulations. Among these other factors are the compatibility of the main purposes of the property with its use for speech, and the availability of other public arenas in the vicinity for expressive activities.

Lamer CJ, however, thought that some balancing of the interests in free speech and the government's interest in effective use of its property was necessary to determine whether the right to freedom of expression was at issue at all; individuals only have a right to expression on government property if the form of expression is compatible with the principal function of that property. Although he rejected L'Heureux-Dubé's approach as too solicitous of free expression interests, he equally strongly rejected the argument that government could exclude speech on its land in the exercise of its property rights. Such an absolutist argument 'fails to take into account that the freedom of expression cannot be exercised in a vacuum and that it necessarily implies the use of physical space in order to meet its underlying objectives'.[66] McLachlin J. proposed a complex test in the third leading judgment. Speech on government property should be covered by section 2(b) if either the government's purpose was to restrict the content of the speech through limiting the places where it may be made, or alternatively, if the claimant could show that expression at the particular place, here an airport terminal, promoted the purposes for which the right to freedom of expression was guaranteed.

The Court found it much easier to apply these tests to reach their unanimous decision. Airport terminals provided thoroughfares to which the public had easy access. It would not hinder their primary purpose to allow individuals freedom to distribute political literature and canvass for membership. The blanket ban on engaging in any political activity could not be justified as necessary to ensure the smooth operation of the airport. In contrast, airline offices and security zones would not be regarded as suitable public arenas for speech.

The judgments contrast quite sharply with the more doctrinal line taken by the majority of the US Supreme Court in the *ISKCON* case, under which an airport

---

[65] [1991] 1 SCR 139; see Moon, 151–71.
[66] N. 65 above, 155, quoted by Lord Hutton in *DPP* v. *Jones* [1999] 2 AC 240, 288.

terminal was not classified as a public forum, largely because the government had not opened it up for speech. The Canadian approach is more flexible and certainly more protective of free speech, but it will be hard to predict how it will be applied in other contexts.

Naturally, the legal difficulties largely fall away if the government opens up or provides access rights to use property for speech. That has happened in the United Kingdom when the Conservative government of Mrs Thatcher became concerned that university authorities had become unwilling to permit, or ensure the safe conduct of, meetings of right-wing groups on their campuses. Section 43 of the Education (No. 2) Act 1986 provides:

(1) Every individual and body of persons concerned in the government of any [university of college] establishment . . . shall take such steps as are reasonably practicable to ensure that freedom of speech within the law is secured for members, students and employees of the establishment, and for visiting speakers.

(2) The duty imposed by subsection (1) above includes (in particular) the duty to ensure, so far as is reasonably practicable, that the use of any premises of the establishment is not denied to any individual or body of persons on any ground connected with—

    (a) the beliefs or views of that individual or of any member of that body; or

    (b) the policy or objectives of that body.

It follows that a university could not prohibit a student club from inviting a leading figure from the British National Party (an extreme right-wing party considered to support racist policies) to address it, unless it had some evidence that he was going to commit an offence, say, under the hate speech provisions of the public order legislation.[67] University authorities are required also to draw up codes of practice to regulate the procedure at, and the conduct of people attending, meetings to be held on their premises; this duty enables them to take steps to prevent disorder and reduce the chance that speakers will infringe the law.[68]

The provision is in some ways anomalous.[69] First, there is no very persuasive reason of principle why strong access rights should be afforded in this context, when they are not provided in others, where the interest of both speaker and prospective audience might be thought stronger: outside the context of elections, a political party or group has no access right, say, to use a town hall or other public space for a meeting to address an issue of current importance. Secondly, the 1986 Act confers rights on members, staff, and students of universities and on visiting speakers, but not on other members of the public who might want to hear the speaker. The university remains free to deny them access, even though their free speech interest as recipients is surely as strong as that of university

---

  [67] See ch. V, s. 4 above.

  [68] But the risk of disorder outside the university premises cannot be used as a ground for refusing permission to a visiting speaker: *R v. University of Liverpool, ex p Caesar-Gordon* [1991] 1 QB 124, DC.

  [69] See E. M. Barendt, 'Free Speech in the Universities' [1987] *PL* 344.

employees and students. The measure was, of course, framed to deal with a particular problem, rather than to show commitment to a coherent free speech principle.

(iv) Freedom of speech on private property

Quite different issues of principle arise if rights are claimed to hold a meeting or to engage in protest activity on private property against the wishes of the landowner. This presents a genuine conflict between the rights of the speaker and the audience on the one hand and the property rights of the individual owner on the other. Further, in many constitutions, rights are only guaranteed against infringement by a public authority. The refusal of a private landowner to allow a meeting to take place on his private property would then not infringe freedom of expression and freedom of assembly. That view was taken by McLachlin J. in the *Committee for the Commonwealth of Canada* case,[70] though other members of the Court reserved their position on the point. On the other hand, as a matter of principle, it should not matter if, say, a large airport or railway terminal is private property, rather than vested in a public authority. The space is as open to the public and as appropriate for the distribution of leaflets and the communication of views by other means, whether it is controlled by a public or by a private corporation. The scope of freedom of speech should not be dependent on the extent to which a state has privatized its transport system and other facilities.

The changing jurisprudence in the United States has for the most part involved claims to speak in shopping centres and malls. In the first case, *Marsh* v. *Alabama*,[71] distribution of literature in a private company town was held constitutionally protected by the First Amendment. It was argued successfully that the company town performed an essentially public function, and, therefore, should be equated with an ordinary municipality. Twenty years later *Marsh* was applied to a case involving the picketing of a store in a private shopping centre,[72] but this latter ruling was subsequently distinguished on very similar facts,[73] and was overruled in *Hudgens* v. *NLRB*.[74] Picketing in front of an employer's store in a private shopping centre was not to be protected under the First Amendment. The Court held the picketing ban did not involve 'state action' and so did not infringe freedom of speech. Stewart J. who gave the majority opinion emphasized that no redress is provided by the Constitution against a private person or corporation who abridges the free expression of others; only statute or common law could provide a remedy.

However, in an odd twist to this story, the Court has held it is permissible under the First Amendment for a state constitution to require a right of access to a private

---

[70] N. 65 above, 228.   [71] 326 US 501 (1946).
[72] *Amalgamated Food Employees Union* v. *Logan Valley Plaza* 391 US 308 (1968).
[73] *Lloyd Corpn* v. *Tanner* 407 US 551 (1972).   [74] 424 US 507 (1976).

shopping centre for the exercise of free speech rights.[75] The California Supreme Court's construction of the 'liberty of speech' clause in the state constitution to this effect did not constitute a 'taking' and hence a violation of the shopping-centre owner's property rights under the Federal Constitution. Further, the US Supreme Court emphasized that the owner of the shopping centre had invited members of the public to enter his land. He was also free to dissociate himself from any message communicated there. That point is important. The recognition of a right to use another person's property for speech might violate not only the latter's property rights, but also his own free speech rights, insofar as he was compelled to transmit and be associated with another's ideas.[76] But that difficulty did not arise in the California case.

What emerges from this case is that there is no overwhelming libertarian objection to the recognition of some right of access in this context, although the US Supreme Court is not prepared now to construe the First Amendment as generally demanding such recognition. Each state may determine the character and scope of free speech beyond the minimum established by the Supreme Court. State courts have sometimes construed their own state constitution as conferring rights to use private property, in particular shopping malls[77] and private universities[78] for speech. Relevant factors are the normal use of the property, the extent to which in practice the public is free to come on it for a range of purposes, and the character of the expression. The owner of a shopping mall—in effect, equivalent to the traditional city centre—should be required to tolerate leafleting and canvassing, though not perhaps a mass protest. But a claim of access to use a football stadium, a theatre, or a cinema for such a purpose would be much weaker. For unlike a shopping mall these premises are only open for one reason—to show a particular type of entertainment, and it would be wrong to compel their owner to allow speech there. Another device to broaden access is to find an element of 'state action'. If, say, a private property owner has leased land from the state to run a market, it may be possible to infer that he is exercising a public function or that the state is a participant in the venture; there is a strong case, then, for the conclusion that land is to some extent a public forum and expressive activity should be allowed, provided it does not disrupt the market.[79]

There has been less authority on these points from other common law jurisdictions. In a pre-Charter case, the Supreme Court of Canada held by a majority that the owner of a shopping centre was entitled to prohibit leafleting and picketing on

[75] *Pruneyard Shopping Center* v. *Robins* 447 US 74 (1980), affirming 592 P 2d 341.

[76] For the right to silence, perhaps implicated in this situation, see ch. III, s. 4 above.

[77] *Shad Alliance* v. *Smith Haven Mall* 484 NYS 2d 849 (1985); *New Jersey Coalition against War in the Middle East* v. *JMB Realty Corp* 650 A 2d 757 (NJ, 1994).

[78] *State* v. *Schmid* 423 A 2d 615 (NJ, 1980), upholding a right to distribute political literature on Princeton campus.

[79] *Citizens to End Animal Suffering* v. *Fanuell Hall Marketplace* 745 F Supp 65 (D Mass, 1990), upholding right to picket a market business on land leased from Boston city council.

its pavements, and use the law of trespass to exclude anyone who engaged in such activity.[80] There was a strong dissent from Laskin CJ, who pointed out that shopping malls have much more in common with public roads than they do with private houses and land to which trespass law was appropriately applied.[81] No English case yet has resolved a conflict between private property rights and freedom of speech, though it is likely that a court here would give primacy to the former, unless, of course, a statute such as the Education (No. 2) Act 1986 had provided speakers with access rights.[82] It is, of course, easy for a private owner to refuse groups permission to canvass or hold a meeting in a shopping centre and its car parks, and it would then be for the latter to challenge the refusal as infringing their freedom of speech and assembly rights.

When the owner of a private shopping centre in Washington, England, refused an environmental group permission to set up a stall and canvass support on its passageways, the group referred the matter to Strasbourg. The European Court held there had been no breach of Article 10 (or of Article 11, not considered in this case to raise separate issues).[83] Regard had to be paid to property rights; the Court was not persuaded that freedom of expression necessarily required recognition of entry rights to private property (or even to all public property). It did admit that Article 10 may require a state to take positive measures to protect effective exercise of the right to freedom of expression; further, it envisaged that a duty to allow access should be imposed, where otherwise there would no effective exercise of freedom of expression, as where meetings had been banned in a company town. But that was not, in the Court's view, the position here. The applicants might have obtained permission from a business within the shopping centre, and they were free to campaign in the old town centre, call on people at home, or write to the local newspaper.[84] This was a very poor decision. As the dissenting judgment of Judge Maruste pointed out, the shopping centre occupied a huge area and had been partly financed with public money. It was tantamount to a traditional city centre and was indicated as such on local maps. It had been privatized at the end of 1987. It was absurd to treat the mall as if it were a private home. Moreover, there was no suggestion that the applicant's stall would be disruptive or inconvenience shoppers. The Court in effect gave greater weight to private property rights over freedom of expression. But that preference is misconceived, for it allows a degree of private control of expression rights, which would not be countenanced if comparable restrictions were imposed by a public authority.

---

[80] *Harrison* v. *Carswell* [1976] 2 SCR 200.   [81] Ibid., 207–8.
[82] See the comprehensive survey by K. Gray and S. F. Gray, 'Civil Rights, Civil Wrongs and Quasi-Public Space' [1999] *EHRLR* 46. Their article is based on the decision of the Court of Appeal in *CIN Properties Ltd* v. *Rawlins* [1999] 2 EGLR 130, which upheld the right of the owner of a shopping complex to exclude young 'troublemakers' from the complex, although no charge of any criminal offence had been proved.   [83] *Appleby* v. *United Kingdom* (2003) 37 EHRR 38.
[84] Ibid., paras. 47–8.

(v) Conclusions

Access to public fora problems occur in contexts other than that of public meetings and demonstrations. In the *Lehman* case,[85] the city of Shaker Heights, Ohio, refused the applicant, a candidate for election to the state assembly, advertising space on municipal buses. Advertising by commercial bodies, churches, and civic groups was permitted, but there had been a consistent policy of barring political notices. The Court upheld the refusal by a 5–4 majority. The transit system was not regarded as a public forum analogous to streets and parks; further, the decision to limit the available space to commercial and non-controversial advertising was reasonable. If the city had permitted political advertising, it would have had to take sensitive administrative decisions, for example, whether to allocate limited space on a 'first come, first served' basis, or perhaps to distribute it on the basis of votes in previous elections, so that minority party candidates could only advertise on fewer or less well-patronized routes. (Of course, discrimination between types of speech would not be countenanced in other circumstances; a law would infringe a free speech clause if it restricted the type of advertisement allowed in newspapers or on billboards.[86]) Public lamp-posts and utility poles are not regarded as public fora, so there is no First Amendment right to use them for election slogans, even though their location makes them highly useful places to communicate views which might otherwise not reach the electorate.[87]

Arguably, the application of public fora analysis in these cases was very strained. The real question is surely whether the rule prohibiting the posting of the advertisements, whether political or commercial, is directed at the contents of the speech or is intended to serve some other legitimate end, such as the protection of the environment or to preserve the character of an area against unsightly notices. But the same point has been made of many public forum cases, including those involving a right to demonstrate in public on the streets and other open spaces.[88] Indeed, it is quite possible to decide public protest cases without recourse to public forum analysis. A good example of this was the ruling of the High Court of Australia in *Levy* v. *Victoria*.[89] It held that a state regulation prohibiting persons, other than the holders of valid game licences, from entering the permitted

---

[85] *Lehman* v. *City of Shaker Heights* 418 US 298 (1974).

[86] In *Metromedia* v. *City of San Diego* 453 US 490 (1981), a majority of the Court struck down an ordinance banning outdoor 'offsite' billboard advertising, whether commercial or political, but permitting 'onsite' advertising and some public notices, while in *Cincinnati* v. *Discovery Network* 507 US 410 (1993) it invalidated a city regulation allowing news racks on pavements for the sale of conventional newspapers, but not for the distribution of commercial advertising. In both cases the Court found the restrictions an impermissible content-based limit on speech.

[87] *City of Los Angeles* v. *Taxpayers for Vincent* 466 US 769 (1984).

[88] See the classic articles by R. C. Post, 'Between Governance and Management: The History and Theory of the Public Forum' (1987) 34 *UCLA Law Rev* 1713 and by D. A. Farber and J. E. Nowak, 'The Misleading Nature of Public Forum Analysis: Content and Context in First Amendment Adjudication' (1984) 70 *Virginia Law Rev* 1219.   [89] (1997) 189 CLR 579.

hunting areas could be applied to protesters against duck shooting who had entered such an area without a licence. The Court ruled, sensibly enough, that the regulations were valid, as they were intended to safeguard public safety, although of course they inhibited the exercise of freedom of expression in circumstances when it might have been particularly effective. Only Kirby J. pointed out that the protest hardly occurred in an area traditionally used for free speech: '[i]t was no Hyde Park'[90] The point is that the Court could have decided the case on the basis that it did not involve freedom of expression at all, given that the state had in effect determined that only those with a valid game licence could enter the shooting areas during the hunting season; the protesters were trespassers. But it made little of the point, preferring to examine the justifications for the regulation in the context of the right to free expression.

The place where the speech occurs is only a factor in determining whether it was legitimate to restrict exercise of the freedom. The government's interest as landowner is rarely, if ever, crucial, whether the case concerns a meeting or the distribution of literature on the streets or in an airport terminal, or posting notices on lamp-posts. What may, however, be important are the range of other public concerns at stake, for example, the passage and comfort of passengers waiting for their flight or the managerial prerogatives of, say, a local authority which is surely entitled to determine that the offices and corridors in a town hall are inappropriate venues for a public meeting or for the distribution of literature unrelated to its business.[91] While, therefore, it is wrong always to regard the location of a speech or a meeting as decisive, it would be equally misconceived to ignore it altogether when deciding whether the exercise of the free speech right should be protected.

4. Public Order

(i) General principles

One perspective is that the law has to deal with a conflict between two rights: the right of free speech and the right of the public to order and tranquillity. This view was expressed in the statement of principles prefacing Lord Scarman's Report on the Red Lion Square Disorders of June 1974:

A balance has to be struck, a compromise found that will accommodate the exercise of the right to protest within a framework of public order which enables ordinary citizens, who are not protesting, to go about their business and pleasure without obstruction or inconvenience... the fact that the protesters are desperately sincere and are exercising a fundamental human right must not lead us to overlook the rights of the majority.[92]

---

[90] (1997) 189 CLR 579, 642.   [91] Post (n. 88 above), esp. 1765–84.
[92] Scarman Report (Cmnd 5919, 1975).

Of course in English law, neither right may be a legal right in the sense that its holders have a claim enforceable in the courts. As the previous section of this chapter has shown, there are considerable difficulties to the argument that free speech entails wide claim-rights, for example, to demonstrate in the streets or to hold meetings in public places. But if arguments about the character of the free speech or assembly right are controversial, the view that the majority, or any member of the majority, has a competing moral *right* to order and tranquillity is surely misconceived. Quite apart from doubts about whether it ever makes sense to talk of the rights of a group or society as a whole, it is difficult to give this particular 'right' any coherent content. In many circumstances it will be unclear what it is a right to be free from: does it make sense, for instance, to refer to a 'right to order' which is infringed by an affray a few streets away? In truth, a proposition about the right of the majority in this context is little more than the sensible statement that there is an important public interest in preserving order. But there are some cases where it is possible to point to a right which competes with free speech in this context. A demonstration may create an intolerable level of noise or other nuisance, which infringe residents' property and privacy rights. Demonstrations outside hospitals and abortion clinics may interfere with the freedom of women seeking pregnancy advice and medical intervention not to be harassed or intimidated when exercising those legal rights.

While reference to competing rights in this area may be problematic, there can be no doubt that the law does have to strike compromises. The difficulty is to formulate and apply clear principles, on the basis of which courts may protect the public interest in preserving peace and good order or the right of individuals not to be intimidated, without sacrificing freedom of speech and of assembly. Admittedly, where there is a real breakdown in public order, clearly attributable to the violence of demonstrators, there is no reason why political protesters should be treated more benevolently than mere vandals. The Court of Appeal in *R* v. *Caird*[93] was right to reject the argument, put forward as a plea in mitigation, that the appellants had only committed the offences of unlawful and riotous assembly from political motives; they had demonstrated against a 'Greek week', the staging of which, they contended, supported the military regime in that country. But in situations falling short of an outbreak of actual violence attributable to the protesters, courts in England, the United States, and in other systems, may try to accommodate the demonstrators' claim to exercise free speech and assembly rights, even though that exercise did bring about or create a clear risk of disorder.

Before we examine the different approaches to balancing free speech and public order, attention should be paid to two related arguments denying that there is really any free speech problem at all in this context. The first is that public protest involves conduct rather than 'pure speech', and therefore falls entirely outside the free speech principle. Secondly, it is said that the powers of the police to stop a

---

[93] (1970) 54 Cr App Rep 499.

meeting if they fear an imminent breach of the peace, or the laws penalizing obstruction of the highway and nuisances, are not primarily aimed at the suppression of speech; any effect on the communication of opinion is incidental to the principal object of preserving public order. Further, it is argued that the political positions and attitudes of demonstrators can equally well be disseminated by more peaceful means—by writing letters to the newspapers or distributing leaflets. Restrictions on holding meetings involve restraints on the manner and form, rather than on the content of speech.

In some US cases in this area, remarks have been made that street demonstrations and meetings, and *a fortiori* all forms of picketing and sit-ins, should really be regarded as conduct, outside the protection of the First Amendment.[94] It is a position which naturally commended itself to absolutists, like Black J., who otherwise would have had considerable difficulty in approving any restrictions on such demonstrations. But, as the argument both in Chapter II and in the second section of this chapter has shown, freedom of speech and expression provisions have been interpreted to cover expressive conduct, including protest activity. Further, meetings, processions, and other demonstrations may be covered by the right to freedom of assembly, where the distinction between pure speech and expressive conduct is immaterial. This position is taken by the German Constitutional Court. It has held that Article 8 covers conduct; it covered the chaining together of demonstrators which blocked the entry of lorries to a nuclear energy plant. It did not follow, however, that it gave demonstrators an unlimited freedom to injure the interests and rights of others or justified criminal behaviour.[95]

Fred Schauer has argued that free speech is implicated whenever the purpose of the governmental restriction is to restrict expression, rather than to achieve some other end, such as public order, safety on the streets, or quiet in residential areas. He takes as an example the prohibition of a Communist march. This raises free speech issues if the ban was imposed because extremist demonstrations are considered undesirable, but does not implicate them if it was imposed because the street is to be repaired on the day in question or if it is imperative for traffic on that route to move freely.[96] But, as this example itself shows, the argument can be used only to remove from scrutiny on free speech grounds a temporary ban or a ban confined to a particular street—what is known in United States First Amendment jurisprudence as a 'time, manner, and place' restriction. A permanent prohibition on all processions in a community can hardly be supported by reference to this argument. Further, a provision which permitted the discriminatory treatment of some groups and political parties would clearly show an illegitimate purpose on its face. These points justify the very limited scope of the power to ban processions under the UK public order legislation: in certain carefully defined circumstances

---

[94] See e.g. Black and Douglas JJ in *Gregory* v. *Chicago* 394 US 111, 118 and 124 (1969), and Black J. in *Cox* v. *Louisiana* 379 US 536, 577 (1965). [95] 104 BVerfGE 92 (2002).

[96] Schauer, 203–5.

all processions, or processions of 'any class', may be banned for up to three months.[97] But permanent or discriminatory bans on particular marches may not be imposed. That is right because such restrictions would clearly abridge free speech rights.

As Schauer himself admits,[98] his distinction only carries real conviction if the primary reason for giving free speech legal protection is suspicion of government. On that assumption, it is relevant whether speech is restricted because the government dislikes its content or because it wishes to achieve some other legitimate end, for example, free traffic flow or a quiet environment. However, if free speech is guaranteed for a more positive reason, such as its role in promoting an effective participatory democracy or individual self-fulfilment, then the government's object in restricting its dissemination seems less relevant.[99] From that perspective, it appears immaterial that speech is restricted incidentally as an aspect of regulation intended to achieve some legitimate social or public goal. If a community were to ban all leafleting and demonstrations on the streets to keep them clean and free of litter, there would be a significant interference with freedom of speech and assembly, even though the regulations were on their face content-neutral and could not be applied selectively to allow some types of protest in preference to others. Similarly, public order arguments should not be used to remove regulations limiting free expression from scrutiny. These arguments may justify significant restrictions on the exercise of speech in some circumstances, for example, where the danger to public order is clear and imminent; but it does not follow that they will always do so. Further, the argument that demonstrators could make their case by other means is not entitled to much weight. Protest on the streets may be the only effective way to communicate their feelings. That is why freedom of speech is valuable in this context, and why constitutions generally guarantee freedom of assembly.

There are perhaps three general approaches which can be taken to striking a balance between the concerns of free speech and those of public order. First, the law may treat as decisive the character of the speech made during a demonstration or at a public meeting. On this approach, inflammatory speech, for instance, a direct incitement to commit disorder or crime, might be proscribed without free speech difficulties; it would be immaterial whether in the circumstances disorder occurred or even whether it was likely. In contrast, speech which is merely offensive should be protected under a free speech or freedom of expression clause, even though disorder occurred or the police feared it might break out. A difficult question is whether the proscription of provocative or intemperate language on political matters is compatible with freedom of expression, on the argument that the state has a compelling interest in ensuring the civility of public discourse. It can be argued that insults and other provocative remarks about these matters in public,

---

[97] See now the Public Order Act 1986, s. 13, discussed in detail in s. 5 of this chapter.
[98] Schauer, 204.   [99] See the arguments in ch. I, s. 2 above.

particularly those addressed to particular individuals, are more than offensive. They may be deeply wounding to the individuals concerned, and in the long term may make disorder more likely. As will be seen in section 4(ii), the US Supreme Court, and recently a majority of the High Court of Australia, have rejected this rationale for the proscription of public speech.[100] (Political insults should be distinguished from the personal insults discussed in section 4 of Chapter VI which may fall outside the coverage of free speech provisions altogether.)

Under the second approach, more weight is given to safeguarding public order: police officers, for example, may be given power to break up a public meeting if they fear that a breach of the peace is likely, even though the speakers at the meeting have not intended to provoke violence and their speeches could not be characterized as inflammatory or insulting. This premium on public order considerations to the cost of free speech has been reflected in some case-law in England and, to a much lesser extent, the United States. Aspects of the UK public order legislation also reflect this second perspective. The third approach is more eclectic. It combines elements of the others, in that, for example, a statute may make it an offence to use insulting or abusive (but not offensive) language with intent to incite violence or a breach of the peace, or in circumstances likely to lead to such violence or breach of the peace. The prosecution must then show both that extreme language is used and that disorder is intended or likely.

The difference between these approaches is best shown in the hostile audience or hecklers' veto cases. Peaceful protest or speeches may be disrupted by groups determined to stop the meeting. If the police fear violence, they may try to take steps to ensure that the protest is not interrupted by arresting troublemakers and safeguarding the speaker, unless he begins to use provocative language: that is the first approach outlined above. Alternatively, they may require the speaker to stop immediately the audience becomes restless, however temperate and moderate his speech. That second approach preserves good order to the detriment of free speech. Or the law may allow the police to intervene, or a prosecution to be brought, only when demonstrators use insulting or abusive language intended to provoke a violent reaction from the audience or in circumstances when it is probable the audience will react in this way: that is the third approach.

The rest of this section for the most part explores how statute and case-law in England and in the United States have adopted these various approaches in public order cases. Unfortunately, the law in both jurisdictions has been inconsistent. Whichever perspective is taken, either free speech or public order must give some ground to the concerns of the other. Legislatures and courts have, therefore, used other techniques in an attempt to reduce the risk of disorderly reaction to public protest and so resolve the conflict between the right to free speech and public order considerations. These methods are considered in section 5 of this chapter.

---

[100] *Cohen* v. *California* 403 US 15 (1971); *Coleman* v. *Power* [2004] HCA 39 (1 Sept. 2004).

(ii) Inflammatory and offensive speech

In 1942 a unanimous Supreme Court held that to address a city marshal, 'You are a God damned racketeer' and 'a damned Fascist and the whole government of Rochester are Fascists or agents of Fascists', was to use insulting or 'fighting' words, wholly unprotected by the First Amendment.[101] Such words 'which by their very utterance inflict injury or tend to incite an immediate breach of the peace' did not communicate any ideas and were so valueless that, like libel and obscenity, they could not be regarded as speech for the purposes of constitutional protection. In the *Chaplinsky* case, therefore, the Court approved the idea that a line should be drawn between, on the one hand, protected propositional speech and, on the other hand, provocative and insulting epithets.

Unfortunately the judgment of the Court, given by Murphy J. is open to two interpretations. It is unclear whether 'fighting words' fall outside the First Amendment only when they endanger public order, or alternatively whether some extreme insults may be proscribed, irrespective of their tendency to lead to a breach of the peace. In the case itself an imminent breach of the peace was very unlikely, though police officers have been known to retaliate to such unfriendly remarks in a hostile manner. Murphy J. adopted the interpretation given the statute by the state courts, holding that it covered only the use of annoying words plainly likely to cause an average addressee to respond violently. The alternative interpretation which would emphasize the character, rather than the likely consequences, of the words gives rise to difficulties. In what sense might words per se inflict injury, unless they amount to a libel or an invasion of privacy? Notions of 'verbal assault' or 'hitting with words' are far from helpful. Some people claim that they have been wounded by speech, but anyone who has been physically injured would recognize the difference between these types of hurt. It is far from clear that the Court was holding that *offensive* remarks directed at a particular individual may be constitutionally proscribed simply because they hurt his sensibilities.

The proscription of the use of unpleasant, offensive, or annoying words is easily understandable. Few people enjoy the sound of foul language, particularly when directed at them, any more than they like the sight of ugly buildings. But acceptance of the special value of freedom of speech entails that we should be more prepared to tolerate the former than the latter type of unpleasantness. It is at any rate important to explore the justifications for imposing restrictions on the use of intemperate or offensive language. Some of the points made in Chapter V in the course of discussing freedom of political speech are relevant here. It is hard to see how the proscription of remarks at a political meeting or demonstration could be justified on public order grounds, unless the prosecution is required to prove that they were likely to lead to an imminent breach of the peace. On the *Brandenburg*

---

[101] *Chaplinsky* v. *New Hamphire* 315 US 568 (1942).

test a conviction would be incompatible with free political speech.[102] An argument that it is right to ban offensive language to protect the sensitivities of the audience would substantially undermine freedom of expression. The general public, or perhaps the particular audience, would in effect be able to impose a veto on the language used by speakers. The implications for freedom of political speech and the arts would be considerable. As the European Human Rights Court said in its first major pronouncement on the scope of Article 10 of the ECHR, freedom of expression is applicable to ideas which '... offend, shock or disturb the State or any sector of the population', as well as those which are regarded as inoffensive.[103]

Whatever the merits of the decision in *Chaplinsky* on the facts, during the 1970s the US Supreme Court narrowed the scope of the principle it established: it applies now only to words likely to incite the person addressed to physical violence.[104] Emphasis is given to the actual or likely consequences of the words during protests and demonstrations, the second general approach identified earlier. Statutes which had been construed by the state courts to cover abusive and offensive language, falling short of a tendency to provoke a breach of the peace, were ruled unconstitutional; it was immaterial that the appellant might have been properly convicted under a more narrowly drafted ordinance. Thus, in one leading case, the defendant, picketing an army induction centre, addressed a police officer: 'White son of a bitch, I'll kill you', and 'You son of a bitch, I'll choke you to death'.[105] The Court held it was wrong to convict him under a Georgia statute proscribing the use of 'opprobrious words or abusive language, tending to cause a breach of the peace', as the state courts had interpreted it to proscribe the use of offensive language, irrespective of whether it provoked violence. In effect the Court ignored that part of the *Chaplinsky* judgment which held unprotected by the First Amendment words 'which by their very utterance inflict injury'.

In other cases the Supreme Court has narrowed *Chaplinsky* by requiring strict proof that an outbreak of violence is likely to occur; in the absence of such proof, a conviction for the use of inflammatory speech at a public meeting will be held incompatible with freedom of speech.[106] Among the relevant factors to be taken into account are the character of the audience and the extent to which it might reasonably have anticipated the use of insulting or scurrilous language. According to Powell J., as the police are trained to use a high degree of restraint in the face of verbal provocation, abuse directed to them may not be punished, while identical language addressed to a hostile audience at a public meeting might constitutionally be outlawed.[107] A similar optimistic view of the capacity of police officers for

---

[102] See *Brandenburg* v. *Ohio* 395 US 444 (1969), considered in ch. V, s. 3 above.
[103] *Handyside* v. *UK* (1976) 1 EHRR 737, para. 49.
[104] See *Gooding* v. *Wilson* 405 US 518 (1972); *Rosenfeld* v. *New Jersey* 408 US 901 (1972); *Brown* v. *Oklahoma* 408 US 914 (1972); *Lewis* v. *New Orleans II* 415 US 130 (1974).
[105] *Gooding* v. *Wilson* 405 US 518 (1972).
[106] See e.g. *Terminiello* v. *Chicago* 337 US 1 (1949); *Edwards* v. *South Carolina* 372 US 229 (1963); *Hess* v. *Indiana* 414 US 105 (1973).   [107] *Lewis* v. *New Orleans I* 408 US 913 (1972).

self-control has been taken in a Canadian case,[108] and recently by members of the High Court of Australia.[109] In contrast, an English court has, perhaps more realistically, held that a person can be convicted of insulting a policeman in such a way that a breach of the peace was likely.[110] Although on public order grounds, it makes sense to consider the propensity of the audience to react violently to inflammatory or offensive speech, this has the unfortunate result that it may give aggressive hecklers a veto on what may be said at a public meeting—the hostile audience problem. Moreover on this approach, the same remarks could be made with impunity if the audience consisted largely of women or old people, who are unlikely to react violently, but who are perhaps more likely to be alarmed or distressed by inflammatory language.[111] Any approach which emphasizes the tendency of speech to cause a breach of the peace, without any regard to the character of the speech itself, may give rise to these difficulties.

But the Supreme Court has clearly held that states cannot, compatibly with freedom of speech, regulate the quality of public debate by outlawing the use of indecent or offensive language. In *Cohen v. California*[112] the appellant was convicted under a statute proscribing offensive conduct which disturbed the peace, when he wore a jacket bearing the words 'Fuck the Draft' in a courthouse corridor. Harlan J. in the Court's opinion rejected the application of the 'fighting words' doctrine, because there was no insult directed to any particular person. And there was no evidence that the appellant intended to provoke disorder or that violence was at all likely on the facts. He then went on to consider whether offensive words could be constitutionally purged from public display and discourse. A vague fear that their use might induce some people to respond violently could not constitute any justification for such a prohibition; this would in effect confer a de facto power of veto on the most sensitive or aggressive members of the public. The general argument that the state has a legitimate concern to regulate the quality of the language used in public was also rejected. Harlan J.'s contention was that the style of speech cannot easily be divorced from its content; language conveys emotions as well as ideas, and it is as impermissible for the state to regulate the communication of the former as the latter.

The significance of this ruling extends far beyond the limits of public order jurisprudence. In the present context, however, it shows, in conjunction with other decisions narrowing the 'fighting words' doctrine, that the Court will only tolerate the prohibition of *inflammatory* speech likely to cause an outbreak of violence and disorder. Admittedly Harlan J.'s judgment does leave open the

---

[108] *R* v. *Zwicker* (1938) 1 DLR 461, 463, CC Nova Scotia.

[109] *Coleman* v. *Power* (n. 100 above), para. 200 (Gummow and Hayne JJ) and para. 258 (Kirby J.).

[110] *Simcock* v. *Rhodes* (1977) 66 Cr App Rep 192, DC.

[111] See F. M. Lawrence, 'Violence-Conducive Speech: Punishable Verbal Assault or Protected Political Speech?', in D. Kretzmer and F. Kershman Hazan (eds.), *Freedom of Speech and Incitement against Democracy* (The Hague: Kluwer, 2000), 11, 29–30.

[112] 403 US 15 (1971), discussed by D. A. Farber, 'Civilizing Public Discourse: An Essay on Professor Bickel, Justice Harlan, and the Enduring Significance of *Cohen v. California*' [1980] *Duke Law Jo* 283.

possibility that, if there had been evidence that a large number of citizens were likely to react violently to Cohen's protest, the application of the statute might have been upheld. This interpretation would not, however, be consistent with the overall spirit of his ruling, nor would it be in line with the 'heckler's veto' cases to be discussed later in this section. The justification for the Court's approach in *Cohen* v. *California* is that any wider prohibition would unduly restrict political protest. Protesters should be free to use offensive language, whether this is done, as in *Cohen,* by a lone individual, or in the course of a march or meeting. The law should only penalize speech which is inflammatory, rather than offensive or shocking, when that speech is intended or likely to provoke violence from an average audience. In other words, elements of both the first and second approaches identified earlier should be adopted. Otherwise, freedom of political speech and protest may be seriously eroded, and the hand of the hostile audience determined to break up meetings it dislikes unduly strengthened.

    Much the same perspective has now been taken by a 4–3 majority of the High Court of Australia in *Coleman* v. *Power.*[113] It upheld an appeal of a protester in Queensland who had been convicted of the statutory offence of using 'threatening, abusive or insulting words to any person' when he publicly accused a police officer in his presence of corruption. Three members of the majority reasoned that the statutory provision should be narrowly construed to cover only speech which was intended or likely to provoke a breach of the peace; it would be incompatible with freedom of political expression to construe it as proscribing provocative remarks of this type.[114] Kirby J. was particularly clear on this point. He said that if 'insulting' were interpreted to cover such remarks, as favoured by two other members of the Court, 'the potential operation on political discourse... would be intolerably over-wide.' Political debate in Australia had always been characterized by insults and invective.[115] On the other hand, strong dissents of Gleeson CJ, Callinan and Heydon JJ held there are good arguments for regulating insulting or provocative remarks; even if they are covered by the implied freedom of political communication, the need to protect vulnerable people and to preserve the civility of public discourse justify their proscription. But the civility rationale for proscription of abusive or insulting speech is hard to reconcile with the rules of defamation law; if the law may properly outlaw abusive remarks as hurtful to their victim, taking the view that they fall outside the scope of free political speech, it is hard to see why libel law requires them to be *defamatory* of a claimant, rather than merely abusive, and why it allows a defence of qualified privilege (and fair comment) when they concern a matter of public or political importance.[116]

---

[113] [2004] HCA 39 (1 Sept. 2004).

[114] McHugh J., the fourth member of the majority, reached this conclusion on constitutional grounds; the Queensland law did proscribe insulting remarks, even though they were unlikely to cause disorder, and that was incompatible with the implied constitutional freedom of political expression.   [115] N. 113 above, paras. 237–9.

[116] See the judgment of Gummow and Haynes JJ in *Coleman* (n. 113 above), para. 199.

We should now consider how successfully the UK Parliament and courts in England have tackled these issues. Under section 5 of the Public Order Act 1936, it was an offence to use in a public place or at a public meeting 'threatening, abusive or insulting words or behaviour...with intent to provoke a breach of the peace or whereby a breach of the peace is likely to be occasioned'. In one leading case, *Jordan* v. *Burgoyne*,[117] the defendant made a speech to a meeting of several thousand people in Trafalgar Square. When he suggested that 'Hitler was right' and that 'our real enemies, the people we should have fought, were not Hitler and the National Socialists of Germany but world Jewry and its associates in this country', there was complete disorder among the audience which included many Jews and Communists who were keen to stop the defendant's meeting. The Divisional Court allowed the prosecutor's appeal against Jordan's acquittal. The lower court had taken the view that ordinary, reasonable people would not have reacted to the speech in a hostile manner. But the fact that an audience of a different character (an assembly of professors or divines?)[118] might have reacted in an entirely peaceable way—perhaps by taking notes—was irrelevant. A speaker must take his audience as he finds it, and cannot argue that elements in the crowd are disposed to break up his meeting. Arguably, the decision allowed the hostile audience a veto and, as Jordan contended, infringed free speech principles. However, Lord Parker CJ emphasized that the speaker had to 'insult' his audience in the sense of 'hit [them] by words' for the offence to be committed. The idea is similar to that of the US 'fighting words' principle, albeit it is very doubtful whether on these facts Jordan could constitutionally have been convicted in the United States. It was clear that Jordan had insulted the audience earlier in his speech, when he had referred to it as a 'red rabble' and 'far from wholesome', though it was unclear whether it was these remarks, rather than the later non-insulting, comments on the Second World War, which brought about the unrest.

In contrast, the House of Lords decision in *Brutus* v. *Cozens* on the meaning of 'insulting' in the public order legislation was more solicitous of freedom of speech.[119] The appellants had interrupted a tennis match at Wimbledon involving a South African player in order to protest against the evils of apartheid. The disruption had prompted some spectators to react angrily. The magistrates held there had been no insulting behaviour, but on appeal the Divisional Court ruled there was an offence under section 5 of the 1936 Act because the appellants' conduct had affronted and offended the spectators. Lord Reid considered this approach misconceived. There is a distinction between 'insulting' a person on the one hand, and evincing disrespect or contempt for his rights on the other. The lower court's view, he pointed out, would have led to an undue restriction on vigorous public debate, merely because it offended some people. The meaning of 'insulting' was a question of fact for the magistrates, and the Divisional Court was

---

[117] [1963] 2 QB 744, DC.   [118] See Coleridge J. in *R* v. *Aldred* (1909) 22 Cox CC 1, 3.
[119] [1973] AC 854.

wrong to give the term such a broad interpretation. However, there is a drawback to this ruling. It is difficult to appeal from magistrates' rulings on the meaning of statutory provisions, if they are treated as determining questions of fact. Free speech is only securely protected if magistrates follow the approach indicated by Lord Reid.

The Public Order Act 1986 has replaced much of the legislation of 1936. It is an offence under section 4 of the 1986 Act to use towards another 'threatening, abusive or insulting words or behaviour' with intent to cause that person to fear immediate unlawful violence against him or others, or with intent to provoke such violence, or in such a way that the other is likely to fear such violence or that it will be provoked. The defendant is only guilty if he intends his words to be threatening, etc. or is aware that they may be.[120] Further, the words or behaviour must have been intended to cause a fear of, or to provoke, violence, rather than a breach of the peace or general disorder. The prosecution must show that *immediate* violence is feared or provoked. It is not enough to show that it may occur at some indeterminate time in the future, though equally it need not be instantaneous.[121] (This is comparable to the insistence by the US Supreme Court that advocacy of illegal action could only be proscribed, compatibly with the First Amendment, if it is directed to produce imminent lawless action and is likely to lead to it.[122]) On the other hand, section 4 is broader than its predecessor, section 5 of the 1936 legislation, in that it is now an offence to use threatening, etc. words which lead the audience to fear violence, as well as to use such words in such circumstances that violence may be provoked. So insults addressed to a police officer or elderly people who are themselves unlikely to retaliate will be covered, as long as it is established that they or others present fear violence.

The Public Order Act 1986 also introduced a new offence of broad scope with serious implications for freedom of speech. Under section 5 it is an offence to use threatening, abusive or insulting words or behaviour, or disorderly behaviour, 'within the hearing or sight of a person likely to be caused harassment, alarm or distress thereby.' The prosecution must show the defendant knew his words were threatening, etc., or his behaviour disorderly,[123] and the defendant is not liable if he shows that 'his conduct was reasonable'.[124] The provision was primarily intended to deal with hooligans who, say, pester and alarm people late at night,[125] but it can be used to penalize the exercise of protest rights. Demonstrators who use abusive or insulting language commit an offence if the audience is likely to be alarmed or distressed. The term 'disorderly behaviour' could be applied to symbolic speech such as the burning of flags or effigies. Admittedly, a majority of the Court of Appeal of the Northern Territory in Australia has held that holding aloft

---

[120] Public Order Act 1986, s. 6(3).
[121] *R* v. *Horseferry Road Metropolitan Stipendiary Magistrate, ex p Siadatan* [1991] 1 QB 260, DC.
[122] *Brandenburg* v. *Ohio* 395 US 444 (1969); *Hess* v. *Indiana* 414 US 105 (1973).
[123] Public Order Act 1986, s. 6(3).   [124] Ibid., s. 5(3)(c).
[125] White Paper, *Review of Public Order Law* (Cmnd 9510, 1985), paras. 3.22–3.26.

burning flags in a demonstration outside the Indonesian Embassy should not be regarded as disorderly conduct; there was no evidence that anyone had been frightened or had been inconvenienced while the demonstrators were exercising their freedom of speech and assembly by protesting in a theatrical manner against the occupation of East Timor.[126] It is unclear whether an English court would come to the same conclusion on comparable facts: the UK statute does not require proof that anyone was actually alarmed or distressed, only that it is likely that someone might be.

The recent judgment of Hallett J. in *Percy* v. *DPP* shows a welcome sensitivity to freedom of speech and protest in this context.[127] The appellant had been convicted under section 5 of the 1986 Act when she defaced and then stood upon a US flag outside an American airbase in Suffolk in protest against its 'Star Wars' policy. US servicemen gave evidence that they were distressed at the treatment of their flag. Ms Percy had been convicted because in the view of the trial court she could have expressed her view in other ways which were not 'insulting' to the servicemen and their families. Hallett J. for the Divisional Court found this approach too narrow, and allowed the appeal. There is a presumption in favour of freedom of speech, guaranteed by the Human Rights Act 1998, so it was necessary to consider all relevant factors to determine whether, in the context of this case, section 5 of the 1986 Act imposed proportionate restrictions. The trial court should have asked, for instance, whether the desecration of the flag was gratuitous or formed part of the appellant's legitimate protest and open expression of views, and whether she appreciated the impact it might have on the audience.

The implications of section 5 for free speech are also shown in cases concerned with anti-abortion protests, an increasing phenomenon in a number of countries in the last two or three decades since the liberalization of the abortion laws.[128] In *DPP* v. *Clarke*[129] the defendants had been prosecuted under the provision in respect of a demonstration outside the entrance to a clinic, when they carried placards with photographs of aborted foetuses. A police officer had apparently found these pictures 'insulting' and felt distressed. The magistrates acquitted the protesters because the prosecution had not shown beyond reasonable doubt that they were aware that their placards were insulting and abusive. The Divisional Court dismissed the appeal on that point. But it also upheld the magistrates' conclusions that the placards were 'insulting', a matter for them to decide under *Brutus* v. *Cozens*, and that the protest should not be regarded as 'reasonable', for the purpose

---

[126] *Watson* v. *Trennery* (1998) 145 FLR 159.

[127] [2002] Crim LR 835, DC. Contrast *Norwood* v. *DPP* [2003] EWHC 1564 (Admin), which upheld a conviction for a religiously aggravated breach of the Public Order Act 1986, s. 5, when the defendant displayed a poster in his flat window with, among other words and images, the words 'Islam out of Britain'. For commentary, see A Geddis, 'Free Speech Martyrs or Unreasonable Threats to Social Peace: "Insulting" Expression and Section 5 of the Public Order Act 1986' [2004] *PL* 853.

[128] See the note, 'Safety Valve Closed: The Removal of Nonviolent Outlets for Dissent and the Onset of Anti-Abortion Violence' (2000) 113 *Harvard Law Rev* 1210.

[129] (1992) 94 Cr App Rep 359, DC.

of the defence provided by section 5. The conclusion that the placards were 'insulting' to the police officer was, as Nolan LJ said, surprising. They did not abuse or amount to a verbal assault on him; at most he might have found them annoying, in much the same way that the spectators at Wimbledon must have found the disruption of the tennis match. In another case the Divisional Court upheld the conviction of anti-abortion protesters; there was evidence that their demonstration made it difficult for patients and staff to enter the clinic.[130] The argument that the protest was 'reasonable' was rejected, as it had been in *Clarke*. Insofar as abortion protests do harass or intimidate women attending abortion clinics, and their doctors and other staff, they do much more than occasion alarm and distress, the interests protected by section 5 of the Public Order Act 1986. Arguably, they infringe privacy interests and rights. How these rights may be accommodated with the right to free speech and to freedom of assembly is discussed in the final section of this chapter.

The UK public order legislation adopts the third approach to balancing free speech and public order identified earlier: it penalizes speech or language which is threatening, abusive, or insulting, rather than merely offensive or annoying, but at the same time it requires the prosecution to show that it was intended or likely to cause violence or alarm or distress. It pays due regard both to the character of the speech and to its consequences. However, unless it is appropriately interpreted and applied by the courts in conformity with the right to freedom of expression, the legislation significantly restricts freedom to protest.[131] The decision in *Percy* shows how it can be construed to respect that freedom; anti-abortion protest of the kind at issue in *Clarke* should be tolerated, unless it interferes with the rights of women and clinic staff not to be harassed. But the conviction of protesters on the ground that their offensive language or disorderly expressive conduct does no more than alarm or distress members of the public who hear or see it should be held incompatible with freedom of speech and assembly.

(iii) The problem of the hostile audience

Something should be said about the hostile audience, or heckler's veto, problem, as it raises acute difficulties for freedom of speech. Any attempt to impose a simple solution is bound to cause dissatisfaction. The law must preserve the peace, but if it is preoccupied with that objective, it will inevitably confer de facto censorship powers on individuals and groups who are determined to break up a public meeting. The fear of disruption from the hostile audience may induce the police to disperse a demonstration when the risk of violence or disorder is in fact relatively slight. Further, if the convenor is prosecuted on a charge of obstruction of the

---

[130] *Morrow, Geach and Thomas* v. *DPP* [1994] Crim LR 58.
[131] See Geddis (n. 127 above) who rightly argues that English courts often fail to give adequate weight to freedom of expression when determining whether the protest was 'reasonable' under the Public Order Act 1986, s. 5(3)(c).

police for failing to comply with their order to stop the demonstration or meeting, he may only be acquitted if the court holds the police action unreasonable. Courts, particularly magistrates, are reluctant to uphold challenges to the exercise of police discretion in circumstances of apparent emergency. In any case, an acquittal does not enable the defendant retrospectively, as it were, to exercise his free speech rights; the time for the protest may have passed, the occasion for demonstration may be no longer relevant. But equally the law should not ignore public order. It is perfectly sensible for the authorities to take precautionary steps to safeguard the peace and other important interests such as residential tranquillity, the free flow of traffic and the use of shops and other commercial premises. Moreover, to require the police in all circumstances to protect the rights of demonstrators when it is clear that the protest will lead to disorder may impose too heavy a burden on their resources. In the face of these dilemmas, the law should look for imaginative solutions to reconcile the competing interests and values as far as possible.

English law can in fact boast one decision which adopts an uncompromisingly pro-free speech position in these circumstances: *Beatty* v. *Gillbanks*.[132] The Divisional Court refused to uphold binding-over orders which had been imposed on leaders of the Salvation Army in Weston-super-Mare for holding an unlawful assembly. On a number of previous occasions their procession had been broken up by their opponents, the Skeleton Army; on this occasion Beatty and some other leaders of the Salvationists were arrested when they refused to disperse a procession which, the police feared, would also be violently obstructed. Field J. held that the appellants had not caused any unlawful acts; the disturbances had not been the intended, nor were they the natural and necessary consequences of their processions. In a passage which has perhaps not received the attention it deserves, he added that the Skeleton Army would be less inclined to intervene when they appreciated that their obstruction would not terminate the Salvationist processions, but that if they did continue with their violent opposition, it was the police's duty to deal with them rather than with persons exercising lawful rights.[133]

The case remains good law. But the decision is controversial in that it is legitimate to question whether the Salvationists' intention was rightly characterized as entirely innocent. In any case, it is clear that the decision will be distinguished where the speeches or general behaviour of the defendant show an intention to provoke violence from opponents.[134] In those circumstances the speaker could be prosecuted under section 4 or section 5 of the Public Order Act 1986, which have just been discussed. More importantly, preventive powers of the police to keep the peace may provide a basis for a criminal prosecution, even though the organizers of the meeting and the speaker had no desire to provoke disruption. The authority

---

[132] [1882] 9 QBD 308, (1882) 15 Cox CC 138.
[133] Ibid., 146 per Field J. (The passage does not appear in the official law reports.)
[134] *Wise* v. *Dunning* [1902] 1 KB 167, DC.

for this is the unsatisfactory decision of the Divisional Court in *Duncan* v. *Jones*.[135] The appellant had started to address a small meeting outside an unemployed training centre in Deptford, London. Disturbance of an unspecified sort had followed a previous meeting conducted by her on the same spot a year before. Fearing a repetition of these troubles, the police asked her to move her meeting to a place 175 yards away; when she refused, she was charged with obstructing a police officer in the execution of his duty. Her conviction was upheld by the Divisional Court.

The judges in *Duncan* v. *Jones* refused to see the case in the context of any right of freedom of public assembly or to reconcile their conclusion with *Beatty* v. *Gillbanks*.[136] The decision in effect outflanked that earlier decision upholding a right to hold a public meeting, provided the speaker did not provoke or incite his audience to violence. Once a police officer intervened, reasonably apprehending a breach of the peace, it was the duty of the speaker to stop and a criminal offence not to do so. The court did not say whether a breach of the peace had to be apprehended as likely or only possible, or whether a *serious* breach had to be contemplated for the police intervention to be justified. The relevance of the previous disturbance which had occurred over a year before these events was not discussed; in the United States the fact of a previous incident would be an inadequate ground for refusing a permit to hold a meeting.[137] The police intervention was, of course, a prior restraint.

Although this obstruction charge is now frequently used in demonstration cases, there was until recently little subsequent authority on these points. In one case,[138] the Divisional Court made it clear that there must be a 'real possibility' of a breach of the peace before intervention is justified. Lord Parker CJ went on to suggest that oppressive and hostile picketing was enough to constitute a breach of the peace; it did not matter that there was no clear threat of violence. One reason for the relative shortage of reported decisions is that appellate courts are reluctant to challenge the findings of magistrates, who are themselves, it may be conjectured, generally prepared to accept police evidence that there were good grounds to fear disorder if the demonstration continued. The result is that hecklers are allowed to impose an effective veto on what might otherwise be peaceable public meetings.

However, the decision of the Divisional Court in *Redmond-Bate* v. *DPP* shows how a different approach can be taken.[139] Three Christian women preachers were speaking from the steps of Wakefield Cathedral. When they were heckled, a police officer, fearing an outbreak of violence, asked the women to stop, and arrested

---

[135] [1936] 1 KB 218.
[136] Lord Hewart CJ and Humphreys J. both denied, albeit in slightly different terms, that the case had anything to do with the right to hold a public meeting or the law of unlawful assembly.
[137] See *Kunz* v. *New York* 340 US 290 (1951).
[138] *Piddington* v. *Bates* [1961] 1 WLR 162, DC.
[139] (1999) 7 BHRC 375, [1999] Crim LR 998.

them for obstruction when they refused to do so. The Divisional Court allowed their appeal. Sedley LJ held that it was for the court itself to determine whether, in the light of the evidence available to the officer at the time, it was reasonable to fear an imminent breach of the peace. Further, it was incumbent on the police, and on the court, to assess whether the threat to the peace came from the speaker or from the audience. Preventive action must be directed to the source of that threat. The police had no right to stop citizens engaging in lawful conduct, unless there were grounds to fear that it would, by interfering with the rights or liberties of others, provoke violence which in those circumstances might not be unreasonable. The women preachers were entitled to speak in terms which some of their audience might find irritating or controversial, but they did not threaten or provoke violence. Consequently, the police officer was not acting in the execution of his duty when he directed them to stop. The exact implications of the decision are uncertain. It is unclear whether it would, say, allow anti-abortion protesters freedom to make their case outside abortion clinics, where demonstrations might interfere with the liberties of the women attending the clinics and anger their supporters. If there were evidence that some of the latter were inclined to react violently, the police might find it easier to stop the protest rather than require supporters of the women to move on. Sedley LJ suggested the police could stop a protest if it provoked violence which, though unlawful, would not be altogether unreasonable. So the decision is far from conferring on speakers a wide right to engage in provocative behaviour, especially when they appreciate it will be offensive to the audience. But the police must now at least be sensitive to the rights of speakers in this context.

The leading Supreme Court ruling is that in *Feiner* v. *New York*.[140] A speaker at a street corner in Syracuse gathered a small crowd of both whites and blacks around him. He certainly provided them with good invective and entertainment: the President was described as a 'bum' and the local mayor as a 'champagne-sipping bum' who 'does not speak for the Negro people'. But when he advocated that the blacks should fight for equal rights, members of the crowd became restive. The police feared that a fight would break out, and after two requests to the speaker to stop, he was arrested for disorderly conduct. The majority of the Court upheld his conviction; he had incited riot, and there was a clear and present danger of disorder. This is perfectly acceptable law, even though the majority's interpretation of the facts seems questionable. The importance of the case lies in the dissents of Black and Douglas JJ who did not think the record showed an intent on Feiner's part to cause violence. They thought the police's primary duty in the situation was to protect the speaker, if necessary by arresting members of the hostile audience. By adopting the opposite course, police censorship had been imposed. Sedley LJ's approach in *Redmond-Bate* shares the spirit of these dissenting judgments.

[140] 340 US 315 (1951).

There is perhaps no Supreme Court decision which clearly delimits the powers and duties of the police where there is a hostile audience intent on breaking up violently a lawful meeting.[141] But at least two Circuit Court cases indicate that their initial responsibility is to protect First Amendment rights so far as possible.[142] If a community has advance notice of a demonstration which is likely to be confronted by political opponents, it should ensure there are adequate police present at the meeting to safeguard freedom of speech and assembly. An order to disperse can only be justified as a last recourse when there is a clear and present, or imminent, danger of physical violence. It has also been suggested that the police officers should observe certain procedural steps. The speaker should be warned before the final order to stop is issued (as happened in *Feiner*) and an explanation should be given for the police action.[143] This may be a counsel of perfection. In many cases it would be absurd to expect hard-pressed officers to behave with deliberation and courtesy. But the case-law in the United States is impressive in its commitment to preserve the values of free speech until it is clear beyond doubt that it should be subordinated on the occasion to public order. The UK offence of obstructing a police officer in the execution of his duty, at least as construed in *Duncan* v. *Jones*, would be incompatible with the free speech guarantee of the First Amendment, since it plainly enables the suppression of speech in circumstances which do not warrant it. Sedley LJ's approach in *Redmond-Bate* would be required to impose acceptable limits on the use of the offence in this context.

5. Notice and Buffer-Zone Requirements

(i) Notice requirements

If the hostile audience problem cannot be satisfactorily solved at the moment when it becomes most acute, the law can try to prevent difficulties arising. One possibility is for the authorities to insist on advance notice of processions and public meetings, so that appropriate steps may be taken to ensure they take place peacefully. This has been a feature of German law, which requires at least 48 hours' notice of the object of a procession or meeting.[144] The police then have ample time to call up reinforcements, if necessary from neighbouring forces, for attendance along the route. Moreover, they can impose conditions with regard to the particular time and route (or place) of the demonstration to minimize the risk of disorder by,

---

[141] See *Gregory* v. *Chicago* 394 US 111 (1969), where the Court held that demonstrators could not constitutionally be convicted of 'disorderly conduct' for refusing to obey police requests to disperse when they were confronted by hostile opponents, since that was not the basis of the charge.

[142] *Sellers* v. *Johnson* 163 F 2d 877 (8th Cir, 1947); *Wolin* v. *Port of New York Authority* 392 F 2d 83 (2nd Cir, 1968).

[143] See the note 'Hostile-Audience Confrontations: Police Conduct and First Amendment Rights' (1976) *75 Michigan Law Rev* 180, 196.

[144] Law on Assemblies and Processions of 15 Nov. 1978, BGBl I, S 1789, s. 14.

for example, preventing its entrance into an area where its opponents are likely to gather in large numbers. A general notice requirement also enables the police (or other suitable authority) to ban formally organized counter-demonstrations, though it would be naive to claim this step will always prevent clashes between rival groups.

The UK Public Order Act 1936 gave the police some powers to take preliminary steps to avert disorder during street demonstrations. Passed largely to deal with violence resulting from fascist marches in London in the early 1930s, it enabled a chief officer of police to impose conditions on the organizers of a procession, including conditions as to its route, if he reasonably believed it would 'occasion serious public disorder'.[145] If he did not consider use of that power adequate to prevent disorder, he was able to apply to the district council for an order prohibiting all or any class of public procession for a period up to three months. In practice the power to ban processions was exercised very rarely. There was no notice requirement in this legislation. The scope of police powers was reviewed during the 1980s to tackle incidents of disorder during protest activity. Under the Public Order Act 1986, the senior police officer is now able to impose conditions on the organizers of a procession if he fears serious damage to property, serious disruption to the community, or the deliberate intimidation of others with regard to the exercise of their rights, as well as to avert disorder.[146] For the first time directions may be imposed on the place, duration, and numbers attending a public meeting,[147] now defined as a meeting of two or more people in a public place, open at least partly to the air.[148]

The most important change made by the 1986 legislation in this context is the imposition of a compulsory requirement to give written notice to hold any public procession with what may be termed political objectives or to commemorate an event.[149] The requirement, it may be noted, does not extend to customary parades or funeral processions. Nor does it apply to marches where it is not reasonably practicable to give notice, because of their spontaneous character; this exemption has been required by the German Constitutional Court, in order to safeguard the freedom of assembly in these circumstances.[150] This new national requirement replaces obligations previously imposed only by some local statutes. At least six clear days' notice must be given, and the notice must specify the date of the procession, the time at which it is intended to start, its proposed route, and details of the organizer.[151] It is a criminal offence not to observe the notice requirements

---

[145] Public Order Act 1936, s. 3.

[146] Public Order Act 1986, s. 12. If these powers are insufficient, the police may apply to a district council for a three-month ban on all, or any class of, processions; this may be imposed with the consent of the Home Secretary. In London, the Commissioner of the Metropolitan Police may make an order with the Home Secretary's consent: s. 13. The provisions considered in this paragraph do not apply in Scotland. [147] Public Order Act 1986, s. 14.

[148] Ibid., s. 16 (as amended by the Anti-social Behaviour Act 2003, s. 57).

[149] Ibid., s. 11(1). [150] 69 BVerfGE 315, 350–1 (1985); 85 BVerfGE 69, 74–5 (1991).

[151] Public Order Act 1986, s. 11(3).

imposed by the legislation, or for a procession to depart from the notified time and route.[152]

These notice requirements should not be equated with a permit system, under which the police or other authority may choose to grant or refuse permission to stage a protest on the streets.[153] Even mandatory permit systems have been upheld in the United States as compatible with the First Amendment, provided they do not allow the licensing authority wide discretion to pick and choose which meetings to allow; such a system is acceptable as long as it only enables the authority to provide proper policing and impose time, manner, and place conditions.[154] Authorization procedures, and indeed a temporary ban on all public meetings, have also been approved by the European Human Rights Commission.[155] So there should be no legal objection to the imposition of a general notice requirement. It enables the police to take steps to avoid disorder and disruption, and to negotiate with the organizers of the procession conditions with regard to its route, duration, and stewarding.[156]

Nevertheless, some reservations should be expressed about the scope of the notification provisions in the Public Order Act 1986. First, they are aimed at political marches. Funerals and traditional processions are exempt. Moreover, crowds leaving a concert or soccer game pose as great a risk of disorder and inconvenience to the general public as political demonstrations, but they are not subject to the same types of control. There is a sense, therefore, in which the notice requirement, as well as other provisions in the legislation, discriminate against demonstrations which, however troublesome, are intended to raise matters of public and social concern. Secondly, the legislation is inconsistent, in that it does not require the convenors of static meetings, as distinct from processions, to give advance notice, and incoherent, in that there is an exemption for spontaneous demonstrations. If the law tolerates instantaneous protests, it is hard to see why it insists on six days' notice of others planned perhaps only a day or so in advance. Notice requirements, of course, attempt to strike a balance between the interests of public order and the freedom to engage in peaceful protest. While it may be unreasonable to expect complete consistency of approach, the requirements in the UK public order legislation should be reconsidered.[157]

(ii) Buffer zones to regulate anti-abortion protest

Anti-abortion protests outside hospitals, clinics, and doctors' homes pose a number of complex free speech and protest issues. Protesters may carry placards with

---

[152] Public Order Act 1986, s. 11(7).

[153] For consideration of these systems, see ch. IV, s. 4 above on prior restraints.

[154] *Cox* v. *New Hampshire* 312 US 569 (1941).

[155] 8191/78, *Rassemblement Jurassien* v. *Switzerland* 17 D & R 93.

[156] See the White Paper, *Review of Public Order Law* (Cmnd 9510, 1985), paras. 4.2–4.6, and for general discussion, see P. A. J. Waddington, *Liberty and Order* (London: UCL Press, 1994), ch. 4.

[157] For a fuller criticism, see Barendt (n. 3 above), 173–6.

pictures of aborted foetuses and shout slogans which are very distressing to patients as they enter a clinic for consultation or an operation. These demonstrations raise a conflict between freedom of speech on the one hand, and on the other the rights of women to have a lawful operation and of the doctors and staff to enter their place of work, free from harassment or intimidation. Patients, and perhaps doctors, may also argue that their privacy has been invaded, even if it is unclear whether a legal right to privacy could be asserted in this context.[158] These protests therefore contain elements additional to those contained in conventional public order cases involving a clash between freedom to protest and the public interest in a peaceful and tranquil environment. Anti-abortion protests may, of course, give rise to violence or general disorder. In those circumstances prosecutions may be brought in the United Kingdom against the protesters if they have used insulting words or engaged in disorderly behaviour likely to provoke violence or cause alarm or distress.[159] Alternatively, the police might be able to use their preventive power to keep order by requiring anti-abortion protesters who provoke unrest to move away from the clinic or to move on, though they could not properly do this if the protest was conducted peacefully and without the use of insulting language.[160]

Some US cases and one Canadian decision show an alternative approach. Courts have been asked to enforce criminal law regulations which prohibit demonstrations within a certain distance of a doctor's residence or a clinic or which prohibit protesters in that area from approaching close to any person, without her consent, to hand her a leaflet or to offer counselling. In other cases, courts have granted injunctions on nuisance grounds to stop demonstrations or unwanted approaches. In both types of case, the object of the measure is primarily to protect women from harassment as they enter the premises, but it may also be to lower the level of noise outside a hospital or to safeguard the privacy of the medical staff. A majority of a strongly divided US Supreme Court has generally upheld these measures. It has recognized that the state has a legitimate interest to safeguard the right of women to seek lawful medical services, public order, and the residential privacy of doctors.[161] Two cases may be mentioned. In *Madsen* v. *Women's Health Center*[162] the Court partly approved, and partly struck down, the terms of an injunction granted in Florida to restrain protests outside an abortion clinic. Terms imposing a thirty-six-foot buffer zone between protesters and the entrance to, and pavements around, the clinic and limiting the amount of noise they could make were upheld. On the other hand, a provision prohibiting

[158] In *A-G of Ontario* v. *Dieleman* (1994) 117 DLR (4th) 449, Adams J. emphasized that the privacy of both patients and doctors was implicated by anti-abortion protests. Even in the absence of a legal privacy right, these interests could be protected by actions in nuisance.
[159] See s. 4(ii) above.
[160] See the discussion of *Redmond-Bate* v. *DPP* [1999] Crim LR 998 in s. 4(iii) above.
[161] In *Frisby* v. *Schultz* 487 US 474 (1988), the Court upheld a total ban on the targeted picketing of the home of a doctor who performed abortions.   [162] 512 US 753 (1994).

protesters from physically approaching anyone, without prior consent, within 300 feet of the clinic to communicate a message was invalidated, in the absence of evidence that their speech would amount to a threat or 'fighting words'.[163] Scalia J., a consistent opponent of abortion rights, considered all the terms of the injunction should be subject to strict scrutiny. The state did not show that it had a compelling enough interest to justify an infringement of the demonstrators' right to protest at the exact place of their choosing, the pavements outside the clinic. For the majority, on the other hand, the injunction was a reasonable time, manner, and place regulation, rather than one aimed at the protesters' objects.

A similar disagreement characterized the decision in a more recent case, *Hill* v. *Colorado*.[164] A state statute made it an offence, within 100 feet of a hospital, to approach within eight feet of anyone, without that person's consent, to hand her a leaflet or handbill or to engage in verbal protest, education, or counselling. A majority, 6–3, upheld the statute. For the Court Stevens J. admitted that the statute restricted speech in a public forum—the streets and pavements outside hospitals—but emphasized that it imposed a minor restriction on the manner and place of communication. It protected unwilling listeners from harassment, and could not be regarded as content-based. The restrictions concerned the particular places where attempts were made to speak to women patients, namely the entrances to hospitals; in principle, they applied to all forms of protest and to expressions of support for abortion rights. Speakers were free to communicate an anti-abortion message by displaying signs or by shouting at the women from outside the eight-foot zone. For Scalia J. and the other dissenters, Thomas and Kennedy JJ, the statute was content-based, in that it was intended to limit the offering of protest, education, or counselling rather than any message ('Have a Nice Day'). Moreover, it infringed the First Amendment freedom of the protesters to approach anyone without that person's permission and attempt to communicate a message. There was no right to be left alone on the streets or other places.[165]

There can be no doubt that the approach of the majority in both these cases is preferable to the more absolutist position taken by Scalia J. He stretched the concept of content-based regulation subject to strict scrutiny unacceptably, by holding that a law prohibiting counselling or protest, but not other types of speech, is caught by the principle. The injunction in *Madsen* and the Colorado law were content-neutral measures, limiting the *precise place* of protest activity. More importantly, the state does have a compelling interest to protect the rights of patients to take advantage of lawful medical services, free from harassment which

---

163 However, in *Schenk* v. *Pro-Choice Network of Western New York* 519 US 357 (1987), a majority approved an order requiring demonstrators not to approach women, if they had indicated they did not want counselling, because previously 'counsellors' had yelled in patients' faces, and there was evidence this had provoked men accompanying the patients to violence.

164 530 US 703 (2000).

165 Scalia J. argued, ibid., 751–3 that the cases where the Court has upheld a right not to be a 'captive audience' are confined to the protection of the audience in the home, for example, a right not to be sent unsolicited pornographic magazines (*Rowan v. Post Office* 397 US 728 (1970)).

may well exacerbate their medical condition and psychological welfare. There is a real difference between a right to be let alone when entering a hospital or clinic, and a general right to be free of offensive or distressing messages when out shopping on a high street. In any case, there is surely no free speech right to approach someone to hand out leaflets, etc., when that person has indicated that this is without her consent. Buffer-zone provisions and other restrictions designed to respect the privacy of hospital patients amount to sensible regulation of the place for speech.

This conclusion does not mean that courts should necessarily uphold such restrictions. Their judgment should be sensitive to the facts. The Canadian case is instructive on these points. In *Attorney-General of Ontario* v. *Dieleman*,[166] Adams J. declined to grant an injunction to restrain anti-abortion protests within a particular distance of any public hospital: that would impose a significant restriction on protest activity outside large premises with many entrances. It could not be regarded as necessary to protect the privacy interests of women patients entering a hospital for abortion services or for its medical staff. On the other hand, he was prepared to restrain the picketing of abortion clinics within a sixty-foot radius of these clinics, which were much smaller than the public hospitals. The institution of a buffer zone, and a prohibition on close physical approaches within a broader regulated area, reduced the difficulties of those patients who would otherwise be a 'captive audience' for the crowds engaged in picketing the clinic.

The merit of buffer-zone provisions is that they accommodate the rights of both anti-abortion protesters and of women and medical staff. Neither freedom of speech (and assembly) nor the right to privacy is unlimited. It is only if an absolutist approach is taken to either right that this balance cannot be struck sensitively. In their object and effects they are similar to the conditions which may be imposed in English law on the route to be taken by processions. Indeed, buffer zones could certainly be imposed by the police in England as a condition on the holding of a static assembly under the Public Order Act 1986.[167] They might be necessary to prevent the intimidation of patients and doctors engaged in lawful conduct.

[166] (1994) 117 DLR (4th) 449.   [167] S. 14(1).

IX

Free Speech and the Judicial Process

1. Introduction

We know from one of Lord Atkin's most memorable pronouncements that: 'Justice is not a cloistered virtue: she must be allowed to suffer the scrutiny and the respectful even though outspoken comments of ordinary men.'[1] Indeed, it might appear obvious that speech should be particularly securely protected when it publicizes or examines the workings of the legal process. But in fact this is a complicated area of law where the values of free speech compete with other rights and interests, both individual and public. Moreover, English law and the common law in other Commonwealth countries often contrast sharply with the approach in the United States of America. This is particularly apparent in the scope of contempt of court, that 'Proteus of the legal world, assuming an almost infinite diversity of forms'.[2] The media in England and other common law jurisdictions may be liable for contempt of court if they reveal that someone facing a criminal trial has several previous convictions. But in the United States the media would generally be entitled to disclose this information under the First Amendment. Divergent solutions also emerge in the treatment of other issues in this context. To what extent is it permissible to penalize vitriolic criticism of the judiciary? Is it ever proper to prohibit publication of the names of parties to legal proceedings? Do the press have a right of access to attend legal proceedings and should the televising of criminal trials and other prominent cases be allowed?

Civilized societies have for a long time attached paramount importance to the fairness of legal procedure. Whether or not the rules of natural justice (or due process) can be traced back to the hearing accorded Adam and Eve before the expulsion from the Garden of Eden,[3] they were enshrined in the common law well before it attached any significance to freedom of expression. Inevitably, practising lawyers and judges are much concerned with these rules. They are now commonly incorporated in bills of rights and written constitutions. The Sixth

---

[1] *Ambard* v. *A-G for Trinidad and Tobago* [1936] AC 322, PC. For a comprehensive academic commentary on the law of contempt, see C. J. Miller, *Contempt of Court*, 3rd edn. (Oxford: OUP, 2000).

[2] J. Moskovitz, 'Contempt of Injunctions, Civil and Criminal' (1943) 43 *Columbia Law Rev* 780.

[3] See *R* v. *University of Cambridge* (1723) 1 Str 557.

Amendment to the US Constitution confers on the accused in a criminal prosecution a 'right to a speedy and public trial, by an impartial jury . . . and to be informed of the nature and cause of the accusation'. Article 6(1) of the European Convention on Human Rights and Fundamental Freedoms (ECHR) provides: 'In the determination of his civil rights and obligations or of any criminal charge against him, everyone is entitled to a fair and public hearing within a reasonable time by an independent and impartial tribunal . . .'. It also permits the exclusion of the press and public from legal proceedings in certain circumstances, indicating, therefore, that access rights to attend such proceedings are not absolute and may give way to the requirement of a fair trial.[4]

There is, therefore, traditional and constitutional authority in many jurisdictions for protecting the right to a fair trial. It is hardly surprising that it has often been given precedence when it conflicts with the claims of the media to attend and report legal proceedings or with other free speech interests which have only been granted constitutional protection by the courts, even in the United States, in the last sixty or seventy years. Conceivably the constitution itself might indicate how these conflicts should be resolved, although it is rare for the text to provide much help in this way. In practice the judiciary resolves these issues. An important preliminary question here is to what extent there is a genuine conflict between two rights: the right to a fair trial and to freedom of speech. Is it necessary sometimes to restrict speech in order to honour the guarantee of a fair trial by an impartial judiciary, or to serve some other interests connected with the proper administration of justice?

In fact the law reports are full of observations to the effect that usually the interests of free speech and a fair trial, so far from conflicting, are quite compatible. This conclusion may indeed be considered implicit in the constitutional protection of a right to a *public* trial. The public and the media should be free to attend legal proceedings to ensure they are conducted fairly and to provide a check against the abuse of judicial power. Moreover, the press should be entitled to report the proceedings for the benefit of the public who cannot, for one reason or other, attend them. Equally, comment on the conduct of a particular trial or on the general administration of justice may promote, rather than impede, the fairness of legal proceedings. These arguments explain the common law's strong commitment to the principle of open justice: the right of the public and press to attend legal proceedings and to report them fully. Formulated by the House of Lords in *Scott* v. *Scott*,[5] the principle 'provides a safeguard against judicial arbitrariness or idiosyncrasy and maintains the public confidence in the administration of justice'.[6]

But in some situations the exercise of free speech or press rights might be incompatible with the administration of justice. A newspaper might, for instance,

---

[4] See further s. 4 below.
[5] [1913] AC 417, discussed below in s. 4.
[6] Lord Diplock in *A-G* v. *Leveller Magazine Ltd* [1979] AC 440, 450, HL.

damage the chance of an accused receiving a fair trial by giving publicity to prejudicial evidence or to his confession or previous convictions. Or a newspaper might engage in a sustained press campaign intended to influence the course of prospective litigation, as occurred in the famous *Sunday Times* case considered in section 3 of this chapter. In these cases the publicity is clearly covered by freedom of speech and of the press, but at the same time it may well interfere with fair trial rights.

But Hans Linde, a state judge as well as a noted First Amendment scholar, has argued that there is no real conflict between the right to freedom of speech and of the press on the one hand and the right to a fair trial on the other.[7] Both rights are only guaranteed under the US Constitution against the state. The law must not interfere with press freedom and must not violate the right to a fair trial. But fair trial rights cannot be invoked against the press or other private media institutions. So while a court, as a branch of government, may violate the right to a fair trial by allowing a case tainted by media publicity to proceed (or by rejecting an appeal in these circumstances), it cannot impose duties on the press to respect fair trial rights by holding it liable for contempt. From an American perspective, this point is well made, for it is the case that constitutional rights in the United States generally only bind the state. But there is no reason why constitutional rights need be understood in this way. Germany, and to some extent other jurisdictions, have a different understanding of basic rights: they represent values which affect the whole legal order and may therefore limit the scope of permissible private behaviour.[8] Powerful private institutions, such as the press and other media, should respect fundamental constitutional rights such as the right to a fair trial, a perspective which may require the courts to balance that right against freedom of speech and of the press. On that approach, it does make sense to refer to a conflict between two fundamental rights, the weight of which must be assessed in the context of the particular facts.

Even if the notion of a constitutional right to a fair trial enforceable against the media is dismissed, the law has at least to resolve a conflict between two strong public interests: that in the freedom of the media to cover and report legal proceedings, on the one hand, and on the other in the fairness of those proceedings. It may be clear, for example, that a witness will not give evidence if he knows that the media are present and will fully report what he says.[9] In that situation there is surely a clash between two important interests. In other situations, admittedly, restrictions on free speech and freedom of the press may be imposed, which are more difficult to justify. One example is the variety of contempt of court known as 'scandalizing the court', to be discussed in section 2 of this chapter. Another is the

---

[7] H. A. Linde, 'Fair Trials and Press Freedom: Two Rights against the State' (1977) 13 *Willamette Law Jo* 211.

[8] See ch. II, *passim* above, and ch. IV, s. 5 above for discussion of the extent to which free speech rights may be claimed against private persons.

[9] For further discussion of this point, see s. 4 below.

prohibition in United Kingdom law of any disclosure of jury deliberations imposed by the common law and extended by the Contempt of Court Act 1981.[10] At common law the disclosure of deliberations amounted to a contempt of court only if it tended to imperil the finality of jury verdicts or adversely to affect the attitude of prospective jurors.[11] Under section 8 of the 1981 Act it is a contempt of court to disclose or solicit any details of opinions or arguments, or votes cast, by members of the jury during the course of their deliberations. It covers disclosure of these matters by the media and other third parties, as well as by members of the jury themselves;[12] it inhibits bona fide research into jury deliberations and informed public discussion of the merits of the jury system.[13]

Free speech may conflict with interests (or rights) other than the right to a fair trial. For example, contempt of court proceedings were successfully taken when a newspaper, contrary to the judge's direction, published the names of blackmail victims who had given evidence under pseudonym.[14] The court made the point that to allow identification might deter victims from giving evidence in criminal proceedings; equally, it is plausible in these circumstances to justify contempt proceedings as necessary to protect the safety and privacy interest of the persons whose identity was concealed.[15] Similar factors also underlie the statutory provisions prohibiting the publication of any matter identifying a complainant of rape or other sexual offence during her lifetime. There was considerable evidence to suggest that women had been deterred from taking complaints to the police because they did not wish to attract publicity when the trial took place.[16] The trial judge has a limited discretion to remove the restriction, if, for instance, it is clear that identification of the complainant is necessary to persuade potential witnesses to come forward. In these circumstances, the interests of a fair trial would exceptionally outweigh the protection of the complainant's privacy.

Usually, however, the protection of privacy is thought more important in this context than the right of the press and other media to identify the complainant or the interest of the public in receiving that information. Interestingly, the Supreme Court of Canada has rejected a challenge on freedom of expression grounds to an equivalent prohibition.[17] It upheld an absolute ban on the identification of the victim of a rape or sexual assault, whether it was imposed at the request of the

---

[10] The relationship of the common law and statutory rules is fully considered by Lord Hope in *R v. Mirza* [2004] 1 AC 1118, paras. 78–93.   [11] *A-G v. New Statesman* [1981] 1 QB 1, DC.

[12] *A-G v. Associated Newspapers* [1994] 2 AC 538, HL. The House of Lords rejected the argument that application of the provision to the press would be incompatible with the guarantee of the right to freedom of expression under ECHR, art. 10.

[13] See J. Jaconelli, *Open Justice: A Critique of the Public Trial* (Oxford, 2002), ch. 7 for a critique of this provision.   [14] *R v. Socialist Worker Printers and Publishers, ex p A-G* [1975] QB 637, DC.

[15] Courts now have statutory power to issue directions to forbid the publication of the name (of a witness) or other matter which has been withheld from the public in proceedings before it: Contempt of Court Act 1981, s. 11.

[16] Sexual Offences (Amendment) Act 1992, s. 1(1). The restriction was originally imposed in 1976, to implement the recommendations of the Report of the Advisory Group on Rape (1975, Cmnd 6352).   [17] *Canadian Newspapers v. A-G of Canada* [1988] 2 SCR 122.

complainant or prosecutor or at the discretion of the judge; without anonymity, many victims would be too inhibited to report offences. The limit on the freedom of the media was minimal in that they remained free to attend the trial and report all aspects of the case, save for facts disclosing the claimant's identity.

English law provides in fact for a number of restrictions on the reporting of judicial proceedings.[18] Some of them are imposed under the general law of contempt, others by specific legislative provision. In some instances the objective is to ensure a fair trial or to protect the authority of the judiciary, while in others the aim is to safeguard the privacy or security of a person who might otherwise be deterred from taking part in legal proceedings. But in almost all situations the law does take freedom of speech and freedom of the press into account. It is now rare for an English court to ignore the importance of freedom of speech in this context, as it did in *Home Office* v. *Harman*.[19] In that case, a majority of the House of Lords held that a solicitor committed contempt of court when she had allowed a journalist to see documents disclosed to her on discovery. The journalist used them as the basis for a newspaper article on conditions in a special prison unit. Lord Diplock denied that the case raised any free speech issue. But, as Lord Scarman pointed out in dissent, the case plainly demanded a balancing of freedom of expression and the interest in keeping the documents confidential. The papers had been read in open court, so there was little, in Lord Scarman's view, to put in the scales against freedom of expression. (The European Human Rights Commission held admissible a challenge to this ruling under Article 10 of the ECHR;[20] the Rules of Court were changed to permit wider use of documents disclosed to a party in certain circumstances.[21])

This chapter will discuss two types of contempt which clearly raise major free expression issues: attacks on the judiciary (section 2) and publications which are thought likely to prejudice the fairness of future legal proceedings, particularly criminal trials (section 3). Section 4 concerns the open justice principle, under which the press and public are free to attend and report legal proceedings. Among other issues, it raises the questions whether freedom of speech entails rights of access to attend, and to film and broadcast, legal proceedings.

2. Attacks on the Judiciary

Almost all legal systems afford the judiciary some protection against vicious criticism.[22] The variety of contempt, colourfully described as 'scandalizing the

---

[18] See further, s. 4(iv) below.　　　[19] [1983] AC 280.

[20] 10038/82, *Harman* v. *UK* 38 D & R 53.　　　[21] For details, see Feldman, 1006.

[22] For a comparative study of the law in a number of European countries, see M. K. Addo (ed.), *Freedom of Expression and the Criticism of Judges* (Aldershot: Ashgate, 2000). Also see Miller (n. 1 above), ch. 12, and I. Cram, *A Virtue Less Cloistered: Courts, Speech and Constitutions* (Oxford: Hart, 2002), ch. 5.

court', can be traced back in English law to the celebrated judgment of Wilmot J. in *Almon's* case.[23] It is a contempt of court to mount a scurrilous or vicious attack on the judiciary by, for example, accusing it, or a particular judge, of arbitrary and corrupt conduct. Such an attack is considered to undermine the authority of the judiciary and public confidence in the proper administration of justice. The object is not to protect the judges personally, so comment on the character of a judge unrelated to his performance on the bench falls outside the scope of the offence. Proceedings have always been rare. At one time during the last years of the nineteenth century the view was expressed that this form of contempt procedure was obsolete.[24] Its use was also subject to criticism in Parliament. In 1883 Lord Fitzgerald in the House of Lords argued that the offence unduly fettered press freedom; he pointed to its absence from the criminal codes of the states in the USA.[25] But successful proceedings were taken on a handful of occasions in the first three decades of the twentieth century. For example, in one leading case, the editor of a Birmingham newspaper was fined for writing a stinging article on the 'terrors of Mr Justice Darling', who had warned the local press not to publish details of any indecent matter given in evidence in an obscenity trial.[26] When the *New Statesman* published an article suggesting that Dr Marie Stopes, the birth control advocate, could not expect a fair hearing in a libel action presided over by Mr Justice Avory, a Roman Catholic, Lord Hewart CJ held it had committed a contempt.[27] The allegation of unfairness and lack of impartiality lowered the judge's authority, even though it seems to have been conceded in argument that the article was not suggesting any deliberate bias on his part.

It is clear, however, that reasonable and moderate criticism of judicial decisions does not constitute contempt. In the leading Privy Council ruling in *Ambard* v. *Attorney-General for Trinidad and Tobago*,[28] Lord Atkin distinguished the imputation of improper motives and malicious comment on the one hand from good faith criticism on the other. Both in his opinion, and in that of Lord Denning MR in a more recent Court of Appeal case,[29] emphasis was placed on the importance of the freedom, particularly of the press, to comment on the administration of justice. In the latter case, the Court of Appeal also observed that the factual accuracy and good taste of the article were irrelevant; in this respect contempt law is not as restrictive of hostile and inaccurate criticism as the law of libel. In fact no successful application to commit for this type of contempt has been made in England since 1930.

---

[23] (1765) Wilm 243, 97 ER 94. For a critical account of the background to the case, see Sir J. Fox (1908) 24 *LQR* 184 and 266, and for a history of scandalizing, see D. Hay, 'Contempt by Scandalizing the Court: A Political History of the First Hundred Years' (1987) 25 *Osgoode Hall Law Jo* 431.   [24] *McLeod* v. *St Aubyn* [1899] AC 549, 561 per Lord Morris, PC.
[25] 277 HL Deb (3rd ser.), cols. 1612–13.   [26] *R* v. *Gray* [1900] 2 QB 36, DC.
[27] *R* v. *New Statesman, ex p DPP* (1928) 44 TLR 301, DC.   [28] [1936] AC 322.
[29] *R* v. *Metropolitan Police Commissioner, ex p Blackburn* [1968] 2 QB 150.

However, proceedings in cases have been brought with success in Australia, Canada, and South Africa.[30] The High Court of Australia, declining to allow an appeal from a contempt conviction, held it was important that public confidence in the administration of justice should not be shaken by baseless attacks on the integrity of the judiciary.[31] In this case an allegation had been made that the Federal Court had changed its mind in an earlier contempt case because of trades union pressure. A Canadian case nicely illustrates an important aspect of this type of contempt.[32] A Minister of Transport in Manitoba accused a magistrate of political bias in refusing to quash a criminal information laid against him: 'The fact that he [the magistrate] is a loyal Conservative and had been appointed by the Conservative administration can't be overlooked.' These remarks, coupled with a threat to take steps to have the magistrate removed, were regarded as calculated to lower his authority and therefore constituted contempt of court. In these circumstances the attack on the judiciary could be considered particularly dangerous because it came from a member of the government and therefore might be regarded as a threat to its independence. However, from another perspective, the comments of this kind, though outrageous in tone, form the stuff of political debate and should be fully covered by freedom of speech; it is wrong, it might be thought, to insulate the judiciary from criticism, even by politicians.

The Privy Council has also upheld convictions for scandalizing in two cases from Mauritius. In this context it is salutary to remember that at the end of the nineteenth century, Lord Morris had said that the offence might still have a place in less developed communities where there was a need to foster and defend the independence and authority of the judiciary.[33] In *Badry* v. *DPP*[34] it declined to interfere with a ruling of the Supreme Court of Mauritius that the appellant had committed contempt. He had suggested that a judge had been improperly influenced in treating a compensation claim by the fact that the defendant was an important business on the island. But the Privy Council did hold that contempt of court did not protect bodies other than courts, so the appellant had not committed the offence by vigorous criticism of a judicial commission of inquiry. In a more recent decision, the Privy Council explicitly accepted that it was easier to see the need for an offence of scandalizing on a small island, where the authority of the judiciary may be relatively vulnerable to challenge.[35] Where publication created a real risk of undermining confidence in the administration of justice, a contempt conviction, as in this case, could be regarded as a necessary restriction on freedom of expression. However, the Privy Council did intimate that in some

---

[30] See e.g. *A-G for New South Wales* v. *Mundey* [1972] 2 NSWLR 887, NSW Sup Ct; *R* v. *Murphy, ex p A-G of New Brunswick* (1969) 4 DLR (3d) 289, New Brunswick Supreme Court; *State* v. *Van Niekerk* (1970) 3 SA 655 (T), Claassen J.   [31] *Gallagher* v. *Durack* (1983) 152 CLR 238.
[32] *Re Borowski* (1971) 19 DLR (3d) 537, Manitoba QB.   [33] N. 24 above.
[34] [1983] 2 AC 297.
[35] *Ahnee* v. *DPP* [1999] 2 AC 294. The case concerned false allegations that the Chief Justice of Mauritius had chosen the judges to hear libel proceedings brought by him.

circumstances a suggestion that a court had acted from improper motives would not amount to contempt, in this way qualifying the distinction drawn by Lord Atkin in *Ambard*.

French law seems to take a particularly strict view of criticism of the judiciary. The Penal Code was amended in 1958 to create a new offence of abuse of courts and tribunals, similar to the common law's 'scandalizing the court'.[36] Proceedings were brought under this provision when a Marxist journal published an attack on an arbitration board which had upheld the termination of the employment contracts of Peugeot workers; the decision was characterized as 'justice de classe'.[37] The state won the case. It appears that there is no need to show an intention to bring justice into disrepute, and moreover, in contrast to the position in modern English law, the form and extravagance of the article's wording may well be material.

The penalization of attacks on the judiciary is surely challengeable on free speech grounds. An attack on the judiciary is clearly covered by a free speech or freedom of expression clause. It is hard to distinguish it from political speech which lies at the core of freedom of speech. Indeed, just as the offence of sedition is in itself incompatible with any serious commitment to free speech, so it can be argued that a vituperative onslaught on the judiciary as a whole or on an individual judge should be regarded as protected speech.[38] Moreover, the judiciary, unlike the legislature and executive, is not politically accountable. Sustained criticism of the performance of a particular judge might be the only way to induce his resignation.

The best argument for the retention of some specific offence to protect the standing and authority of the judiciary is that it may need protection against a mixture of political and public pressure. This may be particularly true where judges are career civil servants, as is generally the case in civil law jurisdictions, or do not enjoy security of tenure. The criminal law provides the judiciary with the necessary protection to resist sustained media criticism of a line of decisions; such criticism might threaten their independence if it were supported by members of the government or other prominent politicians.[39] As Stephen Sedley has pointed out, there is a difference between public criticism of the judiciary which seeks to improve its quality and 'judge-bashing, an easy but foolish activity...'.[40] Moreover, it is usually thought inappropriate for judges publicly to defend their decisions, let alone to take libel proceedings to protect their reputation against

[36] Art. 226. See L. Neville Brown, 'Outrage au tribunal' (1974) 15 *Les Cahiers de Droit* 741, 752–3; B. van Niekerk, 'The Cloistering of Virtue: Freedom of Speech and the Administration of Justice' (1978) 95 *South African Law Jo* 363 and 534; M. Chesterman, 'Contempt: In the Common Law, but not the Civil Law' (1997) 46 *ICLQ* 521, 532–6.

[37] Schroedt case, *Gazette du Palais* 1963(2) 350.   [38] See ch. V, ss. 2 and 3 above.

[39] In *State* v. *Mamabolo* (2001) 10 BHRC 493, the South Africa Constitutional Court held that prosecutions for scandalizing were in some circumstances compatible with freedom of expression. But it was wrong to punish a state official for this offence, when he was in no position to interfere with a judicial order.   [40] Foreword to Addo (n. 22 above).

unfounded allegations of bias or corruption. These points perhaps explain why civil law jurisdictions such as France are willing to protect the judiciary through specific criminal law offences. The arguments may also explain the Privy Council decisions from Mauritius. Judges in common law jurisdictions such as England, Australia, and Canada enjoy security of tenure. Moreover, chosen from independent legal professions, they are relatively impervious to criticism, and are in less need of the protection afforded by contempt laws.

The Phillimore Committee on Contempt of Court, which reported in 1974, did question the need for the offence of scandalizing in English law. It did not think it was acceptable to require a judge to bring a private action for libel to protect his reputation against intemperate criticism.[41] As Arthur Goodhart had pointed out in an article in 1935,[42] the prospect of a judge being cross-examined before a jury on his political attitudes is hardly an enticing one. Instead the Committee recommended that a new strictly defined offence should replace 'scandalizing the court', the advantages of this reform being the achievement of more certainty in the law and the abolition of the summary contempt procedure in this area. The Canadian Law Reform Commission made similar proposals in 1977.[43] A further problem then arises on which the Phillimore Committee and the English Law Commission came to different conclusions: should the truth of a specific allegation concerning the integrity of a judge be a defence to a prosecution for the proposed offence? The Committee thought it should not, unless the defendant also showed that publication was for the public benefit, while the Law Commission felt that a true allegation of judicial corruption should never be penalized.[44] There are difficulties in both solutions. The former would require a jury to decide when it is in the public interest to make a true allegation about the integrity of a judge; some jurymen might find it easy here to adopt Mill's position that revelation of the truth is always for the public good. On the other hand, the Law Commission's proposal would lead to potentially embarrassing inquiries into the accuracy of the allegation every time contempt proceedings were brought.

A better approach might be that suggested by two judges in the Ontario Court of Appeal when it considered the compatibility of the scandalizing offence with the right to freedom of expression guaranteed by the Charter.[45] In their view proceedings could only be taken for the offence where the Crown could show that the attack on the judiciary posed a real danger to the fair administration of justice. Otherwise the restriction on freedom of expression could not be regarded as a necessary and proportionate restriction on freedom of expression. (A third judge would have gone further and held the offence in all circumstances an unwarranted

---

[41] Report of the Phillimore Committee on Contempt of Court (1974, Cmnd 5794), para. 162.

[42] 'Newspapers and Contempt of Court in English Law' (1935) 48 *Harvard Law Rev* 885.

[43] Working Paper No. 20 (1977).

[44] Report of the Phillimore Committee (n. 41 above), paras. 165–6; Law Commission Report No. 96, *Offences Relating to Interference with the Course of Justice* (1979), para. 3.68.

[45] *R* v. *Kopyto* (1987) 47 DLR (4th) 213.

infringement of free expression.) This requirement goes much further than the traditional requirement that the attack must be calculated to undermine the authority of the judiciary; in effect, it would seem that this variety of contempt is now a dead letter in Canada.

This approach is strikingly similar to that adopted in the United States. In federal cases, the relevant statute has been narrowly construed so as to confine contempt to misbehaviour in or physically near to the courtroom.[46] In *Bridges* v. *California* Black J. observed *obiter* that loss of respect for the judiciary was not a serious enough evil to justify abridgement by the states of free speech.[47] Even Frankfurter J., a consistent admirer of the English law of contempt, held unconstitutional proceedings initiated in Florida when a newspaper had published articles criticizing a judge for undue sensitivity to defendants accused of rape;[48] only comment affecting a *pending* decision could properly be proscribed without violating the First Amendment. American judges plainly reject the argument that public confidence in their authority and in the fair administration of justice will necessarily be shaken by hostile comment. It is the truth of the comment, not the mere fact that it is made, which might in some circumstances undermine such confidence. If the remarks are true, the public should certainly be allowed to digest them.

The decisions of the European Human Rights Court in this area are inconsistent. Two cases have upheld the application of national libel laws to penalize the publication of serious allegations against members of the judiciary. In *Barford* v. *Denmark*,[49] the Court refused to hold incompatible with the Convention the conviction of a journalist for the publication of an article suggesting that two part-time lay judges in Greenland had been prejudiced in their handling of a tax case because they were employed by a local authority. A closely divided Court also upheld the convictions of Austrian journalists for alleging bias and bullying by some judges in their conduct of criminal trials.[50] In contrast, in a more recent case from Belgium the Strasbourg Court was prepared to treat allegations of political bias by judges handling sensitive custody disputes as the expression of political opinion, and therefore entitled to strong protection under the Convention, unless there was no factual basis at all for the comments.[51] Although these were strictly libel cases, from the perspective of freedom of speech they raise the same fundamental question as that posed in common law scandalizing cases: should attacks on the integrity of a judge or on the entire judiciary be equated with political speech, or is it right to give judges stronger protection from such attacks because they are less able to defend themselves and as a result more vulnerable to strong criticism?

The offence of scandalizing the court is now so unimportant in practice, at least in English law, that it may appear fruitless to spend much space in debating its

---

[46] *Nye* v. *US* 313 US 33 (1940).   [47] 314 US 252, 270–1 (1941).
[48] *Pennekamp* v. *Florida* 328 US 331, 365–9 (1946).   [49] (1989) 13 EHRR 493.
[50] *Präger and Oberschlick* v. *Austria* (1995) 21 EHRR 1.
[51] *De Haes* v. *Belgium* (1998) 25 EHRR 1.

justification. But it is possible that newspaper editors are occasionally deterred from vigorous comment because of a slight risk of prosecution. In theoretical terms criticism of the judiciary should almost certainly be treated as a form of political speech, and therefore enjoy the highest degree of legal protection. The difference between the approaches adopted on the one hand in the United States and now in Canada, and on the other in continental Europe and some Commonwealth jurisdictions, partly reflects divergent perceptions of the functions and importance of the courts; it is easier for a society which fully accepts the political role of the judiciary to tolerate abusive criticism of it. It is unclear which perspective is reflected in English law, where the offence of scandalizing still exists, but is never used. It is pertinent perhaps to point out in this context that abusive criticism of the legislature and its members remains, in theory, subject to the contempt powers of the Houses of Parliament. In principle, however, exercise of this contempt power would be as incompatible with freedom of political speech as sedition laws.[52] So another explanation for the odd position of the scandalizing variety of contempt of court in England is that respect for established institutions remains an important social value, which might in some extraordinary circumstances be given more weight than freedom of expression.

3. Prejudice to Legal Proceedings

In this section of the chapter we move into deeper waters. While the offence of scandalizing the court can only be justified by reference to the public interest in the administration of justice, proceedings to restrain or punish the publication of matter which might prejudice a fair trial appear to involve conflicts between two fundamental individual rights or interests. This is most obvious in the case of criminal prosecutions, where the life or liberty of the accused may be at stake. Moreover, the verdict in common law countries is determined by a jury. Juries are a priori more likely to be prejudiced by damaging newspaper articles about the accused than are judges. Connected with this point is the argument that to tolerate publication in the press of incriminating information is to make nonsense of the rules of evidence (particularly important in criminal cases) which exclude the admission of testimony which is prejudicial rather than probative. These relatively precise contentions are, however, frequently coupled with a broader argument that newspaper trial, or trial by media, is inherently undesirable.

English law, as will be seen, has been relaxed by the Contempt of Court Act 1981, but it still imposes restrictions on the media which are more onerous than those imposed in some other Commonwealth jurisdictions and which would certainly be regarded as incompatible with freedom of speech and of the press in the United States. Indeed, courts in the United States adopt a radically different

---

[52] See ch. V, s. 3 above.

approach, apparently denying that the conflict of values is as acute as it appears, or alternatively seeking to resolve it by other means. In any case free speech and press rights are not subordinated to competing rights to fair trial.

(i) Arguments of principle

The English law of contempt is concerned with the potential effect of the publication on the subsequent trial.[53] It is irrelevant whether it did in fact prejudice the jury or the court.[54] Indeed, the actual impact on juries of publications discussing, say, the previous convictions of the accused or his general character, or assessing the legal merits of forthcoming legal proceedings, is impossible to determine in England, given that research into their deliberations is precluded by the Contempt of Court Act 1981.[55] (Some reliance can be placed on findings in other jurisdictions where research may be conducted on how juries work;[56] moreover, inferences can be drawn from studies involving simulated cases, though there is some scepticism whether they do justice to the impact of publicity in actual cases.[57]) In the absence of persuasive research data concerning the actual impact of prejudicial media publicity, the law must make assumptions about its likely impact.[58] English law assumes first, that certain types of publication may cause a serious prejudice to future legal proceedings, and secondly, that it is desirable to deter the press and other branches of the media from publishing material where that risk is particularly acute, despite the impact the law has on press freedom and freedom of speech. These two assumptions should be considered in turn.

While it may be difficult, or even impossible, to determine the actual impact of media publicity on juries or judges, the conclusion that in some circumstances it may have considerable impact is a reasonable one. The arguments for freedom of speech itself assume that speech may persuade and influence.[59] Politicians, the media, and advertisers all operate on this assumption. The burden of proof is surely on sceptics to show that media publicity is unlikely to have any, or any significant, impact on readers, listeners, and viewers. Their most powerful point is that juries can be directed to exclude from consideration anything they have read

---

[53] See Miller (n. 1 above), para. 5.41.

[54] There is no requirement under the ECHR that state law must require proof of actual influence on the proceedings: *Worm* v. *Austria* (1997) 25 EHRR 454, para. 54.

[55] Under s. 8 it is a contempt to disclose particulars of jury deliberations, itself a restriction on freedom of speech: see s. 1 of this chapter.

[56] See the research in New South Wales, M. Chesterman, J. Chan, and S. Hampton, *Managing Prejudicial Publicity* (Law and Justice Foundation of NSW, 2001), suggesting that in a small minority of cases publicity might have had an impact on jury verdicts—though even then it did not follow that the verdict was 'unsafe'.

[57] T. M. Honess et al., 'Empirical and Legal Perspectives on the Impact of Pre-trial Publicity' [2002] Crim LR 719, 721–2.

[58] See Sedley LJ in *A-G* v. *Guardian Newspapers Ltd* [1999] EMLR 904, 926.

[59] This is certainly true of the arguments from truth and democracy considered in ch. I, s. 2 above.

or heard outside the context of the court proceedings and to consider only the evidence given, and arguments made, to the court. That point can be met. It is probably right that in some, perhaps most, cases the risk of prejudice can be reduced by an appropriate direction from the trial judge; the suggestion, however, that in all circumstances a direction will entirely remove the impact of a welter of prejudicial material in the media is implausible. Indeed, it seems inconsistent to argue that members of a jury will be influenced by a judicial direction, but never by what they might have read or seen over the previous weeks or months. This view is consistent with recent English decisions on the exercise of contempt powers,[60] and the important ruling of the Supreme Court of Canada in *Dagenais* v. *Canadian Broadcasting Corpn.*[61] They hold that juries will generally comply with a judicial direction to consider the case on the evidence given in court and disregard extraneous matter. But they do not suggest that a direction will necessarily cure the impact of sustained pre-trial publicity.

Of course, the degree of influence from media publicity will vary from one case to another. In some circumstances—in particular, the publication of strongly prejudicial publicity *during* the course of the trial itself—the impact may be enormous. In other cases—the publication in a local newspaper far removed from the likely place of trial—the risk of adverse impact can be assumed to be so insignificant that the law should discount it. Specific publicity disclosing previous convictions or misconduct will usually create more prejudice than general publicity about the type of offence at issue in the pending proceedings. Indeed, as we will see, the law in England and other jurisdictions has evolved a number of criteria to assess whether the risk is sufficiently significant to justify legal intervention.

The second assumption underlying and justifying English contempt law is that it is more important to avert a real risk of injustice from the impact of media publicity than it is to allow full freedom of the press in this area. Fair trial rights are given priority over freedom of speech. This traditional preference has now been challenged, notably in Canada where the majority of the Supreme Court in *Dagenais* held that the common law rule allowing a judge to impose a ban on media publicity should be modified, consequent on the guarantee given to freedom of expression by the Charter. Publication bans should only be ordered when they are necessary to prevent a real and substantial risk to the fairness of the trial and when the beneficial impact of the ban outweighs the damage done to freedom of expression.[62] A similar approach had been taken by the European Human Rights Court in the famous *Sunday Times* case when it assessed the compatibility of the common law with freedom of expression guaranteed by Article 10 of the Convention: in its view it was not called on to balance two competing rights—freedom of expression and the right to a fair trial—but to determine only whether

---

[60] *Ex p Telegraph plc* [1993] 1 WLR 980, CA; *A-G* v. *BBC, Hat Trick Productions* [1997] EMLR 76, DC.   [61] [1994] 3 SCR 835.

[62] The Court held that it was necessary for a judge to consider whether other measures, less restrictive of freedom of expression, could be used to avoid the risk of injustice: see s. 3(iii) below.

the restriction on the former imposed by the common law was really necessary.[63] Indeed, that approach gives precedence to freedom of expression and press freedom over other goals. The Court in Strasbourg was almost certainly influenced by the context of the case, a press campaign assessing the merits of a civil action which would be decided by a judge without a jury. There was therefore no suggestion that the publications would influence the result of the action.

Of course, it is clear that contempt law necessarily penalizes or deters the exercise of press freedom and free speech, while the infringement of the right to fair trial is assumed, albeit that assumption may be reasonable. For that reason the US Supreme Court has in effect ruled that this type of contempt of court is precluded by the First Amendment. On the other hand, in defence of the common law it can be said that a defendant's right to a fair trial will be seriously violated if he is wrongly convicted as a result of media publicity, while contempt proceedings will generally lead at most to a fine on the newspaper, or their threat may induce an editor to postpone publication of material concerning an accused until after legal proceedings have been concluded. There is infringement of the right to freedom of speech and of the press, but it has much less serious consequences than those which might flow from denial of the right to a fair trial.

A second, quite different justification for the common law of contempt is that 'trial by newspaper' or 'media trial' is intrinsically abhorrent. This was put forward by some of the Law Lords in the *Sunday Times* case.[64] As mentioned above, the case involved civil proceedings, which would (in England) not be tried by a jury, but heard before a judge. The House of Lords unanimously held that publication of a newspaper article, assessing some of the issues in a pending (though dormant) negligence action against Distillers for the deformities caused by its thalidomide drug, would be in contempt of court. The grant of an injunction to restrain publication was primarily justified by the argument that it purported to prejudge the questions which would come before the trial court.[65] Subsequently this ruling was held by the European Court to be a breach of Article 10 of the Convention,[66] and the law in the United Kingdom has accordingly been amended. There has been some debate whether the technical changes made by the Contempt of Court Act 1981—in particular, the rule that there may only be a contempt if the proceedings prejudiced are *active*, that is, in civil cases, set down for trial—adequately meet the requirements of the European Court's ruling. The more interesting question of principle remains, however, what was the basis for the House of Lords finding of contempt.

The point of law was one on which there was very little authority. Some of the members of the House admitted that there was no real risk of the article influencing a High Court judge, or the witnesses, so that the conventional 'prejudice'

---

[63] *Sunday Times* v. *UK* (1979) 2 EHRR 245, 281.
[64] *A-G* v. *Times Newspapers Ltd* [1974] AC 273.
[65] The prior restraint aspect of this case is discussed in ch. IV, s. 4(i) above.
[66] *Sunday Times* v. *UK* (n. 63 above), considered in s. 3(ii) below.

argument applicable in criminal cases was irrelevant. Lords Diplock and Simon found it was a contempt to put pressure on a party to litigation to settle to the other's advantage, particularly where the pressure took the form of a press campaign which held that party up to obloquy and abuse. This principle was perhaps only repudiated by Lord Cross. But the majority ground for the decision was that the offending article would lead to public prejudgement of the negligence issue. In other words, trial by newspaper as such should be proscribed by English law. Some of the Law Lords tried to find rational justifications for what appears to be almost an intuitive conclusion on their part. In their view, trial by the media would lead to disrespect for the law; the functions of the courts would be usurped by newspapers and television; unpopular people and causes would fare badly if there were widespread press campaigns. Lord Morris put it in these rhetorical terms: '... is it not contrary to the fitness of things that there should be unrestricted expressions of opinion as to whether the merits lie with one party to litigation rather than with another?'[67]

One or two of these arguments on close scrutiny collapse into the 'prejudice to a fair trial' justification, hard to support in the context of a civil case, or the 'pressure principle', openly advocated by only two members of the House. The view that the press is usurping the functions of the courts will rarely be sustainable. A typical newspaper campaign will employ a range of moral and social, as well as legal, arguments; it will rarely attempt to formulate arguments in the way in which they would be put to the court which has to resolve the matter. The campaign against Distillers was as much directed to the moral issues as it was designed to draw attention to questions of legal responsibility. Further, the press cannot make a legally binding award, so in that precise sense the functions of the courts cannot be usurped. There are perhaps two better arguments, touched on in one or two of the speeches, but never fully developed. The first is that in the long term trial by newspaper will undermine the authority of the judiciary; the second is that parties have some sort of right to a dispassionate assessment of their litigation, wholly free from public discussion. I will take the latter of these arguments first.

Lord Diplock referred to litigants' 'constitutional right to have their legal rights and obligations ascertained and enforced in courts of law'; the exercise of this right would be inhibited by public discussion of the merits of the case before the court pronounced on them.[68] He might have had in mind the risk of prejudice to the outcome of the proceedings resulting from such discussion, or the risk that the court's functions will be usurped. But both these points have already been found unconvincing. Alternatively, Lord Diplock might have been suggesting that media discussion infringes an independent right of access to the courts. But this also is unpersuasive. For it is far from clear how this right would be infringed by press discussion of the legal and moral issues involved in litigation; no matter how prejudiced the treatment of the issues by the media, the parties remain free to go to the courts for an authoritative and binding resolution.

---

[67] [1974] AC 273, 303.   [68] Ibid., 310.

This leaves the argument that trial by newspaper undermines the authority of the judiciary, the central theme of Lord Reid's speech in the House of Lords and the justification for its ruling given in the subsequent proceedings in Strasbourg. The European Court itself accepted in the *Sunday Times* case,[69] and later in *Worm* v. *Austria*,[70] that in appropriate circumstances legal restrictions may be imposed on the press and other media to protect the authority of the judiciary: states are entitled to ensure that the public has confidence in the capacity of the courts to provide a proper forum for the settlement of litigation. The claim is that public confidence in the administration of justice and resort to the courts might seriously decline if it were widely believed that judges were influenced by press campaigns. Conceivably, the media rather than the legal process might be used to resolve disputes. While not absolutely far-fetched, the claim is surely exaggerated. The press has no inclination to take up more than a handful of causes, and in any case, as has been pointed out, it cannot do more than persuade. Litigants will always resort to the courts if they want a coercive order to protect their rights. In fact the reason for the campaign in *Sunday Times* was that recourse to the courts had hitherto proved to be futile; in some of the cases, the writs in the negligence actions had been issued several years before the offending article was written and there was no immediate prospect of satisfactory settlements or trials. For this reason, as well as the intense public interest in the saga, the *Sunday Times* case was an unfortunate one in which to invoke, as Lord Cross did, an absolute contempt rule, applicable no matter how remote the risk of prejudice, for the purpose of preventing 'a gradual slide towards trial by newspaper or television.'[71]

There is really no strong justification for treating as contempt of court a publication prejudging the issues in a forthcoming *civil* case, where there can be no suggestion that the tribunal might be prejudiced by it. In the first place, it is difficult to identify what public interest is served by the imposition of penal sanctions, let alone the grant of an injunction, a judicial prior restraint, as in the *Sunday Times* case itself. Perhaps it is impossible to point to anything more than a general fear that sustained press campaigns might in the long term undermine confidence in the courts as institutions for resolving legal disputes. But the argument then resembles that already canvassed in the context of the earlier discussion of scandalizing the court: is it right to restrict freedom of speech in order to protect the standing and authority of the judicial branch of government? As we saw in section 2 of this chapter, commitment to free speech means that such restrictions, except in extremely unusual circumstances, should not be sustained, any more than they should be in the context of hostile criticism of government and the legislature. Indeed, one valuable function of the type of campaign conducted by the *Sunday Times* is to arouse public interest in the legal process and its apparent inability (in that case) to provide speedy compensation to a group of vulnerable claimants.

[69] (1979) 2 EHRR 245.   [70] (1997) 25 EHRR 454, para. 40.
[71] [1974] AC 273, 323.

These arguments do not apply with the same force to criminal cases, particularly those tried by a jury. The fear in that context is not the general abhorrence of trial by newspaper, but that the jury (or perhaps lay magistrates) may be influenced, consciously or unconsciously, by media publicity which predisposes them to convict the defendant. The next part of this section is concerned with rules of contempt law which try to avert this danger.

(ii) Legal restrictions on prejudicial publicity

The English law in this area has been significantly modified by the Contempt of Court Act 1981. It was enacted to implement the recommendations of the Phillimore Committee on Contempt of Court and to bring the law into line with the decision of the European Human Rights Court in the *Sunday Times* case. The Strasbourg Court had held that the common law strict liability rule under which it was a contempt to publish any material which tended to prejudice the outcome of pending legal proceedings, irrespective of any intention to bring about such prejudice, could not be sustained as a restriction on freedom of expression, necessary to maintain the authority of the judiciary. It was, therefore, essential for Parliament to reformulate the rule. Under the 1981 legislation this variety of contempt is only committed by a publication 'which creates a substantial risk that the course of justice in the proceedings in question will be seriously impeded or prejudiced'.[72] Further, the strict liability rule is to apply to a publication from the time when proceedings are 'active', that is in criminal cases, after the accused has been arrested or a warrant for arrest has been issued;[73] there are defences where the publisher or distributor against whom proceedings are brought was not negligent, for example, the publisher did not know and had no reason to suspect that the proceedings were active.[74].

These changes loosen the constraints imposed on the media. Admittedly, Lord Diplock has said that the legislation was designed to exclude from the strict liability rule only publicity which creates a *remote* risk of prejudice to a fair trial.[75] It might have been thought that the reform confined contempt to really damaging and incriminating publications, but Lord Diplock's interpretation, based on the understandable view that any prejudice to the accused is serious, implied that this goal had not been achieved. However, subsequent decisions show that the reformulation of the strict liability rule has had significant impact. The broadcast of a news bulletin, reporting that an arrested suspect was an escaped IRA terrorist, for example, was held not to amount to a contempt; the transmission occurred nine months before the trial, and it was not repeated in later bulletins.[76] On the other hand, a clear imputation of guilt in a high-profile case, broadcast in a popular

---

[72] Contempt of Court Act 1981, s. 2(2).

[73] Ibid., s. 2(3) and Sch. 1. Civil proceedings are not active until the case has been set down for trial, so for that reason the strict liability rule could not now be applied in the *Sunday Times* case.

[74] Ibid., s. 3.　　　[75] *A-G v. English* [1983] 1 AC 116, 142, HL.

[76] *A-G v. ITN and Others* [1995] 2 All ER 370, DC.

BBC programme and repeated in a second showing of the programme on the following day, did result in successful contempt proceedings.[77] Everything depends on the particular facts. Major considerations are the interval of time between publication and the likely date of the proceedings, the prominence of the 'offending' article in the publication, and the character of the allegations concerning the accused or other prejudicial publicity.[78] For example, courts should in principle be more willing to hold in contempt a publication which discloses the criminal record of a defendant in active criminal proceedings than, say, a television drama containing criminal episodes similar to those in respect of which actual prosecutions have been brought. A programme of that sort might at most create a general climate of hostility to defendants charged with crimes similar to those staged in the drama, but does not imply that anyone in particular is necessarily guilty.[79] That directions will be given to the jury to exclude from their mind such extraneous matter is one factor to take into account in determining whether contempt proceedings under the strict liability rule will succeed, but unlike other factors its weight would not appear to vary from case to case.

The reformulation of the strict liability rule, so that it applies only to publications creating a 'substantial' risk of prejudice to the parties to legal proceedings, does not seem to be directly linked to freedom of speech arguments. The effect of the reform has undoubtedly been to give the media, particularly in practice the tabloid press, wider immunity from contempt proceedings. Nevertheless, the publication, shortly before his trial, of serious allegations about the integrity of a politician or other public figure will probably still be treated as a contempt of court, even though it could be regarded as the exercise of free political speech.

However, another reform in the Contempt of Court Act 1981 does afford some, albeit limited, protection for the freedom of speech and of the press. Section 5 provides that a publication which forms part of a bona fide discussion of public affairs is not to be treated as a contempt if the risk of prejudice to particular legal proceedings is merely incidental to the discussion. Thus, in the *English* case,[80] the House of Lords held that an article endorsing the candidature at a by-election of a 'pro-life' candidate and implying that the tendency of modern medicine is to terminate the life of babies born with mental or physical handicaps did not amount to a contempt, when it was published during the trial of a doctor on a charge of murdering a boy with Down's syndrome. Crucially, Lord Diplock rejected the argument that, as the article could have omitted the prejudicial passages without losing its effectiveness, the protection of the section was forfeited; the test was not

---

[77] *A-G* v. *BBC, Hat Trick Productions* [1997] EMLR 76, DC.

[78] For a comprehensive discussion of these factors, see Schiemann LJ in *A-G* v. *MGN Ltd and Others* [1997] 1 All ER 456, DC.

[79] That was the issue in *Dagenais* v. *Canadian Broadcasting Corpn* [1994] 3 SCR 835, where the Supreme Court of Canada lifted a ban on the showing on television of a fictional account of abuse of children in Catholic institutions at a time when criminal proceedings had started against members of Catholic orders on such charges.   [80] *A-G* v. *English* [1983] 1 AC 116.

whether it was necessary to run the risk of prejudice, but whether the risk was incidental to the wider discussion of mercy killing. However, there is a strong suggestion in his speech that if the trial of the doctor had been specifically mentioned in the article, it would not have enjoyed the protection of the section.[81] But surely the risk of prejudice would have been just as incidental to an important public discussion, which would have taken on a sharper focus in that event?

From the perspective of freedom of speech, section 5 of the Contempt of Court Act provides rather a limited reform, because it protects good faith discussion of public affairs or other matter of public interest only where the risk of prejudice to legal proceedings is *incidental*. It would not have helped the *Sunday Times* in the thalidomide case, for instance, as the very object of the article, subject to the injunction, was to discuss the legal proceedings; the risk of prejudice was not incidental.[82] In this respect, the UK statute falls short of the common law as developed in Australia. As long ago as 1937, the High Court held that it would not be a contempt to continue the discussion of public affairs, merely because an incidental consequence of the discussion might be to prejudice the chances of someone who happened to be a litigant in civil proceedings at the relevant time.[83] Subsequently, this principle was extended to publications prejudicial to criminal proceedings. The question in *Hinch*,[84] now the leading case in Australia, was whether it was necessarily a contempt if in the course of a discussion of public concern the author explicitly suggested that the accused in particular legal proceedings was guilty. The High Court ruled that in these circumstances courts must balance the competing interests in public discussion and the fair administration of justice. The more closely the discussion is concerned with the outcome of the trial and the more clearly it suggests the guilt of the accused by, for example, as in *Hinch* itself, revealing an accused person's previous convictions, the more likely it is that freedom of discussion should give way to the administration of justice. In this case, the High Court upheld the conviction of a radio journalist who in three broadcasts had clearly implied the guilt of a Catholic priest arrested on sexual offences charges, even though the likely date of trial was over eighteen months away. Nevertheless the approach of the High Court is more protective of freedom of discussion than that taken in England; under *Hinch* it is immaterial law whether the publication initiated a discussion or merely continued it, or whether the prejudice to the legal proceedings was an incidental consequence of the discussion. These points are merely factors to be considered when weighing freedom of discussion and the interests of the accused or parties.[85]

---

[81] *A-G* v. *English* [1983] 1 AC 116, 143.

[82] It is arguable that the *Sunday Times* would still be liable for common law intentional contempt preserved by the Contempt of Court Act 1981, s. 6(c).

[83] *Ex p Bread Manufacturers: Re Truth and Sportsman Ltd* (1937) 39 SR (NSW) 242, 249–50.

[84] *Hinch* v. *A-G (Victoria)* (1987) 164 CLR 15.

[85] See S. Walker, 'Freedom of Speech and Contempt of Court: The English and Australian Approaches Compared' (1991) 40 *ICLQ* 583.

(iii) Alternatives to contempt of court proceedings

Before it decides whether to uphold contempt of court proceedings, a court may consider whether other measures, not entailing a restriction on the media, might be taken to avoid the risk of serious prejudice to legal proceedings. Indeed, the Supreme Court of Canada held in *Dagenais* that a ban on the broadcast of a television series which might prejudice legal proceedings should only be upheld as a necessary restraint on the right to freedom of expression, guaranteed by the Charter, if alternative measures are not available to prevent the risk.[86] In England the point has been considered in the context of the courts' powers to order the postponement of the reporting of legal proceedings; they have statutory power to take this step, when this is necessary to prevent a substantial risk of prejudice to the administration of justice in those proceedings or other pending or imminent proceedings.[87] The Court of Appeal has stressed that juries will be directed by the trial judge to determine the case on the basis of the evidence and to ignore what they have heard or read outside the courtroom; that point should be considered before a postponement order is made.[88]

A court should certainly consider whether directions to the jury will cure the impact of prejudicial publicity before deciding whether to grant a discretionary order banning or postponing a publication or whether to uphold a motion for contempt of court. It is more controversial whether they should consider the effectiveness of other steps which could be taken to reduce the risk of prejudicial media publicity. Among them are putting questions to prospective members of the jury before selection about the impact on them of such publicity, postponing the date of trial until its impact has worn off, or changing its venue, and sequestration of the jury during the trial so that they do not read or hear any media comment and reports of the proceedings while they are taking place.[89] These alternative measures are popular in the United States and have been advocated by the Supreme Court as preferable to publications bans which are incompatible with the First Amendment.[90] But it is unclear whether they really work in that country,[91] or whether they should be used in England or other comparable jurisdictions. For example, moving the place of trial is unlikely to avert the risk of prejudice from a national newspaper or broadcasting channel, though it might help

---

[86] *Dagenais* v. *Canadian Broadcasting Corpn* [1994] 3 SCR 835. The Alberta Court of Appeal has doubted whether the principle in *Dagenais* applies to contempt proceedings brought after the trial, although the existence of alternative measures is a factor in determining whether the publication creates a substantial risk of prejudice to the legal proceedings: *R* v. *Edmonton Sun* (2003) 221 DLR (4th) 438.

[87] Contempt of Court Act 1981, s. 4(2).   [88] *Ex p Telegraph plc* [1993] 1 WLR 980.

[89] Lamer CJ in *Dagenais* v. *Canadian Broadcasting Corpn* [1994] 3 SCR 835, 881.

[90] *Sheppard* v. *Maxwell* 384 US 333, 358–63 (1966) per Clark J; *Nebraska Press Association* v. *Stuart* 427 US 539, 563–5 (1976) per Burger CJ.

[91] For a criticism of these techniques and an unfavourable comparison of US with English law, see S. J. Krause, 'Punishing the Press: Using Contempt of Court to Secure the Right to a Fair Trial' (1996) 76 *Boston Univ Law Rev* 537.

where it was only a local newspaper which created the danger. Postponing the date of trial interferes with the right to a prompt trial, guaranteed under the Sixth Amendment to the US Constitution and by Article 6 of the ECHR. Jury sequestration imposes burdens on jurors; in any case, it does not remove any prejudice they may have as a result of pre-trial media publicity. It is therefore a measure of only limited effectiveness. The New Zealand Court of Appeal was therefore right in its leading decision[92] in this area to reject the approach in *Dagenais*; it concluded that the alternatives suggested by Lamer CJ in the majority judgment of the Canadian Supreme Court do not afford defendants adequate protection against the risk of prejudice or they created more problems than they resolved.

The most radical alternative to a ban on prejudicial publicity is the suggestion that counsel can argue at the outset of criminal proceedings that the prosecution case should be stopped, because the welter of publicity infringes the defendant's fair trial rights. Until the last decade or so courts in England have generally been unsympathetic to this argument from defendants (although the US Supreme Court has accepted it in a handful of cases). They were also reluctant to allow an appeal on the ground that a conviction was unsafe in these circumstances.[93] Their view was that the risk of injustice could be corrected by appropriate directions to the jury who should be trusted to follow them and to disregard the impact of prejudicial media publicity.[94] At first glance, this position seems hard to defend. The courts were apparently prepared to convict, say, a newspaper of contempt of court in respect of a publication creating a risk of prejudice to legal proceedings, but were then reluctant to hold in a criminal appeal that it had actually occasioned any prejudice. In the former proceedings judges were in effect accepting that speech about legal proceedings may have a real impact on the jury, while in the latter they were denying that it did have any such impact.

However, in the last few years English courts have sometimes ordered criminal trials to be stayed, when they have been persuaded that the defendant cannot receive a fair trial after exceptionally prejudicial publicity in the media before or during the legal proceedings.[95] They have also on occasion upheld appeals on the ground that in the light of this publicity the conviction should not be regarded as safe.[96] The question has arisen whether in either of these circumstances later contempt proceedings must inevitably succeed. Of course, at that stage an application to stay proceedings or an appeal against conviction is not an alternative to contempt proceedings; instead the stay or successful appeal is a factor in determining whether contempt proceedings should be upheld. The courts have also considered

---

[92] *Gisborne Herald* v. *Solicitor-General* [1995] 3 NZLR 563.

[93] See *R* v. *Malik* [1968] 1 WLR 353, CA, and *R* v. *Savundranayagan* [1968] 1 WLR 1761, CA, discussed in the first edition of this book, 225.

[94] See e.g. the judgment of Lawton J. in *R* v. *Kray* (1969) 53 Cr App Rep 413.

[95] Miller (n. 1 above), paras. 7.10–7.20.

[96] As in *R* v. *McCann* (1991) 92 Cr App Rep 239, CA and *R* v. *Taylor* (1994) 98 Cr App Rep 361, CA.

the converse question: whether it makes sense to uphold an application to commit a newspaper for contempt, when the trial judge, or the Court of Appeal, had rejected the defendant's contention that a fair trial was impossible.

It has been said that courts should speak with one voice or apply a single standard when considering criminal appeals and contempt applications (although the standard of substantial risk of prejudice to the fairness of the proceedings should be applied differently in the two types of case).[97] But this may not be right. The point is that in contempt proceedings, the issue is whether the publication created a substantial or real risk of prejudice to the proceedings (at the time of publication, future or current), while the Court of Appeal (or judge on an application to halt the trial) must assess whether the fairness of the proceedings has been (or will be) irredeemably prejudiced by the publicity, so that a safe verdict was not (or could not) be reached. Contempt proceedings are concerned, in short, with the assessment of risk, criminal trials and appeals with the actual fairness of the proceedings.

From that perspective, the leading decision of the High Court of Australia in *The Queen* v. *Glennon* seems correct.[98] It rejected the argument that an appeal from a criminal conviction must inevitably be allowed because a successful application for contempt of court had already been brought (in *Hinch*)[99] in respect of radio broadcasts which had created a real risk of prejudice to the trial resulting in that conviction. If the Court had accepted the defendant's argument, it would have meant, as Brennan J. pointed out, that no trial could ever properly be held once successful contempt proceedings had been brought. The media could effectively sabotage a criminal prosecution by publishing extremely prejudicial material, certain to be held in contempt of court. Equally, the approach taken by some English judges in recent cases seems to lead to the unfortunate conclusion that a contempt application will almost always fail, whenever the criminal court has rejected an application to stay the trial or the Court of Appeal has held that the conviction was not unsafe.

A good example of their approach is that of the Divisional Court in *A-G* v. *Guardian Newspapers Ltd.*[100] Towards the end of the trial of the defendant, Kelly, on a charge of theft of body parts (used to make casts for artistic exhibition), *The Observer* published an article suggesting Kelly was a necrophile with a perverted personality. Only one juror read the article; she undertook not to reveal its contents to her colleagues. The judge also directed them not to read it. No application was made to discharge her or the whole jury, who then convicted the defendant. The Divisional Court rejected a motion to commit the newspaper publisher for contempt, though Collins J. agreed with Sedley LJ's judgment with hesitation.

---

[97] See Simon Brown LJ in *A-G* v. *Unger* (1998) 1 Cr App R 308, 318–19, DC, and in *A-G* v. *Birmingham Post and Mail* [1998] 4 All ER 49, 57–9, DC, and Sedley LJ in *A-G* v. *Guardian Newspapers Ltd* [1999] EMLR 904, 924.   [98] (1992) 173 CLR 592.

[99] N. 84 above.   [100] [1999] EMLR 904.

The latter said, referring to a hypothetical case where an application to discharge a jury who had read prejudicial material had been rejected: 'If... an appeal on the ground of prejudice would not succeed, no more should the publisher be guilty of contempt. The prospective risk of serious risk cannot be any greater than the actual possibility... that it has occurred.'[101] This is unpersuasive, though that does not mean that the actual decision in this case was wrong. It would surely be coherent for a court to assess the risk of prejudice as substantial *at the time of publication* and so uphold the motion for contempt of court, even though the Court of Appeal considered that in light of the evidence in the case and the judge's directions to the jury the verdict was safe. This point is easier to appreciate, when (as in *Hinch*) contempt proceedings are brought before the trial takes place. It is because they are normally brought after the trial and appeal have been concluded that it may appear odd, as it did to the Divisional Court in the *Guardian Newspapers* case, to contemplate upholding the contempt motion when no stay had been ordered (or even asked for). Indeed, it may make sense sometimes to hold that a publication creates a substantial risk of prejudice to legal proceedings, although the judge had refused to halt them because he was satisfied that with a suitable direction to the jury prejudice need not materialize.[102]

It may seem strange to allow a contempt application to succeed, when the decision of the criminal courts was that the prejudicial publicity had not led to an unsafe verdict. In fact, it is no more odd than it is to convict someone under public order legislation for making an inflammatory speech at a meeting, even though no actual violence or disorder resulted. In that context, the law may restrict speech where it is intended or likely to cause imminent violence or it creates a clear and present danger of unlawful conduct.[103] It is in principle irrelevant to the commission of such an offence whether disorder actually occurred, though in its absence it is improbable that proceedings would be brought. Equally, the Attorney-General in England will be less inclined to bring contempt proceedings when an application to halt the trial has been rejected and the Court of Appeal has dismissed any appeal. But it does not follow that in these circumstances an application should necessarily fail.

(iv) The law in the United States

The law in the United States contrasts strongly with that in England and most other Commonwealth jurisdictions. The Supreme Court has consistently applied the 'clear and present danger' test to contempt proceedings, holding that comment

---

[101] [1999] EMLR 904, 924–5.

[102] That happened in *A-G* v. *BBC, Hat Trick Productions* [1997] EMLR 76, where the contempt motion in respect of a BBC programme containing a clear suggestion that the Maxwell brothers were guilty of fraud was upheld, although the trial judge had refused to halt their trial.

[103] See for instance the US *Brandenburg* principle discussed in ch. V, s. 3 above.

on a pending case is constitutionally protected unless it poses an imminent danger to the administration of justice. So a newspaper editorial urging a sentence of imprisonment on union members who had been convicted of assaulting non-union employees was held to be protected speech, despite a strong dissent by Frankfurter J.[104] Although prejudicial comment before a grand jury investigation has similarly been held protected by the First Amendment, there has, it seems, been no Supreme Court ruling on such comment published immediately before or during a jury trial.[105] It is, however, clear that a prior restraint, forbidding the press and the other media from disclosing details of a defendant's confessions and incriminating statements to the police, will rarely, if ever, be countenanced.[106] Giving the Supreme Court's unanimous judgment, Burger CJ denied that pre-trial publicity, even of an adverse and pervasive character, necessarily led to an unfair trial. Without strong evidence that a jury would be prejudiced, conclusions about the impact on jurors of such publicity were merely speculative. Moreover, before issuing a 'gag order', a court should consider other alternative ways of protecting the defendant's rights, which would not interfere with freedom of the press: postponement of the trial, changing its venue, or questioning jurors to determine whether they were influenced by the pre-trial publicity. Although the question remains open in theory whether a penal sanction for an already published article might be held constitutional on otherwise identical facts, the stronger argument is surely that it would be treated in the same way as a prior restraint.[107] It is incompatible with the First Amendment to hold a publication in contempt of court on the ground that it is likely to prejudice the outcome of legal proceedings. The Court recognizes a privileged position for the press and other media in this context, for it has held compatible with the First Amendment a state rule prohibiting lawyers from making statements outside the court which are likely materially to prejudice legal proceedings.[108] The rule reflected a constitutionally permissible balance between the free speech rights of attorneys and the administration of justice.

However, the Supreme Court has sometimes allowed an appeal against conviction on the ground of violation of the Due Process Clause of the Fourteenth Amendment, where the trial has been accompanied or preceded by significant prejudicial publicity. The best-known applications of this principle occurred in two television trial cases, *Estes* v. *Texas*[109] and *Sheppard* v. *Maxwell*,[110] where there had been saturation coverage, held to have harassed the conduct of the defence

---

[104] *Bridges* v. *California* 314 US 252 (1941).

[105] See *Wood* v. *Georgia* 370 US 375 (1962). There is some state authority for extending this principle to jury trials: e.g. *Baltimore Radio Show* v. *State* 67 A 2d 497, 508–11 (Maryland CA, 1949).

[106] *Nebraska Press Association* v. *Stuart* 427 US 539 (1976).

[107] See D. A. Anderson, 'Democracy and the Demystification of Courts: An Essay' (1995) 14 *The Review of Litigation* 627, 637–9.

[108] *Gentile* v. *State Bar of Nevada* 501 US 1030 (1991). The rule was, however, held void for vagueness.   [109] 381 US 532 (1965).

[110] 384 US 333 (1966).

and to have inevitably prejudiced the jury. A strong dissent by Stewart J. in the former case (where the evidence of prejudice on the facts was much thinner than in the latter) did point out the indirect impact this ruling might have on the exercise by the press of its First Amendment rights; it is now established that there is no absolute ban on broadcast coverage of a criminal trial merely because there is a risk the jury will be prejudiced.[111] The legal position is therefore virtually the opposite of that which has generally prevailed in English law: the courts in the United States cannot use contempt of court to restrain or punish publications which imperil the fair administration of justice, but have been relatively ready to reverse criminal convictions.

The United States position has not been without its critics in that country. Frankfurter J., generally in dissent, preferred the more pragmatic English approach.[112] This may be partly attributable to his general hesitation in applying the Bill of Rights against state decisions; in his view, a state judge was in a better position than the Supreme Court to determine what was necessary to ensure the proper administration of justice. But he was also more sceptical than his colleagues about the ability of the judiciary, let alone jurors, to resist media pressure. Further, some commentators have doubted the adequacy of the alternative steps which, in the view of the Supreme Court, should be taken to insulate juries from prejudicial publicity.[113] These doubts appear warranted in the case of the *voir dire* procedure under which jurors are asked questions concerning the impact on them of any publicity concerning the case. In *Mu'Min* v. *Virginia*[114] the Court, by a bare majority, held that the trial judge was not required under the Sixth Amendment to question individual jurors closely about what they had read about the case in the media; it declined to interfere with the conviction on a murder charge of a defendant about whom there had been substantial publicity in the local media, including articles about a previous murder conviction and indications of a confession to the second murder charge. If the alternative courses are indeed ineffective, it seems that there is no real safeguard in the United States against the dangers to the fair administration of justice posed by prejudicial media publicity—unless, of course, the Supreme Court were to reconsider its strong attachment to the First Amendment in this context.

(v) Balancing free speech and the administration of justice

Once it is agreed, as it should be, that media publicity may pose a danger to the fairness of proceedings, free speech must be balanced against the important public

---

[111] *Chandler* v. *Florida* 449 US 560 (1981): see s. 4(iii) below for televising legal proceedings.

[112] See his dissent in *Bridges* v. *California* 314 US 252, 294–5 (1941) and his judgment in *State of Maryland* v. *Baltimore Radio Show* 338 US 912 (1950), where he appended a survey of the leading English cases.

[113] R. C. Donnelly and R. Goldfarb, 'Contempt by Publication in the United States' (1961) 24 *MLR* 239, 245–6; Krause (n. 91 above). [114] 500 US 415 (1991).

interest in the administration of justice. The risks of prejudice to juries, and perhaps also lay judges, may be so substantial that it seems impossible to support, as the law in the United States does, a more or less absolute rule that freedom of media publication should be protected, whatever its impact in the particular circumstances. An unqualified preference for freedom of speech is surely no more warranted than the absolute rule against any prejudgement of the issues by the media that the European Human Rights Court correctly found incompatible with the Convention in the *Sunday Times* case.

The contrary argument suggests wrongly that most, perhaps all, pre-trial publicity should be regarded as a form of political expression and is therefore entitled to strong free speech protection. That may be true of some forms of publicity, capable of prejudicing pending legal proceedings, such as a general discussion of the courts' treatment of, say, rape cases or of City or tax fraud. Even if an article with content of this type were published during the course of a high-profile trial, and named someone about to face a charge of rape or fraud, as the case may be, it would almost certainly be right to acquit its author or publisher of contempt. In these circumstances, the material is a form of political speech and its publication should not be penalized. (The UK Contempt of Court Act 1981 has to some extent come to this conclusion, with its provision that a good faith discussion of public affairs is not to be treated as a contempt, provided the risk of prejudice is merely incidental to that discussion.[115]) But it is misconceived to treat a sensational article in a tabloid newspaper with lurid details about the previous convictions or unsavoury life of someone about to face a criminal trial as straightforward political speech. Indeed, it would be wrong to view as political expression material which states or implies the legal guilt of a particular person. For that reason, the European Human Rights Court was right to hold compatible with freedom of expression the conviction of a journalist for suggesting the guilt of a prominent politician facing charges of tax evasion;[116] the article went well beyond general criticism of the integrity of politicians, and was capable of influencing the lay judges who might well have read it.

It is also misconceived to invoke the right of the public to read such material. For it is the responsibility of the jury to determine guilt on the basis of admissible evidence, not of the general public, some of whom will eventually constitute the jury. The point is that speech in court about the issues to be decided in legal proceedings is bound by rules of evidence and procedure, enforced by the court. No lawyer has a free speech right to evade these restrictions by introducing inadmissible evidence at a press conference held outside the court.[117] It is hard to see why the press or other media should have a right which would be denied to lawyers, judges, and other participants in the legal process.

---

[115] Contempt of Court Act 1981, s. 5, discussed in s. 3(ii) above.

[116] *Worm* v. *Austria* (1997) 25 EHRR 454.

[117] See F. Schauer, 'The Speech of Law and the Law of Speech' (1997) 49 *Arkansas Law Rev* 687, 692–4 for this point.

4. Open Justice

Open justice has often been regarded as a fundamental principle of the common law. In *Scott* v. *Scott*,[118] the House of Lords held that a court should not exclude the press and public from its proceedings merely because one of the parties, as in that case, or a witness argued that it would be embarrassing for him to give evidence in public. It followed that it would be wrong for a judge to issue an order to prevent the press reporting that evidence. Although the open justice principle was not regarded as absolute, the House of Lords held that departures from it should only be recognized when they are clearly necessary in the interests of the administration of justice and are based on statute or an established precedent. In short, courts have no general discretion to exclude the press and public. The principle formulated in *Scott* v. *Scott* has been adopted in other Commonwealth countries, while the United States Supreme Court has held the press and other media have a First Amendment right to attend legal proceedings.[119] Article 6 of the ECHR guarantees that 'everyone is entitled to a fair and *public* hearing...', although it explicitly provides that the press and public may be excluded from judicial proceedings in a number of specified circumstances. There seems then to be a strong, if not an absolute, right of access to attend legal proceedings and to report them.

(i) Arguments of principle

The familiar arguments for open justice are certainly strong.[120] Witnesses are more inclined to give full and accurate evidence if their testimony is exposed to public scrutiny; open proceedings may encourage other witnesses to come forward and elicit new lines of enquiry. Publicity enables the performance of judges and lawyers to be monitored by the press and general public. In other words, open justice is conducive to the fairness of proceedings and the administration of justice. It safeguards the rights of the parties to a fair trial. But open justice also satisfies the interest that members of the public have, and should have, in the conduct of legal proceedings. Although for reasons of space only a limited number of people will be able to exercise their right by physical attendance, everyone should be able to follow a trial by reading reports in newspapers or, it has been argued, by watching its broadcast on television.

But it is important in this context to distinguish the interests and rights of the parties to legal proceedings on the one hand from those of the public on the other. The former have a fundamental right to a fair trial, recognized, as we have seen, in many constitutions and by the ECHR. This right is safeguarded by the openness of legal proceedings. Moreover, open justice enables the public to be satisfied,

---

[118] [1913] AC 417.   [119] *Richmond Newspapers* v. *Virginia* 448 US 555 (1980).
[120] See Jaconelli (n. 13 above).

for example, that lawyers can freely represent the parties and have effective opportunities to examine and cross-examine witnesses, and that the judge's conduct of the trial is fair. On this perspective, the rights of the public and the press may be regarded as instrumental to secure the fundamental right of the parties to a fair trial.[121] The latter are the principal beneficiaries of the right to a public trial, although the right can be claimed by the press or members of the public on their behalf.

This perspective, however, suggests that the law's adherence to the open justice principle is qualified, and not absolute. In the first place, as the House of Lords recognized in *Scott* itself, it would be wrong to insist on observance of the principle when that course would defeat the administration of justice or conflict with fair trial rights. If the argument for open justice is utilitarian or consequential, it makes no sense to invoke it when publicity would be inimical to the ends of justice it is supposed to promote. Secondly, if the parties are the primary beneficiaries of the right to a public trial, then they should be entitled to waive it. In many cases defendants to criminal proceedings, or the parties to civil litigation, may feel seriously inhibited at giving full evidence in public or for some other reason prefer the public and media to be excluded from the courtroom and its reporting to be restricted. Sometimes, the law allows parties to opt out, as it were, of open justice, as when civil disputes are resolved by arbitration conducted in private; that is not regarded as an infringement of open justice, which in this context is regarded as a matter for the parties to choose. But this is not permitted in other contexts. Criminal cases cannot be heard in private merely because the defendant would find it embarrassing for the public and press to be present. The same principle applies generally to divorce proceedings, even though both parties would prefer them to be conducted privately.[122] Nor are adult defendants entitled to anonymity; the media are free to identify them even though they might be innocent and might eventually be acquitted of all charges, and publicity might spell economic disaster.[123] Open justice, therefore, allows the public and media access and reporting rights in the context of legal proceedings, where the parties, particularly the accused in a criminal trial, might with good reason (so far as they are concerned) wish to dispense with publicity. In these circumstances, the open justice principle would appear not to rest on purely utilitarian grounds or to be incidental to the parties' right to a fair trial.

What is the basis for recognition of such rights apart from the argument just considered that they safeguard the right of the parties to a fair trial? The question is difficult, particularly as the law rarely upholds positive free speech rights of access outside this context. The Supreme Court of the United States has, for

---

[121] Ibid., 112–13.

[122] The Supreme Court of Canada emphasized the importance of an open procedure and full reporting in divorce proceedings in *Edmonton Journal* v. *A-G of Alberta* [1989] 2 SCR 1326.

[123] See *R* v. *Dover Justices, ex p Dover DC* [1992] Crim LR 371, DC, where it was held that magistrates had wrongly granted anonymity to a trader charged with a public health offence.

instance, rejected press claims to a First Amendment right to attend prisons to interview prisoners or investigate conditions there.[124] More generally, freedom of information is only recognized under statute, not as an aspect of freedom of speech or expression. The European Court of Human Rights, for instance, has declined to uphold a right under Article 10 of access to official information.[125] There is no clear explanation why the law should be more willing to uphold free speech access rights to attend legal proceedings, even against the objection of the parties, than they are to uphold rights to attend meetings of government committees and public bodies, in the absence of statutory provision. Arguably, the public has as strong a claim to attend the proceedings of political and administrative authorities as it has to attend legal proceedings.

Moreover, there are hard questions about the scope of any right to attend legal proceedings and to report them. If there is something special about the administration of justice, should not the open justice principle require a right to attend hearings before bodies such as the Parole Board and a right to observe plea-bargaining and the consideration of important ancillary matters such as the decisions of the police or magistrates to grant or extend the time for the detention and questioning of suspects? But these matters usually fall outside the open justice principle.[126] It is hardly an adequate answer to say that these matters are traditionally heard in private, while full trials have for centuries been heard in public. For then we would have to conclude that the open justice principle applies whenever the courts normally sit in public and not when they do not. The scope of this aspect of the principle—the right to attend legal proceedings—would depend on custom, rather than rational argument.[127] Nevertheless, some members of the Supreme Court of the United States argued that the press had a First Amendment right to attend trials, even where the defendant, prosecution, and trial judge had agreed to closure, because historically the courtroom has been open to the public.[128] That seems an inadequate basis for the recognition of a constitutional right.

The numerous qualifications and exceptions to aspects of the open justice principle arguably undermine its coherence and significance. For example, England and other jurisdictions in derogation from open justice afford the complainants in rape and sexual assault cases anonymity, which may only be lifted by the trial judge in a narrow range of circumstances. There are significant limitations on the freedom of the press to publish any material which may identify young people under the age of eighteen involved in criminal proceedings, particularly in the youth court. There are, of course, powerful utilitarian arguments for these exceptions to the general principle of open justice. Moreover, they can also sometimes

---

[124] *Pell* v. *Procunier* 417 US 817 (1974): see ch. XII, s. 3(iii) below.

[125] *Gaskin* v. *UK* (1989) 12 EHRR 36: see ch. III, s. 7 above.

[126] See Jaconelli (n. 13 above), 52–68.

[127] For criticism, see R. M. Dworkin, 'Is the Press Losing the First Amendment?', in *A Matter of Principle* (Cambridge, Mass.: Harvard UP, 1985), 381, 390.

[128] See Burger CJ and Blackmun J. in *Richmond Newspapers* v. *Virginia* 448 US 555 (1980).

be justified as necessary to protect competing privacy interests, an argument particularly pertinent in family cases where statutes impose a number of restrictions on free access to and reporting of judicial proceedings. But the existence of these exceptions seems to show that the law's commitment to open justice is hesitant and qualified; the principle may easily be displaced when insistence on it might prejudice other interests or values, such as the rehabilitation of children and young persons into society after their conviction.[129] It may be difficult, therefore, to speak of *rights* of access to the courts, or even a *right* to report judicial proceedings. Rather, it seems more accurate to refer to a general principle of open justice which may be departed from in a wide range of circumstances.

Two other points should be made at this juncture. First, it should be emphasized that there are two distinct aspects to open justice: a requirement that legal proceedings are open to the press and public and a freedom to report those proceedings. It might be thought that these two limbs of the principle would go hand in hand; when proceedings are open, the media would necessarily be free to report them, and conversely when restrictions are imposed on access, reporting also is forbidden. But in fact in both Britain and the United States the two issues may be kept distinct, either by legislation or by decisions of the courts. It is not necessarily, for instance, a contempt of court in English law for the media to disclose what happened in proceedings held in private.[130] Conversely the press and public may be able to attend proceedings, the reporting of which has been forbidden by court order.[131] As we have seen, details identifying young persons involved in criminal proceedings may not be published. But the press and public are generally free to attend their trial in adult courts, while 'bona fide representatives of newspapers or newspaper agencies' are entitled to attend hearings before the youth court.[132]

Secondly, in this area of free speech law, the law may, and sometimes does, give the press and other media privileged rights of access to attend courts. While every individual, on a rights-based rationale for free speech, has an equal right to exercise the freedom to say and write what he thinks, it would be difficult to infer a similar right of access to the courtroom. It is rather hard to see how the theoretical basis for rights-based theories—the entitlement of all individuals to self-expression and self-development—could justify granting equal rights for everyone to attend courts. Quite apart from this point, it would be quite impracticable for everyone to exercise such a right.[133] However, if free speech and free press guarantees rest on

[129] Jaconelli (n. 13 above), 212–14.

[130] Under s. 12 of the Administration of Justice Act 1960 it may be a contempt of court to publish information relating to proceedings conducted in private in certain prescribed circumstances; the provision would be unnecessary if it were generally illegal to report closed proceedings.

[131] The press and public may attend criminal trials, the reporting of which may be temporarily prohibited under a postponement order granted under the Contempt of Court Act 1981, s. 4(2).

[132] Children and Young Persons Act 1933, s. 47(2).

[133] In *R* v. *Denbigh Justices, ex p Williams* [1974] 1 QB 759, DC, Lord Widgery CJ said that it would be difficult to conclude there had been a public trial if there were no room for the press, but that the duty to accommodate the public had to have regard to the number of seats and the possibility of disorder.

the need for an informed citizenry in a participatory democracy, the case for conferring some special privileges on the press may be stronger. Newspaper and broadcasting journalists have the time and experience to attend and report legal proceedings on behalf of the public. Their case may alternatively be based on a separately protected freedom of the press, as it has been in Germany. Its Constitutional Court has upheld a right of the press, exercisable by the editor or the paper's employees, to attend criminal trials, free from arbitrary exclusion.[134] The right to obtain information about the judicial process is necessary to enable the press to discharge its special responsibilities, though its exercise may be limited under Article 5(2) of the Basic Law, for example, in order to preserve good order in the courtroom.[135]

(ii) Access to the courts

Whatever the coherence of the theoretical reservations discussed in the previous pages, it remains true that many legal systems are committed to open justice as a matter of fundamental principle. In some jurisdictions it is a matter of constitutional right. The traditional enthusiasm of the common law in England for the rule is a little surprising in view of the cautious attitude of its courts in related areas of contempt law discussed earlier in this chapter. *Scott* v. *Scott*, decided by the House of Lords in 1913, is still the leading case; it was held that the High Court had no power, even at the parties' request, to hear a nullity or other family suit in camera because of the embarrassing or indecent nature of the evidence. The Lords were only prepared to countenance a few exceptions to the general rule of open justice: wardship and lunatic cases, where the court's jurisdiction was administrative rather than judicial, and trade secrets litigation. Lord Loreburn considered that a hearing might be conducted in private where otherwise parties would reasonably be deterred from coming to court,[136] but this suggestion was not supported by other members of the House and has since been held to be wrong. The decision in *Scott* has subsequently been reversed, so that courts do have discretion under statute to hear evidence of sexual incapacity in private.[137] But the principles formulated by the House of Lords remain good law. There is a strong presumption in common law that courts should sit in public; it should not be displaced merely to suit the convenience of the parties or reduce embarrassment.

Nevertheless, in some instances, the presumption may give way to the fundamental need to secure the administration of justice. The Court of Appeal upheld the decision of the trial judge to clear the public gallery (though not the press) to allow crucial evidence to be given by a young witness who had earlier adamantly refused to give evidence in public.[138] It was considered compatible with the

---

[134] 50 BVerfGE 234 (1979).   [135] Ibid., 241–2.
[136] [1913] AC 417, 446.   [137] Matrimonial Causes Act 1973, s. 48(2).
[138] *R* v. *Richards* (1999) JP 246.

ECHR to take this step, as it is permissible under Article 6 of the Convention to exclude the press and public insofar as that is, in the court's view, 'strictly necessary' in the interests of justice. The Divisional Court has ruled that magistrates have jurisdiction to allow a plea in mitigation to be given in closed court, where it raised some sensitive personal matters, although it clearly disapproved of the decision to exclude the press in these circumstances.[139] Courts may alternatively take the lesser step of allowing a witness to give evidence anonymously, where disclosure of his identity may imperil his life or safety or for reasons for national security.[140] What emerges from these decisions is that the trial judge does have discretion to depart from the open justice principle, provided it can be shown that otherwise it would be impossible to do justice.

Moreover, there are a number of statutory provisions requiring or enabling courts to conduct proceedings in private. Some of them concern proceedings before magistrates; they have a discretion not to hear committal proceedings in public where 'the ends of justice would not be served by their sitting in open court.'[141] Members of the public are excluded by statute from family proceedings before these courts; journalists have a right to attend, but the magistrates may exclude them to protect any child involved.[142] There is a strong presumption that county court proceedings involving children are heard in private.[143] The High Court may sit in camera for the whole or part of proceedings involving the official secrets and emergency powers legislation or the Defence Contracts Act 1958. Further, the public may not attend the hearing when a judge hears a case or application in chambers, as he may properly do in a variety of cases under the Rules of Court.[144]

There are so many common law and statutory exceptions to the open justice principle, that it is difficult to regard it as much more than that: a principle which may be displaced when there is a strong reason to conclude that it works against the administration of justice. Both the European Commission[145] and Court of Human Rights have treated it in much the same way, despite the explicit guarantee of a 'right to a fair and public hearing' afforded by Article 6 of the Convention. It is not necessarily an infringement of that provision for a state to allow a witness to give evidence anonymously, if there are good reasons to fear reprisals if his identity is revealed.[146] The Court has held compatible with the Convention the UK

---

[139] *R* v. *Malvern Justices, ex p Evans* [1988] QB 540.

[140] As in *R* v. *Socialist Worker Printers and Publishers, ex p A-G* [1975] QB 637, DC (witnesses in blackmail case otherwise unwilling to give evidence); *A-G* v. *Leveller Magazine Ltd* [1979] AC 440, HL (army officer allowed to give evidence anonymously in the interests of national security).

[141] Magistrates' Courts Act 1980, s. 4(2).   [142] Children Act 1989, s. 97(1).

[143] See *Re P-B (A Minor) (Child Cases: Hearings in Open Court)* [1997] 1 All ER 58, CA.

[144] For discussion of these circumstances, see Jaconelli (n. 13 above), 74–80.

[145] In 13366/87, *Atkinson, Crook, and The Independent* v. *UK* (1990) 67 D & R 244, it held that the interest of the media in reporting arguments about the sentencing of a convicted defendant could be outweighed if, for good reason, the defendant himself, the prosecution, and the judge wished to hear them in private. It was feared that points made in open proceedings might put the defendant's family at risk.   [146] *Doorson* v. *Netherlands* (1996) 22 EHRR 230.

statutory provisions, mentioned in the previous paragraph, under which family proceedings concerning children are held in private, subject to a judicial discretion to hear a case in public when this is merited by its special features. It has even upheld rules under which judgments are given in private, as in its view the public pronouncement of a court's decision would undermine the objective of a private hearing: to enable the parents and other witnesses to express themselves openly without a fear of public curiosity or comment.[147]

At first glance, a different perspective has been taken in Canada. In a major decision, the Supreme Court held that measures limiting the access of the media to the courts do restrict freedom of expression guaranteed by the Charter.[148] Open justice enables the press to gather information about judicial proceedings, to which the public is entitled in order to enable it to understand and critique the courts. There was therefore a close link between access to the courts and freedom of reporting. However, the Court entered two qualifications to these broad principles. Freedom of expression did not confer 'a right to be physically present in the courtroom'. In view of the shortage of space, members of the public and the press may be denied access. Secondly, it did not follow that there was a right of public access to all public institutions, or even to all places where criminal justice was administered—such as the jury room or the judge's chambers. The point is that only the courts, and not these other venues, have from time immemorial been arenas to which members of the public have been admitted. (This is the argument from tradition which, as mentioned, has attracted members of the United States Supreme Court.) As a result it was wrong for the trial judge in New Brunswick to exclude the press and public during the sentencing of the accused who had pleaded guilty to sexual assaults. He had taken this step on the broad ground that evidence would be given which might be disturbing to the young girls who were victims of the assault. The order was unnecessary to the proper administration of justice. The qualifications significantly reduce the significance of this ruling; it is difficult to read it as clearly supporting an access right for the media. Rather, it should be taken as evidencing support for a stronger open justice principle than that recognized in the common law.

Since its landmark ruling in 1980 in the *Richmond Newspapers* case,[149] the US Supreme Court has upheld First Amendment rights for the press to attend trials. In an earlier decision the majority of the Court had scrupulously refrained from determining whether there is a general First Amendment right to attend trials, when denying access rights to a pre-trial judicial proceeding.[150] Four members of the Court had dissented on the basis of the Sixth Amendment's 'public trial' provision which, in their view, conferred a right on the *public* to attend trials; the accused was not always entitled to waive his right to a public trial. In *Richmond*

---

[147] *B* v. *UK, P* v. *UK* (2001) 11 BHRC 667, approving in effect the decision of the CA in *Re P-B (A Minor)* (n. 143 above). [148] *CBC* v. *A-G for New Brunswick* [1996] 3 SCR 480.
[149] N. 119 above. [150] *Gannett* v. *De Pasquale* 443 US 368 (1979).

Newspapers, however, the Court ruled, with only Rehnquist J. dissenting, that the press did have a right of access, implicit in the First Amendment, to attend a criminal trial. The defendant had argued, without objection from the prosecution, that removal of the press was necessary to avoid irrelevant information being communicated to the jury, but the Court reasoned that other steps, for example, removal of the jury from the courtroom during argument about the admissibility of evidence, could be taken to safeguard the administration of justice. Burger CJ for the Court did envisage circumstances in which not everyone who wanted to attend a trial could be accommodated, but the media would be entitled to preferential seating. Some other members of the Court, notably Stevens and Brennan JJ, characterized trial attendance rights as falling under a broad First Amendment access right to newsworthy events. For Stewart J., press presence served to guarantee the integrity of the proceedings.

Subsequently, the Court has extended the scope of the principle established in the *Richmond Newspapers* case. For example, a majority struck down a Massachusetts statute requiring judges to exclude the press and public from the courtroom when a victim under eighteen gave evidence at a trial for specified sexual offences.[151] Interestingly, Burger CJ dissented on the ground that historical tradition did permit proceedings to be closed to the public when a minor victim is concerned. Further, the Court has held the principle covered a press right to attend examination of prospective members of the jury,[152] and even more radically a right of access to the transcripts of a preliminary hearing in criminal proceedings, despite the objections of the trial judge, prosecutor, and defendant.[153] In this latter case, the Court was not impressed by the argument that the resulting pre-trial publicity would jeopardize the defendant's rights to a fair trial. Although the access right was not absolute, the Court insisted that a trial judge must make specific findings that closure was imperative to preserve fair trial rights. As a prominent commentator has concluded, '[t]he constitutional right of access to court-rooms, though qualified in theory, is close to absolute in practice.'[154]

The key question remains, is there a strong argument for holding a right to attend trials implicit in the First Amendment, when free speech rights to acquire and gather information from government departments and other public authorities have been rejected?[155] For the same arguments about the role of the press and the importance of an informed electorate can also be deployed in these circumstances, but they have not been found persuasive enough to extend the scope of freedom of speech. Doubts concerning the correctness of the *Richmond* decision are reinforced by the point that it will often be impracticable for more than a few people to exercise this First Amendment right to attend trials; in many

---

[151] *Globe Newspaper Co* v. *Superior Court* 457 US 596 (1982).
[152] *Press-Enterprise Co* v. *Superior Court* 464 US 501 (1984).
[153] *Press-Enterprise Co* v. *Superior Court* 478 US 1 (1986).
[154] Anderson (n. 107 above), 638.   [155] See ch. III, s. 7 above.

circumstances press and broadcasting journalists in effect enjoy special or privileged access rights, albeit exercised on behalf of the public. The case for the open justice principle is certainly a strong one; further, the accused, or the parties to civil proceedings, have a right to a public trial as an aspect of their right to a fair trial. But these points do not make an overwhelming case for recognition of special free speech or press access rights in this context.

(iii) Televising court proceedings

The most lively issue in the open justice context concerns the introduction of cameras into the courtroom to permit the broadcast of legal proceedings.[156] The impact of the continuous coverage of notorious trials in the United States, notably those of O. J. Simpson and Louise Woodward, has been particularly controversial. In England, it is generally considered that the filming of court proceedings is caught by the provision in the Criminal Justice Act 1925 which bans the taking of photographs or drawing of sketches of any person involved in the proceedings, or the publication of photographs, sketches, or portraits taken or made in contravention of this ban.[157] Proposals to allow the televising of court proceedings have hitherto been resisted.[158] On the other hand, there has been a limited experiment in Scotland (where the 1925 legislation does not apply) to allow cameras into the courtroom. But the consent of each person to be filmed is required, while the judge retains an overall power to refuse or withdraw permission for cameras to be used. More importantly, in view of the risks to the administration of justice, the televising of current criminal or civil proceedings is not permitted until they have been concluded. In effect, only appellate proceedings may be televised.[159] These principles were applied recently, when the BBC application to televise the trial of the 'Lockerbie bombers' was rejected; it was immaterial that cameras had been allowed into the courtroom to facilitate broadcast of the proceedings to families of the victims who could not be accommodated within the court.[160] Lord Kirkwood also held that there was no right under Article 10 of the Convention to televise legal proceedings.

It is clear from both the English statute and the terms of the limited experiment in Scotland that there are two issues here, reflecting the distinction between access

---

[156] For general discussion, see M. Dockray, 'Courts on Television' (1988) 51 *MLR* 593; A. Biondi, 'TV Cameras in the Courtroom: A Comparative Note' (1996) *Yearbook of Media and Entertainment Law* 133; Jaconelli (n. 13 above), ch. 9.

[157] See Jaconelli (n. 13 above), 315–28 for a comprehensive review of this provision. It has been questioned whether interpreted in the light of the Human Rights Act 1998, s. 3, the provision now precludes filming and broadcasting of legal proceedings: see Robertson & Nicol, 482–5.

[158] In Nov. 2004, cameras were allowed into the Royal Courts of Justice in London to film judges and lawyers, under a pilot project to determine whether eventually the filming and broadcast of legal proceedings in England might be permitted. Under the experiment the film is to be viewed by judges and MPs, but not broadcast. [159] Jaconelli (n. 13 above), 329–33.

[160] *Petition No. 2 of the BBC* [2000] HRLR 423, High Court of Justiciary.

and reporting restrictions which has often been mentioned in this chapter: is there a right to film proceedings and is there a right to televise them contemporaneously with the trial when viewer interest will usually be greatest? Strong arguments can be made for and against recognition of either of these rights. The broadcast of criminal trials, and also some civil proceedings, notably libel actions, would, at least initially, be of enormous interest to many members of the general public who otherwise lack any real opportunity to attend them. Moreover, there is an argument that the right to televise legal proceedings is now necessary to enable the public to understand and be fully informed about the administration of justice. Obviously, cameras must be allowed into the courtroom to facilitate television coverage.

On the other hand, the intrusion of cameras, though much less physically disruptive than they used to be, might be disturbing to the parties and to witnesses. Even the knowledge that proceedings are being filmed might have some impact; it would of course be inconceivable for witnesses not to be informed and therefore not be aware that their evidence was being filmed. The presence of even unobtrusive cameras would add to the pressure on witnesses. There are obvious risks in allowing live broadcasting of criminal proceedings tried by jury. Unless sequestered, jurors would be exposed to media coverage, which might emphasize, through its repeated showing, a crucial piece of testimony. Inevitably, lawyers will play to the camera, as clearly happened during the O. J. Simpson trial. Most significantly, it seems monstrously unfair to the defendant, particularly if eventually acquitted of all charges, that he should be exposed to public scrutiny for weeks, in addition to facing the prospect of loss of liberty. There must be some strong argument of free speech principle to trump these objections to live television coverage of criminal proceedings, an argument which is more persuasive than the utilitarian case for this form of open justice canvassed in the previous paragraph.

But the case for recognition of a right to televise as an integral aspect or consequence of free speech is very weak. First, we should recall the doubts expressed earlier concerning the coherence of access rights for the press and public to attend legal proceedings (as distinct from the right of the defendant to a fair public trial or a weaker open justice principle). Even if access *rights* are accepted, it would not follow that they confer rights to film and to televise proceedings. For the arguments which can be deployed to support access rights do not justify recognition of these further rights. It is difficult to see why and how public confidence in the legal system and judicial accountability would be enhanced by the provision of rights beyond the freedom of the public and press to attend legal proceedings and the media right to report them. Further, a right to film and televise would necessarily give the broadcasting media privileges which could not practicably be enjoyed by others, say, by amateur film-makers who wanted to record trials for educational purposes. Another point is that in practice broadcasters would choose the trials they wished to cover and which parts or extracts to broadcast; that discretion is far removed from an access right which in principle belongs to the members of the general public as it does to the institutional media.[161]

The constitutional arguments have been fully considered by the German Constitutional Court, which rejected complaints by a news broadcaster to the constitutionality of provisions of a federal law banning recording and filming within the courtroom for the purpose of broadcasting.[162] Neither freedom of information (*Informationsfreiheit*) nor broadcasting freedom conferred access rights unless the source of information was generally open. The legislature had properly decided to limit the openness of judicial proceedings to persons physically present during the trial. Broadcasting journalists were perfectly free to attend and report proceedings, but live coverage was prohibited. The ban took account of the parties' rights to privacy, guaranteed by Article 2 of the Basic Law, and the importance of a fair procedure and the correct finding of facts. The Court added that television coverage might inhibit the reintegration of the accused into society after trial and lead to distortion of testimony (through the broadcast of edited highlights) which would itself infringe the freedom of the witnesses to express themselves in words of their own choosing (*informationelle Selbtsbestimmung*). Finally, a majority of the Court held that the law need not give courts a discretionary power to allow television coverage in exceptional proceedings; media pressure would place an impossible burden on the courts if they were given that discretion.[163]

The German Constitutional Court stated that the Bundestag is entitled, but not required, to limit the openness of proceedings to those present in the court. The implication is that German law could be amended to permit television coverage and filming, though then a party might be able to claim that his fair trial rights had been prejudiced. If that step were taken, the legal position would not be altogether dissimilar from the position in the United States. The broadcast of legal proceedings there is widely permitted under state laws, though not in federal trial courts, or most surprisingly before the Supreme Court.

In two cases in the 1960s, the Court held that saturation television coverage infringed the defendant's right to a fair trial;[164] it was inherently likely to prejudice their fairness, and the trial judge should take active steps to minimize this risk, short of imposing direct restraints on the media. But in *Chandler* v. *Florida* the Court ruled that a state could permit television filming and coverage over the objections of the accused, provided it took suitable steps where necessary to safeguard his interest in a fair trial, for example, by sequestrating the jury.[165] Cameras in the courtroom are now commonplace in the United States, though the furore over the O. J. Simpson case shows their use remains highly controversial.

---

[161] See M. D. Lepofsky, 'Cameras in the Courtroom: Not Without My Consent' (1996) 6 *National Jo of Constitutional Law* 161, arguing against the right to televise proceedings as an aspect of free expression.   [162] 103 BVerfGE 44 (2002).

[163] On this point, three members of the Court dissented.

[164] *Estes* v. *Texas* 381 US 532 (1965); *Sheppard* v. *Maxwell* 384 US 333 (1966).

[165] 449 US 560 (1981).

But television coverage is not a matter of constitutional right under the First Amendment. The case for recognizing such a right has yet to be established; it is much weaker than the argument for a free speech right of access to the courts.

(iv) Reporting restrictions

Perhaps the most robust defence of a right to report details of court proceedings is to be found in the decision of the Canadian Supreme Court in *Edmonton Journal* v. *A-G of Alberta*.[166] The newspaper challenged the validity of a statutory provision banning the publication of any particulars of divorce or separation proceedings, except the names and addresses of the parties and witnesses, a concise statement of the charges, any legal submissions, and the summing-up and court judgment.[167] Cory J. for the Court emphasized the vital role of the press in communicating details of legal proceedings to people who are unable to attend them. The public could not take advantage of the fact that divorce proceedings are open to it. Informed comment on the working of the courts is dependent on the provision of comprehensive information about them. The restrictions therefore infringed the free expression rights of readers and listeners. They had been imposed for legitimate objectives: principally, to protect the privacy of the parties going through the divorce proceedings and to safeguard the access to the courts of people who might wish to litigate matrimonial disputes, but who would be deterred from doing so if media publicity were unregulated. But the provisions went further than necessary to achieve those objectives. A discretionary power for the court to allow parties anonymity or to ban publication in certain circumstances would have been less restrictive of freedom of expression. What was objectionable were rules which applied to all matrimonial causes irrespective of the sensitivity of the facts.

As already discussed in section 4(i) above, it does not follow from the fact that a hearing is conducted in private, that there is no right to publish a report of these proceedings. The media may be free to report proceedings on the basis of information they have picked up from the parties or their lawyers or by obtaining relevant papers, even though they and the public had been excluded from attending the proceedings. In *Scott* v. *Scott* itself,[168] the Lords ruled that even if the nullity case had been properly heard in camera, a subsequent report of the case would not necessarily constitute a contempt. Freedom to publish might be asserted not only by the press, but by one of the parties seeking to correct a damaging impression created by the proceedings. On the other hand, it would undermine the confidentiality of a hearing conducted in private if the press were free to report it simultaneously or shortly after it concluded.

The law in England has been clarified to some extent by section 12 of the Administration of Justice Act 1960, which provides that: 'The publication of

---

[166] [1989] 2 SCR 1326.
[167] The provision is similar to that of the UK Judicial Proceedings (Regulation of Reports) Act 1926, s. 1(1)(b), for which see Miller (n. 1 above), paras. 10.37–10.40.   [168] [1913] AC 417.

information relating to proceedings before any courts sitting in private shall not of itself be contempt of court', except in a number of specified cases, including wardship, adoption and other proceedings affecting the upbringing of children, trade secrets litigation, and cases where the court has sat in private for security reasons. The courts have refused to hold that these provisions enable contempt proceedings to be taken in respect of such a publication where they could not have been taken under the common law; further, the Court of Appeal has ruled that it must be proved the press was aware its publication related to proceedings from which the public had been excluded.[169] The judgments contained ringing declarations of the importance of a free press, and the undesirability of placing more restrictions on newspaper reporting than the strict wording of the Act justified.

The courts have refused to ban reports of (aspects of) legal proceedings heard in private, in the absence of any clear proof that publication would prejudice the administration of justice and so amount to contempt. In *A-G* v. *Leveller Magazine Ltd*,[170] the House of Lords held that the publication of the name of a witness who had been allowed to give evidence to magistrates anonymously was not a contempt of court; there was no evidence that the disclosure threatened the administration of justice, as the witness himself had indirectly revealed his identity in the course of giving evidence. It was not a contempt to publish details of a private hearing (or the name of a witness who had given evidence anonymously) merely because the publication violated a court order. Similar principles were adopted by the Court of Appeal in *Hodgson* v. *Imperial Tobacco Ltd*[171] when it lifted 'gagging orders' to stop the parties and their advisers from making comments to the media on procedural directions given by the judge in chambers. These proceedings had been held in private as a matter of practice and convention, but were not, unlike the cases covered by the 1960 legislation, secret proceedings.[172]

Conversely, there are circumstances where it is forbidden to publish reports of proceedings conducted *in public*, or to publish particulars other than the names of the parties, legal submissions, and rulings. There are, for example, significant, and controversial, restrictions on reporting matters relating to young persons under eighteen involved in criminal proceedings, if the publication is likely to identify them.[173] The courts have a general power under the Contempt of Court Act 1981 to order that reporting of proceedings should be postponed when this step is necessary to avoid a substantial risk of prejudice to the administration of justice in the particular proceedings or in any other pending or imminent proceedings;[174]

---

[169] *In re F (orse. A) (A Minor) (Publication of Information)* [1977] Fam 58.

[170] [1979] AC 440. But see now the Contempt of Court Act 1981, s. 11 which permits courts to restrict reporting of details withheld from the court.   [171] [1998] 1 WLR 1056.

[172] Also see *Clibbery* v. *Allan* [2002] 1 All ER 865, CA, where it was held that it was wrong automatically to ban the reporting of family proceedings not involving children which had been held in private.

[173] See the provisions in the Children and Young Persons Act 1933 and other legislation discussed by Miller (n. 1 above), paras. 10.06–10.30 and by Cram (n. 22 above), ch. 4.

[174] Contempt of Court Act 1981, s. 4(2).

this would almost certainly be treated as an unconstitutional prior restraint on the media in the United States. These statutory provisions illustrate the point that there is no invariable correspondence between limits on access and reporting restrictions. In these cases restrictions are imposed on the (immediate) reporting of proceedings which are open to the press and members of the public.

Some US cases similarly reflect these distinctions. In *Landmark Communications* v. *Virginia*,[175] the Court unanimously invalidated a statute making it a crime to publish details of confidential proceedings before a state judicial review commission which investigated complaints about members of the judiciary. The newspaper published an accurate report on pending proceedings, identifying a particular judge. The Court agreed that the confidentiality of such proceedings served legitimate state interests, but held that the penal sanctions against third parties went further than necessary to protect them. Internal procedures to safeguard confidentiality should have been adequate. While the press might have properly been denied access to the commission proceedings, it could not constitutionally be punished for publishing information about them. The same result has been reached in several controversial decisions allowing the press or other media to disclose the identity of rape victims or juvenile offenders.[176] In the *Florida Star* case the majority judgment of Marshall J. said that, in the absence of a state interest of the highest order, publication of true information which had been lawfully obtained could not properly be punished.[177] In that case, a rape victim's name had been mentioned in a police report, albeit by mistake; although it could have been kept confidential, the report was available for inspection in a press office open to the public.

It is not surprising that the US courts are reluctant to countenance restrictions on media reporting of true information, even where there was a clear state policy to preclude disclosure of the rape victim's name before trial and where the courts have power to prohibit disclosure of her name and other identifying details during the proceedings. Direct restrictions on press reports more clearly implicate First Amendment rights than rules which hinder newsgathering by the media. But a report by a popular newspaper or on television will have enormous impact on the privacy of the victim, and may well deter other women from reporting rape to the police.[178] In contrast, the impact of inadvertent mention of her name in a public report or to those physically present in the courtroom will be relatively trivial. There are in fact sometimes stronger arguments for restrictions on media reporting than there are for limits on access to the trial itself, even though these restrictions clearly engage the free speech rights of the press to report legal proceedings.

---

[175] 435 US 829 (1978).

[176] *Cox Broadcasting Corpn* v. *Cohn* 420 US 469 (1975); *Oklahoma Publishing Co* v. *District Court* 430 US 308 (1977); *Smith* v. *Daily Mail Publishing Co* 443 US 97 (1979); *Florida Star* v. *BJF* 491 US 524 (1989).

[177] Ibid., 541: see ch. VI, s. 5(iii) above for discussion of the case in the context of free speech and privacy.

[178] P. Marcus and T. L. McMahon, 'Limiting Disclosure of Rape Victims' Identities' (1991) 64 *Southern California Law Rev* 1020.

X

Pornography

1. Introduction

The legitimacy of legal controls on pornography may have elicited more academic commentary than any other topic covered in this book. This phenomenon reflects our abiding interest in anything connected with sex. It is also attributable to the wide range of controversial questions of principle and policy raised in any consideration of reform of this area of law. Happily, this chapter is not concerned with all the issues discussed by bodies such as the US Commission on Obscenity and the United Kingdom Committee chaired by Bernard Williams, both of which recommended the relaxation of legal controls, particularly on written publications.[1] Neither body found it easy to reconcile the suppression of pornography with the value placed on freedom of speech. This chapter will show that the application of free speech principles to pornography is far from straightforward. In particular, it examines the extent to which total bans and partial restrictions on its availability rest on arguments which are compatible with freedom of speech.

At the outset, something should be said about the terms 'pornography' and 'obscenity'. In the previous edition of this book this chapter was titled 'Obscenity', largely because that is the principal term used in the law—in England, other Commonwealth jurisdictions, and the United States—to refer to sexually explicit material, the dissemination of which is forbidden. But it is better to employ the word 'pornography', which is conventionally used to refer to sexually explicit representations, whether in the form of a book, film, photograph, or other image.[2] The term 'obscenity' is narrower, in that it often refers to the category of sexually explicit material which may be proscribed, because it has harmful effects. In the United States it denotes hard-core material which falls outside the First Amendment and is not covered by freedom of speech. On the other hand, the term is wider in that other types of publication may be treated as 'obscene', insofar as they are harmful. Books or films advocating the use of hard drugs may, for example, be considered obscene. Moreover, articles such as sex toys may be regarded as

---

[1] Report of the US Commission on Obscenity and Pornography (Washington, 1970); Report of the Committee on Obscenity and Film Censorship ('Williams Committee') (Cmnd 7772, 1979).

[2] Williams Committee (n. 1 above), para. 8.2. Literally 'pornography' means a description of the acts of harlots.

obscene, but hardly as pornographic. It is better to speak of pornography in this chapter, because the questions explored in it concern the application of free speech principles to publications which are sexually explicit.

A crucial threshold question is how far pornography should be immune from legal control because it is a form of 'speech'. In the United States, Canada, Germany, and many other countries, this is a legal issue. If a pornographic magazine is 'speech', then it is covered by the First Amendment, or other freedom of expression clause, and its publication can properly be regulated only if the state is able to adduce powerful reasons for this course. In the United Kingdom the relevance of the free speech principle to the control of pornography has until recently been a matter for philosophical argument and political debate; with the incorporation of the European Convention on Human Rights and Fundamental Freedoms (ECHR), English and Scottish courts must consider how far freedom of expression extends to sexually explicit material. The report of the Williams Committee, for example, discussed how far Mill's free speech theory applies to pornography. Resolution of the question requires some reference to the arguments for free speech protection considered in Chapter I. Moreover, some points made in Chapter III on the meaning of 'speech' may also be relevant. But one or two other points should be made before these ideas are developed.

There may be constitutional arguments other than the claim that pornography is covered by a general free speech clause. Claims may be made on the basis of specific provisions for freedom of artistic expression or for the free development of personality.[3] Arguments from these freedoms may reinforce the case for immunity from regulation based on a general free speech provision. But more radical claims frequently made to support a right to obtain and read pornography extend beyond the limits of freedom of speech. For example, it has been urged that the suppression of pornography, including live sex shows, violates general rights of moral autonomy or more specific rights to choose one's sexual lifestyle.[4] Hitherto, courts have been reluctant to recognize such broad rights. The US Supreme Court has upheld a privacy right to read pornography in one's own home, but later cases show a marked reluctance to extend this right to other situations.[5] It may be that these wide arguments provide a better basis for upholding claims to look at pornographic material. But such arguments fall outside the scope of this book.

So far as possible free speech arguments here, as in other contexts, should be distinguished from privacy and general libertarian claims. They should not be confused, as they may have been by commentators, particularly in the

---

[3] See German Basic Law, art. 2 (right to personality) and art. 5(3) (freedom of art and science, research, and teaching).

[4] See in particular R. M. Dworkin, 'Is there a Right to Pornography?' (1981) 1 *OJLS* 177.

[5] *Stanley v. Georgia* 394 US 557 (1969) upheld a constitutional privacy right to read pornography in the home, but the Court has declined to uphold privacy rights to receive such material through the post (*US v. Reidel* 402 US 351 (1971)) or to import it for personal use (*US v. 12 200 Ft Reels* 413 US 123 (1973)).

United States, when making their case for the unconstitutionality of pornography bans imposed to protect the moral tone of society. It is one thing to object to a ban on the ground that it infringes freedom of speech, but another to argue that it invades the right of individuals to take their own moral decisions, say, to embrace pornography as an aspect of a particular sexual life. The former claims that pornography is 'speech' and its distribution should not be limited, because speech is special. A privacy (or general libertarian) claim rests on other arguments, such as the importance of an activity, for instance, sexual behaviour, to individual identity. It may be made in circumstances where free speech arguments are difficult to sustain: where conduct, rather than communication, is in issue or where the object of government regulation is to avert the consequences of action, rather than change attitudes.[6] Of course, it is not always easy to disentangle free speech and privacy arguments. In *R* v. *Sharpe*[7] the Supreme Court of Canada was concerned with a challenge to the constitutionality of a provision of the Criminal Code penalizing the possession of child pornography. It held that freedom of expression was engaged. A right to possess material, which might be communicated, was covered by section 2(b) of the Charter; the Court noted that the Charter provision guarantees freedom of thought and belief, as well as freedom of expression. But the Court also considered the Code provision intruded on personal privacy. That might be considered a better basis for a challenge to the law, as it is far from clear that child pornography is properly characterized as speech.[8]

A common confusion is that between the *constitutionality* and the *wisdom* of legislation to control pornography. A judicial ruling that sexually explicit material is not constitutionally protected does not mean that it is sensible to ban its distribution.[9] The decision is simply left to the legislature. There are a number of good arguments against attempting to suppress such material which have nothing to do with constitutional rights: obscenity laws are difficult to enforce, the task may distract the police from more pressing matters, and intervention does interfere with privacy and other personal liberties, whether or not they have constitutional status.

Conversely, the conclusion that even hard-core pornography is covered by freedom of speech does not exhaust the legal argument. The state may nevertheless be entitled to restrict its availability, or even to ban it altogether, insofar as there are compelling justifications for taking that step. Only absolutists would deny this. But the assessment of the weight of these arguments against a presumption in favour of free speech poses difficult problems for judges. If it is sometimes legitimate to ban pornography, the decision which particular books or films should be proscribed might be better left to juries under general guidance from the trial judge or perhaps, as in New Zealand, to a specialist tribunal rather than to the ordinary courts.

---

[6] See ch. III, s. 2 above for the speech–conduct distinction.   [7] (2001) 194 DLR (4th) 1.
[8] See s. 4(iv) below.
[9] On the other hand, a refusal to strike down legislation may have the effect of legitimizing it: see A. M. Bickel, *The Least Dangerous Branch* (New York: Bobbs-Merrill, 1962), 29–33.

A similar institutional consideration of this character seems to have persuaded the Supreme Court in the leading case, *Roth* v. *United States*,[10] to rule that obscenity is outside the area of constitutionally protected speech. On this approach, the majority of the Court held there was no need to assess whether the *particular* publication presented a clear and present danger of likely anti-social conduct, an inquiry which would probably have entailed assessment of the book and of empirical evidence. But Harlan J., dissenting, thought the Court could not so easily escape scrutiny of the facts. For the trial judge must still determine whether a particular book or other work is 'obscene' under the criteria laid down by the Supreme Court. It was wrong, therefore, to hope that courts could entirely evade an assessment of particular material merely by treating 'obscenity' as outside the area of protected speech. Indeed, for that reason, in a later case, Brennan J. suggested that any proscription of pornography inevitably required judges in state courts to apply an inherently vague standard, creating uncertainty and deterring the release of non-obscene material which is covered by freedom of speech.[11]

Although, therefore, its resolution does not remove all difficulties, it is important to answer the threshold question whether sexually explicit material should be regarded as speech. If the free speech principle does cover hard-core pornography, then the legislature must produce compelling reasons to justify its proscription; put another way, courts must subject obscenity laws to strict scrutiny to ensure that free speech rights are not infringed. If, on the other hand, hard-core pornography is not 'speech', the legislature has greater freedom to ban it, although it may decide that is not, all things considered, a sensible course to take.

2. Is Pornography 'Speech'?

(i) Arguments of principle

One answer to this question denies there is any difficulty. Granted that speech includes all forms of representation, pornographic books, films, and videos fall under free speech or freedom of expression clauses. The only relevant distinction is the familiar one between speech and conduct. In fact, the Supreme Court has adopted a relatively broad view of speech in the context of this difference: nude dancing, for example, has been held 'expressive conduct' covered by the First Amendment, albeit entitled to less protection than standard modes of communication.[12] There would still be a number of borderline cases. Live sex shows accompanied by a verbal commentary might be hard to classify. But hard-core verbal and pictorial pornography would enjoy full protection.

---

[10] 354 US 476 (1957).   [11] *Paris Adult Theatre* v. *Slaton* 413 US 49, 83–93 (1973).
[12] See *Barnes* v. *Glen Theatre, Inc* 501 US 560 (1991) and other cases discussed in ch. III, s. 2(iii) above.

This is not the position, however, in the United States or in the vast majority of other liberal democracies where political and other types of speech are fully protected. The point is that 'speech' is not in a legal context given its broad dictionary meaning, but is treated as a term of art. Certain types of expression, though literally 'speech', are not so regarded for the purpose of constitutional coverage. As stated in Chapter III, perjury, bribery, and contractual promises, for example, have never qualified for constitutional protection.[13] The scope of 'freedom of speech' can only be determined by looking at the reasons for its special constitutional position.

The justifications for according freedom of speech a degree of special constitutional protection were discussed in Chapter I. We saw that there are considerable difficulties in basing a free speech principle on arguments concerning fundamental rights to self-fulfilment and self-development.[14] These claims are too wide to establish free speech as a discrete and special right, for they equally support other liberties. A background right to dignity or personal moral autonomy might appear in this context to justify the recognition of constitutional rights to unregulated sexual behaviour as well as of rights to distribute or read pornography. If the rationale is unhelpful in justifying the case for a special free speech principle, it follows that it is useless for determining the meaning of speech. Indeed it does not matter much on this argument whether pornography is characterized as speech or not, for its consumption would be immune from regulation on broad libertarian grounds.

It may not be any easier to invoke the other principal arguments for the free speech principle. The argument from democracy applies more obviously to political and social speech than to sexually explicit material without information or ideas. Admittedly, radical political speech about, say, the reform of laws concerning sexual conduct may have some pornographic content. But it would be ludicrous to claim of all hard-core pornography, particularly pictorial literature, that it is implicitly saying something about politics or social relationships. Most pornography is essentially non-cognitive; it does not make claims which might be true. So it is also hard to apply Mill's truth arguments. Rather, the intention of its publishers, and its effect, is to create sexual excitement, to provide material for the indulgence of fantasy. It is an aid to masturbation. Indeed, there is little significant distinction between the impact of a picture magazine, depicting sexual intercourse in close detail, and that of a plastic sex aid or a visit from a prostitute. Now it may be that the public availability of all three means of taking pleasure should be immune from regulation. But that is not a free speech argument. A pornographic picture magazine no more involves communication than these other two means of achieving sexual satisfaction.

[13] See ch. III, s. 1 above, and Schauer, 92. The discussion in this section is indebted to ch. 12 of Schauer's book, and also to his article, 'Speech and "Speech"—Obscenity and "Obscenity": An Exercise in the Interpretation of Constitutional Language' (1977) 61 *Georgetown Law Rev* 899.

[14] Ch. 1, s. 2(ii) above.

Powerful though this case is, a number of points may be made against it. First, it is clear in the United States and other jurisdictions that freedom of speech is not confined legally to intellectual and political discourse, but also includes literature and the visual arts. A constitution may expressly recognize a right to artistic expression which would certainly cover pornographic pictures, statues, and films, as well as novels and drama. Although the argument from truth suggests that speech can only cover the enunciation of propositions which might be true or false, the scope of constitutional protection is much wider. If emotive political epithets ('Fuck the Draft') are treated as covered by the First Amendment,[15] why should it not also cover hard-core pornography which similarly reveals no truths, but which may be presented elegantly and artistically? The assumption underlying this point is questionable: no line can be drawn between literature or other imaginative discourse on the one hand, and the truly pornographic on the other. A literary critic might disagree with that view. 'Writing conceived as art is in most ways the antithesis of pornography. It implies detachment, a rigorous exercise of the critical faculty, and the constant reference to observable realism.'[16] From that perspective, serious literature does appeal to reason and the intellect; no matter how erotic its content, it should be regarded as 'speech', rather than liable to proscription as pornography. Various definitions of 'obscenity' discussed later in this chapter show how courts have attempted to draw this distinction.

Another difficulty is, of course, that serious works of literature and films may be banned under laws aimed at hard-core pornography of no merit whatsoever. Prosecutions have been brought against such significant works as Joyce's *Ulysses* and Lawrence's *Lady Chatterley's Lover*.[17] This danger influenced the conclusions of the Williams Committee which in 1979 proposed several changes to the obscenity laws in England. It found Mill's arguments for freedom of speech hard to apply to pornography, particularly explicit pictorial matter. Nevertheless, it accepted that even in this context there is a strong presumption in favour of free expression, and it feared that serious literature would likely be caught by vague obscenity laws.[18] The Committee therefore suggested the abandonment of all controls on written matter where 'the argument about the survival of new ideas and perceptions applies most directly'.[19] It may be noted that the US Supreme Court has treated only hard-core pictorial pornography as obscene, and therefore as falling outside the scope of 'speech' for the First Amendment, although it has not totally excluded the possibility that extreme hard-core written pornography could be treated in the same way.[20]

---

[15] *Cohen* v. *California* 403 US 15 (1971).

[16] W. Allen, 'The Writer and the Frontiers of Tolerance', in J. Chandos (ed.), *To Deprave and Corrupt...* (London: Souvenir Press, 1962), 146.

[17] See *US* v. *'Ulysses'* 5 F Supp 182, aff'd 72 F 2d 705 (2nd Cir, 1934); *R* v. *Penguin Books* [1961] Crim LR 176. [18] Williams Committee (n. 1 above), paras. 5.15–5.25.

[19] Ibid., para. 5.25. [20] *Kaplan* v. *California* 413 US 115, 119 (1973).

There is, of course, a danger that serious innovative literature may be suppressed under obscenity laws, or more likely that it will not be published because of their 'chilling' or deterrent effect. Such a danger is inevitable, in the absence of absolute protection for all material which might be regarded as speech for the purposes of constitutional protection. Naturally, one may doubt the ability of the legislature or the courts to formulate sufficiently precise standards to ensure that only hard-core pornography is caught by obscenity laws. Such scepticism played a part in the dissent of Brennan J. in the *Paris Adult Theatre* case.[21] One limb of the Court's test for 'obscenity' is whether the publication depicts in a patently offensive way ultimate sexual acts. If it does, then it might not be regarded as 'speech' and could be regulated by state obscenity laws. In Brennan J.'s view, this standard imposed an impossible task on the judiciary. Its application to picture magazines would inevitably be unpredictable. Moreover, there would be a grave risk of abuse if it were applied to written material.

The issue is whether these risks can be minimized so that they can be regarded as trivial. Perhaps legislation can be framed with sufficient precision to catch hard-core pornography without imperilling the free speech rights of authors and publishers. Further, the courts, particularly courts with power to review the constitutionality of legislation, should ensure that these rights are respected. The presumption in favour of free speech means that pornography laws should be interpreted restrictively, so works of literature, art, and films of any quality will not be affected—even if that course means that some hard-core material will escape prosecution.

The last few paragraphs have considered the argument that it is difficult and dangerous to draw a line between erotic literature, fully covered by freedom of speech, on the other hand, and hard-core pornography on the other. We now consider a more radical argument. It is that all, or at least virtually all, pornography should be treated as speech, because sexually explicit material does convey ideas—that sex is fun, that it need have nothing to do with permanent relationships, that it is good to be erotically aroused whenever one wants, and so on. The message of such material can only be put across effectively by the distribution of hard-core pornography.[22] Another way of putting the case is to suggest that one of the purposes of pornography, whether gay or straight, is to explode the distinction between the private and the public in the discussion and portrayal of sexual activity; on this view, the proscription of hard-core material artificially excludes one perspective from public discourse. This novel use of 'The Medium is the Message' line of thought is buttressed by precedents from other areas of free speech jurisprudence. In particular, Harlan J.'s support for the protection of emotive political speech in *Cohen* v. *California* is frequently cited: '... much linguistic

[21] *Paris Adult Theatre* v. *Slaton* 413 US 49, 83–93 (1973).
[22] D. A. J. Richards, 'Toward a Moral Theory of the First Amendment' (1974) 123 *Univ of Pennsylvania Law Rev* 45.

expression serves a dual communicative function: it conveys not only ideas of relatively precise, detached explication, but otherwise inexpressible emotions as well'.[23] Admittedly, that case dealt with a mode of communicating political speech. Moreover, much pornography does not involve linguistic expression at all, but the graphic depiction of intimate sexual activity or close-up shots of genitals. But the radical case is not far-fetched. If it is wrong to outlaw certain forms of expression in the context of political speech, is it not equally incompatible with freedom of speech to distinguish acceptable and unacceptable modes of communication about sexual matters?

Freedom of speech does not always entail a right to communicate an idea by the most effective method. Otherwise there could be no objection to the use of loud-speakers and sound-trucks, a mode of communication which may be the easiest way to spread information to a small community, but which may be subject to local regulation.[24] The decisive objection, however, is that to concede a right to *effective* communication risks blurring the line between speech and action. In some circumstances, violence may be used to protest against a political policy or to communicate the strength of feelings on particularly controversial issues, for example, the abortion laws or participation in a war. But an argument that violence in those circumstances amounts to speech cannot be upheld; its acceptance would make nonsense of any distinction between speech and conduct.[25] Similarly, hard-core pornography does not qualify as speech merely because it portrays sexual activity more explicitly and, in a sense, more effectively than the most accurate medical or literary account.

It is much more useful to enquire why governments wish to suppress pornography. Some commentators argue that hard-core pornography should be treated as 'speech', because government restricts it out of a dislike for its radical message.[26] As we saw in Chapter III,[27] freedom of speech may be engaged whenever the intention of the ban is to hinder the dissemination of an idea or the spread of information. Application of this principle to pornography may not be straightforward. Clearly, bans on the use of drugs, tobacco, or alcoholic drinks would not be subject to scrutiny on free speech grounds; government is entitled to regulate the consumption of products it regards as harmful. Equally, a government may claim that it restricts the availability of pornography because its unrestricted consumption is harmful, rather than because it communicates subversive ideas. But that claim seems very implausible. In the first place, pornography usually assumes the same forms—books, magazines, and films—as other types of speech which are plainly covered by freedom of speech. It differs in that respect from the supply of drugs and tobacco. More importantly, it is hard to see what reason a government

---

[23] 403 US 15, 26 (1971).
[24] *Saia* v. *New York* 334 US 558 (1948); *Kovacs* v. *Cooper* 336 US 77 (1949).
[25] See the argument in ch. III, s. 2(i) above.
[26] See e.g. L. Alexander, 'Low Value Speech' (1989) 83 *North Western Univ Law Rev* 547.
[27] Ch. III, s. 2 above.

might have for banning pornography, other than a dislike of its message about, say, the position of women or a fear that readers and viewers might assault women or children as a result of looking at it. The availability of sexually explicit material, unlike tobacco or drugs, is not restricted in order to safeguard public health. On the other hand, restrictions on the location of outlets for selling pornography can be justified for reasons other than dislike of its content: sex shops spoil the character of residential areas and might attract prostitutes and drug pushers.[28]

There is another dimension which has not been fully explored in discussion of the status of pornography. Almost all of it is written and published simply to make money. Its publishers have no intention of communicating information or opinions. While even the shabbiest politician wants his audience to believe what he has to say or to vote for him, a porn merchant simply wants consumers to purchase his wares. As far as he is concerned they can throw them away afterwards. This feature of pornographic publication was emphasized by Warren CJ in the leading obscenity cases, *Roth* v. *United States* and *Alberts* v. *California*, decided together in 1957.[29] Subsequent cases have treated the distributor's marketing methods as an important factor: erotic literature advertised in an obscene way may fall outside the First Amendment.[30]

As a matter of principle, typical purveyors of pornography can hardly claim they are exercising a right of free speech. That is why more emphasis is placed on the rights of consumers in this context.[31] Elsewhere in this book it is argued that the recipient's interests in obtaining access to information (or the public interest in its communication) may justify the recognition of free speech rights in circumstances where the speaker has forfeited, or is not in a position to protect, them.[32] But it may be difficult to characterize pornography as speech solely because of the recipient's interest in its purchase, when the speaker's claim to exercise freedom of expression is so transparently bogus. Of course, this characterization is a little crude. There are some cases, particularly of sexually explicit writing or films disseminated to shock or disturb or to buttress radical political claims, where the speaker's interest seems quite strong. But it would then be wrong to characterize the writer or film-maker as a pornographer; rather he is engaged in a form of public discourse, as are protesters who employ indecent language to make a political point.

This last point can be illustrated by referring to an early US decision in this area. The Supreme Court held that the film *Lady Chatterley's Lover* which advocated the desirability (in some circumstances) of adultery could not be constitutionally proscribed as 'obscene' under the test it had formulated two years earlier; the film was covered by the First Amendment.[33] The Court majority considered

---

[28] These undesirable secondary effects are considered in s. 6 below.
[29] 354 US 476 (1957).
[30] e.g. *Ginzburg* v. *US* 383 US 463 (1966). But under the English Obscene Publications Act 1959 commercial motive is irrelevant on a charge of publishing obscene material.
[31] As by Dworkin (n. 4 above).   [32] See ch. I, s. 3(ii) above and ch. XIV, ss. 3 and 5 below.
[33] *Kingsley International Pictures Corp* v. *Regents* 360 US 684 (1959).

that the New York statute, requiring the state to refuse a licence for the exhibition of a film which portrayed acts of sexual immorality as desirable or acceptable, improperly restricted the circulation of ideas; it therefore struck at speech. 'Ideological obscenity', as it has sometimes been called, is rightly characterized as 'speech', because it does appeal to the intellect or artistic sensitivity.[34] Whether the ideas canvassed in the work are abhorrent or offensive to the vast majority of people is no more relevant than it would be in the case of political or social speech.

The characterization of hard-core pornography is more difficult. The positive arguments for extending free speech protection are weak or exaggerated. It is grotesque, for example, to suggest that a film containing only close-up shots of sexual activity necessarily communicates an idea, or that neither the legislature nor the courts can distinguish between it and a film of artistic merit. Nevertheless, it would be wrong to exclude publications or displays with sexually explicit content, falling short of the most extreme hard-core material, from the coverage of a free speech or expression clause. Sometimes their explicit content will be coupled with a cultural or educational message, or have some artistic merit. And it is hard to see that there is any reason for suppression, which is not related to the sexually explicit content of the publication. Free speech is put in danger if courts too readily deny pornography the protection afforded by the First Amendment or other constitutional provision.

(ii) Pornography which falls outside 'speech'

Freedom of speech provisions certainly cover some sexually explicit publications. The more interesting constitutional questions concern the scope of their protection, given the arguments the government advances to justify proscription or restriction on their availability. These questions are considered in later sections of this chapter. Something should be said now about the approach taken by courts, notably the US Supreme Court, under which a small category of hard-core publications falls wholly outside the coverage of freedom of speech.

In accord with their general approach to questions concerning the scope of freedom of expression, some courts have no difficulty in holding that freedom of speech covers hard-core material without literary or other merit. For instance, the Supreme Court of Canada in *R* v. *Butler*[35] ruled that such material does convey or attempt to convey meaning and, therefore, has expressive content. It should not be equated with conduct. Moreover, it is irrelevant whether the meaning expressed in it had any 'redeeming' qualities. Nor was the Court impressed by arguments that in this context films should be treated differently from written work. Sopinka J. for the Court even said purely physical activity, including sexual acts, might amount to expression. He was on somewhat surer ground when he

---

[34] See H. Kalven, 'The Metaphysics of the Law of Obscenity' [1960] *Supreme Court Rev* 1, 28–34.
[35] [1992] 1 SCR 452.

added that, in any case, the selection of images of these acts entails the creation of meaning. But it does not follow, as we will see shortly, that the proscription of material treating sexual matters in a degrading or dehumanizing manner is necessarily unconstitutional. In Germany, too, the Constitutional Court has been reluctant to exclude pornography from the coverage of Article 5, in particular from the first sentence of Article 5(3) guaranteeing the freedom of art (*Kunstfreiheit*). The fact that a novel is pornographic does not remove its character as art.[36] Again, exercise of this freedom may be restricted by laws safeguarding interests and values of constitutional importance, in particular, the welfare of children.[37]

In contrast, in the United States, the Supreme Court has in a number of cases wrestled with the question whether all pornography, no matter how hard-core its character, is covered by freedom of speech. In the *Roth* and *Alberts* cases[38] decided in 1957, it held obscenity fell outside the First Amendment, as it was 'utterly without redeeming social importance'; it did not form part of any exposition or discussion of ideas. But only material appealing predominantly to a prurient interest in sexual matters, judged by contemporary community standards, should be regarded as obscene. In later cases, the constitutional threshold was refined. Only hard-core material appealing to that prurient interest, portraying 'sexual conduct in a patently offensive way', and entirely lacking literary or other merit, is regarded as obscene, so failing to qualify as 'speech' for the purposes of the First Amendment.[39] Some types of extreme hard-core pornography may constitutionally be outlawed by the states or the federal government. But it will be very difficult for them to ban, or even to restrict the distribution of, less objectionable matter, given the strong protection afforded to the exercise of speech rights. For instance, the Court held unconstitutional two provisions of the Communications Decency Act of 1996 which banned the sending of indecent messages on the Internet to recipients under eighteen years old or the sending and display of patently offensive messages to them.[40] Though intended to protect children and young persons, the ban inevitably limited the freedom of adults to transmit and receive messages fully covered by freedom of speech. But the transmission of obscene material could be prohibited.

Indeed, it is almost certainly the Supreme Court's reluctance to sustain limits on free speech that explains why it may feel compelled, at least in theory, to isolate some categories of extremely unpleasant or damaging material—in particular child pornography—and exclude it from the coverage of the First Amendment. Other courts do not have this problem. They can allow the free speech or expression provision wide scope, in the knowledge that the state may be able to justify the imposition of some limits on the publication of sexually explicit material.

---

[36] 83 BVerfGE 130 (1990).   [37] See s. 4 below.
[38] *Roth* v. *United States; Alberts* v. *California* 354 US 476 (1957).
[39] *Miller* v. *California* 413 US 15, 24 (1973).
[40] *Reno* v. *American Civil Liberties Union* 521 US 844 (1997).

The following sections of the chapter are largely concerned with the bases or grounds on which pornography may be restricted. In the United States, these points are instead relevant to the definition of sexually explicit material entirely outside the scope of free speech, for it is the disposition of that question which in effect determines whether pornography may be banned. Three principal grounds for control are examined here. First, the unlimited availability of pornography might be considered inimical to the general moral tone of society; a community should be free, it may be argued, to decide its dissemination affects moral attitudes for the worse. Secondly, there are arguments from specific harms attributed to pornography, for example, that it is responsible for increased violence against women, or that it damages their self-esteem, or other feminist arguments. A third ground for regulation is that the material offends people. In its more defensible form, this is an argument for restrictions on the *public display* of pornography, rather than its total suppression, and is, therefore, one which free speech liberals find relatively acceptable.

3. Obscenity and the Moral Tone of Society

Some liberals argue that it is important to outlaw incitement to racial hatred and other hate speech in order to show society's commitment to integrated and harmonious communities and its abhorrence of discrimination. It does not matter very much whether there are many prosecutions, nor does it trouble the law's advocates that there is little evidence to show that this type of speech causes immediate outbreaks of violence or racial tension. In the long term an unchecked flow of propaganda makes more likely the development of racist attitudes with the incalculable dangers to the cohesion of society. The defenders of hate speech laws argue that free speech should be compromised to promote other fundamental values.[41]

Equally, proponents of anti-pornography laws may defend them on the ground that they reinforce balanced attitudes towards sexuality and reduce the risk of a decline into sexual anarchy and licentiousness. This view is taken not only by unthinking moral conservatives. It has been entertained by such a distinguished constitutional lawyer as Professor Alexander Bickel. In 1971 he wrote in a passage quoted by Burger CJ in the *Paris Adult Theatre* case: '[The problem] concerns the tone of society, the mode, or to use terms that have perhaps greater currency the style and quality of life, now and in the future.'[42] Moreover, just as great books reflect the values of a civilized community and may ennoble and inspire generations, so the very existence of pornography lowers (it may be claimed) our sensitivities and debases society's moral outlook. The state has every right to eradicate it.

[41] See ch. V, s. 4 above.   [42] 22 *The Public Interest*, quoted 413 US 49, 59 (1973).

The broad terms of this argument or, if one prefers, its imprecision constitutes its greatest strength. Unlike some of the arguments concerning specific harms canvassed in the following section, it is difficult to puncture it by reference to the lack of evidence establishing a connection between pornography and moral change. The incidence of rape or individual moral corruption may be no greater now than in Victorian times, but the wider availability of pornography reflects and reinforces attitudes to sexual morality different from those held in the nineteenth century. A community in which it was commonplace for people to read hard-core pornography (whether inside plain covers or not) when riding home from work on a bus would have a distinctive character, alien even to that of modern Britain or the United States. If the overwhelming majority of the people want to prevent the emergence of such a society, does adherence to the free speech principle stop it?

The obvious objection to this argument is that commitment to freedom of speech precludes legislation outlawing sexual expression. Free speech, as one Canadian judge put it, protects challenges to established ideas about sexual matters, just as it guarantees the freedom to challenge political orthodoxy.[43] Some pornographic material represents an attempt to persuade readers or viewers of the attractiveness of radical sexual lifestyles, or to reinforce the sexual identity of gays and lesbians.[44] Insofar as legislation precludes communications intended to produce those effects, it is clearly contrary to free speech principles. More strongly, it may be said that broad anti-pornography rules cannot be justified by recourse to moral tone arguments, because the commitment to free expression on sexual matters itself represents an integral aspect of a liberal community's morality.

The only escape from this argument is to deny that hard-core pornography, or perhaps some types of it, amount to speech, the case considered in outline in the previous section of this chapter. It is now appropriate to examine in detail the approach taken by the US Supreme Court in an attempt to isolate a category of sexually explicit material which falls outside the First Amendment. Insofar as that approach is coherent, the publication of such material may constitutionally be proscribed without raising free speech objections, just as the state is entitled to preserve its moral tone by outlawing, for instance, the use of drugs or gambling.

Under the formulation in *Miller v. California* (1973), still the leading case in modern US law, 'obscenity' is limited to:

works which, taken as a whole, appeal to the prurient interest in sex, which portray sexual conduct in a patently offensive way, and which taken as a whole, do not have serious literary, artistic, political, or scientific value.[45]

The first ingredient here—appeal to a prurient interest in sex—captures those non-rational, almost physical, features of pornography which may take it outside

[43] Iacobucci J. in *Little Sisters Book and Art Emporium* v. *Minister of Justice and A-G of Canada* [2000] 2 SCR 1120, paras. 247, 274.
[44] See the argument of Joseph Raz in 'Free Expression and Personal Identification' (1991) 11 *OJLS* 303, considered in ch. I, s. 4 above.   [45] 413 US 15, 24 (1973).

the scope of freedom of speech. Yet the term is curiously ill-defined in the case-law of the Supreme Court. In the earlier *Roth* case,[46] Brennan J. had given it the dictionary meaning of 'having a tendency to excite lustful thoughts', but that is clearly too wide. Lust may be one of the seven deadly sins, but its experience is virtually universal. Moreover, serious works of literature may arouse such feelings. What seems to be indicated is material which is purely designed to excite sexual fantasies, largely as an aid to masturbation. Stewart J. preferred the simple term, hard-core pornography, 'without trying further to define it';[47] in another case he had said, 'I know it when I see it'.[48]

The formula in the Canadian Criminal Code may be as good an attempt as any to describe material which does not communicate ideas or information and which treats sexual matters in a degrading manner: 'any publication a dominant characteristic of which is the undue exploitation of sex...shall be deemed to be obscene.'[49] But the Canadian Supreme Court has held the overriding object of this provision is to prevent harm to society, rather than to express moral disapproval or to maintain conventional social standards.[50] Indeed, the latter objectives would not be consistent with the Charter's commitment to freedom of expression. The coherence of the distinction drawn by the Court can be doubted, given that it did not require clear proof of any particular harm resulting from the availability of hard-core pornography, and is prepared to accept that exposure to it brings about 'changes in attitudes and beliefs'. At any rate, it does not consider this material as standing on an equal footing with public discourse on political and social matters.

If the United States Supreme Court has not said enough about the first limb of its obscenity definition, it has arguably written too much about the second: matters 'which portray sexual conduct in a patently offensive way'. Although in theory an additional requirement, in practice it assumes more importance than the 'prurient interest in sex' condition. Originally formulated by Harlan J. in *Manual Enterprises* v. *Day*,[51] it first enjoyed the approval of a Court majority in the *Memoirs* case, where it upheld the right of Americans to read *Fanny Hill*.[52] The justification for the use of this formula is probably that it enables contemporary moral judgements to be incorporated in the 'obscenity' test. At any rate the Supreme Court in *Miller* gave as examples of what could properly be regulated by the states under this head, 'patently offensive representations or descriptions of ultimate sexual acts, normal or perverted, actual or simulated', and 'patently offensive representations or descriptions of masturbation, excretory functions, and lewd exhibition of the genitals'. The desirability of precision, properly underlined by the Court, has of course encouraged states to formulate what is proscribed in embarrassing detail. Laws outlawing the

---

[46] 354 US 476 (1957).   [47] *Ginzburg* v. *US* 383 US 463, 499 (1966).
[48] *Jacobellis* v. *Ohio* 378 US 184, 197 (1964).   [49] S. 163(8).
[50] *R* v. *Butler* [1992] 1 SCR 452: see Moon, 106–17.   [51] 370 US 478 (1962).
[52] *Memoirs* v. *Massachusetts* 383 US 413 (1966).

depiction in film or photograph of the erect male organ, but implicitly permitting it to be shown flaccid are on one view rather ridiculous. Their object is, however, commendable. The only alternative, short of abandoning any attempt to regulate extremely obscene material, is to leave it to juries to determine what is patently offensive.

The Supreme Court has consistently emphasized that the *average person* must find the material offensive under *contemporary community standards* for this limb of the obscenity definition to be satisfied. It is right to assess a publication by reference to its impact on an average person rather than on a particularly vulnerable or sensitive person (a sex maniac or a nun, for example), for otherwise the availability of reading matter would be determined by the standards of a small minority. In this respect United States law contrasts strongly with the requirement in the English Obscene Publications Act that only a significant proportion of likely readers need be depraved and corrupted. Theoretically, therefore, it is possible for a publication to be successfully prosecuted in England merely because a large number of the sexual deviants at whom it is aimed are liable to be further corrupted by looking at it; it is immaterial that ordinary people would find it inoffensive or just ridiculous.[53] This result cannot occur in the United States if the law is applied properly.

The meaning of 'contemporary community standards', relevant to both the first two limbs of the obscenity formula, has, however, given rise to considerable difficulty. In *Miller*, it was decided that state law need not require the jury to assess the publication by reference to *national* standards, since this might compel a relatively conservative community to accept publications found tolerable in more permissive areas. The reasonable man on the Boise, Idaho omnibus is not the same person as the man who takes the last subway home in Manhattan. Later cases show that the states are not obliged to apply local or state-wide standards; the jury may assess the material, it seems, by the standards of more or less any community it chooses.[54] The juryman must not, however, decide on the basis of his own subjective reaction to the material. The state court may admit evidence of local community standards, though it is not obliged to do so. But evidence of what happened when other comparable publications were prosecuted is not admissible, though, of course, in principle it provides a good indication of what a section of the community thinks about such material. This rule incidentally also applies in England, where it has long been held that the character of other publications which are freely available is irrelevant to the question whether a particular article is obscene.[55]

The Internet poses problems in this context. Communications on the Internet circulate easily nationally (and internationally); conversely, in contrast with postal

---

[53] Contrast the 'aversion' defence (s. 4(ii) below) where concern with the reaction of the likely readers of pornography may allow pornographic material to escape conviction.

[54] *Hamling* v. *US* 418 US 87 (1974); *Jenkins* v. *Georgia* 418 US 153 (1974).

[55] *R* v. *Reiter* [1954] 2 QB 16, DC; *R* v. *Elliott* (1996) 1 Cr App R 432, CA.

communications, or even dial-a-porn services on the telephone,[56] it may be impossible to stop their receipt in particular areas or communities.[57] The assessment of pornographic content on this medium of communication by reference to local standards would create serious dangers for freedom of speech, since the most conservative community would be able to impose their standards on the rest of the country. Web publishers would be inhibited from hosting sexually explicit material or messages, for fear that in some community it would be regarded as obscene or injurious to children. The issue has been considered recently by the Supreme Court.[58] It held that the reliance of the Child Online Protection Act on community standards to determine what material was harmful to children was not as such unconstitutional. But several judges questioned whether the variation in community standards might pose constitutional difficulties, and O'Connor J. explicitly, and other members of the Court by implication, said that adoption of a national standard was necessary for any regulation of Internet obscenity to withstand scrutiny under the First Amendment.

It is in fact difficult to justify a 'local community standards' approach to the application of any federal statute, whether it is concerned with the regulation of the Internet or the traditional postal service. The posting of indecent material across state boundaries may be illegal in some parts of the country, but not in others, because of the different attitudes of particular communities; the result, as Brennan J. has pointed out, is to reduce what may safely be distributed to the highest common factor of what is acceptable throughout the United States.[59] More fundamentally, it is hard to justify the use of variable standards in the context of a federal constitution, under which citizens of all the states enjoy the same First Amendment rights. Burger CJ's argument that the meaning of 'prurient interest' and 'patently offensive' involves issues of fact, and that, therefore, a uniform approach is not required by the national Constitution seems a little naive. The Canadian courts in contrast have adopted a national standards test to determine what is to be tolerated in the community.[60] Expert evidence which only shows local attitudes must be rejected. But in the recent *Little Sisters* case,[61] it was emphasized that the national standards test should be applied to respect the interests of particular minorities, including gays and lesbians.

Some of these issues, admittedly in a radically different context, have come before the European Court of Human Rights.[62] The *Handyside* case raised the question whether the forfeiture proceedings taken in London under the Obscene

---

[56] In *Sable Communications of California* v. *FCC* 492 US 115 (1989), the Court held that local community standards could be applied to determine whether these telephone services were obscene.
[57] See ch. XIII, s. 5 below.
[58] *Ashcroft* v. *American Civil Liberties Union* 535 US 564 (2002).
[59] See his dissent in *Hamling* v. *US* 418 US 87, 141 (1974).
[60] *R* v. *Butler* [1992] 1 SCR 452.
[61] *Little Sisters Book and Art Emporium* v. *Minister of Justice and A-G of Canada* [2000] 2 SCR 1120.
[62] *Handyside* v. *UK* (1976) 1 EHRR 737.

Publications Act 1959 against the publishers of *The Little Red Schoolbook* violated Article 10 of the Convention. The publication urged the young people, to whom it was primarily addressed, to adopt a liberal attitude to sexual matters, and certain passages could be construed as advocating early sexual experience, which would be illegal in the case of children under sixteen. After deciding that the publication was covered by Article 10—it was really 'ideological obscenity', rather than hard-core pornography—the Court went on to consider whether the proceedings were necessary to protect morals. On this point it ruled each state has a margin of discretion in determining whether to restrict or suppress the circulation of books and magazines. National authorities were in a better position to decide what steps are necessary to safeguard the morals of their community, although the European Court could review their determinations to ensure that restrictions were proportionate. There is therefore no uniform degree of free expression throughout the states which are parties to the Convention—at least in this particular area. Publications which circulate freely in Sweden or Denmark are, and may legitimately be, banned in the Republic of Ireland or in Malta. Indeed the Court considered it irrelevant that *The Little Red Schoolbook* was circulating freely in many member states. Perhaps more surprisingly, it also did not take very seriously the contentions that the book had not been prosecuted in other parts of the United Kingdom (while a prosecution in Scotland had failed), and that hard-core pornographic magazines, often available to children, were tolerated by the law enforcement authorities. Implicit in the Court's approach is the view that the standards applied by each member state need not be *national*, but may be *local*.

The *Handyside* case raises broad questions on the desirability and feasibility of common standards throughout the member states. In effect the Court ruled that it would only require a minimum common level of free speech protection; beyond that level it was open to each state to determine its own standards. This approach is more understandable in an international scheme for human rights protection than it is in the context of a federal constitution. More pertinently, the decision also raises the question whether this flexible approach is inevitable in areas such as obscenity law. Perhaps it is difficult to avoid. Any definition of 'obscenity' in terms of 'offensiveness to contemporary community values' necessarily raises questions about the size and character of the *community* whose judgement is to be considered, as well as about the more obviously contentious concept of 'offensiveness'. The larger the community, the less likely that its members will share common values, except the fashionable faith in the virtues of pluralism. Small may be beautiful, but liberals should remember that it is easier for tiny communities to adopt restrictive attitudes on matters of moral and social behaviour.

The problem is then to find a coherent role and meaning for the concept of 'contemporary community standards', on the assumption that it is relevant to the control of pornography. The US Supreme Court's approach, which employs the concept in the *definition* of obscenity and, therefore, as a factor in determining the scope of speech, together with its interpretation as referring to local standards, is hard to reconcile with a national Bill of Rights which should be applicable uniformly throughout the country. The concept may be more helpful in determining whether pornography causes harm or is so offensive that its dissemination should be restricted. (These questions are considered in sections 4 and 6 below.) A broad definition of obscenity in terms of sexually explicit material, designed purely to appeal to a prurient interest in sex, can hardly be improved. Hard-core pornography, moreover, can be identified without reference to (temporarily) prevailing standards. Schauer has in any case argued convincingly that the question whether the material is offensive to the majority of society is really irrelevant.[63] If it is wrong for the Court to take into account the degree of offensiveness or hurt occasioned to people when determining whether intemperate political discourse enjoys the coverage of the First Amendment, so it should be in the case of sexually explicit material. The constitutional question is whether such material is 'speech' at all, and the degree of offensiveness is irrelevant to its answer; what matters is whether there is a genuine communication of ideas or information.

But where sexually explicit material is not treated as 'speech', legislatures may constitutionally incorporate an offensiveness test into their obscenity statutes. It does not matter then that it is formulated or applied differently from one area to another, since this is irrelevant to the question whether rights of free speech have been invaded. This reasoning incidentally provides an explanation why the European Court's approach in *Handyside* does not create the same problems as the apparently similar stance of the Supreme Court. The Strasbourg judges were not concerned with defining 'freedom of expression'—they were satisfied that it included this sort of obscene literature—but with balancing the state's interest against that freedom. This process may properly entail weighing one state's interests differently from another's. Just as political speech may be inhibited in *times* of emergency, so *place* may be relevant when deciding whether to prohibit or restrict other types of speech.

One consequence of a *constitutional* definition of 'obscenity', with the deletion of the formula 'offensive to contemporary community standards', is that a fixed, more or less permanent, meaning is attached to the concept. But views on what is acceptable vary substantially over periods of time and from one community to another. Most legal systems adopt a flexible definition of pornography, whether in terms of its tendency to cause individual harm (as in English law) or in terms of its impact on the moral tone or values of society. The explanation lies, of course, in the difference between constitutional and legislative rules. A supreme court with powers of judicial review should frame a precise and restrictive definition of 'obscenity'; in that context the court must take into account the meaning of 'speech' and the purposes for which it is guaranteed. Naturally the meaning of constitutional terms changes, but it should not alter as rapidly as the formulation

---

[63] F. Schauer, 'Response: Pornography and the First Amendment' (1979) 40 *Univ of Pittsburgh Law Rev* 605, 610.

and construction of legislative provisions. Phrases such as 'contemporary community standards' are particularly ill-fitted for use by constitutional courts. But they are perfectly acceptable in valid obscenity legislation.

4. Specific Harms

(i) Introduction

The Williams Committee admitted that any presumption in favour of freedom of speech applicable to pornographic publications would be displaced if it were shown that they cause harm.[64] But the difficulty is to identify the harm they cause, and then to determine whether its prevention is compatible with any serious commitment to the protection of free speech. English law seems never to have formulated a coherent answer to these questions. In the leading common law decision in *R* v. *Hicklin*, Lord Cockburn CJ stated the familiar test for obscene libel: whether there is a tendency 'to deprave and corrupt those whose minds are open to... immoral influences, and into whose hands a publication of this sort may fall'.[65] The essence of corruption, according to this judgment, is the suggestion of impure thoughts; moreover, the publication would be ruled obscene if it had this impact on any young or other vulnerable people who were likely to read it. The literary or other merits of the book were at that time considered wholly irrelevant, though Blackburn J. in *Hicklin* itself appreciated that many great works of literature on the test in this case might be exposed to prosecution.[66]

One major weakness of the *Hicklin* formula was that the standard of acceptability might be assessed by reference to the effects a book would have on children. While few people, either then or now, doubt that young people should be protected from exposure to obscene literature, it is, as the Supreme Court has ruled, intolerable that this risk should determine what adults can read.[67] (The same principle now applies in the context of the Internet. Bans on the transmission of indecent material over the Net to recipients under eighteen will inevitably circumscribe the freedom of adult recipients, insofar as it is impossible for the sender to prevent minors gaining access to it, without also denying the access of adults.[68]) Following the recommendation of a House of Commons Select Committee,[69] the Obscene Publications Act 1959 substantially removed this possibility. The law now is that a work is obscene if it is 'such as to tend to deprave and corrupt persons who are likely, having regard to all the circumstances, to read, see or hear the matter...'.[70] As interpreted by the Court of Appeal, the test requires the jury to consider the effect on a *significant proportion* of the likely readers; the fact that the

---

[64] N. 1 above, para. 5.26.   [65] (1868) LR 3, QB 360, 371.   [66] Ibid., 374.
[67] *Butler* v. *Michigan* 352 US 380 (1957).
[68] *Reno* v. *American Civil Liberties Union* 521 US 844 (1997): see ch. XIII, s. 3(ii) below.
[69] (1958) HC 123.   [70] S. 1(1).

work may corrupt a few young or particularly vulnerable people who gain access to it is ignored.[71] A significant proportion may be much less than a half of the relevant group.[72] It is, therefore, a radically different test from that determining obscenity by reference to its impact on the typical man in the street, or as one American judge put it, 'a person with average sex instincts—what the French would call *l'homme moyen sensuel*...'.[73] English law, therefore, emphasizes that there is no absolute test to determine 'obscenity'; rather there is a variable standard, the application of which depends on the probable readership or audience. The significance of the harm is assessed by reference to these particular people, not ordinary people in general.[74] In principle, the acceptability of gay literature should not be determined by asking whether it might deprave and corrupt heterosexual readers; its impact on the gay community should be assessed, unless there is evidence that it enjoys wider circulation. Equally, it would be wrong to carve out a special exception for gay and lesbian material, on the argument that it is addressed to groups whose interests are closely linked to particular sexual practices. It is not absurd to conclude that gays and lesbians can be harmed, as can heterosexuals, by exposure to material depicting cruel and violent sexual practices.[75]

(ii) The character of the harm

Of more importance, however, is the character of this harm. In fact there is some evidence that the courts paid little attention to the *Hicklin* formula before the passage of the 1959 legislation, and instead asked whether the publication was 'offensive' or 'indecent' in the ordinary meaning of these terms. Moreover, some Australian decisions suggest that the courts there have been unconcerned with whether the consumption of pornography really leads to the commission of crime or encourages evil thoughts; rather they asked themselves whether the publication crossed the limits of decency, so it became right to characterize it as obscene.[76] Lord Wilberforce in the leading English case, *DPP* v. *Whyte*,[77] has, however, suggested that the Obscene Publications Act 1959 re-established the 'tendency to deprave and corrupt' formula as the central issue for decision. Now this phrase might refer to the mental and moral corruption of the publication's consumers, as Lord Cockburn CJ had ruled, or alternatively denote the instigation of anti-social acts, in particular sexual crimes. After *DPP* v. *Whyte* it is clear that the former is

---

[71] *R* v. *Calder and Boyars Ltd* [1969] 1 QB 151.

[72] Lord Cross in *DPP* v. *Whyte* [1972] AC 849, 870, HL.

[73] Woolsey J. in *US* v. *'Ulysses'* 5 F Supp 182, 184 (1933).

[74] Where magazines are kept for export, courts must decide whether they tend to corrupt foreigners: *Gold Star Publications* v. *DPP* [1981] 1 WLR 732, HL.

[75] See Binnie J. for the Court in *Little Sisters Book and Art Emporium* v. *Minister of Justice and A-G of Canada* [2000] 2 SCR 1120, paras. 66–8.

[76] *R* v. *Close* [1948] VR 445, Full Ct of Vict Sup Ct; *Crowe* v. *Graham* (1969) 121 CLR 375, 392 per Windeyer J., HC of A; *Romeyko* v. *Samuels* (1972) 19 FLR 322, SA Sup Ct.

[77] [1972] AC 849, 861.

the correct interpretation. In that case the principal purchasers of what were admitted to be hard-core pornographic magazines were 'inadequate, pathetic, dirty-minded men, seeking cheap thrills—addicts to this type of material'.[78] The justices had acquitted the respondents because such addicts could not be further corrupted; moreover, there was no evidence that the impact of the magazines went beyond the arousal of sexual fantasies. The majority of the Lords, allowing the prosecutor's appeal, concluded that the magistrates' decision was incompatible with the purpose of the 1959 Act. The legislation was designed to prevent corruption of the mind and to stop the already depraved from further corruption. The argument that bad conduct must be induced was firmly rejected, though actual behaviour might provide evidence to show mental corruption. The law, in this respect, has therefore not really advanced from the *Hicklin* ruling.

Some members of the Lords were clearly unhappy with the interpretation they felt compelled to place on the 1959 legislation. There are, for example, considerable practical difficulties in applying the notion of mental corruption. More pertinently from the free speech perspective, it seems an extraordinarily broad basis on which to justify the suppression of publications, whether written or pictorial. Some great literature and works of art stimulate erotic fantasies, but should nonetheless be treated as 'speech'. The 'sexy thoughts' argument would justify the regulation of a much wider range of matter than the extreme hard-core pornography which may plausibly be excluded from the category of speech. But it is surely in any case incompatible with freedom of speech to prohibit the publication of material just because it arouses sexual fantasy or mentally corrupts people. The state is not entitled to stop the distribution of ideas because it disapproves of them or because it considers they validate an undesirable lifestyle.[79]

The Williams Committee concluded that in practice courts still tend to assess publications in the light of contemporary standards of acceptability, despite the use of the 'deprave and corrupt' formula in the Obscene Publications Act.[80] Some decisions in England and Australia suggest that the term 'obscene' denotes merely a higher degree of offensiveness than 'indecent', a concept also often used in legislation designed to control the distribution of pornography.[81] On the other hand, it has been held by the Court of Appeal that the offences under the Obscene Publications Act and under the common law crime of outraging public decency are quite distinct.[82] Moreover, one major feature of English obscenity law suggests that the notion of harm to the consumer through his moral corruption is still taken seriously. It may be a defence to an obscenity prosecution that the publication is so repulsive and disgusting that readers will be discouraged from indulging in the practices it depicts. Failure to put the 'aversion' defence to the jury results in

[78] [1972] AC 849, 870.

[79] See the discussion of Scanlon's Millian Position in ch. 1, s. 2 above, and of Raz's argument for freedom of expression as validating diverse forms of life: ibid., s. 4.   [80] N. 1 above, para. 2.6.

[81] *R* v. *Stanley* [1965] 2 QB 327, CA; *Phillips* v. *Police* (1994) 75 Aust Crim R 480, Ct Crim Appeal, SA.   [82] *R* v. *Gibson* [1990] 2 QB 619, 624.

reversal of a conviction.[83] Now this argument should be irrelevant if English law is really concerned, as some suggest, with the general decency of the material. In the United States the contention that the pornographic material will sicken the average person has been rejected in circumstances where it was clearly designed to appeal to the perverse interests of a deviant group.[84] It is still treated as hard-core pornography, offensive to the community, and therefore outside the area of constitutionally protected speech. English law rather surprisingly may in this respect (at least in theory) be more protective of freedom of speech.

(iii) Sexual crimes

It is often argued that the frequent consumption of (some types of) hard-core pornography makes more likely the commission of sexual crimes, in particular rape and violence to women. These may, therefore, be the harms that justify rebuttal of the presumption in favour of freedom of speech. Conceivably, legislatures have this in mind when deciding to enact anti-pornography statutes. But according to the House of Lords in *DPP* v. *Whyte* this was not the main object of the Obscene Publications Act 1959. Nor has this argument played much part in decisions in the United States defining 'obscenity' for First Amendment purposes; there is no suggestion that the statute concerned must suppress only publications, the availability of which may instigate the commission of sexual offences. Admittedly Burger CJ referred to the 'arguable correlation between obscene material and crime', when he gave the Court's judgment in the *Paris Adult Theatre* case.[85] He considered that, although there was no conclusive proof of any causal connection between pornography and anti-social conduct, it was reasonable for a state legislature to act on the assumption that a link existed. A similar approach has been taken by the Supreme Court of Canada. In *Butler* it held that a direct link between obscene material and harm may be difficult, if not impossible, to establish, but it is reasonable for the courts to assume there is a causal relationship between its publication and the development of negative attitudes and conduct towards women.[86] Social science evidence suggesting that connection can be supported by experience and common sense.[87]

Any view about such a connection is of course highly controversial. Neither the United States President's Commission on Obscenity nor the Williams Committee found there was sufficient evidence to establish a causal relationship.[88] The latter body examined the arguments extremely carefully, including the claim that there had been a marked fall in the incidence of sexual offences in Denmark, where restrictions on pornography had been abolished in the late 1960s. The Committee, however,

---

[83] *R* v. *Anderson* [1972] 1 QB 304, CA.   [84] *Mishkin* v. *US* 383 US 502 (1966).
[85] 413 US 49 (1973).   [86] [1992] 1 SCR 452, 502–4.
[87] *R* v. *Sharpe* (2001) 194 DLR (4th) 1, para. 94.
[88] US Commission on Obscenity (n. 1 above), 26–7; Williams Committee Report (n. 1 above), paras. 6.1–6.59.

thought it premature to conclude there was a link between these phenomena. Indeed its twenty-five pages on the topic are a masterpiece of scepticism about anything that can be said in this area. On the other hand, the 1986 US Attorney-General's Report on Pornography found a causal link between sexually violent materials and the incidence of sexual violence, but not between other pornographic material and such violence. The degree of sexual explicitness seems to be irrelevant to this link.

What perhaps can be stated with confidence is that the relationship (if any) between pornography and conduct is better determined by a legislature than by a court, even by a court accustomed to considering sociological evidence. One advantage of the Supreme Court's refusal to classify extreme hard-core pornography as 'speech' is that then it does not have to rule whether the connection between the material and crime is sufficiently fully established to justify its proscription. This is a purely legislative question, subject perhaps to judicial review under the 'reasonable classifications' test of the Fourteenth Amendment. Moreover, constitutional courts should not define 'obscenity' as explicit hard-core pornography which causes or is likely to cause criminal conduct or other anti-social behaviour. Any link between pornographic material and crime is quite independent of the degree of its explicitness; a court may take the character of the material into account in determining that it is not covered by freedom of speech, but it would then be for the legislature to assess whether there is a close enough link to violence to justify its proscription.[89]

(iv) Harm to children

It is generally agreed pornography may harm children. Three types of harm can be identified. One is that early exposure to sexually explicit material might endanger the upbringing of young people, unable to place it in perspective and tempted, perhaps, to regard it as a normal portrayal of sexual relations. The protection of young people from this type of harm is the principal aim underlying the German law restricting the availability of general, soft-core pornography. Section 184 of the Criminal Code prohibits the offer or supply of such material to all persons under eighteen, and further bans publication and sale by means or in premises to which the young have access. This makes it harder for adults to obtain the material, but these restrictions are justified in view of the difficulty that a supplier or retailer may have in checking the age of customers. Moreover, under special legislation, works endangering children and young persons are to be placed on a restricted list of publications, though these are not confined to sexually explicit material. Listed material may not be supplied or made accessible to young people.[90] The Constitutional Court has upheld the ban imposed under this law

---

[89] See F. Schauer, 'Causation Theory and the Causes of Sexual Violence' (1987) 4 *American Bar Foundation Research Jo* 737, 767–70.   [90] Law of 12 July 1985, BGBl 1, 1502.

on the supply by mail order of listed pornographic magazines.[91] But the Court agreed with the lower court's conclusion that a comparable ban on the distribution of pictorial magazines advertising naturism was contrary to freedom of expression, which covered this type of 'ideological obscenity' (to use the American phrase). In a later decision the Court said that, in the absence of any generally agreed scientific assessment of the impact of pornography on children and young people, the legislature was free to determine the extent of the danger for itself and take what it regarded as suitable measures. The Court would only intervene if it were clear that scientific knowledge ruled out any danger to youth from exposure to the material.[92]

A second type of harm emerges in decisions of the United States and Canadian courts emphasizing that the distribution of child pornography is integrally linked to the sexual abuse of children in its production. It is therefore essential to ban its distribution, and promotion through advertising, in order effectively to control the abuse. Indeed, the US Supreme Court in *New York* v. *Ferber* on one view appears to have suggested child pornography falls entirely outside the scope of the First Amendment.[93] Another, less persuasive reading of the decision, however, is that it simply allowed bans on the dissemination of what the Court regarded as a type of low-value speech.[94] At all events, it is clear that child pornography need not be characterized as obscene under the *Miller* tests. Its artistic or other value is irrelevant, while material with serious literary or artistic value could not be held obscene.[95] The Court upheld a conviction under a New York child pornography statute for the sale of two films depicting boys masturbating. Subsequently, the Court has held it was constitutional for a state to criminalize the possession of photographs of nude children, where the state court had construed the law to apply only to material which was lewd or focused on the genitals.[96] The Court did not apply the principle established in an earlier case that it is unconstitutional to proscribe the simple possession of obscene material.[97]

Further, paedophiles may use child pornography to seduce children. This third type of harm has been taken into account by the Canadian Supreme Court. It unanimously upheld in *Sharpe* the constitutionality of a provision of the Criminal Code penalizing the possession of 'child pornography', defined to include visual representations of any person who is, or is depicted as, under eighteen engaged in sexual activities.[98] Although such material was treated as falling under the free expression clause of the Charter, several types of harm were identified; it fuelled fantasies and created a distorted image of children, was used in the grooming and seduction of child victims, and damaged children used in its production.

---

[91] 30 BVerfGE 337 (1971).   [92] Mutzenbacher decision, 83 BVerfGE 130 (1990).

[93] 458 US 747 (1982).

[94] F. Schauer, 'Codifying the First Amendment: *New York* v. *Ferber*' [1982] *Supreme Court Rev* 285.   [95] See s. 5 below.

[96] *Osborne* v. *Ohio* 495 US 103 (1990).   [97] *Stanley* v. *Georgia* 394 US 557 (1969).

[98] *R* v. *Sharpe* (2001) 194 DLR (4th) 1.

Six members of the Court were prepared to read two qualifications into the provision, in order to hold it did not amount to a disproportionate interference with freedom of expression: it should not apply to journals, drawings, or pseudo-photographs created by a defendant for his private use, nor should it cover a private recording of lawful sexual activity held by a young couple for their personal use. The law did not extend to the possession of material held for educational, scientific, or therapeutic purposes; nor would it criminalize families taking photographs of nude children playing on a beach, since it only covered indecent, sexually explicit material.

United Kingdom law contains a number of statutory provisions designed to combat child pornography. The Protection of Children Act 1978 proscribes, among other things, the taking of any indecent photograph of a child under the age of sixteen, distributing or showing indecent photographs, and having such photographs in possession with a view to their distribution or display.[99] Under later legislation it is a summary offence to possess such material, whether the possessor intended to distribute them or not.[100] Both sets of statutory provisions have been amended to cover the making of pornographic computer images (pseudo-photographs) of young children.[101] The legislation has been interpreted as covering the storing of photographs in digital form on computers, or downloading them onto a disk.[102] It is immaterial that the photographs or pseudo-photographs were taken or made entirely for the defendant's own private use; the Court of Appeal also rejected an argument that, so interpreted, the provision is incompatible with the right to respect for private life guaranteed by Article 8 of the ECHR and now protected under UK law.[103]

Hitherto, there has been no challenge to this legislation on the ground that it infringes freedom of expression. It is unlikely that a challenge would succeed. But the provisions penalize the possession of photographs and self-created computer images which are kept for purely personal use; they go further than the comparable Canadian statute, which was interpreted by the Supreme Court in *Sharpe* not to cover such possession to avoid infringement of the right to freedom of expression. The UK legislation is also open to challenge, in that it does not take account of the motives of the person taking the photograph; it is for the jury simply to decide whether it is 'indecent' in accordance with general standards.[104] This might create difficulties for naturists, and for medical or other researchers, although the latter might be able to take advantage of the statutory defence that they have a legitimate reason to possess the material.[105] In these circumstances, the grounds for holding child pornography unprotected by free speech may not apply. The creation of pseudo-photographs for purely personal pleasure does not

---

[99] S. 1(1).   [100] Criminal Justice Act 1988, s. 160.

[101] Criminal Justice and Public Order Act 1994, s. 84 amending both the 1978 and 1988 Acts: see ch. XIII, s. 3(iii) below.   [102] *R* v. *Fellows, R* v. *Arnold* [1997] 2 All ER 548, CA.

[103] *R* v. *Bowden* [2000] 2 All ER 418.   [104] *R* v. *Graham-Kerr* [1988] 1 WLR 1098, CA.

[105] Protection of Children Act 1978, s. 1(4).

involve the abuse of children in its production; naturists and researchers do not possess or distribute such material to seduce child victims. The UK legislation is too broad, and should be construed restrictively to bring it into conformity with the requirements of free speech.

The US Supreme Court has recently held unconstitutional the provision of the Child Pornography Prevention Act of 1996 prohibiting the depiction of minors who are engaged or who appear to be engaged in sexually explicit conduct.[106] The provision covered computer-generated images and other non-representational images of children, so *Ferber* was distinguished. No actual children would have been harmed in their production. Any harm would flow from the use made of the images, rather than their means of production, so the provision was a content-based restriction on speech. Moreover, the Court did not think the link between child pornography and the sexual abuse of young persons was clearly established; it was not enough, on general principles of free speech law, to show that this material had a tendency to encourage violence against children. This approach clearly differs from that of the Canadian Supreme Court, which was prepared in *Sharpe* to accept, on the basis of evidence and common sense, a link between child pornography and harm to children.

The Supreme Court has also ruled unconstitutional legislation designed to shield children from indecent (though not obscene) material on the Internet or on cable television, if its effect is to inhibit adults receiving that material. In *Reno* v. *American Civil Liberties Union*[107] it held the strong state interest in protecting children from access to unsuitable, even harmful, messages on the Internet did not justify statutory provisions which would inevitably curtail the freedom of adults to gain access to pornographic websites, or even to provide children with information on contraception, which some communities might find indecent. The provisions in the Communications Decency Act of 1996 made it an offence to transmit any indecent message on the Internet to anyone under eighteen or to display patently offensive messages in a manner available to such recipients. The government was required to show these broad content-based rules were narrowly tailored to prevent harm to children, without impeding adult use of the Internet, and that no less restrictive measure would be equally effective; it had not discharged these burdens. Less persuasively, a bare majority of the Court invalidated section 505 of the Telecommunications Act of 1996 which required cable operators providing sexually-oriented programming channels either to scramble them or to block their transmission between 6.00 a.m. and 10.00 p.m. when children might be viewing.[108] Kennedy J. for the majority held that other less restrictive means could be used, such as blocking the transmission of these channels at the request of subscribers who wished to protect their children. The provision curtailing the

---

[106] *Ashcroft* v. *Free Speech Coalition* 535 US 234 (2002).
[107] 521 US 844 (1997): see ch. XIII, s. 3(ii) below.
[108] *US* v. *Playboy Entertainment Group* 529 US 803 (2000).

right of adults to watch hard core porn before 10 p.m. could not, therefore, survive challenge under the First Amendment. But it should have been upheld as a reasonable time, manner, and place regulation of speech. Unlike the rule in the *Reno* case, it did not ban any type or means of communication.

(v) Harm to women

Quite apart from any link between pornography and violence, it is frequently urged that women generally are harmed or insulted by the mass availability of sexually explicit material.[109] The feminist case for its proscription is now the most hotly discussed argument in this context, as shown by the debate between the leading exponent of the feminist perspective, Catharine MacKinnon,[110] and one of its most prominent critics, Ronald Dworkin.[111] The feminist case has been put in a number of ways. One argument is that pornography amounts to a sexual assault on women. It does not communicate ideas. As MacKinnon puts it, '[p]ornography is masturbation material. It is used as sex. It therefore is sex.'[112] Like bribery and an agreement to fix prices, it constitutes verbal crime. Her argument in this form is a version of the case that sexually explicit material is conduct, rather than speech, and therefore falls outside the scope of the First Amendment.[113] But this perspective ignores the representational character of some pornography—that it describes or depicts sexual conduct, and is not equivalent, say, to a live sex show. More importantly, it moves from the reasonable premise that pornography may be used as an aid for masturbation to the unacceptable conclusion that this is its only function or that it *is* sex. In fact, pornography may elicit a number of responses, including boredom and disgust, as well as (solitary) sexual pleasure. Moreover, it often works through the senses even when it has no intellectual and only minimal aesthetic merit.

Another argument is that pornography silences women by rending them speechless or by implicitly suggesting that their views are worthless.[114] (This case is also made to justify broad hate speech laws; they are necessary to protect the voice of disparaged minority groups.[115]) Paradoxically, therefore, freedom of speech itself is used to support laws which on their face infringe the freedom. This argument, however, is a weak one. In the first place, the fact that pornography now (rightly) elicits so much counter-argument and protest by women

---

[109] For a balanced consideration of the arguments in the context of US constitutional principles, see J. Weinstein, *Hate Speech, Pornography, and the Radical Attack on Free Speech Doctrine* (Boulder, Col.: Westview Press, 1999), esp. 78–92.

[110] See 'Pornography, Civil Rights, and Speech' (1985) 20 *Harvard Civil Rights–Civil Liberties Law Rev* 1, and *Only Words* (London: HarperCollins, 1995).

[111] See the essays, 'Pornography and Hate' and 'MacKinnon's Words' in Dworkin, 214 and 227.

[112] *Only Words* (n. 110 above), 12.   [113] See s. 2 above.

[114] F. I. Michelman, 'Conceptions of Democracy in American Constitutional Argument: The Case of Pornography Regulation' (1989) 56 *Tennessee Law Rev* 291.   [115] See ch. V, s. 4 above.

suggests that it does not have a significant silencing effect. Secondly, while much pornography is objectionable insofar as it represents women purely as sexual objects rather than people entitled to political and social views, that does not mean that its intent or effect is to silence them. Even if pornography does have that intention or effect, freedom of speech does not entail a right for women (or any other group) to favourable circumstances for speech, let alone any right that others, in this case men, must listen to them.[116]

The better feminist arguments are those which try to meet the objection that pornography may communicate ideas, albeit they demean and disparage women. One argument is that pornography denies the right of women to equality, itself guaranteed in the United States and many other constitutions.[117] But it is far from clear that this is what pornography does or is intended to do. Rather, much of it may convey the idea that women are as sexually uninhibited as men, an expression of their equality rather than the converse. Pornography typically does not say anything explicit about the right of women to equal opportunities or pay. It certainly says far less than conservative political speech, encouraging women to marry, stay at home, and look after children. Nobody, I think, would argue that the expression of those views should be suppressed, so it is hard to see how feminists can argue that pornography should be banned because it can be interpreted as supporting inequality between men and women. Finally, the equality argument can be used to defend free speech rights for pornographers. They are as entitled as feminists to put their views across, and it infringes their right to equality totally to deny them any opportunity to communicate their ideas.[118] Of course, it can be said that much pornography does not communicate any idea or contribute to public discourse. But if we raise that point, we have moved away from the equality argument.

The central feminist claim is that pornography presents women purely as objects for men's sexual needs and so demeans and disparages them. In its most extreme forms, where sexual violence is portrayed or promoted, pornography is a variety of hate speech, with women, rather than racial or religious minorities, as the victims. These claims were reflected in a model ordinance drafted by Catharine MacKinnon and Andrea Dworkin in 1983 and enacted by Indianapolis in the following year. Under it pornography was outlawed as discrimination against women. 'Pornography' was defined as 'graphic sexually explicit subordination of women', including the presentation of women as sexual objects, enjoying pain or humiliation, or for domination, conquest, exploitation, etc., or through postures or positions of servility or submission. But the Court of Appeals for the Seventh Circuit considered this definition of pornography unconstitutional, for it attempted to restrict the dissemination of ideas about women.[119]

---

[116] Dworkin, 232.   [117] N. 110 above, ch. III.   [118] Dworkin, 236–8.
[119] *American Booksellers Ass'n* v. *Hudnut* 771 F 2d 323 (7th Cir, 1985) affirmed 475 US 1001 (1986).

Public authorities may not establish what views of women are acceptable, any more than they are entitled to prescribe political opinion. Even if, as the Court was prepared to accept, these ideas perpetuated the subordinate status of women, they did so through their impact on the mental states of their readers. In that way, pornography is no different from unpleasant political speech. Indianapolis could not argue the First Amendment was inapplicable, because in its view there was no chance that healthy or enlightened views about women would emerge in 'the marketplace'; the city would then be arrogating to itself the right to determine truth.

In contrast, the Canadian Supreme Court in *R* v. *Butler* has held that the degrading portrayal of women in hard-core videos can amount to harm which the state may outlaw compatibly with freedom of expression.[120] In its view, harm is occasioned by the reinforcement of sexual stereotypes and the feelings of humiliation and injury to self-worth resulting from the dissemination of material depicting explicit sex in a dehumanizing manner. Such material is quite different from erotic literature or 'good pornography' celebrating female sexuality.[121] The Court's decision in the *Little Sisters* case has clarified aspects of the ruling in *Butler*.[122] It applies to books and magazines as it does to videos and other media. More importantly, the harm principle not only protects women, but may be invoked to protect gays and lesbians from sexually explicit material which disparages and demeans them.

The Canadian Supreme Court has also denied that the harm rationale is really moralism in disguise. It drew a distinction between the enforcement of the moral tone of society, which is incompatible with any commitment to freedom of expression, and the prevention of harm to women occasioned by their portrayal as sex objects, an aim which can be pursued in conformity with that freedom. Arguably, however, this is a distinction without any real difference. The portrayal of women in, say, sexually submissive poses is treated as a harm society is entitled to avert, precisely because it is wrong to regard women in this light. That is a moral view or perspective, reflecting contemporary standards of gender equality. In comparison, speech disparaging, say, vegetarians or meat-eaters would not be treated as occasioning harm, because there is no conventional moral view that such attacks infringe any widely shared moral perspective concerning the position of vegetarians or their opponents. It is hard in fact to see how this version of the harm rationale adds anything to the inadmissible argument that society is entitled to preserves its moral values against challenge.[123]

---

[120] [1992] 1 SCR 452.

[121] Ibid., 500, quoting R. West, 'The Feminist–Conservative Anti-Pornography Alliance and the 1986 Attorney-General's Commission on Pornography Report' (1987) 4 *American Bar Foundation Research Jo* 681, 696.

[122] *Little Sisters Book and Art Emporium* v. *Minister of Justice and A-G of Canada* [2000] 2 SCR 1120.

[123] See B. Ryder, 'The *Little Sisters* Case, Administrative Censorship, and Obscenity Law' (2001) 39 *Osgoode Hall Law Jo* 207, 216–19. Also see Moon, 108–13.

In short, the feminist case does not provide a persuasive justification for the proscription of pornography.[124]

(vi) Conclusions

It is difficult to identify the harms which may in appropriate circumstances overcome the presumption in favour of free speech in this area. The arousal of libidinous or sexy thoughts is hardly harmful, and certainly does not justify the proscription of pornography. It would legitimize the suppression of some great literature; more fundamentally, it runs counter to the free speech principle protecting the communication of ideas or perceptions which might influence what people believe and feel. There is too little evidence that the availability of pornography causes violent sexual offences to warrant its regulation on that ground, though few would dispute that this is potentially a harm which should be taken into account. On the other hand, it seems legitimate to criminalize the distribution of child pornography as a measure to stop the abuse of children involved in its production. Free speech concerns should not be excluded, but they may be trumped to prevent risks to the welfare of children. The feminist arguments for a ban on pornography are less persuasive. It is difficult to distinguish them from the moral tone of society argument considered in the previous section or from the arguments used to justify restrictions on the availability of offensive pornography to be canvassed in section 6. Before that, we consider the significance which should be attached to the artistic or literary character of pornography.

5. Pornography, the Arts, and Learning

How should the law treat pornography for which artistic, literary, or other merit or value is claimed? This may be regarded as a non-problem. On one view, hard-core pornography necessarily lacks artistic or other merit. It merely describes or depicts sexual activity, without placing it in context; claims that, say, explicit images have artistic quality can be dismissed as spurious. On the other hand, writers and artists assert that their work inevitably communicates ideas or appeals to the senses. Novels, poetry, plays, and films are covered by free speech clauses, as are the traditional visual arts and contemporary forms of artistic expression.[125] They do not forfeit free speech protection merely because they have significant, even explicit, sexual content. It would surely be wrong to deny that some works may contain both hard-core pornographic elements and yet claim the status of art.

---

[124] The New Zealand High Court has held that the term 'denigration of all women' is too vague to afford a coherent basis for holding a publication indecent: *Comptroller of Customs* v. *Gordon & Gotch* [1987] 3 NZLR 80.

[125] In Germany freedom of the arts, science, and learning are explicitly covered by Basic Law, art. 5(3).

That seems most likely to be the case with a novel, play, or film, which may present different dimensions in various passages and moments. Equally, paintings may contain explicit, perhaps obscene, sexual images, but their exhibition might be regarded as a display of art. It is better to admit that there is a real difficulty here.[126] However, as the Williams Committee concluded, its importance should not be exaggerated.[127]

The question, therefore, is whether freedom of speech requires some degree of special protection for works of literary, artistic, or similar value which would otherwise be regarded as so pornographic that their publication and dissemination could be banned. The literary character of a work might, for example, be treated as a factor to be taken into account in determining whether overall it should be regarded as 'speech' and not obscene, or alternatively as providing a defence to a charge of publishing an obscene or indecent book. It is easy enough to decide that explicit descriptions of intimate sexual acts are an exercise of free speech (and so not obscene) when made in the course of a novel, but it might be a little harder to treat in the same way the same combination of words in leaflets distributed house to house or left in restaurants. While a medical textbook showing close-up pictures of male and female genitals is obviously 'speech', the same conclusion would not be so straightforward if they are published in a hard-core magazine. The *Roth* definition of 'obscenity' in the United States did not in fact incorporate any reference to the literary or scholarly value of the pornographic material, though Brennan J. stated that the entire absence of any social importance was one of the reasons why obscenity was not constitutionally protected.[128] It was not until the 1960s that the phrase, 'utterly without redeeming social value', became an essential element of the constitutional formula.[129] Its subsequent development will be discussed briefly after the comparable English law has been outlined.

The original Obscene Publications Bill introduced in 1956 and later bills envisaged that literary, artistic, or scientific merit would be relevant to the general issue whether a publication was obscene or not. But after an amendment introduced at the Committee stage of the final bill, these factors were incorporated in a special 'public good' defence, which is only relevant once a book has been found obscene.[130] Section 4(1) of the 1959 Act provides:

A person shall not be convicted of an offence . . . if it is proved that publication of the article in question is justified as being for the public good on the grounds that it is in the interests of science, literature, art or learning, or of other objects of general concern.

Expert evidence on the literary or other merits of the article is frequently admitted, almost always on the side of the defence. As construed by the courts, the

---

[126] In *Mutzenbacher*, 87 BVerfGE 130 (1990), the German Constitutional Court held that a novel could be both pornography and art for the purposes of Basic Law, art. 5(3).
[127] N. 1 above, para. 8.18.   [128] 354 US 476, 484 (1957).
[129] *Memoirs* v. *Massachusetts* 383 US 413 (1966).
[130] For discussion, see G. Robertson, *Obscenity* (Weidenfeld & London: Nicolson, 1979), 160–6.

jury must first rule on the 'obscenity' issue—does the article have a tendency to deprave and corrupt?—and then determine whether on balance publication is for the public good if the work has literary or other merits.[131] A familiar criticism is that this requires mental gymnastics of Olympic proportions: the jury must balance the literary or other merits of a work against its obscene character and determine whether publication is justified.

This aspect of English obscenity law is hard to defend. The US approach, also to be found in New Zealand and New South Wales, is much more coherent:[132] it requires the court to consider the literary and other value of the work in the course of determining whether it is obscene. The best explanation is that English law is concerned (probably wrongly) with the specific harm that may be done to particular individuals, or groups of individuals, by the publication of pornography. It is then plausible to ask the courts to balance this harm against the general good (to the rest of the community) which will flow from publication. Another related criticism of the law in England is that it assumes two readerships: those who are likely to be depraved and those wiser heads capable of appreciating the publication's merits. These elitist assumptions are also borne out by the use of expert witnesses, a feature of the law much attacked by the Williams Committee: 'It is as though informed persons, literary and artistic experts, are supposed to appear from the world of culture and inform the jury of how things stand there with the work under trial.'[133] Their testimony might suggest there could be general agreement about the importance of works of art, when in this context their value is likely to be controversial. In contrast, it is for the jury to decide, generally without expert evidence, whether a work has a tendency to deprave and corrupt a significant proportion of its likely readers or viewers, although such evidence may be admissible to show its impact on a special group, for example, children.[134]

A major difficulty with section 4 is the meaning of 'other objects of general concern'. The House of Lords has ruled that the phrase refers to merits similar to those of science and literature, etc.; evidence that the publication might have beneficial effects in relieving sexual tensions could not be admitted, since a conclusion to that effect would be incompatible with the finding that it was obscene.[135] This is an inevitable consequence of the two-stage test the courts are required to apply. If the merits of a publication were considered in conjunction with its possible corrupting effects, it would be somewhat easier to argue that pornography, far from tending to deprave, had some therapeutic value.[136] Such a claim might be no

---

[131] *R* v. *Calder and Boyars Ltd* [1969] 1 QB 151, CA.

[132] See the New Zealand Indecent Publications Act 1963, s. 11, and NSW Indecent Articles and Classified Publications Act 1975, s. 24.　　　　　　　　　　　　　[133] N. 1 above, para. 8.23.

[134] *DPP* v. *A & BC Chewing Gum Ltd* [1968] 1 QB 159, DC.

[135] *R* v. *Jordan* [1977] AC 699.

[136] In *R* v. *Sharpe* (2001) 194 DLR (4th) 1, para. 64, McLachlin J. for the Court suggested that the possession of child pornography for therapeutic purposes might fall under the 'artistic merit' defence.

more far-fetched than the argument that the material has the very opposite consequence of sickening and disgusting its readers—the so-called 'aversion' defence.[137]

US Supreme Court Justices have rarely suggested that a work might have redeeming value because it satisfied a pressing, psychological need of its consumers.[138] The suggestion is most unlikely now to commend itself to a majority of the Court. It formulated this aspect of the 'obscenity' test in the following terms: does the work, taken as a whole, lack *serious* literary, artistic, political, or social value (emphasis added).[139] This question represents a considerable tightening of the previous requirement that the work must utterly lack redeeming social value for it to be characterized as obscene. Arguably, it should be sufficient for the publication to have any non-trivial intellectual or artistic content to qualify as speech, rather than obscenity. The seriousness of that content is surely irrelevant to the question whether it is legally obscene. The subsequent decision of the Court that the value of a work is to be determined by the standards of a reasonable person makes matters worse.[140] Radical, challenging art is unlikely to be held 'serious' by those standards. Indeed, on this approach, the *Miller* test creates real difficulties for sexually explicit postmodern art which challenges traditional standards of seriousness.[141]

But it would go too far in the other direction automatically to exclude from the reach of pornography laws any material for which the status of literature or art can be claimed. Some assessment of that claim is inescapable. Otherwise the law must abandon the attempt to control the dissemination of sexually explicit material. As the Supreme Court of Canada has said, the courts should be generous in their application of the defence of artistic merit.[142] Any work which can *reasonably* be treated as art or literature should be entitled to the defence. Such a work is covered by a freedom of speech or expression clause, even though otherwise its sexually explicit content would take it outside the scope of that provision. In this context, it should be noted that the 'public good' defence provided by the English Obscene Publications Act 1959 does not apply to a charge of outraging public decency. That was established in *R* v. *Gibson*,[143] when the Court of Appeal upheld the conviction on that charge of the artist and art gallery owner who had exhibited, attached to a model, a pair of earrings made from a freeze-dried foetus of three to four months gestation. Lord Lane CJ thought it unlikely that a defence of public good could possibly arise. He could not have meant that it would be wrong in principle to allow a free speech argument in a case of this kind. Freedom of expression certainly covers art exhibitions. The particular display in *Gibson* might have been intended and understood as a form of protest

---

[137] See s. 4(ii) above.

[138] But see Douglas J. in *Memoirs* v. *Massachusetts* 383 US 413, 432 (1966).

[139] *Miller* v. *California* 413 US 15, 24 (1973).   [140] *Pope* v. *Illinois* 481 US 497 (1987).

[141] A. M. Adler, 'Post-Modern Art and the Death of Obscenity Law' (1990) 99 *Yale Law Jo* 1359.

[142] *R* v. *Sharpe* (n. 136 above), paras. 63–4.   [143] [1990] 2 QB 619.

against the inadequate protection of foetuses.[144] *Gibson* was a classic case, where the artistic character of the display should have led to the conclusion that it was not indecent.

6. Pornography and Offensiveness

Most liberals find wholly unacceptable the idea of banning pornography on the grounds that it harms its readers or that it undermines the moral fabric of society. But they may find more tolerable the proposition that the display of some types of pornography may be controlled insofar as they offend reasonable people. On that basis, the exhibition of pornographic magazines would be regulated as if it were a public nuisance. Pornographic material could still be obtained by the enthusiastic consumer, but he must be prepared to shop around for it. The key point is that the availability of obscene material is *restricted* by this method of control, but it is not entirely *suppressed*. It is important to draw this distinction, because it would clearly be contrary to freedom of speech principles totally to outlaw the publication or dissemination of pornography on the ground that it is offensive to the majority of the community. The harder question is whether a good case can be made for restrictions on its availability.

One argument for an offensiveness principle which surely does not work is that the display of pornographic material on street bookstalls or hoardings invades a right of privacy which people somehow carry around with them when they are shopping or go for a Sunday walk.[145] A right of privacy may protect people against being photographed in public without consent,[146] but it hardly extends to protecting them against exposure to the display of pornographic, or indeed other unpleasant, material. The public nuisance argument proves too much. Many of us object to the appearance of skinheads or of people with tattoos or wearing fur coats, but nobody suggests these objections justify confining their movements to certain areas. Moreover, it would clearly not be compatible with free speech for a local authority in a predominantly conservative area to outlaw political advertising or leafleting by a left-wing minority on the ground that it is offensive to residents or amounts to a public nuisance. It is hard to see why restrictions on the distribution or appearance of pornography should be treated more benevolently.

Yet the Williams Committee was prepared to recommend restrictions on the availability of pornography, even though it was strongly imposed to a total ban. It suggested a restriction on material *offensive to reasonable people* by reason of the manner in which it portrays or deals with violence, sexual functions, or the genital

---

[144] See Feldman, 935–7 for criticism of the decision.

[145] See D. N. MacCormick, 'Privacy and Obscenity', in R. Dhavan and C. Davies (eds.), *Censorship and Obscenity* (London: Martin Robertson, 1978), 76.　　[146] See ch. VI, s. 5 above.

organs.[147] This confines the control to pornography and ensures that the law does not interfere with the availability of political speech. But the formula assumes there is more reason to protect the public from offence by sexually explicit material than from distress occasioned by other types of speech. The Committee offered two arguments: first, a restriction on pornography is not directed against the advocacy of any opinion, and second, it does not defeat the publisher's aims if sexually explicit matter is only available to willing consumers.[148] Both points, however, imply that pornography is not really 'speech'; similar arguments were considered earlier in this chapter.[149] Whatever the purpose of the restrictions proposed in the Williams Report, they would in fact inhibit the availability of sexually explicit speech; moreover, no other mode of expression can be restricted in order to ensure that it is received only by enthusiasts. Publishers want to have access to as wide a market as possible, even if only to make more money.

If pornography is entitled to benefit from a presumption in favour of freedom of speech, it is little easier to justify its restriction on the basis of an offensiveness principle than it is to uphold a total ban. Implicit in the Williams Committee's conclusions is the view that the public has a right to be protected from the offence caused by pornography, though it does not enjoy equivalent protection from exposure to controversial political communication. Moreover, the Committee wanted to prevent more than aesthetic or visual offence. 'The problem lies not with indecent displays, but with displays of the indecent, and to control these, one needs to go beyond the content of the mere display itself to the character of the item being displayed.'[150] The offence is really moral, and it becomes a nice question whether this offensiveness principle does not collapse into the 'moral tone of society' argument canvassed in section 3. This same ambiguity appears in the basis of the statutory power granted local authorities to control the number of sex shops in their area, which is discussed shortly.

However, there is a difference between the total suppression of material and its restriction to separate premises which adults enter only after due warning of the wares on display and from which children are excluded. This second approach may be equally hard to justify in terms of free speech principles, but there are some practical arguments to support it. It enables addicts to satisfy their craving, while society is able to combine in this way muted moral disapproval of pornography with a measure of tolerance. Moreover, a law based on the offensiveness principle is probably easier to enforce than a total ban, the imposition of which encourages an underground market. One respect in which it is more liberal is that it is difficult to justify any restraint on purely *written* publications on this basis. In the absence of a lurid cover, a pornographic novel does not appear different from, say, the driest legal textbook; it cannot give visual offence and it is hard to see what other types of offence it could give rise to. (As most written pornography has some

---

[147] N. 1 above, paras. 9.29–9.38.   [148] Ibid., paras. 7.16–7.23.   [149] Above, s. 2.
[150] N. 1 above, para. 9.08.

ideological content, or perhaps some literary value, it would probably also not be suppressed on any of the bases considered in this chapter.) At any rate neither the Williams Committee nor the United States President's Commission on Obscenity thought there was any room for prohibiting the display of purely written material.

The offensiveness approach to the control of pornography has been adopted in countries such as France and Denmark, where it has more or less replaced bans on publication of obscene or immoral material. In Germany too, apart from the absolute prohibition of hard-core pornography, criminal law is designed to prevent the unwanted intrusion of pornographic material on the public. Thus, it is an offence to provide or to send such matter unsolicited through the post, or to display it on news-stands or in shops, other than those specializing in pornography. It is also an offence to exhibit pornographic films for payment charged exclusively or principally for their performance.[151] There is, however, no prospect that the English Obscene Publications Act will be replaced by such laws. Instead it has been supplemented by further restrictions such as that imposed by the Indecent Displays (Control) Act 1981 which could be regarded as a partial enactment of the Williams Committee's proposals. This measure, introduced by a Conservative MP, prohibits the display of any indecent matter in a 'public place'; this term is defined to include shops, except those to which admission is obtained by payment and those which display an adequate warning that the material inside may be regarded as indecent. The Act does not attempt to define 'indecent'. But the term is familiar to both the common law and in other legislation, and is clearly broader in its scope than 'obscene'.[152] The measure has obviously induced porn shops to conceal their wares from passers-by. Further, it has reduced the importance of the obscenity law as the primary means for protecting the public from exposure to sexually explicit publications.

Another method of implementing the offensiveness principle is restricting the number of outlets which sell pornographic magazines and other similar material. This can be achieved by the use of planning or licensing laws to preserve the character of residential neighbourhoods or to prevent the development of seedy, red-light districts. Broadly, two alternative tactics may be employed: outlets for the sale of pornography may be confined to commercial areas or they may be dispersed throughout a community. However, there is a danger that this type of restriction over a wide area will amount to a total suppression of the availability of such material. Some United States cases nicely illustrate these problems. In *Young v. American Mini Theatres* the Court was asked to rule on the validity of a Detroit ordinance prohibiting 'adult motion picture theaters' and 'adult bookstores' within 1,000 feet of any two other 'regulated uses', which included these theatres and bookstores, as well as liquor stores and pawnshops; in effect the ordinance was

---

[151] Criminal Code, s. 184(1) 5–7. These provisions do not infringe freedom of expression: see 47 BVerfGE 117 (1977).

[152] See *R* v. *Stanley* [1965] 2 QB 327, CCA, interpreting these terms in the post office legislation.

intended to prevent the development of a red-light district. Although the ordinance clearly affected the availability of sexually explicit literature and movies, which would enjoy constitutional protection from total suppression, the Court by a bare majority held that this zoning ordinance was a valid measure for their regulation. Four members of the Court thought that it was proper to draw content-based distinctions in framing these regulations:

> ... even though the determination of whether a particular film fits that characterization turns on the nature of its content, we conclude that the city's interest in the present and future character of its neighborhoods adequately supports its classification of motion pictures.[153]

The Court would have come to a different conclusion if the ordinance had the effect of suppressing or significantly restricting access to pornographic, though not obscene, material. The fifth member of the majority, Powell J., denied there was any content-discrimination in the Detroit measure, and in essence treated it as a land-use regulation which only incidentally affected First Amendment freedoms. On the other hand, Stewart J. for the four dissenting members of the Court saw it as impermissibly distinguishing between sexually explicit material and other types of offensive speech. Whether he exaggerated in viewing the decision as 'an aberration', it is unusual in approving a restriction on the availability of speech by reference to its content.[154]

Perhaps the central question is whether there was any significant overall restriction on the showing of adult films. If Detroit residents had experienced difficulty in gaining access to adult movies, there would have been an improper abridgement of freedom of speech. This is shown by *Schad* v. *Borough of Mt Ephraim*, where a 7–2 majority invalidated a local ordinance which had been construed as prohibiting all live entertainments in the town, including nude dancing.[155] The *Young* ruling was distinguished because it had upheld only a measure to stop the concentration of pornography outlets; it had not banned a mode of speech altogether. It is not clear whether the majority in *Schad* would have come to the same conclusion had there been evidence that this entertainment was freely available in neighbouring communities.[156] Whether it should have done largely depends on the size of the town. A small community, entirely residential, should probably be free, as two members of the Court suggested, entirely to ban certain types of entertainment on environmental grounds. On the other hand, it is surely illegitimate

---

[153] 427 US 50, 71–2, per Stevens J. (1976).

[154] For the hostility of the US courts to content-based restrictions, see ch. II, s. 2 above.

[155] 452 US 61 (1981). In later cases the Court has upheld restrictions on nude dancing: see ch. III, s. 2(iii) above.

[156] Blackmun J. repudiated any implication that the case should be decided differently if a neighbouring community allowed nude dancing. The same issue was raised in debates on legislation in England on sex shops. T. Higgins, MP, argued that a local authority should take the character of neighbouring areas into account when determining the suitability of these outlets in its area: 17 HC Deb (6th ser.), cols. 423–4.

for a large town, with a variety of commercial businesses, to outlaw adult films (or other forms of entertainment) and argue that residents can drive twenty miles into the suburbs or to another town for that sort of amusement. The test should be whether there is in substance a significant restriction on the ability of the public to obtain access to films of their choice.

The principle in *Young* was applied when a 5–4 majority of the Court upheld a city ordinance which prohibited adult film theatres within 1,000 feet of any residential area, park, church or school.[157] Unlike the rule in the earlier case, it was intended to concentrate such cinemas in the commercial area. Although a substantial part of that area, itself barely 6 per cent of the city, was already occupied by a shopping centre and industrial uses, the Court held the ordinance was a valid zoning measure intended to avert undesirable secondary effects of adult cinemas—crime, diminution of property values, and damage to general quality of life—rather than to suppress free speech. For that reason, it was not, in the view of the majority, a content-based restriction on speech. That argument is difficult to sustain; the zoning ordinance on its face clearly distinguished between adult film theatres and other cinemas. Kennedy J. was, therefore, right to admit in a later case[158] that zoning ordinances dispersing or concentrating adult cinemas and sex shops are content-based. But in derogation from the general hostility of the US courts to any content-based treatment of speech, zoning ordinances of this type may be upheld if they are directed to the prevention of undesirable secondary effects.

The secondary effects or consequences principle is a significant qualification to free speech doctrine in the United States. It justifies restrictions on the availability of pornography, even though these are inevitably framed in terms of content-based rules. The supply of sexually explicit material may create attendant harms, for instance, prostitution, drugs, and related crime, which a community is entitled to prevent and which do not flow from any beliefs readers may form from looking at the material. The secondary effects are unrelated to the impact of pornography on its consumers. Planning or zoning ordinances indirectly achieve the objective of diminishing the offensiveness of pornography by, say, keeping outlets away from residential areas, but they are not framed in terms of the offence its display, or even its existence, may cause the majority of the community. However, points often made in this context may be hard to distinguish from general offensiveness arguments. For instance, the argument that a community is entitled to restrict the availability of pornography in order to preserve property values or the general character of residential areas really amounts to a somewhat more acceptable form of the 'moral tone of society' argument which is hard to square with freedom of speech.[159]

---

[157] *Renton* v. *Playtime Theatres, Inc* 475 US 41 (1986).
[158] *City of Los Angeles* v. *Alameda Books, Inc* 535 US 425, 448–9 (2002).
[159] See s. 3 of this chapter.

Planning law in the United Kingdom does not allow local authorities to control the number of sex shops; a grocery store can be changed overnight into a pornography shop without planning permission.[160] The Williams Committee did not think the law should be reformed to enable local authorities to refuse permission for these developments, largely (it seems) because it feared they would exercise this power to exclude all porn shops under public pressure. Nor did it consider that any special licensing system should be instituted.[161] But in 1982 powers to control 'sex establishments' were given to local authorities by legislation.[162] It enabled local councils to exercise licensing powers over sex shops and cinemas. A 'sex shop' is defined as premises used to a significant degree for sale of articles which are concerned primarily with the portrayal of, or designed to stimulate, sexual activity. If a local authority passes a resolution to this effect, all such premises will require a licence, which may be refused if the council thinks there are too many premises of this kind in the locality or they are unsuitable in view of its character or the particular use of neighbouring property. A council may even pass a resolution that there are to be no sex shops in its locality; there is no appeal from a decision to this effect. Although the Minister responsible for the bill did not think authorities should exercise this power merely because it disapproved of sex shops, they are entitled to take account of the strength of local feeling in deciding whether it is appropriate for such shops to be situated in the area.[163]

These provisions nicely illustrate the dangers to free speech of 'nuisance' legislation in this area. A measure, which was primarily concerned with limiting the numbers of outlets for pornographic material to preserve the character of particular localities, can easily be used to ban all outlets because of popular hostility to this type of communication. This reflects the essential ambiguity of the 'offensiveness' principle: is it concerned with aesthetic distaste for publications, the display of which is visually unattractive, or does it really evince moral disapproval? Insofar as it permits a total ban on sex shops and cinemas, the 1982 legislation probably infringes freedom of speech. It could be applied by a local authority to preclude the availability of pornography (not only really hard-core material) in the area, without requiring it to show that the premises caused undesirable secondary effects such as crime or prostitution. It is enough that residents dislike, or are uncomfortable with the existence of, these outlets.

Local authority control is at least exercised by a politically responsible body, which should be aware of local standards. Another remedy which may be used to redress offence is a civil action for nuisance. In one English case an interlocutory injunction was granted to restrain the use of premises as a sex shop and cinema in

---

[160] But it is a change of use requiring planning permission for a shop to show sex films and become a cinema: *SJD Properties Ltd* v. *Sec of State for Environment* [1981] JPEL 673.

[161] N. 1 above, paras. 9.12–9.13.

[162] Local Government (Miscellaneous Provisions) Act 1982, s. 2 and Sch. 3.

[163] See T. Raison, MP, Minister of State for Home Office, 17 HC Deb (6th ser.), cols. 340–1.

a predominantly residential street in Victoria, London.[164] Vinelott J. held that a hard-core pornography business could amount to a nuisance because it was deeply repugnant to reasonable people, even though it was carried on in a relatively decorous way. There was evidence that the premises attracted undesirable people to the neighbourhood and produced nuisance or, in American terms, secondary effects. More controversially, however, the decision also appears to support use of the tort action to restrain behaviour which is offensive to property owners who merely *know* about it.[165] However, unlike the 'sex shops' legislation, the tort remedy could hardly achieve a total ban in a wide area, and is less likely to be used to curtail the availability of pornography in commercial districts.

In this section, I have been rather critical of the coherence of the 'offensiveness' principle. There are admittedly persuasive arguments for attempting to restrict rather than wholly to suppress material which meets the needs of a minority, although most people find its display very disagreeable. But both case-law in the United States and the 1982 legislation in England show it is easy to use the 'offensiveness' rationale to achieve bans over wide areas. Moreover, legitimate concerns over the undesirable secondary effects of pornography outlets need to be distinguished from the claim that they reduce the quality of life in residential areas, a claim which may be hard to distinguish from the argument that pornography lowers the moral tone of society. Restrictions based on a 'quality of life' argument are vulnerable to challenge on free speech grounds, except insofar as they concern only hard-core material which falls outside the scope of the free speech guarantee.

[164] *Laws* v. *Florinplace* [1981] 1 All ER 659.   [165] Ibid., 666.

XI

Commercial Speech

1. Introduction

For a long time it was thought that commercial and professional advertising fell outside the coverage of free speech provisions. Not surprisingly the theoretical issues have rarely been discussed in the United Kingdom, where advertising and other forms of commercial speech are sometimes strictly regulated by statute. Advertising in newspapers, magazines, and on hoardings and billboards is further controlled extra-legally by the Advertising Standards Authority. It enforces the British Codes of Advertising and Sales Promotion which are drafted by the Committee of Advertising Practice, a body drawn from advertisers, agencies, and trade organizations; this system of self-regulation works effectively, and reduces the need for legal intervention.[1] Commercial advertising on radio and television is similarly controlled by Codes issued and enforced by OFCOM, the broadcasting regulatory authority.[2] As it is a requirement of their licences that broadcasters comply with advertising rules, observance can be enforced by a fine, or ultimately by the extreme sanction of withdrawal of the permit to broadcast.

Professional advertising is governed by the rules of the relevant professional bodies. For example, doctors, lawyers, architects, and accountants are all subject to rules of varying strictness which regulate their freedom to market their services. In recent years there has been considerable relaxation of these restrictions, so solicitors are free, for example, to indicate in newspaper advertisements the areas in which they offer advice and help. The advertising of drugs and medicines is tightly regulated,[3] while it is an offence to publish a false or misleading advertisement with regard to the quality of food.[4] It is illegal to publish an advertisement indicating that a parent wishes to have a child adopted or indicating a desire to adopt.[5] On the other hand, there do not seem to be any restrictions in the United Kingdom on publicizing the availability of advice about contraception

---

[1] C. R. Munro, 'Self-regulation in the Media' [1997] *PL* 6.

[2] Communications Act 2003, ss. 319(2)(h)–(i) and 321. From Nov. 2004 OFCOM has contracted out responsibility for regulating the content of broadcast advertising to the Advertising Standards Authority, though it retains ultimate authority for enforcement of the Codes.

[3] Medicines Act 1968, ss. 92–7.   [4] Food Safety Act 1990, s. 15.

[5] Adoption Act 1976, s. 58.

or abortion facilities; prohibitions of such publicity have given rise to litigation in the United States and under the European Convention on Human Rights and Fundamental Freedoms (ECHR).[6]

In the 1970s the US Supreme Court began to reconsider the traditional exclusion of commercial speech from the coverage of the First Amendment. The justification for its exclusion had never really been explored. In *Valentine* v. *Chrestensen* the Court, almost without discussion, upheld the application of a New York city ordinance—forbidding distribution on the streets of commercial advertising—to the owner of a submarine who was touting for visitors.[7] It made no difference that the circular also contained a protest against the city's refusal to allow his boat mooring facilities. In the circumstances it was right that this feature did not affect the result, for otherwise it would have been too easy to evade the commercial speech exclusion. On the other hand, where the speech was primarily political in character, the fact that it was incorporated in an advertisement did not remove the protection it was entitled to enjoy under the First Amendment.[8] In 1975 the Court reversed a conviction under a Virginia law which made it an offence to encourage or promote an abortion in the state.[9] The law had been applied to an advertisement for abortion services in New York. The Court rejected the argument that all commercial publications fell outside the First Amendment. But the subject matter of the advertisement in that case was a matter of great public interest; further, the Court itself had recently held that in some circumstances there is a right to have an abortion,[10] so the advertisement related to an act itself protected under the Constitution.

In the following year the Court upheld a challenge to a state ban on the publication by pharmacists of the price of drugs available only on prescription. It held unequivocally in *Virginia State Board of Pharmacy* v. *Virginia Citizens Consumer Council* that pure commercial advertising, at least when it provides accurate information about a product or service, is covered by freedom of speech.[11] The Supreme Court of Canada has reached the same conclusion,[12] while the German Constitutional Court and the European Human Rights Court are prepared to hold some advertisements or commercial speech covered by freedom of expression.[13] These conclusions are generally accepted by writers on freedom of speech; it is even argued that advertising should enjoy much the same degree of protection as political speech, with an exception being made only for false claims.[14] But some commentators argue strongly that the decision in *Virginia Pharmacy* was wrong.

---

[6] See s. 2 below for discussion of these cases.   [7] 316 US 52 (1942).

[8] As in *New York Times* v. *Sullivan* 376 US 254 (1964); it is immaterial for free speech purposes whether the defamatory allegations are published in an editorial or in an advertisement.

[9] *Bigelow* v. *Virginia* 421 US 809 (1975).   [10] *Roe* v. *Wade* 410 US 113 (1973).

[11] 425 US 748 (1976).   [12] *Ford* v. *A-G of Quebec* [1988] 2 SCR 712.

[13] 102 BVerfGE 347 (2001); *Markt Intern & Beerman* v. *Germany* (1990) 12 EHRR 161.

[14] Notably M. H. Redish in 'The Value of Free Speech' (1982) 130 *Univ of Pennsylvania Law Rev* 591, 630–5, and in 'Tobacco Advertising and the First Amendment' (1996) 81 *Iowa Law Rev* 589.

In their view the arguments for freedom of speech simply do not apply to advertising or other forms of commercial speech.[15] The merits of these rival claims are considered in section 3 of this chapter.

Section 2 examines a threshold question to which comparatively little attention has been paid: what is 'commercial speech'? Some definition of the term is necessary, if distinct free speech principles are applied to it, which differ from those governing political speech or general 'public discourse'. In the United States, as will be seen throughout this chapter, special principles have been developed for commercial speech, under which it enjoys a significant degree of immunity from regulation, but protection falls short of that enjoyed by political speech or literary and artistic work. These principles can only be applied properly when it has been established that the case concerns commercial, rather than, say, political, speech. In two cases the Supreme Court considered whether advertisements for contraceptive devices should be treated as commercial speech, or should be entitled to fuller protection because information on sexuality and venereal disease was included with the promotional material;[16] the material in one of them, *Bolger* v. *Youngs Drug Products*, was characterized as 'commercial speech', because it had primarily been sent to persuade recipients to buy particular products.

In other jurisdictions the courts may appear less concerned with the characterization of the speech. In theory, their decision whether a particular restriction on expression is justified involves determining whether it meets a 'pressing social need' and is proportionate to achievement of that aim.[17] Much the same principles are applied in commercial speech as in non-commercial speech cases. But in practice the application of these principles by the European Human Rights Court and the Supreme Court of Canada varies according to the type of speech at issue. Courts are generally more willing to uphold restraints on commercial speech than they are comparable restrictions on political speech; while political speech lies at the heart of a free speech guarantee, commercial speech, or at least some forms of it, may be regarded as peripheral. Some commentators, however, argue, that commercial speech cannot be satisfactorily defined, or demarcated from political and social speech; if that is right, it should enjoy the same degree of coverage and protection as the latter categories.[18] For this reason alone, it is important to say something about the question.

After considering the arguments for the *coverage* of commercial speech by freedom of expression (section 3), some types of advertising regulation are considered

---

[15] See in particular R. A. Shiner, *Freedom of Commercial Expression* (Oxford: OUP, 2003) and C. E. Baker, 'Commercial Speech: A Problem in the Theory of Freedom' (1976) 62 *Iowa Law Rev* 1.

[16] *Carey* v. *Population Services International* 431 US 678 (1977); *Bolger* v. *Youngs Drug Products Corp* 463 US 60 (1983).

[17] See the discussion of the approach of the courts in Canada and of the European Human Rights Court in freedom of expression cases in ch. II, ss. 3 and 5 above.

[18] For this view, see A. Kozinski and S. Banner, 'Who's Afraid of Commercial Speech?' (1990) 76 *Virginia Law Rev* 627, and C. R. Munro, 'The Value of Commercial Speech' (2003) 62 *CLJ* 134, 148–55.

in section 4 of this chapter. That section is concerned in effect with the *protection* of advertising, the quintessential type of commercial speech. Section 5 deals with tobacco advertising, a controversial topic which has led to important cases in jurisdictions on both sides of the Atlantic and which nicely brings out some of the difficulties in this area of free speech law.

2. What is Commercial Speech?

The US Supreme Court has itself provided two classic definitions of commercial speech. In *Virginia Pharmacy*, Blackmun J. said the question before the Court was 'whether speech which does "no more than propose a commercial transaction" . . . is so removed' from the expression of ideas about politics, morality, the arts, and science that it should be without protection. The 'idea' the pharmacists wanted to communicate was simply: 'I will sell you the X prescription drug at the Y price'.[19] Commercial speech in effect is defined as the provision of information, through advertising, about the price (and other aspects) of goods and services to induce a commercial transaction. This is a narrow definition. For a start, it is unclear whether it covers 'lifestyle' advertising, like the Marlboro County cigarette advertisements, which promote a favourable image associated with the product, but which provide no information about it.[20] Other types of speech are problematic: on the *Virginia Pharmacy* definition, statements in a company prospectus or in its annual report about its trading plans would appear to fall outside the scope of commercial speech, but it would equally be difficult to characterize them as political or social discourse. The Supreme Court has in fact held the commercial speech principles are applicable to a variety of types of communication which might not be covered under *Virginia Pharmacy*. For instance, personal solicitation of customers,[21] references to professional credentials and certificates in letter headings,[22] and the use of news-racks on streets for advertising journals[23] have all been characterized as commercial speech, although the expression in these instances went beyond the mere provision of information to promote a sale or other commercial transaction.

---

[19] 425 US 748, 761–2 (1976), quoting *Pittsburgh Press Co* v. *Pittsburgh Commission on Human Relations* 413 US 376, 385 (1973).

[20] For criticism of the application of freedom of expression to lifestyle commercials, see R. Moon, 'Lifestyle Advertising and Classical Freedom of Expression Doctrine' (1991) 36 *McGill Law Jo* 76.

[21] *Edefield* v. *Fane* 507 US 761 (1993) (personal solicitation by accountants); *Board of Trustees* v. *Fox* 492 US 469 (1989) (personal solicitation by Tupperware salesmen). But restraints on personal solicitation have often been upheld: see s. 4(ii) below.

[22] *Ibanez* v. *Florida Department of Business and Professional Regulation* 512 US 136 (1994) and *Peel* v. *Attorney Registration and Discipline Commission* 496 US 91 (1990) (lawyers' use of professional designations on letterheads and business cards).

[23] *Cincinnati* v. *Discovery Network* 507 US 410 (1983) (unconstitutional for city to allow news-racks on pavements for newspapers and magazines, but not for advertising journals).

Another definition given by the Supreme Court may, therefore, be preferable. In *Central Hudson Gas and Electricity Corporation* v. *Public Service Commission*, the leading case on the regulation of commercial speech, it was defined as 'expression related solely to the economic interests of the speaker and its audience.'[24] This is a much broader definition, encompassing it is suggested, all the problematic cases mentioned in the previous paragraph. On this test, speech inducing one party to a contract to break it would also be treated as commercial speech; on the *Virginia Pharmacy* test, its status seems less clear, since the persuasion may not communicate any information and may only be intended to terminate, rather than bring about, a commercial transaction.[25] The *Central Hudson* definition rightly emphasizes the economic interests of *both* parties as necessary elements of commercial speech. It would be wrong to attach decisive weight to the profit motive of the speaker or publisher, for on that approach all newspapers, magazines, and books should probably be regarded as commercial speech; they are all published for profit, though of course they are read because they contain (sometimes) material of real political, literary, or other public interest.

Even more important is the point that the expression relates *solely* to economic interests. On that criterion, advertising by a family planning centre might not be regarded as commercial speech, since it provides information of real importance, which does not primarily, let alone solely, concern the recipients' economic interests. Equally, advocacy of a boycott of particular traders for political reasons, for example, to induce them to employ more workers from racial minorities, is political expression,[26] while advocacy intended purely to persuade the audience to terminate its contracts with the traders for economic reasons should be treated as commercial. Arguably, professional advertising, drawing attention to the services offered, say, by lawyers, accountants, and dentists, should also not be treated as commercial speech, since there are good health and welfare reasons why members of the public should have access to that information from the firms and practices which supply these services. Advertising features ('advertorials') in newspapers and magazines frequently combine valuable information about, say, the attractions of holiday resorts, with the promotion of services; it is a nice question whether they should be characterized as commercial or as public interest speech.[27] On the *Central Hudson* test, they should probably be treated as the latter.[28] That is how they would be treated in Germany. In one of its leading rulings in this area,

---

[24] 447 US 557, 562 (1980) per Powell J. for the Court: see s. 4(i) below for discussion of this case.

[25] For a full discussion of the position of speech inducing breach of contract, see D. A. Anderson, 'Torts, Speech, and Contracts' (1997) 75 *Texas Law Rev* 1499.

[26] See *NAACP* v. *Claiborne Hardware Co* 458 US 886 (1982).

[27] In *R* v. *Advertising Authority, ex p Charles Robertson Ltd* [2000] EMLR 463 Moses J. held that the ASA had jurisdiction over the contents of columns ('advertorials') appearing alongside advertisements, even though they might amount to 'political expression' for the purpose of ECHR, art. 10.

[28] But in *Bolger* v. *Youngs Drug Products Corp* 463 US 60 (1983) the Court treated leaflets which provided information about venereal disease and family planning and also promoted the company's contraceptives as 'commercial speech'.

the Constitutional Court held that advertisements are covered by freedom of expression, insofar as they take a line on a political question or make a contribution to the formation of public opinion.[29] The civil courts were, therefore, wrong to interpret Benetton pictorial advertisements protesting against environmental damage, the employment of children, and the spread of AIDS as solely intended to promote the company's economic interests.

Two leading decisions of the European Court of Human Rights show that expression is not to be characterized as commercial, when it has significant public interest. In *Barthold* v. *Germany*[30] a vet had been disciplined for advertising his services in breach of professional rules, when he gave an interview to a Hamburg evening paper drawing attention to the absence of a proper veterinary night service in the city, and highlighting his own comprehensive service. The Court held that application of the German advertising restrictions would deter a professional person from contributing to public debate on a matter of importance to the community whenever the expression might boost the advertiser's own business. It declined the invitation of the German government to treat the interview as commercial expression, outside the scope of Article 10 of the Convention. In *Open Door Counselling and Dublin Woman* v. *Ireland*[31] the Court appeared unconcerned with the characterization of advertisements for abortion services, when it held incompatible with Article 10 the restrictions imposed by Irish law on the provision of information concerning such services in the United Kingdom. The US Supreme Court, applying the test in *Central Hudson*, would probably have reached the same conclusion in these cases: in neither was the speech made solely for economic reasons, so it would have been wrong to treat it as commercial speech.

It is particularly difficult to classify statements which, on one view, adopt a position on a matter of current controversy, but which are intended also to promote sales. A Circuit Court of Appeals has held that press releases issued by the National Commission on Egg Nutrition, a producers' consortium, denying there was scientific evidence to link egg consumption to heart disease amounted to commercial speech: the Federal Trade Commission could issue an injunction to stop this misleading advertising.[32] But it is not clear these press releases related only to economic interests. The US Supreme Court has recently declined to give full consideration to a case from California, which would have given it an opportunity to clarify the meaning of commercial speech.[33] The Supreme Court of

---

[29] 102 BVerfGE 347, 359–60 (2001). For a more straightforward case from Germany, see 21 BVerfGE 271 (1967), where press adverts detailing employment opportunities abroad were held protected by art. 5 of the Basic Law.   [30] (1985) 7 EHRR 383.

[31] (1992) 15 EHRR 244.

[32] *FTC* v. *National Commission on Egg Nutrition* 517 F 2d 485, and on remand 570 F 2d 157 (7th Cir, 1975).

[33] *Nike Inc* v. *Marc Kasky* 123 S Ct 2554 (2003). See J. Weinstein, 'Speech Categorization and the Limits of First Amendment Formalism: Lessons from *Nike* v. *Kasky*' (2004) 54 *Case Western Law Rev* 1091.

California, reversing lower court decisions, had held that responses by Nike to allegations that it was mistreating and underpaying workers outside the United States might be categorized as commercial speech, as made by a commercial speaker to a commercial audience with a view to promoting sales of its products.[34] Nike had responded to the allegations with press releases, and letters to newspapers, university presidents, and athletics directors. (Characterized as commercial speech, these responses would not enjoy First Amendment protection if found false or misleading, a matter which had not yet been resolved by the state courts.) The majority of the Court held the case was not yet ripe for full consideration. Breyer J. strongly dissented from the majority decision not to consider the state court decision, arguing that there were no further questions of fact to be resolved, so it was right for the Supreme Court to take the case. In his view, the responses were in form and content public, rather than commercial, speech; in that event to hold false statements a breach of state unfair competition law would 'chill' speech of public importance. The key points in Breyer J.'s opinion are that Nike's responses were not made in an advertising format, did not propose sales, and concerned an important matter of public controversy, the criticism of its employment practices.

In summary, the *Central Hudson* test is more illuminating than that formulated in *Virginia Pharmacy*. First, it is not confined to advertising or other forms of sales promotion, but can be applied to a variety of types of speech which appear commercial in character. Secondly, it puts forward a criterion—the economic interests of speaker and audience—for distinguishing commercial speech from political, artistic, and other forms of discourse, sometimes unhelpfully labelled simply as 'non-commercial'. Of course, there will be difficulties in applying this criterion. But that does not mean that we should abandon any attempt to distinguish between commercial and other types of speech.[35] Courts should not find it any harder to identify commercial speech, or to differentiate it from political or social discourse, than they do to reach similar decisions in other contexts such as hardcore pornography. Borderline cases should, it is suggested, be resolved with the help of a presumption that the speech is non-commercial, rather than commercial, at least if the consequence of classification as the latter would lead to less intensive scrutiny of the speech restrictions. Courts may classify particular expressive acts mistakenly, holding that an advertisement, say, like that in the German Benetton case is commercial speech entitled to less protection than speech concerning political and social issues, or even that it falls outside the coverage of the free speech guarantee altogether. A wrong classification would lead to underprotection of speech. In order to avoid that risk, it would be right to hold, for instance, a producer's or retailer's advertisement fully covered, unless it is clear, as will generally be the case, that it solely serves the economic interests of advertiser and consumer. This argument is similar to that made by Frederick Schauer for some coverage of commercial speech by constitutional free speech guarantees, the

---

[34] 45 P 3d 243 (2002).   [35] But see Munro (n. 18 above).

issue to be considered in the following section of this chapter.[36] Just as it should be incumbent on sceptics to show why commercial speech should be *excluded* from coverage, so in hard cases the burden should be on the party arguing that speech is commercial, rather a contribution to public discourse, to justify that argument.

3. Should Commercial Speech be Covered by Free Speech Clauses?

(i) Introduction

In dissenting from the Court's judgment in *Virginia Pharmacy*, Rehnquist J. (as he was then) rejected the view that the First Amendment had anything to do with 'the decision of a particular individual as to whether to purchase one or another kind of shampoo'.[37] Such a decision was not to be equated with public decision-making on political and social questions, which are the concern of the free speech clause. This is a succinct statement of the sceptics' case that commercial speech, in particular advertising, falls outside the coverage of a free speech or expression clause. In their view, it is really more appropriate to classify advertising as a trade practice or commercial *conduct*, rather than *speech* entitled to some immunity from regulation. The arguments discussed in Chapter III are relevant to this issue.

It is not easy to apply any of the classic arguments for a free speech principle to commercial speech. The argument that bases the principle on the desirability of a fully informed population, able to play an intelligent active role in the working of democracy, hardly seems applicable; commercial advertising induces consumers to buy products and use services, but does not equip them to think about social issues or the conduct of government. The argument from truth is also difficult to apply. In political, social, and moral inquiry, we can never be certain that the right answer has been obtained. If we prescribe what can be said and written, and prohibit alternative views, we make an 'assumption of infallibility', as Mill put it, which is never warranted.[38] This reasoning does not work for advertising and other types of commercial speech, for instance, statements in a company report or its accounts. We can often be sure that a particular product does or does not possess certain qualities. A claim that the daily consumption of, say, baked beans guarantees 'long life' is so obviously false that Mill's theory is quite irrelevant. The Court in *Virginia Pharmacy* recognized that the truth or falsity of commercial speech can easily be determined.[39] In fact, very little commercial advertising is intended to assert anything which could be regarded as a truth, rather than persuade consumers to do something.

---

[36] 'Categories and the First Amendment: A Play in Three Acts' (1981) 34 *Vanderbilt Law Rev* 265, 281–2.　　　　　　　　　　　　　　　　　　　　　　　　[37] 425 US 748, 787 (1976).

[38] Ch. I, s. 2(i) above.　　　[39] 425 US 748, 771, fn. 24 (1976).

The coverage of commercial speech is, however, most open to question when self-development and self-expression arguments are considered.[40] Admittedly, it is not decisive that a commercial speaker almost always has a purely economic motive for advertising its goods or for announcing its trading plans. A profit motive does not disqualify the publication of newspapers, books, or other material from coverage by a free speech or expression clause. But this point does not establish a positive self-expression case for the coverage of advertising and other types of commercial speech. In order to make out such a case, we must focus on the free speech rights or interests of recipients, an argument which will be canvassed shortly. It is generally difficult to argue that advertisers and other commercial speakers themselves have free speech rights, grounded or based on their interests in self-development and self-fulfilment. For the most part they are corporations or firms to which this argument is inapplicable. It is nonsense to contend that advertising is vital to a corporation's sense of its ability to develop or achieve self-fulfilment, in the same way that the freedom to write or to paint is essential to the identity and self-fulfilment of authors and artists. It is interesting in this context to point out that the challenge to the advertising restrictions in the seminal *Virginia Pharmacy* case was brought by the state Consumer Council, not by the pharmacists themselves, though in subsequent cases courts in the United States have had little difficulty in ascribing free speech rights to corporations when they advertise or otherwise seek to maximize their profits.

One further point should be made at this juncture. The argument is not whether it is right, all things considered, to ban or impose restrictions on advertising and other forms of commercial speech. Many restrictions may be silly, inhibiting quite unnecessarily members of the professions, manufacturers, and traders, from giving information which customers might find helpful. But that is a matter for legislative and administrative judgement, unless the provision of such information and other forms of advertising is covered by freedom of speech or expression. (Some forms of advertising may be covered by other constitutional guarantees, notably in Germany the right of citizens freely to choose their trade, occupation, and profession;[41] much constitutional litigation in this context has concerned the propriety of limits on the exercise of this right.[42]) Even if the arguments for the coverage of advertising by the free speech guarantee are unsound, it would not follow that it is right to ban or restrict it. It means solely that there is no good free speech case for outlawing that course.

In *Virginia Pharmacy* Blackmun J. gave a number of reasons for holding pure commercial speech covered by the First Amendment. The first focused on the interest of consumers in the free flow of commercial information: '. . . that interest may be as keen, if not keener by far, than his interest in the day's most urgent political debate.'[43] Secondly, society has a strong interest in the unimpeded flow of

---

[40] See ch. I, s. 2(ii) above.   [41] Basic Law, art. 12.
[42] e.g. 40 BVerfGE 371 (1976), 94 BVerfGE 372 (1996).   [43] 425 US 748, 763 (1976).

commercial information, partly because that information may have a public interest component, but more generally because the flow is important in enabling consumers to make informed choices, which cumulatively are essential to the working of a free-enterprise economy.[44] Thirdly, for the state to justify its ban on the publication of drug prices with the argument that otherwise consumers would be attracted to go to low-cost, low-quality pharmacists is unacceptable paternalism.[45] The status of this third argument is unclear. It should probably be regarded as a counter to a common justification for the imposition of restrictions on advertising, rather than an independent argument for the coverage of commercial speech. But it is treated here as an aspect of a common free speech argument that it is intrinsically wrong for the state to deprive people of information because they might use it improperly.[46] Blackmun J., in effect, said that the state necessarily infringes freedom of speech when it prevents people acquiring information, even though the state justifies its ban on welfare or other paternalist grounds.

These points will now be considered in turn. The Supreme Court has considered the case for commercial speech coverage in many subsequent cases, but has not significantly added to the arguments it deployed in *Virginia Pharmacy*. Courts in other jurisdictions have contributed little to the theoretical debate. The Supreme Court of Canada, for instance, has generally been content to say that advertising falls within the scope of 'expression' for the purposes of section 2(b) of the Charter. It conveys meaning. There is no reason to *exclude* it from its coverage.[47] The academic literature, particularly in the United States, is vast, but it either refines, rather than adds significantly to, the case made by Blackmun J. for coverage of commercial speech, or is very critical of it.

(ii) The interest of consumers in commercial information

It is correct to say that most people are more interested in the price of drugs and other commercial information than they are in political news. But this does not remotely establish that there is a *free speech right* to receive, or impart, this information. People are also interested in cheap medicine, adequate housing, reliable transport, and many other goods, but that does not mean they have a free speech right to them. A normative right to a good does not follow from even the most acute interest in its enjoyment. So much more must be said for the argument to become coherent.

One line of argument is that the unimpeded receipt of commercial information is important to the *autonomy* of consumers, their right to make fundamental choices concerning their life. This was intimated by the Supreme Court of Canada when, in its first ruling in this area, it said that commercial expression leads to

---

[44] Ibid., 764–5.   [45] Ibid., 769–70.

[46] See Scanlon's Millian argument, discussed in ch. I, s. 2(ii) above. Also see D. A. Strauss, 'Persuasion, Autonomy, and Freedom of Expression' (1991) 91 *Columbia Law Rev* 334, 343–5.

[47] *Irwin Toy* v. *A-G of Quebec* [1989] 1 SCR 927: see s. 3(v) below for discussion of this point.

informed economic choices, an important aspect of individual self-fulfilment.[48] But it is easy to see weaknesses in the argument.[49] It is unclear what conception of autonomy is held by its proponents. They may take the view that informed economic choices lead to self-fulfilment. But the making of informed or better economic choices seems to be neither necessary nor sufficient to individual self-fulfilment. Many people are perfectly content and feel self-fulfilled without worrying much about their economic choices, while the most scrupulous care in this area does not appear to guarantee happiness, let alone personal maturity. Alternatively, proponents may believe that informed economic choices are intrinsically good, or, put another way, that this is what individual autonomy means. But that belief, as Shiner points out, takes a very thin view of the concept of autonomy.[50] Not all economic choices are good. Let us imagine a society where tobacco advertising is unrestricted. A manufacturer engages in an advertising campaign which provides accurate information about a new brand of cheaper, apparently safer cigarette, and which persuades many people to take up smoking or to smoke more. Would it be right to resist any attempt to restrict tobacco advertising with the argument that such a move would curtail the making of informed economic choices such as those made in this case, choices which are somehow essential to the purchasers' autonomy?

There is another difficulty. Even if it is accepted that informed economic choices foster self-fulfilment or somehow instantiate autonomy, it is far from clear that this makes a *free speech* argument. Informed economic choices enable consumers to make better purchasing decisions, not to develop their capacities for free speech. The argument from the interest of the recipients of information is much weaker here than it is in the context of claims of access to government information, or freedom of information, as it is generally known.[51] In that context, it is plausible to argue that freedom of information enhances the capacity of its recipients to contribute more effectively to public discourse. No comparable case can be made here. The autonomy argument is unpersuasive, at least in this form.

(iii) The public interest in the free flow of commercial information

Unlike the previous argument, this one is not based on the interests, let alone the rights, of consumers and other recipients. It is a utilitarian argument. It claims there are sound utilitarian reasons for the free flow of commercial information: in particular, the free flow is economically efficient, it reduces the costs which consumers would otherwise incur in their search for bargains and good-quality goods, and it promotes competition by facilitating the entry of new products and manufacturers into the market. All these are good points. But there are difficulties in

---

[48] *Ford* v. *A-G of Quebec* [1988] 2 SCR 712, 767.
[49] In particular, see the criticisms of Shiner (n. 15 above), ch. 11.   [50] Ibid., 230–3.
[51] See ch. III, s. 7 above.

using them to construct an overall case for free speech coverage of commercial advertising. In the first place, any utilitarian argument for free flow of information may be met by the contention that, in the *particular case*, the welfare or other arguments for regulation trump the general case for free commercial speech. Government or specialist regulators may make an apparently persuasive case that in some circumstances, for instance, on the introduction of new drugs, it is better to restrict advertising to consumers to protect their health or to deter them from putting pressure on their doctors to prescribe them unnecessarily. It is difficult for the courts to assess these arguments.[52] Further, it would often be wrong for them to try to do so, rather than defer in these circumstances to the expert judgement of the regulator.

Another objection is that it is wrong for a court to attempt to protect the values of a market economy through interpretation of a free speech clause.[53] When Blackmun J. related the free flow of commercial information to the working of a market economy, he appears to be protecting values on which courts should remain neutral. It is legitimate to hold public interest advertising, for example, for contraceptive advice and services, covered by freedom of speech because that is linked to political and social discourse, entitled to constitutional immunity from governmental restriction. In contrast, courts should not interfere with regulations introduced by an interventionist government, anxious to protect people from what it considers to be the dangers of excessive or misleading advertising. The government's view may be misguided, but it is entitled to restrict advertising, just as it is entitled to outlaw harmful trade practices.

(iv) Paternalism

In *Virginia Pharmacy*, Blackmun J. rejected the state argument that the ban on price advertising was justified in order to prevent consumers buying drugs from low-cost, low-quality pharmacies and so to keep high-quality pharmacists in business. That approach was regarded as 'highly paternalistic'. It should be assumed 'that people will perceive their own best interests if only they are well enough informed, and that the best means to that end is to open the channels of communication rather than to close them.'[54] This argument certainly underlies the coverage, and indeed strong protection, for political speech. Restrictions cannot be imposed on such speech, as that would be incompatible with a fundamental

---

[52] *Thompson* v. *Western States Medical Center* 535 US 357 (2002) is in point here. The Court, by a 5–4 majority, invalidated a provision in the Food and Drug Administration Modernization Act of 1997 which in effect banned the advertising of compounded drugs made for particular patients. Once advertising, as in this case, is characterized as 'commercial speech', courts inevitably have to assess complex arguments put forward to justify its restriction, in this case the argument that unrestricted advertising pressures doctors to prescribe compound drugs inappropriately. It is difficult for courts to assess these arguments.

[53] See R. C. Post, 'The Constitutional Status of Commercial Speech' (2000) 48 *UCLA Law Rev* 1, 8.

[54] 425 US 748, 770 (1976).

commitment to a participatory democracy, which recognizes that people are entitled to engage freely in public discourse and make their own political choices, wise or foolish. Thomas J, now the leading proponent in the Supreme Court of free commercial speech, would apply the same principles to bans on truthful commercial advertising. In his view they are imposed to manipulate consumer choices by keeping them ignorant.[55] This argument echoes the Millian Principle of Thomas Scanlon that government is not entitled to suppress speech because recipients will form false beliefs if exposed to it, or because they will as a result engage in harmful acts.[56] Otherwise it denies their autonomy.

This argument is open to the same criticisms as those levelled at the argument from consumers' autonomy rights or interests. Consumers may have a strong desire for price and other commercial information, but frustration of that desire does not mean that free speech is infringed. It must still be established that individual autonomy requires an ability to make informed economic choices, and that this is a free speech argument.[57] Further, it is far from clear that government bans or restricts advertising in order to keep consumers ignorant, let alone to influence public opinion. Such restrictions are quite different from restraints on political speech, and seem to have more in common, say, with packaging requirements or with noise pollution regulations. The concern of government is to discourage consumption, to promote health, or to protect the environment. When government regulates advertising to achieve one of these legitimate ends, it acts from paternalism; but the paternalism is directed to the protection of the environment or other policy goal. The Court was, therefore, wrong to charge the state in *Virginia Pharmacy* with the imposition of an unacceptable paternalist restriction on speech. Virginia had reasonable arguments for its ban on price advertising. It was intended to maintain professional standards and keep high-quality pharmacists in business, rather than keep consumers ignorant. (There was no ban, as Rehnquist J. pointed out, on third parties publishing drug prices.) These arguments suggest that the case for holding commercial advertising covered by the First Amendment was not made really made out by the Court; freedom of speech is not engaged when the state acts to safeguard a substantial interest unrelated to the suppression of free expression.[58]

(v) Conclusions

The *positive* arguments for holding advertising and other forms of commercial speech, as defined by the *Central Hudson* test, covered by freedom of speech or expression guarantees are, therefore, unconvincing. The standard justifications for a free speech principle, even as developed in *Virginia Pharmacy*, do not apply. Further, the arguments in that case only apply to informational advertising, and

---

[55] *44 Liquormart* v. *Rhode Island* 517 US 484, 522–3 (1996).   [56] See ch. I, s. 2(ii) above.
[57] See s. 3(ii) above.   [58] See ch. III, s. 2 above.

not to 'lifestyle' commercials, which provide no facts about the price, availability, or quality of the goods. But that is not the end of the argument. Advertising is 'speech' in the dictionary sense—it conveys information or an idea of the good life. That is also true of other forms of commercial speech, such as statements in a company prospectus or at a shareholders' meeting. It is not clearly excluded from the meaning of 'speech' for the scope of a free speech clause, in the same way as, say, perjury or blackmail.[59]

Frederick Schauer has argued that it is wise to take a broad view of the scope of a free speech guarantee, in order to avoid difficult arguments of principle and the risks of the denial of coverage to speech which should be covered, because it is of public importance.[60] Even if we think that the case for the coverage of commercial speech is thin, it is better not to *exclude* it from the scope of the relevant guarantee. That indeed is how Blackmun J. treated the matter in *Virginia Pharmacy*.[61] The Supreme Court of Canada has also usually approached the question in the same way. In *Irwin Toy* v. *Attorney-General of Quebec*, it held that advertising aims to convey a meaning, and so it falls within the scope of section 2(b) of the Charter. It 'cannot be excluded as having no expressive content.'[62] The courts must still examine whether there is expressive activity, rather than commercial conduct; an Ontario court was rightly doubtful whether margarine producers have a free expression right to use the same colour for their packing as butter manufacturers.[63]

This argument makes perhaps the best case for coverage of commercial speech: all things considered, it is too much trouble to require courts in every case, where the point is argued, to consider whether a particular advertisement (or other instance of speech made and received exclusively for economic ends) merits coverage. This is not a strong case. As I argued in the previous section, it is not too difficult to distinguish the public interest and professional adverts and other types of commercial speech which should clearly be covered, from purely commercial material, for which the case for coverage is much weaker. Courts might, therefore, not be burdened by too many hard cases, once it is granted that this distinction can be made easily enough in practice. But in cases of doubt, there should be a presumption that the advert is covered.

At all events, the coverage of commercial speech is narrower than that of political speech or of 'public discourse', the term used by Robert Post to identify the type of expression which is central to the First Amendment.[64] False and misleading claims about products and services are not covered at all. In contrast, false political claims could not be penalized, without infringing free speech. Further, as will be discussed later,[65] companies and professional firms may be required to

[59] See ch. III, s. 1 above.   [60] N. 36 above, 281–2.

[61] 'Our question, then, is whether this communication is wholly outside the protection of the First Amendment': 425 US 748, 761 (1976).

[62] [1989] 1 SCR 927, 971. Also see *Ford* v. *A-G of Quebec* [1988] 2 SCR 712, 767.

[63] *Institute for Edible Oil Foods* v. *Ontario* (1989) 64 DLR (4th) 308, Ontario CA.

[64] See Post (n. 53 above).   [65] See s. 4(iii) below.

disclose particular information when they advertise their products or services; freedom of commercial speech does not include a negative freedom not to provide information. For some reason, it is unclear how far the commercial speech principles cover the provision of financial advice in stock market journals. A Circuit Court of Appeals has upheld the power of the Securities and Exchange Commission to require a magazine to reveal the consideration received from a company for featuring its securities; an injunction against the magazine was considered permissible as an aspect of regulation of economic activity.[66] There is little or no case for allowing company promoters or directors to argue free speech as a defence to legal proceedings for making inaccurate or misleading statements. But even when commercial speech is covered, it should enjoy much less protection than political expression. As will now be discussed, governments have generally had considerable power to regulate this aspect of commercial enterprise to protect consumers, public health, safety, and the environment.[67]

4. The Regulation of Advertising

(i) General principles

Courts are usually more prepared to countenance the regulation of advertising than they are restrictions on other types of speech. In the United States they apply a somewhat more lenient standard of review than the strict scrutiny given content-based regulation of political speech. The European Court of Human Rights and the Supreme Court of Canada may in theory apply much the same tests to commercial as to other forms of speech; there is no distinctive 'commercial speech doctrine' as there is in the United States. But the latter court takes the value of the expression into account when determining whether its restriction is justified under section 1 of the Charter; commercial expression is entitled to less weight than political speech.[68] Moreover, the leading ruling of the European Human Rights Court suggests that states may enjoy more discretion, or a greater margin of appreciation, in determining whether to restrict commercial speech than they are allowed in other contexts. In *Markt Intern & Beerman* v. *Germany*, it held that an article in a trade bulletin reporting allegations of bad practice by a mail order firm 'conveyed information of a commercial nature' which did not fall outside the scope of freedom of expression.[69] However, with regard to commercial matters and unfair competition, the Court should limit its review to the question whether the national measures were in principle justifiable and proportionate; it should

---

[66] *SEC* v. *Wall St Publishing Institute, d/b/a Stock Market Magazine* 851 F 2d 365 (DC Cir, 1988).
[67] See Breyer J. dissenting in *Thompson* v. *Western States Medical Center* 535 US 357, 388 (2002).
[68] See the judgment of McLachlin J. in *Royal College of Dental Surgeons of Ontario* v. *Rocket* (1990) 71 DLR (4th) 68, 75, 79.   [69] (1990) 12 EHRR 161, para. 26.

not intervene when the national courts 'on *reasonable grounds*, had considered the restrictions to be necessary' (emphasis added).[70]

The United States standard of review in commercial speech was formulated in the *Central Hudson* case, where the issue was the constitutionality of a ban on promotional advertising for gas and electricity services, which had been imposed to further energy conservation.[71] The Court held that commercial speech should be subject to a complex four-part analysis. Provided: (i) the speech concerned lawful activity and was not misleading, it could only be restricted (ii) where the government interest in its regulation was substantial; if those tests were satisfied, courts must determine (iii) whether the regulation directly advanced the government's interest, and (iv) whether it was not more extensive than necessary to serve that interest. (This is a more lenient test than strict or heightened scrutiny applied to speech of public concern, where the Court requires the state to show that compelling interests justify the restrictions on speech and that they are the least onerous restraints which may be imposed to protect that interest effectively.[72]) In the *Central Hudson* case itself, the ban was invalidated under the fourth test, because it was too broad; it caught promotional advertising for products, the use of which might in fact have saved energy consumption. Three members of the Court, Brennan, Blackmun, and Stevens JJ, would have gone further and have held that any ban on truthful, non-misleading advertisements should be struck down, whether it fell foul of the four-part test or not. There is little difficulty about the first two parts of the test. False and misleading advertising falls outside the coverage of the First Amendment. The courts have usually been prepared to find a substantial state interest which may justify the regulation, though there have been some difficulties in satisfying this requirement in professional advertising cases.[73] The protection of health, the environment, and the reduction of consumption have been regarded as legitimate objectives for the state to pursue in this context. Advertising restrictions have met greater difficulties under the third and fourth parts of the test.

Despite some criticism, particularly from Thomas J. that it is insufficiently protective of commercial speech, the Court continues to use the *Central Hudson* test. It has been applied to strike down, for example, a ban on brewers' advertising the alcoholic strength of their beers,[74] and recently a ban on advertising and promoting compounded drugs.[75] The fullest discussion of the test is to be found in *44 Liquormart* v. *Rhode Island*,[76] where the Court unanimously invalidated a total

---

[70] Ibid., paras. 33, 37.

[71] *Central Hudson Gas and Electricity Corporation* v. *Public Service Commission* 447 US 557 (1980).

[72] See ch. II, s. 2 above for strict scrutiny of speech restrictions in the United States. The state does not have to show that restraints on commercial speech are the 'least restrictive [of speech] means' to achieve the desired end: *Board of Trustees of the State University of New York* v. *Fox* 109 S Ct 3028, 3035 (1989) per Scalia J.   [73] See the following section, s. 4(ii).

[74] *Rubin* v. *Coors Brewing Co* 514 US 476 (1995).

[75] *Thompson* v. *Western States Medical Center* 535 US 357 (2002).   [76] 517 US 484 (1996).

ban on advertisements providing information about the prices of alcoholic drinks. Emphasizing that the test was to be applied particularly stringently to *total* bans of truthful, non-misleading speech, Stevens J. in the leading judgment found that the state had not shown its legitimate objective of moderating alcohol consumption would be significantly advanced by the ban on price advertising. He required a clear evidential basis for the state's argument. In other words, the third part of the *Central Hudson* test was not satisfied. Moreover, the ban also failed the fourth part. Other steps could have been taken which would have been more likely to achieve the state's objective and would have been less restrictive of commercial speech; the imposition of higher prices through taxation, a requirement that alcohol is only available on prescription, or the launch of state educational programmes to draw attention to the dangers of excessive drinking would all have achieved the state's temperance objective. This part of Stevens J.'s opinion seems to have been shared by all members of the Court. It amounts to a significant tightening of the fourth part of the *Central Hudson* test. In effect, a state is not free to ban, or perhaps even restrict, advertising to achieve a legitimate goal, but must choose some other means of accomplishing that end, less intrusive on speech.

Stevens J. also considered, but with three other members of the Court, rejected another argument often used in support of advertising bans. If a state is free to ban an activity, such as smoking or the use of drugs, without constitutional objection, there should be no difficulty in conceding that it has the lesser power to ban the promotion of that activity by advertising: the 'greater-includes-the-lesser' argument. That argument had succeeded when the Court had upheld a Puerto Rico law permitting gambling in casinos, but forbidding them from advertising their facilities to state residents.[77] But Stevens J. considered that decision and the underlying argument wrong. First, in his view, as a ban on speech may sometimes be more inhibiting on freedom than a ban on the activity, it should be not be assumed that the power to ban the activity is 'greater' than the power to proscribe speech about it. But that cannot be right in all cases. A ban on, say, the sale of alcohol would have far greater impact on the life and liberty of individuals than a ban on advertising alcoholic drinks, the primary impact of which would be on drinks companies. Indeed, that is why governments are much more reluctant to outlaw smoking than tobacco advertisements. Other courses open to the state to encourage temperance, such as imposing higher taxes, would also have greater impact on individual liberty than the advertising ban.

There is more to Stevens J.'s second point: the 'greater-includes-the-lesser' argument is inconsistent with the First Amendment assumption that speech is entitled to more protection than conduct, and that government cannot suppress speech to achieve its ends.[78] It is certainly true that under the free speech principle

---

[77] *Posadas de Puerto Rico Associates* v. *Tourism Co of Puerto Rico* 478 US 328 (1986).
[78] 517 US 484, 512 (1996). Also see on this point, *Greater New Orleans Broadcast Assoc* v. *US* 527 US 173 (1999).

speech must be tolerated when it creates the same or similar risks of harm or damage as conduct. The commitment to free speech requires us to tolerate, say, the display of sexually explicit material, when we are not required to tolerate the aesthetic offence given by, say, ugly buildings or unpleasant conduct. But it surely does not follow that we must tolerate speech promoting conduct which government wants to discourage, but which for prudential reasons it does not make illegal. On Stevens J.'s view, if society decided to decriminalize the consumption of a drug, such as cannabis, it would then have to tolerate advertising promoting its use, even saturation advertising on billboards and in magazines. That is not an attractive conclusion.

The *Irwin Toy* case is typical of the general approach to judicial balancing of freedom of expression and competing social objectives in Canada.[79] Quebec had banned advertising directed at persons under thirteen years old. The Supreme Court accepted its argument that advertising aimed at young people is inherently manipulative. It required the legislature only to exercise a *reasonable* judgement in determining the vulnerable groups which need protection. As advertisers remained free to direct their messages at parents and other adults, the ban was no more than a slight interference with their freedom of expression. In contrast to the US approach, the Supreme Court of Canada allows the government discretion in framing restrictions on commercial speech; it usually intervenes only when the regulations are clearly wider than necessary to achieve the government's end.[80] The European Human Rights Court would most probably adopt a similar approach to restrictions on commercial advertising. In fact, its slender jurisprudence in the commercial speech area largely concerns restrictions on professional advertising, and is therefore discussed in that context.

(ii) Restrictions on professional advertising

The issues arising in connection with professional advertising deserve separate attention. In the first place, it may be hard in this context to determine whether a restriction limits speech of general public concern or the commercial speech of a lawyer, doctor, or other professional person. As already mentioned, the decision of the European Human Rights Court in *Barthold* shows that an article drawing the attention of the public to an important matter, in that case the inadequacy of night veterinary services, should not be treated as commercial speech, but merits full free expression protection.[81] The German Constitutional Court has held that the application of professional advertising restrictions to penalize a doctor for

---

[79] *Irwin Toy* v. *A-G of Quebec* [1989] 1 SCR 927.

[80] But see its judgment in the tobacco advertising ban case, *RJR-McDonald Inc* v. *A-G of Canada* [1995] 3 SCR 199, discussed in s. 5 below.

[81] *Barthold* v. *Germany* (1985) 7 EHRR 383. Also see *Hertel* v. *Switzerland* (1998) 28 EHRR 534 (views of scientist in journal article about health dangers of microwaved food treated as expression on matter of public interest and could not be restricted by unfair competition law).

writing a book of medical interest about his treatment of ageing infringed freedom of expression.[82] Similarly, it was wrong to apply the rules to a doctor for cooperating with the press before publication of a newspaper article concerning his services.[83] In these cases the doctors were contributing to public knowledge concerning medical issues; any promotion of their professional standing in this way was incidental to the main point of the publication.

Secondly, professional advertising restrictions are often justified by distinctive arguments. It is said that they are necessary to uphold general standards or to preserve the integrity or dignity of the profession. And it may be argued that professional advertising is inevitably misleading, because prospective clients or patients are unable to assess the claims made by lawyers, accountants, doctors, or dentists. The United States Supreme Court has generally been unsympathetic to these arguments. In its first professional advertising case, when it struck down a ban on price advertising by lawyers, it was unimpressed by the argument that such advertising had an adverse impact on their professionalism and was inherently deceptive or misleading.[84] It has also invalidated a ban on the illustration of intrauterine contraceptive devices in literature sent by lawyers to women who might claim compensation for injuries occasioned by their use: the Court rejected the argument that the ban was necessary to protect the dignity of the profession.[85]

The European Court has been much more sympathetic to these arguments. It has upheld a broad (though not absolute) ban on advertising by lawyers imposed to protect the dignity of the profession, the proper administration of justice, and the protection of clients; it was for the state to decide whether these restraints were necessary to protect 'the rights of others' to meet the requirements of Article 10(2).[86] In *Stambuk* v. *Germany* it did rule incompatible with freedom of expression the imposition of sanctions against a doctor who had featured in a newspaper article concerning his use of laser treatment for eye problems. But it emphasized that even objective, truthful advertising by professional people could be restricted in order to protect health and to ensure respect for the rights of others, in this context the interests of the doctor's professional colleagues.[87] The Supreme Court of Canada, in the leading case in this area, held that maintenance of high professional standards and the protection of the public from misleading advertising were sufficiently important aims to justify a ban on professional advertising; but a more or less total ban on advertising by dentists was held too broad to pass constitutional muster, because it would have prevented the provision of information concerning their hours of work and the languages they spoke.[88]

---

[82] 71 BVerfGE 162 (1985).   [83] 85 BVerfGE 248 (1992).
[84] *Bates* v. *State Bar of Arizona* 433 US 350 (1977).
[85] *Zauderer* v. *Office of Disciplinary Counsel of Ohio* 471 US 626 (1985).
[86] *Casado Coca* v. *Spain* (1994) 18 EHRR 1.   [87] (2003) 37 EHRR 845, paras. 29–31.
[88] *Royal College of Dental Surgeons of Ontario* v. *Rocket* (1990) 71 DLR (4th) 68.

Challenges may be made to restrictions on professional people engaging in personal solicitation for custom. These limits can be justified as necessary to protect personal privacy, and to protect clients from pressure which leads to hasty decisions. The US Supreme Court has upheld the suspension of a lawyer who engaged in personal solicitation of accident victims.[89] This sort of speech was treated as a subordinate element in a business transaction, and, though not considered to be entirely outside the scope of the First Amendment, was afforded a low degree of protection. However, the Court struck down a state rule which prohibited certified public accountants from engaging in direct, personal solicitation for clients; it was not satisfied that the ban was necessary to protect privacy and stop fraud.[90] It also invalidated a comprehensive ban on direct solicitation by mail targeting specific people.[91] But it upheld, by a 5–4 majority, a rule which prohibited personal injury lawyers from sending targeted mail to solicit custom from victims and their relatives for thirty days following the accident.[92] The majority and the dissenting Justices disagreed whether the state had done enough to show the rule advanced the privacy and peace of mind of victims and their families. The Florida Bar Association had produced a 106-page report of a study, which had been conducted over two years in an effort to establish the link. The majority was satisfied that it substantiated the connection, but Kennedy J. in dissent found the report inadequate; it gave no explanations of its methodology and provided no statistical guidance. This point nicely brings out one of the difficulties of intensive judicial review in this area; the courts question a matter on which they have little competence, certainly less than government.

Advertising by doctors, lawyers, and others such as insurance agents or stockbrokers should be distinguished from the information and advice they provide within the context of relationships with their patients or clients. Bodies such as the UK Financial Services Authority or the Securities and Exchange Commission in the United States lay down the terms and conditions on which investment advisers act.[93] Equally, doctors may be disciplined if they provide wholly inaccurate information or their advice falls short of required professional standards. In these circumstances, arguments that sanctions for breach of professional rules infringed the adviser's or doctor's freedom of speech or expression should be rejected. Professional advice to a particular person is not part of any public discourse, nor should it enjoy even the lower level of protection conferred on commercial and professional advertising. Governments and regulatory bodies are entitled to ensure that members of the professions meet certain minimum standards in the interests of the public they serve.[94]

---

[89] *Ohralik* v. *Ohio State Bar Association* 436 US 447 (1978).

[90] *Edenfield* v. *Fane* 507 US 761 (1993).

[91] *Shapero* v. *Kentucky Bar Association* 486 US 466 (1988).

[92] *Florida Bar* v. *Went for It, Inc* 515 US 618 (1995).

[93] See the judgment of White J. in *Lowe* v. *SEC* 472 US 181, 232 (1985).

[94] D. Halberstam, 'Commercial Speech, Professional Speech, and the Constitutional Status of Social Institutions' (1999) 147 *Univ of Pennsylvania Law Rev* 771, 834–49.

(iii) Disclosure requirements

In a footnote to his opinion in *Virginia Pharmacy*,[95] Blackmun J. indicated that the objectivity of commercial speech may make it appropriate to require advertisers to provide additional information and warnings to prevent consumer deception. That is something of an understatement. Drug manufacturers and food producers, for example, are commonly obliged to disclose the chemical ingredients or dietary qualities of their products and (in the case of the former) warn of any risks from taking the medicine. The best-known rule is the obligation imposed by governments on tobacco companies to state on cigarette packets the dangers of smoking:[96] 'SMOKING KILLS'. Company reports must contain prescribed information, while life assurance companies, building societies, investment advisers and others must say something about the risks of entering into agreements with them or buying shares. Professionals may be required to give a precise description of their fees and any hidden costs involved in the use of their services. Disclosure requirements in this context were considered by the US Supreme Court in *Zauderer* v. *Office of Disciplinary Counsel of Ohio*.[97] The state required attorneys, who advertised they would work on a contingency fee basis, to disclose whether clients would have to pay costs if their actions were unsuccessful. The requirement was upheld by a 7–2 majority, White J. for the Court stating that it did not infringe the attorneys' right of silence or negative freedom of speech. In the *Ford* case the Supreme Court of Canada struck down requirements that commercial advertising must be in French, but said that there would be no objection to an obligation to use French in addition to other languages or to give French greater visibility than that accorded others.[98] The obligation would not infringe advertisers' rights of silence.

Disclosure requirements are hardly controversial. They do not impinge on any right to silence of corporate manufacturers or producers, because it is unclear whether a right grounded on conscience and belief can be asserted by corporations exercising their commercial speech rights. Moreover, negative freedom of speech covers a right not to be forced to subscribe to opinions one does not hold, not a right to withhold information.[99] Since the best arguments for freedom of commercial speech are based on the interests of consumers in finding out attributes of the goods and services they want to buy, rather than speakers' rights, there is no good reason for holding that advertisers have any right not to provide information. The recipient interests here do justify a limit on the speakers' rights, for the latter are derivative from the former. Disclosure requirements reveal the peculiar character of commercial speech rights. Unlike free speech in the context of politics and the arts, they are primarily not the rights of the speaker, but of the consumer or client.

---

[95] 425 US 748, fn. 24 (1976).   [96] See s. 5 of this chapter.
[97] 471 US 626 (1985).   [98] *Ford* v. *A-G of Quebec* [1988] 2 SCR 712, 780.
[99] See ch. III, s. 4 above for discussion of this point.

5. Tobacco Advertising

No topic in this area arouses so much controversy as the regulation of tobacco advertising. It also highlights the range of commercial speech questions, as well as showing a stark contrast between the approaches in Europe on the one hand, and in the United States and in Canada on the other. Many European countries, notably France and the United Kingdom, have imposed a comprehensive ban, under which all advertising for tobacco products is prohibited, with a few exceptions.[100] The European Union introduced a directive in 1998 requiring states to introduce a comprehensive ban on tobacco advertising.[101] The measure was successfully challenged before the European Court of Justice on the ground that it fell outside the sphere of Community competence,[102] but the Advocate General also considered whether it infringed the guarantee of freedom of expression in the ECHR, with which EU legislation must comply. He submitted the ban was a proportionate measure to safeguard health, one of the aims which can justify restrictions under Article 10(2) of the Convention. He was persuaded that lesser bans, say, on advertising directed at children and young people, would be ineffective. Advertisers were free to argue that smoking was safe, so their freedom of expression was not wholly curtailed. Implicitly rejecting an argument accepted by the US Supreme Court,[103] it was immaterial in his view that smoking and marketing tobacco products are lawful; there might be good libertarian and practical reasons for deciding not to proscribe certain activities, but instead to outlaw advertisements which promoted them.[104]

The UK legislation allows the Secretary of State for Health to permit, subject to regulation, advertising at the point of sale: at retail premises, on vending machines, or on a website.[105] Tobacco manufacturers challenged the validity of the regulations which, among other things, limited the size of the advertisements and their place of display. They argued that these restrictions infringed their freedom of commercial expression. Rejecting the claim, McCombe J. pointed out that the government was not required to allow point of sale advertising at all; the legislation contemplated a comprehensive ban. The restrictions could not be regarded as disproportionate means for achieving the legitimate goal of the protection of public health; moreover, freedom of commercial expression was of less

[100] Tobacco Advertising and Promotions Act 2002; French law of 9 July 1976, as amended by Law of 10 Jan. 1991. For an analysis of the UK law (before its enactment) see E. Barendt, 'Tobacco Advertising: The Last Puff' [2002] *PL* 22.

[101] Directive 98/43 of 6 July 1998. A narrower directive has now been enacted to proscribe advertising of tobacco products in the media: Directive 2003/33 of 26 May 2003.

[102] *Germany* v. *European Parliament and European Council* [2000] 3 CMLR 1175.

[103] In *Lorillard Tobacco Co* v. *Reilly, A-G of Massachusetts* 533 US 525, 564 (2001), O'Connor J. for the Court emphasized that the sale and use of tobacco products is a legal activity.

[104] N. 102 above, paras. 157–66.

[105] Tobacco Advertising and Promotion Act 2002, s. 4(3).

significance than freedom of political or artistic speech.[106] The applicants had not challenged the legislation itself, but a clear implication of the decision is that such a challenge would not be upheld.

After its ruling in *44 Liquormart* v. *Rhode Island*[107] it is likely that the US Supreme Court would reject a comprehensive ban on tobacco advertising. It would take the view that there are other means, less restrictive of commercial speech, for a state to reduce smoking levels and so promote public health. Nor would it be sympathetic to an argument that, if a state can proscribe smoking altogether or ban it in public, it could take the lesser step of outlawing cigarette and tobacco advertising. As we have seen, it now rejects the 'greater-includes-the-lesser argument'.[108] It has even invalidated restrictions falling well short of a total ban. Massachusetts introduced regulations banning outdoor advertising of cigarettes and other tobacco products within 1,000 feet of a school or playground, and requiring indoor 'point of sale' adverts to be placed no lower than five feet from the floor. The object was to prevent the use of tobacco products by minors. Insofar as the rules restricted cigarette advertising, they were unconstitutional since they were pre-empted by federal legislation which covered this area.[109] Their application to the advertising of cigars and smokeless tobacco products was held incompatible with the First Amendment. While O'Connor J. for the Court was satisfied that the state had a substantial interest in reducing underage smoking, the ban on advertising within 1,000 feet of a school or playground would completely stop the provision of information in many urban areas to adults and children alike. It was also too broad in that it would preclude verbal advertising on the streets. The ban therefore failed the fourth part of the *Central Hudson* test, as it was much more extensive than necessary to advance the state's goal. The 'point of sale' requirement failed the third part of that test; many teenagers are now more than five feet tall, so it would be completely ineffective in limiting their exposure to tobacco advertising. Thomas J. would have gone further. In his view all restrictions on truthful, non-misleading commercial speech should be subject to the same strict scrutiny as, say, political speech. The restrictions were content-based, singling out tobacco advertisements, as compared, say, to adverts for fast food, and to the dissemination of dangerous political ideas.

However, the most interesting decision in this area is that of the Supreme Court of Canada in *RJR-McDonald Inc* v. *A-G of Canada*.[110] By a 5–4 majority, it invalidated a comprehensive ban on all forms of tobacco advertising (save at the point of sale) as an unjustified restriction on freedom of expression. McLachlin J. for the majority accepted that the ban had a rational objective, the reduction of

---

[106] *R (on the application of British American Tobacco and others)* v. *Secretary of State for Health* [2004] EWHC 2493 (Admin).   [107] 517 US 484 (1996).

[108] See s. 4(i) above.

[109] The Federal Cigarette Labelling and Advertising Act of 1965, amended in 1969, imposed mandatory health warnings for the packaging and advertising of cigarettes, and prohibited state regulation covering the same ground.   [110] [1995] 3 SCR 199.

smoking-related risks to health. She was willing to accept as a matter of common sense, in the absence of convincing proof, that promotional, lifestyle cigarette advertising had an impact on consumption. But the link was much less clear with regard to informational advertising of the price, tar content, and other attributes of particular tobacco products. The fatal flaw in the legislation was that it deprived consumers of this information. It failed the 'minimal impairment' test, under which a ban on the exercise of expression rights should not be wider than necessary to achieve its object. That test was not satisfied in this case, because the government had not shown that a prohibition confined to lifestyle advertising would have been less effective. It was relevant that smoking and marketing cigarettes were lawful, and consumers had a right to information about new brands which might perhaps have lower tar or nicotine contents. In a long dissenting judgment, La Forest J. argued that commercial advertising was only entitled to a low level of protection, and that in this context it was unreasonable to require irrefutable scientific evidence for the link between advertising and consumption. Parliament could have banned smoking altogether, so it was entitled to take the more moderate step of outlawing advertising for the activity: this is the 'greater-includes-the-lesser' argument now rejected in the United States.

The Court also invalidated the statutory requirement for cigarette packets to contain specified health warnings about the risks of smoking. McLachlin J. would have upheld an obligation to print a warning attributed to a government health officer, as has been required in the United Kingdom and other European countries,[111] and since the 1960s in the United States. The Canadian provision requiring packets to contain unattributed warnings infringed the manufacturers' freedom not to speak. The German Constitutional Court has also held that it would be an infringement of negative freedom of expression for tobacco manufacturers to be required to print warnings which would be understood by consumers as representing their own views; but it was clear that the warnings printed on cigarette packets could not be, and were not, so regarded.[112] There should not be any difficulty with regard to this issue. It is most unlikely that consumers will understand a health warning, particularly one such as 'SMOKING KILLS' or 'SMOKING CAUSES CANCER' as representing the producers' own view. The argument that it does is one of the many clever arguments made by tobacco manufacturers to defend their rights.[113]

As a result of the decision in *RJR-McDonald*, the government introduced a more narrowly drawn ban on 'lifestyle' advertising for tobacco products. Informational advertising is, however, allowed in publications with an adult readership of

---

[111] A health warning has been required under EU law by Directives 89/622 of 13 Nov. 1989 and 92/41 of 15 May 1992.   [112] 95 BVerfGE 173, 182–3 (1997).

[113] A standard argument is that cigarette advertising does not persuade people to smoke, but merely to change brands. The fact that monopoly tobacco manufacturers advertise suggests the argument is not a serious one. Further, if it were sound, they should have no objection to a ban on 'lifestyle' advertising which applies equally to all brands.

85 per cent or on signs to which young people are not exposed.[114] There can be little objection to a ban on lifestyle advertising, though that conclusion would be strongly contested by advocates of full free speech coverage for commercial advertising. They argue that such a ban would inhibit the freedom of the tobacco manufacturer to speak as it wants to do; it would be wrong to confine it to the issue of 'tombstone' notices, stating only the name, price, and contents of its product.[115] But that argument assumes that all forms of advertising are fully covered by freedom of speech or expression. If that is the case, it would, of course, be wrong to permit only 'tombstone' notices. But the assumption is wrong.

This chapter has argued that the case for free speech coverage of commercial speech in general, and advertising in particular, is weak. The best argument derives from the interests of consumers in product information, coupled with the disinclination, in this area as in others, to exclude from coverage communications which convey a meaning.[116] But lines can be drawn between pure commercials on the one hand, and on the other advertisements, say, for contraceptive advice or facilities, which may be regarded as on the margins of public discourse. Again, lines should be drawn generously not to exclude anything of more than purely commercial content.[117] These arguments do not remotely apply to lifestyle advertising for cigarettes (or for that matter other products). Even if such advertising is covered, the case for its proscription is very strong. Commercials like the Marlboro County ads are not banned because government fears that people will consider their argument and come to false conclusions, but to protect public health. Insofar as they suggest obliquely that smoking is healthy or life-enhancing, and so can be said to have free speech content, they are inherently misleading. On either interpretation the case for their protection under a free expression provision is weak. The personal autonomy arguments for freedom of speech are distorted when they are used to preclude sensible advertising limits.[118]

---

[114] Tobacco Act 1997, s. 22 (Canada). 'Lifestyle' advertising is defined as material which associates a product with, or evokes an emotion concerning, a way of life, which includes, for instance, glamour, vitality, or excitement: s. 22(4).

[115] See M. H. Redish, 'Tobacco Advertising and the First Amendment' (1996) 81 *Iowa Law Rev* 589. The author admits his research was financed by R. J. Reynolds.   [116] See s. 3 above.

[117] See s. 2 above.

[118] See T. M. Scanlon, 'Freedom of Expression and Categories of Expression' (1979) 40 *Univ of Pittsburgh Law Rev* 519, 531–4, and the discussion in ch. I, s. 2(ii) above.

XII

Freedom of Speech in the Media

1. Introduction

Traditional free speech arguments often assume that we are concerned with the freedom of *individuals*, in particular the rights of speakers to express their opinions to others. This is reflected in the early cases in the United States involving claims by politicians and others to distribute leaflets, address meetings, or demonstrate on the streets, and in more recent cases concerning acts of protest such as draft-card burning and flag desecration. But free speech rights are now more usually asserted by newspapers, broadcasting companies, and other media corporations, as well as by commercial institutions engaged in promoting their business. Such speech may be characterized as 'mass' or 'institutional' speech'.[1] It differs significantly from the speech contemplated by Mill in his essay, *Of the Liberty of Thought and Discussion*. It is generally the work of a production team, rather than of an individual, and, therefore, may not reflect the ideas or perspective of anyone in particular. It rarely invites dialogue or discussion. Insofar as mass speech is published to satisfy popular curiosity and prurience, it is not too cynical to say that it is produced for public consumption. News is just another commodity.

But speech emanating from the mass media is covered by constitutional free speech guarantees. Admittedly, it may be hard to justify coverage by recourse to the arguments concerning the importance of speech to the self-development and fulfilment of the speaker. In some circumstances, for example, in the case of television documentaries, it may even be impossible to identify a particular speaker whose views the programme represents. Further, it may be difficult for, say, tabloid newspapers to claim immunity from legal restraint on the ground that their stories contribute to the search for truth. Mill's arguments for liberty of discussion easily apply to scientific and learned journals, but fit the entertainment media much less comfortably.

But other arguments do establish an overwhelming case for extending the coverage of freedom of speech to the mass media. The media provide readers, listeners, and viewers with information and that range of ideas and opinion which

---

[1] See L. A. Powe, 'Mass Speech and the Newer First Amendment' [1982] *Supreme Court Rev* 243, and R. P. Bezanson, 'Institutional Speech' (1995) 80 *Iowa L Rev* 735, 806–15.

enables them to participate actively in a political democracy. Put shortly, the media perform a vital role as the 'public watchdog'.[2] As the 'eyes and ears of the general public'[3] they investigate and report the abuse of power. So the argument from democracy, overall the most persuasive rationale for the free speech principle, justifies the coverage of mass media communication.[4] Moreover, it would be dangerous to allow distinctions to be drawn between the serious press and public service broadcasters on the one hand and the tabloids and commercial entertainment channels on the other.[5] For a government might use its regulatory power over the latter to proscribe the dissemination of critical or subversive opinion. Consequently, all forms of the media—the press, broadcasting media, and the new electronic media—are entitled to the protection of a freedom of speech or expression clause, though, of course, that does not mean that every article or programme should necessarily be immune from legal restriction.[6]

It is easy to reach that general conclusion. It is much harder to determine what exactly freedom of speech means in the mass media context. It might mean simply that journalists and editors are free, as are all other individuals, to express their views unless there are good grounds for legal restraint. But freedom of speech might also confer on editors a constitutional right to determine the contents of their newspaper or to draw up a programme schedule—a right of editorial judgement or control. Regulations requiring a newspaper or broadcaster to publish a right of reply to a personal attack or to devote some space (or time) to coverage, say, of foreign affairs would be incompatible with such a right of editorial control, and hence with freedom of speech in the media. But it has been contended, on the contrary, that rules of this kind promote the access of readers to information and views which the press should provide as the eyes and ears of the public.[7] From that perspective freedom of speech might justify recognition of the reply or access right. Secondly, it may be difficult to determine who enjoys free speech in the media context: does the law confer free speech rights on individual journalists, on editors, or on owners of newspapers and broadcasting channels? This question becomes particularly pressing when there are conflicts between them: when an owner directs an editor to take a particular editorial line, that could be regarded as an exercise of the owner's free speech and press rights or as an interference with editorial freedom.[8]

Issues may be further complicated by the provision of specific guarantees for freedom of the press (and of the broadcasting media) in addition to freedom of

---

[2] *Observer and Guardian* v. *UK* (1992) 14 EHRR 153, para. 59.

[3] This phrase was used by Sir John Donaldson MR in *A-G* v. *Guardian Newspapers Ltd (No. 2)* [1990] 1 AC 109, 183, CA.   [4] See ch. I, s. 2(iii) above.

[5] The German Constitutional Court has refused to draw distinctions of this kind: see Soraya, 34 BVerfGE 269, 282–3 (1973).

[6] The application of free speech principles to the Internet is discussed in ch. XIII below.

[7] J. A. Barron. 'Access to the Press: A New First Amendment Right' (1967) 80 *Harvard Law Rev* 1641.   [8] See s. 4 below.

speech. In Germany this separate provision has led to the recognition of media rights clearly distinct from the rights to freedom of speech enjoyed by individual members of the public. Some commentators in the United States have argued that similar consequences should follow from the reference to 'freedom of the press' in the First Amendment,[9] though this claim has hitherto not been accepted by the Supreme Court. These different perspectives on the relationship of freedom of speech and freedom of the press (or media freedom) are explored in the next section of this chapter; section 2 also discusses the concept of editorial freedom, arguably the central idea in any discrete right to press freedom. Section 3 examines the legal implications of recognition of special media rights and immunities in a number of different contexts: taxation of the press, competition law, information rights, and the privilege not to disclose the sources of information. Section 4 discusses how different legal systems resolve conflicts between the free speech and free press interests of owners, editors, and journalists. Many of these questions are as relevant to the broadcasting media as to the older print media, but the former have always been subject to a degree of special regulation which has not been countenanced for centuries in the case of newspapers and books. Section 5 discusses whether this regulation is compatible with freedom of speech.

2. Press Freedom and Free Speech

(i) Three perspectives on press freedom

This section outlines three perspectives on the relationship of press freedom to freedom of speech. The first is that the two freedoms are really equivalent. They have broadly the same meaning; freedom of the press simply refers to the free speech rights of owners, editors, and journalists. This traditional approach was, for example, held by Dicey. He treated freedom of speech and liberty of the press as interchangeable terms.[10] It is also implicit in the judgment of Sir John Donaldson MR in the *Spycatcher* case when he said that the right of the media to know and to publish 'is neither more nor less than that of the general public.'[11] It is also held by a majority of American commentators on the First Amendment.[12] They point out that, except perhaps in one or two areas, the Supreme Court has not given the 'freedom of the press' limb of the First Amendment any specific content which is clearly distinct from the coverage afforded by freedom of speech.

---

[9] In particular, see M. B. Nimmer, 'Introduction—Is Freedom of the Press a Redundancy: What Does it Add to Freedom of Speech?' (1975) 26 *Hastings Law Jo* 631, and C. E. Baker, *Human Liberty and Freedom of Speech* (New York: OUP, 1989), chs. 10–11.

[10] A. V. Dicey, *Introduction to the Study of the Law of the Constitution*, 10th edn. (London: Macmillan, 1959), ch. VI.

[11] *A-G* v. *Guardian Newspapers Ltd (No. 2)* [1990] 1 AC 109, 183, CA.

[12] e.g. D. Lange, 'The Speech and Press Clauses' (1975) 23 *UCLA Law Rev* 77; W. W. Van Alstyne, 'The Hazards to the Press of Claiming a "Preferred Position" ' (1977) 28 *Hastings Law Jo* 761.

There are advantages to this approach. It treats ordinary individual speakers and writers in the same way as the press and other media, so avoiding any charge of discrimination in favour of the latter. Secondly, it does not face the definitional problems which are inevitable when a legal regime recognizes special press or media rights: what, for instance, is the 'press' and does it include book publishers or the publishers of circulars and leaflets? Finally, the traditional perspective does make sense in many contexts. If a government bans a television programme or a court awards libel damages against a newspaper, freedom of speech and media freedom are equally implicated. It is immaterial whether the channel controller or editor claims a violation of the right to freedom of expression or a right to press freedom.

But there are shortcomings to this approach. First, it means that any explicit mention in the constitutional text of freedom of the press or freedom of the broadcasting media is redundant, for it does not add anything to freedom of speech. That would seem particularly hard to accept where the constitution covers the press and broadcasting media separately from the individual right to freedom of expression. The German Basic Law, for instance, guarantees press freedom and freedom of reporting by broadcasting and films in the second sentence of Article 5; this suggests press and broadcasting freedom have a different content from the right to freedom of expression guaranteed by the first sentence of the Article. Secondly, the traditional perspective does not meet the powerful argument that the press is entitled to some legal privileges because it performs a vital constitutional role. For instance, newspapers may claim that freedom of the press gives them immunity from taxation and other laws which endanger their existence or which make it impossible for them to perform their function effectively.[13] Equally, the media may argue that, as a matter of constitutional law, they are entitled under the free press guarantee to acquire information or to attend public events, even though the general free speech clause does not give individuals comparable access rights.[14]

From the second perspective, freedom of the press would bear a meaning distinct from freedom of speech (or expression). Press freedom exists to protect mass media *institutions* which may enjoy special rights and privileges going beyond freedom of speech. The guarantee of this freedom is a structural provision of the constitution, giving the media, uniquely among private institutions, protection in recognition of its role as a check on government.[15] In the American context, the case was made in a classic article by Potter Stewart, a Justice of the US Supreme Court.[16] It was perhaps also the perspective of the third Royal Commission on the Press in the United Kingdom, when it defined press freedom as 'that degree of freedom from restraint which is essential to enable proprietors, editors and journalists to advance the public interest by publishing the facts

---

[13] See s. 3 below.   [14] See ch. III, s. 6 above.   [15] See Baker (n. 9 above), ch. 10.
[16] 'Or of the Press' (1975) 26 *Hastings Law Jo* 631.

and opinions without which a democratic electorate cannot make responsible judgements.'[17]

But this argument is open to criticism, at least insofar as it is understood to suggest a privileged position for the press. There are serious objections of principle to giving the traditional print and broadcasting media special rights which are not shared by individual writers and artists on whose work they often rely. Why should a journalist enjoy, say, access rights to interview prisoners or to report prison riots, when a novelist or penal reformer is denied them?[18] Admittedly, the media as a whole may play a more substantial role than any particular individual in disseminating information and ideas to the public. But this seems a thin basis for conferring on every press and broadcasting institution a wide range of privileges and immunities beyond the rights covered by freedom of speech, irrespective of the outlet's contribution to this process. Moreover, all sorts of institutions such as banks, financial services, and credit agencies now provide information to their customers and subscribers, while Internet service providers actually or potentially reach as many people as newspapers and broadcasters. There seems no obvious basis for distinguishing the position of these information providers from that of the traditional media.[19] On the other hand, if the benefit of 'media freedom' were extended to all information providers, the term would really cease to have any clear or distinct meaning.

Another objection to recognition of a broad constitutional guarantee for the institutional media is that it might be interpreted as allowing them to act incompatibly with free speech itself, or at least in a manner prejudicial to free speech interests or values. For example, one likely implication of a distinct press freedom is that the owner of a newspaper has an absolute right to determine its contents. He could exploit that right to damage the readers' interests in pluralism of information—a value underlying freedom of speech—by, say, dictating the political line of the newspaper irrespective of the editor's views, or by arbitrarily refusing to publish readers' letters in reply to what they considered inaccurate allegations printed in the paper. A similar clash might occur if press barons resisted the application of competition and anti-concentration laws with the argument that it would violate their free press rights. In these circumstances, it can be argued, the owner is really exercising a freedom to determine the use of his property, the newspaper, or a commercial freedom, although of course he may claim to be exercising freedom of speech. It would be unfortunate if recognition of an institutional freedom of the press were to be treated as strengthening these claims.

These arguments lead to a third perspective on the relationship of press freedom and freedom of speech. The former is not a right which is distinct from the latter and which is recognized to protect media institutions and their proprietors

---

[17] Royal Commission on the Press (Cmnd 6810, 1977), para. 2.3.
[18] See Lange (n. 12 above), 104–6.
[19] D. A. Anderson, 'Freedom of the Press' (2002) 80 *Texas Law Rev* 429, 435–46.

as such; rather, press freedom should be protected only to 'the degree to which it promotes certain values at the core of our interest in freedom of expression generally.'[20] Media freedom is an instrumental, rather than a primary or fundamental human right. Press claims to special privileges and immunities should only be recognized insofar as they promote the values of freedom of speech, in particular the public interest in pluralism in its sources of information.

This perspective is attractive. In the first place, it fits well with the underlying rationale for extending free speech guarantees to mass media speech: the essential role of the media in disseminating ideas and information to the public. It enables courts to resolve conflicts between the rights of the press and other media, on the one hand, and the claims by individuals to assert their right to free speech against the media on the other.[21] Secondly, it does not involve the drawing of a bright or sharp line between the rights of the institutional media and the rights of other information providers; the claims, say, of both journalists and novelists to interview prisoners or visit hospitals might be recognized, insofar as that step would give the public more information about significant social problems. It is, however, less clear whether recognition of those rights should primarily be a matter for the courts in their interpretation of a free speech or press clause or for the legislature. It may be better for statutes or other regulations to provide for access and other specific press rights. In the first place, the framing of these rights should be sensitive to particular circumstances; secondly, it is easier to introduce or amend legislation to meet new claims or to extend existing entitlements to new media outlets.[22]

Hitherto, as already mentioned, the United States Supreme Court has generally declined to give the free press limb of the First Amendment a distinctive content. For example, it is clear that non-media defendants enjoy the same degree of protection as the press and broadcasters from libel actions.[23] The Court has refused to recognize constitutional rights for journalists to withhold sources of information,[24] and to secure access to prisons to interview prisoners or investigate conditions there.[25] It is only, perhaps, in its decision in *Miami Herald* v. *Tornillo*,[26] recognizing the First Amendment right of newspaper editors to refuse to publish a reply to a personal attack, and more clearly in some newspaper taxation cases, that the Court appears to have endorsed a distinct press freedom.[27] For the most part, it has adopted the first perspective on the relationship of press freedom to freedom of speech. Constitutional protection for the press and other media generally derives from the speech limb of the First Amendment; the press,

---

[20] J. Lichtenberg, 'Foundations and Limits of Freedom of the Press', in J. Lichtenberg (ed.), *Democracy and the Mass Media* (Cambridge: CUP, 1990), 104.   [21] See s. 2(ii) below.
[22] See Anderson (n. 19 above), 515–21.
[23] *Dun & Bradstreet Inc* v. *Greenmoss Builders Inc* 472 US 749 (1985).
[24] *Branzburg* v. *Hayes* 408 US 665 (1972).
[25] *Pell* v. *Procunier* 417 US 817 (1974); *Houchins* v. *KQED* 438 US 1 (1978).
[26] 418 US 241 (1974).   [27] See s. 3(i) below for the tax cases.

though not broadcasters, are treated in the same way as other speakers and writers.[28]

In contrast, the German Constitutional Court has had no hesitation in distinguishing press freedom (*Pressefreiheit*) and broadcasting freedom (*Rundfunkfreiheit*) from freedom of expression. The distinct provision for *Pressefreiheit* and *Rundfunkfreiheit* in the second sentence of Article 5 has made that conclusion almost inevitable. Both branches of the media are constitutionally protected as institutions; their independence from state control is an essential element of a liberal democracy.[29] The independence of the press extends from the acquisition of information to the dissemination of news and opinion; it includes the protection of journalists' sources. Institutional press freedom means, for example, that a newspaper is entitled to be protected against the economic pressure applied by other media companies, when the latter threatened to stop supplying those retailers which had refused to cooperate with their call for a boycott of the newspaper.[30] It also provides constitutional support for state financial subvention through postal subsidies, provided they are allocated neutrally and do not distinguish between publications on the basis of their political slant.[31]

But the Court has made it clear that press freedom does not provide individual journalists with special free expression rights. The dissemination of opinion and information in the press and other print media is covered by the same right to freedom of expression which everyone enjoys. Press freedom is concerned with protection of the organizational and framework conditions necessary to enable the print media to contribute to the formation of public opinion.[32] It is also worth noting that the benefit of the press freedom clause is not confined to the institutional print media. What matters is that the material is used for communication. An employer could therefore invoke press freedom in respect of a news-sheet distributed to his employees.[33]

The German Constitutional Court in effect adopts the third perspective on the relationship of press and broadcasting freedom to freedom of speech: the former is an instrumental freedom which is guaranteed only inasmuch as it promotes the values of freedom of speech. It has taken this view most clearly in the case of *Rundfunkfreiheit*, sometimes described as a *dienende Freiheit*, a subordinate freedom, which is safeguarded to protect the interests of viewers and listeners in the receipt of a wide variety of information and ideas.[34] But the Court referred to press freedom in much the same terms when it affirmed the

---

[28] See Anderson (n. 19 above), 430–2, 506–7. For the constitutional position of broadcasters in the United States, see s. 5 below.

[29] First Television case, 12 BVerfGE 205, 260 (1961); Spiegel case, 20 BVerfGE 162, 174–6 (1966).   [30] Blinkfüer, 25 BVerfGE 256 (1969).

[31] 80 BVerfGE 124 (1989), discussed in s. 3(i) below.

[32] 85 BVerfGE 1, 12 (1991); 86 BVerfGE 122, 128 (1992).   [33] 95 BVerfGE 28 (1996).

[34] Third Television case, 57 BVerfGE 295, 320 (1981) and Fourth Television case, 73 BVerfGE 118, 152 (1986). See s. 5 below.

constitutionality of postal subsidies.[35] Further, it takes account of the underlying rationale of press freedom when it decides whether the limits imposed on its exercise by legislation or to respect other basic rights are constitutional. For example, although press freedom covers both the serious and the tabloid press, the Court is more willing to countenance limits on a fabricated interview in the latter in order to protect personal privacy; a tabloid paper cannot claim free speech or free press rights when its story is made up and contributes nothing of value to public discourse.[36]

The third perspective may be shared in other jurisdictions. The Canadian Charter provides that everyone has the fundamental freedom of expression 'including freedom of the press and other media of communication'.[37] Media freedom is not a right to be enjoyed solely by the media themselves, although of course a press or broadcasting institution is entitled to assert it. But when they do so, they are in effect claiming to exercise a freedom on behalf of everyone. The Charter does not give the institutional media special rights not enjoyed by others.[38] Although the the European Convention on Human Rights and Fundamental Freedoms (ECHR) does not provide any separate guarantee for the press or broadcasting media, the European Court of Human Rights has emphasized the vital function of the press as a 'public watchdog' in imparting information and ideas of public interest.[39] But journalists have 'duties and responsibilities' in performing this role. In *Jersild* the Court held it was an infringement of Article 10 to penalize a journalist for aiding the dissemination of racist speech by interviewing on television members of an extremist group; the interview was one means by which news was reported to the public.[40] The decision does recognize a special reporting right for journalists, which might not be afforded, say, someone who gratuitously repeated the hate speech of others in the course of discussion in a bar or even at a formal meeting. But it is most unlikely the Court would allow a journalist a greater freedom than other members of the public to disseminate his own racist views through a newspaper column.

Free press clauses and other provisions guaranteeing media freedom should, therefore, be understood to confer on all communications media—a term not confined to the established press and broadcasting media—some constitutional rights and immunities which are not conferred on individuals under freedom of expression or speech clauses. But they should be interpreted in conformity with the values of free speech, since it is the importance of that basic right which justifies the further protection of the institutional media.

---

[35] 80 BVerfGE 124, 135 (1989).

[36] Soraya, 34 BVerfGE 269, 283–4 (1973), discussed in ch. VI, s. 5 above.

[37] S. 2(b) of the Charter, discussed in ch. II, s. 3 above.

[38] M. D. Lepofsky, 'The Role of "The Press" in Freedom of the Press' (1992) 3 *Media and Communications Law Rev* 89, 117–18.

[39] *Observer and Guardian* v. *UK* (1992) 14 EHRR 153, para. 59.

[40] *Jersild* v. *Denmark* (1995) 19 EHRR 1, para. 31.

(ii) Editorial freedom

In *Miami Herald* v. *Tornillo*[41] the United States Supreme Court unanimously invalidated a Florida statute providing a mandatory right of reply to election candidates whose character was attacked by a newspaper. One rationale for the decision was that the statute intruded into the function of editors to determine the contents of the paper and the treatment of public issues; they would be compelled to publish a reply whether they thought it appropriate or not.[42] In the United States broadcasters also enjoy editorial freedom to determine programme schedules, including a right to reject political advertisements.[43] Even public broadcasting channels are free to editorialize, that is, to take a distinctive view on controversial public issues.[44] They are also entitled, and perhaps required, to exercise substantial editorial discretion in the selection of programmes, and are free to exclude minority party candidates from televised election debates.[45] Indeed, a prominent American commentator on press freedom has argued that the exercise of editorial judgement constitutes the essence of the freedom. It is equivalent to the exercise of free will, or liberty, which is guaranteed individuals by the free speech clause of the First Amendment.[46] Many courts and commentators in England and other jurisdictions would also accord editorial freedom a central role, without necessarily deriving from it the same implications usually drawn in the United States.

As a German decision shows, press freedom clearly entitles an editor to select the letters for publication in his paper and to allow a writer to contribute anonymously.[47] Equally, he is free to determine its general outlook and its views on particular political and social issues.[48] Under any understanding of press freedom, the editor of, say, a radical newspaper or journal should not be compelled to publish conservative right-wing feature articles in order to balance its contents.[49] But apart from these straightforward cases, there may be problems in determining the scope of editorial freedom. The Canadian Supreme Court held in a pre-Charter case that the *Vancouver Sun* was entitled to reject publication of an advertisement inviting subscriptions to a gay newspaper.[50] Otherwise editorial discretion and

---

[41] 418 US 241 (1974).

[42] Ibid., 258 per Burger CJ. The requirement to publish a reply interferes with an editor's right to silence: see ch. III, s. 4 above.

[43] *Columbia Broadcasting System* v. *Democratic National Committee* 412 US 94 (1973), holding that political groups had no constitutional right to compel a broadcaster to transmit political advertisements: see s. 5 below for restrictions on broadcasting political advertisements.

[44] *FCC* v. *League of Women Voters of California* 468 US 384 (1984).

[45] *Arkansas Educational Television Commission* v. *Forbes* 523 US 666 (1998).

[46] R. P. Bezanson, 'Institutional Speech' (1995) 80 *Iowa L Rev* 735, 806–15, and 'The Developing Law of Editorial Judgment' (1999) 78 *Nebraska Law Rev* 754.

[47] 95 BVerfGE 28 (1996).   [48] 52 BVerfGE 283, 301 (1979); 97 BVerfGE 125 (1998).

[49] But the imposition of such obligations on public service broadcasters is not generally regarded as incompatible with freedom of the broadcasting media: see s. 5 below.

[50] *Gay Alliance toward Equality* v. *Vancouver Sun* [1979] 2 SCR 435: see Moon, 197–9.

press freedom would be compromised. But a strong dissent of Dickson J. argued that application of the provincial non-discrimination legislation to compel acceptance of the advertisement would not interfere with the editor's freedom to determine the news contents of the paper. On the other hand, the US Supreme Court has held that the publication in a newspaper of sexually discriminatory job advertisements was not covered by the First Amendment.[51] So one difficulty is how far editorial freedom covers the advertising sections of a newspaper.

A more complex question is the extent of an editor's discretion with regard to the control of journalists and other staff. According to one decision of the US Supreme Court, an editor is not entitled to claim constitutional immunity from employment legislation, so he is not free to dismiss staff for union membership; but Roberts J. in that case said that Associated Press could discharge any editorial employee who had failed to comply with its editorial policies.[52] Presumably, a newspaper could dismiss a journalist who persisted in writing articles with a different perspective on political issues from that determined by the editor. Under the principle of editorial freedom the Supreme Court of Washington allowed a newspaper to transfer to copy-editing work a journalist who had refused to abstain from radical political campaigning outside her work as a journalist.[53] The paper's constitutional right to protect its editorial integrity and credibility gave it immunity from state legislation which prohibited employers from discriminating against politically active employees. But as the dissenting judgment pointed out, the decision gave preference to the institutional rights of the newspaper over the individual employee's right to political expression.

The most familiar conundrum in this context concerns the constitutionality of laws giving persons attacked by the media a right to reply in the newspaper or in a broadcast. As already mentioned, in *Tornillo* the US Supreme Court held the statutory provision of a right of reply to a newspaper article an interference with editorial freedom and so contrary to freedom of the press.[54] But in an earlier decision it had upheld, again unanimously, the constitutionality of a Federal Communications Commission (FCC) provision of a right of reply to a personal attack on radio and television.[55] Moreover, the German Constitutional Court has rejected a challenge to articles in the Hamburg Press Law which provided, in certain conditions, for a right of reply (*Gegendarstellung*) and a right of correction (*Berichtigung*) to allegations concerning the complainant.[56] In the Court's view, these provisions did not interfere with press freedom, although clearly they required editors to publish material they would prefer not to. The Court held that

---

[51] *Pittsburgh Press Co* v. *Pittsburgh Commission on Human Relations* 413 US 376 (1973). The decision, however, was reached before the coverage of the First Amendment was extended to commercial speech: see ch. XI, ss. 2 and 3 above.   [52] *Associated Press* v. *NLRB* 301 US 103, 133 (1937).

[53] *Nelson* v. *McClatchy Newspapers* 936 P 2d 1123 (1997).

[54] *Miami Herald* v. *Tornillo* 418 US 241 (1974).

[55] *Red Lion Broadcasting* v. *FCC* 395 US 367 (1969). For free speech and the special regulation of broadcasters, see s. 5 below.   [56] 97 BVerfGE 125 (1998).

they protected the personality rights of individuals, guaranteed by Article 2 of the Basic Law, and also the free expression rights of readers to form their own views about a dispute by hearing the perspective of the concerned individual (in this case, Princess Caroline of Monaco) as well as that of the press.[57] The European Human Rights Commission has also rejected a challenge to right of reply provisions. They guarantee pluralism of information and did not amount to a disproportionate infringement of press freedom, for the editor remained free to publish his own version of events.[58]

These decisions prompt reflection on the scope of editorial discretion and of the press freedom, of which it is an essential aspect. There may be conflicts between the interests of an editor on the one hand, and on the other that of an individual journalist, as in the Washington case, or those of readers and persons claiming a right of reply. On one view, the editor's constitutional press right should trump any rights conferred by statute on journalists or on other individuals. But arguably the editors' *free speech* interests in these cases was relatively weak: indeed, in the Washington case it seems more appropriate to characterize the interest as one in the organization of the newspaper's staff than an interest in communicating the editor's or newspaper's own distinctive views. Editorial freedom, like the press freedom of which it is an aspect, is subordinate to freedom of speech, which is arguably better served by recognition of the right of reply with which the editor's right conflicts.

3. The Implications of a Distinct Press and Media Freedom

This section explores four areas of law where the recognition of a distinct press and broadcasting freedom would be important. In these contexts the institutional media may enjoy rights which ordinary individuals do not, and indeed cannot, share.

(i) Taxation and the media

In the eighteenth and the first half of the nineteenth centuries, taxation was used in Britain (and other countries) to hinder the growth of a popular radical press. Imposed initially by the Stamp Act 1712, the duty was frequently a matter of bitter political controversy until its effective abolition by Palmerston in 1855. There followed an immediate rise in the circulation of cheaper popular newspapers.[59] There seems little doubt that legislation similar to the Stamp Act would now be held an unconstitutional abridgement of freedom of the press by the US Supreme Court. In *Grosjean* v. *American Press*,[60] the Court ruled a Louisiana tax imposed on

---

[57] Ibid., 145–8.   [58] 13010/87, *Ediciones Tiempo* v. *Spain* (1989) 62 D & R 247.
[59] See S. Koss, *The Rise and Fall of the Political Press in England* (London: Fontana Press, 1990), 92–4.   [60] 297 US 233 (1936).

the gross advertising revenues of newspapers with a weekly circulation above 20,000 an infringement of the Free Press clause of the First Amendment; it was clear from its history that the tax was intended to penalize higher-circulation newspapers, almost all of which had been critical of the state government. The tax could therefore be treated as discriminating against particular newspapers on the basis of their content.

However, in *Minneapolis Star & Tribune* the Court struck down discriminatory taxation of the press in circumstances where there was no evidence of state hostility to particular newspapers.[61] Minnesota had imposed a special tax on the ink and paper used in the publication of newspapers, though the first $100,000 worth of paper was exempt from the tax. The Court concluded that differential taxation of this kind—it applied only to products used in the production of newspapers and (owing to the exemption) affected only a small number of papers—was presumptively unconstitutional. The Court was unimpressed by the state's argument that the arrangement overall benefited the press which was immune from the general state sales tax: O'Connor J. for the majority said that the selection of the press for special taxation created the risk of '*more burdensome* treatment', adding that the courts were ill-placed to determine whether special tax arrangements were beneficial to it or not.

On this approach the special 'zero rating' for Valued Added Tax (VAT) conferred by a UK statute on a range of publications might be regarded as constitutionally suspect in the United States, for it would equally be open to Parliament to impose a higher rate of taxation on them. At the moment, certain categories of publication, including books, brochures, pamphlets, newspapers, and periodicals are in effect immune from VAT. Nice questions have arisen whether, for instance, a betting guide published at greyhound races and a property guide for estate agents are entitled to zero rating.[62] Rightly, no objection has been taken to the scheme either on the ground that decisions have to be taken (by the VAT Tribunal) whether particular publications are entitled to zero rating or on the more radical ground that it could be amended to prejudice newspapers and periodicals.

It has been quite common for states to allow tax concessions and confer postal or transport subsidies for the benefit of newspapers and other publications. These may be confined to journals and periodicals of general interest in order to avoid the provision of public financial support for pornographic material. Although the US Supreme Court has held that the Postmaster-General was not entitled to deny a magazine a reduced postal rate because, in his view, its contents were vulgar,[63] no constitutional objection was taken to the statutory provision confining the benefit

---

[61] *Minneapolis Star & Tribune* v. *Minnesota Commssr of Revenue* 460 US 575 (1983).

[62] *Evans & Marland Ltd* v. *Commssrs of Customs and Excise* [1988] VATRR 125 (racing card not a 'newspaper', as did not provide information, nor a 'periodical', as published every meeting day); *Snushall* v. *Commssrs of Customs and Excise* [1982] STC 537 (property guide not a 'newspaper', as did not contain news, nor a 'periodical', as not published for sale to public).

[63] *Hannegan (Postmaster-General of US)* v. *Esquire* 427 US 146 (1946).

of lower postal rates to publications providing 'information of a public character, or devoted to literature, the sciences, arts, or some special industry'.

The constitutionality of postal subsidies was fully considered by the German Constitutional Court in 1989.[64] It held that reduced postal rates may be made available to newspapers and other print material, provided the state is neutral in its allocation of subsidies. There must be no discrimination between journals on the basis of their contents or views. But it was constitutional not to subsidize purely or partly commercial and trade journals which made little or no contribution to the formation of public opinion. While it would be incompatible with Article 5 of the Basic Law to ban or limit the distribution of these publications, there was no obligation on the state to extend to them the benefit of postal or other subsidies. Moreover, no newspaper enjoys a constitutional right to state support; press freedom does not require the state to introduce tax or other subsides, but does oblige it to ensure that any subsidies are administered fairly.[65]

The US Supreme Court has recently resiled from its earlier hostility to discriminatory taxation. In *Leathers, Commissioner of Revenues of Arkansas* v. *Medlock*,[66] it held that differential taxation of speakers, including members of the press, is not constitutionally suspect under the First Amendment, unless it is aimed at, or creates a danger of suppressing, particular views. There was therefore nothing objectionable in the decision of the state legislature to apply to cable television services a general sales tax from which, in contrast, newspapers and magazines were exempted. O'Connor J., for the Court majority, argued that the sales tax did not single out the press or other media or hinder discharge of its role as a 'watchdog of government activity'. The Court's decision may be hard to reconcile with its earlier ruling in *Minneapolis Star & Tribune*. But it was surely right to hold that the Free Press clause does not confer any immunity on the media from general taxation or entitle it to special subsidies. Instead, legislation in this area, as in others, is only suspect if its effect is to inhibit the distinctive role of the press in providing the public with information and ideas or if it improperly discriminates on the basis of a journal's views or contents.[67]

(ii) Competition law and the media

The press and broadcasting media are subject to both general and media-specific competition laws. Typical examples of the latter are tighter restraints on press mergers than those governing mergers in other industries and statutory limits on

---

[64] 80 BVerfGE 124 (1989). [65] Ibid., 133–4. [66] 499 US 439 (1991).

[67] A state scheme which exempted newspapers and magazines covering religion, sports, professions, and trades, but not other journals from a sales tax was held to discriminate unconstitutionally on the basis of content: *Arkansas Writers' Project* v. *Ragland* 481 US 221 (1987). But it is permissible to tax *all* magazines, but exempt newspapers from a sales tax, on the ground the latter appear more frequently and provide current news: *Magazine Publishers of America* v. *Pa Dep't of Revenue*, 654 A 2d 519 (Pa, 1995).

the accumulation of radio and television licences. The rules of general competition law are intended to protect consumers against abuse by leading companies of a dominant position within the market, in this case the market for newspapers or for broadcasting services, or perhaps a general media market; these rules also protect the ability of prospective competitors to enter the relevant market by establishing new titles or broadcasting stations. Specific media competition laws are usually justified by reference to the value of 'media pluralism' or 'pluralism of information', the objective of ensuring the access of citizens to a wide variety of opinion and sources of information.[68]

The application of competition laws to the media may be challenged on a variety of constitutional grounds. Insofar as these laws inhibit the growth of a particular newspaper group or other media company, they may, it is argued, fetter property rights or the freedom of commercial enterprise which is recognized in some constitutions. But it can also be argued that they are a restraint on freedom of the press or other media freedom. On the other hand, such laws may be regarded as not only compatible with freedom of the press, but also as mandatory: the state is *under an obligation* to enact such laws in the interests of media pluralism. Another issue is whether commitment to freedom of speech or media freedom means that government may not legally maintain a monopoly such as the public broadcasting monopoly which existed in the United Kingdom until 1954 and which was a standard feature of European broadcasting laws until the 1970s. In one of its leading freedom of expression judgments, the European Court of Human Rights held that the Austrian public broadcasting monopoly should no longer be held compatible with Article 10, as it inhibited the freedom of individuals to communicate their ideas on the audiovisual media.[69]

The resolution of these complex questions may be affected by our understanding of freedom of the press and of other media and how their freedom relates to the freedom of speech (or expression) with which it is linked. If press freedom is understood as a distinct institutional freedom for the press, quite separate from freedom of speech—the second perspective identified in section 2 of this chapter—the restraints imposed by competition law on the conduct and growth of media corporations may be hard to defend. But if media freedom is regarded as an instrumental freedom, to be protected only to the extent it promotes the values of freedom of speech, at least some restraints on, say, media concentrations and conduct may be required to safeguard the values of free speech itself. For among those values is that of pluralism requiring public access to a variety of opinion and sources of information.[70]

These issues have frequently been considered in the United States. In a landmark case the Supreme Court held that general antitrust laws could be applied to

---

[68] See ch. I, s. 4(ii) above for the value of pluralism.
[69] *Informationsverein Lentia* v. *Austria* (1994) 17 EHRR 93: see ch. II, s. 5 above.
[70] See Lichtenberg (n. 20 above), 102–5.

the press; the Associated Press news service was unable to challenge, as an infringement of the First Amendment, the application of the federal antitrust Sherman Act to invalidate the requirement on its members to transmit the news they acquired to the service and not to anyone else. As Black J. for the Court put it, '[F]reedom of the press from governmental interference... does not sanction repression of that freedom from private interests.'[71] In other words, press freedom does not give newspapers or press agencies immunity from any general legislation intended to safeguard that freedom.

This decision was cited by the 1962 Royal Commission in the United Kingdom in support of its conclusion that legislation to regulate press mergers was unobjectionable on free press grounds.[72] Since then, press mergers have been subject to special mergers control. Under a recent revision of the law in this area, the Secretary of State for Industry may intervene and refer a proposed merger to the Competition Commission (formerly, the Monopolies and Mergers Commission) where specified media public interest considerations are present. These are 'the need for accurate presentation of news and free expression of opinion', and the need, so far as reasonable and practicable, for a 'sufficient plurality of views in each market for newspapers in the United Kingdom or a part' of it.[73] Previous provisions of this kind have been widely criticized as ineffective or unnecessary, but it has rarely been suggested that they are fundamentally flawed in that they improperly hinder the exercise of a free press.

Special media concentration laws, including restrictions on links between newspaper and broadcasting companies ('cross-media mergers') have been upheld in the United States. In *FCC* v. *National Citizens Committee for Broadcasting* the Supreme Court unanimously upheld a regulation of the FCC prohibiting a press company from forming links with a broadcasting company to own a radio or television station in an area where the newspaper was distributed.[74] The regulation did not infringe the First Amendment rights of newspaper companies, for it was unrelated to the contents of speech, but was rather intended to promote the diversity of sources of information in a particular community and so enhance freedom of speech. In this case, therefore, a regulation to preserve media pluralism was approved, even though it limited the commercial freedom of newspapers and broadcasters.

Measures to preserve newspaper titles have also been approved. Following a Supreme Court ruling that a joint operating agreement (JOA) between two newspapers in Tucson to provide for common management of their commercial operations and advertising resources was contrary to antitrust law,[75] the Newspaper Preservation Act of 1970 empowered the federal Attorney-General to consent to such arrangements where it was otherwise likely that one paper would

---

[71] *Associated Press* v. *US* 326 US 1, 20 (1945).   [72] Cmnd 1811, para. 337.
[73] Communications Act 2003, s. 375, replacing provisions in the Fair Trading Act 1973, ss. 57–9.
[74] 436 US 775 (1978).   [75] *Citizen Publishing Co* v. *US* 394 US 131 (1969).

close. In these circumstances the JOA would, it could be argued, preserve pluralism, for each newspaper kept its own editorial and news department, so preserving at least two independent voices in the community. Nevertheless, it was arguable that the effect of the Act might be to deter newcomers from entering the particular press market. A Circuit Court of Appeals has, however, rejected a First Amendment challenge to the constitutionality of the Newspaper Preservation Act, holding that the exemption from general antitrust law was an economic regulation which did not affect the content of speech.[76] Of course, it is unclear whether in the long term a measure of this kind will keep an unsuccessful newspaper in business, deter new entrants, and so inhibit the pluralism which it is designed to foster. Understandably the Circuit Court was prepared to defer to legislative and Attorney-General discretion in determining whether to exempt a JOA from the antitrust laws, rather than hold that those challenging the agreement had a free press right to enter the local newspaper market.

Circuit Courts have been more willing recently to entertain First Amendment challenges to restraints imposed by competition law. Telephone companies have argued successfully that a legislative provision prohibiting them from providing video programmes to subscribers within their service areas infringed free speech.[77] The provision was designed to prevent the risk of unfair competition by telephone companies which could subsidize and discriminate in favour of their own programmes if they were free to deliver them over their own lines. The court followed the Supreme Court ruling in *Turner Broadcasting System* v. *FCC*[78] that the provision of cable television programmes was covered by the First Amendment, and held the rule infringed the freedom of telephone companies to engage in this form of protected speech. Secondly, the DC Circuit Court has upheld challenges to FCC rules regulating the ownership and use of cable systems.[79] A rule imposing a 30 per cent limit on the number of national subscribers which may be served by one cable system operator was held outside the FCC's statutory authority, but the court also doubted whether it would survive the First Amendment, as it inhibited the number of viewers to whom a cable operator could speak. But a rule requiring at least two cable operators in the relevant area would, in the court's view, be upheld. Another rule requiring an operator to reserve 60 per cent of its first seventy-five channels for programmes made by firms unaffiliated to the operator was held unconstitutional, as infringing its First Amendment right to exercise editorial control over the selection of programmes transmitted over the system. But these rules were intended to promote competition and pluralism in the provision of

---

[76] *Committee for an Independent P-I* v. *Hearst* 704 F 2d 467 (9th Cir, 1983): see L. A. Powe, *The Fourth Estate and the Constitution: Freedom of the Press in America* (Berkeley: California UP, 1991), 212–21 for criticism of the 1970 Act.

[77] *Chesapeake & Potomac Telephone Co* v. *US* 42 F 3d 181 (4th Cir, 1994), *US West* v. *US* 48 F 3d 1092 (9th Cir, 1994).				[78] 512 US 622 (1994) discussed in s. 5 of this chapter.

[79] *Time Warner Entertainment* v. *FCC* 240 F 3d 1126 (DC Cir, 2001).

cable programmes; moreover, neither impinged on the content of particular programmes. The decisions in these cases suggest therefore that US courts now favour, at least in this context, distinct rights for the institutional media under the First Amendment, even though they seem more closely related to commercial freedom than to the traditional right of individual speakers freely to assert their convictions.

A strong contrast with the recent US decisions is provided by two important rulings of the Conseil constitutionnel in France on press concentration laws. In 1984, the Conseil held the provision of a bill limiting press proprietors to a 15 per cent share of national newspaper circulation was constitutional, provided it was interpreted only to apply in the event of mergers and acquisitions.[80] If the restriction were applied to inhibit the natural growth of circulation over 15 per cent or to stop a proprietor establishing a new title, it would inhibit the free choice of readers. But special merger and takeover restrictions were required to safeguard pluralism, which was treated as a principle of constitutional value. In a seminal passage the Conseil reasoned that effective freedom of expression itself was dependent on the access of readers to a range of publications with different opinions and character. Their free choice was fundamental in this context and should be protected against interference either by government or by private market forces. Contrary to the arguments of the opponents of the measure, there was no infringement of the owners' rights, rightly characterized as an exercise of property rights and of commercial freedom. Two years later, when the press concentration rules were relaxed by the Chirac government, the Conseil held provisions in its bill unconstitutional as infringing pluralism and the interests of readers in a variety of newspapers: the new bill did not effectively preclude acquisitions leading to a group commanding more than the new 30 per cent ceiling on national newspaper circulation, when the acquisition was made by a group which already exceeded that limit or by an associated, though nominally independent, company.[81]

Decisions of constitutional courts requiring the enactment of appropriate competition rules to safeguard pluralism in the broadcasting media are considered in section 5 of this chapter. The French decisions are the clearest expression of this requirement in the context of the print media. In the Spiegel case, the German Constitutional Court intimated that it would adopt a similar approach: *Pressefreiheit*, it said, imposes a duty on the state to take steps to avert the dangers arising from media monopolies.[82] Press freedom is understood in relation to the value of pluralism, itself essential to effective freedom of speech, rather than as a separate institutional right of the media corporation. Special competition laws are not only compatible with, but required by, this conception of press and media freedom.

---

[80] Decision, 84-181 of 10–11 Oct. 1984, Rec 73.
[81] Decision 86-210 of 29 July 1986, Rec 110.   [82] 20 BVerfGE 162, 176 (1966).

(iii) Press rights of access to information

Freedom of speech does not confer on individuals rights of access to information, as distinct from a right to communicate information which they have already acquired. As discussed in Chapter III, freedom of information is often recognized by particular statutes, but courts have usually been unwilling to derive a constitutional right from freedom of speech or expression. But the press and other media sometimes claim that the separate provision of freedom of press gives them positive rights of access to information, at least in particular contexts where their role distinguishes their position from that of the general public. Legal systems do sometimes give journalists privileged access rights to attend trials either for reasons of principle or for practical reasons.[83] But otherwise courts have been hesitant to accept arguments for special press rights to acquire information which would give journalists privileges not enjoyed by members of the general public.

There is no decision of the German Constitutional Court on the point, but the federal Administrative Court has on a number of occasions declined to recognize a constitutional press right to acquire information. Article 5(1) does not, for instance, confer a press right to compel a public broadcaster to disclose detailed information about its finances; it was for the legislature to decide whether there should be a right to acquire information in these circumstances, taking account of the state's general duty to respect press freedom.[84] Similarly, the press had no constitutional right to make a tape recording of an open sitting of a city council meeting; it was better for the chairman to take a decision on this matter in the light of the particular circumstances.[85]

The United States Supreme Court has also been reluctant to recognize special access rights for the press outside the context of legal trials. In a pair of cases it rejected journalists' challenges to California and federal rules prohibiting press interviews with particular prisoners.[86] The majority of the Court denied that 'the Constitution imposes upon government the affirmative duty to make available to journalists sources of information not available to members of the public generally.'[87] (The majority judgment was given by Stewart J., who had argued in a law review for recognition of special press rights.[88]) In a later case the Court refused to uphold an injunction granting a public television station access to a jail, including parts of it not open to the general public, and authorizing its journalists to interview prisoners about their conditions.[89] But a majority of the Court, 4–3, was prepared to grant journalists more effective and frequent access to parts of the jail; they would not be limited to the monthly tours of the prison open to the public. In all these cases, a minority of the Court dissented, arguing that access rights for

---

[83] See ch. IX, s. 4 above.   [84] 70 BVerwGE 310 (1984).
[85] 85 BVerwGE 283 (1990).
[86] *Pell* v. *Procunier* 417 US 817 (1974); *Saxbe* v. *Washington Post* 417 US 843 (1974).
[87] *Pell* v. *Procunier* 417 US 817, 834 (1974) per Stewart J.   [88] N. 16 above.
[89] *Houchins* v. *KQED* 438 US 1 (1978).

journalists should be recognized in these circumstances, not because the press as an institution enjoyed a privileged position, but because recognition of these rights was justified in order to enable it to inform the public about prison conditions. It was the public's right to know which was paramount.

Courts are understandably reluctant to recognize special *constitutional* access rights for the press in these situations. A claim by journalists that they should have access rights to inform the public is really no stronger than a claim by individuals that they have a free speech right of access to acquire information. As we saw in Chapter III that argument is unpersuasive, largely because it imposes duties on public authorities which are difficult to enforce. If the press (or other branch of the institutional media) claims to enjoy special access rights because of its constitutional status as a check on government, courts will have to define which organizations are entitled to claim these rights. Further, upholding constitutional press rights in the context of access to prisons would create powerful precedents for the recognition of such rights in other contexts, say, to attend the meetings of executive bodies or visit army bases.

On the other hand, the Supreme Court has rightly approved the grant by *statute* of preferential access rights to information for the press. It held that California was entitled to ensure that a person requesting the address of anyone arrested by the police wanted the information for journalistic or scholarly, and not for commercial, purposes.[90] It is preferable for the courts to sustain legislative access rights, rather than formulate them as a matter of constitutional entitlement. Statutory grants are more flexible: the scope of the rights can be expanded or contracted by the legislature at its discretion as circumstances change. Access rights could be confined to the established institutional press, or sectors of it, without legal difficulty. On the other hand, constitutionalizing these rights may be counterproductive. If a court holds, say, that bona fide reporters have a free press (or free speech) constitutional right to attend, say, the press conferences of a Prime Minister or President, it would either have to hold that all journalists are equally entitled to claim that right, or more realistically would have to determine on good grounds which journalists can assert it. Governments might prefer to abandon press conferences altogether rather than face the prospect of interminable, costly litigation about access entitlements. Non-constitutional protection for the press avoids these difficulties.[91]

(iv) Privilege not to disclose sources of information

Journalists argue that a source would generally be unwilling to supply information unless he was sure his identity would be kept confidential, since on identification

---

[90] *LA Police Dept* v. *United Reporting Publishing Co* 528 US 32 (1999).

[91] See Anderson (n. 19 above), 509–21, for criticism of *Sherill* v. *Knight* 569 F 2d 124 (DC Cir, 1977), recognizing a journalist's constitutional access right to White House press conferences, which could only be denied for compelling reasons.

he might face prosecution or dismissal from employment. Without respect for the confidentiality of sources, the press claims it would be unable to report fully matters of real public interest and so discharge its responsibilities as a public watchdog. Respect for such confidentiality is, on this view, an integral aspect of freedom of speech and press freedom, as well as a moral obligation. As a result, journalists should not be required to answer questions or surrender documents which would disclose the identity of their source to the police or to any other applicant who wants to take legal steps against him.

The courts in England had been reluctant to uphold a common law right not to disclose the source of information supplied to the press. In the leading common law case, *British Steel* v. *Granada*,[92] the House of Lords denied that the right was an aspect of press freedom: the latter referred to the right to publish information free from censorship, not a right to acquire information. Lord Wilberforce for the majority was only prepared to recognize a judicial discretion to take account of the importance of the free flow of information to the public, which would be promoted by recognition of a press privilege not to disclose its sources. But this right was not absolute, and indeed was not upheld in the case itself; Granada Television was ordered to identify the person who had sent it confidential documents concerning the management of British Steel, which had been quoted in the course of its documentary.

In principle the law has been radically altered by the Contempt of Court Act 1981. Section 10 provides:

> No court may require a person to disclose, nor is any person guilty of contempt of court for refusing to disclose, the source of information contained in a publication for which he is responsible, unless it be established to the satisfaction of the court that disclosure is necessary in the interests of justice or national security or for the prevention of disorder or crime.

However, in practice the courts have still been almost as reluctant to uphold a press claim not to disclose its sources as they had previously been at common law. An applicant's argument that disclosure should be ordered to enable dismissal of the employee who leaked the story has usually been accepted on the ground that this is 'necessary in the interests of justice'.[93] The House of Lords has also decided that the Secretary of State for Defence could require the editor of the *Guardian* to return confidential documents discussing how the government might handle any controversy which might arise on news of the arrival of Cruise missiles in Britain.[94] (From marks on the documents the government could discover which officials might have leaked them.) The House accepted that disclosure was necessary in the interests of national security, since it was reasonable to fear that a civil servant prepared to leak these documents might on a future

---

[92] [1981] AC 1096.
[93] See *X Ltd* v. *Morgan Grampian Ltd* [1991] 1 AC 1, HL; *Camelot Group* v. *Centaur Ltd* [1999] QB 124, CA.   [94] *Secretary of State for Defence* v. *Guardian Newspapers* [1985] AC 339.

occasion supply the press with information, the publication of which would seriously imperil national security.

Three points should be emphasized. First, the courts do now recognize that the right not to disclose sources is an aspect of press freedom which should be protected, unless the applicant makes a persuasive case for disclosure. As Lord Woolf CJ put it in a recent case, '[T]he fact that journalists' sources can be reasonably confident that their identity will not be disclosed makes a significant contribution to the ability of the press to perform their role in society of making information available to the public'.[95] In other words, the confidentiality of sources is protected because it enables the press to serve the interest of the public. The second point brings out implications of the first. The right is not confined to the press and other branches of the institutional media. It may be asserted by anyone responsible for any publication, whether a national newspaper or a privately prepared leaflet. That is why it is wrong to label the freedom not to disclose the source of information as a journalists' privilege, although the media are its principal beneficiaries.[96]

The third point concerns how the courts balance the right to freedom of expression and freedom of the press, on the one hand, and the interests which militate in favour of disclosure on the other. One factor which the courts may take into account is the nature or character of the information supplied by the source and subsequently published by the press. The courts are more likely to order disclosure of the source's identity if the information concerns the financial problems of a company, and is of no general interest to the public, than they would be if it concerned a political matter of real public interest.[97] Whether this particular distinction should be made may be open to question. But the fact that sometimes it is made is important. The courts are concerned with the character of the speech made possible by the confidentiality of the source, not simply with the fact the newspapers regard confidentiality as an integral aspect of their right to press freedom.

The reluctance of the English courts to uphold newspaper claims to keep the identity of sources confidential was, surprisingly, shared by the US Supreme Court in *Branzburg* v. *Hayes*,[98] still its leading ruling in this area of press law. By a majority, 5–4, it rejected the argument of three journalists that they should not be required to testify to a grand jury and to answer questions which would identify their sources of information about serious drugs and other offences. White J. for

---

[95] *Ashworth Hospital Authority* v. *MGN Ltd* [2002] 4 All ER 193, 210, HL. But an order was made to enable a mental health hospital to identify and dismiss the employee who had disclosed medical records and so protect patient confidentiality.

[96] See Lord Diplock in *Secretary of State for Defence* v. *Guardian Newspapers* [1985] AC 339, 348.

[97] See *X Ltd* v. *Morgan Grampian Ltd* [1991] 1 AC 1, 45 per Lord Bridge. In *Interbrew SA* v. *Financial Times* [2002] EMLR 446, paras 54–7, Sedley LJ suggested that the court's assessment of the importance of the story was immaterial, but the privilege could not be claimed where the information provided by the source was false. [98] 408 US 665 (1972).

the Court was sceptical whether the obligation to disclose sources in fact significantly limited the flow of news; history suggested that a free press could flourish despite the imposition of this obligation. In short, the media's argument was exaggerated. Even if there was evidence that some people are deterred from talking to journalists through fear of the consequences, it would be wrong to place much weight on the possible loss to the public of important information, measured against the certain loss of valuable information to the police or other applicant.

Another point made by White J. was the familiar one that the courts would eventually have to determine which types of reporter would be entitled to claim a constitutional privilege. There was no obvious reason, he suggested, why it should be confined to journalists from the established press; individual authors had just as strong an entitlement, for they also contributed to the flow of valuable information for the public. In support of *Branzburg* it has been persuasively argued that to confer a privilege only on representatives of the institutional media would increase the risk of arrogance and separate them from the public they purport to serve.[99]

Some of the points made by the Supreme Court in *Branzburg* were also expressed by the Supreme Court of Canada when it denied reporters a right not to disclose their sources under section 2(b) of the Charter.[100] Sopinka J. was unsure whether freedom of expression under the Charter conferred a right to gather information. He was even more doubtful whether a compulsion to disclose sources of information really restricted the ability of journalists to gather information. It was for the press to show that there was a link between a privilege and their freedom to gather and report information concerning stories of public importance. There was no evidence on this point in the case, nor is there generally any evidential support for the proposition that without promises of confidentiality sources will not talk to the media.

As the Supreme Court concluded in *Branzburg*, it is better for a privilege to be formulated by legislation than recognized as a constitutional right. In fact, many states in the United States have enacted generous 'shield' statutes conferring qualified, or in some instances absolute, privilege on the press not to disclose sources of information. Federal legislation also followed the decision of the Court in *Zurcher* v. *Stanford Daily*,[101] rejecting a claim of a student newspaper for constitutional protection against the search of its offices for photographs which would identify participants at a violent demonstration. Permission had been granted for the search by an *ex parte* warrant, rather than by issue of a subpoena to produce the material, a procedure which could be contested in court. Again, White J. for the majority doubted whether the procedure for obtaining a search warrant really inhibited the freedom of the press. The Privacy Protection Act of 1970 subsequently

---

[99] See A. Lewis, 'A Preferred Position for Journalism?' (1979) 7 *Hofstra Law Rev* 595. He also argued that the absence (at that time) of even a qualified immunity for the press in England had not inhibited it from investigative journalism.
[100] *Moysa* v. *Alberta (Labour Relations Board)* (1989) 60 DLR (4th) 1.
[101] 436 US 547 (1978).

established that normally subpoenas should be issued to the communications media for the production of documents to the police; search warrants should only be issued in exceptional circumstances.

The Police and Criminal Evidence Act 1984 (PACE 1984) in England confers similar procedural privileges. Normally the police may obtain from a magistrate a warrant to search for evidence; but access to 'journalistic material', defined as material acquired or created for the purposes of journalism and in the possession of a person who acquired or created it for these purposes, may only be secured from a circuit judge.[102] Moreover, the police must show in these circumstances that it is in the public interest that the material should be produced.[103] Although the legislation does not spell out what factors should be considered as relevant to the 'public interest', the judge should consider the danger to freedom of speech and of the press which would follow if the police secured access to material outside the strict conditions laid down in the legislation; the Divisional Court has accepted that legal proceedings brought to seize a journalist's papers or search press or broadcasting offices tend to deter exercise of these freedoms.[104]

In comparison with the caution of courts in England, Canada, and the United States, the German Constitutional Court has held without hesitation that press freedom covers the confidentiality of sources; it also confers on the media some protection from search of their offices and seizure of documents insofar as those procedures might disclose a source's identity. These principles were established in the famous Spiegel case,[105] although an evenly divided Court upheld the constitutionality of the search of the magazine's premises in order to look for evidence relevant to a charge of publication of state secrets. All members of the Court regarded the confidentiality of sources as an essential aspect of *Pressefreiheit*; the press would not, in its view, be able to acquire information unless its sources could rely on their identity being kept secret.[106] However, this right was not absolute; it could be limited by general laws which might have been enacted to implement other constitutional rights and values such as the right to a fair trial. Four members of the Court held it was legitimate in this case to impose a restriction on press freedom in the interests of national security.

Later decisions have clarified the scope of this press privilege in Germany. It is primarily a matter for legislative judgement how press freedom should be balanced with other relevant rights and values. It was reasonable to distinguish material produced by journalists themselves, such as film of a demonstration, from documents sent them in confidence by third parties; in the case of the latter, respect for the relationship of confidence between informant and the press justified a wider immunity than was warranted for self-produced or researched

---

[102] PACE 1984, s. 13. See Robertson and Nicol, 270–4, and D. J. Feldman, 'Press Freedom and Police Access to Journalistic Material' (1996) *Yearbook of Media and Entertainment Law* 43.

[103] PACE 1984, Sch. 1, para. 2(c).

[104] *R (Bright)* v. *Central Criminal Court* [2001] 1 WLR 662, paras. 91–5 per Judge LJ.

[105] 20 BVerfGE 162 (1966).   [106] Ibid., 176.

material.[107] In the Spiegel case the Court had made it plain that journalists' privileges, such as the immunity from disclosing sources, should not be regarded as their personal entitlements; rather they existed solely to enable the press to discharge its public role. Subsequently it rejected a claim by a journalist that he was not obliged to identify a tax adviser who had placed an anonymous advertisement contrary to the law.[108] The placing of advertisements of this kind could not be regarded as an important contribution to public debate, so it followed that press freedom was of little weight when balanced against the investigation of a criminal offence. This decision shows an approach similar to that of the English courts in cases where they have ordered disclosure of a source who has leaked commercially sensitive information of little importance to public discourse. Equally, it shows that in Germany, as elsewhere, this aspect of press freedom should be understood as serving the overall values of free speech, rather than as an exercise of a distinct institutional right.

The European Court of Human Rights has also recognized the protection of journalistic sources as a basic condition of press freedom. It accepted that without such protection sources might be deterred from helping the press with its investigation of stories of real public interest. The press would then no longer be able to discharge its role as a public watchdog. It is for the state to justify a disclosure order by an 'overriding requirement in the public interest'.[109] The Court has ruled that the order issued by the English courts (in the *Morgan Grampian* case)[110] to a journalist to reveal the source of a story about a company's financial difficulties was incompatible with the terms of the Article 10 guarantee of freedom of expression; it was not necessary to order disclosure of the sources, given that the company was able to stop publication of the story itself by a breach of confidence injunction. When eight virtually simultaneous searches of Belgian newspaper offices and journalists' homes were conducted by 160 police officers to discover the source of a leak by investigating judges, the European Court held that Article 10 had been infringed; the Belgian government had not shown that such a draconian operation was necessary to establish the source.[111]

One further US case should be mentioned to highlight the problematic character of the privilege not to disclose their sources. A consultant employed by the Republicans had told reporters that the Democratic candidate for Lieutenant Governor in Minnesota had a conviction for shoplifting. The reporters promised not to identify the consultant, but their editor decided it would strengthen the story to name him. The issue in *Cohen v. Cowles Media* was, therefore, whether a newspaper had a First Amendment right to break its promise to its source and reveal his identity as an aspect of its story.[112] The paper argued that to allow the

---

[107] 56 BVerfGE 247 (1981); 77 BVerfGE 65 (1987).   [108] 64 BVerfGE 108 (1983).
[109] *Goodwin* v. *UK* (1996) 21 EHRR 123, 143.
[110] *X Ltd* v. *Morgan Grampian Ltd* [1991] 1 AC 1, HL.
[111] *Ernst* v. *Belgium* (2004) 39 EHRR 35.   [112] 501 US 663 (1991).

consultant to bring an action (in promissory estoppel) against it would inhibit truthful reporting, where, as here, the source's identity was newsworthy. This argument was accepted by Souter J. in dissent, but the majority rightly held that the general law of promissory estoppel bound the press, just as employment, antitrust, and non-discriminatory taxation laws do.[113] Another argument for the decision might have been that, if the newspaper were free to identify their source in this case, no one else would trust it to keep a promise of confidentiality, with the result that in the long term the public would be deprived of information of political importance. The decision rejects, albeit implicitly, the second perspective on press freedom canvassed in section 2 of this chapter. The media do not have special First Amendment rights and immunities which set them apart from ordinary individuals. The privilege not to identify their sources can only be justified by the argument that, without it, sources would dry up to the loss of the public. The media are not free to discard that argument whenever they choose.

4. Whose Right to Press and Media Freedom?

The third Royal Commission on the Press in Britain pointed out that press freedom has different meanings for journalists, editors, and owners.[114] More cynically, it has been observed that, '[f]reedom of the press is guaranteed only to those who own one.'[115] Certainly, some aspects of press and media freedom are best asserted by proprietors, notably the freedom to establish a newspaper or to operate a media business free from discriminatory taxation. But it would be unfortunate to conclude that *only* the proprietors of a newspaper or a broadcasting channel are ever entitled to exercise a constitutional right to media freedom. It would be inconsistent with the claim that editorial judgement is the essential element of press freedom. If proprietors are the sole holders of press freedom, an editor would not be able to claim a right to editorial freedom against an owner who directed him to take a particular line in the newspaper's leading articles or to publish material against his judgement.[116]

How should conflicts between the claims of proprietors, editors, and journalists to exercise press or media freedom be resolved? The problem is one of internal press or media freedom: who is entitled to exercise freedom of speech within a media organization? Conflicts between press owners and editors will often be governed by the terms of the latter's contract and employment law. Sometimes special undertakings are given, or independent directors appointed to the newspaper directors' board, to safeguard editorial independence against arbitrary interference

---

[113] See s. 3(i) and (ii) above.   [114] N. 17 above, para. 2.2.

[115] A. J. Liebling, *The Press* (New York: Ballantine Books, 1964), 30–1.

[116] Max Hastings, editor of the *Daily Telegraph* for nearly ten years, observes that editorial independence is rare: see *Editor* (London: Macmillan, 2002), xv, 67, 81–2, 384.

or dismissal.[117] The editors' position (and also that of other journalists) could be safeguarded by legislation, perhaps incorporating terms into their contracts of employment. A prominent American commentator, Edwin Baker, has argued that legislation of this kind should be upheld, as it would be framed to promote the values of editorial independence and media pluralism. There would be no unconstitutional interference with the owners' First Amendment rights, provided they remain free to communicate their individual views in their newspaper.[118] Owners do not have a free speech right to compel their editors to take a particular line.

The one significant German case on internal press freedom (*innere Pressefreiheit*) is equivocal. The Constitutional Court refused to decide whether legislation limiting owners' prerogatives and protecting editors would be compatible with *Pressefreiheit*, when it held that a statutory obligation to consult a works council before dismissing an editor did not infringe press freedom.[119] The law was interpreted to allow the council to consider objections to dismissal on social, non-editorial grounds. However, the Court suggested that to allow the council influence on the political direction of a newspaper would be incompatible with press freedom.

The attribution of free press, and for that matter free speech rights, may be also crucial to the resolution of conflicts between owners or editors and individual journalists. Suppose the owner of a newspaper or magazine (or its editor) decides to suppress a journalist's story because he finds its contents embarrassing, perhaps because it reveals misconduct by an enterprise associated with the press organization. A court might decide that the journalist has a free speech right in these circumstances to have it published elsewhere. Alternatively, it might hold that the press proprietor has a property (or even a free press) right not to have the story published. The US Supreme Court has held that commercially sensitive information acquired by a journalist for use in his financial column is the property of the newspaper owner, so the journalist could be convicted for the theft of confidential information when he disclosed unpublished material to personal contacts.[120] In this situation, the owner's right should probably be regarded as a property right which may be trumped by the journalist's own First Amendment right and the free speech interest of readers in access to information.

The Wallraff/Bild decision of the German Constitutional Court is particularly pertinent to these issues.[120a] A well-known publicist, Günter Wallraff, infiltrated the tabloid paper, *Bild*, working as a journalist under a disguised name. He wrote a book about his experiences; it reported in detail an editorial conference, quoted

---

[117] See T. Gibbons, 'Freedom of the Press: Ownership and Editorial Values' [1992] *PL* 279.

[118] N. 9 above, 262–6. Max Hastings invited his proprietor, Conrad Black, to write in the Letters column in his papers: n. 116 above, 82.

[119] 52 BVerfGE 283 (1979). See I. von Münch and P. Kunig (eds.), *Grundgesetz-Kommentar*, 5th edn. (Munich: Beck, 2000), 412–13 for the view that ultimately it is the prerogative of the owner to determine the direction and editorial line of a newspaper.

[120] *Carpenter* v. *US* 484 US 19 (1987).   [120a] 66 BVerfGE 116 (1984).

instructions he had received from the chief reporter, and reproduced a report he had written, showing manuscript changes made by the latter. The publisher, Axel Springer, took proceedings to stop publication of these disclosures and of allegations in the book that the paper distorted presentation of the news from a right-wing perspective. The Federal Supreme Court rejected the action on the ground an injunction would interfere with Wallraff's freedom of expression. Springer brought a constitutional complaint that the decision infringed his right to freedom of the press, in that it allowed publication of confidential editorial discussions and internal workings of the paper. The Constitutional Court held that the confidentiality of editorial proceedings was covered by *Pressefreiheit*; otherwise sources might be reluctant to produce stories and free discussion between editors would be inhibited. On the other hand, while there was no right under Article 5 of the Basic Law to acquire information by deception, as Wallraff had done, the disclosure of unlawfully acquired information was covered by freedom of expression. That was implicit in the journalist's right not to disclose the source of such information which had already been recognized as an integral aspect of press freedom.[121] The case, therefore, raised a conflict between the publisher's press freedom and the freedom of speech of the bogus journalist.

The Court required the competing rights to be balanced. The relevance of the particular disclosures to a matter of public concern and the means by which the information was acquired were both taken into account in this process. The Federal Supreme Court had not attached sufficient weight to the gross deception practised by Wallraff, while it had exaggerated the significance of the reports of the editorial conference, which did not reveal any unlawful conduct by the paper. So its decision infringed press freedom. But the Constitutional Court was divided whether the same conclusion should be reached with respect to the reproduction of the altered report. Four members of the Court held that this had less impact on editorial confidentiality, while the other four found that the contents of the altered page were confidential.[122] As well as providing guidance on the scope of press freedom, the Wallraff decision is significant in recognizing that an individual reporter's rights may prevail over the right of a newspaper owner to suppress a story about abusive press practices. Had the information not been acquired by deception or the report of the editorial conference revealed impropriety, that result would have been reached in this case.

There is no single right answer to the question: who enjoys press freedom rights? Nor is there to the resolution of conflicts between the interests of the owners and the competing free speech rights of individual journalists. One factor is whether there is any relevant legislation: it would usually be easier for a court to conclude that legislation, say, formulating the rights of editors against owners

---

[121] Spiegel case, 20 BVerfGE 162 (1966), discussed in s. 3(iv) above.
[122] The Federal Supreme Court's decision on the point was upheld, as a majority of the Constitutional Court is required to sustain a complaint.

(or journalists) is compatible with press freedom and freedom of speech, than it would be for it to hold editors have *constitutional* free press rights to be protected against the claims of owners. Hard cases concerning the resolution of free speech conflicts within a media organization can most satisfactorily be resolved by the court determining which result enhances the values of freedom of expression, in particular, the public interest in the dissemination of information of political or social significance and the values of pluralism—the diversity of sources of information and the range of opinion available to the public. Press and media freedom exist to serve the values of freedom of expression, rather than to boost the commercial interests of media institutions; courts should take this consideration into account when they decide whether to ascribe rights to the owner, editor, or individual journalist.

5. Freedom of Speech and Broadcasting

The issues discussed in this chapter have been discussed for the most part in the context of the press and other print media. But they also concern the broadcasting media, whether terrestrial, cable, or satellite. Broadcasters have been more tightly regulated than newspaper publishers and editors. This is particularly true in Europe and Canada, where channels are, for example, usually required to be impartial in their presentation of news and treatment of political issues; they are also subject to stricter controls than the press with regard to the use of bad language and the portrayal of sex and violence.[123] Moreover, public service broadcasters are typically under positive obligations to show current affairs and other serious programmes, so they are not completely free to determine their own schedules. Even in the United States regulations used to provide until recently for a mandatory right of reply to personal attacks on radio and television;[124] further, there are restrictions on indecent programmes,[125] although private commercial channels are not subject to the range of 'public service obligations' often imposed in Europe on some private channels as well as on public broadcasters like the BBC.

Another difference concerns political advertising. In the United Kingdom paid-for political advertising, whether by political parties or by pressure groups,

---

[123] See E. M. Barendt, *Broadcasting Law* (Oxford: OUP, 1995), esp. chs. II and V for a full treatment of these topics from a comparative perspective.

[124] In *Red Lion Broadcasting* v. *FCC* 395 US 367 (1969), the Court unanimously held a mandatory right of reply to broadcast attacks compatible with the First Amendment. Compare the ruling in *Miami Herald* v. *Tornillo* 418 US 241 (1974). However, the FCC no longer enforces the Personal Attack rule, and has been ordered to repeal it in the absence of any attempt to justify it: see 229 F 3d 269 (DC Cir, 2001).

[125] *Action for Children's Television* v. *FCC* 58 F 3d 654 (DC Cir, 1995) upholding a ban on the broadcast of indecent material from 6.00 am until 10.00 pm.

is totally banned on broadcasting channels.[126] But newspapers are free to publish it. It seems hard to justify this position, given that most channels carry commercial advertising. The ban on political advertising appears to privilege commercial speech against political or other public interest communications which groups and political parties may be willing to pay for. The distinction has been successfully challenged before the European Human Rights Court in *Vgt Verein gegen Tierfabriken* v. *Switzerland*.[127] An association for the protection of animals was denied the opportunity to broadcast a commercial on Swiss television protesting against cruel methods of pig rearing; it had prepared the advertisement in reaction to commercials for meat. The broadcast would have contravened the Swiss ban on the broadcast of adverts with a political character. In one of its boldest decisions, the European Court held this restriction on free political speech could not be sustained. The prohibition on political advertising did not apply to other media; moreover, an advert on national television was the only practicable means of communicating a message to the whole population. While appropriate regulations could be framed to ensure that political (or indeed other) commercials did not excessively interrupt programmes, it was incompatible with freedom of expression to deny the association the opportunity to broadcast its message merely because of its political content.[128] The Court has, however, subsequently rejected a challenge to the ban in Ireland on religious advertising, holding that the total ban was sustainable, given the practical difficulties in determining which groups should be free to buy time for evangelizing. It accepted the argument that in the absence of the ban dominant religions would enjoy greater freedom than those with fewer members and resources.[129] The distinction drawn by the Court in this case between political and religious advertising is unconvincing. What really requires examination is whether any restrictions of this kind should be tolerated in broadcasting, when they would clearly be regarded as incompatible with freedom of speech in the context of the press and other print media.

A number of arguments have been used to justify the special regulation of broadcasting. The most important historically has been the scarcity of frequencies; they have been too scare to allow everyone who wanted to broadcast an opportunity to do so. It was therefore reasonable to impose conditions on those who were given a licence to broadcast.[130] This argument has become impossible to sustain with the advent of cable and satellite broadcasting and, more recently, of digital broadcasting. As a result, courts in the United States have generally held that cable operators cannot, compatibly with the First Amendment, be subject to

---

[126] Communications Act 2003, s. 319(2)(g).The UK rules are criticized by A Scott, ' "A Monstrous and Unjustifiable Infringement"?: Political Expression and the Broadcasting Ban on Advocacy Advertising' (2003) 66 *MLR* 224. For election broadcasts, see ch. XIV, s. 2(ii) below.

[127] (2002) 34 EHRR 4.   [128] Ibid., paras 74–8.

[129] *Murphy* v. *Ireland* (2004) 38 EHRR 13, paras 77–8.

[130] *Red Lion Broadcasting* v. *FCC* 395 US 367 (1969).

the same legal regime as terrestrial broadcasting channels.[131] On the other hand, in its major decision in the *Turner Broadcasting* case,[132] the Supreme Court decided it would be wrong to treat cable in the same way as the press. Cable operators exercise 'bottleneck' or gateway control, in that they decide which programmes are available to viewers on their system. That puts them in a much more powerful position than press proprietors who are unable to cut off the access of readers to other newspapers in the same way. Moreover, rules requiring cable operators to carry local terrestrial and public television channels, or to make some channels available for educational programmes, do not interfere with the operators' own First Amendment freedom; they can still make and transmit their own programmes.

It is now more common to put forward other arguments for the special regulation of broadcasting. In a decision upholding the entitlement of the FCC to apply sanctions against a California radio station for broadcasting 'indecent' language in the afternoon,[133] Stevens J. for the Court said that the broadcasting media were uniquely pervasive and powerful. It was also difficult to limit the access of children to unsuitable programmes. These points are far from persuasive. It is not clear that broadcasting is really very different from 'dial-a-porn' telephone lines or the Internet, both of which have been held by the Supreme Court to enjoy full First Amendment protection.[134] Nor does it seem consistent with general free speech principles to impose greater restrictions on a mode of speech merely because it is thought more effective than other media or means of communication. Parental control on the access of children to broadcasting is almost as feasible as it is in the case of the Internet.

A more promising argument for the special regulation of broadcasting emphasizes its relatively recent evolution.[135] In Europe and many other countries radio and television were originally public monopolies. Listeners and viewers have relied on the audiovisual media for objective news and for a comprehensive range of programmes which introduced them to topics and ideas they might not otherwise have chosen to consider. In the last fifty years that monopoly position has been eroded by the introduction of private commercial channels. But it has only been in the last twenty years, with the advent of cable and satellite broadcasting, that more than a handful of television channels have become available; even now almost 50 per cent of households in the United Kingdom actually receive four or five channels, although many more are available on cable, satellite and through digital systems.

[131] See *Midwest Video Corp* v. *FCC* 571 F 2d 1025 (8th Cir, 1978); *Time Warner Entertainment* v. *FCC*, 240 F 3d 1126 (DC Cir, 2001).

[132] *Turner Broadcasting System* v. *FCC* 512 US 662 (1994).

[133] *FCC* v. *Pacifica Foundation* 438 US 726 (1978).

[134] *Sable Communications of California* v. *FCC* 492 US 115 (1989) (telephone censorship unconstitutional); *Reno* v. *American Civil Liberties Union* 521 US 844 (1997) (legislation proscribing indecent messages on the Internet unconstitutional: see ch. XIII, s. 2 below).

[135] See L. C. Bollinger, 'Freedom of the Press and Public Access: Toward a Theory of Partial Regulation' (1976) 75 *Michigan Law Rev* 1.

Consequently, broadcasting policy, and in some countries the constitutional courts, have emphasized the importance of pluralism in this context.[136] First, the public should have access to a wide variety of types of programme and a range of diverse opinion within the public broadcasting channels: internal pluralism. This is particularly important, when these channels enjoy a dominant position within the overall system. Secondly, once private commercial broadcasting is permitted, competition law must supplement programme regulation to ensure the access of viewers and listeners to a multiplicity of voices within that sector: external pluralism. Otherwise commercial television might be dominated by a handful of media corporations. These principles have been developed by the Constitutional Courts in Italy and Germany,[137] as well as by the French Conseil constitutionnel. In its leading ruling on these points in 1996,[138] the Conseil said that pluralism was itself a principle of constitutional status and that respect for it was necessary for democracy. Freedom of speech within the audiovisual media would be ineffective unless the public enjoyed access to a wide variety of views and programmes. Pluralism justified limits on the broadcasters' own freedom of speech.

In theory, the Italian jurisprudence is particularly striking, although it has, unfortunately, had little practical impact. In 1981 the Court held that private broadcasting at the national level should be permitted, provided that adequate antitrust laws were introduced to ensure that this step did not lead to commercial broadcasting monopolies or oligopolies.[139] It affirmed this view in 1988 when it called for comprehensive regulation of commercial broadcasting to ensure media pluralism.[140] However, a clause in legislation enacted in 1990 allowed a media company to own three national networks (or 25 per cent of the available channels), a provision which was clearly intended to allow Silvio Berlusconi, then just an ordinary media mogul, to keep his three commercial channels. Four years later the Constitutional Court held this provision contrary to the guarantee of freedom of expression in the Constitution and the requirement of external pluralism.[141] (Unfortunately, it did not also invalidate another law which allowed Berlusconi's channels to continue to broadcast for the time being; by now Berlusconi had become Prime Minister and has been able, with the enactment of subsequent legislation, to hold on to his media holdings.) The Court has also held that external pluralism may not be enough to provide citizens with that range of opinion to which they are entitled, particularly during election campaigns. It, therefore, upheld the constitutionality of legislation providing for fair access of all political

---

136 Barendt (n. 123 above), ch. VI, s. 2; R. Craufurd-Smith, *Broadcasting Law and Fundamental Rights* (Oxford: OUP, 1997), 148–68.

137 See the rulings of the German Constitutional Court in the Third Television case, 57 BVerfGE 295 (1981) and the Fourth Television case, 73 BVerfGE 118 (1986).

138 Decision 86–217 of 18 Sept. 1986, Rec 141.

139 Decision 148/1981, [1981] *Giur cost* 1379.

140 Decision 826/1988, [1988] *Giur cost* 3893.

141 Decision 420/1994, [1994] *Giur cost* 3716.

parties to televised debates and precluding the expression of political views by the broadcasters themselves.[142] The interests of the latter could properly be subordinated to those of the general public; the legislation did not infringe the free speech rights of broadcasters.

It may be objected that the arguments from pluralism hardly now distinguish broadcasting from the press and other print media, where there are similar risks of oligopolies. The point, however, is that the more recent evolution of broadcasting has meant that the public has different expectations of the audiovisual media than it has of newspapers or magazines. While it expects the print media to be biased or to have selective coverage, it has relied on radio and television to provide objective news and a comprehensive range of programmes to inform as well as to entertain. These expectations may now be changing, at least with regard to cable and satellite. As far as those channels are concerned, it is increasingly difficult to justify the imposition of constraints on freedom of speech which would not be countenanced in the case of newspapers and magazines. The arguments from pluralism, however, remain persuasive for the principal private terrestrial channels and networks, and, of course, for public broadcasters.

Nevertheless, the awkward questions posed earlier in this chapter about the meaning of press freedom, and its relationship with free speech, are equally pertinent in the broadcasting context. What, for example, does editorial freedom mean and who is entitled to exercise it within a broadcasting organization? How should conflicts between the board of a broadcasting company and the channel controller or the programme producer be resolved? These issues are even more complex in the case of cable or satellite where programmes are made by one company for transmission on a system operated by another. In the *Denver Area* case some members of the US Supreme Court thought that the providers of access channels on cable systems enjoyed First Amendment rights,[143] while others would have ascribed an editorial freedom to the cable operators, so allowing them to refuse access to patently offensive or indecent programming prepared by independent providers. Breyer J. for the Court rejected the view that all media should be treated in the same way: cable broadcasting should not be equated with terrestrial broadcasting or regarded, like a telephone company, as a common carrier of the message of others. In the *Red Lion* case White J. had said, in the context of limits imposed on the freedom of terrestrial radio broadcasting stations, '[i]t is the right of viewers and listeners, not the right of the broadcasters which is paramount'.[144] There seems no good reason why that is less true for cable or satellite programmes.

This perspective does not mean that broadcasters have no freedom of speech. Within the confines of general programme standards, they are entitled to draw up schedules for their channels and to determine the contents of particular

[142] Decision 155/2002, [2002] *Giur cost* 1303.
[143] *Denver Area Educational Telecommunications Consortium* v. *FCC* 518 US 727 (1996).
[144] *Red Lion Broadcasting* v. *FCC* 395 US 369, 390 (1969).

programmes. Government censorship of programme material or a direction to give, say, more airtime to speakers favouring one view rather than another clearly infringe the free speech rights of broadcasters. For example, the direction of the United Kingdom government not to broadcast the words of supporters of pre-scribed Northern Ireland bodies was incompatible with free speech in broadcast-ing.[145] But respect for the interests of listeners and viewers means that legislation enacted to protect the values of pluralism is compatible with freedom of speech, even though it does limit the freedom of broadcasting corporations. Broadcasting freedom, like press freedom, is recognized to promote the values of freedom of speech, rather than to protect the interests of proprietors and editors.

6. Conclusions

A lot of nonsense is written about freedom of the press. Newspapers themselves are responsible for much of it. On the basis of these freedoms they claim the right to publish gossip and trivia about the private lives of celebrities, as well as the right to investigate and report stories of clear relevance to the conduct of public life. They are proud of their ability to influence political attitudes, especially during election campaigns. Equally, newspapers are free not to cover, say, foreign affairs or debates in Parliament or Congress, if editors think their readers would find such coverage boring. An obligation to cover these matters would generally be regarded as incompatible with press freedom, just as the US Supreme Court held in *Tornillo* that an obligation to publish a reader's right of reply infringed the First Amendment.[146] Newspaper proprietors and editors would be dismissive of any argument that the imposition of these obligations might serve the free speech interests of readers or be better for democracy. (On the other hand, broadcasters, particularly public broadcasters such as the BBC, are required to provide compre-hensive news bulletins and to include documentaries and arts programmes in their schedules.) Newspapers also often claim that, owing to their 'public watch-dog' position, they are entitled to special access rights to acquire information, to the privilege not to disclose their source (unless perhaps it would enhance their story to identify him,[147]) and perhaps even to immunity from competition laws.

These claims assume that the press and other media enjoy a unique, or at least a special, constitutional status. They might have that position because the constitu-tion confers a privileged position on the media, so they can check government effectively. That was the argument of Potter Stewart. As we have seen, it is open to a number of objections and for the most part is not supported by decisions of the Supreme Court.[148] Alternatively, the press and other media might claim special

[145] Regrettably it was upheld by the House of Lords: *R* v. *Home Secretary, ex p Brind* [1991] 1 AC 696.
[146] See s. 2(ii) above.
[147] See *Cohen* v. *Cowles Media* (n. 112 above) discussed in s. 3(iv)above.
[148] See s. 2(i) above.

rights and privileges to enable them better to serve the public: giving citizens information and ideas, and providing fora for public discourse—correspondence columns and televised Presidential debates. On that perspective, press and media freedom is, as we have argued in this chapter, protected because it promotes the values which underlie freedom of speech. But on that perspective it seems legitimate to ensure that the press, as well as the broadcasting media, serves freedom of speech by enriching public discourse. National newspapers might be subject to the modest 'public service' requirements imposed on the principal terrestrial channels in most European countries. Of course, newspaper owners and editors will protest that these requirements would inhibit their freedom of speech. But then they lay claim to a freedom of speech which in practice is enjoyed only by that handful of people who own or edit a national newspaper. That is an unattractive position.

XIII

Freedom of Speech and the Internet

1. Introduction

Dramatic claims are made for the Internet: it represents the most important development in communications technology since the printing revolution of the fifteenth century, and so heralds a new and more democratic information age.[1] A rich variety of content is made immediately available to everyone who can afford the relatively minimal (at least in developed countries) cost of access to the Web. Individuals can communicate their views to others by setting up a website, by participating in discussion groups, and by e-mail. The Net certainly affords much more equal opportunities for communication than the traditional press and broadcasting media, where the entry costs are high and which are in practice for the most part available only to professional journalists and to the political and social elite. It is therefore, as a District Court judge said in a leading United States case, *Reno* v. *American Civil Liberties Union*, 'the most participatory form of mass speech yet developed'.[2] The clear implication drawn by both the District Court and the Supreme Court[3] in the *Reno* case was that it would be wrong to restrain speech on the Internet, except for the dissemination of obscene messages and of other material wholly outside the coverage of the First Amendment.

The effective regulation of Internet communications is, of course, made much harder by their instantaneous availability over a wide geographical area. It is difficult, for example, to apply obscenity laws to electronic communications sent from, say, New York or Boston which can be read immediately in Tennessee and Texas: should it matter that the message is 'offensive' to communities in those states, if it would be regarded as acceptable to the vast majority of the residents of cities on the east coast of the United States?[4] These difficulties are magnified when the global character of the Internet is considered. Unless it takes draconian measures to restrict use of the Internet altogether, a state may be unable to prevent its citizens accessing material which is available from websites under the jurisdiction

---

[1] For general discussion, see G. Graham, *The Internet: A Philosophical Inquiry* (London: Routledge, 1999); Y. Akdeniz, C. Walker, and D. Wall (eds.), *The Internet, Law and Society* (Longman, 2000), ch. 1; the Symposium, 'Emerging Media Technology and the First Amendment' (1995) 104 *Yale Law Jo* 1613–1850.   [2] 929 F Supp 824, 883 (ED Pa, 1996) per Dalzell Dist J.
[3] 521 US 844 (1997), discussed in s. 2 below.   [4] See s. 3(ii) below.

of other countries. This creates real problems, particularly with regard to the regulation of pornography and hate speech. French and German law, for instance, penalize the dissemination of hate speech which would circulate freely in the United States, where its proscription would be incompatible with the First Amendment.[5] Courts in those countries may levy a fine on an Internet service provider (ISP) based in the United States for the publication of hate speech or pornography which it makes available in Europe, but the US courts may refuse to enforce their judgments as contrary to US public policy. Similar problems occur in the context of libel and privacy actions, where, say, a resident in England might be awarded damages by the High Court in London for the injury to his reputation caused by an item on a US website, but would then find it difficult to enforce the award in the US courts.[6]

These problems have led to the suggestion that cyberspace should not be subject to national or state laws at all. Arguably, the differences between free speech law in the United States, on the one hand, and in European jurisdictions or Australia on the other, are too difficult to reconcile. Even within the United States, it is unclear whether in principle a sexually explicit website or e-mail should be assessed by the moral standards of the community in the state of trans-mission or those of the community in the state where the prosecution is brought. If electronic messages were assessed by the standards of the most conservative community in which they could be accessed, ISPs and website operators might censor communications under their control, as they would be anxious to mini-mize the risk of prosecution or legal action. Website operators and other senders may have no idea who picks up their messages and which jurisdiction they live in, so the law imposes a great burden of them if they can be prosecuted whenever, say, a sexually explicit communication is accessed by a child, or extremist speech is accessed by anyone living in a country with strict hate speech laws.[7] It would be better, it may be argued, to abandon control by national laws which are necessarily inimical to the development of Internet communication, and replace them with systems of self-regulation. Eventually, a common cyberlaw might emerge.[8]

Whether that development is feasible at some time in the future, it has not yet happened, although much greater reliance is placed on self-regulation than is usual for more traditional media. In any case, it would be wrong to abandon legal controls altogether. Internet communications do have an impact in the real world. Reputations may suffer and privacy may be invaded. Consumers of pornography may use computer images of children engaged in sexual activity for the purposes of 'grooming' and for sexual abuse. Racists and other extremists can use the Net as

---

[5] See ch. V, s. 4(ii) above.   [6] See s. 5 below for discussion of these issues.

[7] See Kirby J. in *Dow Jones and Company Inc* v. *Gutnick* (2002) 210 CLR 575, paras. 84–6, HC of A. The difficulties are explored by L. Lessig and P. Resnick, 'Zoning Speech on the Internet: A Legal and Technical Model' (1999) 98 *Michigan Law Rev* 395, who discuss technological solutions to enable senders of messages to appreciate that their recipients are children.

[8] The classic exposition of this case is by D. R. Johnson and D. Post, 'Law and Borders: The Rise of Law in Cyberspace' (1996) 48 *Stanford Law Rev* 1367.

easily as liberals or Democrats to canvass support. Indeed, the Net poses greater dangers to, say, safety and public order than the conventional mass media. While the extremist speech of racists or anti-abortion campaigners is unlikely to find a place in the correspondence columns of national papers or in television programmes, it can easily be disseminated on the Net. Unlike speech on the mass media, Net communications are not controlled or modified by professional editors. The directness and immediacy of Internet communication is both its strength and its weakness.[9]

These considerations are relevant to fundamental questions of legal policy. One of these concerns the general treatment of the Internet under constitutional free speech principles, in particular whether it should, like the broadcasting media, be subject to a measure of special legal regulation. Another question is whether the Internet should be regarded as a public forum, with the result that limits on access to it in public libraries and universities would be incompatible with freedom of speech, in the absence of compelling reasons for denying access. There are now Supreme Court and other US decisions on these points; they are considered in section 2 of this chapter. The regulation of indecent material and child pornography is discussed in section 3, while section 4 is concerned with aspects of libel law, in particular the different treatment of ISPs under English and US law. Section 5 briefly examines some of the legal questions posed by the global character of Internet speech.

A broader question is whether the Internet should lead to a reconsideration of some free speech principles discussed in this book. Perhaps, for example, there should be a re-evaluation of the arguments for freedom of speech discussed in Chapter I. More weight might be accorded to the argument from self-fulfilment, given the ease and increasing frequency of Internet use. Free expression on the Net and open access to websites is crucial for many people. The Net might also have implications for the argument from democracy. Some commentators argue that its arrival makes possible greater participation in public discourse and politics, enabling everyone to share their views with others and to communicate them to the authorities.[10] It might be easier to hold frequent polls and referendums. A system of representative government, under which people vote for Members of Parliament or of Congress every few years, could be replaced by something like a direct democracy.

The advent of the Net may have implications for media regulation. As was explained in the last chapter,[11] it may be legitimate to regulate the broadcasting media and (probably) also the press in order to safeguard pluralism. Without regulation of ownership and also, to an extent, content, the interests of the public in access to a wide variety of opinion and sources of information will not be adequately protected. But the Internet may eventually lead to a shift in perspective.

[9] Graham (n. 1 above), ch. 5.
[10] For a discussion of the implications of the Net for democracy in Britain, see C. Walker and Y. Akdeniz, 'Virtual Democracy' [1998] *PL* 489. [11] Ch. XII, ss. 5 and 6 above.

If the Internet were *in practice* to provide most people with adequate news and other information to enable them to participate fully in public discourse, and involvement in Net discussion groups concerned with political issues became widespread, we would become less concerned with pluralism in the traditional media. But it is unclear whether the electronic media will ever play that role in public discourse. The optimists believe the Net will create a genuinely free and open market for the exchange of ideas, making realistic Holmes J.'s famous metaphor.[12] Others are more sceptical: they argue that the new technologies cater for consumers who seek out the information and messages they want, rather than the ideas they ought to consider as citizens.[13] The Internet will not provide a new public forum for general political debate, but rather will lead to further fragmentation or balkanization of speech. If that is the case, its growing use should have no effect on the arguments for media regulation considered in the previous chapter.

It is perfectly reasonable at this stage to remain unsure about the long-term impact of the Internet. In that event, it is legitimate and prudent for legislatures and courts to be cautious. First, that means it would be wrong to remove legal guarantees of media pluralism on the optimistic, perhaps facile, assumption that the Internet renders them unnecessary. Secondly, it is surely wise at least to retain those controls on Internet speech which are justifiable in the case of speech disseminated by other means. The mere facts that the Internet is easy and cheap for most people to use, and that they enjoy equal access as speakers and receivers on it, does not constitute an argument for a bonfire of controls. Moreover, as Kirby J. said in the High Court of Australia's important decision in *Dow Jones and Company Inc* v. *Gutnick* (discussed in section 5 of this chapter), the difficulty in exercising effective legal control 'does not mean . . . that the Internet is, or should be, a law-free zone.'[14] Arguably, the ease with which everyone can gain access to the Net suggests rather that we should be more hesitant to remove reasonable controls. Speech on the Net which spreads rumours and scandal round the world instantaneously may cause much greater damage, say, to an individual's reputation than could any article in the press or television broadcast. It is not surprising that advocates of absolute free speech protection argue for the removal of all restraints on Internet communication, but it does not make much sense for others to adopt that position. The important questions are whether the legal standards regulating, say, the publication of pornography or defamatory allegations by the traditional media need modification for the Internet.

---

[12] See Dalzell Dist J. in *ACLU* v. *Reno* (n. 2 above), 880–1, commenting on Holmes J.'s 'market-place of ideas' argument in *Abrams* v. *US* 250 US 616, 630 (1919). For similar perspectives, see J. Berman and D. J. Weitzner, 'Abundance and User Control: Renewing the Democratic Heart of the First Amendment in the Age of Interactive Media' (1995) 104 *Yale Law Jo* 1619, 1621, and E. Volokh, 'Cheap Speech and What It Will Do', ibid., 1805, 1846–7.

[13] O. M. Fiss, 'In Search of a New Paradigm', ibid., 1613, 1617, and C. R. Sunstein, 'The First Amendment in Cyberspace', ibid., 1757, 1785–7; Graham (n. 1 above), 80–3.

[14] (2002) 210 CLR 575, para. 87.

2. How Should the Internet be Treated?

(i) Rejection of the analogy with broadcasting

The United States Supreme Court considered the appropriate treatment of the Internet in *Reno* v. *American Civil Liberties Union*.[15] The American Civil Liberties Union, among others, challenged provisions of the Communications Decency Act of 1996 (CDA) which made it an offence knowingly to transmit by telecommunications devices 'obscene or indecent' messages to persons under eighteen, or to communicate or display by interactive computer services 'patently offensive' messages to such persons. The government argued it was entitled to protect children from exposure to harmful materials on the Net. It relied, in part, on the Supreme Court decision in *FCC* v. *Pacifica Foundation* that regulation of indecent broadcasts did not infringe the First Amendment guarantee of free speech.[16] In *Reno* the Court held it would be wrong to apply that precedent. There was no tradition of special regulation of the Net, as there has been for the audiovisual media. Further, the Internet could hardly be thought a 'scarce' commodity, so an important factor often used to justify broadcasting regulation did not apply. Most importantly, it does not invade the home in the same way as radio and television; users do not come across indecent (or other) items by accident. In that sense, the Net resembles telephone message services, which also, unlike radio and television, require listeners to take positive steps to gain access.[17]

It is also surely clear that the Internet is dissimilar to cable broadcasting. Cable operators act as 'gatekeepers', determining, subject to any statutory requirements that may be imposed on them, the programme services allowed access to the system, as well as transmitting their own programmes. Conceivably, the Internet could have been set up that way. ISPs might have been licensed by government or by some regulatory authority, and might have been legally required to exercise control over individuals and institutions given access to their system. That did not happen. (Even television services provided over the Net fall outside the licensing and regulatory powers of OFCOM, the broadcasting and telecommunications authority in the United Kingdom.[18]) The Internet allows open access, and operates without a system of centralized control operated by a handful of gatekeepers.[19]

(ii) Similar, but not identical, to the press

The Court in *Reno* did not explicitly bracket the Internet with the press and other print media for the purposes of the First Amendment. But it applied the same

---

[15] 521 US 844 (1997). Other aspects of this case are considered in s. 3 below.

[16] 438 US 726 (1978): see ch. XII, s. 5 above.

[17] In *Sable Communications of California* v. *FCC* 492 US 115 (1989) the Court held that a ban on sending 'indecent messages' over telephone lines was incompatible with the First Amendment.

[18] Communications Act 2003, s. 233.   [19] Berman and Weitzner (n. 12 above), 1621–9.

principles of review it had developed for print, and indeed for all communications media other than broadcasting. It required the government to show that it could not achieve the legitimate interest of protecting children from exposure to harmful material by less restrictive means than those contained in the CDA. The Court in effect adopted the same approach that it does to the application of indecency or offensiveness laws to books or magazines. Moreover, it is inconceivable that the Supreme Court in the United States, or other constitutional courts, would countenance the imposition of general standards or editorial constraints on, say, the contents of a website or bulletin board, similar to those which have been upheld in Europe on public broadcasting channels. To that extent, the Internet is treated in the same way as the press and other print media.

But their position should not be regarded as identical. The Internet has not yet assumed the role which the press performs when it reports and investigates public affairs. Claims for an editorial freedom for website operators or ISPs would appear even more extravagant than they are when they are made on behalf of newspaper editors.[20] There is even less justification for rejecting a right of reply to personal attacks on a website or made in the course of an Internet discussion group than there is to attacks in newspaper columns. A newspaper can at least argue that the space devoted to a reply cannot be used for its own material; no such claim could be advanced in the context of electronic communications.[21] Further, as will be discussed in section 3, there is a case for modifying obscenity laws in this context to take account of the global character of communications on the Net. In summary, the Internet is not to be equated with the institutional press and other print media, but, in principle, speech on it should be as free from regulation; the print model is certainly closer than the 'broadcast model'.[22]

(iii) The Internet is not a public forum

One issue which has been discussed in the United States is whether in some contexts the Internet should be treated as a 'public forum', so that individuals can claim access to it. Clearly, that argument is not generally sustainable, since access to the Net is organized by private ISPs. If an ISP for some reason denies an individual or company access to it, there is no state action; the First Amendment is not engaged.

For this reason District Courts have denied companies a free speech right to send unsolicited advertising messages over the Internet; ISPs are entitled to stop

---

[20] See ch. XII, s. 2(ii) above.

[21] A. W. Branscomb, 'Anonymity, Autonomy, and Accountability: Challenges in First Amendment Cyberspace' (1995) 104 *Yale Law Jo* 1639, 1671–2, argues for rights of reply in cyberspace as a sensible remedy for defamatory allegations.

[22] See T. G. Krattenmaker and L. A. Powe, 'Converging First Amendment Principles for Converging Communications Media', ibid., 1719.

spam messages.[23] But it has been argued that when a local authority installs computers in libraries, or a public university provides them for its staff and students, government is operating a public forum and it, therefore, cannot deny individuals access, say, to sexually explicit material which they have a free speech right to look at.[24] It would be as wrong for a public library to refuse a member of the public access to that sort of material, as it would be to forbid him to borrow a pornographic (non-obscene) book.

This argument has, however, now been rejected by the Supreme Court. In *US* v. *American Library Association*[25] it held, by a 6–3 majority, that the US government was entitled, as a condition for the receipt of federal assistance, to require public libraries to install software blocking obscene or indecent images and preventing the access of children to harmful material. Rehnquist CJ for the Court said that Internet access in public libraries was neither a 'traditional' nor a 'designated' public forum, in which users could claim a First Amendment right of access to view any material available on it.[26] The Internet could hardly be equated with long-standing traditional fora such as parks and streets. Neither were libraries places where any material could be read or viewed; a librarian could determine what material could be viewed on the Net, just as he could determine what books to make available for loan.[27] He pointed out that adults could request a librarian to unblock sexually explicit material which they were in other circumstances free to look at.

These arguments are unpersuasive. The access conditions might well deter some members of the public from looking at material covered by the First Amendment which they would be fully entitled to view on a computer at home. Souter J. in dissent correctly pointed that blocking sexually explicit sites which the public is normally free to visit is equivalent to the removal of books from a library on the basis of their content, an act which, according to the *Pico* decision, is incompatible with the First Amendment.[28] It is worth noting that the Court did not decide that the government could direct libraries to block material, access to which it wanted to discourage. In any event, the argument that access rights to the Net in public libraries and universities should be recognized is an attractive one. The Internet enables ordinary individuals to speak to each other on an unlimited range of topics without significant cost. It can be, and has been, used by radicals and dissenters who lack access to the traditional mass media. It would be unfortunate

---

[23] *Cyber Promotions* v. *AOL* 948 F Supp 436 (ED Pa, 1996); *Compuserve Inc* v. *Cyber Promotions* 962 F Supp 1015 (SD Ohio, 1997).

[24] S. G. Gey, 'Reopening the Public Forum: From Sidewalks to Cyberspace' (1998) 58 *Ohio State Law Jo* 1535, 1631–3.

[25] 539 US 194 (2003): see ch. III, s. 8 above for other aspects of this case.

[26] See ch. VIII, s. 3 above for 'traditional' and 'designated' fora for speech and public meetings.

[27] In *Loving* v. *Boren* 956 F Supp 953 (WD Oklahoma, 1997), a District Court ruled that university-owned computers and Internet services are not a public forum, so the state could restrict their use to academic and research purposes.

[28] *Board of Education, Island Trees Union School District* v. *Pico* 457 US 853 (1982), discussed in ch. III, s. 7 above.

if, as a result of the decision in the *American Libraries* case, members of the public without access to the Net at home are unable to make full use of it free of charge in libraries or other appropriate places.

A Court of Appeals has rejected a 'public forum' claim in a quite different context.[29] A city in Tennessee refused the request of a local tabloid paper to allow a hyperlink from the city website to that of the paper; it only allowed links to the sites of non-profit organizations which would promote the commercial interests of the city. The Court held the city website and its hyperlinks did not amount to a public forum, since they had not been set up for unrestricted dialogue between users; the site was instituted purely for the city's benefit, and it could determine the character of the sites to which links could be made. But the Court remanded the case back to the District Court for it to determine whether the hyperlink had been refused because the city disliked the tabloid editor's views. Access even to a non-public forum cannot be denied on the basis of the claimant's viewpoint.[30] A public library could not, therefore, deny a member of the public access to the Internet because it thought, even with good reason, that he would visit the websites, say, of far-right or racist groups.

3. Pornography on the Internet

(i) The application of obscenity laws

The availability of pornography on the Internet, in particular to children, has posed considerable legal problems. It is clear that obscene publications legislation applies to the Net as it does to other media outlets. Some prosecutions have been brought in England under the Obscene Publications Act 1959. But there have not been many cases, and it is clear that in practice greater reliance is placed on self-regulation through the Internet Watch Foundation (IWF), an organization established by ISPs, which directs service providers to remove material against which a complaint has been made from the Net. This system has obvious advantages of flexibility and informality compared with legal control. On the other hand, it can lead to the removal, and in effect the censorship, of material which might survive an obscenity prosecution. The IWF might effectively protect the public, including children, from exposure to hard-core pornography, but equally it might curtail the free speech rights of website operators and other communicators on the Net, whose interests do not appear sufficiently protected. The IWF is unaccountable.[31] From the perspective of free speech, its de facto jurisdiction is open to the same objections as those which may be made to the power of the British Board of Film Classification to censor films.[32]

---

[29] *Putnam Pit* v. *City of Cookeville* 221 F 3d 834 (6th Cir, 2000).
[30] See ch. VIII, s. 3 above.   [31] Akdeniz, Walker, and Wall (n. 1 above), 224–5, 244–7.
[32] See ch. IV, s. 2 above.

There is no constitutional objection in the United States to the application of tightly drawn obscenity laws to the Internet. The Sixth Circuit Court of Appeals affirmed the defendant's conviction for the federal offence of the inter-state transportation of obscene materials, when he transferred hard-core computer-generated images from his bulletin board in California to a personal computer in Tennessee.[33] The Court rejected the argument that the relevant 'community standards' for determining whether the images were 'obscene' were those in cyber-space, rather than those of the locality in Tennessee where the trial took place. In this case the defendant knew the request for transmission from his bulletin board came from Tennessee, a conservative state, and could have refused to send them. The question of whose standards to apply is a complex one: see section 3(ii) below.

(ii) The protection of children

The protection of children is at issue in two types of case in the Internet context. The first concerns laws intended to protect children from the harms occasioned them by viewing sexually explicit images on the Net; this type of case is considered here. The second involves legal restrictions on the making and distribution of indecent computer images of children: see section 3(iii) below. The difficulty with the first type of law is that, unless it is very tightly drawn, it inevitably curtails the freedom of adults to view sexually explicit material on the Net. In *Reno*[34] the Communications Decency Act of 1996 was held too broad by the Supreme Court, in that it penalized the communication of 'indecent' and 'patently offens-ive' communications to persons under eighteen without specifying what these terms meant. More fundamentally, in the absence of a reliable process by which senders of messages on the Net could determine the age of their recipients, they must inevitably be taken as 'knowing' that any sexually explicit message they sent could be received by children. It would have been prohibitively expensive to verify whether a user was an adult. The provisions would have had the effect, therefore, of deterring the communication of this material to adults, merely because chil-dren would be likely to view it. The government had not established that there were no other means less restrictive of speech to protect children. There was evi-dence that software was available by which parents could prevent children from accessing sexually explicit material; its use would not interfere with the free speech interests of adults to look at this material on the Net.

Following this decision, Congress enacted the Child Online Protection Act (COPA). In a number of respects, it was more narrowly drawn than the 1996 legislation. It applied only to material displayed on the World Wide Web and communicated for commercial purposes. Most importantly, it covered only the

---

[33] *US* v. *Thomas* 74 F 3d 701 (6th Cir, 1996).
[34] *Reno* v. *American Civil Liberties Union* 521 US 844 (1997).

communication of material harmful to minors, defined primarily in terms similar to the *Miller* test of 'obscenity', that is, that the average person, applying *contemporary community standards* would find it of prurient interest with respect to minors, patently offensive with respect to them in its depiction of sexual activity, and without serious literary or other value.[35] However, the Court of Appeals for the Third Circuit held that COPA's reliance on 'community standards' to define harmful material to children rendered it incompatible with the First Amendment.[36] Web publishers could not comply with that standard, given that they could not control the geographic areas in which their messages circulated. The Supreme Court allowed the government's appeal and sent the case back to the Circuit Court.[37] But only three of its members thought it right to assess Internet messages by the 'local standards' rule which had been formulated in earlier cases for postal and telephone communications.[38] They did not think the particular characteristics of the Internet justified a departure from the approach adopted for other media. Other members of the Court, notably O'Connor and Stevens JJ, thought it was unconstitutional to assess the obscenity of Internet communications by reference to local standards. National standards would be much more appropriate. In their view, the application of local standards would inevitably lead to self-censorship, as senders would play safe and avoid the communication of messages that would be regarded as harmful to minors, or obscene, in conservative communities. Adoption of a national standard does seem preferable. Within a continent such as the United States, it is also feasible; the Internet itself has to some extent led to greater homogenization of standards. But this approach would not resolve conflicts between the standards in, say, the United States or Europe on the one hand, and Asia on the other; the global character of Internet communications creates enormous difficulties with regard to the application of pornography and other laws restricting freedom of speech.[39]

On remand the Circuit Court of Appeals again held that COPA was likely to be held invalid, but this time on the ground that the government had not shown that the measure was the least restrictive intrusion on speech to prevent minors accessing harmful communications on the Internet. It approved the District Court's grant of an injunction to stop enforcement of the legislation. The Supreme Court upheld this decision by a 5–4 majority.[40] Kennedy J. for the Court reasoned that the employment of blocking and filtering software was a viable alternative to the imposition of criminal sanctions. Its use would prevent children viewing unsuitable items, while adults could gain access to sexually explicit material without having to identify themselves by producing a credit card or digital certificate of age: under COPA, website operators had a defence if they restricted children's

---

[35] For the *Miller* test of 'obscenity', see ch. X, s. 3 above.
[36] *ACLU* v. *Reno* 217 F 3d 162 (3rd Cir, 2000).　　　[37] *Ashcroft* v. *ACLU* 535 US 564 (2002).
[38] *Hamling* v. *US* 418 US 87 (1974) (postal communications); *Sable Communications of California* v. *FCC* 492 US 115 (1989). For discussion of these issues in the context of obscenity, see ch. X, s. 3 above.　　　　　　　　　　　　　　　　[39] See further s. 5 below.
[40] *Ashcroft* v. *ACLU* 159 L Ed 2d 690 (2004).

access by requiring adults to produce such a card or certificate. Filters would, in his view, be more effective than criminal penalties, in that they would prevent children accessing pornographic material posted from outside the United States, and could be used for all forms of Internet communication, not just access through the World Wide Web. With improving technology, it was likely that filtering techniques will evolve to become even more effective, and the government could encourage their use. In the principal dissenting judgment, Breyer J. pointed out that filtering software was already available, but Congress had decided it was inadequate for a number of reasons; in particular, its effectiveness depended on its correct use by parents. In his view, it was wrong for the Court to question the legislature's assessment of these issues. The majority required the government to show in effect that it was impossible to achieve its aim of protecting children by promoting filtering software. This was an unreasonable requirement. Of course, government could throw money at the problem and instruct every parent in the land in the proper use of filtering software, but it was entitled to choose the more realistic and less expensive option of using the criminal law.

As Breyer J. argued,[41] Congress had attempted to meet the objections raised by the Supreme Court to the earlier 1996 legislation. He felt that the Court was unreasonable to reject Congress's second attempt to balance the right of adults to view sexually explicit material on the Net against the effective protection of children. The criminal law cannot now be used in this context. As a result of the Court's decision, parents must be relied on to use software effectively to protect their children from exposure to this material. Few decisions show so well the lengths to which the US Supreme Court will go in the context of the Internet to protect speech, which in other contexts has been treated as of 'low value'.[42]

(iii) Indecent images of children on the Internet

The publication of indecent photographs of actual children is proscribed to stop sexual abuse. For that reason the proscription has survived free speech challenge in the United States; the ban is not imposed to penalize the communication of ideas, but rather to protect the physical welfare of children whose involvement in sexual activity might be captured on film.[43] In the United Kingdom, the taking, making, distribution, or possession (with a view to distribution) of such material is proscribed by the Protection of Children Act 1978. It is also a summary offence even to possess it.[44] These offences have been extended to cover the Internet. 'Photographs' include data stored on a computer disk or electronically, capable of being converted into a photograph. The legislation proscribes the taking, distribution, or

---

[41] Ibid., 716–17.
[42] See Stevens J. in *Young* v. *American Mini Theatres* 427 US 50 (1976), considered in ch. X, s. 6 above.　　　　　[43] *New York* v. *Ferber* 458 US 747 (1982): see ch. X, s. 4(iv) above.
[44] Criminal Justice Act 1988, s. 160.

possession of 'pseudo-photographs': computer images which appear to be photographs. These provisions have now been considered in a number of reported cases and no exception has been taken to them either on freedom of expression or privacy grounds.[45] (The Supreme Court of Canada has also held legislation proscribing the possession of virtual child pornography compatible with freedom of expression.[46]) In its most important ruling in this area, the Court of Appeal in England held that a defendant who downloaded images on to a disk or who printed them out for his own purposes could be convicted of the offence under the 1978 legislation of 'making' an indecent photograph or pseudo-photograph.[47] It accepted the prosecution's argument that the legislation was not only concerned with criminalizing the production of original material, but also proscribed the proliferation of matter which might have come from outside the United Kingdom.

The US Child Pornography Prevention Act of 1996 contained a similar ban on the distribution of 'virtual child pornography', images which appear to depict children under eighteen years old engaging in sexual activity, actual or simulated. Resolving a conflict of view among Circuit Courts concerning the compatibility of this provision with the First Amendment, a majority of the Court struck it down as infringing freedom of speech.[48] It could not be defended as necessary to protect children against abuse, since it covered computer images. They did not depict harm being done to actual children. Kennedy J. for the Court also dismissed the argument that the legislation was necessary to prevent the use of this material by paedophiles for grooming or corrupting children. Applying the *Brandenburg* principle,[49] he held the government had to show more than a remote connection between virtual pornography and child abuse; the link must be close and direct. But it is doubtful whether it is right to apply a general principle formulated in the context of political speech in this context.[50] As O'Connor J. pointed out in a persuasive dissent, the weight of expert evidence shows that child pornography, including computer images, is widely used in grooming young children for sexual abuse.

Congress has now enacted more tightly drawn legislation to proscribe the distribution of images of children engaged in sexual activity or of images indistinguishable from such images. It is unclear whether this will survive First Amendment challenge.[51] If it were held incompatible with free speech, responsibility for protecting children from exposure to computer images depicting underage sexual activity would fall entirely on parents and schools. The criminal law could not be used in the United States in this context, any more than it can

---

[45] For discussion of these cases, see ch. X, s. 4(iv) above.
[46] *R* v. *Sharpe* (2001) 194 DLR (4th) 1.   [47] *R* v. *Bowden* [2000] 2 All ER 418.
[48] *Ashcroft* v. *Free Speech Coalition* 535 US 234 (2002).
[49] *Brandenburg* v. *Ohio* 395 US 444 (1969), discussed in ch. V, s. 2 above.
[50] I. Cram, 'Beyond Madison? The US Supreme Court and the Regulation of Sexually Explicit Expression' [2002] *PL* 743, 754–5.
[51] S. H. Kosse, 'Virtual Child Pornography: A United States Update' (2004) 9 *Comm Law* 39.

now be employed to penalize the distribution to children of other sexually explicit messages or pictures on the Net.

4. Defamation and the Internet

(i) General principles

Libel law clearly applies to communications on the Net, whether these take the form of a website or a bulletin board, contributions to a discussion group, or e-mails. This area of law amounts to a significant restraint on the freedom to use a means of communication which is characterized by its ease and informality. Just as writers of e-mails are often prepared to depart from the rules of grammar and syntax they would observe in a letter or in a newspaper article, they may feel instinctively that the complexities of libel law are out of place in this context. Further, Net users do not generally have access to legal advice when they participate in a discussion group or circulate e-mails to friends and colleagues. So it can be argued that the rules of libel law should be significantly modified to cater for the characteristics of the Internet and its users.

On the other hand, Internet communications may do serious injury to individual and corporate reputations.[52] Indeed, the ease with which messages on it can be sent and forwarded around the world means that the most ludicrous allegations can immediately gain widespread currency. It is then very difficult for the individual concerned to defend his reputation without taking legal proceedings; there is no equivalent to the letter to a newspaper or a broadcast interview which may put matters right when a false story has been circulated by the press, radio, or television. The risks of a libel action may certainly chill or deter the exercise of free speech on the Net, but that is surely desirable, if it prevents the dissemination of wholly unsubstantiated rumours, which are either known to be false or which have not been checked before they are put on a website or sent in an e-mail. Only proponents of absolute free speech rights or of the view that the Internet should be altogether immune from legal regulation can argue coherently that libel law has no place in this context. Neither view is defensible.

This conclusion does not, however, mean that the usual principles of defamation law should be applied without modification. Questions of meaning should be approached with regard to the context; a statement in an e-mail may appear innocuous at a casual glance, but might bear a defamatory meaning if read in conjunction with a statement in an attachment or in a website to which it makes a link. The cyberspace community, or the participants to a particular discussion group, might not regard a particular epithet or allegation as defamatory, when an identical allegation in a daily paper would be regarded by its readers as lowering

---

[52] For examples, see the cases mentioned by M. Hadley in 'The *Gertz* Doctrine and Internet Defamation' (1998) 84 *Virginia Law Rev* 477, 491–8.

the standing of the claimant. It may be right in the context of messages on the Net to modify the usual principle in English law that communications are assessed by general community standards; it might be more appropriate to assess them by the standards of those using the Internet. Under the normal principles of defamation law, a publisher is liable for the injury to reputation occasioned by any foreseeable republication of the allegations. That may create real difficulties for Net communications, in view of the ease with which e-mails can be forwarded. Another issue is whether a website operator, or even a search engine could be regarded as a publisher of an allegation on a site to which they create a link. These are all complex questions of libel law, but they do not raise significant free speech issues.[53]

Three issues of libel law are discussed in this chapter. The first is the treatment of ISPs: are they entitled for free speech reasons to some immunity from defamation liability? The second is whether freedom of speech considerations might also justify some modification of the defences available to the authors of defamatory allegations. The third question concerns jurisdiction to entertain libel actions: should only the courts of the country where the allegations were originally made have jurisdiction, or may courts in any state where they are published entertain a libel action, at least where the claimant enjoys a reputation there? This question is considered in the following section when discussing the special problems raised by the global character of Internet communications.

(ii) The immunity of Internet service providers

Section 230 of the Communications Decency Act of 1996 states that '[n]o provider or user of an interactive computer service shall be treated as the publisher or speaker of any information provided by another information content provider'. US courts have held that this provision gives an ISP total immunity from defamation actions, even though a complainant has given notice that it is carrying an unfounded defamatory allegation and it has failed to remove it. The leading decision is that of the Court of Appeals for the Fourth Circuit in *Zeran* v. *America Online (AOL)*.[54] A week after the bombing of a federal building in Oklahoma, someone posted anonymously on an AOL bulletin board an advertisement for 'Naughty Oklahoma T-Shirts'; the shirts carried vulgar, tasteless slogans. Prospective purchasers were invited to call 'Ken' at Zeran's home number. It was a complete hoax. As a result of this and subsequent messages, Zeran received a number of angry and abusive telephone calls, some of them threatening death. As a matter of policy, AOL declined to post a retraction of the original message, and it failed for several days to remove it and the subsequent messages. The Court of Appeals held that Zeran could not bring libel proceedings against the ISP. In its view Congress had intended not to deter online speech by imposing defamation

---

[53] For a full treatment of these (and other) issues concerning libel law and the Net, see M. Collins, *The Law of Defamation and the Internet* (Oxford: OUP, 2001), chs. 5–7.

[54] 129 F 3d 327 (4th Cir, 1997).

(or other) liability on ISPs; another purpose of the provision was to encourage them to self-regulate the transmission of defamatory or offensive material over their services, though on the facts it was clear that AOL had made no attempt to do this promptly. In another well-known case,[55] a District Court dismissed an action against AOL for a scurrilous allegation in a Drudge Report available to all its subscribers. The item alleged that a new White House recruit had 'a spousal abuse past that has been effectively covered up'. The judge in this case reached the decision with understandable reluctance, as it was clear that AOL had rights under its contract with Matt Drudge to require changes in the content of his reports and it had affirmatively promoted him as a source of unverified gossip. But he recognized that Congress had granted ISPs immunity, 'even where the interactive service provider has an active, even aggressive role in making available content prepared by others.'[56]

This approach has been rejected in *Godfrey* v. *Demon Internet Ltd*, the only reported case in England concerned with the extent of ISP defamation liability.[57] An unknown person made a posting to a newsgroup in the United States, which was carried by the defendant ISP from an American service provider. It was defamatory of the claimant, though purporting to originate from him. He notified Demon's managing director of the forged posting and asked for it to be removed. This was not done; it remained available for another ten days until the end of the period for which Demon carried the newsgroup messages. The question for the judge concerned the application of the UK Defamation Act 1996 which appears to have conferred a limited immunity on ISPs. Section 1 provides that a person has a defence to defamation proceedings if he shows that he was not the author, editor, or publisher of the statement and that he took reasonable care in respect of its publication.[58] An ISP can establish that he is not the publisher, etc., of a statement, because he is only involved 'in operating or providing any . . . service by means of which the statement is retrieved, copied, distributed or made available in electronic form.'[59] Morland J. held that Demon was not a 'publisher' under section 1 of the Act, but it could not claim immunity after it had received notice of the defamatory allegation, since it had not removed it from its service. It had therefore failed to take reasonable care with respect to its publication. He considered the position in the United States, but did not think it relevant to English law. A court would now have to consider the application of regulations implementing the European Union e-commerce directive, which confer immunity from civil liability on ISPs.[60] (The extent of the immunity depends on whether the ISP is acting as a mere conduit of information, is caching it temporarily, or stores it as a host site.[61]) It is unlikely that it would lead to a different result on the facts in the *Demon* case.

---

[55] *Blumenthal* v. *Drudge* 992 F Supp 44 (DDC, 1998).
[56] Ibid., 52, per Paul L. Friedman Dist. Judge.   [57] [1999] 4 All ER 432, Morland J.
[58] S. 1(1).   [59] S. 1(3)(c).
[60] Electronic Commerce (EC Directive) Regulations 2002, S.I. 2002/2013, regs. 17–19, implementing Directive 2000/31/EC of 8 June 2000.   [61] Collins (n. 53 above), ch. 18.

The general practice of ISPs in England is to remove a site from their service once they are informed that it contains defamatory material. Otherwise they may be exposed to a libel action, which they have no interest in defending. Allegations may be removed, even if they are true. The ISP has no idea whether the material is accurate. Even if it considered on good grounds that it was, it would have no defence under the 1996 legislation which allows liability to be imposed on a secondary publisher who has not taken reasonable care in relation to a defamatory publication, irrespective of whether it could be justified as true. As the Law Commission found, '[t]he crux of the problem is that the present law results in internet service providers removing material that may be in the public interest and well-researched. They may also remove material that is true.'[62] The Commission considered the US approach and other more limited reform without making a firm recommendation.

Defamation law may have a greater chilling effect on Internet speech in England than it does on speech by the press and broadcasting media. The latter are generally committed to defending libel actions brought in respect of material they publish or transmit, particularly when they are confident that it is accurate or that it is covered by qualified privilege.[63] It is unlikely that an ISP would take the same attitude when faced with a solicitor's letter that proceedings will be started if material is not withdrawn. But it would be wrong to adopt the US approach. That may leave individuals without an effective remedy to protect their reputation against wholly unfounded, and perhaps malicious, allegations. A claimant such as Zeran suffered enormous damage as a result of a hoax perpetrated by someone who was never identified. The speech which the court protected in that case was completely worthless, as was the forgery in the English *Demon* case which similarly came from an unknown speaker. It would be quite wrong to confer unconditional immunity on ISPs in these circumstances, though there is a case for allowing them a defence if they have reason to believe that the allegations they carry are true.[64]

(iii) Wider defences for individuals?

As a result of the complete immunity of ISPs, libel claims in the United States are now brought against the authors of defamatory allegations on the Net. Actions are brought against the unknown 'John Doe' defendant, and a subpoena issued against the ISP to require it to identify him.[65] They are typically brought by corporations whose stock value has collapsed following allegations on the Net about their financial position or trading prospects. The object of the litigation is

---

[62] *Defamation and the Internet*, Scoping Study No. 2 (Dec. 2002), para. 2.41.
[63] For this defence, see ch. VI, s. 3 above.   [64] N. 62 above, paras. 2.55–2.65.
[65] L. B. Lidsky, 'Silencing John Doe: Defamation and Discourse in Cyberspace' [2000] *Duke Law Jo* 855, 881–3.

to silence the author and to deter other rogue commentators, rather than to secure an award of damages which the defendant would probably be unable to pay. Some pundits may be deterred from using the Net, while others may be careful about the terms in which they speak on it. Free speech may be chilled, but fewer reputations will be damaged.

The question is whether the defences to libel actions developed to protect the press and other branches of the traditional media are adequate to safeguard the legitimate free speech interests of individual speakers on the Net. In the United States it has been argued that all claimants should be treated as 'public figures' for the purposes of defamation on the Net, with the result that they would be required to prove actual malice to recover damages.[66] Everyone, it may be said, has the opportunity to use the Internet to reply to defamatory allegations and anyone who uses it can be taken to have entered into public debate. It was these factors which distinguish a public figure from a private person according to Powell J.'s judgment for the Court in *Gertz* v. *Robert Welch Inc.*[67] But the Internet hardly provides an effective right of reply for the victims of defamatory attacks, while it is far-fetched to suggest that anyone who accesses information on a website or sends e-mails has thereby entered public debate.[68] Moreover, the case-law holding that no libel action can be brought compatibly with the First Amendment, in respect of hyperbole or other incredible claims concerning a claimant, is particularly pertinent to Netspeak.[69] US free speech principles, therefore, already constrain libel actions so much that it is very doubtful whether there is any justification for widening the existing defences further in the case of defamation on the Net.

With regard to the law in England and other countries, there is a case for generous application of the existing defences, particularly the qualified privilege formulated in *Reynolds* v. *Times Newspapers*.[70] Ordinary individuals do not have the same resources as the press and other media to verify stories and contact the claimant for his comments before publication. They may be less culpable than the traditional media for the spread of what turn out to be baseless rumours. While it is legitimate to require the media to produce reliable sources for their stories, less can be expected of most Web publishers who in any case lack access to legal advice. But this argument does not warrant different legal rules, only the sensitive application of principles which have been developed in contexts other than the Internet. Defamation on the Net spreads rapidly and can cause enormous damage. It would be wrong to allow individuals a freedom to defame by e-mail, which they do not enjoy when they write a letter or publish a leaflet.

---

[66] J. S. Weber, 'Defining Cyberlibel: A First Amendment Limit for Libel Suits Against Individuals Arising from Computer Bulletin Board Speech' (1995) 46 *Case Western Law Rev* 235.
[67] 418 US 323 (1974), considered in ch. VI, s. 3(i) above.   [68] See Hadley (n. 52 above).
[69] See ch. VI, s. 4 above for these cases.
[70] [2001] 2 AC 127, discussed in ch. VI, s. 3(iv) above.

5. The Problems of Global Communication

(i) Introduction

Internet communications cross national territorial boundaries. Their global character is one of their principal characteristics, so much so that, in the view of some commentators, effective regulation by state authorities is impossible.[71] Moreover, it is arguably undesirable to attempt it. Website operators and ISPs might not know which legal systems they will become subject to. As a result they might be prosecuted under the obscenity or hate speech laws of, say, France or Germany, for communications intended for computer users in the United States or England. Communicators in cyberspace, it has been argued, would have to be aware of the libel laws in every country from Afghanistan to Zimbabwe, if the courts in any state where a defamatory message was accessible could claim jurisdiction and apply its law.[72] Attempts by one jurisdiction to regulate communication on the Net would inevitably chill the exercise of free speech rights in others, particularly in the United States where speech is very strongly protected. Conflicts may occur, arising from the inconsistency between the decision of a court in one country regulating speech on the Net and that of a court in another state refusing to enforce that judgment.

Some of these fears are probably exaggerated.[73] In many circumstances it is no harder for cyberspace communicators to determine the impact of their speech than it is for broadcasters and publishers whose communications may also cross national boundaries. There is little evidence that courts have imposed liability on content providers for unforeseeable loss in unpredictable jurisdictions.[74] Software technology may develop to enable communicators more easily to control the geographical destinations of their messages. At present, they can ensure that services with clear significant legal risks are only available on subscription. They can exclude, or at least make more difficult, the receipt of, say, sexually explicit material in jurisdictions where it is banned or where civil liability is imposed. Most importantly, communications on the Net may cause as much harm as expression in the traditional mass media. Indeed, in the absence of editorial and legal control, cyberspace speech is free of internal restraints, so it is more likely than press or broadcasting material to damage reputation, to prejudice a trial, or to incite serious crime. The interests of individuals harmed by Net communications are entitled to as much respect as the interests of communicators.

The problems of global communication on the Net have now been considered by courts in a number of jurisdictions. An important question has been whether it

---

[71] See in particular Johnson and Post (n. 8 above).
[72] *Dow Jones and Company Inc* v. *Gutnick* (2002) 210 CLR 575, para. 54 per Gleeson CJ, HC of A.
[73] See J. L. Goldsmith, 'Against Cyberanarchy' (1998) 65 *Univ of Chicago Law Rev* 1199.
[74] Ibid., 1221.

is proper for a court to apply the law of the state where it sits to speech which has an impact in that state, but which has been communicated from another country. There are important decisions of the High Court of Australia in a defamation case and of a French court in what may loosely be termed a hate speech case. Their decisions are considered shortly. The second issue is whether the courts can enforce their judgments in these circumstances. That poses real problems, particularly where the ISP or other Net defendant does not have assets in the country. These difficulties are considered in section 5(iii). The final pages of this chapter consider how conflicts arising from the global character of communications on the Net might be resolved.

(ii) The appropriate forum for the regulation of Internet communications

The issue in *Dow Jones and Company Inc* v. *Gutnick*[75] was whether the courts of Victoria could properly consider a defamation action brought by a resident of the state in respect of an allegation of money laundering, which had been published on *Barron's Online*, available on a website operated by Dow Jones. Access to the site was available to subscribers and to others who registered with a user name and password. The defendant argued that the publication of the article containing the allegation occurred in New Jersey, where it had been put on the Web servers. It was, therefore, wrong in its view, for the courts in Victoria to exercise jurisdiction, even though the allegation concerned a resident of that state. Alternatively, Dow Jones argued it would be improper for a court in Australia to apply the law of Victoria, given that publication had occurred in New Jersey. That was the place where the tort of libel had been committed.[76] New Jersey law should, therefore, govern the case. Otherwise, Dow Jones argued, Web publishers would have to take account of the law of any country where their information could be downloaded.

These arguments were rejected by the High Court. It affirmed the decision of the judge in Victoria that the defamatory allegations were published when subscribers downloaded the article. It was only then that the damage to the claimant's reputation was done, so it was right to hold that publication occurred in Victoria, where the claimant, Gutnick, lived and enjoyed a reputation. The courts in Victoria had jurisdiction and should apply the law of that state. Victoria could not be regarded as an inappropriate forum to determine the libel action. Indeed, it was surely the most appropriate forum, given that the allegations about Gutnick were

---

[75] N. 72 above. See U. Kohl, 'Defamation on the Internet: Nice Decision, Shame about the Reasoning: *Dow Jones & Co Inc* v. *Gutnick*' (2003) 52 ICLQ 1049.

[76] Strictly, there are two issues of private international law: jurisdiction and choice of law. But courts often apply their own law (the law of the forum) once they have decided they have jurisdiction, so the two issues may easily be conflated.

clearly directed to subscribers in the state.[77] The High Court applied common law principles which have been developed in libel actions brought against the press and broadcasting media: every publication of a libel amounts to a distinct wrong or tort, and publication occurs when the allegations are read or heard.[78]

The free speech issue is whether it would have been right to depart from these principles, given the character of the Net. Five members of the High Court did not consider that Internet communications should be treated any differently from speech on the traditional media for this purpose. It was doubted whether 'the World Wide Web has a uniquely broad reach'.[79] Satellite broadcasting, for instance, enjoys a similarly wide dissemination. Only Kirby J., in a long judgment concurring with the decision, thought it right to reconsider the traditional common law principles in view of the global character of the Net.[80] He sympathized with the appellant's submission that the Internet required new principles to determine the appropriate forum and choice of law rules for global communications. But he rejected its argument for replacing the common law principles with a 'single publication' rule, specific to the Internet, under which a libel would be published at the place of uploading—in this case, New Jersey. It would be wrong for a court, rather than the legislature, to reform long-standing common law principles for the benefit of a particular technology. Moreover, in view of the vast numbers of Web servers in the United States, the practical impact of the change would be to extend the reach of US media-friendly libel law principles to actions brought by citizens of other countries, with the result that they would have great difficulty in protecting their reputation.[81] Kirby J. recognized that the common law approach might lead to unsatisfactory results in some instances, for example, where a claimant has a reputation in a number of countries and brings an action in all of them in respect of allegations on the Net. But the costs of bringing proceedings would deter most litigants; moreover, only legislation and international agreement could resolve the difficulties.[82]

Similar issues arose in a very different context in the famous proceedings taken in France against Yahoo! Inc. in respect of its auction site advertising the sale of Nazi memorabilia and propaganda. A court in Paris held the display of this material on the Net infringed the French Penal Code. It rejected Yahoo!'s argument that its services were primarily directed at surfers in the United States and that, therefore, the French courts lacked competence to rule on the matter. The display clearly had an impact in France, and Yahoo! was aware that French surfers

---

[77] If Victoria had been a state in the United States, a court there would have held it entitled to consider the case: see *Young* v. *New Haven Advocate* 315 F 3d 256 (4th Cir, 2002).

[78] The leading case in England is *Berezovsky* v. *Michaels* [2000] 1 WLR 1004, where the House of Lords held 3–2 that the English courts were an appropriate forum to hear a libel action brought by Russian citizens, with a reputation in England, in respect of allegations in the US business magazine, *Forbes*. The principles have now been applied to an Internet libel, emanating from websites in California, and downloaded in England: *Lennox Lewis* v. *Don King* [2004] EWCA Civ 1329.

[79] N. 72 above, para. 39 per Gleeson CJ and three other members of the Court.

[80] Ibid., paras. 113–19.   [81] Ibid., para. 133.   [82] Ibid., paras. 164–6.

visited the site: when they made a link to it from a French server, Yahoo! transmitted advertising in French.

The court ordered Yahoo! to make it impossible for surfers from France to access the site via Yahoo.com. It also ordered it to post a warning on its French site, Yahoo.fr, that any search through its system might lead to sites containing this material and so expose the Internet user to criminal proceedings. Yahoo! had no difficulty in complying with this second order, but argued that it could not prevent French citizens gaining access to the sites through Yahoo.com. Alternatively, it contended that the costs of taking the necessary steps might jeopardize the company's existence. The court then commissioned consultants to advise on the feasibility of denying access to the auctions site to French surfers and surfers from France. They found that over 70 per cent of surfers residing in France could be identified as French through their ISPs, while visitors from other ISPs could be asked to declare their nationality. With a combination of the two procedures, almost 90 per cent of French surfers could be successfully filtered. On the basis of this report the court in Paris confirmed its order, imposing a significant daily fine if Yahoo! did not comply within three months.[83] In response, Yahoo! continued to claim it could not technically comply with the order; it withdrew many, though not all, of the materials from its auction site, so denying access to US as well as other surfers. It took proceedings in a US District Court for a declaration that the French court's orders are not enforceable in the United States.

(iii) Enforcement of judgments

Judgment can only be enforced against a defendant when it has assets within the country where the decision has been given, or if courts in another jurisdiction where it does have assets are required or are willing to enforce the judgment. With regard to the latter alternative, there is no problem if a constitution or international convention provides for mutual enforcement of judgments; for example, states in the US are required to enforce the proceedings of other states in the federation.[84] But otherwise courts may refuse to enforce a foreign judgment, if that course would conflict with a requirement of its public policy. US courts have declined to enforce English libel rulings against a defendant who would have been able successfully to claim a First Amendment defence if the action had been brought in the United States.[85] Yahoo! was therefore able to claim that the judgment of the Paris Court should not be enforced. The District Court for Northern California held the order was far too broad and imprecise to survive

---

[83] *La Ligue contre le racisme et l'antisemitisme* v. *Yahoo! Inc*, Order of TGI Paris of 20 Nov. 2000: see www.juriscom.net/txt/jurisfr/cti/tgiparis20001120.htm.

[84] Full Faith and Credit Clause, US Constitution, art. IV, s. 1. The Brussels Convention on Jurisdiction and Enforcement of Judgments in Civil and Commercial Matters of 1968 requires recognition and enforcement of judgments in other member states of the European Union.

[85] *Bachchan* v. *India Abroad Publications Inc* 585 NYS 2d 661 (NY Sup Ct, 1992); *Matusevitch* v. *Telnikoff* 877 F Supp 1 (D DC, 1995).

scrutiny under the First Amendment, in that it required Yahoo! to make it impossible for users in France to access sites which defended the Nazis or contested their crimes. The order discriminated against speech on the basis of its viewpoint.[86]

The Court emphasized that normally the judgments of foreign courts would be recognized. But they would not be enforced where that step would prejudice the exercise of rights guaranteed by the US Constitution. However, that result would surely have occurred only if Yahoo! had been right to claim that it could not comply with the Paris court order by denying French users access to the auction site. If it could have done this, without excluding Nazi material from its site altogether, it is hard to see that there was any interference with the exercise of free speech rights in the United States. Admittedly, it can be argued that Yahoo!, and US citizens and corporations, have rights under the First Amendment to speak freely over the Net to audiences in a foreign country, even though the courts there have decided the speech infringes its law.[87] But the District Court did not make that explicit ruling. It left it unclear exactly how the French ruling infringed the First Amendment.

The difficulties of enforcing court judgments against US defendants unless they have assets, or subsidiaries with assets, in France, Germany, or Australia, as the case may be, lessen the chilling effect of defamation, pornography, hate speech, or other laws.[88] Kirby J. in *Gutnick* even suggested the difficulties reinforced the argument for amending the choice of law rules in global libel cases; there would be little point in allowing a court in Victoria to determine a defamation action on the basis of its law, if its judgment would be ignored in the United States.[89] But it would have been wrong for the High Court of Australia to have paid much attention to the enforcement problem. The French court rightly rejected Yahoo!'s argument that enforcement difficulties justified the plea that it lacked jurisdiction. If it had been accepted, US courts and jurisprudence would have been given a decisive voice on the application of the law in other jurisdictions with regard to the appropriate balance between freedom of speech and, say, reputation rights or the protection of public order. US courts are perfectly entitled not to enforce the judgments of foreign courts when they clearly infringe First Amendment rights. Equally, those courts in France and Australia are right to apply their own free speech laws when speech on the Net is directed or aimed at residents in those countries.

(iv) Legal and technical solutions to the regulation of global communications

In the context of communications on the Net, the profound differences between the approach taken in the United States and that normally found in other countries

[86] *Yahoo!* v. *La Ligue contre Le Racisme et L'Antisemitisme* 169 F Supp 2d 1181 (ND Cal, 2001).
[87] M. S. Van Houweling, 'Enforcement of Foreign Judgments, the First Amendment, and Internet Speech: Notes for the Next *Yahoo!* v. *Licra*' (2003) 24 *Michigan Jo Internat Law* 697.
[88] Goldsmith (n. 73 above), 1216–22.   [89] N. 72 above, para. 121.

to free speech issues have important practical consequences. Courts in the United States are unwilling to enforce judgments in other countries which, in their view, infringe the First Amendment rights of American citizens and corporations. This refusal makes it more difficult for European countries, Australia, Canada, etc. to protect, say, reputation or fair trial rights, or to safeguard other interests which may conflict with the exercise of free speech rights. This is an unsatisfactory position. It is most unlikely to be wholly resolved by international conventions, though the Cybercrime Convention of the Council of Europe shows that agreement can be reached on the policing of child pornography, copyright infringement, and computer fraud.[90] It would be fanciful to imagine that a comparable convention could be agreed on the use of the Net for the transmission of sexually explicit material, hate speech, or defamation.

It is possible, however, that a combination of improved technology and legal restraint might reduce the scale of the problem identified in the previous pages. The first point is that courts are only entitled to apply their law to communications on the Net which are clearly directed or aimed at residents in the jurisdictions. The decisions in the *Gutnick* defamation case and in the Yahoo! Nazi memorabilia case can be defended, as the speech was deliberately communicated to the cyberspace audience in Victoria or France, as the case may be; Dow Jones need not have sent the defamatory allegations to subscribers or callers from Victoria, and Yahoo! could, according to the experts' report, have stopped the access of French surfers to the auction site. Moreover, it is reasonable to assume that the defendants were aware that they were taking legal risks. Interestingly, a US District Court has ordered an injunction to stop an Italian website granting US subscribers access to images on the site which infringed the US plaintiff's trademark rights; the order did not stop the publisher from maintaining the site in Italy, but safeguarded important intellectual property interests.[91] Albeit in a different context, the court's approach was similar to that of the High Court of Australia and the Paris court. But courts should not attempt to regulate speech on the Net, unless it targets the jurisdiction. It would be wrong, for example, for a court to hear libel proceedings when the allegations communicated on the Net were primarily addressed, or of concern, to the public in another country, or to hear a case, similar to the Yahoo! proceedings, where the (Nazi) propaganda had little or no impact on the public within the jurisdiction.[92]

The development and use of software enabling website operators and ISPs to control the geographical destination of communications on the Net should reduce the scale of the problem. Of course, surfers may find ways to evade these restrictions. But its use would show that the defendant was not targeting the public in another state; it would be much less reasonable for a court in, say, France to claim jurisdiction over the dissemination of hate speech from a website in the

---

[90] See S. Room, 'Criminalising Cybercrime' (2004) 154 *New Law Jo* 950.

[91] *Playboy Enterprises Inc* v. *Chuckleberry Publishing Inc* 939 F Supp 1032 (SD NY, 1996).

[92] But the recent decision of the Court of Appeal in *Lennox Lewis* v. *Don King* (n. 78 above), paras. 33–4 rejected the 'targeting' approach as uncertain.

United States, if the operator indicated it had taken steps to confine its spread to the United States and other countries where such speech is not proscribed. With the development of geographical location programmes, cyberspace is not now as naturally borderless, as has sometimes been argued. Indeed, it may be technically easier to prevent cross-border flows on the Net with improved filtering techniques than it is to enforce limits on the reception of broadcasts from neighbouring countries. The question is then whether the costs of preventing access to, say, the hate speech should be borne by the ISP or by the state which is concerned to restrict its availability.[93]

The final question is much the most difficult to answer: should courts in the United States (or in other countries) enforce foreign judgments restricting the freedom of their citizens and corporations to communicate ideas abroad, when their ideas are directed at the foreign audience? An answer may be attempted, on the assumption that it is easy and cheap for an ISP, say, in the United States to take technical measures to deny the access of computer users in other countries to speech on the Net prohibited in the latter.[94] The court in the United States must apparently resolve a conflict between its general duty under comity principles to recognize and enforce a foreign judgment and its obligation to uphold the First Amendment. But it is far from clear that the First Amendment (or other freedom of expression clause) is really engaged here, unless of course it confers a global freedom to speak, no matter what other courts have ruled with regard to the impact of that speech for their country. That conclusion would be sustainable if a court in the United States, Germany, or wherever were asked to enforce the judgment of, say, a court in China or Zimbabwe which had convicted a defendant for publishing material critical of the government there. Such a ruling could not be sustained on any view of freedom of speech, and its enforcement would surely be repugnant to the values of any liberal society. But the same could not be said with regard to the enforcement of, say, a libel judgment of a court in England or Australia, or of the order of the Paris court in the Yahoo! case. Respect for both the courts of other liberal democracies and for the divergent views which may be taken of the scope of freedom of speech requires enforcement of their judgments. These views should be respected unless they are plainly illiberal or incoherent.

---

[93] See H. M. Watt, '*Yahoo!* Cyber-Collision of Cultures: Who Regulates?' (2003) 24 *Michigan Jo Internat Law* 673, to which the argument in these paragraphs is indebted.

[94] If it is not easy to take these measures, then any requirement to do so as a result of a foreign judgment will inevitably deter protected speech in the United States.

XIV

Freedom of Speech in Special Contexts

1. Introduction

In some special contexts it may be appropriate to depart from standard principles of free speech law and regulate speech more strictly. For example, particularly tight constraints may be imposed on speech in courts, during legislative debate and at public meetings. Limits may appropriately be imposed not only on the time allocated for overall debate and on the length of individual contributions, but also on their contents; it is legitimate for a chairman (or judge) to ensure that an address is relevant to the theme of the debate or the argument. Clearly these are contexts or environments where some special regulation is acceptable, although naturally the application of a particular restriction may be contested.

This chapter examines four special contexts where the case for tight regulation of speech has been extensively discussed: election campaigns, the employment relationship, schools and universities, and prisons. To some extent it develops general points made earlier in the book about the meaning of speech and the character and scope of the freedom. For instance, the issue whether ceilings on election expenditure should be characterized as restrictions on 'speech' or merely as limits on the spending of money has already been discussed in Chapter III, while the question whether there is a positive right to speak on university campuses was canvassed in Chapter VIII when discussing access to public fora to exercise freedom of speech and assembly.[1] This chapter is concerned with the arguments of principle and policy why free speech questions should be treated in a distinctive way because they are raised in one of a number of particular contexts.

There are some similarities to the free speech issues raised in these contexts. It may be said, for example, that employees, students, and prisoners are not entitled to claim the same rights to freedom of speech as ordinary citizens. Or, more precisely, that employees and prisoners should be deemed to have waived their ordinary rights, while students, at least those at school, are not fully entitled to assert them. Alternatively, it may be argued that governments, or other public authorities, have stronger interests in regulating the speech of employees, students, or prisoners, and that these interests justify the formulation and application of

[1] Ch. VIII, s. 3(iii) above.

discrete principles to regulate speech in these contexts. Speech within the secluded environments of the workplace, school, or prison may be considered inherently more likely to occasion disruption than speech outside them. Moreover, such speech does not form part of the public discourse to which the fullest free speech protection should be given. Generally, it is not disseminated to a wide audience, let alone all citizens, for public discussion.

Initially, it may appear hard to apply these points to election campaign speech. On one view, this is a species of political expression, which lies at the core of freedom of speech.[2] On the other hand, there are, as will be discussed shortly, powerful arguments of principle for regarding election campaigns as a special environment, in which it may be right to modify the application of standard free speech principles. Candidates may be treated as having *waived* their standard free speech rights, in much the same way as civil servants may be, in return for the conferral of certain benefits and privileges, such as free use of television and radio for election broadcasts. There are difficulties, of course, in accepting these arguments; they are stated here to illustrate that there are common themes running through these apparently diverse contexts.

2. Election Campaigns

(i) Limits on expenditure and contributions

Many jurisdictions limit the sums that may be spent by political parties, candidates, and their supporters during and in preparation for election campaigns. Restrictions take a number of forms. In the United Kingdom there have for a long time been limits on the expenditure which may be incurred in individual constituencies by, or on behalf of, candidates. It also used to be a statutory offence for unauthorized persons to spend more than £5 on the communication of information for the purpose of promoting the election of a particular candidate.[3] On the other hand, there were no limits on expenditure by political parties or by their individual supporters at national or regional level,[4] so they were free, for instance, to spend whatever they chose on advertisements in newspapers and on hoardings. This difference reflected a nineteenth-century political perspective, according to which the significant electoral battles were fought in local constituencies rather than nationally. Political advertising on radio and television has always been, and still is, completely outlawed by statute,[5] a draconian ban which covers any advertisement placed by a body whose objects are mainly of a political character.[6]

---

[2] See ch. V, s. 2 above. [3] Representation of the People Act 1983, s. 75(1)(c).
[4] See *R* v. *Tronoh Mines Ltd* [1952] 1 All ER 697, McNair J.
[5] See now the Communications Act 2003, s. 319(2)(g).
[6] *R* v. *Radio Authority, ex p Bull* [1998] 2 QB 294, CA, upholding the ban imposed by the Radio Authority on advertisements by Amnesty International.

But political parties are allocated times for political and election broadcasts, and have been free to spend as much as they like on them.

Following recommendations of the Committee on Standards in Public Life under the chairmanship of Lord Neill,[7] legislation now imposes a ceiling on party expenditure at the national level, as well as on spending in individual constituencies and by third-party individuals and groups.[8] There must be full disclosure of the source of donations of more than £5,000 to a registered political party. But there are no limits on the amount that an individual or corporation may give; this is odd, given the opportunities for political influence that large donations may provide the donor.[9] On the other hand, following the recommendations in the Neill Committee Report, the prohibition on broadcast political advertising continues; in contrast, the content of newspaper and hoardings advertising is entirely unregulated, though the national party expenditure limits of course affect the amount of money that may be spent on them.

A further legal change has been made following the ruling of the European Court of Human Rights in *Bowman* that the strict limit of £5 on the expenditure by third parties to communicate information with a view to promoting a candidate's election amounted to an unjustified restriction on freedom of expression.[10] The Court held that this limit had been imposed for legitimate purposes, in particular to ensure fairness between candidates and to prevent wealthy pressure groups distorting election campaigns by concentrating voters' attention on single issues. However, given that there were no limits on expenditure by national parties or on press advertising, the restriction was, in the view of the Court majority, disproportionate. As the Neill Committee rightly concluded, this was not a radical decision; the Court accepted it was legitimate for the United Kingdom to restrict expenditure and, to that extent, freedom of expression, in order to ensure a 'level playing field' between the parties. So United Kingdom law has been changed, but only to allow expenditure of up to £500 by third parties within particular constituencies.[11]

The Neill Committee did at least consider the arguments of free speech principle in this context, albeit not with the same rigour with which they have been addressed by the Strasbourg Court and courts on the other side of the Atlantic. For the majority of the Committee favouring the imposition of national expenditure limits, the argument from equality or, put another way, for a 'level playing field' between the parties, trumped the objection raised by John McGregor, MP, that limits would restrict freedom of speech. It was right to point out that it made

---

[7] 5th Report of the Committee (Cm. 4051, 1999).

[8] Political Parties, Elections and Referendums Act 2000 (PPERA 2000), on which see K. D. Ewing, 'Transparency, Accountability and Equality: The Political Parties, Elections and Referendums Act 2000' [2001] *Pub Law* 542.

[9] For criticism, see J. Rowbottom, 'Political Donations and the Democratic Process: Rationales for Reform' [2002] *Pub Law* 758. But only those individuals registered to vote, and UK (not foreign) companies are entitled to make donations: see PPERA 2000, s. 54.

[10] *Bowman* v. *UK* (1998) 26 EHRR 1.   [11] PPERA, s. 131; see Ewing (n. 8 above), 560–2.

little sense now to limit spending in constituencies, but to allow circumvention of these limits by unrestricted national expenditure. On the other hand, from the perspective of free speech, it may be argued that all limits should be struck down, rather than that they should be extended to the national level.

What then should we make of the arguments of principle in this context?[12] First, it should be accepted that a limit on the expenditure of money, whether by an individual or by a political party, in the course of an election campaign (or of course outside that context) does amount to a restriction on freedom of speech. This also applies to ceilings on the size of permissible contributions to party funds, or other types of regulation such as a requirement to disclose their size or the identity of donors. As the Supreme Court pointed out in its landmark ruling in *Buckley* v. *Valeo*,[13] virtually every type of communication in a modern mass democracy is dependent on expenditure, so restrictions on the money that may be spent, say, on printing election literature or placing an advertisement are tantamount to restrictions on speech. The restrictions limit the quantity of speech. Moreover, they are clearly intended to influence the conduct of election campaigns, by, for example, limiting the opportunities for richer parties and candidates to pay for more advertising than less well financed rivals. They, therefore, are aimed at speech, while, say, income or wealth tax laws serve other ends— although indirectly these laws may also have the effect of inhibiting the ability of the rich to disseminate their views as effectively as they would like.

The case for campaign finance laws cannot therefore rest on a denial that they are designed to restrict freedom of speech. They must be justified by other arguments. In particular, it may be claimed that, in the context of elections and other democratic procedures such as referendum campaigns, considerations of citizen equality trump the right of more wealthy individuals and groups to spend as much as they like on political debate and advertising. Proponents of these laws may start from the point that each citizen has an equal right to vote. Modern democracies do not give more votes to the rich or better educated. So it may be equally legitimate for the law to ensure that all citizens, so far as possible, have an equal voice in the democratic process. It should be conceded that this aim can never be fully achieved; political journalists and pundits inevitably exercise disproportionate influence on the conduct of an election. But it may be right to frame campaign finance laws in general, and expenditure limits in particular, to limit the electoral influence which money can buy.

One version of this argument contends that electoral speech is institutionally bound or constrained, in much the same way as speech within a courtroom or legislative proceeding or at a public meeting. Analogies may also be drawn between campaign speech and speech within a classroom or prison, or on an army base, where government (or other public authority) may similarly limit freedom

---

[12] For a recent discussion of these arguments in a US context, see J. Weinstein, 'Campaign Finance Reform and the First Amendment: An Introduction' (2002) 34 *Arizona State Law Jo* 1057.

[13] 424 US 1 (1976), discussed above in ch. III, s. 3 above.

of speech in order to safeguard, say, discipline and harmonious relationships, ends which would rarely justify restrictions on public discourse.[14] Government may, it is concluded, legitimately impose some restrictions on the quantity of speech during election campaigns in order to safeguard their fairness. This argument distinguishes campaign speech from general public debate, where considerations of fairness do not justify limits on freedom of speech.

As already mentioned, an argument of this kind has been accepted by the European Court in the *Bowman* case.[15] The Canadian Supreme Court has also come to a similar conclusion. In *Libman* v. *Attorney-General of Quebec*,[16] it upheld the legitimacy in principle of restrictions imposed by Quebec legislation on spending by individuals unaffiliated to official 'umbrella organizations' during the course of a referendum campaign. The object of the legislation was egalitarian. Spending limits were related to this end, in that they prevented the most affluent individuals and groups from dominating debate. In a particularly pregnant aside, the Court added that these limits reinforced one of the values underlying freedom of expression itself: the ability of the voters to make informed choices.[17] Moreover, it was justifiable to limit spending by independent third parties, as otherwise constraints on party and candidate expenditure would be ineffective. Indeed, the Court added that, in the context of an election campaign, it would be reasonable to impose stricter limits on third parties' spending than on that of political parties and candidates, since an election is essentially a party contest. However, the Court concluded that the Quebec rules in effect silenced the voice of independent third parties, since individuals could not incur any expenditure to influence voters during a referendum campaign unless they were affiliated to one of the official organizations. Freedom of expression was significantly impaired. Recently in *A-G of Canada* v. *Harper*,[18] the Court by a 6–3 majority upheld strict limits on third-party advertising expenditure during election campaigns: C\$3,000 in particular districts and C\$150,000 nationally. The Court accepted that the aim of these restrictions was to safeguard electoral fairness and the confidence of the electorate in the electoral process. While the majority was prepared to defer to Parliament's judgement that the limits were a justified restriction on freedom of expression, the dissent of McLachlin CJ argued that there was no evidence to support a link between them and electoral fairness. They amounted, in her view, to a disproportionate restriction on the freedom of an individual to communicate his views effectively during an election campaign; it would be impossible to pay for an advert in a national newspaper.[19]

The approach of the Canadian Supreme Court assumes that a sensible line can be drawn between campaign expenditure on the one hand and expenditure on general political and social discussion outside this particular context on the other.

---

[14] C. E. Baker, 'Campaign Expenditures and Free Speech' (1998) 33 *Harvard Civil Rights–Civil Liberties Law Rev* 1; Weinstein (n. 12 above), 1082–4.   [15] N. 10 above.

[16] [1997] 3 SCR 569; see Moon, 96–9.   [17] See ch. I, s. 2(iii) above.

[18] (2004) 239 DLR (4th) 193.   [19] Ibid., paras. 4–9.

Two criticisms may be made of this approach. First, even if it is assumed that the distinction between campaign and general political expenditure can be defended in principle, it may be difficult for legislation satisfactorily to draw it; as a result spending on general political expression, and hence speech itself, may be curtailed. Courts may find it impossible to police the line between spending on what is sometimes termed 'issue advocacy', say, by a pro-life or environmental pressure group on matters not associated with a particular candidate or party, and spending to promote the electoral chances of candidates who support the outlook of that group.[20] But the major point is that the distinction is in principle unwarranted; speech and associated expenditure during the course of an election campaign is political speech in one of its purest forms.[21] Even if a line could be drawn between expenditure on general 'issue advocacy' and on election campaigns, it cannot be right to impose limits on what parties, candidates, and their supporters consider necessary to spend in order effectively to communicate their political messages.

However, these arguments ignore the crucial point that elections themselves are often governed by constitutional principles. The First Protocol to the the European Convention on Human Rights and Fundamental Freedoms (ECHR) provides for the right to free elections.[22] In *Bowman* the Strasbourg Court indicated that this right had to be balanced against freedom of expression in determining the compatibility of expenditure limits with the Convention. Similarly, the Canadian Supreme Court has derived a principle of electoral fairness from the constitutional guarantees of equality rights and the right to vote,[23] so there was a rational basis for regulations designed to ensure that electoral debate was not dominated by the most affluent. The constitution itself may, therefore, justify a distinction between the regulation of expenditure on campaign speech and the regulation of expenditure on speech outside that context, when it may be right to give equality considerations less weight.

More radically, campaign finance laws may be defended by the claim that government may constitutionally intervene to protect the equal opportunity of all citizens to participate in political life. Campaign finance laws cannot simply be dismissed as driven by a misguided paternalist 'concept that government may restrict the speech of some elements of our society in order to enhance the relative voice of others [which] is wholly foreign to the First Amendment.'[24] Rather, they are an attempt to realize an ideal of democracy, integrally linked to the underlying value of freedom of speech itself.[25] This claim has radical implications. It would appear to justify a wide range of laws designed to achieve more equal opportunities

---

[20] The provisions in the Canada Elections Act 2000 upheld in *Harper* (n. 18 above) restrict third-party spending intended to promote the chance of a candidate, but not general 'issue advocacy'.
[21] See K. M. Sullivan, 'Against Campaign Finance Reform' [1998] *Utah Law Rev* 311.
[22] First Protocol, art. 3.
[23] *Libman* (n. 16 above), 410–14; also see *Harper* (n. 18 above) paras. 86–7.
[24] *Buckley* v. *Valeo* (n. 13 above), 49.
[25] See R. M. Dworkin, 'The Curse of American Politics', *NY Rev of Books*, 17 Oct. 1996, 19, and *The Sovereign Virtue* (Cambridge, Mass.: Harvard UP, 2000), ch. 10.

for speech, for instance, rules restricting the amount of money which may be spent on political advertising or limiting media monopolies. Rules of this kind are intended to prevent certain groups from dominating the terms of political debate and from reducing the effective participation of less affluent individuals and groups.

Even if this radical argument is unacceptable, more limited regulation confined to election campaigns should be upheld. Quite apart from any justification provided by constitutional provisions concerning elections, there are good reasons why constraints on election expenditure are acceptable. In the first place, there is the obvious point that they are a less intrusive interference with speech than regulations which attempt to ensure equality over a wide field. Secondly, they serve specific ends in the context of electoral campaigns, for which there are no equivalents in other circumstances. For instance, one justification for ceilings on candidate and party expenditure is that they reduce the need for politicians to devote inordinate amounts of time on fund-raising, and consequently to limit their opportunity for reflection on political issues and the consideration of legislative proposals.[26] The protection of candidate time is clearly a point of substance; it supports limits on election expenditure, but does not justify the imposition of limits on expenditure on general political causes. A third point is that constraints on private expenditure may be imposed as a condition of the public funding of an election; in *Buckley* the Supreme Court upheld the constitutionality of the scheme under which presidential candidates could receive federal funding on the condition of accepting limits on private expenditure.[27]

Three other arguments relevant to the constitutionality of campaign finance laws should now be considered. The first concerns the distinction between two types of restriction. Limits on the amount of *contributions* which may be made to candidates and a campaign organization, in contrast to those imposed on independent *expenditures*, have been justified on the ground that they are necessary to prevent corruption. In *Buckley* v. *Valeo*, it was held that the contribution limits should not be treated as a direct restraint on expression; while contributions may result in expression, 'the transformation of contributions into political debate involves speech by someone other than the contributor.'[28] The Supreme Court held the $1,000 ceiling on contributions constitutionally justified to prevent actual quid-pro-quo corruption or its appearance. The distinction between contributions and expenditures has always been controversial, though it retains the support of a majority of the Court.[29] But a minority would now overrule *Buckley*,

---

[26] V. Blasi, 'Free Speech and the Widening Gyre of Fund-raising: Why Campaign Spending Limits May Not Violate the First Amendment After All' (1994) 94 *Columbia Law Rev* 1281. This argument was accepted by Kennedy J. in *Nixon* v. *Shrink Missouri Govt PAC* 528 US 377, 409 (2000).

[27] *Buckley* v. *Valeo* (n. 13 above), 92–104. [28] Ibid., 21.

[29] See *Colorado Republican Campaign Committee* v. *Fed. Election Comm.* 518 US 604 (1996), treating political party advertising expenditure, uncoordinated with a candidate, as independent expenditure rather than a contribution to the latter's funds, and *Nixon* v. *Shrink Missouri Govt PAC* 528 US 377 (2000), holding limits on contributions to candidates for state office compatible with the First Amendment.

insofar as it did not apply strict scrutiny to the limits on campaign contributions. Certainly, the tighter limits on contributions discriminate against those who lack the means, say, to place advertisements in newspapers or to engage in other forms of independent expenditure, but are prepared to contribute to the funds of a candidate or party. Moreover, mandatory disclosure of the size and identity of the source of contributions over a certain limit, as now introduced in the United Kingdom,[30] should be enough to reduce corruption. In any case, the corruption argument does not provide a convincing justification for expenditure constraints, which represent a much more significant attempt to introduce fairness into election campaigns.

A second argument is that ceilings on expenditures, and for that matter contributions, do not discriminate on the basis of viewpoint. Indeed, they could be regarded as content-neutral, in that they are not aimed at any particular views, but simply prohibit expenditure on campaign speech beyond a certain limit.[31] Of course, laws imposing such ceilings may distinguish expenditure on speech promoting the electoral prospects of the candidates or parties, which they do limit, and expenditure on general political speech during an election campaign, which they do not; moreover, such laws do not affect the freedom of the press and other print media to canvass support for a particular party. In that sense they do distinguish between types of speech on the basis of content, treating expenditure on electoral speech less favourably than spending on other types of political speech. But it is hard to see why that sort of distinction should attract the strict judicial scrutiny which is more appropriate to legislation which discriminates between communications on the basis of their subject matter or viewpoint, or the particular identify of the speaker.[32] Moreover, there are good constitutional and other reasons for distinguishing between electoral and general political speech.

But campaign expenditure limits may well have a greater impact on some parties than others. This point has been exhaustively discussed in the United States where limits may favour incumbents who benefit from greater media publicity than their challengers. Moreover, Democrats are more likely to defend expenditure ceilings than Republicans, since the latter enjoy more financial backing from wealthy individuals and corporations. Similarly in the United Kingdom, Conservatives have traditionally been hostile to the imposition of expenditure limits and mandatory disclosure rules for contributions, while the Labour and Liberal Democrat parties have supported their introduction. From the perspective of freedom of speech, however, this point does not amount to a strong argument against the imposition of ceilings on expenditure and contributions. Many types of law produce disproportionate effects on the free speech and press rights of particular groups and individuals. For example, media concentration laws have

---

[30] PPERA 2000, ss. 62–9.

[31] For the classic exposition of this argument, see J. Skelly Wright, 'Politics and the Constitution: Is Money Speech?' (1976) 85 *Yale LJ* 1001, 1009–10.

[32] For the US hostility to content-based restrictions on speech, see ch. II, s. 2 above.

more impact on large press and broadcasting groups, while planning regulations controlling the site of notices and billboards will probably have more repercussions on commercial advertisers than on local shops and pressure groups. Short of a judicial finding that a limit was imposed with the specific aim of reducing the resources of a particular party and with no other justification for its imposition, the fact that a ceiling is more hurtful to one party than to others should not affect its validity.

This last point leads to the crucial third argument. Whatever the merits of campaign finance laws in theory, it must be conceded that governments will be tempted to enact laws to the disadvantage of opposition parties. That is why judicial review of their constitutionality is not just appropriate, but vitally necessary to safeguard the democratic process.[33] For that reason, it is difficult fully to share the view of Breyer J. that courts should be reluctant to question the assessment of the state legislature on contribution limits, as this is a matter on which the latter enjoys greater expertise.[34] However, it does not follow that courts should always or generally invalidate expenditure and contribution limits as interfering with speech. They may conclude that a law should be upheld.[35]

This has now happened in the United States. At the end of 2003 the Supreme Court considered the constitutionality of the Bipartisan Campaign Reform Act of 2002 (BCRA 2002), amending the earlier legislation at issue in *Buckley* v. *Valeo*. By a bare 5–4 majority, it upheld the principal reforms.[36] In the first place, the contribution limits and disclosure requirements were extended to cover the provision of so-called 'soft money' (contributions to party funds for state elections and for general party advertising, as distinct from 'hard money' contributions made specifically to influence federal elections). Stevens and O'Connor JJ, giving the Court's judgment, held the regulation of 'soft money' did not infringe freedom of speech; the governmental interest in preventing actual or apparent corruption justified the new restrictions. Secondly, BCRA 2000 extended the prohibitions on election expenditure by corporations and unions from their general funds, and the obligation to disclose the sponsor of electoral advertising, to cover 'issue advertising', that is advertisements which did not specifically advocate a vote for or against a named candidate, but which drew, for instance, attention to his voting record on particular issues. These changes were also upheld. The form of the advertising is immaterial; what matters is whether it referred to a clearly identified candidate and was addressed to the electorate within the campaign period.

---

[33] See F. Schauer, 'Judicial Review of the Devices of Democracy' (1994) 94 *Columbia Law Rev* 1326.

[34] *Nixon* v. *Shrink Missouri Govt PAC* 528 US 377, 402–4 (2000). In a rare reference by a US judge to comparative law, Breyer J. referred approvingly to the decisions of the European Human Rights Court in *Bowman*, n. 10 above, and of the Canadian Supreme Court in *Libman*, n. 16 above. [35] Schauer (n. 33 above), 1345.

[36] *McConnell* v. *FEC* 157 L Ed 2d 491 (2003).

(ii) Other issues

Elections may raise other freedom of speech questions than those concerning the financing of party campaigns. In many European countries, it is illegal to publish opinion polls in the period immediately prior to polling day, while by convention political parties do not canvass or broadcast in the preceding day or so. The United States Supreme Court has held the application to a newspaper editor of a state law which banned electioneering on polling day incompatible with the First Amendment.[37] A majority of the Canadian Supreme Court invalidated a provision in the federal elections legislation prohibiting the publication of opinion polls within three days of polling day.[38] One justification often given for provisions of this kind is that they give the electorate an opportunity for calm reflection before voting; the Italian Constitutional Court, for instance, upheld a ban on the use of loudspeakers on motor vehicles to canvass support during the thirty days before an election as a reasonable restriction on freedom of expression designed to prevent confusion and so protect effective exercise of that freedom by voters during election campaigns.[39] The Canadian court did not regard this argument as a substantial enough objective to justify a restriction on the dissemination of information which voters might find valuable—the results of late polls. Further, there were other less restrictive means to achieve the more pressing objective of limiting the influence of inaccurate late polls; pollsters could be required to disclose their methodology. More fundamentally, the majority reasoned that voters should be credited with enough judgement to interpret polls intelligently. It is a nice question whether a court should allow a ban on the publication of opinion or exit polls during polling day itself. There is some evidence that publication may deter some people from voting, if they consider that their party is going to win comfortably without their support. The broadcast of inaccurate polls or predictions might influence the result, as may have happened in Florida in November 2000 when television networks at one point announced that Gore was going to take the state. In these circumstances there is a strong argument that it is much too late for serious mistakes to be corrected and that it is better to ban the publication of poll results altogether.

Perhaps the most difficult question is whether a ban on broadcast election advertising is compatible with freedom of speech. Political advertising on radio and television, at election and other times, is banned in the United Kingdom; political parties are, however, allocated a number of free broadcasts, particularly during election campaigns.[40] The ban is justified as necessary to prevent the

---

[37] *Mills* v. *Alabama* 384 US 214 (1966).
[38] *Thomson Newspapers* v. *Canada* [1998] 1 SCR 877.
[39] Decision 138/1985, [1985] *Giur cost* 986.
[40] Communications Act 2003, ss. 319(2)(g) and 321(2)–(3) (ban, and definition, of political advertising), and s. 333 (party political broadcasts). For a review of these arrangements, see Electoral Commission Report, *Party Political Broadcasting* (Jan. 2003).

dominance of political debate in general, and election campaigns in particular, by wealthy individuals and groups or by the richer political parties. Smaller political parties would be unable to afford to advertise on television, and so would be unable to put their views to the electorate. For these reasons, the Electoral Commission has concluded that the ban is in the public interest.[41] Two questions should be distinguished here. A comprehensive ban on all political advertising on television and radio outside the context of an election campaign seems incompatible with freedom of speech. It discriminates against political speech in favour of commercial advertising, which is essential to the financing of private broadcasting. It is also hard to see why a pressure group should be entirely free to advertise in newspapers and magazines, or in the cinema, but be entirely forbidden from disseminating its message to the public by the most effective means. For that reason, the European Court was right to hold the Swiss ban on political advertising incompatible with freedom of expression.[42]

But it does not follow that tighter rules may not be justified during election campaigns. To allow paid-for political advertisements might enable rich individuals or pressure groups to distort the terms of an election debate which should be conducted primarily between political parties and at the local level between their candidates. Unrestricted political advertising would make nonsense of any scheme for free political broadcasts under which time is allocated to political parties on the basis of the number of seats they hold or are contesting. A ban, or at least significant restrictions on paid-for broadcast political advertising at election times, is as justifiable to safeguard the electoral process as are the expenditure limits on press and other advertising upheld by the Supreme Court of Canada in the *Harper* case.[43] Arguably, the European Court in the Swiss case had election broadcasting in mind when it said that in some situations it might be compatible with freedom of expression to ban political advertising.[44]

On the other hand, in one of its initial decisions on the implied right to freedom of political communication, the High Court of Australia invalidated as incompatible with the freedom provisions in broadcasting legislation which prohibited paid-for political advertising on radio and television during campaign periods, but allowed parties and candidates (but not other persons or pressure groups) some free air time for election broadcasts.[45] The High Court recognized that the legislation had serious objectives: the prevention of corruption and dominance of election broadcasting by rich parties and candidates. But the majority

---

[41] Ibid., 15–16.
[42] *VGT Verein gegen Tierfabriken* v. *Switzerland* (2002) 34 EHRR 4, discussed in ch. XII, s. 5 above.
[43] N. 18 above.   [44] N. 42 above, para. 75.
[45] *Australian Capital Television Pty Ltd* v. *Commonwealth* (1992) 177 CLR 106. Recently, the High Court has distinguished this decision when it declined to hold that the requirement that a party had 500 members to be identified on ballot papers burdened the freedom of political communication between candidates and voters: *Mulholland* v. *AEC* [2004] HCA 41. There was no restriction on a pre-existing freedom of speech, as there had been in the broadcasting case, where the legislation curtailed a freedom previously enjoyed by broadcasters and advertisers.

thought that these objects could be met by means less restrictive of freedom of expression, in particular by limiting the amount of money which could be spent and the amount of time which could be purchased. As it stood, the legislation wholly prevented individuals who were not themselves candidates from using the most effective means of putting their views on election issues to the voters.

It ought to be clear that restrictions on what a party can say in its election broadcast, or in any advert it is free to pay for, are incompatible with freedom of speech. While expenditure constraints, or a total ban on paid-for advertising on television and radio, can be defended as necessary to safeguard a fair electoral process, prohibiting a party from communicating its message because it is considered too offensive for the public to consider surely amounts to a clear infringement of free political speech. Yet the House of Lords has held that the BBC (and other broadcasters) were entitled not to transmit the party election broadcast of the ProLife Alliance party, because they were required by a rule of broadcasting law not to show any material which offends good taste and decency or is offensive to the public.[46] The rule should have been interpreted not to infringe freedom of political expression; restrictions on the *content* of what can be said during an election campaign should be subject to the strictest scrutiny.

3. Free Speech in Employment

(i) Preliminary issues

The major question considered in this section is how far freedom of speech may be curtailed in the context of employment: may a public authority or a company dismiss or discipline an employee for his speech?[47] Before considering the relevant arguments of principle, two preliminary issues should be addressed. One is whether the right to freedom of speech is only at stake in the context of *public* employment or is also engaged when a *private* employer dismisses an employee for, say, publishing a letter to a newspaper which it regards as seriously damaging to the firm's interests. From the employee's perspective, it does not make sense to differentiate between the rights enjoyed by, say, a civil servant and those of an employee of a private company. In particular, it would be odd if the constitutional free speech rights of an employee of a public company were affected by its privatization. Yet that is the position in a jurisdiction such as the United States, where rights such as freedom of speech are only guaranteed against state action or interference.[48] Public employees may be entitled to claim the protection of the First Amendment or other free speech provision, but private employees cannot when they are summarily dismissed for saying something at work which their employer

---

[46] *R (on the application of ProLife Alliance)* v. *BBC* [2004] 1 AC 185, considered in ch. II, s. 1(iii) above.   [47] See L. Vickers, *Freedom of Speech and Employment* (Oxford: OUP, 2002).
[48] For discussion of this point, see ch. II, s. 2 and ch. IV, s. 5 above.

dislikes. (Of course, they may claim successfully that they are entitled to compensation for breach of contract or for unfair dismissal.)

In support of this distinction, it can be said, first, that governments have usually been more concerned to stifle criticism over a wide range of issues than have private individuals and corporations. When the government employs citizens, it has a means of control over their speech in addition to use of the criminal law: it can simply deprive them of their livelihood if they say or write things it dislikes. Admittedly, private employers enjoy the same sanction of dismissal. But generally they are inclined only to regulate their employees' speech when its dissemination prejudices their commercial or other immediate interests. A second basis for the distinction between public and private employers is that the latter's own rights, including in some cases their right to freedom of expression, may be compromised unless they are free to discipline an employee. A church school or private hospital should, it may be argued, be free to maintain its own ethical position by dismissing employees who publicly adopt a different stance on, say, the value of a religious education or the morality of abortion.[49] This argument does not apply to government, and other public authorities, as they are not entitled to claim free speech rights.[50]

However, these points surely do not show that a sharp line of principle should be drawn between the treatment of restraints imposed by public employers on the one hand and by private employers on the other. At most the first argument indicates that a public employer—particularly, though not exclusively, central government—may be particularly inclined to use its powers to dismiss (or downgrade) an employee in a wide range of circumstances. Indeed, government may frequently be tempted to abuse its powers to discipline employees who speak wholly outside the employment context. As far as the second point is concerned, while it is true that a private employer may be able to invoke its own free speech interests as a justification for regulating those of its employees, it does not follow that they are without free speech rights in the context of their employment relationship. Both these arguments can, as we will see shortly, be accommodated in the balancing of the employer's interests with the employee's free speech. They do not require a bright line to be drawn between speech in public and private employment, so that speech in the latter environment *necessarily* falls wholly outside the scope of legal protection.

As far as the United Kingdom is concerned, the scope of freedom of expression in the context of employment is governed by the Human Rights Act 1998 (HRA 1998). A 'public authority' is required to act compatibly with Convention rights.[51] This term includes bodies, 'certain of whose functions are functions of

---

[49] See the Commission ruling in 12242/86 in *Rommelfanger* v. *Germany* (1990) 62 D & R 151, discussed in s. 3(ii) below.

[50] The arguments for free speech considered in ch. 1 mean that it cannot be claimed by government itself. ECHR, art. 34 provides that only individuals and non-governmental institutions can claim to be a victim of an infringement of a Convention right.   [51] HRA 1998, s. 6(1).

a public nature', but they are not treated as a 'public authority' in relation to a particular act 'if the nature of the act is private'.[52] The implication is probably that while, say, a local authority must respect freedom of expression when deciding whether to discipline an employee, bodies such as BT or a gas company need not. The decision whether to dismiss someone would probably in most circumstances be regarded as private and so not covered by the legislation.[53]

When applying the HRA 1998, United Kingdom courts must take account of European Court and Commission rulings.[54] The latter held that an employee dismissed from his post with a private immigration association, owing to his active membership of a political party hostile to immigrants, could not bring an application against the association itself;[55] however, it could be brought against the state, as formally the employment relationship had been terminated by a court decision. More significantly, the Strasbourg Court in *Fuentes Bobo* v. *Spain* has held that states have a positive obligation to protect freedom of expression against infringement by private persons. Article 10 may, therefore, be invoked in the context of private employment relations.[56] In that case the employer was the Spanish public broadcaster TVE, which under statute was regulated by private law; the employee's speech savagely criticized the management of the broadcaster, a matter of clear public concern. Clearly no sharp line can now be drawn under the ECHR between speech in the contexts of public and private employment.

Secondly, there is the argument, pertinent to both public and private employment, that the dismissal of an employee for saying something disliked by his employer does not even engage freedom of speech. That right has been surrendered or waived by contract; when an employee has been dismissed in these circumstances, he is really claiming a right to stay in his job.[57] This argument is not now accepted either in the United States or by the Strasbourg Court. Admittedly, some employees do expressly agree not to publish material on particular topics, for example, not to divulge government or trade secrets; or it can be said that such an agreement can be implied from general duties of loyalty to the employer. But for the most part such express (or implied) terms cover only limited categories of speech, and do not amount to a total surrender of the free speech rights the employee

---

[52] HRA 1998, s. 6(3)(b) and (5).

[53] But see Vickers (n. 47 above), 73–8, for the argument that freedom of expression may be indirectly enforceable against private employers, as tribunals are bound by HRA 1998, s. 6 to act in conformity with Convention rights. Also see Sir Patrick Elias and J. Coppel, 'Freedom of Expression and Freedom of Religion: Some Thoughts on the *Glenn Hoddle* Case', in *Freedom of Expression and Freedom of Information*, 51, 58, where it is argued that the dismissal by the Football Association of the manager of the English football team for expressing 'religious' views should be regarded as the act of a public authority.   [54] HRA 1998, s. 2.

[55] 11002/84, *Van der Heijden* v. *Netherlands* 41 D & R 264.

[56] (2001) 31 EHRR 50, para. 38. But compare *Nafria* v. *Spain* (2003) 36 EHRR 36, where the Court held that art. 10 was not infringed by the dismissal of an employee of the Bank of Spain for alleging irregularities in its management.

[57] See Holmes J. in *McAuliffe* v. *Mayor of New Bedford* 25 NE 517 (1892) for a robust expression of this discredited view: 'The petitioner may have a constitutional right to talk politics, but he has no constitutional right to be a policeman'.

enjoys as an ordinary citizen. Apart from these cases, the argument that employees freely waive their right to free speech is patently bogus. Even where the employment contract does explicitly restrict speech, it is a constitutional question whether the right to freedom of speech can lawfully be surrendered. Some rights, for instance, the right not to be tortured or held in slavery, cannot be surrendered by contract. Courts may come to the same conclusion with regard to freedom of speech; at least they should entertain the argument that an employer infringes the freedom if it dismisses an employee for expressing his views.

The European Court of Human Rights did hold in two cases that a state is free not to give permanent employment to probationary teachers who were members of extremist political parties.[58] The Court treated these cases as involving a right of access to the civil service, which is not guaranteed by the ECHR, rather than the Convention rights to freedom of expression and association. But in *Vogt* v. *Germany*,[59] distinguishing these cases, it ruled that the dismissal of a civil servant, in this instance a teacher who had been in post for eight years, for membership of the Communist Party did interfere with the Convention rights. The Court's failure even to consider freedom of expression in the first pair of cases has been convincingly criticized; the exclusion of an individual from consideration for a post, or the decision not to confirm probationary employment, on the grounds that he has expressed particular views, may amount to as significant a restraint on freedom of expression as dismissal.[60] But at least the Court has rejected the argument that employees in post surrender their free speech rights to their employer.

(ii) Balancing the interests of employees and employers

The legal systems discussed in this book adopt a similar approach to speech in employment cases, though the results reached in particular contexts may differ. It is a matter of balancing the interests of employee and employer.[61] A classic statement is that of Marshall J. in *Pickering* v. *Board of Education*:

The problem in any case is to arrive at a balance between the interests of the teacher, as a citizen, in commenting upon matters of public concern and the interest of the State, as an employer, in promoting the efficiency of the public services it performs through its employees.[62]

Similarly, the European Human Rights Court in *Vogt* developed a 'fair balance test' under which the civil servant's freedom of expression should be weighed against the state's interest in achieving the aims, for instance, national security, for which restrictions on speech may be imposed under Article 10(2). The German

---

[58] *Glasenapp* v. *Germany* (1987) 9 EHRR 25; *Kosiek* v. *Germany* (1987) 9 EHRR 328.
[59] (1995) 21 EHRR 205.
[60] See G. S. Morris, 'Political Activities of Public Servants and Freedom of Expression', in I. Loveland (ed.), *Importing the First Amendment* (Oxford: Hart, 1998), 99, 111–12.
[61] Vickers (n. 47 above), 28–62.   [62] 391 US 563, 568 (1968).

Constitutional Court also requires labour courts to balance the employer's contractual freedom with the employee's freedom of expression; they should examine the speech carefully to determine whether it indicated that continued engagement of the employee would lead to disruption in the workplace.[63]

From the side of an employee-speaker, the most important factor in striking a balance between the two interests is surely whether he expressed his views primarily as an individual citizen or primarily within the context of the employment relationship. To discipline an employee, whether public or private, for, say, writing a letter to a newspaper, expressing views on general political questions which have nothing to do with his work, amounts to an unwarranted interference with freedom of speech. Employees retain their interest as citizens in being free to express their views and exchange information with others. What is important is not so much that the speech is on a matter of 'public concern' (to use the test developed by the US Supreme Court), but that it has little or nothing to do with the employment relationship between the two parties.[64] These distinctions are, of course, easier to state than to apply. The views of a teacher or hospital worker on education or health service policy generally, or on the performance of his particular school or hospital, relate to matters of 'public concern' and indeed may represent an especially valuable contribution because of the speaker's inside knowledge of the facts. But equally in these cases there is a close connection between the content of the speech and the employment relationship. It is really only possible to determine whether the employee's speech should be protected, when the strength of the employer's interests has been considered in the context of all the facts.

The US Supreme Court has attempted to draw a sharp line between an employee's speech of 'public concern' and speech as an employee on questions of personal interest. Whether restrictions imposed by an employer on the former category of speech are constitutional is determined by applying the balancing test formulated in *Pickering*; the employee's free speech interest is weighed against the employer's interests in its restriction. But, absent unusual circumstances, the Court decided there should be no judicial review when an employer fires an employee for expression falling under the second category. So in *Connick* v. *Myers*,[65] where this line was drawn, the Court, by a bare majority, declined to intervene when an assistant district attorney's appointment was terminated because she had distributed a questionnaire to her colleagues inviting their views on a number of issues concerning office transfer policy and morale. Brennan J. for the four dissenting

---

[63] 42 BVerfGE 133 (1976); 86 BVerfGE 122 (1992). In the latter the Court held that the labour court was wrong to conclude that the support expressed by the writer, a successful trainee, for violent demonstrations against nuclear plants would necessarily mean that he would support violence at work and that the employer was therefore justified in not offering a work contract.

[64] See D. Gordon Smith, 'Beyond "Public Concern": New Free Speech Standards for Public Employees' (1990) 57 *Univ of Chicago Law Rev* 249.

[65] 461 US 138 (1983). This decision has recently been followed in *City of San Diego* v. *John Roe*, 6 Dec. 2004, when the Supreme Court held the city was entitled to dismiss a police officer for marketing videos which showed him in sexual activity. There was no need to balance as the video did not raise matters of public concern.

Justices argued persuasively that it was wrong to draw a sharp line between speech of public concern and employment speech; it would have been better to decide whether circulation of the questionnaire had a significant impact on the functioning of the District Attorney's Office.

As the United States Supreme Court said in *Pickering*,[66] the employer's primary interest in this context is the efficient performance of the services it provides. Abusive reactions to reasonable directions from an employer and its managers, offensive speech to fellow employees or to members of the public, and the holding of political meetings during work hours, disrupt the working environment. Employers have a legitimate interest in curtailing all these modes of expression, although outside the work environment it would be constitutionally impermissible for the state to restrict them. As O'Connor J. put it in *Waters* v. *Churchill*,[67] the interest of government in ensuring the efficient performance of its functions is treated as substantial when it acts as an employer, though it is entitled to much less weight when it regulates the speech of general citizens. Moreover, reasonable predictions of a public employer that speech will be disruptive will be taken into account. However, the Court will not accept vague claims that restrictions are necessary to support general operational efficiency, and therefore invalidated a Congressional law which prohibited federal employees from accepting fees for making speeches or writing articles, whether or not the expression related to the employee's duties.[68] The German courts adopt a stricter approach, insisting on evidence that the speech brought about actual disruption, not just its threat, before allowing an employer to limit his employees' freedom of expression.[69]

Private and public employers may each have specific interests in addition to the interest in preventing disruption of their work. The former may argue that unrestricted free speech for their employees would compromise their own freedom to pursue a distinctive mission. In *Rommelfanger*,[70] the European Human Rights Commission accepted that a Catholic hospital was entitled to dismiss a doctor who had a letter published in *Der Stern*, expressing sympathy for abortion, because its own freedom of expression was also implicated. It is hard to see how on these facts the hospital's freedom to articulate its distinctive views was compromised, but certainly in some situations publication of an employee's views might weaken the impact of his employer's distinctive political or social position.

Public employers may argue that restrictions on the free speech of their staff are necessary to ensure their political neutrality. The European Court has accepted that restrictions on the political speech and activity of local authority officers[71] and of police officers[72] satisfy the rights of the public to fair and impartial treatment. In these cases it fastened on the phrase in Article 10(2) of the ECHR that

---

[66] N. 62 above.   [67] 511 US 661, 675 (1994).
[68] *US* v. *National Treasury Employees Union* 513 US 454 (1995).
[69] 42 BVerfGE 133 (1976); Decision of Federal Labour Court of 9 Dec. 1982, NJW 1984, 1142.
[70] (1990) 62 D & R 151.   [71] *Ahmed* v. *United Kingdom* (2000) 29 EHRR 1.
[72] *Rekvenyi* v. *Hungary* (2000) 30 EHRR 519.

the exercise of freedom of expression 'carries with it duties and responsibilities'. There is indeed a European tradition of a neutral civil service, and it is right to safeguard public confidence in it. Whether this interest always justifies the restriction on the particular expression is a different matter. That depends on how it is balanced against the employee's free speech interest.

Apart from the content of the speech itself, a number of factors may be relevant to determining whether it was legitimate to restrict it. One of the most important is the position within the authority of the particular employee. Other things being equal, an employer has a stronger interest in restricting political speech by senior staff engaged in policy formation than in limiting speech by clerical assistants or support staff. (On the other hand, in practice employers may be more tolerant of criticism of office working methods and other matters from senior staff, at least if it is not expressed publicly.) In Canada restrictions which banned all public employees, irrespective of their position, from engaging in any type of political activity or speech were held too broad.[73] Narrower restrictions are imposed in the United Kingdom on the speech of civil servants and local authority employees, although even they may be too wide.[74] Civil servants are divided into three groups: first, the politically free group, entitled to engage in any political activity, including speech, when not on duty or on work premises; secondly, an intermediate group, free to engage in political activity, local or national, if given permission; and thirdly, a politically restricted group, wholly debarred from national political activity, but free with permission to engage in local politics. As far as local authority staff are concerned, the Local Government and Housing Act 1989 has created a category of 'politically restricted' posts, the holders of which are forbidden, among other things, from speaking to the public with the apparent intent to affect public support for a political party. The holders of some identified posts, for instance, chief officers and their deputies, are covered by these restrictions, as are others who are in receipt of more than the salary specified by regulations or whose work involves regular contact with councillors or with the media.[75] Teachers are exempt from these proscriptions.[76]

The importance of examining the speech restrictions in relation to the position of the employees affected by them is shown by two decisions of the European Human Rights Court. When holding it was a breach of Article 10 to dismiss a teacher for membership of the Communist Party, the Court emphasized that she taught languages, a position which did not involve security risks; nor was there any evidence that she had attempted to indoctrinate her pupils.[77] Subsequently, it held Article 10 was infringed when the President of the Administrative Court in

---

[73] *Osborne* v. *Canada* [1991] 2 SCR 69; the Supreme Court referred with approval to the more nuanced restrictions in the UK.   [74] See Feldman, 791–3.

[75] The Strasbourg Court has held these restrictions necessary in a democratic society to protect local democracy and the right of councillors to receive independent advice: *Ahmed* v. *UK* (n. 71 above).

[76] Local Government and Housing Act 1989, s. 2(10). For a critical analysis of these rules, see Morris (n. 60 above), 100–8.   [77] *Vogt* v. *Germany* (n. 59 above), para. 60.

Liechtenstein was reprimanded in a letter from the Prince (and later not re-appointed) for expressing in a lecture views about the constitution which the Prince strongly disliked.[78] The reprimand was not for any lapse in the execution of the applicant's duties, the lecture addressed matters of constitutional importance, and judges enjoy more freedom to express their views on constitutional matters than senior civil servants.

It may be material whether the speech was made at the workplace during employment hours, or in the employee's free time. The former is more likely to disrupt working relations, so it is normally easier to justify its restriction. The German Federal Labour Court has held, for instance, that an employee could be dismissed for wearing a political badge at work, as this 'expressive conduct' infringed his obligation not to disrupt harmonious work relations.[79] But the distinction is not decisive. The US Supreme Court held that a clerical officer in a police department could not be fired for remarking to a colleague at work that he hoped a further attempt to assassinate President Reagan might be successful. The remark was treated as speech on a matter of public concern; its expression did not interfere with the effective working of the department.[80] Subsequently, in *Waters v. Churchill*[81] it held that a hospital was entitled to dismiss a nurse for making remarks critical of the administration of the obstetrics department to another nurse who had been contemplating a transfer to that department; the administration was entitled to act on its reasonable belief that the remarks were not of public concern, but even if they had been, the hospital's interest in preventing disruption to its work outweighed their value under the First Amendment. But no importance was attached to the fact that the remarks were made at the hospital itself.

Courts may be more tolerant of sanctions against employees who use the media to criticize their employer. The European Commission rejected an application by a teacher who had been dismissed for suggesting in a television broadcast that she had been passed over for a headship because of her homosexual orientation.[82] It was wrong for her to make her complaint in this way, given its wide and immediate impact. Similarly, the Commission was unsympathetic to an application from a civil servant in the UK diplomatic service who had been dismissed for writing a letter to the *Guardian*, critical of his employer.[83] It has also declared inadmissible applications by a health service employee[84] and by a police officer[85] whose employments were terminated for publishing abusive and offensive criticisms; sanctions imposed for moderate criticism, initially made only to the employer, are

---

[78] *Wille* v. *Liechtenstein* (2000) 30 EHRR 558. [79] NJW 1984, 1142.

[80] *Rankin* v. *McPherson* 483 US 378 (1987) (the remarks were made on hearing the news of an attempt to assassinate the President in 1981). [81] 511 US 661 (1994).

[82] 11389/85, *Morissens* v. *Belgium* (1988) 56 D & R 127. Also see 10293/83, *B* v. *UK* (1985) 45 D & R 41. These and other Commission decisions are discussed by J. Bowers and J. Lewis, 'Whistleblowing: Freedom of Expression in the Workplace' (1996) 6 *EHRLR* 637.

[83] 18957/91, *Haseldine* v. *UK* (1992) 73 D & R 225.

[84] 9336/81, *Tucht* v. *Germany* (unpublished).

[85] 10280/83, *De Jong* v. *Netherlands* (unpublished).

less likely to be upheld. In the context of a comprehensive balancing of the value of the employee's speech and the damage its dissemination does to the employer's interests, these decisions are surely right. English law has also adopted a cautious attitude to the disclosure of confidential information to the media.[86]

Finally, courts take into account that the dismissal of an employee may well represent a more serious sanction for expressing his views than criminal or civil penalties. In *Vogt* the Strasbourg Court emphasized that dismissal was a disproportionate restriction on the teacher's freedom of expression; it would be difficult for her to obtain other work as a teacher, as there were few private schools.[87] Given that dismissal, or its threat, is the most distinctive sanction available to an employer, judicial control of its application represents a valuable degree of protection for speech in the employment context.

(iii) Speech by members of the armed forces

Speech by members of the armed forces may be treated in one of two ways. First, it may be regarded as a distinctive case, where the interests of discipline and morale in the forces warrant a low degree of protection for the speech of their members. The alternative is to apply the principles developed in cases concerning the expression of civilian employees. Even on this second approach, important interests, such as national security and order within the forces, may well make it relatively easy to justify the regulation of, say, the distribution by soldiers of leaflets on army bases advocating non-participation in a controversial war or peace-keeping operation.

Broadly, the former approach has been taken by the United States Supreme Court. In the first case to consider speech rights in this context,[88] it rejected a constitutional challenge to the conviction of an army medical officer who had urged soldiers not to serve in Vietnam, speech which would almost certainly have been protected under the First Amendment if made by a civilian. The Court was unimpressed by the argument that the offences under the Military Justice Code were drawn in such vague terms—'conduct unbecoming an officer and a gentleman'— that they would inevitably proscribe much speech which should be constitutionally protected. Congress had wide discretion when it laid down standards for military life. Subsequently in *Brown* v. *Glines*[89] the Court upheld a regulation forbidding the solicitation, without prior approval, on air force bases or in uniform, of signatures for a petition to be presented to members of Congress and the Defense Secretary. The commanding officer would be entitled to withhold approval, if he

---

[86] See *Francome* v. *Mirror Group Newspapers Ltd* [1984] 1 WLR 892, CA, but cf. *Lion Laboratories* v. *Evans* [1985] 2 QB 526, CA. The Public Interest Disclosure Act 1998, amending the Employment Rights Act 1996, imposes more onerous conditions for the protection of 'whistleblowing' disclosures to the media and the public than it requires for disclosures to employers and other authorized persons: see Y. Cripps, 'The Public Interest Disclosure Act 1996' in *Freedom of Expression and Freedom of Information*, 275.   [87] Also see *Fuentes Bobo* v. *Spain* (n. 56 above), paras. 48–9.
[88] *Parker* v. *Levy* 417 US 733 (1974).   [89] 444 US 348 (1980).

took the view that circulation of the petition endangered discipline or morale, but not because it criticized government policies. In effect the provisions amounted to a prior restraint on speech, without adequate procedural safeguards; there was no right to make representations or to judicial review.[90] The Court was influenced by its earlier decision in *Greer* v. *Spock*,[91] where it had held that *civilians* had no right of access to army bases to distribute leaflets. That case should not have been persuasive. Dr Spock was free to communicate his views in a variety of other ways, for instance, in the media and by post. But the restriction in *Brown* radically inhibited the ability of members of the air force to speak freely within their own community.

In contrast, the European Human Rights Court has taken the second approach. Members of the armed forces are entitled to freedom of expression, though states are allowed more latitude in restricting its exercise than they enjoy with regard to civilian speech.[92] In determining whether the restriction is necessary to achieve one of the ends for which it may be imposed—notably, national security and the prevention of disorder—the Court examines the character of the speech and whether its publication could objectively be considered a serious threat to discipline and order among the armed forces. In accordance with this approach, it has held that Austria was in breach of Article 10 when, under instructions from the Ministry of Defence, a soldier had been prevented from distributing in army barracks copies of a soldiers' association magazine.[93] The Court emphasized that, though its contents were critical of aspects of military life and advocated reform, the magazine did not urge disobedience. More remarkably, it ruled there was a violation of Article 10 when a conscript was convicted of insulting the army for sending a letter to his commanding officer severely critical of life in the services. Some remarks in the letter were strong and intemperate, but they did not amount to a 'real threat to military discipline'.[94]

The approach of the Strasbourg Court is clearly preferable to that of the United States Supreme Court. Quite apart from arguments of principle, there is no need to draw a sharp line between the position of members of the armed forces and civilian public employees. In many circumstances there are good arguments for restricting the speech of members of the armed forces, but that need not lead to the conclusion that they have virtually surrendered the right to exercise this freedom. Courts can assess the cogency of these arguments in the light of the facts, balancing the interests of the government and the services on the one hand and the free speech interest on the other. Further, drawing a sharp line might be thought to raise problems when members of the forces participate in the distribution of speech by civilians, as in the Austrian case mentioned in the previous

[90] See ch. IV, s. 1 above.
[91] 424 US 828 (1976): see ch. VIII, s. 3(iii) above for access to public fora.
[92] For statements of principle, see *Engel* v. *Netherlands* (1979–80) 1 EHRR 647, 683–6, and *Hadjianastassiou* v. *Greece* (1992) 16 EHRR 219, 238.
[93] *Vereinigung Demokratischer Österreichs & Gubi* v. *Austria* (1994) 20 EHRR 56.
[94] *Grigoriadis* v. *Greece* (1997) 27 EHRR 464, para. 45.

paragraph. It would be unattractive to conclude that a soldier could be disciplined for circulating a magazine which its publisher was free to post to members of the armed forces, and which they would, presumably, be free to read, at least when they are at home. Yet that result might be inescapable, if it is held that soldiers abandon their rights to free speech when they enter the army barracks.

4. Free Speech in Education

(i) Introduction

Freedom of speech in the educational context raises a number of related legal issues: among them are questions how far the speech of students and teachers within or outside the classroom may be restricted and to what extent education authorities may control the contents of school libraries and magazines. To some extent the rights of teachers as employees have already been discussed in the preceding section. Both in the United States and under the European Convention they are free, as citizens, to engage in political activity, provided their exercise of the freedom does not interfere with their employment. But there may be stronger reasons for restricting speech in the classroom or lecture hall and perhaps also generally within the school premises. To take a straightforward case, a teacher has no right to decide what subject he teaches a particular class; he is employed to teach, say, mathematics or French, and the syllabus for these subjects is prescribed. So he is not free to discuss general political issues in these classes. Equally, students' freedom of speech in class does not mean they can say anything they like, irrespective of its relevance to the subject.

Quite apart from those obvious points, it is a major responsibility of government to educate children and young people; schools have a duty to determine the information and ideas of value to be taught, a process which inevitably entails selection and discrimination.[95] In short, education is incompatible with unlimited freedom in the school environment. Further, the law should not allow indoctrination of the political values of the party in government, a ruling elite, or indeed of the schoolteachers themselves. It is this concern which explains provisions of the UK Education Act 1996, forbidding the promotion of 'partisan political views' and requiring educational authorities to ensure the balanced presentation of opposing views when political topics are discussed at school.[96] Arguably, these rules promote the free speech value of pluralism in the same way that the standards of impartiality and fairness in broadcasting safeguard the interests of listeners and viewers in a balanced discussion of political issues.[97] To some extent, higher

---

[95] See J. Tussman, *Government and Mind* (New York: OUP, 1977) for a vigorous exposition of this argument.

[96] Ss. 404–7. See Feldman, 787–9 for criticism of the drafting and implementation of these rules.

[97] See ch. XII, s. 5 above.

education is different. Academic freedom means that a university department may choose what it teaches and allows its members freedom of teaching and research. Further, it is legitimate for university students to disagree strongly with their professors; indeed, up to a point they should be encouraged to do this and even, in appropriate settings, to challenge the prescribed syllabus. Legal provisions and court decisions often reflect these arguments, in particular the case for distinguishing speech in primary schools at one end of the scale and in universities at the other.

(ii) The free speech rights of students and teachers

The US Supreme Court held in *Tinker* that high school students could not constitutionally be disciplined for wearing black armbands to school in protest against the Vietnam war.[98] There was no evidence that their wearing was disruptive or in any way interfered with the rights of other students. The ban had been imposed to avoid controversy, and there was evidence to suggest it was aimed at anti-war speech, as the wearing of other badges was not stopped. Fortas J. for the Court said that students' rights were not confined to classroom hours, but extended to communications anywhere on the school premises. Indeed, there are much stronger arguments for curtailing speech within the classroom or during a school assembly than, say, during lunch breaks or in other periods when students talk informally with each other; classroom discussions should be relevant to the subject and coherent, standards which can hardly be applied elsewhere on school premises.

This distinction may explain the Court's decision in *Bethel School District No. 403* v. *Fraser*,[99] where a student had been disciplined for making an indecent speech during a school assembly. The school authority did not infringe the First Amendment. While *Tinker* had involved political protest, this speech was sexually explicit. The school could legitimately conclude that to tolerate the speech would be incompatible with its responsibility to teach the limits of acceptable behaviour. But the particular setting for indecent or offensive speech is also a factor; students should be free to use strong, even indecent, language at play, while during class lessons it is reasonable for the school to inculcate the values of civil discourse.

Similar distinctions should surely also apply with regard to teachers. With regard to their speech and political activity outside the school environment, both the US Supreme Court and the Strasbourg Court have balanced the education authority's interest as an employer against the teacher's interest in freedom of expression. Indeed, the principles governing speech in employment were largely developed in cases concerning teachers.[100] It is less clear whether these principles should be applied when the issue is how much freedom a teacher enjoys to express his political or social beliefs on school premises generally or in the classroom in

[98] *Tinker* v. *Des Moines School District* 393 US 503 (1969): see ch. III, s. 2 above for discussion of another aspect of the case. [99] 478 US 675 (1986).
[100] See *Pickering* (n. 62 above) and *Vogt* (n. 59 above).

particular.[101] Should a teacher enjoy the freedom, recognized for students in *Tinker*, to wear badges or other items indicating a political attitude, or to hand out leaflets at school inviting students to attend a political meeting? How much freedom should a teacher of history or politics have to argue in class that government education policy is flawed or that it was wrong for his country to have invaded Iraq or to defend that action?

The US Supreme Court has not hitherto ruled on issues of this kind, though some Court of Appeals decisions have applied the principle in *Tinker* to cover schoolteachers.[102] On the other hand, the European Commission held inadmissible a complaint by a teacher who had been dismissed from his post at a non-denominational school for displaying religious and anti-abortion slogans on his clothes. As they could be considered offensive to women teachers and disturbing to children, restrictions could be imposed to protect the 'rights of others'.[103] German courts have held that schoolteachers do not have a right to wear badges protesting against nuclear plants while they are on school premises; a display of their political views infringes the requirement of political neutrality and may influence impressionable students.[104] But teachers are free to wear badges and engage in political activity outside their employment. The Canadian Supreme Court appears to be less concerned with this distinction. In *Ross*[105] it upheld the removal from a teaching position of a primary schoolteacher who was notorious for writing anti-Semitic books and pamphlets outside work. There was no evidence that his views had intruded into the classroom. Nevertheless, the Court took account of the educational context, as well as the employment relationship and the character of the speech. It stressed the responsibility of schools to inculcate the values of tolerance and a multicultural society; the teacher was involved with young children who might not find it easy to draw distinctions between comments inside school and those made outside.

The most difficult question is whether a teacher's free speech rights are infringed if he is directed by the school authorities not to cover a particular topic or he is disciplined for teaching what they consider unsuitable material. In the United States, the Fourth Circuit Court of Appeals has divided 7–6 on this question, the majority holding that a drama teacher at a high school had no free speech right to shape the curriculum by choosing to put on a play (concerning the dynamics of a dysfunctional single-parent family) against the objections of some parents and the school authorities.[106] The school, rather than the individual teacher, is entitled to determine the curriculum. On the other hand, the Supreme Court

---

[101] See G. A. Clarick, 'Public School Teachers and the First Amendment: Protecting the Right to Teach' (1990) 65 *New York Univ Law Rev* 693.

[102] e.g. *Keefe* v. *Geanakos* 418 F 2d 359 (1st Cir, 1969) (right to quote dirty words in class); *James* v. *Board of Education* 461 F 2d 566 (2nd Cir, 1972) (right of teacher to wear black armband in war protest).   [103] 8010/77, *X* v. *UK* 16 D & R 101.

[104] Federal Labour Court decision of 2 May 1982, NJW 1982, 2888; 84 BVerwGE 292 (1990).

[105] *Ross* v. *New Brunswick School District No. 15* [1996] 1 SCR 825.

[106] *Boring* v. *The Buncombe County Board of Education* 136 F 3d 364 (4th Cir, 1998).

of Prince Edward Island has held 2–1 that a school board violated a teacher's freedom of expression when it stopped him showing (without conditions) a documentary film concerning the impact of religious fundamentalism on US life in his language arts class for 14–15-year-old students.[107] Following the expression of concern by a number of parents, the principal decided the film should not form part of the language arts programme, or should be shown only after students had been properly prepared. The majority of the Court ruled that the teacher's freedom of expression had been infringed, for it was the purpose and effect of the board's decision to stop him presenting material of his choice to the class. The dissent of McQuaid JA argued that a restriction on the freedom of a teacher to deliver the curriculum as he wanted did not engage freedom of expression; the school board was entitled to control the material used in class and the manner of its presentation: '[a] public school, at the junior high school level, is not a marketplace for ideas where everyone has the right to freely and openly debate all issues in the same manner that each citizen has the right to do in the public square'.[108]

The US decision and the dissent in the Canadian case are persuasive. Teachers are employed to teach a specific subject according to a set curriculum, and the school authorities should be free to prescribe appropriate methods of presentation and other requirements. Within the classroom, teachers enjoy only limited freedom of expression, though its scope may well be wider in other contexts, say, in general school debates, and they may have the same freedom as other citizens with regard to expression outside the school premises. A consequence of the Canadian decision is that principals and school authorities will have to show that there are good educational reasons for limiting, say, a teacher's choice of material, in order to justify a restraint on the exercise of his right to freedom of expression. Courts might become the ultimate arbiters of school curricula.

Questions concerning the scope of school authorities' discretion to control the contents of libraries and school magazines have been raised in the United States. In *Board of Education* v. *Pico*[109] four members of the Court held a school board could not compatibly with the First Amendment remove books from the school library because it wished to deny students access to the ideas expressed in them. Three of them emphasized the particular character of a school *library*, which provided books for optional rather than compulsory reading. But none of them (nor any other member of the Court) doubted that a school board could prescribe certain books as set books for discussion in class or for examination purposes. In contrast, the four dissenting justices denied that there was any significant difference between control over the syllabus or discussion in the classroom and over the contents of the library; a school library, unlike a public or a university library,

---

[107] *Morin* v. *Board of Trustees of Regional Administrative Unit No. 3* (2002) 213 DLR (4th) 17.
[108] Ibid., para. 232.
[109] 457 US 853 (1982); other aspects of the case are discussed in ch. III, s. 7 above.

is not a centre for unrestricted research.[110] There was, therefore, a fundamental difference of view how to resolve the apparent conflict between the free speech interests of school students and the distinctive mission of schools.

In comparison, the *Hazelwood* case[111] produced a clear majority upholding the discretion of a high school principal to control the contents of a magazine produced in the journalism course. He had deleted two features written by students dealing with schoolgirl pregnancies and with the impact of parents' divorces, partly on the ground that they might have been disturbing to younger students. The Court emphasized that a school has wide authority over publications and theatrical productions with which it is associated; in the absence of intervention, parents and the public might think the school itself approved publication of the articles. Control over the magazine was as justifiable as control over the school curriculum. This decision is surely right. No intelligible distinction can be drawn between the prerogative of educational authorities to prescribe the syllabus and determine what may be discussed in class, and their right to control contents of material produced in the context of a school course. But the principal would not have been entitled to censor a magazine produced by students outside that context.

(iii) Free speech in universities

There are good reasons for thinking that speech in higher education should be more generously protected than it is in schools. The purpose of a university is not only, perhaps not even primarily, to inculcate a body of received knowledge and values; rather it is to provide a forum for research and discussion where students are encouraged to think for themselves. This idea is captured by the concept of 'academic freedom' which may not be confined to higher education, but clearly has considerably more resonance in that context than it does in schools.[112] Academic freedom confers on university lecturers some freedom in determining the scope and contents of their courses, if not always its subject, and they are free to choose their areas of research and writing. But academic freedom is an institutional right which ranges far beyond freedom of speech for individual lecturers and students. It confers on universities a degree of organizational independence, for example, to determine their own syllabus and to select their staff, visitors, and students. Analogies may be drawn perhaps with press freedom. A university lecturer may assert freedom of speech and academic freedom if government or some public authority were to prescribe the contents of his course, just as a journalist may claim free speech and press rights against the state. But within the university

---

[110] The ninth member of the Court, White J., agreed with the first group of Justices, affirming on procedural, rather than constitutional, grounds the Court of Appeal decision denying the school board summary judgment.   [111] *Hazelwood School District* v. *Kuhlmeier* 484 US 260 (1988).

[112] In Germany, freedom of research and teaching is guaranteed by a separate clause of the freedom of expression provision, art. 5(3): see ch. II, s. 4 above.

organization, as within a newspaper or broadcasting company, the individual's freedom of expression may be limited: a head of department or course organizer may impose some constraints on how a lecturer teaches, just as the broad terms of a newspaper leader or feature article may be determined at the editors' conference.

Academic freedom has sometimes been articulated as an aspect of the First Amendment by US courts.[113] Differences in the United States between the freedom of speech in universities from that enjoyed in schools is largely a matter of degree. University students need less protection from indecent or offensive speech than children at school. Indeed, they may be expected to be as tolerant of such speech as adults, though the fact that they may live, as well as work, together in a close community might justify campus codes imposing some restrictions. The issue has largely arisen in the context of hate and racist speech provisions which have generally been held too broad and vague to survive constitutional challenge, unless they are narrowly framed to outlaw only speech which is insulting of the individual to whom it is directly addressed.[114] University students should not be expected to tolerate racist abuse in the lecture hall or in leaflets distributed in halls of residence; speech on campus, like speech at the workplace, does not form part of that public debate or discourse to which the fullest free speech protection should be given. But university authorities infringe free speech if they attempt to control the content of student journals,[115] or discriminate against a student society in its allocation of facilities or financial support on the basis of the society's aims or beliefs.[116]

Remarkably, the United Kingdom provides the clearest legal recognition of the distinctive responsibility of universities to promote freedom of speech. The Education (No. 2) Act 1986 imposes an obligation on universities and colleges of further and higher education to take the steps that 'are reasonably practicable to ensure that freedom of speech within the law is secured for members, students and employees of the establishment, and for visiting speakers.'[117] The use of university premises is not to be denied to an individual or body on the ground of his views, or those of any member of the relevant body, or of any of its objectives or policies. But a university may refuse permission for a campus meeting if it reasonably believes that an illegal speech will be made at it. It may therefore outlaw racist hate speech or speech likely to cause disorder on the university premises. But a general fear that the meeting is bad for campus relations or may exacerbate tensions between different groups of students would not be enough to justify its proscription.

---

[113] Frankfurter J. in *Sweezy v. New Hampshire* 354 US 234, 263–4 (1957) and Powell J. in *Regents of the University of California* v. *Bakke* 438 US 265, 312 (1978). For a different perspective, see F. Schauer, ' "Private" Speech and the "Private" Forum: *Givhan* v. *Western Line School District*' [1979] *Supreme Court Rev* 217, 244–9, and T. L.Haskell, 'Justifying the Right of Academic Freedom in the Era of "Power/Knowledge" ', in L. Menand (ed.), *The Future of Academic Freedom* (Chicago: Chicago UP, 1976), 43.   [114] See *Doe* v. *University of Michigan* 721 F Supp 852 (ED Mich, 1989).

[115] *Hosty* v. *Carter* 325 US F 3d 945 (7th Cir, 2003).

[116] *Rosenberger* v. *University of Virginia* 515 US 819 (1995).

[117] S. 43(1). See ch. VIII, s. 3(iii) above.

In contrast, a primary or secondary school would be permitted, indeed would surely be under a duty, to prevent speech which is likely to cause disruption of this kind.

5. Free Speech and Prisoners

Prisoners' rights to freedom of speech may be restricted for a number of reasons. Correspondence discussing plans for escape or insurrection endangers prison security and good order; a prisoner found reading sexually explicit or radical political material may be considered more vulnerable to attack by fellow inmates. Rules may enable prison authorities to restrict prisoners' correspondence, their access to publications from outside, and their freedom to give interviews to the media. Prison governors may have power to act as a censor by denying access to a particular publication which, in their view, poses a risk to prison order. Utilitarian arguments of this kind may be supported by the sweeping argument that prisoners have forfeited basic rights such as freedom of speech, just as in the United Kingdom, for instance, they have had no right to vote.[118]

But jurisprudence in the United States, United Kingdom, and from Strasbourg establishes that prisoners do not lose all their constitutional rights. The Supreme Court, for instance, has said that '[p]rison walls do not form a barrier separating prison inmates from the protection of the Constitution.'[119] The House of Lords has affirmed that prisoners retain all their civil rights unless it is plain by express words or necessary implication that Parliament intended to take them away.[120] Moreover, any curtailment on the rights of prisoners to circulate letters or other material, or to have access to material from outside prison, inevitably restricts the freedom of speech of other persons outside prison. The family, friends, and lawyers of prisoners are particularly affected. There is also a loss to the public insofar as it is deprived of, say, information, or prisoners' views, about their conditions. Equally, if there is an overwhelming justification for a rule restricting communication to or from prisoners, it is impossible to apply separate standards to safeguard the interests of people outside prison who wish to communicate with them. A restriction unavoidably abridges the rights of prisoner and non-prisoner alike.

The approach of the United States Supreme Court in this area appears a little inconsistent. In *Procunier* v. *Martinez*,[121] it invalidated California regulations, for the most part providing for censorship of correspondence from prisoners to relatives and friends outside. The Court formulated a relatively strict standard of review, emphasizing that restrictions should not be too broad and must serve

---

[118] The total ban on voting rights has been held incompatible with the ECHR, art. 3 of Protocol 1 guaranteeing the right to vote: *Hirst* v. *UK* (2004) 38 EHRR 40.

[119] *Turner* v. *Safley* 482 US 78, 84 (1987).

[120] See Lord Wilberforce in *Raymond* v. *Honey* [1983] 1 AC 1, 10.

[121] 416 US 396 (1974).

a substantial government interest in the security, order, or rehabilitation of prisoners. But in later cases, notably *Pell* v. *Procunier*,[122] concerning a claim by journalists of access to prisons to conduct interviews, and *Turner* v. *Safley*,[123] concerning restrictions on the right of prisoners to receive correspondence from other inmates, it adopted a more lenient standard of review. Restrictions reasonably related to legitimate penal interests are to be upheld, as they were in these cases. This standard has now been applied in a case concerning prisoners' freedom to receive books.[124] Stricter scrutiny of rules limiting freedom of speech is reserved for outgoing correspondence; unlike material coming into prison, such correspondence poses no risks for internal order,[125] although it might promote criminal activity outside. The distinction is a coherent one, but it is doubtful whether it justifies different standards of review.

Prisoners' complaints about restrictions on their freedom of communication have usually been considered by the European Human Rights Commission and Court under Article 8 of the ECHR, guaranteeing the right to respect for privacy of correspondence. This is regarded as the more appropriate provision under which to assess whether it is compatible with the Convention to stop letters to and from a prisoner's family, friends, and lawyers. In a leading case the Commission and Court held that blanket prohibitions on writing any letter of complaint and any letter intended for publication were not shown to be necessary to prevent disorder and were incompatible with the ECHR.[126] But Article 10 covers correspondence to the media intended for general publication and the receipt by prisoners of newspapers and books. The Commission has ruled that the denial of access to paper for writing and a blanket prohibition on sending out academic writing for publication could not be justified.[127] But it was compatible with the Convention for prison authorities to deny a prisoner access to a *particular* issue of a magazine which contained anti-Semitic views.[128]

In *Simms* the House of Lords has held that Prison Service Standing Orders should be interpreted to allow prisoners to give interviews to journalists to argue that their convictions were wrong and to give publicity to the case for their review.[129] On a literal interpretation of the rules, no inmate could be interviewed by a professional journalist, except with the governor's permission, and no material could be published except with his approval. But the House held unanimously that the rules should be interpreted in light of the prisoners' fundamental right to freedom of expression to challenge the safety of their convictions. There was no evidence to suggest that interviews conducted for this purpose, and subsequent

---

[122] 417 US 817 (1974).   [123] N. 119 above.
[124] *Thornburgh (US A–G)* v. *Abbott* 490 US 401 (1989).
[125] The German Constitutional Court has made this point: see 33 BVerfGE 1, 16 (1972) when it invalidated broad censorship powers lacking statutory basis.
[126] Report of the Commission in *Silver* v. *UK* (1980) 3 EHRR 475, paras. 344–51. The Court accepted this part of the Commission's decision: (1983) 5 EHRR 347, para. 102.
[127] 8231/78, *T.* v. *UK* 49 D & R 1.   [128] 13214/87, *Lowes* v. *UK* 59 D & R 244.
[129] *R* v. *Home Secretary, ex p Simms* [2002] 2 AC 115.

media publication, would disrupt prison order. Lord Steyn in the leading speech suggested that his approach provided a more generous treatment for prisoners' freedom of expression than the US cases such as *Pell* v. *Procunier*, where deference was shown to the judgement of prison authorities.

But the decision in *Simms* only recognized a freedom for prisoners to speak to journalists to challenge the safety of their convictions. Lord Steyn explicitly denied that they had any right to give interviews to speak about general political issues or the economy, for in those circumstances their freedom must give way to the need to preserve discipline and order in the prison.[130] But it is hard to see how such a blanket prohibition on free speech can be justified. Some political speech might conceivably have disruptive effects, but other interviews, say, concerning prisoners' voting intentions or regarding the circumstances that led to their committing criminal offences might not. Interviews discussing such matters may be as important to the public as a protestation of innocence. Although the decision in *Simms* is bold, the reasoning on the limited scope of the prisoners' right to free speech ignores the audience interest in receiving views and information.[131]

The Court of Appeal has recently distinguished the *Simms* decision in a ruling denying, in effect, the right of Dennis Nilsen to publish the horrifying details of his murders of six homosexual partners in an autobiography.[132] Nilsen had challenged the prison governor's refusal to allow his manuscript to be returned to him, so he could do further work to prepare it for publication; the decision was taken under a Standing Order restricting the communication of material for publication which concerns the inmate's crime or others' offences (except where it contains, as in *Simms*, serious representations about his conviction or about the penal system). The Court of Appeal held the application of the rule did not infringe freedom of expression. In terms of the European Convention, it could be regarded as necessary to protect the families of Nilsen's victims from distress and prevent the outrage which the public would feel if he were free to publish his own account. The fact that a graphic account of the crimes had been published twenty years ago would not diminish that outrage.[133] It is far from comfortable to disagree with this decision. But some of the reasoning is impossible to square with freedom of speech. Much speech (including the previous accounts of Nilsen's horrifying crimes) occasions real hurt and distress but it would clearly be incompatible with freedom of speech to proscribe it for that reason. If that were not true, we would have no difficulty in banning all types of hate speech, including offensive political speech, which is distressing to many. Freedom of speech entails tolerance for the publication of material which shocks and disturbs.[134] It is also hard to accept that a prisoner's account of his crimes may be proscribed merely because the public would feel outraged that he was free to publish it. A terrorist's

---

[130] *R* v. *Home Secretary, ex p Simms* [2002] 2 AC 115, 127.   [131] See ch. I, s. 3(ii) above.
[132] *Nilsen* v. *Governor of HMP Full Sutton* [2004] EWCA 1540.
[133] Ibid., paras 41–3.   [134] *Handyside* v. *UK* (1976) 1 EHRR 737, para. 49.

account of the beliefs and associations which led him to commit the offences for which he was convicted might be of real public interest, though some would think it outrageous that he could publish it. Nilsen is as unattractive a free speech claimant as any identified in this book, but that does not mean that he is not entitled to the right. The only coherent explanation of the decision is that, with some exceptions, prisoners do not enjoy free speech rights.

Select Bibliography

This is a select, rather than a comprehensive, bibliography. It refers primarily to monographs and collections of articles or essays on freedom of speech and aspects of free speech law. A few leading law review articles are also referred to, while other references to helpful literature on particular topics are given in the notes to each chapter.

GENERAL WORKS

Why Protect Free Speech?

John Stuart Mill's essay, 'Of the Liberty of Thought and Discussion', in *On Liberty and Other Essays* (Oxford: OUP, 1991) is essential reading. The best modern discussion of the philosophical arguments is by Frederick Schauer, *Free Speech: A Philosophical Enquiry* (Cambridge: CUP, 1982), though his arguments for a free speech principle are found unconvincing by Larry Alexander and Paul Horton in their review article, 'The Impossibility of a Free Speech Principle' (1983) 78 *North Western Univ Law Rev* 1319. That article is to be found in the two-volume collection of reprinted articles on free speech theory edited by Larry Alexander, *Freedom of Speech* (The International Library of Essays in Law & Legal Theory, Aldershot: Ashgate, 2000). The first volume also contains the seminal article by Thomas Scanlon, 'A Theory of Freedom of Expression' (1972) 1 *Philosophy and Public Affairs* 204, reprinted in R. M. Dworkin (ed.), *The Philosophy of Law* (Oxford: OUP, 1977).

Other books exploring the justifications for free speech include: C. Edwin Baker, *Human Liberty and Freedom of Speech* (New York: OUP, 1989), Kent Greenawalt, *Speech, Crime, and the Uses of Language* (New York: OUP, 1989), and David A. J. Richards, *Free Speech and the Politics of Identity* (New York: OUP, 1999). Some articles in W. J. Waluchow (ed.), *Free Expression* (Oxford: OUP, 1994), and Tom Campbell and Wojciech Sadurksi (eds.), *Freedom of Communication* (Aldershot: Dartmouth, 1994) are concerned with free speech theory, while others discuss aspects of free speech law. The former collection reproduces the classic article by Joseph Raz, 'Free Expression and Personal Identification' (1991) 11 *OJLS* 303. Five chapters of Ronald Dworkin's *Freedom's Law* (New York: OUP, 1996) discuss free speech principles.

England

Two general books should be mentioned. David Feldman's magisterial book, *Civil Liberties and Human Rights in England and Wales*, 2nd edn. (Oxford: OUP, 2002) devotes six chapters to freedom of expression, while Geoffrey Robertson, QC and Andrew Nicol, QC, *Media Law*, 4th edn. (London: Penguin, 2002) discusses free expression rights in the context of press and broadcasting law. The essays in Jack Beatson and Yvonne Cripps (eds.), *Freedom of Expression and Freedom of Information: Essays in Honour of Sir David Williams* (Oxford: OUP, 2000) cover a number of themes, among them free speech theory, the status of political speech, and the relationship of free speech and privacy.

United States of America

Most of the vast literature on the First Amendment is to be found in US law reviews. Reference is made elsewhere to monographs on special topics; Lee C. Bollinger and Geoffrey R. Stone (eds.), *Eternally Vigilant: Free Speech in the Modern Era* (Chicago: Chicago UP, 2002) has essays on free speech doctrine by outstanding US scholars. Ian Loveland (ed.), *Importing the First Amendment* (Oxford: Hart, 1998) contains reflections on US free speech jurisprudence by English lawyers and scholars.

Canada

Richard Moon, *The Constitutional Protection of Freedom of Expression* (Toronto: Toronto UP, 2002) offers a stimulating critique of leading Canadian Supreme Court decisions, as does Jamie Cameron, 'The Past, Present, and Future of Expression under the *Charter*' (1997) 35 *Osgoode Hall LJ* 1.

Germany

The best account in English of the freedom of expression decisions of the German Constitutional Court is in David P. Currie, *The Constitution of the Federal Republic of Germany* (Chicago: Chicago UP, 1994), ch. 4. Also see Edward J. Eberle, *Dignity and Liberty: Constitutional Visions in Germany and the United States* (Westport, Conn.: Praeger, 2002), ch. 7. Readers with German should look at a commentary on the Basic Law, for example, volume 1 of Ingo von Münch and Philip Kunig (eds.), *Grundgesetz-Kommentar*, 5th edn. (Munich: CH Beck, 2000), and at Wolfgang Hoffmann-Riem, *Kommunikationsfreiheiten* (Baden-Baden: Nomos, 2002) (the author is a member of the Constitutional Court).

European Convention on Human Rights

In addition to Feldman's book (see *England*), Mark W. Janis, Richard S. Kay, and Anthony W. Bradley, *European Human Rights Law*, 2nd edn. (Oxford: OUP, 2000) might be consulted for an introduction to the ECHR and the European Court. Chapter 5 contains extracts from leading decisions on freedom of expression, in addition to substantial commentary. Also see Mario Oetheimer, *L'Harmonisation de la Liberté d'Expression en Europe* (Paris: Éditions A. Pedone, 2001), chs. I–II and VI for a discussion of the influence of the ECHR on English freedom of expression law.

France

Jean Morange, *La Liberté d'Expression*, in the series 'Que Sais-je?' (Paris: Presses Universitaires de France, 1993) provides an elegant introduction to free speech principles in France. Laurent Pech, *La Liberté d'Expression et sa Limitation* (Presses Universitaires de la Faculté de Clermont-Ferrand, 2003) is a stimulating comparative study of French, German, and US law.

Italy

The classic account of freedom of expression in Italian law is by Carlo Esposito, *La Libertà di Manifestazione del Pensiero nell'Ordinamento Italiano* (Milan: Giuffrè, 1958). The leading modern treatment is by Alessandro Pace, *Problematica delle libertà costituzionali, Parte speciale*, 2nd edn. (Padua: Cedam, 1992), with supplement in 2002, ch. 11.

Australia

George Williams, *Human Rights under the Australian Constitution* (Melbourne: OUP, 2002), ch. 7 chronicles the High Court decisions on freedom of expression, while Michael Chesterman, *Freedom of Speech in Australian law* (Aldershot: Ashgate, 2000) is a collection of critical essays on these decisions and on comparative free speech law.

WORKS ON SPECIFIC TOPICS

Political Speech, Hate Speech, and Pornography

Many of the articles in David Kretzmer and Francine Kershman Hazan (eds.), *Freedom of Speech and Incitement against Democracy* (The Hague: Kluwer, 2000), and in Raphael Cohen-Almagor, *Liberal Democracy and the Limits of Tolerance* (Ann Arbor: Michigan UP, 2000) are concerned with how far a democracy should tolerate speech which advocates its violent overthrow.

Lee C. Bollinger, *The Tolerant Society: Freedom of Speech and Extremist Speech in America* (New York: OUP, 1986) defends the US tolerance of hate speech, while Richard Delgado and Jean Stefancic, *Must We Defend Nazis? Hate Speech, Pornography and the New First Amendment* (New York: New York UP, 1997) is critical of the US approach to hate speech and pornography. In a balanced discussion of the arguments, James Weinstein, *Hate Speech, Pornography, and the Radical Attack on Free Speech Doctrine* (Boulder, Col.: Westview Press, 1999) points out the risks to public discourse of attempts to ban hate speech and pornography. Catharine A. MacKinnon, *Only Words* (London: HarperCollins, 1995) defends bans from a feminist perspective; for criticism of her arguments, see Ronald Dworkin, 'Pornography and Hate' and 'MacKinnon's Words' in *Freedom's Law* (New York: OUP, 1996), 214, 227.

For the regulation of official secrets in the UK and Australia, see Pauline Sadler, *National Security and the D-Notice System* (Aldershot: Ashgate, 2001).

Libel and the Invasion of Privacy

Anthony Lewis, *Make No Law* (New York: Random House, 1991) is a graphic account of the historic decision in the *New York Times* case. A sympathetic view of the US approach to free speech and libel is taken by Ian Loveland, *Political Libels* (Oxford: Hart, 2000).

On privacy and free speech, see Raymond Wacks, *Privacy and Press Freedom* (London: Blackstone, 1995), Eric Barendt, 'Privacy and the Press' (1995) *Yearbook of Media and Entertainment Law* 23, and Basil Markesinis (ed.), *Protecting Privacy* (Oxford: OUP, 1999).

Copyright and Freedom of Speech

Two recent books contain articles dealing with the relationship of copyright and freedom of expression: Paul L. C. Torremans (ed.), *Copyright and Human Rights* (The Hague: Kluwer, 2004) and Jonathan Griffiths and Uma Suthersanen (eds.), *Copyright and Free Speech* (Oxford: OUP, 2005).

Freedom of Assembly and Public Order

David Feldman, *Civil Liberties and Human Rights in England and Wales*, ch. 18 provides a full account of English law. P. A. J. Waddington, *Liberty and Order* (London: UCL Press, 1994) examines the use of police powers to control demonstrations.

The most comprehensive analysis of the complex US 'public forum' doctrine is by Robert C. Post, 'Between Governance and Management: The History and Theory of the Public Forum' (1987) 34 *UCLA Law Rev* 1713.

Freedom of Speech and the Judicial Process

C. J. Miller, *Contempt of Court*, 3rd edn. (Oxford: OUP, 2000) is the leading academic book on the law of contempt in England, with some reference to leading Commonwealth cases. Joseph Jaconelli, *Open Justice: A Critique of the Public Trial* (Oxford: OUP, 2002) explores the open justice principle and its limits, while Ian Cram, *A Virtue Less Cloistered: Courts, Speech and Constitutions* (Oxford: Hart, 2002) discusses a number of restrictions on the freedom of the media to report legal proceedings. Barend van Niekerk, *The Cloistered Virtue* (New York: Praeger, 1987) is a classic: written by a radical South African academic lawyer, it examines the restrictions which common law and civil law jurisdictions impose on the freedom to report and comment on legal proceedings. Also see Michael K. Addo (ed.), *Freedom of Expression and the Criticism of Judges* (Aldershot: Ashgate, 2000).

Commercial Speech

Roger A. Shiner, *Freedom of Commercial Expression* (Oxford: OUP, 2003) is critical of the protection of commercial advertising in US and Canadian decisions. Alex Kozinski and Stuart Banner, 'Who's Afraid of Commercial Speech?' (1990) 76 *Virginia Law Rev* 627, and Robert C. Post, 'The Constitutional Status of Commercial Speech' (2000) 48 *University of California Law Rev* 1 are important contributions to the rich American literature, while Colin R. Munro, 'The Value of Commercial Speech' (2003) 62 *Camb LJ* 134 discusses the law in England and under the European Convention.

Freedom of Speech in the Media and on the Net

Eric Barendt (ed.), *Media Law* (International Library of Essays in Law & Legal Theory, Aldershot: Dartmouth, 1993) reprints a number of important articles on freedom of speech in the media. Among them is the article by Potter Stewart, 'Or of the Press' (1975) 26 *Hastings Law Jo* 631, arguing that freedom of the press gives the media rights beyond those covered by freedom of speech. Judith Lichtenberg, 'Foundations and Limits of Freedom of the Press', in J. Lichtenberg (ed.), *Democracy in the Mass Media* (Cambridge: CUP, 1990) provides a different perspective on the relationship of freedom of speech and press freedom. David A. Anderson, 'Freedom of the Press' (2002) 80 *Texas Law Rev* 429 is a major contribution to recent debate on the meaning of press freedom in the United States. One of the themes of Rachael Craufurd-Smith, *Broadcasting Law and Fundamental Rights* (Oxford: OUP, 1997) is the guarantee of freedom of expression and pluralism in broadcasting laws in Europe, notably the UK, France, and Italy. Also see Andrew Scott, ' "A Monstrous and Justifiable Infringement"?: Political Expression and the Broadcasting Ban on Advocacy Advertising' (2003) 66 *MLR* 224.

The Symposium, 'Emerging Media Technology and the First Amendment' (1995) 104 *Yale LJ* 1613 has articles on the implications of the Net for freedom of speech. Eugene Volokh, 'Cheap Speech and What It Will Do', ibid., 1805 offers perhaps the most optimistic perspective on the Net's impact. For English views, see the essays in Yaman Akdeniz, Clive Walker, and David Wall (eds.), *The Internet, Law and Society* (Longman, 2000).

Free Speech and Elections

For a justification of restrictions on election expenditures in terms of an egalitarian, partnership conception of democracy, see Ronald M. Dworkin, *The Sovereign Virtue* (Cambridge, Mass.: Harvard UP, 2000), ch. 10. The Symposium, 'Campaign Finance Reform' in (2002) 34 *Arizona State Law Jo* 1017 contains a range of views on the compatibility of expenditure restrictions with freedom of speech; James Weinstein's article, 'Campaign Finance Reform and the First Amendment: An Introduction', ibid., 1057 provides a clear survey of the complex Supreme Court jurisprudence and the free speech arguments. Little of the English literature on election expenditure considers free speech arguments, but see Jacob Rowbottom, 'Political Donations and the Democratic Process: Rationales for Reform' [2002] *PL* 758, 771–6.

Free Speech and Employment

Lucy Vickers, *Freedom of Speech and Employment* (Oxford: OUP, 2002) provides a comprehensive discussion of the issues of free speech principle and European Court and Commission rulings in this area.

Free Speech and Education

Joseph Tussman, *Government and the Mind* (New York: OUP, 1977) argues that freedom of speech does not preclude government intervention in education and in providing support for the arts. Essays in Louis Menand (ed.), *The Future of Academic Freedom* (Chicago: Chicago UP, 1996) explore the relationship of academic freedom to freedom of speech; in particular see Ronald Dworkin, 'We Need a New Interpretation of Academic Freedom', also published in the author's *Freedom's Law*.

Index